COLLECTED WORKS OF ERASMUS

VOLUME 29

❧ LINGVA

PER ERASMVM ROT.

Icturus non de aſini, quod a/
iunt umbra, ſed de his quæ
præcipuum habent momen/
tum ad humanæ uitæ uel feli
citatē uel perniciem, precor
ut omnes, quandoquidem ad
omnes hæc oratio pertinet,
his auribus atque animis auſcultetis, quas in rebus gra
uiſſimis maximisq̃; bene conſulenti præbere ſoletis.
Atq̃; illud in primis ſuo quiſq̃; cum animo perpendat,
ſi quis ueſtrum uenenum deferat præſentaneum, quod
uel ipſo contactu ſubitam mortē adferret, idq̃; ſic de/
ferat incluſum uaſculo ut nō poſſet abijcere, nónne is
quamlibet alijs in rebus incurius, hic ſumma ſolicitu=
dine caueret, ne per imprudentiam aut incuriam exi/
tium conſciſceretur, uel ipſi qui teneret, uel alijs qui/
bus bene uellet, ucluti liberis aut uxori? Quanta cura
ſeponeret eam pyxidem, quàm religioſe caueret ne
quid effluerct, aut ne quis ſpiritus letalis exhalaret, ne
quis imprudēs attingeret. Rurſus ſi quis pharmacum
circunferret, aduerſus omnia morborū genera præ /
ſens habens remedium, quo uel iuuentus reuocari poſ
ſet, uel mors iam urgens propelli, an nō is anxie ſolli
citus

Exordiū ab attentiōe & beneuolētia.

Simile.

Erasmus *Lingua*, the beginning of the text
Basel: Froben, February 1526
Centre for Reformation and Renaissance Studies,
Victoria University, University of Toronto

COLLECTED WORKS OF
ERASMUS

LITERARY AND EDUCATIONAL WRITINGS 7

DE VIRTUTE / ORATIO FUNEBRIS / ENCOMIUM
MEDICINAE / DE PUERO / TYRANNICIDA /
OVID / PRUDENTIUS / GALEN / LINGUA

edited by Elaine Fantham and Erika Rummel

with the assistance of Jozef IJsewijn

University of Toronto Press

Toronto / Buffalo / London

The research and publication costs of the
Collected Works of Erasmus are supported by the
Social Sciences and Humanities Research Council of Canada.
The publication costs are also assisted by
University of Toronto Press.

©University of Toronto Press 1989
Toronto / Buffalo / London
Printed in Canada

ISBN 0-8020-5818-3

Printed on acid-free paper

Canadian Cataloguing in Publication Data
Erasmus, Desiderius, d. 1536.
[Works]
Collected works of Erasmus

Includes bibliographical references.
Partial contents: v. 29. Literary and educational
writings, 7. De virtute. Oratio funebris. Encomium
medicinae. De puero. Tyrannicida. Ovid. Prudentius.
Galen. Lingua / edited by Elaine Fantham and Erika
Rummel; with the assistance of Jozef IJsewijn.
ISBN 0-8020-5818-3 (v. 29)

1. Erasmus, Desiderius, d. 1536. I. Title.

PA8500 1974   876'.04   C74-006326-x

Collected Works of Erasmus

The aim of the Collected Works of Erasmus
is to make available an accurate, readable English text
of Erasmus' correspondence and his
other principal writings. The edition is planned
and directed by an Editorial Board, an Executive Committee,
and an Advisory Committee.

Contents

Introduction

The pieces that make up this volume form a suitable conclusion to the series of literary and educational writings in the CWE. While the commentaries on Ovid and Prudentius undoubtedly come under the heading of educational writings, and the *Lingua* may be regarded primarily as a literary composition, the rest of the works included here straddle the two categories. Moralizing in content and paradigmatic in form, they appeal to the reader's Christian conscience as well as his literary tastes and provide for his moral as well as his stylistic guidance. As works of literature, the compositions are impressive witnesses to Erasmus' classical scholarship; as school texts they fit well into the overall framework of his philosophy of education and, more specifically, his theory of the development of writing skills.

Erasmus describes the most accomplished writer as one who has mastered the classical style, but whose *imitatio* of classical models is of a kind that does not simply 'incorporate into its own speech any nice little feature it comes across, but transmits it to the mind for inward digestion.' Filtered through the writer's personal experience and transformed through his imagination, it takes on the 'force of [his] own mind and personality' – becomes 'a child sprung from his own brain.'[1] In his definition of *imitatio* Erasmus recognizes the three stages traditionally discerned in the educational process: information gathering, internalization, and creative development. He is also aware of the corresponding steps in the teacher's method of instruction. First 'he must see that sources are available from which [the student] may draw topics,' next he must encourage the student 'to elaborate on commonplaces,' finally he will require him to produce his own composition, and 'it will suffice to indicate the bare subject-matter.'[2]

As educational writings, the pieces in this volume may be grouped according to these three levels of skill development. The translations from Galen and the commentaries on Ovid and Prudentius belong to the first stage, at which source material is explored; the *Lingua* represents an advanced stage, at which the source material is applied in context; the remaining pieces belong to the most accomplished stage, at which the writer has entered into the classical heritage and made it his own intellectual property.

Erasmus thought of translation as a highly beneficial exercise in developing a good style of writing. 'We shall add greatly to our linguistic resources,' he said, 'if we translate authors from the Greek, as that language is particularly rich in subject-matter and vocabulary.'[3] Erasmus himself wrote and published versions of a number of classical authors – Euripides, Lucian, and Plutarch, among others. The translations from Galen are a sample of his mature work, when he had abandoned his earlier, somewhat anxious, care and approached his subject with the easy confidence of an experienced craftsman.

The Greek *editio princeps* of Galen's *Opera* was published in Venice in 1525, but Erasmus was probably familiar with Galen's works from the Latin edition (Venice 1490). He chose for his translation the first three pieces in the Aldine edition. Since they treated non-medical topics, they appealed to the lay audience Erasmus had in mind. The *Exhortation to Study the Liberal Arts* and *The Proper Physician* are particularly suitable for young readers because of their edifying character and their moral lessons. The former proclaims education, especially medical training, the supreme good; the latter offers a highly idealized picture of the physician as philosopher and philanthropist. The third essay, which discusses the possibility of absolute knowledge, is less suitable as source material for students because of its rather technical nature, yet somehow appropriate because it deals with a question fundamental to education.

Erasmus' purpose in publishing the three essays was twofold. He wished both to make a Greek source accessible to a Latin readership and to present a model translation to students of Greek. Neophytes might compare his version with the original, thus acquiring a better understanding of the Greek text as well as gaining insights into the process of translation.

When the scope of the CWE was determined, a decision was made not to include Erasmus' versions of classical Greek authors except for a sample illustrating his methods as a translator. The Galen pieces have been chosen for a number of reasons. The essays in question are not available in a modern English translation. True to Erasmus' purpose, therefore, the works of a classical writer are being made accessible to a wider audience. Moreover, the versions represent Erasmus' mature work. The means he used to preserve the literary qualities of the original, to explain difficult passages in the Greek text, and to protect the morals of youthful Christian readers through a form of censorship can readily be documented in the pieces selected here. Finally, the reader is able to observe the process of *imitatio*, that is, the adaptation and creative development of a classical theme, by comparing the Galen pieces with Erasmus' own oration in praise of medicine, a tract included in this volume among the rhetorical compositions.[4]

The Aldine edition of Galen contained many corrupt passages, and Erasmus was therefore obliged to provide not only a translation but textual criticism as well. Through his conjectures he exercised considerable influence on the history of the text – an influence that can still be traced in modern editions of these essays.

Introducing readers to source material is also the function of the commentaries on Ovid's *Nux* and Prudentius' hymns, published in 1523. They were originally composed for, and dedicated to, members of Thomas More's family. The *Nux* commentary was written for John More, then a lad of fifteen, with the direction to share it with his sisters, and the Prudentius for Margaret, the eldest and most studious of the More children.

The *Nux* is a poetic parody of a forensic speech: the nut-tree brings an action against the general public for throwing stones at it. Erasmus expresses no doubts about the authenticity of the poem, attributing it to the Augustan poet Ovid, but modern philologists are inclined to regard it as spurious and dating from a later period, perhaps the end of the first century AD. In his commentary Erasmus draws the reader's attention to philological points, explaining the significance of single words and phrases and citing parallel expressions and structures in other classical authors. He also puts the arguments presented into the context of the rhetorical theories familiar from Quintilian's and Cicero's handbooks, categorizing them according to the rules of forensic oratory. In addition, he provides background information where necessary, especially on the subjects of natural science and mythology.

Prudentius' hymns are a poetic interpretation of the Nativity and Epiphany, presented in an allegorizing fashion. Erasmus' commentary on the hymns differs substantially from that on the *Nux* in that it is predominantly exegetical. Expositions of biblical allegories take up the greater part of the commentary, although there are some notes of a philological nature, especially on metre and poetic usage, and noteworthy explanations of astronomical matters. The format adopted is the same as in the *Nux*: after a brief general introduction Erasmus quotes the text in full, dividing it into portions of two to six verses and adding his comments and explanations.

The commentaries first appeared together in Froben's edition of 1524 and remained twinned in reprints over the next twenty years. They immediately found a readership far beyond the one addressed in the dedication and remained in use until the end of the sixteenth century.

Both the translations of Galen and the commentaries belong to the first

stage of instruction, the presentation of classical sources. On a more
advanced level this raw material is abstracted into historical anecdotes, *bons
mots*, arguments, and examples for use in composition. The *Lingua*
illustrates the process of adapting classical sources to a new use, employing
them to embellish, dramatize, and add conviction to a discourse.

A critical disquisition on contemporary vice, the *Lingua* shares in the
satirical mode of Erasmus' most famous work, the *Moria*, but lacks its
sparkling quality and is less successfully executed. Composed and published in 1525, the *Lingua* is a rambling, loosely structured work on the uses
and abuses of the tongue, with a disproportionate emphasis on the latter.
Clearly it reflects Erasmus' frustration with the theologians and monks who
harangued him relentlessly, associating him with, and indeed blaming him
for, the rise of the Lutheran faction. These rabble-rousers, slanderers, and
backbiters, as Erasmus saw them, needed admonition. The *Lingua* serves
this purpose. It is, so to speak, a polemic against Erasmus' critics, and the
autobiographical element is transparent despite the author's stated intention to say nothing about himself.[5]

The literary quality of the *Lingua* is uneven. The first half is little more
than a patchwork of classical and biblical quotations strung together without
discernible plan, as Erasmus himself admits, saying: 'I have found it
difficult to avoid confusion, all the more so since I had no leisure to polish all
the material which I have brought together' (261 below). The Book of Sirach,
the Pauline Epistles, and Plutarch are among the most heavily exploited
sources. In fact, the latter's essay 'On Talkativeness' offered a convenient,
ready-made collection of arguments. Their availability led Erasmus to
burden his text with unseasonably long and frequent quotations from it.
One feels that he is spending far too long on this display of classical learning
before embarking on the serious protreptic, the exhortation to use language
to express the *philosophia Christi*. The first half of the *Lingua*, then, evinces a
disappointing lack of creativity even by the standards of Renaissance
rhetoric, in which less emphasis is placed on originality than in contemporary literature. Thus, while the content of the *Lingua* invites comparison
with the *Moria*, its execution links it with the *Parabolae* or *Apophthegmata*,
works in which Erasmus' stated purpose was to collect and elaborate on
classical material.

The second half of the work is more satisfying to the reader looking for
Erasmian thought expressed with characteristic flair. Here we find not only
commonplaces but also statements of personal opinion and recollections of
personal experiences. Should the reader's attention flag, it is rekindled with
anecdotes introduced in the storyteller's time-honoured fashion: 'I once
knew a man who ...'[6] Pursuing his main topic vigorously, Erasmus lectures

the reader with candour and self-assurance. The long diatribe against Franciscans and Dominicans (350–62 below) is a vintage piece repeating many of the complaints familiar from Erasmus' correspondence and apologiae of the same period. He points a finger at the tyranny of monks, their slanderous sermons, disparaging dinner conversations, and abusive drinking-bouts, their superstitious adherence to man-made laws, their hypocrisy and self-righteousness, and their readiness to label any critic a heretic and a Lutheran.

The appeal to all Christians to adopt a speech worthy of Christ, which forms the concluding section of the *Lingua*, also displays the eloquence that is Erasmus' hallmark. It has a ringing oratory that might be put to good use by a preacher wanting to rouse his congregation. Thus, after a slow and staid beginning, Erasmus finally brings to bear the fire of his rhetoric. All the familiar techniques are present here: synathroismos, urgent interrogatives, and a crescendo of balanced and gradated clauses leading up to the climactic appeal: 'Sing hymns to the Lord in your hearts.'[7] Thus the *Lingua*, which is at some times a display of Erasmus' learning, at others an indictment of his critics, ends with a prayer epitomizing the truly Christian use of the tongue.

After reading the classics and practising his writing by quoting or paraphrasing the sources in a new context, the student must progress to a higher level of writing, at which he demonstrates that he has not only internalized the classical precepts of style and invention, but is also capable of developing them independently and creatively. To this level belong the speeches in this volume, the homily on the child Jesus, the funeral oration for Berta Heyen, the exhortation to embrace a life of virtue, the speech in praise of medicine, and the plea against the tyrannicide. Representing *imitatio* at its best, they illustrate three categories of rhetoric: protreptic, eulogy, and forensic speech.[8]

The *Concio de puero Iesu*, composed for the students of St Paul's cathedral school and published in 1512, sets before its young listeners the example of Jesus and exhorts them to adopt him as their model. Though composed according to the rhetorical rules of antiquity, the homily is a conscious effort to put classical rhetoric into the service of Christ, a concept first propagated by St Augustine, who encouraged Christians to enlist rhetoric in the battle for truth.[9] In Erasmus the idea of 'spoiling the Egyptians' appears first in an early poem, where this advice is put into Jerome's mouth: 'When you take away gleaming Egyptian vessels, prepare to build a noble shrine to the Lord.'[10] The theme recurs in a letter of 1496 to Henrik van Bergen and in the *Ciceronianus*, where Erasmus writes: 'To take away the wealth of Egypt is to transfer wealth to the adornment and use of our faith.'[11] Erasmus felt confident that rhetoric could be employed as a means of drawing the listener to God, to transfix and transform him, 'to send him away a different man.'[12] This was the power of the Christian orator described in the *Ciceronianus*. He did not slavishly imitate pagan writers but applied the technique learned from them to a new purpose, the glorification of God. 'This is the purpose of studying the basic disciplines ... to know Christ, to celebrate the glory of Christ.'[13]

Among the works in this volume the homily offers the most striking example of rhetoric in the service of Christ, but in the *Lingua*, too, there is a noticeable interplay of pagan and Christian thought, demonstrating that suitable precepts might be drawn equally well from Old Testament prophets and classical authors, especially from Plutarch, of whose writings Erasmus said that he had 'read nothing outside Scripture with such a high moral tone.'[14] Christian and pagan culture are also coupled in the commentaries on Ovid and Prudentius, externally by their joint publication and internally by the application of classical philology to a religious text, an aim that Erasmus had already pursued on a grander scale in his annotations on the New Testament.

The funeral oration for Berta Heyen, written by the young Erasmus for a motherly friend and patron, brings to life another classical genre[15] in a new, Christian context. Though Erasmus professes himself indebted to both Jerome and Cicero,[16] Berta Heyen is clearly a Christian heroine. The classical funeral speech celebrated the national heritage and praised the physical prowess and courage of soldiers. Erasmus dwells almost exclusively on the moral qualities of his subject. In fact, he declares that it is 'unchristian' to draw arguments from the subject's ancestral glory (20 below). Instead of his patroness' noble descent, he praises her good works and charitable spirit. Obedient to the precepts of the gospel, she had cared for orphans, fed and clothed the poor, and comforted the sick. And although shining examples drawn from ancient history are not lacking in the oration, the pious widow is compared specifically to Christian saints.[17] The speech concludes with the consoling thought that a devout Christian dies only to be rewarded with eternal life and with the Pauline exhortation to rejoice with the joyful (29 below).

A Christian slant is also given to the *Encomium medicinae*. Classical ideas are presented, then reshaped to fit the Christian philosophy. Aesculapius, the mythical founder of the art of medicine, was revered as a god by the ancients. Erasmus concurs with their high estimate of the first physician, but not with his deification: 'I do not personally approve of such actions by the ancients' (37 below). The statement that the physician displays godlike qualities in preserving and prolonging life is similarly qualified: '... though we owe this art, as we do everything else, to Almighty God'

(38 below). In advocating sobriety and moderation, Erasmus agrees with the classical notion that the physician cares for the whole man, not only for the patient's body, but adds that questions of ethics are more specifically the domain of theologians (39 below). Thus the oration, though classical in form, is unmistakeably addressed to a contemporary Christian audience. The transformation of the traditional argument from authority culminates in the endorsement of medicine by Christ. Undoubtedly it is a praiseworthy art, for 'Christ himself, the author and originator of all branches of knowledge ... professed to be a physician' (45 below).

The Christian tone is less pronounced in the *Oratio de virtute amplectenda*. It is replete with classical *exempla* and quotations, notably from Homer and Virgil (the former quoted in Greek, since the young addressee had just begun to study this language), and allusions to classical literature. The youngster's teacher is credited with a 'Nestorian' eloquence; the boy himself, though interested in 'Martial' pursuits, has already become a promising 'nursling of the Muses' and governs his 'Pegasus' well.[18] In the concluding paragraph, however, Erasmus turns to a Christian theme: secular and religious studies must go forward hand in hand. Accordingly, together with the oration, which was a showcase of classical learning, he sent some prayers, 'so that you may already begin to learn Christian doctrine along with your basic literary education' (13 below).

The Christian element is, however, completely lacking in the *Tyrannicida*, and with good reason: Erasmus had set himself the task of composing an oration in reply to Lucian's plea on behalf of a tyrannicide. It was to be a companion piece to the ancient forensic speech that he had translated from the Greek. The fictitious setting was a Greek court, and it was imperative for the literary success of the oration that the speaker, a pagan, stay in character. The speaker in the *Tyrannicida* argues against giving the state bounty to a man claiming to have slain a tyrant. This is Erasmus' only foray into the genre of forensic oratory, the most prominent branch of rhetoric in ancient literature.[19] Closely modelling himself on Lucian, Erasmus produces a masterpiece, well structured and well argued. He places the emphasis on *ethos*, the speaker's character, which, according to ancient theory, contributed significantly to the persuasiveness of a speech. Erasmus and Thomas More had translated a number of Lucian's works. Seeking a new challenge, the two friends decided that each of them should compose a retort to Lucian's *Tyrannicida*. It was a demonstration of *imitatio* at its best. The authors devised their own arguments but observed the classical norms of speech-writing. It was a friendly competition with gratifying results for posterity, for each man created a speaker after his own heart, Erasmus a dramatic wordsmith and More a level-headed advocate.

mainly produced ingratiating or plaintive letters and poems, but – as Bainton said – 'Let not those with university tenure or grants from foundations cast the first stone.'[23]

The bishop of Cambrai, whose Latin secretary Erasmus became a few years later, sponsored his studies in Paris, where the *Encomium medicinae* was written. The story behind its belated publication in 1518 illustrates another chapter in Erasmus' quid-pro-quo relationship with patrons. In August 1517 Henricus Afinius, a physician from Lier near Antwerp, promised Erasmus a present of silver cups. Erasmus in turn hinted that he might dedicate to him the second book of Gaza's grammar, which he had then in hand, or a composition on a more suitable subject at a later time (Ep 638). When the present was not forthcoming, Erasmus dedicated the grammar to Johannes Caesarius. Meanwhile he wrote a pressing letter to Afinius, urging him to make good his promise. 'Send me the cups you have so often promised,' he pleaded.[24] Any failure to do so promptly would make them both look like fools. Two months later Erasmus published the *Encomium medicinae*, with a laconic dedication to Afinius. The work, which had apparently lain buried and forgotten among some papers, was unearthed by Erasmus for the occasion. It represented, as he said rather ambiguously, a token of his feelings for the physician. We do not know whether Erasmus ever received the promised cups in return.

The year 1499/1500 was a turning point in Erasmus' career. He accompanied his pupil Lord Mountjoy to England, where he was introduced to a circle of like-minded humanists, many of whom became his lifelong friends and supporters. Among them was John Colet, who opened up to Erasmus an approach to theology more palatable than the scholastic method taught at Paris. Just as the humanists were appealing for a return to the literary sources of antiquity, Colet was advocating a return to scriptural sources. Erasmus had always felt a distaste for the medieval glosses, summaries, and commentaries that were the staple of scholastic teaching and considered them muddy pools compared to the golden river of Scripture. He now discovered a kindred spirit in Colet. When Colet founded St Paul's school, which offered a curriculum that was to Erasmus' liking, combining intellectual with spiritual instruction, he wrote for its pupils a number of textbooks and inspirational works, among them the *Concio de puero Iesu*.

On his first trip to England Erasmus also made the acquaintance of Thomas More, whom he described in a biographical sketch as so pleasant and agreeable that he dispelled any sorrow and lightened any task.[25] The *Moria* was written on his inspiration, and the translations from Lucian, composed during Erasmus' second visit to England in 1505/6, may also have been initiated by him. As Erasmus reports, More 'has taken delight especially in declamations, and, in that department, in paradoxical themes ... He wrote an answer to Lucian's *Tyrannicida*, on which topic it was his wish to have me as an opponent.'[26] The compositions appeared in 1506 in a joint publication of translations from Lucian. One can hardly imagine a more fitting tribute to their intellectual bond than this scholarly collaboration or a more satisfying consummation of their friendship than this sharing of a common interest in the witty Greek essayist.

Erasmus' friendship extended also to More's family, and the commentaries on Ovid and Prudentius are a token of his concern and affection for More's children. The commentaries were composed in 1523, however, during a darker period in Erasmus' life. In 1516 Erasmus had published the Greek text of the New Testament and his own Latin version. The text and annotations accompanying it immediately became the focus of a prolonged debate on the place of philology in theological studies and on the authority of the Vulgate, which had no official standing as yet but was nevertheless the *textus receptus*. Conservative theologians objected to Erasmus' enterprise on principle. They accused him of undermining the authority of the church by altering dogmatically significant passages, of casting doubts on the inspiration of the evangelists by criticizing their grammar and style, and of meddling in a subject-area that was the exclusive domain of professional theologians – Erasmus being in their eyes a mere *grammaticus*. Lengthy apologiae, justifications, and rectifications added to subsequent editions of the New Testament did nothing to silence Erasmus' opponents, who saw in him the inspirational source of the reform movement. When he composed the *Lingua* in 1525, Erasmus was under investigation by the Sorbonne. A few years earlier he had been obliged to defend himself against a series of acerbic attacks by the Complutensian scholar Diego López Zúñiga and had to answer criticism from the theologians at Louvain, where he resided between 1517 and 1521. The *Lingua* was the outpouring of a man who had experienced the abuses of the tongue and had suffered his share of backbiting, gossipmongering, and slander.

If one considers for a moment the psychological dimension of Erasmus' writings, it would appear that the *Lingua* was an attempt to externalize feelings of frustration, a sort of catharsis, while the translations of Galen, composed the following year, were an exercise in escapism. At least this is the motive given by Erasmus for undertaking the versions of Plutarch, a product of the same period. 'At this time,' he wrote, 'I gladly exercise myself in such fields, all the more because I see that the affairs of

Christianity have reached such a tumultuous state that it is no longer safe to speak of Christ.'[27] Erasmus' works reflect not only his writing skills and his learning, but also his circumstances and moods. Because the pieces included here span a considerable length of time in Erasmus' life, they present a many-faceted picture of the author, both as seeker of patronage and as patron of learning. They reflect his emotions and intellect, his idealism and cynicism, his craftsmanship and creativity – a tableau of qualities suitably illustrating the complex character and manysided talents of the author.

ACKNOWLEDGMENTS
The editors would like to express their gratitude to Craig Thompson for his valuable advice and to Jacqueline IJsewijn and Christopher McDonough for their many helpful suggestions. The copyeditor, Mary Baldwin, gave the text unstinting and meticulous attention. The index was prepared by Kim Kippen. Finally, the editors thank the Social Sciences and Humanities Research Council of Canada, without whose generous assistance the *Collected Works of Erasmus* could not be published.

EF and ER

Erasmus and the Greek Classics

Erasmus grew up in an era that was a turning point for Greek scholarship. During the latter half of the fifteenth century the rediscovery and publication of a number of classical texts had generated a new wave of interest in Greek studies. Erasmus himself was eager to acquire a knowledge of Greek, but his efforts were frustrated by lack of funds, unsympathetic advisors, and a scarcity of texts and teachers north of the Alps. Yet he persevered and ultimately succeeded in his quest. He was inclined to ascribe his success to a 'mysterious force of nature'[1] that had guided him in his studies, but external influences also contributed to his interests and shaped his goals.

Because of the circumstances of Erasmus' birth and the premature death of his father, direct parental influence may not have been a factor of great importance, but one cannot overlook the admiring tone in which Erasmus spoke of his father and the pride he took in his accomplishments: the fact that he had a knowledge of Latin and Greek and had copied out the classical authors with his own hand.[2] This memory may well have served as an inspiration to the young Erasmus. We must also assume that some of his teachers played a role in directing his interests. The schoolmaster Pieter Winckel, who taught the boy in Gouda and was later on to become his guardian, proved to be an obstacle rather than a source of inspiration to Erasmus, who described him as boorish and averse to scholarly ambitions.[3] At the age of nine, however, Erasmus entered the school of the Brethren of the Common Life in Deventer, where Alexander Hegius was promoting humanistic studies, giving his students a first taste of Greek.[4] It was at Deventer that Erasmus got his first instruction, although it may have consisted of little more than learning to write the characters and memorizing the meaning of individual words or, as Erasmus put it, sampling Greek 'with the tip of the tongue.'[5]

After the death of his father Erasmus was sent to a school of the Brethren in 's Hertogenbosch and, two years later, he entered the priory of Steyn to take the vows.[6] It was an unhappy period in his life and one that contributed little to his academic progress, for the Brethren were 'suffering from a lack of the best authors and living by customs and rites of their own in a darkness of their own making.'[7] It is clear that Erasmus' studies could not prosper in this stifling and oppressive atmosphere.

In 1492 Erasmus entered the service of the bishop of Cambrai. For some time he entertained the hope that his new position would afford him the opportunity to visit Italy, the centre of Greek learning, but his plans came to nothing. On the contrary, Erasmus found that his duties kept him from furthering his knowledge.[8] It was not until he was sent to Paris in 1495 that he could devote himself again to his scholarly interests. Although he found life at the Collège de Montaigu uncongenial, it seems that his Greek studies progressed. Greek occurs in his letters as early as 1489, but the practice cannot be used as conclusive evidence of his linguistic progress, since the phrases may well have been inserted at the time of publication.[9] Letters dating from the period between 1496 and 1499, however, show increasing evidence of Erasmus' familiarity with Greek as he put his newly acquired skills to use, joking with Thomas Grey, whom he called 'Leucophaeus,' and displaying his knowledge by quoting Homer in Greek.[10]

We do not know who, if anyone, was Erasmus' mentor in Paris, but Robert Gaguin is a most likely candidate for this role. Gaguin had acquired a knowledge of Greek on his travels to Greece and Italy, had published translations from the Greek, and taught Greek at the University of Paris from 1458 on. An exchange of letters between Erasmus and the ageing scholar indicates that he consulted the master on philological matters and had access to his well-endowed library.[11] A chance remark throws further light on the relationship between the two men. In the preface to the second edition of the *Adagia* Erasmus mentions that Gaguin was critical of the original text because Greek sources had not been consulted.[12] The remark may well be indicative of Gaguin's influence and of the advice, challenge, and encouragement provided by the French scholar for Erasmus, who was then at the beginning of his career.

In the summer of 1499 Erasmus accompanied his pupil, Lord Mountjoy, to England, where he was brought into contact with a number of humanists. He met William Grocyn, who was teaching Greek at Oxford, Thomas Linacre, who had published a translation of Proclus' *Sphere*, and Thomas More, who was to become his lifelong friend. Describing the atmosphere in England in a letter to Robert Fisher, Erasmus wrote: 'I find here a climate at once agreeable and extremely healthy and such a quantity of intellectual refinement and scholarship, not of the usual pedantic and trivial kind either, but profound and learned and truly classical in both Latin and Greek.'[13]

The society of his English friends made a deep impression on Erasmus and fired him with a new zeal for Greek studies. The letters written to Jacob Batt on his return to Paris bear witness to his dedicated efforts to improve his Greek.[14] As usual, he laboured under a lack of funds, but he placed a greater value on his studies than on his physical needs and professed a willingness to sacrifice comfort to higher goals, declaring: 'The first thing I shall do, as soon as the money arrives, is to buy some Greek authors; afterwards I shall buy clothes.'[15] He also spoke of engaging the services of a teacher by the name of Hermonymus, a native of Sparta, who supported himself by copying Greek manuscripts and giving instruction in Greek.[16] It seems, however, that Hermonymus lacked professional skills as well as ethics, for Erasmus describes him in retrospect as a 'hungry Greekling' who 'babbles Greek; a man who couldn't have taught even if he wanted to and wouldn't have wanted to if he could have.'[17]

Threatened by an outbreak of the plague, Erasmus left Paris in 1501 and returned to his native Holland, where he continued his Greek studies on his own. At various times he tried to kindle in his friends an interest in the subject. Thus he wrote to Batt: 'I am very anxious that you should know Greek, both because I find that a Latin education is imperfect without it, and also to heighten the pleasure we take in each other's society, as would happen if we both enjoyed precisely the same range of study.'[18] But soon Erasmus reported that his mission had failed, that Batt had neither the time nor the inclination to study Greek. An effort to interest Willem Hermans proved similarly ineffective, as Erasmus recounted in a letter to Jacob de Voecht: 'I have gone as far as Haarlem ... on purpose to visit my friend Willem, or rather to make a Greek out of him, taking a huge bundle of books with me; but all my trouble and all my money were wasted. By making the journey I lost twelve couronnes, and one friend along with them.'[19]

Erasmus not only promoted Greek studies but also sought contact with fellow scholars: In 1501 he wrote to a former pupil, Nikolaus Bensrott, inviting his co-operation; in England he encouraged Andrea Ammonio's work and expressed hopes of joining him in his efforts; but it was More above all who provided him with scholarly companionship.[20]

Erasmus' self-professed goal in Greek studies was modest. He wished to acquire a reasonable command of the language, a 'certain limited competence,' and in the fall of 1502 he was able to report with satisfaction: 'I have made such good progress that I am capable of expressing my meaning in Greek with reasonable proficiency and, what is more, extempore.'[21] By the end of 1506 he had published several translations from the Greek and thus concluded his apprenticeship,[22] but any account of his studies would be incomplete without mention of his Italian journey, undertaken *Graecitatis causa*, for the sake of Greek studies.[23] The beginning of his journey was inauspicious, as warfare disrupted all scholarly pursuits, but later on he was able to enjoy more peaceful times in Venice, where he spent eight months doing editorial work for the famous publishing house of Aldus Manutius. There he was in daily contact with the scholars of the 'Aldine Academy' and had at his disposal both texts and learned colleagues with whom to exchange ideas and opinions. Erasmus' career in Greek studies was rounded off by a lectureship at Cambridge and reached its zenith with the edition and annotation of the New Testament.[24]

In his quest for proficiency in both of the ancient tongues, Erasmus followed humanistic and philological interests as well as theological considerations. He was, no doubt, charmed by the 'Greek Muses, whose gardens bloom even in the depth of winter.'[25] He was greatly attracted by the poetic quality of a language whose wealth of expression could not be matched or paralleled in Latin. In fact, he took such pleasure in the Greek language and was so enamoured of Homer in particular than on one occasion he all but refused to part with a borrowed copy, exclaiming: 'Though I should fail to understand him, I should still derive refreshment and sustenance from the very sight of his work':[26] Self-gratification was not the main objective of his Greek studies, however: there were other, more compelling, reasons for the young scholar. Erasmus contended that without Greek 'a Latin education was imperfect' and 'liberal studies lame and blind.'[27] Apart from the immediate benefits of learning a language and gaining new rhetorical and linguistic skills, Greek literature offered an abundance of ideas and a wealth of factual information that was best absorbed in the original: 'For ... whence can one draw a draught so pure, so easy, and so delightful as from the very fountain-head?'[28] Moreover, the attentive reader would find these sources not only instructive but also edifying. Although Christian writers were the primary sources of spiritual guidance, pagan authors too could benefit the reader through their moral content. Among the classical Greek authors whose ideas could serve as an inspiration to the reader Erasmus singled out Plutarch, the most uplifting writer 'outside Scripture,' Xenophon, whose *Hiero* could serve as a model to Christian princes, and Lucian, whose characters spoke 'with a wisdom exceeding that which divines and philosophers commonly attain in the schools.'[29] The main significance of Greek studies, however, lay in their value for the interpretation of scriptural works.

Erasmus emphasized that, whatever other purpose was served, his studies were ultimately undertaken for the sake of theology. In 1500 he indicated the direction and final aim of his studies in a letter to Batt, saying that he had devoted himself to learning Greek so as to be better equipped for theological studies.[30] He reiterated this view in a letter to Warham, explaining that he translated Greek authors 'in order to restore or promote, as far as I could, the science of theology.'[31] His work on Jerome, on Romans, and on Galatians had convinced him that a knowledge of Greek was indispensable for the interpretation of Holy Scripture, that it was of the utmost importance to consult Greek manuscripts and to collate Greek and Latin versions in order to establish the correct text and to understand its meaning.[32] Erasmus' position on the role of Greek in Bible studies is expressed in a letter to Antoon van Bergen:

> I can see what utter madness it is even to put a finger on that part of theology which is especially concerned with the mysteries of faith unless one is furnished with the equipment of Greek as well, since the translators of Scripture, in their scrupulous manner of construing the text, offer such literal versions of Greek idioms that no one ignorant of that language could grasp even the primary, or, as our own theologians call it, literal, meaning.[33]

It was Erasmus' ambition to offer a clearer, more readable, and idiomatically correct translation. He wished to 'adorn the Lord's temple, badly desecrated as it has been by the ignorance and barbarism of some, with treasures from other realms, as far as in [him] lay.'[34]

In a letter to Colet he sounded an apologetic note, explaining that he was only spending time on secular Greek authors because he expected to gather 'by the way many flowers that will be useful for the future, even in sacred studies.' For the editor, interpreter, and textual critic a knowledge of Greek made the difference between conjecture and certainty, 'for it is one thing to guess, another to judge; one thing to trust your own eyes, and another again to trust those of others.'[35]

In this area Erasmus encountered much opposition from traditional theologians who considered any change in the wording of the Scriptures sacrilege and who associated the very study of Greek with doubts concerning the authority of the Bible. Erasmus strenuously combatted this attitude and eloquently defended the study of the ancient tongues against his reactionary colleagues. His struggle to make them recognize the merits of Greek scholarship and its useful function developed into a lifetime campaign. In 1505 he pointed out the value of collating manuscripts so as to reveal 'internal disagreements, or a nodding translator's plainly inadequate renderings of the meaning, or things that are more intelligibly expressed in Greek, or, finally anything that is clearly corrupt in our texts.' He concluded that 'those who venture to write, not merely on the Scriptures, but on any ancient books at all, are devoid of both intelligence and modesty if they do not possess a reasonable command of both Greek and Latin.'[36]

A letter written in 1515 and addressed to Dorp serves as a protreptic as well as an articulate defence of Greek studies. Erasmus' advice is summed up in his statement that 'a knowledge of [the ancient tongues] is so important for our understanding of Scripture that it really seems to me monstrous impudence for one who knows none of them to expect to be called a theologian.'[37]

In 1520 Erasmus reiterated his concerns in a letter to Campeggio, calling Latin and Greek the handmaidens of theology, the queen of the sciences,[38] and ten years later we find him still engaged in the battle against those who believe that 'there is no difference between knowing Latin and Greek and being a heretic.'[39] The relationship between philology and theology continued to occupy him in his *Annotationes* and in the polemics that followed his edition of the New Testament, but the dispute about the respective functions of philology and theology remained unresolved in his lifetime.

In examining Erasmus' editions and translations of classical Greek authors it is important to understand his views of the translator's task, to consider his stated aims, and to observe his own practices.

The translator's task, Erasmus says, 'demands exceptional skill, and not only the richest and readiest vocabulary in both languages but also an extremely sharp and alert intelligence.'[40] He set a high standard for himself, expecting the ideal version to reflect the stylistic qualities of the original without being deficient in accuracy or deviating from its meaning.

Erasmus' views underwent a certain change during the first phase of his publishing activity, in which he produced translations of three of Libanius' declamations and two of Euripides' plays. In his preface to Libanius he invoked Cicero's rule that the translator should 'weigh the meaning, not count the words,' but wanting to forestal any criticism he added that he 'preferred to err on the side of accuracy rather than of boldness.'[41] A few years later he modified this statement, now expressing mild criticism of 'the freedom in translating authors that Cicero allows others and (I should almost say excessively) practises himself.' He ridiculed in particular those who would hide their incompetence by terming their translations 'paraphrases,' thereby shirking the responsibilities of a translator.[42] The statement of his own aims remains equivocal, however, as he promises to preserve figures and texture, to recapture the force and effect of the Greek, and at the same time, to render the text 'verse for verse and almost word for word.'[43] To combine these elements and produce an accurate translation while recreating the style and duplicating the rhetorical or poetic form of the original was an ambitious undertaking for a novice and a challenge even to an experienced translator. His first venture was, however, crowned by success and added to the growing reputation of the young scholar.[44]

In the revised preface to *Hecuba* we find Erasmus gradually moving towards greater freedom in translation for the sake of clarity, smoothness, and rhetorical colour, but we also see him holding fast to the demand for *fides*, faithfulness to the original. He did entertain the idea of venturing beyond the proper role of a translator, saying that he 'would not be reluctant to alter the style and topics of the choruses,' but he never put the idea into practice.[45] As Erasmus became more proficient and experienced as a translator he saw less need for remarks explaining or defending his techniques, so that we are reduced to studying his practices in order to learn more about his methods.

Despite the fact that Erasmus' work was often completed in a hurry and that he is known to have dashed off a hundred verses in one bout or prepared a translation in a day or two,[46] his versions are generally accurate and closely parallel the meaning of the original. Misunderstandings, errors, and omissions do occur, but their number and significance is relatively small. Erasmus' most impressive quality as a translator is his versatility, the wealth of expression that allows him to recapture the desired nuance of a complex Greek term, to substitute or even create a suitable phrase where Latin lacks an equivalent, and to supply the appropriate Latin idiom for a unique Greek expression. For example, in one of Libanius' declamations he uses no less than five different expressions to translate the various meanings of Greek δίκαιον 'just,' rendering it according to the context as *justum rectumque, aequi bonique ratio, rectum, ius* and *quod par est*.[47] Greek composite words are occasionally imitated in Latin, but more frequently rendered by circumlocution. Thus ὑψιπετής 'high-flying' is paralleled by *altivolus*, but δυσκαταμάθητος 'hard-learned' becomes *perdifficile cognitu* 'hard to learn,' ἀνουθέτητος 'unwarned' is rendered as *admonitore carent* 'they lack an advisor,' συνδοκιμάζοντες 'discussion-partners' as *cum quo rem expendere possis* 'one with whom you can discuss the matter.'[48] For phrases that are idiomatic and cannot be translated literally Erasmus finds an appropriate substitute. Greek εἰ μὴ τοὺς προσήκοντας λόγους τὰ πράγματα λάβοι (literally 'if matters do not get an appropriate account') is suitably rendered as *nisi negotium, ut gestum est, narratur* 'if the matter is not told the way it happened.' Elsewhere the Greek interjection ὦ τᾶν 'my dear sir' is translated by the Latin idiom *quid ais* 'what is this you are saying?'[49] Generally speaking, Erasmus' version is rather more elaborate and wordy than the original. He is fond of using two Latin words for one Greek expression,[50] and on occasion adds phrases for explanatory or stylistic reasons.[51] On the other hand, we find instances of censorship, notably on the topic of divine power and, in one case, on a homosexual relationship.[52] This editorial interference, though perhaps justified by the demand for clarity and purity or motivated by moral considerations, is, however, restricted to translations of secular authors. It must be noted that in editing the New Testament, Erasmus applied different standards, frowning on displays of *copia* and stylistic niceties and, in general, rejecting all forms of unnecessary paraphrase and circumlocution.[53] From the translator of the Scriptures Erasmus demanded a closer, more scrupulous version that could do without rhetorical flourish as long as it was grammatically and idiomatically correct.

A few words may be added here on verse translations, which constitute a special case. Citing the practice of Horace and Seneca, Erasmus restricted the variety of metres found in Euripides.[54] He did so because it facilitated his task but also because he felt that 'such a mixture of kinds [of metres] yielded a result not very far removed from prose.'[55] In dealing with the composite words that characterize poetry he adopted the various methods already discussed. In addition, he took the liberty of replacing names by patronyms or circumscribing them by epithets, a practice which is, of course, in keeping with the genre.[56] As in prose, he often employed two terms to translate one Greek word and did not hesitate to coin new words, although he emphasized that he did not wish to imitate the grandiloquence of Latin tragedy and preferred to 'reproduce the concise clarity and neatness' of his original.[57]

Erasmus' activities as a translator of classical authors span almost thirty years, from 1503 when he presented a copy of his Libanius translations to Ruistre to 1530 when he published Xenophon's *Hiero*. Considering the length of this period it is surprising to note the absence of distinct stages in the development of Erasmus' skill in translation or in his methods. All of his translations, regardless of their date of publication, exhibit similar character-istics. There may be a slight shift from conservative, safe choices to more imaginative or daring versions, but Erasmus' basic skills are present even in his earliest translations, just as errors and omissions, the consequences of hurried execution, plague even his mature work. And whatever period of his life they belong to, Erasmus' translations are graced by the clear and lucid style that is his own.

The declamations of Libanius are Erasmus' first formal attempt at translating a classical Greek author. He considered the task a challenge to his skills and an opportunity to give a practical demonstration of his progress in Greek studies. These were his *progymnasmata*, his first exercises, on which he had chosen to gamble his reputation.[58] The expressions of uncertainty with which he describes his enterprise indicate that he was not at all sure of its reception. In 1503 he presented a copy of the three declamations to

Nicolas Ruistre, bishop of Arras and chancellor of the University of Louvain, who received the gift kindly and rewarded Erasmus' efforts with an invitation to dinner and a gift of ten gold pieces.[59]

Why did Erasmus choose Libanius as his practice ground? It seems that he selected the declamations not so much for the qualities of their author as for the availability of the Greek text.[60] Although Erasmus felt obliged to sing the praises of the author 'to whom the verdict of scholarship awards a leading place among the practitioners of Attic style,' he admitted that his subject was, after all, 'somewhat trivial.' The undemanding character of the declamations made them suitable practice-pieces for a novice translator who did not want to risk 'learning the potter's art on a great jar.'[61] The translations were not published until 1519, a delay which can be explained by the fact that the work would have made up only a very small book and that Martens, Erasmus' publisher at the time, was not as yet able to print Greek.[62]

Euripides' *Hecuba* and *Iphigenia* were the first of Erasmus' translations to be published and proved to be happy auspices for his literary career.[63] Some of the work or at least its conception may have pre-dated the translations of Libanius, for we know that Erasmus sent 'a Euripides and an Isocrates' to Nikolaus Bensrott in July of 1501 and invited his co-operation without, however, specifying a project.[64] We know for certain that Erasmus completed his translation of Euripides' *Hecuba* while residing in Louvain, that is, in the years 1502–3, and that the task occupied him for 'a few months.'[65] He presented a copy of the finished translation to William Warham, archbishop of Canterbury, during his visit to England in 1506, and was rewarded with a modest gift. The suggestion, made by Grocyn in jest, that the archbishop had kept the amount low because it was the custom of authors to tender their works to more than one patron embarrassed Erasmus and stung his pride. To prove his sincerity, while still in England he completed the translation of a second play, *Iphigenia*, and dedicated this work to Warham as well.[66]

Erasmus had several reasons for choosing Euripides as a testing ground for his skills. He felt challenged to the task by an earlier (in his opinion, inadequate) attempt by Francesco Filelfo to render Polydorus' speech as a funeral oration; he was urged on by Jean Desmarez, his former host and public orator at the University of Louvain; and he was encouraged by his English friends, to whose judgment he submitted the first draft.[67] He was also attracted by the poet's ideas, his masterful portrayal of human emotions, and his skill in argumentation. He was impressed by the playwright's 'rhetorical ability in marshalling arguments on one side or the other of a question' as well as by his style, his 'remarkably succinct, delicate, and exquisite' diction.[68] He did, however, find fault with the lyrics of the chorus, which he characterized as affected and obscure, a judgment that he extended to other classical authors as well: 'for nowhere did the ancients write more foolishly than in choruses of this sort, where, through excessive striving for novelty of utterance, they destroyed clarity of expression, and in the hunt for marvellous verbal effects their sense of reality suffered.'[69] Erasmus did not approve of this 'confusion or freedom (whichever it is)'[70] and considered the metric restrictions he had imposed on his own translation an improvement over the original.

Erasmus' work on Euripides was not confined to translating, but was also his first attempt at textual criticism involving Greek manuscripts. He therefore listed among the problems that he encountered 'poor texts, shortage of manuscripts, and a lack of commentators.' In a letter to Aldus he pointed out a number of passages that he suspected of being corrupt and made suggestions for emendations that have subsequently been adopted by modern editors.[71]

Erasmus' translations of Euripides were well received by his readers. Bade sold out the first edition within a year, and the popularity of Erasmus' translations may well account for the fact that the two plays were published more frequently than any other of Euripides' tragedies in the sixteenth century.[72]

Hecuba and *Iphigenia* were followed by translations of Lucian's dialogues. The date of these compositions is somewhat uncertain, although the publication date, November 1506, provides the *terminus ante quem*.[73] In his letter to Botzheim Erasmus mentions an attempt to translate Lucian's *Podagra*, an undertaking that he abandoned, however, because he was deterred by the abundance of epithets in the choruses and despaired of his ability to 'duplicate in Latin the felicity of expression found in Greek.'[74] During his visit to England in 1505–6 Erasmus returned to the task of translating Lucian, this time enjoying the companionship of More, who, like Erasmus, was attracted by Lucian's wit and biting humour. The result of the friends' co-operation or friendly competition was the translation of a number of dialogues, which Erasmus presented to friends and patrons 'on various occasions, as is the custom among the English.'[75] The dialogues were first published in 1506 under the title *Luciani opuscula*, but additions were made at each subsequent edition, with work on the translations spanning more than a decade.[76]

In the preface to *Gallus* Erasmus discusses Lucian's merits and explains what characteristics he finds most attractive and useful in the sophist's writings:

Recalling the outspokenness of the Old Comedy, but lacking its acerbity, he satirizes everything with inexpressible skill and grace, ridicules everything, and submits everything to the chastisement of his superb wit ... He possesses such grace of style, such felicity of invention, such a charming sense of humour, and such pointedness in satire; his sallies arouse such interest; and by his mixture of fun and earnest, gaiety and accurate observation, he so effectively portrays the manners, emotions, and pursuits of men, as if with a painter's vivid brush, not so much inviting us to read about them as to see them with our own eyes, that whether you look for pleasure or edification there is not a comedy, or a satire, that challenges comparison with his dialogues.[77]

Erasmus considered Lucian one of the most entertaining classical authors, but he valued him even more for the didactic element in his writings. The possibility of combining pleasure with profit is a recurring theme in Erasmus' prefatory letters. Lucian, he said, charmed his readers with his style and moulded their character with his satirical description of human vice and the evils of his age. His criticism applied not only to his own time but also to Erasmus' generation.[78]

Although Erasmus acknowledged these merits, he assigned to Lucian his proper rank in the hierarchy of authors. He did not neglect to point out that translations of secular authors were of slight importance compared to theological studies, that he pursued such pastimes in his leisure 'rather than do nothing.'[79] Here as elsewhere we find Erasmus torn between the scale of values applied by the theologian and the humanist respectively, a dichotomy expressed succinctly in a letter to Warham: 'You will say that the things I send are trifles. Why yes, they are: but scholarly trifles.'[80]

There was a lull in Erasmus' activities as a translator of Greek authors until the autumn of 1512, when we find him occupied with Plutarch. The first selection of *Moralia* was published in London in July 1513, with subsequent editions containing additional discourses.[81] Erasmus, who based his translation on the Aldine edition, found that his task included textual criticism, which was made difficult by a lack of manuscripts for collation. He repeatedly complained that the text he had in his hands was corrupt and admitted that he was not always successful in dealing with the problems involved, saying: 'I have overcome quite a number of them; a few, though only a small number, I have glossed over rather than removed.'[82]

Erasmus describes Plutarch's style as more difficult than Lucian's, mainly it seems, because of the many quotations inserted throughout, which gave the work the appearance of a literary mosaic. Plutarch's unique combination of elaborate style and recondite knowledge made him a challenging as well as an instructive author. Erasmus' view of the benefits and difficulties inherent in Plutarch is best summed up in his dedicatory epistle addressed to Alexius Thurzo:

> It is not easy for the translator to discover Plutarch's sources, especially since the majority of authors from whom he has plucked his flowerets and woven his garlands are no longer extant. Moreover, his concise and sometimes abrupt style, which transposes the reader's mind suddenly from one subject-matter to another, causes additional difficulties. It requires from the reader not only universal learning, but also attention and concentration.[83]

Erasmus was impressed by the learning displayed in Plutarch's writing and by the author's common-sense approach to ethics, which made moral ideas accessible to the general reader: 'Socrates brought philosophy down from heaven; Plutarch introduced it into our bedrooms.'[84] In his dedicatory epistles to individual discourses he emphasized time and again the moral benefits accruing to the reader. Plutarch provided a 'technique' for good living and could be used as an 'antidote' to man's natural faults.[85] Erasmus also drew on the stylistic and gnomic aspects of Plutarch's writings and used them extensively as a source for his *Parabolae*, *Lingua*, and *Apophthegmata*, published in 1514, 1525, and 1531 respectively.[86]

The qualities that attracted Erasmus to Plutarch are also present in Isocrates, whose rules for good government Erasmus published together with his own *Institutio principis christiani*.[87] The juxtaposition of the two works allowed Erasmus to complement the advice given by Isocrates in his *Ad Nicoclem* and to compete as a Christian with the precepts of a pagan author.[88] He approached the topic of political ethics once more when he undertook a translation of Xenophon's *Hiero*. He abandoned a first attempt because of seemingly insurmountable textual difficulties, but returned to the task a few years later and completed the translation. It was published in February of 1530 with the recommendation that 'it contained many ideas that would be useful even for our princes to know.'[89]

Some years before, Erasmus had translated three discourses by Galen, two of which are concerned with the study of medicine, a subject whose praises Erasmus had sung before.[90] The third essay is concerned with problems of epistemology. The *editio princeps* of Galen's *Opera omnia* published by Aldus in 1525 provided the impetus for Erasmus' enterprise. Once again he had to come to grips with textual problems and was obliged to edit and emend as well as to translate the treatises, but the work provided him with an opportunity to pay tribute to his physician friends, in particular to Jan Antonin, to whom the translation was dedicated.[91] Galen's subject and the questions he raised were matters of concern to Erasmus, and the treatises supported his views on the importance of liberal education.

In addition to translating, Erasmus was also involved in the editing of classical Greek texts. He prepared a critical edition of Isocrates' *Ad Demonicum*, together with a translation by Agricola, and wrote spirited prefaces to editions of Aristotle, Demosthenes, and Ptolemy.[92]

Although Erasmus enjoyed the fruits of his own labour, it was the reading public that profited most from his work. His translations were often undertaken for his own benefit, that is, to practise his skills or to provide suitable presents for his patrons. They were often by-products of larger enterprises, stepping-stones in Erasmus' career, yet it was of great advantage to Greek scholarship that he shared the products of his workshop with fellow students and, more importantly, that he made Greek literature accessible to those who had insufficient or no knowledge of the language. His unselfish attitude and sincere interest in aiding Greek studies by his publications is seen in his reflection on the declining popularity of his translations of Lucian: 'These trifles were snapped up at first by those who wished to learn, and warmly welcomed; but when the knowledge of Greek began to be widely shared, as happened most successfully in our part of the world, they began to fall into neglect, which I knew of course would happen, and am very glad it has happened.'[93] Far from resenting any personal loss, Erasmus rejoiced in the good fortune of the young generation who enjoyed the opportunities denied him in his own youth and who benefited from the revival of letters promoted by him throughout his life with such zeal and eloquence.

ER

Erasmus and the Latin Classics

The relationship of Erasmus' thought and works to the classical authors is matter for a book, even several books. This brief essay concentrates on three aspects of it: the use made by Erasmus of different authors and the value he ascribed to them, his changing interests from youth to old age, illustrated by the preparation of editions of Latin writers and translations of the Greek, and the balance kept during his creative years between the demands of his biblical and theological studies and his continuing loyalty to the classics. It requires an effort of the imagination for any twentieth-century student, even one who began early to specialize in classical studies, to conceive the role of the classical Latin authors in the consciousness of a young Renaissance scholar. Erasmus' first surviving letters, written from the monastery of Steyn, show that the twenty-year-old had absorbed many of the major Latin authors into his thought and expression and had acquired a lasting enthusiasm for others. Although his conscience as a Christian and his early devotion to the Bible and its great interpreters led him at times to relegate the classical authors to a marginal place in his reading and active scholarship, the writers whom he loves and quotes as a studious young novice are the same, indeed his favourite allusions continue unchanged, into his last years.

Probably before any other Latin authors Erasmus had read, reread, and learned by heart the plays of Terence: many phrases in his own Latin idiom occur first in Terence, and quite a few are rare outside the playwright. The schoolboys read the plays to form their own Latin speech; hence in an early letter Erasmus lists Terence with Cicero, Quintilian, and Sallust as one of his authorities in *prose*,[1] although he knew better than many of his contemporaries the many forms of verse in which Terence composed. Erasmus copied out the complete text of Terence by hand for an unidentified friend,[2] praising his style as 'wonderfully pure, choice, and elegant' and defending the plays for their moral goodness and their value in 'showing up men's vices.' Scarcely a letter passes without allusion to the archetypal flatterer Gnatho and his vain master[3] or to the contrasted lenient and severe fathers of Terence's play *Adelphi*.[4] This affection persists as late as 1532, when he dedicated his edition of Terence to the young sons of his Polish friend Jan Boner.[5]

Erasmus' student letters also reflect his rhetorical training; he quotes freely from all of Cicero's rhetorical works and dialogues on moral philosophy, with or without acknowledgment. Indeed many statements about Greek authors in Erasmus' writings were made before he learned Greek and concern works not extant in his own time; he merely repeats Cicero's verdict on the lost works. But although Erasmus practised and also preached in his works on composition (*De copia*, *De conscribendis epistolis*, *De recta pronuntiatione*[6]) the principles advocated by Cicero and Quintilian, he did not consider it urgent to edit the texts of any of their works. Indeed he seems to have begun with a prejudice against Cicero, for in a later letter, he admits that as a boy he found Seneca more attractive[7] and was twenty years old before he could tolerate prolonged reading of Cicero. Even so, his early letters quote often from *De officiis*, and when Willem Hermans recommends that this work be read repeatedly and carried everywhere as a constant companion he is certainly echoing Erasmus, who makes the same claim in his edition of 1501[8] – the first pagan work that he is known to have edited.

The third component in Erasmus' early classical reading was the poets, but unlike the modern student he read the Latin poets as much for their moral utility as for their aesthetic merits. In the list of poetic authorities he quoted to Cornelis Gerard only Virgil and Horace won his admiration on both counts;[9] then we can distinguish between the stylistic appeal of Ovid, Statius, Claudian, Lucan, and the elegists, on the one hand, and the moral or applied value of Juvenal, Persius, and Martial on the other. But from the beginning Erasmus is most likely to quote and incorporate into his argument Horace's *Satires* and *Epistles*, with their strong concern for individual morality and self-discipline; almost as frequent are his citations of maxims from the *Ars poetica* or the letter to Augustus on the criticism of contemporary poetry (*Epistles* 2.1); less common are quotations from the *Odes*, although these have been the most cited part of Horace's works for the last century and more.[10]

Yet Erasmus, if he had been asked at any time between 1489 and 1495 how he wanted to employ his gift for writing, would probably have acknowledged that he thought of himself as a poet.[11] A letter from Cornelis Gerard is our source for the genesis of Erasmus' poem 'lamenting the neglect of the art of poetry,' which Cornelis and Erasmus recast in the form of a dialogue.[12] This and many other poems in classical diction and metres were later published 'without his consent' in *Herasmi silva carminum*.[13]

A faint hint that Erasmus was still relatively unskilled can be drawn from Cornelis' tactful words: 'In order to make the poem ... give still greater pleasure to all and sundry, I took pains to see that it could be recited aloud with pleasant effects of sound ... and in order to achieve this more readily without impediment, I carefully excised all hiatus of vowels.'[14]

In representing their correspondence as 'based on a single bond of brotherhood, single devotion to the literary pursuits we share,'[15] Cornelis and Erasmus no doubt saw themselves as another Catullus and Calvus, though Erasmus enjoyed a closer relationship with young Willem Hermans. In the disguised autobiography written to Lambertus Grunnius, Erasmus speaks of nights spent with his friends in secret reading of the poets and in contests at composing verse.[16] The years from 1489 gave birth to Erasmus' first dialogue, the *Antibarbari*, in which, through the speeches attributed to his friend Batt, Erasmus proclaims a passionate vindication of good letters. He blames upon the Christian enemies of pagan literature not only the loss of many great works of the classical authors but the degeneration of theology, of grammar, and of contemporary writing in prose and verse.[17] The modern *barbari* hate what they have not read, not realizing how much the Christian Fathers owed their thought and expression to their pagan predecessors: if men cannot live without the practical inventions of the pagans, why try to live without their intellectual discoveries?

> It was Greece, devoted to study, which discovered the arts; then Latium entered into rivalry with her, and was the victor as far as concerns war, but barely equalled her achievements in literature and oratory. Some concerned themselves with searching out the hidden causes of things; others, bound by the fetters of Prometheus, observed the regular revolutions of the heavenly lights. There were those who tried to explore divine mysteries; one discovered methods of argument and another laws of oratory; some portrayed the customs of men with great sagacity, and for some their great concern was to hand on to posterity the memory of past deeds. In law, in philosophy, how the ancients laboured! Why did all this happen? So that we on our arrival could hold them in contempt? Was it not rather that the best religion should be adorned and supported by the finest studies?
>
> Everything in the pagan world that was valiantly done, brilliantly said, ingeniously thought, diligently transmitted, had been prepared by Christ for his society ... their age produced this harvest of creative work, not so much for them as for us.[18]

Both in this manifesto on behalf of the classical heritage and in Erasmus' correspondence with Gerard and Hermans we see the partisanship and purist arrogance of youth. But letters such as Ep 23 (to Gerard) also reflect the commitment of the young Erasmus to Latin as a living language and his sense of a renewal of taste and clarity in both prose and verse. In it he champions the pioneers of this stylistic renaissance, starting from his hero Lorenzo Valla[19] and including the Italian humanists Rodolphus Agricola and his pupil, Erasmus' own teacher Alexander Hegius; the letter adds now forgotten contemporary poets in the continuing tradition that Erasmus ardently desired to advance.[20] Even in 1496, when he published the volume named after the devotional poem *Carmen de casa natalitia Iesu*,[21] he will include complimentary poems for Gaguin and Andrelini; and in his preface to his Scots friend Hector Boece,[22] like a Propertius or Horace imitating Callimachus, he disclaims any desire to thrust his verse upon the public but protests his contempt for bad poets and his indifference to the envy of the ignorant. With the exception of the *Carmen de casa natalitia Iesu*, the late poems lack the feeling of his passionate Horatian poems to Servatius, but Reedijk remarks on his increasing mastery of the metres, which can be seen for instance in the four-hundred-line Sapphic ode to the Blessed Virgin.[23]

The influence that drew his interest away from poetry was Jerome, whose letters are quoted repeatedly even in the early exchanges with Cornelis Gerard. In a letter of 1497 Erasmus excuses himself from having no poetry to offer his patron, because he has followed Jerome's advice and busied himself with theology in order to learn what he intended to teach.[24] He relishes Jerome's literary richness (even claiming that Jerome put Cicero in the shade)[25] and praises him in the dedicatory letter of the first version of the *Adagia*.[26] By this time he was already preparing a commentary on Jerome's works, and a begging letter to Batt justifies his importunity by his plans for the years ahead. He must pursue his studies in Greek, which he had begun in Paris, but above all he needs money in order to buy the complete works of Jerome: the 'limited competence' he is hoping to acquire in Greek is to enable him to devote himself entirely to sacred literature.[27] This is the first reference to the work on Jerome that was to preoccupy Erasmus for the next fifteen years. It is not within the scope of this essay to trace the course of this work, but simply to indicate the dominant role played by Erasmus' devotion to Jerome during the period of his own prime, from 1501 to 1516, when Erasmus' studies have to be divided between the Latin and Greek *ethnici* on the one hand and the gospel and the Christian Fathers on the other.

Very shortly after his return to Paris at the end of 1500 Erasmus published his first textual edition of a Latin author, Cicero's *De officiis* (Paris: J. Philippi, probably late in 1501). The prefatory letter to Jacob de Voecht, which was somehow omitted from the original publication, was instead printed with a second preface to de Voecht in Erasmus' augmented edition of 1519.[28] He knew the fully annotated text by Pietro Marso (Venice: de Tortis 1481) but offered to de Voecht a neat pocket edition with brief notes, to be carried always with him as a talisman, a herbary, and a spring, granting its drinker eloquence and immunity to misfortune. As for the text, though he complains of its flaws, Erasmus gives no hint that he has sought out rare manuscripts. He has merely tried to counter scribes' miscopyings and displacement of words, partly by collating editions, partly by informed guesswork based on Cicero's style. If we measure this comment against his prefatory letter to the *Tusculan Disputations* (1523),[29] it is apparent that his critical methods increase in refinement, but we must also allow for the limitations of his early working environment, in contrast with the greater access to manuscripts for collation that fame, his residence in Basel, and his association with the house of Froben brought to him.

During the thirteen years from 1501 to 1514, years which included two visits to England (from late 1505 to spring 1506 and from 1509 to 1514) and time in Italy (from 1506 to spring 1509), Erasmus produced educational works for Colet, the *Moria*, the *Adagiorum chiliades*, and an expanded version of the *Adagia*, delivered by Birckmann to Froben in 1513 and printed in 1515. He also composed the *Enchiridion* as part of the *Lucubrationes*.[30] He had begun to use his knowledge of Greek to respond to the increased public demand for reading Greek in translation generated by the new availability of printed books,[31] and it is small wonder that he had little time to spare for editions or annotation of Latin authors. While the work on Jerome and the New Testament undoubtedly dominated Erasmus' thoughts until the publication of his editions,[32] he was always plunging into new enterprises and might leave aside virtually completed works (such as *De copia*, begun in 1499) when diverted by his absorption in new projects. Something of the variety of his activity during his second visit to England can be gauged from Ep 264 to Pieter Gillis (autumn 1512). He reports that he has just completed work on his collection of proverbs (the enlarged *Adagiorum chiliades*); he is bent on finishing his revised Latin version of the New Testament and his edition of the letters of Jerome; he hopes for time to undertake emending the text of Seneca.[33] He also mentions the Plutarch works that he had recently translated, and he is anxious for news from Bade of the second publication of the *Moria* and of his enlarged collection of Lucian's dialogues.

Only in 1514, thirteen years after the publication of his edition of Cicero's *De officiis*, does Erasmus again edit ancient, non-Christian texts, publishing two very different types of writing with different printing-houses. The *Opuscula* are a set of school texts chosen chiefly for their moral content and brevity. The most important of these is the *Disticha Catonis*, a

at that time to Cato the Censor, for
ed the Greek translation of Maximus
collection as the *Cato* or *Catunculus*
oned only in April of the year of
comments, 'the *Cato*, with the other
ince been finished, but for want of
opy.'[34] A later letter claims that the
a day,[35] but this statement should
casual boast necessary in a letter to
Martens, September 1514), entitled
igatore, included the one-line maxims
liani), the sayings of the Seven Sages
ome excerpts from Aulus Gellius and
Erasmus, however, who calls himself
preface to Jan de Neve,[36] probably
ly gesture towards Gonnell or other
ession. Then as now there was a
nd it is significant that the *Opuscula*
inor adjustments). Of the forty-four
p to the year of Erasmus' death, we
er of Strasbourg, reprinted them in
per 1517, and September 1518, while
d by five different printers: by Mast
gne, Gryphius in Lyons, and in Paris

al text that Erasmus published in this
when Erasmus had sent to Bade his
Moria, translations from Lucian and
tragedies, Bade had written a rather
uished scholar and author who might
rks he had offered the publisher were
rs. Bade was both afraid of provoking
case of the Seneca because one text of
ed at Paris by Petit (1511, printed by
Keysere was printing the text of the
eared in this year. Nevertheless Bade
tragedies 'accompanied by your brief
sed and partly annotated by Erasmus,
re is no reference to it in the ensuing
ds, and it seem to have attracted little
came on the market too late. In this

decade the pressure on publishers to print editions of popular ancient authors must have been a crucial negative factor in the sequence of the publications of Erasmus, as of his contemporaries. Even the letters of Jerome, which he offered to Bade at this time, could not be completed by Erasmus swiftly enough for the publisher to satisfy his customers and so came to be offered to Froben, by whom they were given their first edition in 1516.

Erasmus' first catalogue of his compositions, the letter to Botzheim written in 1523 and expanded in 1524,[38] suggests that he had first worked on the Senecan tragedies when he stayed with Aldus in 1508 'after the appearance of my *Proverbia*.' (He had at that time also contributed to the Aldine editions of Plautus and Terence, but only in clarifying the colometry of the lyric and non-dialogue metres.) He had benefited by ancient manuscripts for the Senecan tragedies and originally left the material under Aldus' control, but subsequently, after a second scrutiny, he sent the tragedies to Bade. There were (and are) fine manuscripts of Seneca at Cambridge, and Erasmus credits to the stimulus of these manuscripts his new work on Seneca. In Erasmus' day it was common to attribute all the philosophical writings of the younger Seneca to the author of the *Controversiae* and *Suasoriae*, so that Erasmus edited the prose of father and son together for the *Senecae Lucubrationes* published by Froben in 1515.[39] We know from several letters that he left his material for the text with Beatus Rhenanus and a young untried reader, Wilhelm Nesen,[40] and while the letters immediately after publication hold Rhenanus responsible for the many errors of this edition, Erasmus later transferred his reproaches to Nesen, reporting that the young man had either lost the notes and concealed their loss or tried to introduce his own readings into the text. Certainly Erasmus came to realize that it was not safe to leave such an enterprise before it was seen through the press, and he remedied the mistakes of his first edition by his preparations for and supervision of the later full-scale edition of 1529. But he had extreme difficulties with the text; for instance he reports that he had access to no manuscript of the *Quaestiones naturales* (none is now extant) and had to base his text on a printed edition, probably one of the four Aldine editions of 1490, 1492, 1495, or 1503. He adds that he edited conservatively, correcting only obvious scribal errors and adding his own conjectures in the margin.[41]

Erasmus did not rest content with the first edition of the New Testament (*Novum instrumentum*, Basel 1516) but spent the bulk of the years before the second edition (*Novum Testamentum*, Basel 1519) in reworking and refining his text. At this time, however, he was also working on the Latin historians in response to a new public interest that had been intensified by the discovery of manuscripts containing lost parts of the major historians. In 1517 he sent to Matthias Schürer of Strasbourg his text and annotations to the *History of Alexander the Great* of Quintus Curtius Rufus, dedicated to Ernest of Bavaria[42] and published in the following year. Froben himself was preparing an edition entitled *Historiae Augustae scriptores* but containing, besides the later writers now known under that heading, Ammianus Marcellinus and Suetonius' *Lives of the Caesars*. Despite the general attribution to Erasmus on the title-page, he edited only the Suetonius.[43] As often, he considered the dedication an investment in material patronage and so transferred the original homage from the ungenerous Albert of Brandenburg to Dukes Frederick and George of Saxony. In this as in other dedications to princes he emphasizes the value of the historical texts in teaching statecraft, with their cautionary example of the bad princes and models of good ones, but this emphasis is perhaps more a gesture towards the addressees than a true indication of the value of historical works in Erasmus' eyes.[44] He might relish a historian like Sallust, whom he had almost certainly read as a school-text, for his pungent style (Sallust is among the authors whose phrases are most frequently commended in the *Copia*); no doubt he also relished Sallust for his moralizing and his delineation of character; and he constantly draws on historians and biographers such as Suetonius or Plutarch for examples of virtuous or heroic action and for cautionary anecdotes. But he does not discriminate between the systematic historian and the collector of edifying tales like Valerius Maximus.[45]

It may seem that Erasmus is indifferent to the preoccupation of history with factual accuracy, and Bietenholz has stressed how Erasmus diverges in this respect from the tradition of humanists like Politian, whom he admired, by leaving aside the Ciceronian principles of truth and clarity of explanation in historiography. But he was moved to give less honour to the truthfulness of history by two factors: scepticism, born of his own researches, about the capacity of historians to discern the truth and a concern, drawn from his study of the Fathers, for a higher level of truth than particular fact. Aristotle had given to secular rhetoric a tradition whereby *fabula*, poetic fiction, depicting what was likely to happen, was nearer to the truth of human nature than *historia*, which merely reported events, however arbitrary or coincidental. So too from a Christian point of view the value of historical narrative lay beyond the factual level and came from its anagogical counterpart, the moral or theological truth (*historia mystica*) that it represented.

Thus, as Bietenholz has shown, Erasmus grew to be more pessimistic about the power of secular history either to retrieve the truth or to improve the morality of its readers. In his considered judgment, expressed in his commentary on Psalm 33, he sets aside Livy and the great Greek historians as fallible and at best concerned with the surface of events.[46]

For all his familiarity with the ancient historians, Erasmus seldom rises to the same faith in history as a guide to principles of government that dominates his preface to Suetonius; generally he uses history, not for historical purposes, but as a moralist, for its illustration of individual characters and its inspiring examples.

A special reason can be advanced for Erasmus' scant use of Tacitus. Major portions of his work, the first six books of the *Annals* and the *Germania*, were only rediscovered during Erasmus' prime. The manuscript on which scholars depend even now for *Annals* I–VI was found at Korvei in 1508,[47] and the *editio princeps* of the *Annals* is as late as March 1515. Although Erasmus uses the later books as his source for the life of Seneca in the 1529 edition of Seneca's works, and seems to know the *Dialogus* quite well, he appears indifferent to Tacitus,[48] and may never have been really familiar with his work; perhaps the historian's disillusionment offended him, or perhaps his subject-matter: the immorality of the Neronian court offered less edification than Livy's republican worthies to the impressionable reader. Froben published the second edition of the complete *Annals*, with the addition of the newly found *Germania*, edited by Rhenanus, at almost the same time that Erasmus wrote his commendatory letter for the new edition of Livy published by Schöffer of Mainz in 1519, but Erasmus mentions the discovery of 'several books of Cornelius Tacitus' only as a foil to the newest addition to the text of Livy, a large part of the missing book 33 and of book 40, in a manuscript lost almost immediately after it was turned to print.[49] He stresses the difficult demands on the editor caused by the new manuscript, which was 'sketched in with a brush rather than written.' He had loved Livy in his own youth,[50] and perhaps was tempted to recall this period of his life, for he addresses his prefatory letter to 'all antibarbarians and lovers of good literature,' and recommends Livy as a rich source of history which will enable his readers, whom he calls his 'excellent young friends,' to reap a harvest of eloquence in Latin. Did Erasmus believe that only the young student would want to purchase or consult Livy, or is it merely that his love of teaching led him to put these readers foremost?

In Erasmus' last years of retirement at Freiburg two further discoveries prompted him to renew his role as publicist for editions of the Roman historians. In 1531 Simon Grynaeus edited Livy for Froben, incorporating the new manuscript of books 41–5 that he had found at the monastery of Lorsch. Grynaeus had wanted to preface this edition with a letter of dedication to Melanchthon, but, perhaps because Melanchthon was controversial as a reformer, perhaps to do honour to Erasmus, Froben and Herwagen printed a letter from Erasmus to young Charles Blount, giving an account of the new discovery.[51] Erasmus describes the manuscript as 'of marvellous antiquity' but 'written in the old fashion, with the painted letters undivided, so that it was most difficult for anyone but a learned, careful, and practised reader to distinguish word-divisions'; he also stresses both the fidelity of the editor to the text and the splendour of this extensive new find, which far surpassed the discovery of 1518. But he offers no detailed critical appraisal of Livy – after all the author was familiar and much published. There is evidence for one more occasion on which Erasmus was invited to salute a new historical find. In July 1532 he reports a visit from Herwagen urging him to write a letter 'about Ammianus' for Gelenius, who was then editing Ammianus with the newly discovered books 27–30.[52] Erasmus declares that he wrote such a letter on the spot, but Allen does not indicate that this letter found a place in the edition of Ammianus.

It seems that the practical function of ancient texts – as manuals of government for princes or of behaviour in the family or society for citizens – was represented in almost every pagan Latin work edited by Erasmus; he loved Virgil and Horace, but he edited the moralists. So now 1519 saw his enlarged edition of Cicero's *De officiis* with the *Laelius de amicitia* (how to be a good friend and a good citizen) and *Cato maior de senectute* (how to make the best use of old age) and *Paradoxa Stoicorum*. The first edition in this form is 'probably'[53] that of Martens of Louvain, dedicated like the first edition to Jacob de Voecht. The prefatory letter (Ep 1013) extols the amazing power of the pagan Cicero to stir the reader more effectively to virtue than many a Christian is moved by the gospel itself, and praises the work as a personal companion, an ideal means of teaching for the young, and a comfort for the old. So too in the *Convivium religiosum* of 1522, not only Chrysoglottus, the lover of eloquence, but Eusebius, the mouthpiece of Erasmus himself, declares that he cannot read Cicero's *De senectute*, *De amicitia*, *De officiis*, or the *Tusculan Disputations* without kissing the text before him and reverencing Cicero's pure heart for its heavenly inspiration; he does not hesitate to count him among the Christian saints themselves.[54] Even so Erasmus does not forget his old literary training, and adds in the preface to his beloved moral works that his notes are largely designed to vindicate Cicero's Latinity against the charges of linguistic unorthodoxy.

In fact Erasmus found time during his preparation of editions of Arnobius and Hilary to revise his edition of the *Tusculan Disputations*, a work whose praise of virtue as a tool enabling man to face pain, injustice, and death could satisfy the highest principle of Christian self-denial and martyrdom. Erasmus' dedication describes some of his editorial procedure: his servant-pupils were set to compare the manuscripts to which he had access, and then he decided between the variant readings. He reports that where neither of the alternative readings was obviously superior, he preserved both, placing one in the margin. As in his work on the dramatists, he was particularly interested in the correct division of the verse quotations with which Cicero illustrated his argument. He also added a few discreet conjectures and some explanatory notes, 'all at a cost of two or three days' labour taken from [his] work on the Scriptures.' In his praise for Cicero Erasmus again singles out the moral benefits of his teaching, but mentions as well the intellectual merit of Cicero's erudition in contemporary and earlier historical writing and his clarity and skill in expressing in Latin the abstraction of Greek thought. He saw Cicero as extending philosophy from the governing classes reached by the Greeks to make it accessible to the common folk.[55] He goes further than he had in the prefatory letters to *De officiis* in his vindication of the honourable pagan,[56] and expresses his gratitude to the new benefactors, the printers who have made the company of great writers widely available.[57] It is perhaps only human nature that he should not recognize the implications of his own youthful impatience with Cicero[58] but urge his friend to impose the edifying writer upon his young pupils, along with such poets as are pure in thought or at least such chosen passages of poets like Martial as do not offend innocence.[59]

But in spite of his emphasis on the moral benefits of the ancient writers, Erasmus never outgrew his love of style in language, and in the following year he composed an exegesis of two hymns by Prudentius for More's daughter Margaret Roper and presented as a gift to More's son John a rhetorical commentary on the *Nux*, an elegiac poem attributed to Ovid and blending the form of a civil lawsuit with that of self-defence in a criminal court.[60]

Erasmus used the Latin authors as a source of information on lost Greek works and events of the Greek world; they were also for him and his contemporaries a sort of encyclopaedia of geography, natural history, astronomy (and astrology), pharmacology, and medicine. In *De ratione studii* he prescribes Pliny and the Roman antiquarians Gellius and Macrobius for the growing boy as a source of factual knowledge, although he recognizes that the sources of these writers were often Greek, and in particular Aristotle and his school.[61] Since the seventeenth century carried European science beyond the ancient lore, scholars have retained Erasmus' faith in the literary style and rhetoric of classical authors but no longer have his reasons to consult the ancient technical writers. Erasmus' special recommendation of Pliny is borne out by his practice, for he writes to Batt in 1500 that he cannot tell him which jewels are beneficial to poor eyesight, because he does not have his text of Pliny with him.[62] We might also see it as a mark of his easy trust in biological matters that he can quote from Pliny conflicting (and intrinsically improbable) statements,[63] for his chief concern with plant and animal life was as material to point a moral or adorn a tale.

Thus it is not surprising to find Erasmus concerned in Froben's edition of the elder Pliny's *Naturalis historia*. Erasmus had already worked on Pliny, contributing notes to Bérault's Paris edition of 1516, but Allen suggests that the initiative for the edition came from Froben, who had begun to search out surviving manuscripts in the previous year, borrowing a manuscript from Murbach which according to Rhenanus was still in his possession in late 1525.[64] Erasmus will have combined study of the available manuscripts with consultation of the editions of Ermolao Barbaro (to whom he gives special praise in the dedicatory letter), Beraldus, and Johannes Caesarius, the last being printed at Cologne only a year before. The prefatory letter to Stanislaus Thurzo, bishop of Olomouc, uses Pliny's own collection of monuments and marvels to praise the durability of works of the intellect, which outlast all monuments; Erasmus calls Pliny's work a treasure house, declaring that 'Pliny's subject is the whole world' and stressing his achievement despite a life of public service.[65] There is a strong element of advertisement in the preface; the claim, for instance, that no man ever studied this work without becoming distinguished, and the strictures on the carelessness of previous scribes and printers. Erasmus launches an ironic attack on conservative editors who are scandalized by emendations, but protects himself from their retorts by emphasizing the support guaranteed by his *codex vetustissimus* to the emendations that he himself has made.[66] Yet despite his pride in the text and his delight in the curious facts contained in Pliny's massive work,[67] Erasmus left the business of providing textual notes to Rhenanus, who published his *In C. Plinium* separately in the following year. Rhenanus, however, showed himself an arch-conservative, criticizing even Ermolao for relying on conjecture rather than adhering to the reading suggested by collation of the manuscripts.

It may be more illuminating to turn to an 'original' work, composed by Erasmus in the same year, as a sample of the ancient authors Erasmus used and the purposes to which he put them. The *Lingua* is chiefly concerned to deter the reader from irresponsible or malicious speech and redirect his eloquence to prayer and the promulgation of Christian teaching. Erasmus draws extensively on his classical reading for arguments, allusions, and quotations illustrating the many varieties of abuse of language – especially from Plutarch, on whom he had recently been working.[68] One short essay 'On Talkativeness' is dismantled and every story in it reused, and Erasmus draws almost as generously from Plutarch's collection of apophthegms (which he later made the basis of his own *Apophthegmata*). Near the midpoint in his argument Erasmus rises as it were from pagan literature to the holy Scriptures, and produces a catena of denunciations from the Psalms, Ecclesiastes, and the prophets against the venom of a slanderous tongue.

But the work's chief merit lies in its last part, the positive exhortations to speech that is imbued with charity and will draw men towards God; and it is here that Erasmus relies least on his classical learning and offers most of his own wisdom and personal convictions. At first it might seem that the Latin authors contribute little even to the repetitious and undisciplined first section of the book. But Erasmus has not only invoked the rhetorical precepts of brevity and discipline of speech from Cicero and Quintilian or the moral anecdotes of his favourites Gellius[69] and Valerius Maximus, he has, as always, expressed his own argument in quotations and adapted phrases from Terence and from Horace's *Satires* and *Epistles*; he has drawn on encyclopaedic material – which he never challenges – from Pliny, who supplies a series of alleged antidotes for types of venom; he relies on Cicero and Celsus for his physiology; and he takes from other rather less factual sources, notably Lucan and Virgil's *Georgics*, further illustration of medicinal herbs and antidotes.[70]

The years from 1525 were beset with anxiety. Erasmus was committed to biblical exegesis, but was now criticized and attacked from more than one side in the conflict over Luther and the reformers: not only by Luther himself, and by less scrupulous men like Hutten, but also by the theologians of the Sorbonne and of Louvain, not to mention the offended representatives of the friars and of the monastic orders. He describes himself, in Horace's image, as an old gladiator forbidden to retire from the arena; all the time that he would like to give to scholarship is taken by apologetic and polemic.[71] In such circumstances even criticism given in good conscience seemed a hostile act. At this time even his philological interests took on a polemical edge, with the composition of one of his most elegant and lively dialogues, the *Ciceronianus* (Basel: Froben 1528). This was a justified criticism, by one who, in the words of Werner Ruegg, loved Cicero's spirit, and loved his style because it conveyed and illuminated that spirit,[72] of a more pedantic cult of Ciceronian Latin as practised by men like Christophe de Longueil, who would write only such Latin words and phrases as could be attested in the writings of Cicero. Such purism could only frustrate the continued use of Latin to communicate subtlety of thought and genuine personal feeling. Erasmus embodies this self-defeating purism in the character of Nosoponus, the Ciceromane, whose health is suffering from his obsession. The arguments of Erasmus' representative, Bulephorus, are designed to distinguish between proper and improper imitation of Cicero. Most importantly they show the misuse of the Ciceronian ideal by men whose true motive is paganism, making Ciceronian Latin the tool of a counter-culture motivated by resentment against Christianity.[73] Against these Erasmus affirms the Augustinian ideal of Christian eloquence, based on Christian loyalty and belief.[74] To the literal Ciceronians he answers that true eloquence worthy of Cicero depends on more than words or style;[75] the essentials are a sense of propriety, thorough knowledge of one's topic, and sincere commitment; without knowledge this is impossible, without a sense of fitness it is absurd.[76] Mechanical imitation of Cicero's diction provoked Erasmus into what outsiders saw as an attack on Ciceronian Latin, but to Cicero himself Erasmus does full justice: while he reports and apparently endorses the ancient criticism of the orator for lack of brevity, austerity, or vigour,[77] he stresses more than once the thorough rhetorical training, the wide erudition, and the natural gifts that enabled Cicero to achieve excellence, and he uses Cicero's own rhetorical principles to urge on the neophyte.[78] To imitate Cicero is not, he argues, to copy mannerisms or even the general tenor of his style in an alien society with a changed state and church,[79] nor is it possible for a man of one personality to duplicate that of another, especially one so pre-eminent; for the greater the excellence, the worse the failure of the undistinguished imitator.[80] What is needed is imitation, not of Cicero's surface, but of his method of training and preparation and the standards he demanded of himself, which included a willingness to respect and learn from all his predecessors.[81] In refuting the superficial 'apes' of Cicero Erasmus shows how deeply he had absorbed and endorsed the best critical values not only of Cicero but of Horace and Quintilian, and this ostensibly anticlassicizing work is among those which owe most to his familiarity with the classics. What he admired in Cicero was the man's whole nature; so in his recommendations to the would-be writer, the final goal is that the good Christian's speech should be informed and sincere, the living likeness of his own spirit.[82]

The *Ciceronianus* was republished in 1531 with a more technical study of Latin and Greek diction, the *De recta latini graecique sermonis pronuntiatione dialogus*,[83] which again dramatized an educational issue, establishing on the basis of earlier scholarship a consistent pronunciation for the ancient languages and offering a code of symbols very close to the modern system for distinguishing the units and sub-units of the periodic sentence.

A letter of 1527 reflects the literary tasks Erasmus had in hand and their relative priority in his eyes.[84] He was preparing the fourth edition of the New Testament, working on his translations of Chrysostom (published in instalments from 1525 to 1527) and some Athanasius (published in this year with Chrysostom), revising his paraphrases on the New Testament, preparing a new revised and enlarged edition of the *Adagia*, composing his reply to Noël Béda, and going over the text of Seneca's *Moralia* for a fresh edition because of his embarrassment at the errors left or imposed by young Nesen in the earlier edition.[85] This shame explains his care to obtain essentially practical motives behind much of his concern with the classics. The boys are urged to practise every kind of verse, since their own exercises will enable them to receive more pleasure from the poets and to acquire the skill to diagnose scribal errors that violate the metres of a text. As in his earlier work on Plautus and Senecan tragedy, Erasmus specially annotated his Terence to aid the inexperienced in construing the metrical forms, which he describes as rather irregular and freely changing. (Indeed, although Terence uses a smaller range of rhythms than Plautus, he makes far more use of metrical change as a mood modifier within the scenes). Erasmus had always loved to compose manuals and aids to good Latin style; it is appropriate that this edition of Terence should be his last substantial treatment of a secular author, one written from affection for children, and addressed to the generation that would soon replace his own.

EF

ORATION ON THE PURSUIT OF VIRTUE

Oratio de virtute amplectenda

translated and annotated by
BRAD INWOOD

This formal epistle is addressed to Adolph, prince of Veere (1490?–1540), the son of Erasmus' patroness Anna van Borssele (c1471–1518), to whom he wrote Ep 145. Anna was a maternal granddaughter of the Bourbon duke Louis I; hence Adolph could claim French royal blood (4 below). Philip of Burgundy (1453–1498), Adolph's father, was the son of Anthony of Burgundy (8 below) (1421–1504), the bastard son of Philip the Good (1396–1467), the duke who established the Burgundian control of the Low Countries, which later fell to the Hapsburgs when his granddaughter married Maximilian. This justifies the boast of illustrious Burgundian ancestry.

Adolph's father, recently dead when this letter was written, held high office at the court of Philip the Fair (1478–1506), who ruled the Low Countries for his father Maximilian and to whom Erasmus' *Panegyricus* was addressed. Adolph himself had a successful career in the service of the Hapsburg-Burgundian regime. For details, see Adolph of Burgundy in CEBR I.

At the time of this letter (1498), Adolph was living at Tournehem, the seat of Anthony of Burgundy, and was under the tutelage of Erasmus' friend Jacob Batt. Erasmus wrote two other letters to Adolph, Ep 94 and Ep 266, written in 1512 when Adolph was about twenty-three.

The *Oratio de virtute amplectenda*, originally called *Epistola exhortatoria ad capessendam virtutem ad generosissimum puerum Adolphum, principem Veriensem*, is the first work in Erasmus' *Lucubratiunculae* (first edition Antwerp: Dirk Martens 15 February 1503). It appears next under the title *Exhortatio ad virtutem ad Adolphum principem Veriensem* in the *Lucubrationes* (Strasbourg: Schürer 1515 and 1516) and was published with the *Enchiridion militis christiani* (Froben: Basel 1518), and also with the *Liber de praeparatione ad mortem* (Froben: Basel 1535); twice it was included in *Declamationes quattuor* (Cologne: Cervicornus 1525; Cologne: Soter 1536). For further details of publication see Allen Ep 93 introduction. The text used here is LB V 65D–72D, which has been collated against Schürer 1515. There are no significant changes in the text, and only a few minor changes involving spelling, word forms, and punctuation.

The present translation is independent of the excerpts constituting CWE Ep 93.

ORATION ON THE
PURSUIT OF VIRTUE

DESIDERIUS ERASMUS OF ROTTERDAM TO ADOLPH PRINCE OF VEERE

My dearest Adolph, when I consider the matter carefully I do not, as a rule, conclude that the ancients' habit of formally praising kings and emperors with panegyrics,[1] even to their faces, was caused by a vicious tendency to ubiquitous toadying[2] and flattery. Rather, my view is this: intelligent men who had an exceptional understanding of nature and of the human spirit gave up hope that any noble and lion-hearted king with fastidious ears would ever come to tolerate the moral authority of an adviser or the stern censure of a critic. So, acting out of a concern for the public interest, they changed their tack; they kept on towards the same goal, but took a less obvious route. Thus, these wise men showed their princes a sort of image of the perfect prince, almost as though it were a painting on canvas, but under the guise of a panegyric, in order that the princes could examine themselves against the model offered and admit to themselves in the privacy of their thoughts how far they fell short of the standard of the prince being praised, and learn without being shamed or taking offence what faults should be corrected and which virtues should be displayed. One pretext could thus serve two purposes, namely, that good princes might review their deeds and bad ones could be advised of their duties. That sort of eulogy was, then, no more than a pleasing way to give advice, a flattering way to offer criticism, and, in short, a medicine that was necessary but bitter and therefore coated with honey.[3] This practice was a concession made in times past to the violent temper of barbarian kings, not, I think, from some shameful motive, but from prudence. But to foster children's studies and encourage them with flattery as though by giving out little confections is so far from being considered a bad practice that it is recommended even by the great experts.[4]

What is the purpose of all this, you ask? My plan, to be sure, was to use a little preface like this to avert and prevent the charge of flattery, because I had decided to treat with you in a somewhat undignified manner and to play the child again for a while in the company of your childhood. But, noble Adolph, I am not even going to praise you, really. No, what I shall do, rather, is simply to show you to yourself as though in a mirror, so that you can know yourself.[5] I do not, however, want you to go so far as to fall in love with yourself and die on the spot, like Narcissus in the poets' tales;[6] but I do want you to be constantly aware of how great a debt you owe to God, the author of your good fortune, aware of the station you were born to, and aware of the heights you must struggle to if you are to avoid the feeling that you have been something less than a success despite all of heaven's favour.

Unless I am mistaken, this must have been the meaning of that famous mirror of Socrates,[7] which this wisest of men used to send his young friends to look into. His purpose was that those who saw that they were generously endowed with bodily and intellectual gifts and with the blessings of fortune should be incited to a zeal for virtue by the very fact of their good luck, when they realized that so much natural endowment created both a duty and an expectation of a substantial expenditure of effort.

He also wanted those to whom such gifts had been more grudgingly given to be stimulated to correspondingly greater efforts, so that hard work might make up for the deficiency in natural endowment. And although there is no excuse at all for slackness in such an important matter, nevertheless those who have worked hard and been disappointed by fortune are much less blameworthy than people who have had good fortune but are not doing anything with it.

But you, my dear Adolph, have been so generously endowed with all that heaven can provide to help you to acquire complete virtue that unless you display excellence of every kind you will not seem to be living up to either the blessings entrusted to you by God or to the expectations of your friends and family. In the first place, I need hardly mention the exceptional, astonishing generosity shown to you by Fortune. No sooner were you born than she placed you with her own hands, as it were, at the very summit of human affairs. She did not elevate you to greatness, she bore you to it. No, more than that, she made you a most prosperous prince even before you were born, by endowing you with a lineage distinguished on both sides by the most noble ancestors: on your paternal side, your line derives from Philip, duke of Burgundy,[8] a hero fit to be matched with any of the ancients, and on the maternal side from the Bourbons,[9] that is, from the kings of France. I pass over for now the great wealth and splendid power of your family; I make no mention of the marriage alliances formed by both your dear sisters with powerful princes; I do not congratulate you on the great piety of your mother, who is giving you what amounts to a second birth with her almost incredible concern for you and who thinks she has not really given you life unless she has also brought you to the peak of virtue; I will not even refer to the fact that already, although you are a mere lad, most of the chief courtiers and also the illustrious prince Philip[10] himself see an unlimited natural potential in you and so rival each other to show you an auspicious devotion and favour.

There is a blessing more important to you than all the others, one that even that most wise king[11] was not ashamed to boast about, namely, as he phrased it, that you have been granted a good soul; and also that the creator, that true Prometheus,[12] has given you a very fruitful intelligence, which is worthy of your wealth, your high station, your ancestry, and your young body; that in addition Nature, the master architect, has adorned this body most generously, with all the gifts of Venus and the Graces, to be a sort of jewel-case for your virtues, no doubt so that your most beautiful mind might dwell in a home of equal beauty.

And indeed, it is not a trivial matter for a prince to excel the common herd in bodily beauty as well as in virtue, for it is clear to me that, despite the objections of Seneca, notable men have had good reason to approve that maxim of Virgil's: 'virtue is more pleasing when it occurs in a fair body.'[13] But none the less this forbidding old philosopher himself, whom I might almost call the most stoic of the Stoics, mentions as though it were something astonishing that a certain Claranus, a friend of his, was exceptional for his talent and virtue although he was physically ugly; and then he reasons on the basis of this one example that an outstanding mind can hide beneath any sort of exterior. Nor indeed does Virgil deny this; he merely says that a spiritual beauty is more pleasant and satisfying to men's eyes if it occurs together with an attractive body. Now who could be so short of common sense as to think that this could be denied? So I am all the more puzzled that this sensible man should have written that such a widely accepted opinion, expressed by the poet, seemed false to him.

But let us leave Seneca and return to the point. The poets, who have an amazing ability to imitate all things, attribute the most beautiful bodies to godlike minds, whom they certainly wish to appear to be the happiest. Not even Plato himself hesitated to accept this idea, for when he was wrapping wisdom's mysteries (as he usually did) in the cloak of poetry, he assigned to the gods (that is, to the blessed minds that are free from any taint of earthly decay) fair chariots and horses sleek from their diet of nectar and ambrosia.[14]

Homer, who is a sort of Ocean[15] of all the arts and sciences, used to present Achilles, Ulysses, Menelaus, and all the other heroes whom he makes exceptional for their virtue as outstanding in physical beauty, repeatedly calling them 'of form divine and like unto the gods.'[16] On the other hand, Homer gave to Thersites a freakishly misshapen body to go with his base and cowardly character: 'He was bandy-legged and lame in one foot, and his shoulders were hunched round his chest; atop, his head was pointed and scantily covered with fuzz.'[17] Our own Virgil[18] imitated this technique assiduously, as he did so many aspects of Homer's art, when portraying Aeneas, Iulus, Euryalus[19] and many others.

Why, even Socrates, not only the wisest of philosophers but also the most incorruptible man of all time, agrees, in Plato's *Phaedrus*[20] (albeit somewhat obscurely, but still, with more than passing eloquence), with the view that a beautiful body indicates the possession of a beautiful mind or is at least an aid in acquiring it. For he portrays and characterizes the body as a handsome steed and the soul as a handsome horseman. Finally, even Aristotle himself thought that the quality of a mind could be inferred from the evidence of the face and body; he also thought that soft flesh was a mark of an utterly flabby mind.[21]

In the end, though, even these authorities might be doubted, if historians too did not agree in testifying that Pythagoras, Scipio Africanus, and countless others who were thought to be more than mortal because of some godlike moral qualities all had beautiful and pleasing bodies. Indeed, body and soul are so closely connected that the latter corresponds to the condition of the former and the mind's excellence is reflected in a beautiful external appearance; and, on the other hand, the body's condition has a reciprocal effect on that small portion of divine breath (as Horace puts it[22]), since it is seated deep inside the body, is bound to it, and is surrounded by it as though by an oyster's shell. (For this is one of those coarse Socratic comparisons that Alcibiades makes fun of.[23])

But I am afraid to say too much about physical beauty. For despite all this, I by no means exalt bodily gifts or intellectual endowment so much that I would either discourage those who have a smaller share in them from the pursuit of virtue or childishly flatter you, who are a mere child. On the contrary, I am bringing them and you, not to the pool of Narcissus, but to the mirror of Socrates, in order to stimulate in the others a stronger zeal for virtue, as they are less aided by natural gifts, and so that you will realize what an unworthy and ludicrous failing it would be if you let your mind go ugly and unkempt inside such a beautiful body and if your spirit were squalid with decay and filth beneath your handsome exterior. And it would be equally unworthy if you offended by neglecting to cultivate with noble pursuits that part of you which is immortal, despite the fact that nature has given refinement to that other part of you which is the most worthless. Lastly, you should consider no horror more horrible than, as the Greeks put it, a treasure of coal[24] kept in a finely wrought box, or, to put the point in a more Cynic fashion, than keeping filth or something even fouler than filth in a jewelled casket.

Further, my dear Adolph, you must not think that you are being praised when someone says that you are handsome or noble or talented. For there is a maxim of Epictetus that is utterly true and that you must remember tenaciously (if, that is, the delicate ears of the court will tolerate such a Stoic old man): that whatever can be given or taken away by Fortune is completely beyond our power and so, totally irrelevant to us.[25] We have not yet, therefore, praised the real Adolph, but merely entered in the books God's freely given generosity to you, which must be charged to your account unless you make it fit to return a profit. And the rest of the virtues for which a man may earn praise can certainly not be praised in one who is still of such tender years without stooping to the flattery of a greedy parasite.

And yet we are looking forward to the yield those virtues will produce in season, at the harvest-time of your life, and I do not think you will disappoint our expectation. For it is the richly blooming springtime of your youth that arouses in us the highest hopes. Already now your virtues swell like grapes heavy on the vine.[26] At this very moment, though you are still a mere lad, you show the signs of a sort of double excellence; that is to say, that of your father's spirit, which is equally outstanding for the virtues of war and of peace, together with that of your mother's mind, over whose character Fortune herself realizes with wonderment that she has no power. He indeed is borne aloft by his blazing virtue[27] and by the fame of martial glory. But she provides an unparalleled example for us: she has combined with her female sex a masculine strength of mind; with the lofty refinement in her style of life that her station, not her character, requires a self-restraint that passes belief; and with an exceptional nobility and the proudest of lineages a modesty and affability greater, almost, than what is found in a humble commoner; your mother, to sum it up briefly, has combined the Christian and the courtly lives.

Thus, Adolph, this twofold promise that you already show reminds us of both of your parents, the one utterly invincible and the other completely pure[28] and modest; for you are drawn to the martial pursuits and at the same time you are not repelled by the literary leisure of the Muses. You appear, therefore, to have been born and moulded for both sorts of life equally, for the practical life preferred by Dicaearchus and for the theoretical life which was dearer to Theophrastus' heart.[29] This latter is, of course, the one which Plato, in the *Republic*, considers to be both more important and more happy;[30] nevertheless, he says that the wise man should be dragged back to the other life, by force if necessary, for the sake of the public interest.[31] For the private citizen, who lives only for himself, there should be a free choice of which life he will lead; the prince, though, must certainly follow both, since he is born to serve his country and not himself. Homer attributed both forms of life to Ulysses, just as Virgil did to Aeneas. The practical life is seen when the poets harass their heroes with long wanderings and various dangerous adventures and plunge them into the midst of fearful battles; the theoretical life is shown when the poets send Ulysses and Aeneas down to the underworld. I think that Plato is making the same point when he demands that those who are chosen to rule the state must have a balanced and moderate cast of mind, which is neither spirited to the point of ferocity nor listless to the point of sloth. And he thinks, moreover, that this type of mind should be the product of two opposite forms of education, music[32] and gymnastics.

And this, certainly, is just the cast of mind I think I can detect in you; for I see in you a sort of balanced natural talent, blended from the heroic spirit of your father and grandfather[33] and from the gentleness and piety of your mother. Indeed, I can see a reflection of your father's and grandfather's virtue in the way that you already guide in those little hands of yours the reins of an unruly Pegasus,[34] with skill to match your bravery. This monstrous beast can barely feel the weight of your tiny body, and yet he obeys its technique and courage: you can make him run or stop, turn a tight circle, spur him to jump, rein him in to a fixed gait or do a jolting little dance; you can have him race in full gallop across the plain, then climb sharp inclines, then plunge down steep hillsides – obeying every flick of your boyish left hand. There are other signs of this virtue: something regal shines forth on your youthful brow, a mark of heroic majesty; despite your youth you have none of youth's limitations; and you yield to none of your comrades in archery, running, or wrestling.

On the other hand, when I look you over from top to toe[35] in a different light, I see how little there is in you that is unworthy of one destined to be a prince, that is, nothing lowly, dull, or ignoble and, conversely, nothing savage, arrogant, threatening, or insolent. Rather, you have eyes that are neither soft nor stern, but friendly; a brow neither censorious nor wicked, but quick and lively; a kindly face, full of charm; a bashful mouth; cheeks of a most becoming modesty and always more than ready to blush; your speech is unassuming and restrained and your gestures dignified. I note too how devoted you are to your father, how respectful to your grandfather, how obedient you are to your teacher and how accommodating to your comrades, how little disposed to hauteur or moodiness with your servants and far removed from impudence against anyone. In brief, when I reflect on your moral character, I find nothing redolent of the habits of court or of your station; I seem to gaze on the spitting image (as Plautus might say[36]) of your most virtuous mother.

These characteristics in you are, of course, important if we are praising your present youthful character, but vital for our expectations and as it were predictions of your future condition. But what confirms our hopes for you most strongly is the fact that in addition to your natural talents you have in your home an outstanding teacher for each of these kinds of excellence. For military virtue, your tutor is your grandfather, a man who lacks none of the qualities expected of a brave general; for philosophy, that Platonic 'music,' as

it were, that I referred to before, your teacher is Jacob Batt,[37] who is a man –
by Immortal God! – of such outstanding erudition, such exceptional moral
purity, and such unparalleled eloquence!

Is there anything that your homeland could not expect from you, now
that such an outstanding educator has charge of such a promising natural
talent? Indeed, he has charge of a pupil who is not, as so often occurs,
already mature and inflexible because of his age. But just as in Homer that
renowned Phoenix was made tutor to Achilles while he was still a little boy,
almost a mere infant, 'to teach him all things, to be a speaker of words and a
doer of deeds,'[38] so Batt immediately took charge of your infant years, when
you were hardly even weaned. He shared with your nurses the task of
nourishing you; they cared for your tiny body and he trained your mind.

Your mother, as you can see, was even then acting with a purpose: that
your tiny ears should receive the famous precepts of philosophers together
with your very milk; that the new vessel of your mind should be filled with
the unguent of philosophy, whose aroma would be given off for the rest of
your life; that your little tongue should be kept from being corrupted by the
solecisms of the vulgar crowd, but rather steeped in the purest nectar of the
Muses; and that your heart, still unformed and able to adopt any character,
should be guided by her friendly counsels.[39] Some ages are too late for the
introduction of virtue, but none is too early.[40]

Someone else might either ignore the value of these influences or think
that they need only be touched on in passing. I, however, think that they are
practically the only topic worth mentioning, since they are, as the saying
goes, the very stem and stern of a man's true happiness.[41] Not many people
can equal or surpass the nobility of your ancestry and the other gifts given
you by Fortune. But it is a blessing that is yours alone, almost, and one
perhaps not shared with any of the princes in our country, to have been
entrusted, while still in your formative years, to a man capable of filling the
blank page of your mind with pure and salutary opinions. He has the ability,
because of his great erudition; he has the will to do so, because of his great
virtue; and he has the power to accomplish the task, because of his great
diligence. Batt will use excellent philosophy to forearm you against the
courtiers' blandishments and certain men's words that are even more
dangerous to your character, just as an attendant Mercury[42] would use a
powerful charm of moly[43] to ward off the potions of Circe.[44] In our part of the
world, a man with an education better than the ordinary is a rare bird[45]
indeed; even more rare is a man of pure and blameless character; but the
rarest of all and in fact as scarce as the phoenix[46] is someone who has
combined a profoundly learned mind with a character utterly free of
blemish. In Batt you have received a tutor so accomplished in all of these

respects that I do not hesitate to claim that you are more fortunate than Achilles, who had Phoenix as a tutor, than Dionysius, who had Plato, Alcibiades, who had Socrates, Alexander, who had Aristotle, or than Nero, who had Seneca. But really, on this account you are not so much indebted to Fortune as you are to your parents, whose careful selection acquired the services of such a man.

In general, this is virtually the only blessing that great men should wish for, and yet it is the only one they usually lack. For what good is noble birth if you lack a sound education? Moreover, it is hard to train a prince to be virtuous unless you have started at it before he is aware that he is a prince. Philip, the famous king of Macedon,[47] a man praised for many achievements, had sound ideas on this matter and used to congratulate himself, thinking that he was exceptionally fortunate because he had raised his son when Aristotle, who was the only man worthy of having such a pupil entrusted to his care, was teaching philosophy. Should I, then, not congratulate you most heartily, my fortunate Adolph? For at home you constantly see, hear, and have all to yourself a teacher of such calibre that you do not need to balance his character against his learning, or his learning against his character, or some faults against his virtues, but you can safely imitate him in all aspects without qualification. If his erudition is considered, what is more exceptional? if his life, what is more pure? if his eloquence, what is there more admirable? if his sense of humor, what could be more delightful?

Time and again, my dear Adolph, you read in the poets about Phoebus with his golden lyre. You read that Orpheus[48] could stir brute animals, oak trees, and even rocks with his tuneful harp. You read about Minerva, queen of the arts and sciences. You read of staff-bearing Mercury,[49] whose power rests in his magic wand. You read about the famous Nine Sisters,[50] who preside over learning and refined literature; and then there are the Graces, who foster affability and human kindness; and there are the vales of Helicon and its tuneful fountain.[51] Lastly, you read too of the goddess Peitho,[52] whose Latin name is Persuasion. Now, do you think that these are mere nonsense and empty words? They are real things, of exceptional value, all of which are there to be observed in Batt, and not just observed; they are also there for you to benefit from.

What else, I ask you, could it possibly be, this clear sweet voice of his, which can carry over a great distance without any hoarse shouting, if not a lyre of Phoebus[53] producing a godlike tone on its golden strings? And who is there with a wit so dull, so animal, so hard as stone, that he could not be aroused, soothed or subdued by the sweet eloquence of Batt, more honey-tongued even than Nestor?[54] Come, then, what is his discourse, which flows so smoothly from the channels of an honest heart, always pure, always clear, always abundant, if not a bubbling spring from the eternal Castalian fountain?[55] You and your classmates constantly imbibe this voice through your ears and practise imitating it in your own conversation. Does it not make even the other students eloquent and fluent, as though it were a real magic potion they had drunk? Furthermore, who could fail to recognize the presence of the goddess Minerva, as it were, when he so effectively instructs his audience with his erudition, convinces them with his sharp wit, and delights them with his varied style? And then, whenever he soothes and delights everyone's hearts so marvellously with those superbly light and witty jokes of his, don't you feel that every charm and grace just bubbles from his lips? Surely he reminds us a bit of Mercury,[56] when he uses some secret skill to adapt his discourse to each different kind of character and so sweeps anyone at all into whatever emotion he wishes to produce? In fact, that Persuasion who sways the heart[57] seems to sit on his lips alone. To live with him and converse with him is nothing less than to stroll in the groves of Parnassus.[58] Finally, whoever has gazed on that encyclopaedic learning of his, which ranges unrestricted over every discipline, will look no further for the Muses' chorus. Who would not begin to admire, love, and revere either Jacob Batt because of such learning, or learning itself because of this man? Believe me, it would be a serious error and an act of deep ingratitude if you did not count as a special mark of favour this aspect of your good fortune, which is one that even the richest kings do not often receive. And – by the Immortal God! – what else is as important, what else is important at all for the happiness of princes than to acquire a wisdom based on one's own knowledge and not one limited to other men's maxims, and to learn as children from virtuous and wise men those lessons which they will never hear from their flatterers when they are adults? In fact, I have not yet been able to decide which is the more fortunate, you for having such a tutor as he or Batt for having so fine a pupil as you. I think that both of you are most blessed, each for his own reason; and since I love you both, I congratulate him because of you and also you because of him. For you have acquired such an excellent cultivator for the most fertile field of your mind, and he at long last has found a raw talent worthy of the full application of his exceptional skill.

At this point I would go further and say that not just you two, but even literature herself deserves public congratulations. At last literature has now begun to be fostered and written by people who can pay her back with interest for any glory she may bring them, and not just by the likes of Ennius, Plautus, and Caecilius.[59] If works of literature are written by someone of low station, then, despite the brilliance they may have, they are tarnished and somehow obscured by the author's low rank. But when written by men of your nobility, even middling efforts acquire an amazing fame. For learning adorns high rank and, in return, high rank adorns learning. And so literature herself seems to be exultant with joy, and I think I can see the famous sisters upon Helicon congratulate themselves and race to clasp you, their dearest nursling, to their bosoms and kiss and hug you whenever you draw your pen across the page with those gifted little fingers, when you practise your Latin, and your Greek too, with a tongue that is lisping and still barely under control, and when with your pretty and noble little mouth and your dear sweet voice you already declaim in prose and modulate the strains of verse.

All hail to your talent, my lad! I pray to God, greatest and best,[60] to preserve and foster your mind and the outstanding beginning you have made, and to deign to bring your virtue, already, as it were, putting forth tender shoots, to full fruition by the influence of his lucky star. I pray him to grant productive and fertile growth both to your youth and to your noble aims; otherwise, indeed, we may seem to be deluded in taking a short-lived and hollow pleasure in the infancy of your virtues, as though in the gardens of Adonis.[61] We see this frustration befall others often enough and would deplore seeing it in your case too.

Beware: do not let the blessings you have draw you into complacency. For although Nature and Fortune have made you so rich with all their gifts that you could surpass Pandora[62] herself, I would still count it as nothing done if an equal measure of hard work were not added to these advantages. Although hard work is almost crippled without such advantages, yet these too, without the hard work, will be utterly useless if they are neglected, destructive if you turn insolent, and deadly if you abuse them. If the stars of heaven have bestowed on you all they can when at their most favourable, if the Rhamnusian maid has poured out her horn of plenty for you all at once,[63] none the less it is up to you to make the greatest contribution towards developing an excellent mind. So come now, struggle with might and main to prove equal to those gifts, equal to the hopes of your family and friends, equal to the greatness of your ancestors, and equal to the efforts of your excellent teacher. When everything you need is in such plentiful supply, it would be a terrible disgrace if you fell short of your potential. And to help you continue with the fine beginning you have made, my dear Adolph, I shall not stop singing in your ears those words of Homer – but why not in Greek,[64] rather, since you are already studying this language?

And you, my friend, I see that you are fair and tall,
Be valiant, so that even a man in later days will speak of you.[65]

And since, as I have so often said, you have at hand all you need to help you win perfect praise – 'a following wind and the waves'[66] – make that other saying of the same poet true as well: 'And the wind and the helmsman guided straight the ship.'[67] If you do all this, I am sure that you will eventually bring great glory and support to your race, to your country, and to all your family and friends by means of your literary accomplishments, and to literature because of your high station in life.

In closing, I add one point; may you take it as closely to heart as possible, and make it your firmest belief: there is nothing so worthy of the noble and the well-born as religious devotion. I warn you, and not without reason, for I know for a fact that there are some men at court who are irreverent enough to believe and shameless enough to say that Christ's teaching need not concern princes, but is best left to priests and monks. Stop your ears against their deadly incantations and follow the guidance of your mother and Batt. And so that you may already begin to learn Christian doctrine along with your basic literary education, I am sending you some prayers.[68] I wrote them at your mother's request, with the encouragement of Batt, but expressly for you. I have, therefore, adapted the style somewhat, so that they will be appropriate to your age. If you use them regularly, you will improve your style and at the same time learn to scorn those rather warlike little prayers, marred by both a profound ignorance and an abysmal superstition, which generally give pleasure to the common sort of courtiers.

Farewell.

Paris. In the year of our Lord 1498

FUNERAL ORATION

Oratio funebris

translated and annotated by

BRAD INWOOD

This rhetorical address (apparently the one referred to in Ep 28 to Cornelis Gerard) was written by Erasmus when he was about twenty-one (c 1489), in memory of his friend and benefactress Berta Heyen. She was the widow of Baert Jan Heyenzoon, who had been dead at least since 1474. She was prosperous enough to have bought and sold real estate in Gouda in the 1470s and 1480s. By 1484 she was a 'matron' of the hospital of St Elizabeth, which was located near a Minorite convent in Gouda (23–4 below), and had acted on its behalf in 1487. Berta's own house, at which Erasmus and other clerics were entertained, was on the Westhaven.[1] She died on 9 October, the feast of St Bridget (28 below).

Berta's two surviving daughters, nuns resident in Gouda, are other- wise unknown, although one of them has been speculatively identified with the Elizabeth of Ep 2. They were Augustinian nuns (Allen I 74), for whom Gouda boasted four convents at the time. Erasmus himself was still in an Augustinian monastery; indeed, despite the veneer of classical learning, this speech is almost completely formed by the ecclesiastical atmosphere in which the young cleric still lived, quite contentedly to all appearances.

Erasmus' early interest in Jerome (see 19 below) strongly influenced the balance struck between Christian and pagan themes in his eulogy of Berta. He borrowed from Jerome almost unchanged a topos from Cicero's lost *Consolatio* (26 below and n42) – an apt illustration of Erasmus' regard for Jerome as a model of the Christian humanist he himself would become.[2]

The text used for this translation of the *Oratio funebris* is that in LB VIII, which is the first edition, and is based on a single manuscript from the collection of P. Scriverius. On the provenance of this manuscript, see Reedijk 159 and 132. Biblical references are to the Vulgate, and modern numbering for the Psalms is given in parentheses. The inexactness of some of the quotations has necessitated fresh translations of them, rather than the use of a standard version. Significant differences from the Clementine edition are mentioned in the notes, as are the few minor textual errors in LB.

BI

FUNERAL ORATION
FOR BERTA HEYEN

It has been a long time, my dearest daughters and sisters, since I decided to send you some pages with which you could soothe the grief inflicted upon you by the death of your mother. But whenever I take pen in hand in order to set down on paper the praises of our Berta, believe me, I immediately break out in tears, my fingers turn numb, my joints stiffen, my spirit swoons, and I am so overcome by sorrow that I cannot even give a bit of serious reflection to your mother's virtues, let alone write about them. How often have I begun this speech, and how often have I thrown it down, overcome by sobbing and sorrow? How often have I taken it up again, stiffening my resolution and temporarily forcing back my tears, only to throw down again the task just resumed? How many times have I given it up altogether, and stubbornly tried yet again to take up the task? But just when I am making these efforts to apply a salve to the wound of your sorrow, I realize that I myself have been stricken by a much more painful blow; and just when I am beginning to examine your sores so that I may administer a healing ointment, my own wounds break open once again.[1] And what wounds are these? I do not mean bodily ones, I assure you, but wounds much more serious than those, wounds in the spirit. For whenever I imagine the dear, sweet face of Berta, tears immediately burst forth from my eyes, like blood from a wounded soul, as it were; my sobbing is redoubled, I utter groans that reveal the gravity of the pain within, and 'a chill trembling passes right through my bones,'[2] my face turns hideously pale, my tongue sticks in my throat, I am left breathless, and I am so completely seized by dread grief that I cannot bear it. Despite my shame, I confess my weakness; I am overcome by emotion, drowned in sorrow; I have no control over the tears my eyes shed. Now I can share in that mournful song that the lamenting David sang: 'My life has wasted away in grief and my years in groaning. Grief for death has surrounded me, surrounded me like water, at once surrounded me for the whole day. You have taken away from me my beloved, even my dearly beloved.'[3]

Perhaps someone will unjustly find fault with my lament and accuse me of indulging in tears more freely than is proper. Here is my answer for anyone who thinks that my complaints are an offence. First, I do not grieve for Berta's lot; she has made a blessed exchange, trading this earth for heaven and death for eternal life. I grieve, rather, for my own lot. Second, who in his right mind would think it shameful for a man to be stricken by human emotions? I do not deny that I am moved by human feelings, any more than I deny that I am human. 'For I have not a heart of stone,'[4] nor was I born on the harsh rocks of the Caucasus and nursed by Hyrcanian tigers,[5] 'nor,' to use a biblical phrase, 'is my courage the courage of stones or my flesh made of bronze.'[6] Furthermore, only someone totally unaware of the close friendship I had with Berta could accuse me of excessive sorrow. You, dearest daughters, you can easily see that the cause of my complaints is not unreasonable; for you too burned with a love for Berta identical to my own and are now gripped by an equal sense of loss. You, I say, who are fully aware of my relationship with Berta, recognize the justice of my lament.

What else can I do? She is gone, she, my guardian, my benefactress, my refuge in times of need. She took me in as an orphan, supported me in my poverty, helped my when I was in need, consoled me time and time again in my despair, encouraged me when I was faint-hearted and sometimes (although I am ashamed to mention it) aided me with her advice when the situation called for it. She embraced me with the same love, and equal love, as she gave to her own children. She was as fond of me as though she had given birth to me herself. Indeed, she was not related by blood, but no one could be closer spiritual kin. Why shouldn't I have loved her as I would a mother, since she cherished me like a son? She was as much like a mother to me as I could have wished, with the sole exception of the actual blood relationship, which I definitely think is the least important aspect of motherhood. Other than that, she fulfilled every single duty of motherhood with a truly remarkable devotion to me.

Oh, how Berta's death suddenly deprived me of all I had! Whatever hope, consolation, or safety I used to have died with her, passed away with her. Who suddenly snatched you away from me, my mother, dearer to me than my own soul? Is this how you part people from each other, bitter Death? How far will your savage madness range, you fierce beast? You steal brother from brother; cruel and terrible Death, you separate those who are dearest to one another, part the closest blood relatives, sever the bonds that join lovers together, and come between close friends, Death, in your envy of all sweet friendship and your hostility to all that is good. It was you who suddenly snatched away the woman upon whom I was totally dependent – a sad parting, and I wish you had carried me off along with her and not taken her away from me! But now you have torn my heart in two, ripped out of me a part, and the better part at that, of my soul; and I am left, wasted and wounded. Why shouldn't I prefer to die with her than to live as a mere half of my former self?[7] Or perhaps I should consider the time I pass without Berta to be a kind of death and not life at all.

But where has this access of grief swept me to? I set out to soothe the sadness in your heart, and look! I seem to have wakened it again when time had all but put it to sleep.[8] I fear that you may criticize me, and fairly too, in the words of the blessed Job: 'You are a burdensome consoler.'[9] But, my dearest daughters, I am sure that you will easily forgive my weakness because of your exceptional wisdom and your innate compassion, and all the more easily since you know, without a shadow of a doubt, that it stems from a boundless sense of loss for our Berta.

Now, my speech should return to its original intent, since enough time has been granted to emotion and enough indulgence has been given to tears. Although, therefore, I who wish to console you am myself in need of consolation, and I who am endeavouring to be a physician to you do myself need the attentions of a physician, nevertheless, since I have good reason to feel that the death of your mother has inflicted a more painful wound on your hearts (for you were linked to her by a double bond, both physical and spiritual), I decided to use this short speech to portray for you your mother's virtues, as a consolation, such as it might be.

In this I am following the custom of the ancients according to which sons used to give mournful speeches for their parents' funerals at an assembly in the forum.[10] These speeches were designed to induce grief in the hearts of the listeners and to make the ancestral virtues familiar to everyone. Even the famous Jerome used just this literary genre to console Heliodorus for the death of Nepotianus and Eustochium for the demise of her mother Paula.[11] Following this example only as far as the general line of the speech, but not with an equal rhetorical power, I thought it right to set down in literary form the divine virtues of our Berta, both to console you and for the edification of all who might read this work. When you read this commendation of your mother, you will not only forgo grief for the loss of her, but will, rather, rejoice that such a one has been sent on ahead. And the others, when they admire these most outstanding feminine virtues, will for time eternal praise her to the skies in immortal commendations.

What future generation could be so deaf, what report could be so grudging, that people would fail to commemorate with eternal recognition such outstanding deeds done by a woman? Again, I fear that I may serve not so much to adorn her deeds as to detract from them because of this uncouth and crude speech; for they are great deeds and far exceed all the eloquence of her eulogists. And who am I to promise that I will do justice to the task, I who am as much a novice in literature as I am ineloquent in style? But since to remain totally silent would be an injustice, or rather, as far as concerns me, an impiety, let me undertake the task with that eloquence which I do command if not with the eloquence I should desire. Although I am aware that my speech will not add anything to the praises of her glory (which are already so great that they cannot be increased) none the less, there will be no small benefit in simply recalling them to mind.

Before I begin, there is one thing above all of which I would particularly like the reader to be informed: I shall say nothing either to win popular favour or in the hope that I shall profit thereby, nor, certainly, shall I write anything after the manner of those who exaggerate the importance of minor matters and who (as the poet says) 'turn black to white.'[12] But I shall set down either what I myself have seen with my own eyes and heard with my own ears as a first-hand observer or what I have learned in unanimous testimony from everyone, with my conscience called to witness before the eyes of the all-seeing God.

Cicero's instructions on the art of rhetoric advise us to trace far back the virtues and reputation of someone's ancestors, when we wish to eulogize him, and to note the outstanding deeds of his grandfathers and more distant forbears.[13] This was so that he would be considered worthy of more illustrious praise from everyone, since we could show not only that he had not declined from his ancestral virtues, but that he had surpassed the very reputation of his forefathers. But judging someone by another person's merits is foreign to Christian practice. Just as it is unfair for children to pay the penalties incurred by their parents' sins, so we think it unjust for them to gain glory from their parents' efforts. 'For the soul which has sinned shall itself die.'[14]

To avoid, then, adorning our Berta with borrowed plumage (like the crow in Aesop[15]) I pass over the reputation and good character of her ancestors; I will not mention the abundant material wealth and the other advantages bestowed on her by good fortune. This alone I set down as praiseworthy, that she despised all these advantages and, in her mind, embraced only virtue. For although she was abundantly wealthy, enjoyed the bloom of youth and the flower of beauty, had a generous supply of the other luxuries conducive to baneful pleasure, and could have safely passed her time in leisure, dressing too fashionably, dining too luxuriously, and sleeping in excessive comfort, she preferred only to follow in the footsteps of a bride of Christ and chose the rough rigours of the Christian life before the blazing vanity of the world. She did not, as girls usually do at that age, concentrate on adorning her wardrobe or dedicate herself to learning about cosmetics; she did not divert herself with the empty pleasures of dances; she did not, in fact, devote herself to any girlish pastimes. Rather, she overcame the bloom of her playful youth with a kind of premature spiritual gravity found in old age; she subordinated the flesh to the spirit, obeyed her parents' commands, attended church often, and devoted all of her spare time to prayer.

Perhaps some will be puzzled why she did not instead reject the world completely and dedicate herself to the monastic life. I do not deny that this would definitely be the safer course, but I think it is much nobler to live innocent of all vice amid numerous temptations to wickedness and to lead the peaceful life that only virtue can provide amid the great storms and billows of the secular world.

And what better description could I pick for the world today than a sea – tossed by constant tempests, beset by dangers beyond number?[16] How rare it is to see a person who can sail this sea and save his ship, who can make it to the desired port safe and sound, with no loss suffered. There are a thousand ways to die on this sea, a thousand dangerous trials and, as Virgil says, 'On all sides a great fear and everywhere the faces of death.'[17] But our Berta gave no thought to the times she lived in; she conquered dangers of every kind with an admirable strength of spirit. She was not frightened by the terrifying sound of Scylla's barking dogs; the bottomless Charybdis of greed did not suck her under; the jagged Syrtes of ambition did not smash her onto the thundering rocks; and finally, she sailed past the Sirens with her ears stopped against their deadly songs.[18] Moreover, I can well believe that it was the divine will that our Berta, who would have preferred to sit at the feet of our Lord like Mary, should have to be troubled like Martha and disturbed by so many trials[19] – in order to increase the fame of her virtue, which was tested by the constant attacks of evil, and also so that she could be a source of aid not just to herself, but to as many people as possible, and especially to the poor, which someone of her social standing could readily do.

Thus, when she had overcome the temptations that come with the bloom of adolescence (I pass over her girlhood for the sake of brevity) and had reached a marriageable age, she was joined to her husband in the bond of wedlock at her parents' command,[20] although she had always had a remarkably strong desire for celibacy. Her husband himself was as outstandingly virtuous as he was wealthy and above all diligent in his concern for domestic affairs – a worthy husband indeed for such a saintly wife. Furthermore, since she was aware that the marital tie was designed not for physical pleasure but for the production of children, she spared no time for the enticements of Venus, she paid no attention to luxuries, and she did not, as most women do, begin to treat her belly like a god.[21] But she pondered in her troubled heart the message of the Apostle: 'As for the rest, those who have wives should live as though they have them not, etc.'[22] She curbed her fleshly desires with incredible strictness. Whenever she had the opportunity, she withdrew herself from the troubles of this worldly life in order to devote herself more calmly to reading and prayer. Finally, this most blessed woman was so keenly desirous of chastity that it almost seemed as though she lived as a maiden, a wife in name only.

However, one must not think she ignored the Apostle's commands: 'Women, be obedient to your husbands,'[23] and also: 'Let women fear their husbands.'[24] She was so accommodating to him in all matters that you would have believed she was a servant, not a spouse, and she was so modest that you would have thought her a sister, not a wife. They competed with each other by turns in the duties of kindness and modesty, this most saintly of wives and her husband, who was correspondingly happy to have such a wife. What could be more chaste than this relationship? What more pure than this marriage – indeed, what could be more pleasant? Their marriage provided no grounds for that poetic criticism: 'The marriage bed is always filled with quarrels and mutual strife. / Where a bride lies, there is little sleeping.'[25] In their marriage there were no noisy quarrels at night, no screaming wrangles in the daytime – not even the slightest disagreement troubled it. Such a mutual and certainly such a modest love had bound them one to the other that her desires were always his and his were always hers.[26]

I need not refer to the assiduity she showed in the conduct of domestic affairs, to the strictness with which she brought up her children, or to the generosity with which she supported the needy. For if she happened to see some student poor in material goods but rich in learning and good character, she would immediately bring him to her home and set him among her own brood of children, both to relieve his want and to mould her sons' characters and behaviour by his example. And when he had been prepared for the priesthood or some ecclesiastical order, or at least for the religious life, she took the greatest care to see that he achieved his goal just as he wished and as soon as possible.

One thing, however, did cause her considerable trouble in these activities: she could not do exactly as she wished in bringing their noble spiritual efforts to fruition; her generosity suffered from a lack of freedom. She felt she was constrained by the restrictions binding her to her husband; she clearly felt that the marriage bond was holding her back in accordance with the word of the Apostle: 'A woman is bound to her husband as long as her husband is alive.'[27] Therefore, she still had to live in part in an uncongenial manner, since she was not yet independent.

But after her spouse had died and she was free of a husband's authority, she immediately devoted herself with unlimited zeal to every virtuous pursuit, as though she were at last able, after long, misguided delays, to begin a holy life. She vigorously rejected a second marriage, although from all sides a great crowd of suitors, of no humble station I assure you, pressed their intentions on her. This was the answer she used to make to friends and relatives who urged a remarriage: 'Until now, the claims of wedlock have forced me to serve my Lord with only half my efforts. From now on, for all that remains of my life, please allow me to live entirely for the Lord; I belong wholly to him, who has given me everything. Why dissuade me, to no avail, from what I have for a long time greatly desired?'

And this noble woman's words were matched by great deeds. She immediately scorned all worldly pomp and completely rejected beautiful clothing. So great was her modesty of speech, so great her love of frugality, that you would have thought she was not a widow, but a nun (although these virtues were not so much changes in her former way of life as they were complements to it). She was almost constantly at prayer, regular at church, and very seldom in the market-place.

Moreover, she was more eager to work at emptying her purse than other rich people usually are to see their purses stuffed. It is amazing how generously and assiduously she bestowed for the use of the poor all of her wealth, which was quite exceptionally large. What pauper was not dressed in clothing she gave? What poor man ever asked for alms in vain? Who asked a favour of her that he did not receive – or even, to whom did she not offer it unasked, if she happened to see a man burdened by want? The whole crowd of paupers filled her ears with laments as though she were their mother. She was possessed by a concern for them equal to that for her own children. And so that none of you should criticize her unfairly for doing good deeds only with the wealth she had in such abundance, she used to sew clothes for the poor every day by the labour of her own hands so that she would have ready something to give to each one when the opportunity arose.

But why do I go on describing all of her deeds in detail in this speech? They are innumerable and difficult to recall, and also all of Gouda, even today, testifies in admiration to her very great benefactions to the poor, and the entire city cries aloud about her overflowing and profoundly compassionate heart.[28] None the less, this one point can, I think, hardly be passed over in silence: that on the day before Good Friday each year she summoned thirteen people from the ranks of the poor and seated them at her own table; she herself set the serving of food before them, and when the guests had eaten well, she washed their feet with her own hands in an outstanding example of humility.

Moreover, she used to make frequent visits to the almshouse, generally referred to as the Hospital, which is next to the monastery of the

Minorites[29] in the city of Gouda, and which was established for the relief of
the illnesses of the poor (and to which she herself had given considerable
financial support). She visited each one's sick-bed and ministered to each
one's needs. What is more extraordinary than this woman? What more
exceptional than her virtue? Although she was accustomed to delicate
circumstances, she did not shrink from the stench caused by the decaying
rags or avoid the dangers of foul air infected by the breath of the sick,
provided she could earn the right to hear on the Last Day[30] the voice of the
Lord, saying: 'What you have done for one of the least of my people, you
have done for me. I was sick and you visited me.'[31] Do you not think that she
resembled a second Elizabeth?[32] She certainly did, and if you ignore the
difference in names, you will see that they differ in no other respect.

Another point: surely one thinks this incident worth mentioning? One
day she chanced to be giving alms to a woman and criticized her gently for
some fault or other (since Berta thirsted for everyone's salvation); the
woman, demonstrating that she was as bereft of wit as she was of material
goods, took offence somewhat, turned on Berta, and began to shower her
with an endless stream of outrageous abuse. 'Hey you,' she said, 'You hire a
town crier and go around the crossroads and street-corners, boastfully
scattering your alms – do you think you'll get any reward for this?[33] For a
fact, I'll make you this prediction: these expressions of gratitude from
people, which you pursue so eagerly, will be your payment for your good
deeds, if you have in fact done any. But what should be the reward for your
hypocrisy? What garlands should be the payment for such an appetite for
glory? It's none of my affair, but you'll find out soon enough, poor woman.'
That cursed woman, driven by the lash of Tisiphone,[34] bawled out this and a
great deal of similar abuse, which was not fit to be heard by the ears of such a
saintly woman; she shouted words speakable and unspeakable together.
But Berta bore it, not just calmly but even cheerfully; later she told me about
the incident with great joy and promised to give the woman a gift twice as
big, in return for her curses, as soon as she returned.

Finally, who could adequately describe in words the generosity of her
expenditures in aid of the monastery of the sacred brothers, or the kindness
she displayed to all religious people? She had an estate outside the city walls
of Gouda, which contained seven small dwellings; she donated it for the
construction of the monastery of the Brigittine brothers.[35] Of course they did
begin to work on their house there, but somehow or other they felt it would
be more convenient to move from there to the city. And so, when the farm
was sold and the buildings had been put up for sale, they began again to
build their house near the city walls. It can be seen there to this very day. It is
a charming building and is packed with the most saintly company of
brothers and sisters, praising the beneficence of Berta in undying memory.

We ourselves have often witnessed the kindness that she lavished on religious men. Whenever she happened to hear that one had come to Gouda, she would immediately welcome him hospitably; her home was like a wayside inn for them all; her door was open to all of them, even without invitation. As a result, they flocked to her home as though to their mother, and she took them in, each and every one, as though they were her sons – or rather, like Fathers – and then refreshed them with generous meals. She thought it would be to her great profit if she sowed her material seed and reaped our spiritual harvest,[36] if she fed us with material food and was in turn nourished by the example of our virtue or by a word of blessing from us. The situation, however, was just the opposite (although this is shameful for us): most often we went away having learned much more from her modesty than she did from ours. For if during a meal anyone carelessly let slip even one word that suggested that someone was in disgrace, she immediately broke in on the villainous conversation with a frown and said, 'Forbear, dear Fathers, while you sit at my table, forbear to cast abuse at someone who is not present, or to repeat shameful stories about anyone. This sort of talk offends my ears.' She had, indeed, protected her ears with a hedge of thorns, as it were, to avoid hearing whispered words.

I am omitting many of her virtues so that the reader will not weary of a long speech. But why not give at least one example of her extraordinary fortitude? I pass over the strength of spirit she showed in sustaining the attacks of hostile fate; I make no mention of her stout endurance of the misfortunes befalling her children.[37] I myself was an eyewitness of the event I report, so no one should suspect me of fabricating empty fictions.

She had a daughter, one who stood out among all others for her beauty; her name was Margareta,[38] and she was her mother's only dearest darling. She was married to her husband in a ceremony of the most fitting dignity, with a very large crowd in attendance. And oh! how suddenly her mother's joy disappeared! How unreliable is the lot of human life! The newlyweds had not yet enjoyed six weeks together, when suddenly the girl contracted a very grave disease and took to her bed. In a few days the disease began to get worse, and the usual human symptoms began to suggest that death was near. We were summoned to her; we hurried, even ran. All who were present – a very large number of both men and women – wept most bitterly. No one could hold back the tears. Even a man with a heart of stone could not watch dry-eyed as such a virtuous, beautiful girl was so suddenly snatched from human life, in the flower of her youth and in the early days of her marriage. Only her mother, in Virgil's words 'holding her eyes steady and straining to hide the pain in her heart'[39] was able to resist bursting into tears. For a short time we indulged in silent weeping, when suddenly her daughter, the mother's only joy, passed out of this life.

Then suddenly everyone's grief, restrained until now, burst forth, and the tears turned into vocal lament. The wailing of her husband, the moaning of the household, the outcries of the women at her side – they were all extraordinary; the entire house re-echoed with the mournful turmoil.

But the mother was still dry-eyed and absented herself from the grieving throng for a while. My thought was that she was going off to find solitude because of her deep anguish, since there is nothing more congenial to grief or more welcome to misfortune. I watched her and noted what she would do next; but she retired to her couch, propped herself up on her elbows and pondered reflectively on I know not what, her eyes glazed. I thought that she had been overwhelmed by her inner grief (for I will admit to my error) and was considering some bitter savage act, the way madmen often do. I believed that she was only hiding the distress she felt at so great a misfortune; I did not think she could completely conquer the pain, and I applied to her the lines of Virgil: '... and sick with a terrible sadness / She feigned hope on her face and hid deep in her heart the grief'; and these: '... and so, when she was overwhelmed by grief and infected by madness / and concealed her plan behind her expression, showing hope on a peaceful brow, / I became worried and went to soothe the mother's grieving heart / and to divert her sad woe with words.'[40]

When she realized my purpose, she stared at me more sharply than usual and said: 'Father, do you come to console me, as though what happened to me today were an injustice or a proper reason for chagrin? How could I be so shameless as to resent the fact that the Lord has taken away my daughter, except perhaps through ingratitude, forgetting that he also gave her to me? Has not he who granted her to me himself taken her back? And what reason do I have for a legitimate complaint? I have better grounds to be vexed at my own failings, for in my opinion they were the reason that she was snatched away from me by an early death. The fault was mine and she paid the penalty. For indeed, I was perhaps too proud of her at her wedding.'

What could be more amazing than this fortitude in a woman? Do you not think that this woman's words exactly echo those of the most blessed Job, after the loss of his wealth and the deaths of his children? 'The Lord gave; the Lord has taken away. As it pleased the Lord so was it done. Blessed be the name of the Lord.'[41] What worthy precedent for this fortitude can I cite? Surely the histories in Latin do not refer to any of the ancients who is worthy of being compared to her virtue. Mention is occasionally made[42] of Pericles,[43] a man outstanding among the ancients, who donned a garland and spoke in an assembly despite the loss of his two children. Xenophon too, the famous Socratic philosopher, is said to have removed his garland when, during a sacrifice, he learned that his son had died in battle; but he immediately put it on again when he was told that his son had fallen fighting, not like a coward, but with courage and with all his wounds in front. Pulvillus was celebrating the festival of the dedication of the Capitol when he heard of his son's death, but he thought it a matter too slight to justify interrupting the rites. He told them to bury his son in his absence. Lucius Paulus entered the city of Rome in triumphal parade during the seven days separating the funerals of his two sons. I pass over great men like Cato, Gallus, Piso, Brutus, Scaevola, Metellus, Scaurus, Marius, Crassus, and Marcellus – famous examples for future generations. But Anaxagoras, that philosopher of no small repute, was engaged in discussion with the other philosophers in the gymnasium when he learned of his daughter's death. He calmly gave this reply to the messenger: 'What? Am I not aware that I fathered a mortal child?'

These are notable precedents, but in my opinion they are hardly comparable to the virtue of our Berta. For it is one thing to ignore the feelings of family love in order to win glory (or, to be more precise, to conceal one's inner distress behind an insincere expression), but it is altogether different to overcome the love she felt for her daughter by means of her exclusive love for Christ and, moreover, even to give thanks for what happened.

Furthermore, the frailty of the weaker sex is an addition to the full measure of her glory. For who would not deem these characteristics, which we consider worthy of admiration in men accustomed to warfare from the very cradle (as they say) or in philosophers with their universal knowledge, even more glorious in a woman? Who will be able to find a woman who has such courage?[44] Such a woman has definitely been found – unless perhaps we think she should be termed a maiden rather than a woman.[45] Certainly, there is nothing else womanly about her, if you ignore the one difference – that of gender. Why should I not with justice call her a maiden, since she scorned death itself, which terrifies all mortals, with a manly spirit? When she suffered with a grave illness and was worn down day by day by the horrendous pain of the disease, she endured it with such strength of spirit that she did not ask for much attention, not even from the doctors. Yet she did not refuse it either, for fear she would seem to be testing God. She had put all her trust in the Lord; she was totally dependent on his will; she entrusted herself completely to him. She knew that without God even the doctors' efforts were useless.

One day when I went to visit her and asked with concern about the state of her health, she admitted to me that she was tormented by an unbearable pain. But while I was trying somehow or other to urge on her the virtue of fortitude, I got this answer from her: 'I am aware of all that, most honoured Father; I know, I know that my present sufferings are not worthy of comparison with the glory to come which will be revealed in us. I know, I tell you, what prizes will be awarded to us by our judge, if we fight bravely to the end. But although the spirit is willing, so also is the flesh weak.[46] Just let him who set me the trial give me the strength to endure; no, he *will* give me the strength. For God will not allow us to be tried beyond our strength, but with the trial he will bring it about that we shall be able to bear it.'[47]

Then, when the agonies of approaching death had already set in, she forgot about family concerns and was content to take no thought for any of her children; she remembered only the poor, and amid the last breaths of her failing spirit, she repeatedly whispered these words into the ears of the people at her bedside: 'Do as you will about the rest, only remember the needy!' and she repeated this time and again. At the last, she lifted her eyes to heaven, folded her hands, and, free of bodily chains, on the feast of St Bridget[48] (for whom, as I said before, she felt an astounding love) she passed to Jerusalem, the mother of all freedom, borne along by troops of angels. Her body, which had been a dwelling not unworthy of her most saintly soul, was interred in a solemn funeral accompanied by great lamentation from all.

It is hard to describe the grief and tears of the entire city as it marched in her funeral procession. No one's grief, though, seemed more bitter than that of the poor who were once her wards. For when according to the custom of solemn funerals the final alms were distributed, the poor suddenly broke out in such a storm of wailing that it would be hard to describe, difficult to believe, and pitiful to hear. What plaints were not uttered then? What cry of grief did not ring out? What kind of complaint, what laments were not heard? They all competed in crying aloud that they had each lost not just a guardian, but a very mother – no, someone dearer than a mother. Voices broken by sobs were heard, from old women on one hand and from children on another: 'Alas! Who is there to feed us in the future? Who to clothe us against the winter winds? Whose ears shall hear our cries in the future? Who shall be a second Berta to us?'

They at least have a reasonable cause for tears. We, however, dear daughters, ought not to grieve so much as to feel triumphant joy. For we have not lost a mother (and such a mother!) so much as we have sent her on ahead. How long will we go on indulging our tears and wasting away in useless grief? Berta triumphs among the starry thrones in the gleaming ranks of heaven's residents, wreathed in sparkling garlands. And do we lament her death? How I fear that she will quite properly mock our tears with a Democritean laugh[49] and turn against us the words of our Lord: 'If you loved me, you would certainly be rejoicing, for I go to my homeland,'[50] and: 'Do not weep for me but weep for yourselves.'[51] Clearly our lot is more to be lamented than hers. Of course it is: she has cast off the burden of mortal flesh and has entered her heavenly homeland. We are sojourners and visitors in this sad vale of tears,[52] in this exile of misfortune and death, still weighed down by the burdensome load of the body. We are forced to linger here, weeping with David: 'Woe is me! for my sojourn has been lengthened; I have dwelt with the inhabitants of darkness; long has been the sojourn of my soul.'[53]

Berta is in starry sanctuaries, and in the company of the holy prophets, with the sacred assembly of apostles, accompanied by the white-robed ranks of martyrs, protected by a crowd of maidens, surrounded by rows of angels, joining with chaste throngs of widows; she happily sings before the sight of the Lamb: 'As I heard, so have I seen, in the city of the Lord of virtues, in the city of our God.'[54] 'But we sit by the waters of Babylon, and remembering Sion we weep and say: "How shall we sing the Lord's song in a foreign land?"'[55]

So let us rejoice for Berta's own joy, triumph for your mother's triumph, O dearest daughters. Let us dry up our tears, cease our weeping, and put an end to grief. Let us try instead to follow her, with the same determined effort that she used in preceding us. And we will accomplish the task if we too cling to the path of virtue which she has trodden, if we have a zeal for fortitude equal to hers, if we have the same abundance of deep compassion and hold with equal firmness to justice and faith.

And may he who makes blessed your mother with his presence for everlasting time, grant us these gifts according to her merits. Amen.

The end of the speech of mourning for the death of Berta Heyen, widow of Gouda, written by Erasmus of Rotterdam in his twenty-first year.

AN EPITAPH[56] FOR BERTA HEYEN

Stop here, traveller, and read these lines. Behold, this coffin that you see at hand contains the bones of loving Berta; but her soul rests in the lofty sanctuaries of heaven, receiving worthy rewards for her good deeds. For while she was here in this life,[57] she was a devoted mother to orphans and a consolation to the needy; she nourished those oppressed by dread famine and was the sole hope for all unfortunates; she was an assiduous nurse to the sick. To these she generously gave of her riches so that she might win heavenly riches with great interest.

ANOTHER EPITAPH IN ANAPAESTIC METRE

Direct your eyes here, traveller; come read my verses. Tread with gentle foot on the mound you see there; it covers the bones of blessed Berta, who has earned an eternal reward. Future generations will celebrate her name and praise her to the skies in song as long as the earth produces arbutus,[58] while the sky gleams with stars, while the sun brings[59] on the rosy orb of the day and the dewy moon brings night. For while she was alive no woman more devoted to piety and justice lived anywhere in the regions of the vast earth. She was a mother to all whom the rage of pitiless Death[60] had unjustly deprived of their parents' support and love. She nourished all who were oppressed by dread want; she was the sole hope of the suffering; to the sick she alone restored life.[61] Although her bloodless bones lie hidden in a humble mound of earth,[62] deprived of light, nevertheless, some day the time will come when[63] her living mind will visit again its former home, revive it from the mouldering tomb and carry it off with her to heaven.[64]

ORATION IN PRAISE OF
THE ART OF MEDICINE

Declamatio in laudem artis medicae

translated and annotated by
BRIAN MCGREGOR

In his dedicatory letter to Afinius, Erasmus refers to the *Encomium medicinae* as a declamation composed many years earlier, at a time when he was attempting to master various types of literary composition. Those of his readers who had absorbed the educational programme that Erasmus had set forth in his *De ratione studii*,[1] which is heavily indebted to Quintilian, would have fully appreciated that what is being presented in the *Encomium medicinae* is an example of epideictic oratory. The Renaissance attached the highest importance to the art of rhetoric, by which is meant the presentation of a convincing case within well-recognized conventional limits.[2] These conventions are set out in great detail in the *Rhetorica ad Herennium*,[3] a Latin treatise of the first century BC, which became a standard of authority in the Renaissance.

Comparison of the *Encomium medicinae* with book 3 of the *Rhetorica ad Herennium*,[4] which deals with panegyrical or epideictic oratory, reveals how closely the structure of Erasmus' work follows the traditional divisions: introduction (*exordium*); narrative (*narratio*); evidence (*argumentatio*); refutation of opposing views (*refutatio*); close (*peroratio*). Given the artificial nature of such a composition, the temptation is strong to deduct the rhetorical element in order to arrive at Erasmus' 'real' views. Such an approach would be mistaken. The categories of rhetoric were for the humanists a screen through which they approached critical problems, and should be regarded as a cultural as much as a literary phenomenon. The *Encomium medicinae* is, then, a literary, not a technical, treatise on medicine, and should be addressed as such.

This is not to say that Erasmus' work is vacuous in content. On the contrary, in the letter to Johann von Botzheim in which Erasmus characterizes his various works by genre, and which in turn determines their order of publication in his *Opera omnia*,[5] the *Encomium medicinae* is grouped with those works which pertain to instruction (*quae pertinent ad institutionem vitae*). But the instruction Erasmus has in mind is moral rather than medical. In his translations of medical works by Galen and Plutarch he explicitly states that he is attracted to such writings less for their technical content than for their moral instruction.[6] The reader should therefore not be surprised at how little Erasmus tells us of medical practice in his day. For this we have to turn to works such as the *De fabrica corporis humani* of Andreas Vesalius.[7]

The ancient sources upon which Erasmus draws are dominated by the *Naturalis historia* of Pliny the Elder, the inexhaustible quarry of ancient knowledge.[8] Homer, Plato, and the Bible are also explicitly cited. Other sources can be deduced, for instance Galen and Diogenes Laertius. St Augustine is mentioned twice, and there is a reference to the *Corpus Hippocraticum*, which Erasmus is likely to have acquired through his study of Jerome rather than at first hand. Little attention is paid to contemporary medical writings, and no contemporary authorities are cited. Erasmus was well acquainted with medical men such as Listrius, Linacre, and Cop and had sought medical advice from both Linacre and Cop. But his familiarity with such men stemmed in the main from their being fellow humanists rather than their being medical authorities. Like other humanists, Erasmus turned to antiquity for his knowledge of medicine.

The allusions to Pliny, Plato, and Augustine alert us to the strong vein of Platonism running through the *Encomium medicinae*. In his introduction to the ASD edition, Domański isolates four major themes which are central to Erasmus' thought and which find their first systematic development in this work.[9] The *philosophia Christi*, which lay at the heart of his humanism and which had as its aim the restitution of true piety in practical life, required the subjection of the passions to reason, and this, as Erasmus says, was the essence of Plato's philosophy. Erasmus' philology is guided by his concern to approach classical and biblical figures as real people, whose meaning and relevance could be established only by the closest critical attention to the texts. Witness his contempt in the *Encomium medicinae* for the false exegesis of St Paul's weakness. Closely allied to this is Erasmus' expressed intention of penetrating to the sentiments and moral judgments of the ancient world, even where their outward expression was unacceptable to the Christian. This euhemeristic approach, exemplified in his discussion of the divine origins of medicine as recorded in the ancient sources, is typical of Erasmus. Lastly, there is Erasmus' insistence on the need to distinguish clearly between the practitioner and his profession. We are not to condemn the teachings of the church because some priests and monks are adulterers or pirates. In his controversies with the reformers Erasmus was to return to this theme time and again.

This mingling of medical and theological concerns finds further expression in Erasmus' statement in the *Encomium medicinae* that the physician, like Christ, is involved in the treatment of the whole man, not just of his body. The image of Christ as physician ('the wounded surgeon plies the steel') is one that Erasmus brings to bear in later works, for instance in his paraphrase of St Luke's Gospel, dedicated to Henry VIII.[10] He employs it to startling effect in his identification of Christ as the good Samaritan, just as in his colloquy *The Epicurean*[11] he was to make the more sensational comparison of Christ with Epicurus.

The genesis of the *Encomium medicinae* can be traced in Erasmus' letters. In writing to Botzheim on 30 January 1523, he refers to the *Encomium medicinae* as having been written twenty-three years earlier, at the request of a friend who subsequently became physician to the emperor Charles V.[12] Allen's thesis that the friend in question was Ghisbert (Ghysbertus), at that time physician in St Omer,[13] is probably correct. We know from the letters that Erasmus was living at Tournehem close to St Omer in the spring of 1499.[14] The *Encomium medicinae* was therefore probably written early in 1499. The *editio princeps* was published by Martens at Louvain in 1518, nineteen years after its composition.

The recovery of the text would, on the evidence of the dedicatory letter, appear to have been fortuitous – Erasmus chanced upon it while he was sorting through his books. But its discovery came at a most opportune moment. Erasmus had been pressing Afinius for several years to fulfil his promise of sending him silver cups,[15] and had originally intended to mark the gift by dedicating to Afinius book 2 of his translation of Theodorus Gaza's *De linguae graecae institutione*.[16] This translation was subsequently dedicated to Johannes Caesarius, presumably when the promised gift of the cups failed to materialize. The tone of the dedicatory letter of the *Encomium* suggests, although this cannot be stated with certainty, that it was to reciprocate the eventual receipt of this valuable gift of the silver cups that Erasmus decided to dedicate his long-forgotten speech to Afinius. Whether the text recovered by Erasmus in 1518 was the original draft, or whether the latter had been retained by Ghisbert, we do not know. It must, however, have been set up with some haste by Martens at Louvain, since the *editio princeps* of March 1518 contained errors which were to be perpetuated in subsequent editions over which Erasmus had no control. These errors were finally eliminated by Erasmus in 1529. At the same time he took the opportunity to improve the syntax and style, to insert passages that made for smoother transitions in the text, and to refine his exposition of certain themes.[17] This translation of the *Encomium medicinae* is based on the revised 1529 text published by Froben at Basel, and has been checked against the edition of Domański in ASD I-4.

B MCG

ERASMUS OF ROTTERDAM TO THE DISTINGUISHED PHYSICIAN
HENRICUS AFINIUS OF LIER,[1] GREETING

I was lately looking through my library, dear Afinius, my learned friend,
when there came into my hands a speech[2] I composed long ago,[3] when I was
trying my hand at everything, in praise of the art of physic. I thought at once
of dedicating a not very good speech to a very good physician, that the
attraction of your name at least might recommend it to the suffrages of
educated readers. For the time being it shall be a small token of my feelings
towards you, until something is available more worthy of our friendship.
Farewell.

Louvain, 13 March, 1518[4]

ORATION IN PRAISE OF THE
ART OF MEDICINE

Given the frequent occasions on which the art of medicine has been presented to many of you from this platform, in profound and polished speeches by men endowed with consummate eloquence, you will doubtless appreciate, most distinguished listeners, my resulting diffidence in my ability to do justice either to so great a subject or to your expectations of its treatment. For neither will our feeble power of speech easily attain to a subject of almost superhuman dimensions, nor can an ordinary speech[1] hope to avoid boring when dealing with such a well-tried theme. Nevertheless, lest I appear remiss in observing the beneficial custom of our ancestors, who resolved to kindle, fan, and, inflame the minds of our youth with admiration and love and devotion to this excellent branch of learning by means of a solemn eulogy,[2] I too shall endeavour, as far as my abilities allow – only grant me when I speak the favour of your attention and good will, since it is your support which has driven me to undertake this duty – not, I may say, to expatiate on the worth, influence, and application of the faculty of medicine, since this, of course, would be an endless task, but only to touch briefly upon these topics and to set forth before the imaginations of the students, in outline only, as the saying goes,[3] the prodigious riches, as it were, of some fabulously wealthy queen.

Now the principal form of praise attaching to medicine consists in the first place in the fact that she has no need whatsoever of adventitious advertisement, being amply self-sufficient to commend herself to mankind by reason either of utility or of necessity.[4] Second, although her praises have already been sung on many an occasion by outstanding minds, she is ever able to provide from her own abundance new material for her praises to even the most barren imagination, so that there is no need to praise her after the common fashion through those invidious comparisons which involve the denigration of the other arts.[5] On the contrary, it is more to be feared that human speech may not do justice to her natural gifts, her real and intrinsic abundance, her grandeur, which dwarfs the human condition – so far is she from requiring exaltation through the calumny of a sister art, or through the false colouring[6] of rhetoric, or through the illusion of rhetorical amplifications.[7] It is the hallmark of the mediocre to be rendered agreeable by comparison with more deformed shapes or by the meretricious aids of cosmetics. When things are in themselves truly distinguished, they can be revealed as such without any adornment[8] at all.

But let us press on with our subject. The other arts have from the beginning been held in the highest esteem, since there is not one of them which has not brought some great boon to life. But the invention of medicine once upon a time was so wonderful to mankind, the knowledge so sweet, that its authors were clearly taken for gods,[9] for example Apollo and his son Aesculapius; indeed, as Pliny says, 'There are some whom a single discovery has added to the number of the gods.'[10] Or they were, at least, thought worthy of divine honours, as in the case of Asclepiades, whom the Illyrians treated as a god, affording him honours on a par with those of Hercules.[11] While I do not personally approve of such actions by the ancients,[12] I wholeheartedly applaud their sentiment and judgment, which were based on the sound principle that in the case of a learned and trusty[13] physician no honour can be deemed too high.

Indeed, one has only to reflect upon the manifold diversity of the human body; the huge variation in condition resulting from age, sex, country, climate, education, study, or habit; the infinite variety of properties of the tens of thousands of plants that grow in different parts of the world – to confine myself for the moment to herbal remedies; then again, consider the many types of illness, of which Pliny writes that three hundred had been separately identified by his time[14] – to pass over the countless subdivisions within each of them, which will be readily comprehended by someone who has so far got to know the many variations subsumed in the word 'fever' and their differential diagnoses, to say nothing of new strains, which increase daily, just as if they seemed to be deliberately waging war upon our science of medicine. I pass over the thousand and one dangers of poisons, which can cause as many types of death as there are varieties, each requiring its own antidote. I say nothing of the daily hazards of landslides, falling buildings, fractures, burns, dislocations, wounds, and the like, which constitute a danger equivalent almost to the scourge of disease itself. Finally, just consider the great difficulties involved in observing the heavenly bodies, where the application of inexact knowledge can often produce a fatal remedy![15] I omit, for the time being, the frequently deceptive symptoms of disease, whether you are observing the complexion, or examining the urine, or feeling the pulse: it is almost as if the forces of evil are conspiring to deceive and impose upon the physician in this matter. So overwhelming are the difficulties that beset one from every quarter that it would be hard for me to tackle them even in a formal speech.

But, as I had begun to say, to pursue all these types of subject-matter through study; to penetrate obscurities through intelligence; to master difficulties through application; to penetrate the bowels of the earth;[16] to force all nature to unlock her secrets; to seek effective remedies for all the ills of human life from every plant, fruit, tree, animal, gem, and, finally, from poison itself; to pursue the proper application of these in numerous authorities[17] and sciences, yes, even in the stars themselves; to probe scrupulously such esoteric matters; to grasp mentally such profundities; to commit so much to memory; to offer, for the public good, cures vital to the well-being of all mankind – does not all this, I say, appear to have been the work of a force superhuman and clearly divine?[18] May there be no ill construction placed on my remarks, and let it be acknowledged that what is truer than the truth[19] should be frankly proclaimed.

I seek not to sing my own praises, but rather to extol the art of medicine itself. For if the gift of life[20] belongs to God alone, then it must be granted that the next best thing is the art which protects and restores that life. Admittedly antiquity, as credulous as it was appreciative,[21] had already attributed to the art of medicine what we Christians ascribe to God alone. For antiquity believed that Tyndareus[22] and several after him were restored to the land of the living through the art of Aesculapius.[23] We read how a man who lay dead and was mourned was brought down from his funeral pyre and led home alive by Asclepiades.[24] The chronicler Xanthus[25] records that a lion cub, and subsequently a man, had been killed by a snake, and were restored to life by the plant which they call *balis*.[26] So, too, Juba bears witness that a man in Africa was restored to life by means of a herbal remedy.[27] I should not, of course, be unduly upset if some people find such tales lacking in credibility! They at least engender – and this is the point I am making – an admiration for the art of medicine in proportion to their lack of credibility, and compel recognition of the vast import of something which transcends the facts. And yet, as far as the person who is restored to life is concerned, what difference does it make whether life is once again restored to his dead limbs by divine agency or whether the spark of life, though beset by the onslaught of advancing disease, still flickered deep within him and is sustained and nurtured and restored from certain extinction by the skill and care of the physician? Is there not an almost imperceptible dividing line between restoring the dead to life and maintaining the life of one who would soon be dead?[28]

In fact Pliny, in book 7 of his *Naturalis historia*, cites numerous individual cases where men brought out for burial came to life again, some on the actual funeral pyre, others after a few days.[29] What chance granted to a few is treated as a wonder; but how much more so are the examples which our art of medicine furnishes in abundance every day, even if, to forestal accusations of my being more concerned with personal vanity than with the truth, we owe this art, as we do everything else, to Almighty God. Such is the virulence of several diseases that they inevitably prove fatal unless a physician is at hand: for instance, that lassitude to which women in particular are prone,[30] a dead faint, paralysis, and apoplexy. Every age and every nation can furnish its own examples in this matter. Does not the man who by his professional skill holds imminent death at bay and who restores life when it has been suddenly assailed by disease for ever deserve to be treated as if he were some beneficial and propitious supernatural being? How many men, do you reckon, met with untimely burial in the days before medical science had grasped the virulence of diseases and the nature of their cures? How many thousands of people are alive and well today who would not even have been born had not this same medical art discovered treatments for the many crises of childbirth and evolved the science of obstetrics? Witness how at the very onset of birth both mother and baby pitifully cry out for the healing hands of the physician. Even the unborn child owes its life to the skill of these men, which is vital in preventing miscarriages, in enabling the woman to conceive and retain the foetus, and in helping her bring it to birth. And if there is any truth in the saying 'It is godlike for mortal to assist mortal,'[31] then I am convinced that the only true exemplar of that noble proverb of the Greeks 'Man is to man a deity'[32] will be the trusty and virtuous physician who not only assists but also saves.

Accordingly, would he not appear to outdo ingratitude itself and be himself almost unworthy of life who did not love, honour, esteem, and revere medicine as parent, nurse, guardian, and protector of life, second only to God himself? Everyone everywhere needs its protection. For in the case of the other arts our need is neither constant nor universal; whereas the entire life of mankind depends on the utility of this art of medicine.[33] For even if you abolish disease and imagine everyone to be blessed with good health, how shall we be able to protect our health unless the physician instructs us to discriminate between wholesome and harmful food, unless he teaches us the first principles of that entire way of life which the Greeks term dietetics?[34] Old age is a heavy burden for mankind to bear,[35] and one we can no more escape than death itself. Yet thanks to that craft of the physician, the burden of old age can be considerably lightened for many people. For it is no mere myth that man can overcome old age and take on a new lease of life, as it were, by means of what they call the fifth essence,[36] since there are several living witnesses to this fact. Nor is it fair to impugn the profession[37] because some of its practitioners cheat the unwary.

Now the physician is concerned not only with the care of the body, the lower element in man,[38] but with the treatment of the entire man,[39] and just as the theologian takes the soul as his starting-point, the physician begins with the body.[40] And rightly so, because of the very close relationship and connection between them, so that, just as the sins of the spirit recoil upon the body, so likewise the diseases of the body can hinder, or even completely check, spiritual growth.[41] Who can match the physician as a persistent advocate of abstinence and sobriety and of the need to control bad temper, avoid depression, shun drunkenness, abandon passion, and control desire? Who can more effectively persuade the patient that if he wants to be well and benefit from the physician's art of healing, then he must first cleanse his soul of the dregs of sin?[42] Likewise, how often does the physician, either by the science of dietetics or by the use of drugs, reduce melancholia, restore a weak heart, strengthen the functions of the brain, cleanse the organs of the mind, improve the constitution, check loss of memory, change for the better the entire mental outlook, and, by working through the outer man, as they put it, save the inner man as well?[43] When a physician has cured the melancholic, the lethargic, the insane, the ill-starred, the phlegmatic,[44] has he not effected the cure of the entire man? It is the task of the theologian to see that men are saved from sin, but without the physician there would be no men to be saved. The former would be an ineffectual physician of the soul if the soul that he was trying to cure had already departed. When a wicked man is suddenly stricken by a stroke or apoplexy or some other instant form of destruction which would kill him before he had time to renounce his evil ways, surely the effect of the physician in saving such a person, who would otherwise have to be buried doomed by his own crimes, is tantamount to rescuing a body and soul from hell? At least he puts the man in a position where it now rests in his own hands whether he decides to escape eternal damnation. How can a theologian advise a sufferer from lethargy, when the latter cannot hear his advice? How can he move the melancholic, until the physician has purged him of his excess of black bile? I do not deny that piety and the other virtues that make for happiness in the Christian stem for the most part from the conscience; but since the conscience, being bound up with the body, expresses itself willy-nilly through the instrument of the body, it follows that a good conscience depends in good measure upon the state of the body.[45] A bad bodily temperament, which the Greeks term 'mixture,' or sometimes 'system,'[46] drives very many to sin unwillingly and under protest, while the charioteer of the soul[47] draws the reins to no avail, applies the spur to no avail, but is forced to follow after a horse charging in headlong flight. The soul has sight[48] and the soul has hearing, but if the eyes are diseased, if the passages of the ears are blocked, then it is vain for the senses of the soul to be intact. The soul can detest[49] and rage, but it is some malignant humour, distorting the powers of reason, which causes you to hate someone you know is worthy of love and causes you to be angry with someone against your will. According to Plato, the essence of philosophy consists in the subjection of the passions to reason,[50] and the chief ally in that objective is the physician, who sees to it that the element in man which promotes the performance of virtuous acts is kept vigorous and alert. If those who, like cattle, are prey to their desires are deemed unworthy to be called human, we must grant that the dignity which this name confers[51] is due in large measure to physicians. Although that is of great importance in the case of private individuals, how much more beneficial is it when it occurs as an outstanding feature of a ruler! No destiny is more exposed to evils of this kind than that of kings who want for nothing.[52] What tumults can arise from the corrupt brain of one little man! It is vain for his courtiers to protest: 'You are mad, O prince; come to your senses!' unless the physician by his craft restore his sanity, although the prince may neither desire it nor appreciate its absence. If Caligula had been attended by a trusty physician, his insane desire to destroy the human race would never have reached the level of boxes of daggers and poisons.[53] And it was for that very reason that the universal custom was introduced that no ruler of any place or people should perform his duties without having personal physicians.[54]

Consequently, wise rulers never held any profession in higher esteem than medicine. Witness, to take but one example, the case of Erasistratus,[55] descendant of Aristotle's daughter, who was rewarded with a hundred talents by Ptolemy for having cured his father, King Antiochus. Even the Bible tells us that the physician should receive his special honour, not only for reasons of utility, but of necessity as well,[56] so that, while in the case of other benefactors it would be ungrateful for a man not to acknowledge the benefaction, in the case of the physician it would be impious, inasmuch as he protects by his skill and acts in a sense as coadjutor of that heavenly gift which is the supreme sign of God's abundant love for us – I mean, of course, the gift of life. We owe everything to our parents, since it is through them to some extent that we seem to have received the gift of life; but, in my opinion, more is owed to the physician, to whom we owe time and time again what we owe at once to our parents, if indeed we do owe life to them.[57] We should revere the man who overpowers the enemy at our throat; should we not, then, show even greater respect for the physician who daily wrestles for our protection with so many deadly enemies of life? We look up to our rulers as gods, because they are accepted as holding the power of life and death; but, granted that they have the power to kill, they are able to grant life only in the limited sense of not taking it away, just as robbers are said to 'spare' the life of someone they refrain from butchering, and the only life they are able to grant is that of the body. But how much more does the physician's beneficence approximate to the divine charity, when by his art, skill, care, and constant help he saves someone who is already slipping towards the next world and snatches him back, as it were, from the very jaws of death!

Granted that it was his duty to benefit men in other ways, yet to have saved someone whose body and soul were in mortal peril constitutes something beyond duty. Add to these the fact that whatever is great in man, whether it be learning, virtue, natural gifts, or what have you, must be admitted as due in its entirety to the art of the physician, inasmuch as he preserves life, without which not even those talents can exist. If all these qualities stem from there being a man, and the physician saves that self-same man, it follows that thanks is due to the physician on behalf of all of them. If a man wracked by disease cannot be said to be truly living at all, and the physician either restores him to full health or keeps him out of danger, surely it is proper to acknowledge the physician as, in a sense, a giver of life? Now, if immortality is something which is to be desired, then it is achieved as far as is humanly possible by medical research, which can prolong life almost indefinitely. For do I need to cite in this connection the famous examples of Pythagoras,[58] Chrysippus,[59] Plato,[60] Cato the Censor,[61] Antonius Castor,[62] along with countless others who, for the most part, applied medical knowledge to prolong their life, free from disease, well beyond their hundredth year, and without any impairment of mental vigour or weakness of memory or loss or deterioration of their senses? Is not this to illustrate here on earth the immortality we hope for? Christ himself, the sole author and guarantor of immortality, became flesh, mortal it is true, but of a mortality that was not subject to any disease.[63] He shrank not from the cross but from disease. Would it not then be most morally uplifting for us to strive to imitate our Lord in this too? We read that the apostles, almost all of whom lived to a ripe old age, were martyred or slain; but we do not read of their having been ill. However this came about in their case, the art of the physician certainly achieves an effect comparable to that which their beatitude achieved for the apostles. For I do not believe that any attention should be paid to those who, with an ignorance of exegesis matched only by their impudence, are accustomed to cite in refutation the text 'for my strength is made perfect in weakness,'[64] erroneously taking this to mean that Paul was afflicted by a severe physical pain in the head, when in fact what he calls his weakness is either mental temptation or, more probably, a troublesome band of impious persecutors.[65] So, too, that same Paul recorded the gift of healing as being amongst the apostolic gifts.[66]

Now, the glory of medicine receives additional and far from insubstantial enhancement from the fact that the majesty of civil law and the authority of canon law are voluntarily submitted to medical arbitration, for instance in matters of maturity, birth, and sorcery, and likewise in certain matters pertaining to marriage. O new-found dignity of medicine! In the case of a capital offence, even the judge's verdict is dependent upon the prior examination by a physician. If the pope in his clemency grants plenary indulgence to some people at the moment of death,[67] he does so only after weighing the medical evidence; and in his decretals the Roman pontiff forms his decision as to whether a bishop who had been relieved from his office after being stricken by some foul and horrible disease should be removed from or restored to his see only after seeking medical judgment on the case.[68] Likewise St. Augustine decrees that medical opinion should be paramount in deciding what has to be done, even if this goes against the wishes of the patient.[69] So, too, in the matter of rendering the physician his due, that is, the reward for his skill and dedication, he writes that it is just to extract it forcibly from a person who holds it back, whom he equates with an illegal owner and one who holds in bad faith what rightly belongs to someone else.[70] Furthermore, those people also who employ ritual prayers[71] to expel evil spirits from the human body not infrequently call in the help of physicians, for example in the case of those diseases which, for reasons not yet understood, upset the equilibrium of body and mind and produce such a convincing appearance of demonic possession that they can be diagnosed only by the most expert physicians, whether it be the case that there exist certain more gross demons – such is said to be the varied nature of demons – which are also susceptible to medical treatment, or whether disease has so penetrated the innermost recesses of the mind that it appears unrelated to the body.

Grant me your good-natured indulgence[72] while I cite one positive proof from the many known to me of the credibility of the above proposition. I myself when young did eagerly frequent Doctor Panacea of celebrated fame. I bear witness to the fact that he cured a certain native of Spoleto, Raving by name, who, as a result of suffering worms, had developed a new type of madness, such that in his ravings he used to speak fluent German, which it was generally agreed he had never been able to do when sane. Who not skilled in medical science would not have solemnly sworn that this man was a victim of demonic possession? But Doctor Panacea restored his wits with a simple and ready remedy. Once restored in mind he could neither speak nor understand German. But if anyone should maintain that this man was truly a victim of demonic possession, that in itself highlights the skill of the physician whom, it follows, even evil spirits obey, so that, as in the restoration of life, so too in the expulsion of demons, it ministers to and emulates the divine power. Indeed, there were some who would have attributed this deed to the magical arts.[73] But I can turn this slander to the glory and credit of our art of medicine, by which deeds are performed which the vulgar believe to be beyond human powers.

In days of old,[74] therefore, before sordid gain and unnatural pleasure had corrupted everything, it was with consummate judgment that the art of healing above all was held in special esteem by both gods and lords of men, by the wealthiest kings, and by the most distinguished senators, and that no other art was more pleasing to mankind. The great Moses is believed to have chosen his food solely upon the basis of medical science.[75] Orpheus, at the very dawn of Greek civilization, is recorded as having offered some teaching on the medicinal properties of plants.[76] Homer himself, that incontrovertible fountain-head of genius, abounds both in references to plants and in the praise of physicians.[77] It is Homer who has described for us moly as well, that most esteemed of all plants, according to Pliny, and an effective antidote to poisons; he attributes its discovery to Mercury, who forearms his protégé Ulysses with it as a protection against the potions of Circe.[78] Homer also tells us how nepenthes should be administered at banquets to dispel grief and sorrow.[79] Again, he often gives honourable mention to Machaon, Paeon, Chiron, and Polidarius as outstanding physicians,[80] whose skill he records as coming to the aid not only of the heroes but of the very gods themselves,[81] his underlying meaning being, of course, that even the most exalted rulers require the protection of the physician, and that the life of those who are seen to hold the power of life and death over everyone else is in the hands of the physicians. What of the fact that the same poet, in book 11 of the *Iliad*, has dignified this art of medicine with the most noble of eulogies, where he says that a single physician should be held in higher regard than scores of other men?[82] Again, in another passage he goes so far as to designate the physician as a man of universal knowledge,[83] thereby testifying to the established fact that this art comprises not one or two branches of science but an encyclopaedic knowledge of all the arts, and, in addition to fine judgment, requires much practical experience as well. We read that the famous Pythagoras of Samos, who was regarded as a demigod by antiquity, left a celebrated volume on the nature of plants.[84] If I might pass over Plato, Aristotle, Theophrastus,[85] Chrysippus, Cato the Censor, and Varro,[86] who were diligent in the application of medical knowledge both in their studies and in their daily occupations, to Mithridates,[87] king of Pontus, whose claim to fame and standing as a truly great man rested not so much upon his kingdom, abundantly rich as it was in other respects, not so much upon his prodigious mastery of twenty-one languages, as upon his skill in medical matters, and who, according to Pliny, left behind in his memoirs his reflections upon this art, together with experiments and results. Even today a famous type of antidote perpetuates the name of Mithridates.[88] Nowadays the concern of kings in general is held to consist in dicing, hunting, and trifling. But there was once a time when the chief concern of the emperors of the Roman people was to advance medical science by the importation of new plants from abroad,[89] and no service was more acclaimed by that people, who were at the time masters of the world.

What of the fact that Christ himself, the author and originator of all branches of knowledge,[90] professed himself not a jurisconsult, not a rhetorician, not a philosopher, but a physician,[91] when, in referring to his own ministry, he said that they that be whole need not a physician;[92] when, as the Samaritan, he bound up the man's wounds, pouring in oil and wine;[93] when he spat on the ground, and made clay of the spittle, and anointed the eyes of the blind man?[94] What of this, as the most convincing commendation of all: that the same Christ, when still unknown to the world, gradually worked his way into the minds and hearts of men, not by gold, not by authority, but by healing the sick? What he, being God, could do at will, the physician strives to imitate as far as his human powers allow. They too participate in the divine nature of healing, by virtue of the powers conferred by God to this end. The power of healing was all that Jesus granted his disciples for their journey, commanding them from that time forth to bind their host to them through its action, anointing, he said, with oil those that were sick, and healing them.[95] Did not the great apostle Paul, in prescribing for his follower Timothy a little wine to fortify his weak stomach,[96] openly play the role of the physician? But why should this be remarkable in the case of the Apostle, when the angel Raphael cured the blindness of Tobit,[97] and thus even found fame among students of the apocryphal scriptures? O heavenly and truly sacred science of medicine, whose name does honour to holy minds such as these!

Among humankind, different men learn or profess different arts; but everyone should learn this one art which is vital to everyone. But alas for the extreme perversity of human judgment! While no man will remain ignorant of the difference between genuine and counterfeit coin, lest he be cheated in some way in matters of gross materialism, there is no corresponding zeal to discover how he can protect his most valuable possession.[98] In monetary matters he does not trust to somebody else's eyes, but in the business of life and health he is content to follow somebody else's judgment, with his eyes shut,[99] as they say. But if absolute knowledge of the whole art is reserved only to the few who have dedicated a lifetime to this single branch of study, there is no reason why anyone should be ignorant of at least that part which pertains to the maintenance of good health,[100] granted that a good part of the problem stems not from the art itself but from either the ignorance or the self-aggrandizement of disreputable physicians.

Even among wild and barbarous peoples the word 'friendship' was always held in awe and respect,[101] and the friend par excellence is held to be he who shows himself a companion and ally in good times and in bad,[102] because the common run of friends, like the swallows in summer, are present in times of prosperity, but in times of adversity they fly away, like swallows at the approach of winter.[103] But how much more genuine a friend is the physician, he who, after the fashion of the birds of Seleucis (which, they say, are never seen by the inhabitants of Mount Casius except when their protection is needed against a plague of locusts destroying their crops),[104] never intrudes himself upon those who are hale and hearty. But in times of peril, in these adversities in which wife and children often abandon a man, such as in cases of phthiriasis, consumption, or pestilence, the physician alone is constant in his attendance, and he is present, unlike many others, not out of mere sense of duty, ineffective as that is, but is there to give practical help, is there to contend with the disease for the life of the critically ill, and thereby frequently puts his own life at risk. They exceed the bounds of ingratitude who, saved by the good offices of such a friend, can find it in them to hate the physician once the danger has been removed, when they should rather cherish and honour him as they would a parent! They invite to dinner the first fair-weather friend they happen to meet; they express their gratitude to one whose concern for them is that of mere formality;[105] can they really shun such a friend as the physician when they cease to require his services? They do indeed shun him, and for this very reason: they perceive that no degree of gratitude can repay the physician for the service he has rendered.

But[106] if the best type of man is he who renders the greatest service to the state, then this art of medicine should be learned by all the best men, because among the duties of the civil magistrate not the least, and, I am inclined to think, even the principal one, is to see to it that the citizens are in good health. What does it profit to have repelled an enemy from the walls if pestilence steals inside and carries off more of the citizenry than the sword would have done? What good does it do to have striven to avoid loss of property if physical health is lost? The ancients, who arranged the things which make for human happiness on a scale of values, placed good health at the very top.[107] For what does it profit that a possession be intact unless the health of the possessor be intact as well? Consequently, the laws of the ancients, in the time before concern for profit and self-aggrandizement had corrupted everything, had as their objective the promotion of strong, robust, and well-ordered bodies among the citizenry. That is determined partly by birth, partly by education,[108] partly by exercise and diet, and in some degree also by the type of housing.[109] In performing their duties they were, of course, adopting the role of physician when they joined healthy couples in matrimony,[110] when they provided healthy wet-nurses, when they set up baths and gymnasia, when they proposed sumptuary laws,[111] when they prevented disease by rebuilding and by draining the swamps,[112] when they took special measures to ban the sale of food and drink which might be injurious to health. But nowadays princes think it hardly any concern to them if poison is sold as wine, if countless diseases are imported into the country through adulterated wheat and rotten fish. We see, then, that there is no area of life which can be properly conducted without the aid of medicine.

If there really are people who prefer to evaluate things in terms of their utility and profitability, albeit this art is too sacred to be appraised in terms such as these, then not even in this respect does medicine yield precedence to any of the other arts. For no other art has been more profitable or as convenient for providing instant earnings. Erasistratus, whom I have previously mentioned, and Critobulus[113] are recorded as having been presented with huge rewards by King Ptolemy and Alexander the Great respectively. And yet what reward would not in effect seem mere trifling recompense for the man who saves the life of one for whose safety alone so many thousands of men used to do battle? Need I now remind you of the Cassii, Carpitani, Aruncii and Albutii, who, Pliny tells us, enjoyed immensely profitable careers at Rome with both rulers and ruled?[114] And yet, do we need to go back to the distant past for such illustrations, as if several examples would not readily spring to anyone's mind, of men today whom this art has made as rich as Croesus?[115] The arts of rhetoric or poetry support only their most outstanding practitioners; a musician excels or he starves; a man scratches a bare living from the law unless he be pre-eminent in his profession. Medicine alone supports and safeguards a man whatever his level of learning. The science of medicine comprises countless disciplines, an infinite knowledge of things, and yet the quack doctor frequently makes a living on the basis of one or two remedies – so far is this art from deserving condemnation as unprofitable. There is the additional fact that the other arts cannot be profitably pursued everywhere. The rhetorician will be coldly received among the Sarmatians,[116] the expert in Roman law among the British.[117] Wherever in the world the physician goes, he finds that honour and a livelihood are afforded him, such that the well-worn saying of the Greeks that every land supports a trained skill[118] applies to no discipline with greater propriety than to medicine. But Pliny – or rather others whom he records – is offended at the very idea that the medical profession is one of material gain.[119] Now, I admit that this branch of science is too important to concern itself with the slavish pursuit of pecuniary profit: that is the hallmark of the base arts.[120] But for all that it is too much if medicine, which can never receive full recompense, is alone cheated of its reward. The distinguished physician, like some divinity, saves life free of charge, and saves even the recalcitrant patient; but it is impiety not to acknowledge the service of a divinity. The physician may care nothing for payment, but you deserve the full severity of the law for your signal ingratitude.

Now the fact has not escaped me that this outstanding art was once held in bad repute by the ancients, and is so held today by some ignorant persons. Cato disapproved of it, not because he found the science itself reprehensible, but because, as a true son of Rome, he could not bear the blatant ambition of its Greek practitioners.[121] Cato set such store by experience that he refused to acknowledge medicine as an art, but, there again, he recommended that Greek philosophy[122] in its entirety should be banned from Rome. A man of uncompromising austerity, he was of the belief that cabbage and regular vomiting were sufficient to cleanse a man's system;[123] yet this selfsame antagonist of physicians is recorded as having lived to a ripe old age with strength unimpaired through his attention to medicine. They say that physicians alone are allowed to take life with absolute impunity.[124] But in this context good physicians are the more to be esteemed, since, although it lies within their power to take life, not only with impunity but also to their financial gain, they nevertheless prefer to save life. That they have the opportunity is due to their profession; that they decline it, to their moral integrity. Now the old saw is frequently heard, on the lips of the hard drinkers in their cups, that a man who lives according to medical advice lives miserably.[125] As if true happiness consists in being swollen by drink, broken by debauch, bloated with beer, buried in sleep! But what need is there of reasoned argument to refute parasites like these, when they themselves make redress in abundance to medicine for their insolence towards her when they are, in due course, wracked by gout, paralysed by a stroke, when they become prematurely senile, lose their sight in advance of old age, and then, in their misery, like Stesichorus[126] recant their former abuse of medicine – but too late? For all their unworthiness, however, medicine in her compassion does not begrudge them whatever it lies within her power to give. There are those who jeeringly refer to physicians as men who feed on dung,[127] a calumny borrowed from ancient comedy. But the truth is that such abuse of physicians really connotes signal praise, applied as it is to men who descend from the eminence of their calling to basic bodily functions in order to bring relief to the misfortunes of mankind. But if physicians were as censorious as their detractors are impertinent, they would let them die with impunity. But our art of medicine has this in common with good rulers: to do good works and suffer ill repute.[128]

But if, as is the case in medicine, there are many to be found who pass themselves off as physicians although they are not physicians at all, if there are some who administer poisons instead of remedies, if there are some who

from motives of gain or worldly ambition fail to give the sick proper
attention, what could be more perverse than to turn the shortcomings of its
practitioners to the malicious misrepresentation of the art itself?[129] Adulterers
exist even among priests, murderers and pirates among monks; but how can
this detract from the essential goodness of religion itself? No profession is so
pure as to be without its share of rogues. It is, indeed, devoutly to be wished
that all monarchs should be such as to be deemed worthy of the title they
bear. Monarchy as an institution, however, should not be condemned
because some of that title act like plunderers and enemies of the state. I too
would desire that all physicians should acquit themselves as true physicians, and that the saying of the Greeks that there belongs more than
whistling to a ploughman should have no application to them.[130] I too would
desire that they all should bear witness to that solemn oath which
Hippocrates formulated in hallowed terms and exacted from his pupils.[131]
Nor should we cease striving to live up to its lofty demands because we
observe its being neglected by very many. But, since this is so fruitful a line
of argument to pursue that it would be very difficult to know where to stop, I
think it fitting, my masters, lest I fail to fulfil my opening promise, to sum up
all the praises of medicine.

    Although the sanction of antiquity alone commends a great number of
things, consider how necessity has found this art to be the first of all. If its
authors render a science illustrious, bear in mind that the invention of
medicine has always been attributed to the gods.[132] If the honour paid to an
art enhances its prestige in any way, consider how no other art has earned
divine honours on such a scale, and for such a length of time, as medicine. If
great esteem attaches to pursuits that find favour with men in highest
authority, consider how this art has both pleased and added glory to
eminent kings and lords. If excellence comes only through great labour,[133]
consider how nothing is more demanding than the study of medicine,
which comprises so many disciplines, together with the scientific study and
mastery of the most profound matters. If we assess medicine by the criterion
of esteem, what could be held in higher esteem that that which approxi-
mates to the charity of God? If we assess it in terms of capability, what could
be more potent or efficacious than the ability to restore the entire man who
was marked for certain death? If we assess it in terms of necessity, what
could be more necessary that that which is essential for life or birth? If we
assess it in terms of moral excellence, what could be more honourable than
the saving of human life? If we assess it in terms of utility, then nothing can
be admitted to be of greater or more widespread usefulness. If we assess it in
terms of profit, then medicine should be pre-eminent in the rewards it
brings, or else human beings are guilty of signal ingratitude. Accordingly, I

heartily congratulate such talented men as yourselves, who excel in this, the most noble of professions. At the same time, I exhort you, the best of students: embrace medicine with all your heart, apply yourselves to it with every nerve and fibre of your being, since it will win you distinction, glory, prestige, and riches; by its agency you in turn will confer no mean blessing upon your friends and country, nay more – upon all mankind.

HOMILY ON THE CHILD JESUS

Concio de puero Iesu

translated and annotated by
EMILY KEARNS

The *Concio de puero Iesu*, at least in its present form, was written by Erasmus for use in the new school at St Paul's cathedral in London founded by his friend John Colet and opened in 1510.[1] The new foundation, dedicated to the child Jesus and the Virgin, was intended to put into public practice the ideals of humanist educational theory; both its administration, which was independent of clerical control, and its curriculum showed a marked difference from those of the medieval cathedral school.[2] But Colet was a deeply religious man, and the school's educational programme placed its central emphasis on moral and Christian elements. The statutes prescribe the study of 'goode auctors suych as haue the veray Romayne eliquence joyned withe wisdome specially Cristyn auctours that wrote theyr wysdome with clene and chast laten other in verse or in prose, for my entent is by thys scole specially to incresse knowlege and worshipping of god and oure lorde Crist Jesu and good Cristen lyff and maners in the Children.'[3] Clearly Erasmus would have been entirely in sympathy with these aims.

Although little is known of Erasmus' activities between summer 1509 and April 1511,[4] it is certain that he was in England, probably in London, during most of this period, and therefore that the two men would have had ample opportunity for close association as the idea of the school took practical shape. It is therefore not surprising, given their shared enthusiasms, that Erasmus should have been asked to supply some compositions for the new school. *De copia*, although it had been evolving for some years, was finally published in July 1512 with a dedication to Colet and his school,[5] and the same volume, printed by Josse Bade in Paris, contains the first official publication of *De ratione studii*.[6] The volume concludes with the *Concio* and a few poems, some for school use, and one, *Expostulatio Iesu cum homine suapte culpa pereunte*, whose themes relate it very closely to the homily;[7] these last works had first been published by Robert de Keysere, almost certainly the previous September. The connection with Colet in all these works was not merely a piece of honorific publicity for the foundation, although that was, of course, part of the intent; as educational pieces, they had also a practical use. Colet's statutes prescribe the reading of *De copia* at the school (along with the *Institutum christiani hominis*[8]), and the programme of study outlined in *De ratione studii* has a clear relevance to the establishment of a new curriculum. Of the shorter works, most of the poems (*carmina scholaria*) seem to be intended as hymns for the school, or in one case as a programmatic inscription, while the *Concio*, as we know from its full title, was to be delivered by one of the boys to an audience of his schoolfellows.

Both sermon and poems breathe the spirit of devout learning expressed in Colet's statutes, summed up in the inscription designed for the statue of the presiding child Jesus: 'Children, first learn me, and show me forth in pure behaviour: then add pious works of literature.'[9] The child Jesus was to be the model for the boys of the school, a child both holy and learned.[10] With this in view, Erasmus composed his sermon entirely in the persona of the boy who was to deliver it. To some extent, therefore, especially perhaps in its presentation of a Christ particularly well disposed towards children, the *Concio* is a piece of demonstrative oratory, selecting its material to illustrate a point appropriate for a special occasion and audience. At the same time, however, it contains educational, moral, and religious ideas that were clearly extremely important to Erasmus. Central to the piece, and explicitly stated in it, is the conviction that people can be moved by eloquence to love and imitate Christ. The *Concio* is not only a rhetorical exercise on a sacred theme; it is also, and more importantly, a serious attempt to persuade by the skilled use of rhetoric. It is as far from Erasmus' purpose here to construct a literary showpiece entirely for its own sake as it is to expound the articles of faith pertaining to Christ in the orderly manner of dogmatic theology. What counts is the effect on his hearers' lives. At the beginning of the work Erasmus explains the arrangement of his material around the three factors most potent in causing us to follow 'our teacher and general' Jesus, and the reasons for this threefold impact on us as individuals. In his emphasis on the serious and persuasive power of rhetoric Erasmus aligns himself not only with the classical traditions of rhetorical theory but also with the many medieval sermons which, rather than dealing with doctrinal matters, aimed at generating an emotional response in listeners so causing them to amend their lives. Such an aim is of course a central part of the Christian's duty,[11] but in addition medieval preaching was itself dependent to a large extent on classical rhetoric; even the basic form of the late medieval 'thematic' or 'modern' type of sermon, with its clearly defined constituent parts, derived ultimately from the classical analysis of the component parts of an oration, as defined by Cicero and Quintilian.[12] It is this form, shorn of its excesses of subdivision and pedantic over-classification, which Erasmus adopts in the *Concio*, rather than the simple, informal, 'ancient' style typical of patristic homilies, which he used for the most part in his expositions of the psalms. While some of Erasmus' writings adopt the conventions of the sermon only to lose track of them midway and relapse into the form of a written commentary, the *Concio*, being a short piece and composed specifically for oral delivery, never loses sight of its formal rhetorical nature. Even the opening disclaimer of Ciceronian rhetoric, opposing such foibles to true Christian eloquence, is itself a variant of a rhetorical convention, and is marked by elaborate word-play and para-doxes. Among Erasmus' contemporaries were those who felt uneasy with such literary effects: Colet's own attitude to eloquence was somewhat ambivalent.[13] The modern reader, living in a world where 'rhetoric' has become a pejorative word, may also be tempted to dismiss this studied artifice as insincere, the product of an immature religious sense; but such a reaction misunderstands the evangelical nature of Erasmian humanism, devoted as it was to bringing about improved knowledge and above all a change of heart in its public. Undoubtedly Erasmus was interested in questions of style and rhetoric for their own sake; his own creative works make that clear, as do his literary and stylistic handbooks, such as *De copia*, *De conscribendis epistolis*, and to some extent the *Adagia*. But equally clearly he found it entirely appropriate to put such devices to pious ends. The topic continued to preoccupy him, and his last major work, *Ecclesiastes* (1535), is a lengthy treatment of the preacher's task and the literary technicalities he must master. To any who felt that classical rhetoric was an unsuitable vehicle for proclaiming the gospel, Erasmus would no doubt have replied with St Augustine: 'Who would dare to say that truth, in the person of her defenders, should stand unarmed against falsehood, so that while those who try to persuade of what is false know how to make their listeners benevolent or attentive or docile in their introduction, the defenders of truth are ignorant of such things?'[14]

While no one would claim that the *Concio* is one of Erasmus' major achievements, it did enjoy a considerable success in its author's lifetime. Evidently his public understood and appreciated its rhetorical context. The first edition (NK 2887), printed by Robert de Keysere, is dated 1 September, which almost certainly refers to 1511; probably this was printed at Paris, not at Ghent, as was earlier supposed. It seems likely that Erasmus gave the text to de Keysere on his trip to Paris in the spring of that year.[15] This was followed by several reprintings, notably that of Bade in July 1512[16] and that of Matthias Schürer in Strasbourg, who almost simultaneously issued an edition along with *De ratione studii*. Later editions reveal a revised text. After leaving England in the summer of 1514, Erasmus made a leisurely journey to Basel, spending the month of August in Strasbourg.[17] Among his associates here was Schürer,[18] for whom he revised the texts of the *De ratione studii* volume. The result was published in December of the same year; the changes made were mostly in the nature of simple corrections, except in the case of the *Concio*. Here too they incorporate no new material, but they do demonstrate how carefully Erasmus reread the work to remove both infelicities of style and inaccuracies in biblical quotation and interpretation. Almost all the modifications made in 1514 concern either minor but deliberate verbal changes, or else, in two cases, quotations from the New Testament; here Erasmus corrected one quotation (making his argument less cogent in the process) and removed one sentence, which he had come to consider irrelevant (notes 53 and 51 below). This revised text was the basis for almost all further printings of the *Concio*; changes in the many later editions are merely corrections (or further errors).

As Erasmus no doubt hoped, the work attained popularity in circles much wider than those for which it was originally intended. As a short devotional work in 'clene and chast laten,' suitable for school use, it was assured of a reasonably wide success in one context at least, but a popularity outside the schoolroom is suggested by the editions, notably those of Froben in 1518 and 1519, in which it appears not with educational works like *De copia* but following basic works of lay piety such as the *Enchiridion*. A firmer indication is provided by translations into the vernacular – into Spanish (1516),[19] English (about 1540),[20] and Dutch (1607). In later ages, it seems to have been only in England that the *Concio* was even sporadically remembered, obviously because of its connection with St Paul's school.[21]

The basis for this translation is the text of Schürer's 1514 edition, incorporating later corrections; this is substantially the text of LB v. Passages in the earlier editions which were altogether omitted in 1514 and other significant differences in the unrevised text are identified in the notes.

EK

HOMILY ON THE CHILD JESUS

TO BE SPOKEN BY A BOY IN THE SCHOOL
RECENTLY FOUNDED BY COLET IN LONDON

I, a child among children, shall now speak to you of the child Jesus, who cannot be expressed in words; so I should not wish to possess the eloquence of a Cicero, to delight the ears with a short-lived, meaningless pleasure. For Christian eloquence should be as far removed from the eloquence of the world as is the wisdom of Christ from the wisdom of the world, and such a distance is immeasurable. Rather, I should desire you to pray fervently with me to God, the good Father of good Jesus, from whom as from a spring the sum of all good things proceeds, who alone by his fruitful Spirit makes eloquent the tongues of infants, and who often draws out perfect praise from the mouths of sucklings,[1] asking him that as our whole life should express none other but him of whom I shall now speak, Jesus, so may my speech savour of him, reflect him, and breathe him, who is the word of the Father, who alone has the words of life,[2] whose living and efficacious discourse pierces deeper than any two-edged sword,[3] reaching right to the inmost recesses of the heart. Let us also ask him from whose body flow streams of living water[4] that he may not be displeased to pass through the medium of my voice as through a channel, flowing into the souls of all of you present and inundating them with the copious waters of heavenly grace.

I am confident that this will be granted, my dear comrades-in-arms, if in addition to your devout prayers you have ears made pure and truly athirst; such, that is, as the everlasting Word requires from us in the gospel, when he says, 'He who has ears to hear, let him hear.'[5] As for me, why should I lack courage to tackle this task, which, hard though it may be, is yet a pious one; especially with God himself to help me, in whom our mortal weakness is the stronger the less it trusts in its own resources, and in whom Paul boasts that he can do everything.[6] Those who have enrolled in the armies of the world – that is, of the devil – are carried away by ardent enthusiasm as each showers his own general with praises. So for us, what task should be more urgent or important in our eyes than to compete in honouring with pious praises our teacher, our champion, and our general, Jesus, who is indeed the ruler of all people, but yet peculiarly our own, the prince of children? Above all things, let us strive to know him; knowing him let us praise him, praising him let us love him, loving him let us imitate him and show him forth, imitating him let us enjoy him, and enjoying him let us attain everlasting felicity.

But amid such a vast, fertile array of topics, how can my oration find a starting-point, and where may it end? He of whom I shall speak is the fount or, better, the ocean of all good things. And yet although by nature he is infinite and cannot be contained, he has drawn himself in and confined himself within limits. In the same way, although my speech expounds his praises, which know no limit, it must still set limits for itself.[7] It seems to me that there are three principal factors which tend to encourage pupils or soldiers to act with enthusiasm: admiration of their leader, love of him, and the reward that he offers. Consequently, so that we may be the readier to obey our teacher and commander[8] Jesus, let us consider reverently and thoroughly how each of these applies to him. First, we shall consider how he is to be admired and wondered at in every respect; then, how much he is to be loved, and therefore imitated; finally, how great will be the fruit of our love.

[Part I][9]

The usual practice of orators in this type of speech is to produce examples of famous princes, so that the comparison may increase the stature of the man they want to praise. But our commander so far surpasses every peak of human greatness that whatever you adduce, however splendid it may be, you are adding darkness, not light. Is there anyone whose magnificent birth and ancestry would not seem a mere shadow beside that of Jesus, who in a manner we cannot express, cannot even imagine, is continually being born, beyond time, God from God, in all things equal to the highest and eternal Father? And yet surely even his birth as man easily casts into darkness the light shed by any king. At his birth the universe marvelled, as by the Father's command and the Spirit's inspiration, with an angel for bridal messenger, without the agency of a man, he was born a virgin of a virgin who conceived from heaven; he was born a human being and in time, and yet human in such a way that he did not cease to be God, and did not acquire one whit of the filth with which we are polluted. What could one imagine greater in extent than he who is immanent in all things and yet confined to no place, remaining in himself unbounded? What could be richer than he who is that utmost good from which all good things flow, yet which is incapable of being diminished? What could shine more brilliantly than he who is 'the splendour of the Father's glory'[10] and who alone 'lights every man coming into this world?'[11] What could be more powerful than he to whom the almighty Father has given all authority in heaven and earth?[12] Whose will could more prevail than his whose simple command formed the universe, at whose orders the sea grows calm, things change in kind, illnesses disappear, armed men fall to the ground, devils are expelled, the elements are obedient, rocks are split, the dead come to life, sinners repent[13] – in short, all things are made new? What could be more majestic than he on whom the heavens gaze in wonder, at whom hell trembles, and whom this world between entreats and adores, compared with whom the mightiest kings acknowledge that they are but worms? What could be stronger, a mightier conqueror than he, who alone by his own death defeated death, which by others was unconquered, and overthrew the tyranny of Satan through his heavenly prowess? What could be more triumphantly victorious than he who shattered and despoiled hell, and taking with him great numbers of pious souls came victorious to heaven, where he is seated at the right hand of God the Father?[14] What could be wiser than he, who created everything with such amazing order that even in the tiny bees he has left so great and so many wonderful traces of his wisdom, and who binds together, holds, and governs everything with such extraordinary harmony and order, present everywhere without leaving himself, moving everything while himself unmoved, stirring everything while himself remaining still, and in whom the most foolish thing surpasses by far all the wisdom of human philosophers.[15] Whose authority ought we to take more seriously than his, to whom the Father openly gave witness: 'This is my beloved son, in whom I am pleased: hear him.'[16] What should we reverence so much as him whose eyes see all things plainly? And what should we fear so much as him, whose assent suffices to send both body and soul to hell?[17] Yet what could be fairer to behold than he, the contemplation of whose face is the highest of all bliss? Lastly, if the value of many things is increased by their antiquity, what is more ancient than he who has no beginning and who will have no end?

But perhaps it would be more fitting for us as children to marvel at a child. Here too he presents himself for our wonder, so much so that the meanest thing about him is finer than the highest peaks of human achievement. He became a wailing infant, and was bound in rags and laid down in a feeding-trough. Yet how great he was! Angels in the heavens sing his praises, shepherds worship him, as does his mother, the brute beasts acknowledge him, a star points him out, the Magi pay him homage, king Herod fears him and all Jerusalem trembles, holy Simeon takes him in his arms, Anna prophesies,[18] and the devout are raised to hope of salvation. Humble sublimity and sublime humility! If we are impressed by novelty, what was ever done or heard or thought that resembles this? If we respect grandeur, what could be in any manner greater than our Jesus, whom no created being could express in words or conceive in thought? To wish to contain his greatness in speech is much more senseless than to try to drain the huge ocean using a tiny cup.[19] His boundlessness is rather to be adored than explained, and we ought to marvel at it all the more since we cannot aspire to it. Then what prevents us from so doing, when his great precursor[20] proclaimed himself unworthy to untie the fastenings of his shoes? My dearest children, let us then glory with holy pride in this noble child, our teacher Jesus, this illustrious general. Let his sublimity give us the courage for devout enterprises. Let us be content with ourselves only when we realize that everything of his he shares with us; only, moreover, when we consider that we are better than if we had become slaves to the world or to vices, the most disreputable of masters, after having been once enrolled in the army of such a general.

Part II

But amazement and awe are felt even by evil spirits;[21] love is felt only by the devout. For this reason the second part of my oration concerns us more closely and should be heard with greater attention: I mean the reasons for which we ought to love Jesus, or rather reciprocate his love, since when we were not yet made, before time began, he loved us in himself,[22] in whom already all things were in existence. In his own natural goodness when we were nothing he created us, creating not any common animal but man. He made us in his image (that is, capable of the highest good) and with his holy breath he infused into us the spirit of life. In addition to this he ordained that the other animals be subject to our rule, even allocating angels to watch over us, and he gave us this whole immense and marvellous world to use. He placed us therein as though in some wonderful theatre, so that in creation we might marvel at the creator's wisdom, love his goodness, and revere his power, and to heighten this effect he decked us out with all the gifts of our mind, and beautified us with the clear light of the intellect.[23] What more wonderful or fortunate creature could be imagined than this? And yet envy is the constant companion of good fortune. Through the serpent's guile the creature fell miserably into sin, that is, into less than nothing. But here again, good Jesus, with what inexpressible wisdom, what unprecedented action, what incomparable charity you restored your creation! You restored it in such a manner that to fall was almost a benefit, and that 'fault' has not without justification been called 'happy.'[24] We owed everything to our creator, but to our restorer we owe more than everything. From your Father's kingdom you reduced yourself of your own free will to the exile which we endure, so that though we had been expelled from paradise you might make us citizens of heaven. You assumed our humanity so that you might win for us a share in your divinity.[25] You put on our filth so that you might clothe us in the glory of immortality.[26] You desired to take our form upon yourself and pass a number of years with us in this world, so full of disasters, so that thus you might succeed in rousing us to love of you. You came forth naked into the light, or rather darkness, which is ours; with us and for us you gave forth a child's cries, you thirsted, you hungered, you endured cold and heat, toil, weariness, and want, you kept vigils and fasts. You wanted to be subject to all these ills of ours so that you might set us free from all ills and claim for us a sharing in the highest good – that is, yourself.

The whole course of your most holy life serves to fire our minds with inspiring examples. You form and educate us with salutary precepts,[27] you rouse us with astonishing miracles, you draw us to you with gentle counsel, you call us with unalterable promises, so that there is no path to you more easily traversed than that through you yourself; you who are alone the way, the truth, and the life.[28] Yet you did not merely show the way; you opened it, when for our sake you consented to be bound and led by force, to be condemned, mocked, struck, spat upon, scourged, and reviled, and finally to be sacrificed, a spotless lamb,[29] on the altar of the cross. All this so that you might free us with your bonds, heal us with your wounds, wash us with your blood, and with your death bring us to everlasting life.[30] To sum up, you gave yourself over to us entirely, so that by your loss – were such a thing possible – you might save us, who were lost. Restored to life, you appeared many times to your disciples, and in their sight you sought again your Father, to give the members assurance that they would reach the place where they had seen the head go before them.[31] Then when you had made satisfaction to your Father, you wished to supply your friends with further strength, and you sent that wonderful pledge of your everlasting love, the Holy Spirit, so that though dead to the world we might live in a far more real sense and far more happily in you than we can in our own spirit. What more could be added to these proofs of perfect charity? But even these deeds, so great and so many, were not enough to satisfy your ardent love for us. Who could narrate the whole series of martyrdoms by which you fill us with contempt for this life? Or the virgins by whose example you inspire us to chastity, the deeds of the saints through which you encourage us to holiness, or the wonderful sacraments of your church with which you both strengthen and enrich us? Who could describe how you comfort us, cheer us, arm us, teach us, advise us, attract us, take us to you, change us and transform us by your mystical writings? In them you chose to hide living sparks of yourself, destined to light a great fire of love in those who will only make determined and devout efforts to seek them out. And everywhere you come to meet us, so that we may never forget you. Further, how fatherly you are as you bear with sinners, and how merciful as you receive those who return to you. You do not count your benefits to those who please you, nor do you reckon our wrongdoings to our account when we repent. Constantly you rouse us and pull us towards you by secret impulses. You correct us by adversity and encourage us by prosperity; you leave no stone unturned,[32] and your burning love never ceases to cherish us, to defend us, to protect us, and to make us blessed.

My fellow soldiers, we have dealt with only a very few of an unlimited number of things, but even so you see how vast is this pile of benefits. Some may produce elaborate speeches about Pylades and Orestes, Pirithous and Theseus, Damon and Pythias,[33] but such are mere trifles compared with these others. Remember that he freely gave us these benefits when we had done nothing to deserve them – rather, we were traitors and enemies, quite unable to give any good in return. If we human beings can be inspired to love others of our kind by ordinary benefits, can we not at least return the love of this our creator and our redeemer, who so loves us and so deserves our love? He asks from us only those thanks which he pours back into the store of our gain. The diamond softens when it comes into contact with goat's blood.[34] Eagles, lions, leopards, dolphins, and snakes understand when good is done to them, and return it.[35] Then how hard is the human heart, harder than the diamond, if it does not grow tender with such unprecedented love; how ungrateful is man, more so than the beasts, if he can forget such good deeds; how uniquely shameless, or should I rather say insane, if when he has been thus formed, thus restored and enriched, heaped with such kindnesses, and summoned to such hopes, he can love anything but him alone in whom is everything, from whom comes everything, and who shares all things with us.

But although this love extends to all people, still we in particular have a special debt towards him, because on many occasions he showed that he was especially interested in and indulgent towards our part of society – that is, towards children. He showed this first by his choice, in accordance with the prophets' oracles,[36] of being born a tiny child, when he was infinite in extent. And when he was still enclosed and hidden in the Virgin's womb, he took pleasure in being greeted by the movement and delight of another unborn child.[37] Then straightway he wished to consecrate his birth with the blood of innocent children,[38] engaging them as it were for a preliminary skirmish, so that he might enter the war an unconquered leader. And when with his triumphal death upon him he came to Jerusalem,[39] he desired children to come running to meet him for his honour and service, and he wished his praises to be sung by children's voices. Then, what a loving and concerned champion of children he appears when, as the mothers push forward their offspring to be hallowed by Jesus' touch, he is angry with the disciples who prevent their approach and says: 'Let the little ones come to me.'[40] And not only did he bless the children; further, he says that no one is able to enter the kingdom of heaven unless he stoops to resume the state of an infant.[41] Again, how lovingly he acts when he solemnly warns against causing injury to children, saying that it would be better for a man to be thrown into the sea with a millstone round his neck than to harm any of these little ones.[42] Furthermore, he added a fine saying in praise of children: 'Truly I say to you that their angels always behold the face of my Father.'[43] Your flock, the flock dedicated to you, gives you thanks, Jesus our teacher; and I ask that you may be always willing to bring your sacred hands to our help and keep us far from every stumbling-block. Then, was it not a great sign of love when he placed a child in the middle of the gathering and put him forward to the disciples as an example? He said: 'Unless you are changed, and become like this child, you will not enter the kingdom of heaven.'[44] The same is demonstrated by his reply when Nicodemus asks him how he may obtain eternal life: he tells him to be born again[45] – that is, to go back to childhood. The state of childhood was so pleasing to our leader Christ that he compels even old men to become children again if they wish to be admitted to that society outside which there is no hope of salvation. And Peter does not differ from Christ when he tells us to 'desire milk like newborn babes.'[46] Neither does Paul disagree when he says, 'My children, whom I bring to birth again, until Christ is fully formed in you.'[47] He also nourishes children with milk in Christ.[48] There are many passages of this sort in the Scriptures. In fact, to sum up, Christianity is nothing other than a rebirth and a sort of renewed infancy.

The child, then, and childhood, in which Jesus took such pleasure, are great sacraments. Let us not despise our stage of life,[49] when he who gives everything its true value thought so highly of it. Only let us take care to be the sort of children whom Jesus loves: innocent, easily led, and simple. And let us also remember that the childhood which is acceptable to God lies not in years but in disposition; not in age, but in behaviour.[50] Children who have hairless chins but bearded minds, who are young in years, but old in wickedness and cunning, are a perverse sort of child whom we should shun completely.[51] It is then a new kind of childhood which Christ approves: a childhood which is not puerile, a sort of aged childhood[52] consisting not in number of years but in innocence and simplicity of mind. Does not Peter make this quite clear when he says, 'Therefore abandon all malice and all guile and insincerity and envy and slander, and like new-born babes wish for the milk of reason, which is without guile, so that in it you may grow up to salvation.'[53] Why did he add 'of reason'? Clearly, to exclude stupid behaviour, which certainly tends to accompany that stage of life. And why does he counsel against envy, hypocrisy, and other faults of that type, which are particularly characteristic of the old? Obviously so that we realize that Christ's children are so reckoned by their simplicity and purity, not by their date of birth. Paul speaks to the same effect. 'In respect of malice,' he says, 'be children, but in your understanding be perfect.'[54] But in fact there is in childhood itself a natural sort of goodness, a kind of reflection and image of innocence, or rather a disposition which gives hope of uprightness to come. There is a malleable mind, ready to follow any way of life, a sense of shame which is the best guardian of innocence, a nature free from vice, a bodily freshness and as it were a flowering in the springtime of life, and a quality somehow indefinably allied to spiritual beings. It is not simply coincidence that whenever angels appear they present themselves to our eyes in the form of a child.[55] Even magicians, when they invoke spirits with their incantations, are said to summon them into a child's body.[56] How much more willingly the Spirit who is God, when summoned by devout and holy prayers, will journey to such a dwelling-place!

So if to these gifts of nature children can add the imitation of that highest, most perfect child, then they will be revealed as children both grateful to him and worthy of him. Who indeed could not love one so deserving? And yet the effect of true love is that you are eager to become as like as possible to the object of your love. Now if human love can have this effect on us, how great a desire of imitation will be aroused in us by divine love, when the human emotion is in comparison hardly even a pale shadow of love? So if we sincerely love Jesus from our souls, not merely in words, we will try to the best of our ability to express Jesus, or rather to be transformed into him. If we cannot follow in the steps of the man, let us as children at least imitate the child. And yet this too is an achievement not in the least childish, but beyond the resources even of the old; however, it is an achievement which is scarcely ever accomplished better than by children. Whenever a task depends on human resources, then strength, age, and sex come into the balance; but when the matter is one of grace, not nature, then the wonderful operation of the Spirit displays itself more forcefully in inverse proportion to natural resources and the trust placed in the flesh. Then why should we feel doubts and hesitations, when we are shaped, moulded, and transformed by him whom we attempt to express? Who was it who gave the boy Daniel such judgment?[57] Who bestowed such wisdom on the boy Solomon?[58] Who granted the Three Children such powers of endurance?[59] Who made the boy-servant of Eli worthy to hear God's voice?[60] Or the child Nicholas, or Giles, Benedict, Agnes, or Cecilia?[61] Who gave so many defenceless young girls such masculine, invincible courage? Obviously, it was not nature, but grace; and the less assistance is supplied by nature, the more marvellous is the action of grace. Then let us trust in grace, and confidently undertake the task of imitating the child Jesus; let us never take our eyes from him, our aim. We have a perfect model; there is nothing that we need to seek elsewhere. His whole life shouts aloud those things we ought to follow. What lesson was taught by the birth of that most pure child from a most pure virgin, if not that we should avoid all the filth and pollution of this world and even now on earth practise a life like that of the angels, that is, to practise being what there we shall be for ever? Furthermore, although the spirit of Jesus loathes and detests all filthiness, he particularly hates that bestial impulse of lust, quite unworthy of a human being. What lesson was taught by his birth far from home, when he came into the world in a little hut and was put down in a feeding-trough and wrapped in rags, if not that we must remember always that here we are sojourners of a few days only, and that we should tread riches underfoot, reject the world's false honours, and through pious works hasten towards our native land in heaven, in which even now our minds should dwell, though our bodily feet must touch the earth the while? And what teaching did he give us with his flight into Egypt, if not that we must completely avoid dealings with the defiled, who try to eradicate Jesus – that is, innocence – and disregard for the world from within us? What lesson was taught by his circumcision, if not that we should cut off from ourselves all fleshly passions, which stand in the way of our hastening to Christ, and should live as though we were dead in ourselves, being guided and flourishing only in the spirit of Jesus? What lesson was given by his presentation in the temple, if not that we should dedicate and consecrate our entire selves to God and to holy pursuits from our very infancy, and straightway imbibe Jesus while the mind's vessel is still newly formed?[62] No age is too young to learn piety; in fact no age is more suited to learning Christ than that which is still ignorant of the world.

Now consider yourselves, children, how holy were the pursuits in which this child, born in this fashion and thus dedicated to God, spent his whole childhood. He did not spend his time in idleness, food, sleep, silly games, foolish tales, or straying loose, the way that ordinary children behave, but in fulfilling his parents' wishes, or in prayer, or in hearing the discourses of the learned, or in holy meditations, or in devout and serious conversations with children of his age. Surely St Luke includes these and many other similar things in his summary when he says, 'The child grew and became strong, filled with wisdom; and the favour of God was upon him.'[63] Can you not clearly see a new kind of childhood? Of the old sort of child it was written, 'Folly is bound up in the heart of a child,'[64] but of the new child you hear that he was 'filled with wisdom.' How then can we continue to use our youth as an excuse for ignorance, when we hear of a child not merely wise, but filled with wisdom? You see how this child turns

the whole order of things upside-down: it is he who says in the book of
Revelation, 'Behold, I make all things new.'[65] The wisdom of the elders is
destroyed, the prudence of the prudent is reproved,[66] and children are filled
with wisdom. For this reason he gives thanks to his Father: 'For you have
hidden these things from the wise, and revealed them to children.'[67]
Further, so that we do not strive to attain the foolish and specious wisdom of
this world, there follows immediately 'and the favour of God was upon
him.' He is truly wise who is foolish to the world and whose wisdom is in
nothing but Christ. Such a man is not known by philosophers' tomes or from
the subtleties of a Scotus;[68] he is known by heartfelt faith, he is maintained in
hope, and bound by love.

Now consider how much Jesus taught us by his secret disappearance
from his parents at the age of twelve, when after three long days he was
found – but not among acquaintances or relatives.[69] Where then was he
found? at games or dances in streets or market-place? Listen, children, to
where Jesus was discovered when he left his parents like a runaway, and
you will realize where you too should spend your time. 'He was found,' we
read, 'in the temple, sitting among the learned men, listening to them and
asking questions by turns.'[70] What did Jesus mean to teach us by these
marvellous deeds of his? We cannot doubt that the lesson is serious and
important, and one to be practised. What then is it? Surely it is true that
Christ should mature in us, since he is born in us and goes through the
stages of his life in us, until we attain to mature manhood and the measure of
his fullness.[71] Then as he grows up in us, he teaches us to transfer our
natural feelings for parents and friends to God, and to love and admire
nothing in this world unless it is in Christ, and Christ in all things. Let us
remember that our true father, country, family, and friends are in heaven.
But to prevent us from supposing that this unconcern for parents suggests
arrogance or disobedience, the passage continues 'and was subject to
them.'[72] In fact no one loves his parents more truly, no one pays them more
dutiful attention, no one obeys them more scrupulously than he who
neglects them in this manner. And what does it mean 'to be seated in the
temple,' if not to rest in the sacred, and to bring a mind free from all anxieties
to the task of learning? Nothing is more turbulent than sin, while wisdom
loves calm and relaxation. Then how can we object to learning from anyone?
How closely ought we to listen to our teachers, given the example of that
heavenly child, the wisdom of God the Father, who sat in the midst of the
doctors, listening and answering them by turns, and by his answers causing
them all to marvel at his wisdom. This was scarcely surprising, since this
was he compared with whom all worldly wisdom is foolish. Study of the law
is a fine thing, knowledge of philosophy is an outstanding achievement,

attainments in theology are worthy of great respect; but if one hears Jesus, immediately they all seem foolish. Our replies may not be able to produce a miracle of wisdom; they can, however, at least reflect modesty and innocence. Note also, I pray you, how docile and obedient we should be towards our parents and teachers (who are a more important kind of parent to us, in effect the parents of our intellects), when he who is the Lord of all returned under his parents' authority to Nazareth, although they failed to understand him. The duty and respect that we owe to our parents requires that we should sometimes give way to their will, even if we ourselves know better.

But now it is worth your while to hear the suitable conclusion which Luke gives to his account of Jesus' childhood. 'And Jesus,' he says, 'increased in wisdom and in years, and in favour with God and with men.'[73] How much he teaches us in how few words! The first lesson is that an increase in years should be accompanied by an increase in piety, so that no one can have reason to say of us what St Augustine said of the mass of human beings: 'More years, more wickedness.'[74] Further, let us never pause in this finest of all contests, let us never think we have attained the goal, but like those who run in a race let us forget all that we have passed and strive towards what lies ahead.[75] Let us aim to go from good to better and from better to best until we reach the finishing-point, which is the end of this life. When Socrates reached old age, he was constantly desirous to learn from all and sundry, as though he were completely ignorant.[76] It is the same for us: the more completely we are in Christ, the less pleasing we find ourselves, if we have truly made progress in him. Self-love[77] is a terrible threat to both learning and piety. In Quintilian's words, 'that type of headstrong disposition does not readily reach the fruits'[78] either of learning or of a blameless life. I think too that the word-order, 'with God and with men,' is not merely coincidental; it enables us to realize that our first priority is to take care that our life be pleasing to God. When we do this, favour with men will ensue of its own accord. For nothing is finer or more lovable than virtue, and the praise which follows it will come more readily the less it is sought.

I have described briefly, as well as I could, this model of a child whom we should love deeply and imitate diligently. Then assuredly in proportion as we have imitated him, so we shall be seen to love him; also, the more ardently we love him, the more completely we shall imitate him. Then let us daily ask him this very thing in prayers that are pure: that he may grant us to burn with love of him and to become like him – that is, chaste, pure, unspotted, meek, simple, docile, free from deceit, ignorant of guile, unknowing of envy, obedient to our parents, responsive to our teachers, taking no thought for the world, intent on the divine and occupied in the study of Scripture, daily better than our own selves, acceptable to the heavenly host and pleasing to men, drawing as many as we may to Christ by our good repute. Let us ask this without ceasing, I say, let us strive for this with all our resources, while our youth, so soon to leave us, still has such capability. If Quintilian's precept is correct, that 'the best things should be learned first and without delay,'[79] what should be learned before Christ, than whom nothing is better? Or rather, what else should a Christian learn but him alone, to know whom is everlasting life, as he himself declares when in the gospel he prays to his Father?[80] If we are concerned for this, we shall always to the best of our ability give thanks to him who so uniquely deserves them, and in giving him thanks we shall also benefit ourselves. Our thanksgiving will be greater the more passionately we return his love; we shall return his love in greater measure the more we depict him in our way of life; and the more we depict him, the more we shall be enriched by so doing.

Part III

Perhaps the thought will have occurred to some of you that this is hard soldiering, to reject all things and take up the cross with Christ. But bear in mind, dear brothers, that Christ and the world are entirely different in nature. The world is like a painted whore; its first outward appearance strikes us as charming and all gold, but later, the deeper you tread and the closer you look in, the more bitter, foul, and disgusting is every aspect. Christ is quite the opposite: when we see him from far off, the prospect seems somewhat dour, as we look at the crosses and the contempt for pleasures and for life. Yet anyone who in trust throws himself completely on Christ will find that nothing is more pleasant, more beneficial, or more delightful. Unless, of course, the Truth did not speak the truth in the gospel, when he said, 'Take my yoke upon you, and you will find rest for your souls. For my yoke is easy, and my burden light.'[81] This, of course, is that same difficult path of virtue of which Hesiod dreamed, all those years before Christ, 'harsh as you approach, but as you go on always easier and more pleasant.'[82] But what can in the end seem harsh if it is the way to a prize so great and so assured? If we agree with the sage's words that 'the hope of the prize mitigates the whip's force,'[83] who would not judge anything in this brief life desirable or easy to bear if it will bring him that heavenly and unceasing life which is to reign forever with Christ[84] and to gaze continually on that highest good, to associate with the company of angels, and to be far distant from every fear of evil. Who would not wish to purchase such a reward, even at the price of a thousand deaths? Yet this is the largesse promised to his soldiers by our general Jesus, who cannot deceive and does not know falsehood. You can weigh up for yourselves the great and everlasting profit against the little term of our service – no longer than our lifetime, and what is that but smoke which appears for a little while,[85] or the dream of an hour?

But let us now pass over this prize, which exceeds reckoning, and examine the abundant and great benefits with which our leader even in this life rewards the labours of his men. Let us see what different harvests are reaped by the world's soldiers and those who serve under Jesus Christ. We should hear what the wicked themselves say in the book of Wisdom: 'We have grown weary in the path of wickedness and perdition; we have trodden hard paths, but the way of the Lord we have not known.'[86] The world entices them with its painted imitations of good things – nothing but poison glozed with honey. When it has won them over,[87] and as it were enrolled them in its service, dear God! what cares, what anxieties, what turmoil, what losses, what dishonour! What tortures of a guilty conscience, what a miserable end it brings the unfortunates! We can see that they are already punished severely in this world for their wickedness, even if there were no hell to follow. But those who reject the deceptions of the world, placing instead all their love, their attention, and their devotion with Jesus (that is, the highest good), those who are completely dependent on him, will in accordance with the promise made in the gospel not only attain eternal life, but even in this world receive a hundredfold.[88] What does this mean, to receive a hundredfold? Clearly, to receive instead of meretricious benefits, real ones; instead of uncertainty, certainty; instead of the transitory, the eternal; instead of poisoned food, healthgiving nourishment; instead of worries, peace; instead of anxiety, trust; instead of disturbances, quiet; instead of loss, gain; instead of crimes, integrity; instead of an anguished conscience, a secret and unutterable joy; instead of a squalid and miserable end, a glorious and triumphant death. You have scorned wealth for the love of Christ; in him you will find true riches. You have rejected false honours; in him you will gain far greater glory. You have spurned the love of your parents; all the more lovingly will you be cherished by your true Father, who is in heaven. You have regarded earthly wisdom as nothing; your wisdom in Christ will be far more true and more happy. You have despised such pleasures as are pernicious; in him you will find delights which are completely other. In short, when the world's thick clouds are scattered and you see the hidden but real riches of Christ, everything which previously attracted and concerned you will cease to hold excitement for you; more, you will turn from it forthwith, reject it, and fly from it as from some contagion. In some wonderful way it comes about that as soon as the heavenly light touches our souls within, our perception of all things is immediately changed. So things which a little while ago seemed sweet are now bitter; things which were bitter grow sweet; what was loathsome is pleasing; what was pleasing is loathsome; what before seemed sparkling is now filthy; what was strong is weak; what was beautiful is ugly; what was noble is base; what was rich is poor; what was lofty is humble; what was gain is loss; what was wise is foolish; what was life is death; what was sought is shunned, and vice versa. Suddenly the appearance of things changes, so that you will reckon everything as completely the opposite of what it used to seem. Thus in Christ, who is but one, you will find gathered together all truly good things, of which the world shows forth vain and empty shadows and reflections, like magicians' tricks; these the unhappy mass of mortals[89] pursues through good and evil, with such turbulence of spirit, such losses, and such perils. Tell me what happiness can be compared with that of the mind[90] which has gained its freedom from error and from emotion, which is secure and continually rejoicing in the witness of conscience,[91] which is worn by no cares, which is lofty, raised high and next to the sky, already beyond the human lot, which is supported by Christ the highest rock, and which from above sees all the deceits, turbulence, and storms of this world and feels amusement, scorn, or rather pity? For what can one fear who has God for champion? Dishonour? But to suffer dishonour for Christ is the highest glory. Poverty? But anyone hastening towards Christ is eager to cast off his burden of wealth. Death? But that must be the most desirable of events, since we know that we shall pass through it to eternal life. What worry can afflict the man whose heavenly Father has numbered even the hairs of his head?[92] And what can one long for if one possesses all things in Christ – for what is not common to the members and the head? How great is man's happiness – and not only happiness, but also dignity – to be a living member of the most holy body of the church, to be one with Christ, the same flesh, the same spirit, to have a heavenly Father in common with him, to have Christ as brother, to be destined for a common inheritance with him: in short, to be no longer man, but God! Add to this a sort of foretaste of future happiness,[93] which is sometimes experienced by the devout. Surely it was this that the prophet saw, this he perceived, when he said, 'Ear has not heard, nor eye seen, nor has the heart of man perceived that which you have prepared, O God, for those who love you.'[94] And so, my dear comrades, if we take care to be true members of Christ, then as the prophet says, 'the righteous man shall flourish as the palm-tree,'[95] and even in this life we shall be fresh and green in a sort of perpetual youth, not only of mind but of body. As the fair and fruitful spirit of Jesus flows into our spirit, so too our spirit will flow into his body, and as far as may be will be transformed into it. And such a shining soul and body may not wear filthy garments; for our soul is

God's dwelling-place, the soul's habitation is the body, while clothes are in a way a body to the body. Thus it will come to pass that the whole man will reflect the purity of the head, until this life is done and he passes to immortality.

Conclusion

Up then, brave comrades! Let us strive with all our might towards such great happiness. Let us admire only Jesus our commander, than whom nothing can be greater – or rather, without whom nothing is great at all. Let us love him alone, than whom nothing can be better – or rather, outside whom nothing is good at all. Let us model ourselves on him, who alone is the true and perfect model of piety, outside whom all wisdom is folly. Let us cling to him alone, embrace him alone, delight in him alone, in whom is true peace, joy, rest, delight, life, and immortality. Why prolong the list? He is the sum of every good. Let us respect nothing, love nothing, desire nothing outside him, let us be eager to please him alone. Let us remember that whatever we do is done under his eyes and with his angels for witnesses. He is jealous, and will not tolerate any of the world's pollution. Therefore let us live a pure life in him like that of the angels; let him be in our hearts, on our lips, in all our lives. Let us know him inwardly, let us speak him, let us express him in our way of life. Let us find all our work, our leisure, our joy, our consolation, our hope, our defence in him. May he never leave our minds while we are awake; may he come to meet us as we sleep. May our studies and even our play bear his imprint; may we grow through him and in him, until we attain perfect manhood,[96] and when we have bravely completed our service, may we enjoy with him the everlasting triumph in heaven. My speech is at an end.

THE TYRANNICIDE, ERASMUS' REPLY TO LUCIAN'S DECLAMATION

Tyrannicida, declamationi Lucianicae respondens

translated and annotated by

ERIKA RUMMEL

In 1506 Erasmus and Thomas More published a volume of translations from Lucian to which each of them had contributed a number of pieces.[1] Lucian, a professional rhetorician of Samosata in Syria (c 125–90 AD), left a large corpus of writings, including model speeches, and essays in popular philosophy, dialogues containing literary and social criticism, and fiction. Famous in antiquity for his brilliant wit, biting satire, and penetrating criticism of traditional beliefs, Lucian had a new vogue in the Renaissance. Manuscripts of his writings in the original Greek were first introduced into Italy in the early fifteenth century, Latin translations began to circulate soon thereafter, and by the end of the century his works were available in print.[2]

Erasmus appreciated Lucian's literary gifts and recommended him as a school author.[3] He admired not only his stylistic excellence, but also the substance of his writings, which he considered both entertaining and morally instructive. Accordingly, he described Lucian's works as a mirror of life, 'useful and pleasant to read,' 'most serviceable for the detection and refutation of ... impostures,' and raising a 'civilized laughter, not without art.'[4] The collection of Lucian's writings thus recommended to the reader was an immediate success. Erasmus later recalled that the book 'was snatched up at first by those who wished to learn, and warmly welcomed.'[5] It was reprinted many times and remained for generations the standard Latin translation in northern Europe.[6]

Among the pieces in the collection, the forensic speech *Tyrannicida* is of special interest. It is the only work translated by both Erasmus and More, and it prompted them to compose retorts, that is, to lay aside the role of translators for a time and to present their own specimens of forensic oratory in competition with Lucian and with one another.[7]

Lucian's *Tyrannicida* belongs to the class of court speeches that were used as models in schools of rhetoric, and the retorts composed by Erasmus and More preserve the generic characteristics of the original. Exercises dealing with fictitious – and often improbable – court cases were supposed to develop the skills of aspiring lawyers and to further their dexterity in manipulating arguments. In antiquity, opinion about the usefulness of such exercises was divided. Seneca and Quintilian were among their defenders, Tacitus voiced doubts about their efficacy.[8] Erasmus himself regarded them as profitable and expressed the hope that they would some day be revived in schools. He went so far as to blame his generation's linguistic inadequacies on a lack of such exercises: 'If we were to follow the precepts of Cicero and Quintilian, and also the general practice of antiquity, and carefully train ourselves from boyhood onwards in exercises of this kind, I believe there would be less of the poverty of expression, the pitiful lack of style, and the disgraceful stammering we see even among public professors of the art of oratory.'[9]

Tyrannicide was a stock theme among rhetorical exercises. Its hack-
neyed character was noted by Tacitus and mocked by Juvenal.[10] Lucian's
variation on the theme is the speech of a claimant who demands a reward for
tyrannicide although the circumstances surrounding the case make his title
appear doubtful. The events leading up to the tyrant's death are as follows:
The claimant, entering the citadel secretly and at night, had surprised and
killed the tyrant's son. He then withdrew, leaving his sword at the scene of
the murder. Upon discovering his son's body, the tyrant committed suicide,
using the assassin's sword. The petitioner claims that he left his sword
behind for this very purpose, that he foresaw this development, and in fact
refrained from killing the tyrant in order to let him die a more wretched
death. He acknowledges that he has not fulfilled the letter of the law, which
provides a reward for tyrannicide, but insists that there is no substantial
difference between killing the tyrant and causing his death. Thus he
considers his claim to the reward a valid one.

In his retort, Erasmus observes the traditional rules of forensic oratory
as set out by Cicero and Quintilian.[11] According to their handbooks a court
speech consists of six parts: the exordium, which captures the audience's
good will and attention; the narration or statement of facts; the division,
which explains the speaker's procedure; the proof, which is divided into
assertion and refutation; and the peroration.

In a lengthy exordium Erasmus establishes patriotism as the speaker's
motive, rejects the suggestion that he is acting out of envy or partiality to the
tyranny, and discredits the motives of his opponent in turn, accusing him of
greed and selfish ambition. He briefly refers to the tyrant's death, and then
summarizes the points on which the petitioner bases his claims: he had good
intentions, he made a valiant attempt, he caused the tyrant's death, and he
killed the heir apparent, who was already ruling *de facto*. In his proof
Erasmus refutes these arguments, asserting that good intentions cannot
serve as legal grounds for a claim, since they cannot be verified. An
unsuccessful attempt does not qualify a man for a reward. He insists,
moreover, that the claimant could not have foreseen the outcome of his
action and that he was arrogating to himself what was due to his good
fortune and the grace of the gods. Finally, he establishes that the removal of
the son, that is, the future tyrant, does not satisfy the legal definition of
tyrannicide. On the contrary, it sets a dangerous precedent, since a liberal
interpretation would allow murderers to escape punishment by pleading
that their victim was somehow a 'tyrant.' Producing counter-arguments of
his own, Erasmus then establishes three conditions to be met by anyone
claiming the reward: the tyrannicide must show that he had a worthy
motive, that he proceeded in a manner conforming with the city's moral
conventions, and that he was successful in his undertaking. Since the

petitioner meets none of these conditions, he has no valid claim to the reward. In the peroration, Erasmus introduces the laws, the state, and the gods as imaginary supporters of his cause, pleading with the petitioner to abandon his claim.

A comparison between Erasmus' composition and that of his friend and rival Thomas More affords us an opportunity to examine their respective literary qualities and patterns of argumentation.

Erasmus' composition is the more elaborate of the two. In a speech that is almost three times as long as More's, he illustrates each point with a number of examples, dwells on the general principles underlying his arguments,[12] and in accordance with traditional rhetorical precepts supplements his refutation of the opponent's claims with counter-propositions of his own. This last element in particular gives Erasmus' speech a more assertive and, at times, aggressive tone than More's oration, in which the speaker projects quiet determination, keeps to the specific issues at hand, and restricts himself almost completely to defensive arguments. Moreover, while Erasmus speaks with great flourish, employing a full register of rhetorical devices ranging from majestic declamation and dramatization to direct appeal and sarcastic asides, More presents sober, pointed, and precise legal arguments enlivened only by the occasional dramatic note. Thus, while the arguments presented by the two men are similar, the manner of their presentation is markedly different. Erasmus delights in *copia*, More knows the virtue of brevity. As a speech to be delivered before a live audience, More's is perhaps more effective. Unlike Erasmus' lengthy discourse, which strains the listener's patience and taxes his understanding, More presents his case clearly, concisely, and within an easily recognizable structure. Erasmus' flow of arguments, though an impressive demonstration of resourcefulness, is channelled into so many examples and supplementary proofs that its force is diluted; his composition is better read than heard. But although this may not suit its dramatic purpose, it accords well with its actual purpose, that of a model speech exploring and demonstrating to students of rhetoric the possibilities inherent in a given topic.

It has already been stated that the two authors took a similar approach to their topic. Both used the exordium to establish the speaker's motive and to discredit the opponent's. Both refuted his claims by saying that attempted tyrannicide did not qualify a man for a reward, that the son's murder did not constitute tyrannicide, and that the father's suicide could not have been anticipated by the claimant but was the result of divine intervention. Some coincidences in argumentation are to be expected, for certain approaches are suggested by Lucian's speech and develop naturally from his presentation of the case. Whether or not all the parallels between More's and Erasmus' speeches can be explained in this manner remains a question to be explored.

In his introduction to More's composition, Craig Thompson points out that the idea of composing the retort was More's. He also refers to the fact that while Erasmus was accustomed to improvise and reluctant to revise, More generally produced draft outlines.[13] The parallels in the two men's speeches, which are not confined to broad themes but extend to details in thought and word patterns, suggest that More showed such an outline to Erasmus or at any rate discussed certain points with him when he proposed the competition. For example, both men in their exordium deny that the speaker is motivated by partiality toward the tyrant. This is what Lucian's speaker alleges, and it is natural that the allegation should be denied; it is not quite as natural that the refutation should take the same form. 'My opponent ought rather to have shown,' says More, 'that I was connected with the tyrant by blood or marriage ties, or obligated to him for favours, or leagued with him in crimes.' Erasmus makes the same point: 'There existed between myself and the tyrant neither kinship nor relationship by marriage, neither close contact nor a profitable association.'[14] In rejecting the petitioner's title to a reward both men cite an empty treasury. Pointing out the 'meagre resources of our treasury, the present scarcity of funds,' More's speaker cannot bear 'that the state be drained of money by this extra and unnecessary expenditure.' In a similar vein Erasmus contends that 'the treasury is too depleted ... to allow the withdrawing and handing out of prize-money rashly and to undeserving men.'[15] It is difficult to believe that this somewhat circumstantial argument of doubtful validity should have occured to each man independently.

Rejecting the claimant's argument that the son was a tyrant *de facto* and that his assassination therefore constituted tyrannicide, both Erasmus and More state that it was impossible to have two tyrants, one *de facto* and one in name, coexisting in one city. 'Who would believe, jurors, that one city satisfied two tyrants?' asks More. And Erasmus, in similar fashion, exclaims: 'What do I hear? Was this city sustaining two tyrants, then?'[16] Far from accepting a co-regent, the tyrant eyes his son with suspicion. 'No one is more suspect to tyrants than the heir,' explains More. 'The more he gives vent to his savage nature and tyrannical practices, the more he terrifies his parent.' Erasmus makes the same point: 'No follower is less useful to the tyrant than his son,' and 'a violent and insolent son is a cause for concern to the tyrant.'[17] As for ruling *de facto*, no follower, however tyrannical his bearing, can be called a 'tyrant.' In legal terms, he is seen as the tyrant's deputy, acting on his authority, or as both More and Erasmus say, 'in his shadow.'[18]

Other arguments that occur in similar form in both compositions are the comparison between the claimant's attempt to rid the state of a tyrant and the physician's attempt to rid his patient of an illness, the idea that the

tyrant was driven to suicide by the Furies,[19] and the exploration of the hypo-
thesis 'What would have happened if the tyrant had not committed suicide?'
In that case, More contends, the claimant 'would not be alive today ... to
seek this reward, nor would we have a commonwealth of which it could be
sought.' Or as Erasmus puts it: 'You would not be around to lay the claim,
nor the state to grant it.'[20]

Conceptual and structural parallels are also found. More's impatient
exclamation 'Shameless man, if you are lying! Insane, if you are not!' is
echoed in Erasmus' 'A simpleton, if he really conceived such hopes! An
arrogant fellow, if he claims what he cannot hope for!'[21] Verbal parallels are
scattered throughout the respective descriptions of the events leading up to
the tyrant's suicide. More's account runs as follows:[22]

> He [the assassin] had rashly broken into the citadel (*perrepsisset*; Erasmus:
> *irrepseris*) ... and there suddenly attacked and overpowered the young man,
> who, with the carelessness of youth (*ut est iuventa semper incautior*; Erasmus:
> *ut est ea nimirum aetas securior*), was alone, off guard, and not in the least
> suspicious (*solum, securum, ac nihil minus expectantem*; Erasmus: *solum atque
> incustoditum ... periculique minus cogitans*). Then fright took hold of him, lest he
> be betrayed ... by the cry and groan of the dying youth (*voce vel gemitu morientis
> audito*; Erasmus: *exaudito videlicet morientis gemitu*) ... He did not dare to carry
> the sword with him for fear his flight would be slowed down (*ne esset fuga
> tardior*; Erasmus: *ne te redderet in fuga tardiorem*).

While it might be argued that the scenario was suggested by the arguments
put forward in Lucian's speech, the verbal resemblances cannot be
explained in this manner. The number of parallels, which occur throughout
the two speeches, not only singly but also in clusters and sequences,
strongly suggest the existence of an outline that was accessible to both men.
Such an outline may have been composed by More prior to his proposing the
composition, or jotted down in a joint preparatory session to provide what
Quintilian calls *primas lineas* or *praeformata materia*, basic guidelines or a
rough sketch of the subject-matter.[23]

The *Tyrannicida* is a typical piece of Erasmian rhetoric replete with
characteristic virtues and vices. At its worst the style is overdone and, in the
words of a contemporary arbiter, 'chokes the crop with a rich growth of
weeds'; at its best it is 'richly endowed with language, in arrangement
workmanlike and elegant at the same time, full of examples and close-knit
arguments and agreeable sallies.'[24]

ER

THE TYRANNICIDE

A DECLAMATION BY DESIDERIUS ERASMUS

This is not a translation, but a reply
to the preceding declamation translated from Lucian

Gentlemen of the jury! If I had to plead this case before the popular assembly, which is usually guided by its inclinations rather than by an accurate assessment of the facts – if I did not rather plead my case before a jury selected from the most respected ranks, before men, obviously, of the gravest authority and of supreme wisdom,[1] I should certainly feel some concern that, while everyone's heart is jubilant and, so to speak, leaping at this new and unexpected joy, I might not have a suitably attentive and receptive, much less a well-disposed and favourable audience.[2] Indeed, to those who consider only the façade masking this business, as it were, and do not scrutinize its proper features, I may appear, amid the universal joy of the whole community and, moreover, in such a popular case, to be raising objections and stirring up trouble at a rather inopportune moment.

Correct judgment has no use for any kind of emotion, least of all for excessive, uncontrollable, and overwhelming joy, which is wont not only to eradicate all judgment but often also to rob us of our senses entirely, especially in a situation like ours, when after grievous and prolonged misfortunes resembling a savage storm, suddenly and beyond all hope a haven presents itself. For what is harsher for a free people than slavery? What sweeter and more longed for than liberty? Thus not only the actual conditions themselves, but even the empty words denoting them can rouse a people's spirits to any course of action, especially in these first few days, when jubilation, like some uncontrollable tide, confounds everything and turns it upside-down, when a kind of drunken joy enters the heart, and a sweet, congratulatory mood intoxicates it, keeping the mind from composing its thoughts. But your singular wisdom and insight, gentlemen of the jury, not only relieve me of such misgivings, but also give me the confidence to hope that my dutiful objection – which I have undertaken, not out of envy or out of partiality toward the tyranny (as the claimant has insinuated),[3] but because of my habitual and, I think, well-known love for the republic[4] – may be regarded by you not only as unexceptionable, but even as deserving your support and approval.

When I saw that we had at last, after that long and wretched servitude, and by the manifest grace of the gods, obtained the liberty so often sought in public prayers, I thought we should take care before all else to show our gratitude to those who were the source of our surpassing joy, that they may be willing to make their gift a lasting possession of this city, that they may strengthen and secure the liberty they willingly bestowed on us. Let us remember that they in whose power it was to grant our prayers also have it in their power to withdraw the favour if we prove ungrateful.[5]

Now the most important element of gratitude is understanding who ought to be credited with the favour received. And the only form in which we mortals can return thanks for divine favours is by acknowledging them, by proclaiming them, and by giving credit for them to the authors of that blessing. And I think we must avoid the mistake of being found ungrateful and irreverent towards the gods in our eagerness to be overgenerous to a citizen. For my present effort has not only the objective of preventing the treasury from losing the reward and this man from increasing his profit (although this too is at stake, for the treasury is too depleted after long years of tyranny to allow the withdrawing and handing out of prize-money rashly and to undeserving men) – the purpose of my action is to keep the immortal gods who turned this ill-planned venture to our advantage from demanding the return of this great gift when they see that we are depriving them of the honour, praise, and thanks that they alone deserve, and are bestowing them on a human being. And what sort of human being, I ask you?[6] A private citizen who, in violation of the laws, killed a young man, and by this bold deed merely created a risky opportunity for our freedom being restored, who did so unintentionally (as I shall presently demonstrate), and who has no qualms about taking the most noble title of tyrannicide away from the gods, claiming it for himself, indicting the republic, summoning the very laws to the bar, and accusing the citizens of ingratitude should they fail to attribute this good fortune to him in its entirety.

No deed, gentlemen of the jury, is more splendid than tyrannicide, none more worthy of the gods – the more impudent is it to usurp so eminent an honour without deserving it. No reward is more respected, none more distinguished than that owed to the tyrannicide – the more earnest and rigorous must be your examination, lest the prize be rashly conferred on an unworthy man. A great deal, a great deal indeed, is required from the man who would be worthy of so eminent a title, so divine a prize. This man fulfils none of the prerequisites, as I shall prove shortly. Accordingly, I consider it an unsufferable act of dishonesty that a man liable to punishment by the laws for his murderous and rash deed should seek from the laws the greatest of all rewards. I used the term 'seek,' whereas in fact he makes demands, demands such that, according to his judgment, the laws would remain in his debt and owe him a great deal more,[7] even after having paid out one reward.

By rights he could have demanded the whole lot, but being a modest man, he preferred to be paid a single prize[8] and be owed the rest – no doubt so that he may have grounds for making the state's obligation a reproach whenever he so desires.

As for his conduct, I know not whether to consider it deserving of laughter or indignation, when he appeared here in court before the most dignified council of stern jurors, acting like Thraso,[9] a character straight out of comedy. You noticed, gentlemen of the jury, how many in the audience were unable to contain their laughter when that fellow adopted the pose of a Hercules and recited his tragedy for us, calling himself tyrant-slayer thrice and four times over, telling us about that clever sword of his, that companion in arms which, in its wisdom and unaided, slew the old man and deserved therefore to be placed among the stars while its master was to be counted as one of the gods.[10] Good heavens, how he decked out that deed of his with ornaments, false colours, and bombastic words! How he boasted about it, how he exaggerated! How like a braggart soldier, with stentorian voice, with foolish expression, with raised eyebrows, and with staring eyes he trumpeted his own praises before you!

I beg you, gentlemen of the jury, take a close look at the man's expression even now: does he not seem to threaten you, does he not seem to say, 'If you do not confer the prize on me, you will not get away scot-free as long as that divine and valiant sword of mine is intact, for it will act on my behalf when and where it pleases me, without my raising a finger.' Who would suffer such boastful talk, even in a man who had actually killed a tyrant?

Another thing, too, prompted me to object to his claim (for I must not deny it, gentlemen) or rather to check his excessive pride and his hateful imputation of wrongdoing.[11] Right from the start, when the whole community vied in giving thanks to the gods as the authors of our freedom, I observed how this man pushed himself forward, how he was bursting with anger, suffering with ill grace the sacrifices offered to our divine saviours. He loudly asserted that this honour was being taken away from him, that he alone was the author of our restored freedom, that laws, altars, and places of worship – public or private – all owed their preservation to his right arm, to his magnificent sword. Well then, gentlemen of the jury, what do you foresee will happen if his intolerable boasting is given the added weight of your authority, the seal of your approval, and, as its token, the reward? What else but that another tyrant will be foisted on this city, replacing the one that has been removed, a new tyrant exercising his rule with boastful tongue and vainglory, who every day would rehearse before us that tiresome tragedy, every day threaten us with his Herculean fists and marvellous sword? Is this to be delivered from a tyrant, citizens, or is it to exchange one tyrant for another? You can see for yourselves how he glowers at me with threatening mien.

Why are you angry with me?[12] Why do you threaten me with your glance? Why do you frighten me with knitted brows? Shall I not be granted freedom of speech in opposing you (on your own invitation) while you abuse your rights, thinking yourself entitled to impute to a citizen such a serious and capital offence (something the law prohibits even on stage);[13] to bring this accusation at a mere whim and before sworn jurors, in the presence of an assembly of citizens, and without being able to prove it by even the slightest of arguments; to assert – as bold in your accusation as you were boastful in the rest of your speech – that I had no other motive for acting as your adversary than to avenge the tyrant's death, which caused me grief? If I wanted to adopt your example and use such arguments against you in turn, you would soon realize what atrocities could be hurled back at you, with even greater plausibility. For that hateful reproach (or at least that is what you considered it to be) intimidated me much less than the proverbial thunder in a basin![14] Apart from the fact that there existed between the tyrant and myself neither kinship nor relationship by marriage, neither close contact nor a profitable association, nor any other reason why his survival should concern me – and in the absence of such motives you cannot cast any suspicion or fasten any accusation on anyone, as you too should know, unless you have never seen the inside of a courtroom or unless hope for gain has made you a foolish counsel today[15] – apart from this, I think my trustworthiness, integrity, sense of duty, and my whole life's conduct are so well known in this community that your accusation is more likely to bring ill will upon yourself because of its injustice than to cast any suspicion on me.[16]

You see how many reasons prompted me to take a stand against you. Finally, if you want to know, a good number of citizens earnestly pressed me to take up their cause against you, saying that they did not consider themselves delivered from tyranny unless I prevented you from obtaining the reward for tyrannicide. Not that they had misgivings about owing this happy outcome to a man – though this too is hard to bear, to be indebted to a man making his claim in this fashion. To feel indebted to an arrogant fellow is irksome enough, but to feel indebted to a man to whom you owe nothing is not only most painful, but also very foolish. I would not say a word in opposition, not even against a pimp, if he truly deserved the reward – but to be under obligation to such a churl, who thinks so highly of himself yet has made no contribution, is doubly wretched – indeed, is doubly foolish. For no one carries on more insolently about his good services than the man who has not rendered them but wishes to give the impression of having done so.

Assuming that I have no reason for opposing you except that it so pleased me, you have absolutely no justification for being angry with me. Indeed, since the case is before such respected jurors, I am not depriving you of any honour if you have truly earned a reward; rather I am adding great lustre to it, for it is nobler by far to have fought and won the prize for tyrannicide than to have been given it. At the very least you will be fair enough to pardon me if I perform a good citizen's duty[17] when I, without gaining any advantage for myself, defend the state, which is accused of owing the reward, if I prevent this community from being charged with folly and acquiring a reputation for ignorance, if I prevent this city from being ungrateful to the gods at our common peril, and, finally, if I plead the case of the immortal gods whom you attempt to defraud of their due honour – an attempt which makes clear how much respect you will show in conducting the rest of this suit, having begun with such impudent slander: 'He is taking the stand against me, therefore he is against the republic and in favour of the tyranny.'[18] Not but that I consider this too the mark of a free city, to have the right to come here and speak with impunity, even on behalf of tyrants. Nor do I ask you, gentlemen of the jury, to let me benefit in the trial from my good will toward the state or to let this man be encumbered by his insolent pride. Indeed, I will not deprecate his suggestion that I acted out of envy, I will not even dodge that harshest of accusations, the odious motives he tried to impute to me, that I would appear to have favoured the tyrant. On the contrary, I will prove him wrong with arguments too sound to be refuted and in the end persuade even my adversary (provided he does not withdraw his claim) to admit that no prize is owed him – if one acted in the kindest possible manner – and that he himself owes a fine – if one was a more exacting and severe judge. As I shall do this in the shortest possible time,[19] I beg of you, gentlemen of the jury, to listen to me with attentive ears and minds.

You will recall,[20] gentlemen, that in his speech the claimant continually tried to parade before our eyes and asked us to consider exclusively the many evils of which we were relieved when the tyranny ended. He impressed this upon us throughout, he took up the better part of his speech with this theme, he wanted us to consider nothing but this: that we had been suffering grievous servitude and were now enjoying the longed-for freedom. In truth, he wanted us to consider only what was of no relevance to this investigation. For the question is not how wretched is tyranny or how desirable liberty. Your investigation, gentlemen of the jury, concerns another matter: now that the city's freedom has been restored, what portion of this laudable enterprise is due to this man's valour? And should this event, which is linked with his deed, be regarded as linked with his merit?

Let me go over the steps which he himself followed in introducing the case,[21] for I believe this is the simplest method of disproving his claim. I shall follow his division of the subject into parts, for he proceeded like cunning party-hosts who prepare and spice the same meats in different ways, thus creating the impression that there are many and varied dishes. Just so this man created multiple tyrannicide out of a single murder. I shall therefore review in order the steps by which he decided to extol his deed so wonderfully and on which he likewise rested his case. If he can resist my thrust and maintain even one of his points, he may pronounce himself victorious.

'How many tyrants were slain?' he says. 'How many rewards do I deserve,[22] first because I had good intentions, secondly because I tried, then, too, because I killed the son who was more than a tyrant, and finally because the father committed suicide on account of the son's death?'

As for the first point, his good intentions, gentlemen of the jury, who would not consider this an argument too feeble to need refuting? Yet he thundered away ever so loudly and repeated ever so often that he had intended to kill the tyrant, asserting that this in itself without further ado was worthy of reward. But what can be more ridiculous than demanding a reward from the law for a mere act of volition, when the law considers nothing less pertinent to its business than what men want to do or conceive in their hearts, so that it neither exacts punishment for wanting to do what is wrong, nor offers a reward for wanting to do what is right, but judges a man's intent solely by what he has brought to pass without coercion? 'Well,' you will say, 'does not intent constitute the better part of a deed, and is it not generally considered sufficient by itself in the case of difficult tasks?'[23] Quite right. But only before the gods, who alone can see what you do or do not intend to do. Expect to be rewarded by them if you have conceived in your heart a noble plan. The law represents the human aspect: it does not consider its business what men pursue in the dark recesses of their hearts' maze.[24] It does not even accept what is public opinion and widespread rumour, let alone secret and disputed matters. In fine, the law admits only what is certain knowledge, and therefore listens only to evidence established, corroborated, and proved by the firmest arguments. Tell me, is there a deed so heinous that the mere intent to perpetrate it has ever been admitted as grounds for an accusation? Trials of this sort are reserved for the courts of Aeacus and Rhadamantus.[25] In this court tell me not what you intended to do, but what you have accomplished.

Since there is no law threatening punishment for a crime resolved only in your mind, what impudence is this – to demand from the law a reward for services you merely intended to render, as if you had in fact rendered them? Indeed, since laws are specifically designed for the purpose of deterring or checking crimes, it would be much more in accordance with their role to exact punishment from evildoers than to bestow rewards on benefactors (a point I shall soon demonstrate in more detail). When the law does not admit the charge of mere intent among the grounds for accusation, will it, pray, admit the display of good will in the claim for a reward? Who is there among the common people, however sluggish he may be, who would not form an intent to kill a tyrant if it could be done safely?[26] What pimp would not want to do it, at least for the sake of profit? Finally, who could not easily pretend that he had had the intention so that he might carry off the prize gratuitously? Shall I tell you, then, how much this whole argument of 'intended murder' is worth? About as much as if you had killed in your dream.

It is fitting that like be requited with like. The law rewards the benefactor with a benefit; as for the man who merely showed good will, what is he owed by the state but good will in return? Go ahead now and ask us to dwell on this point. You say: 'I have considered, resolved, and decided upon such a splendid deed. Will you deny me the reward?' You will not be cheated of your reward if you ask for it on such terms, but the reward you reap will be of this kind: being an unbearably shameless fellow you will depart ridiculed, jeered, and hissed out of this court. You were not ashamed to demand from the law what no pimp ever dared to ask of anyone: to be paid for his intentions. No one is so foolish as to pay a prize for some sort of intent, that is, something less tangible than words.

'But I not only formed an intent,' you say, 'I also ventured forth. I went up to the citadel and drove off the guards.' In the first place, you did well to abandon the original point, on which you certainly rested uneasily – though you will find the new position hardly more comfortable. For whereas it may appear a little less absurd, it is barely less impudent to demand a reward for a mere attempt when the law clearly ordained it for the man who had accomplished the deed. Will you thus deny to the laws the basic right granted to private citizens in their transactions? Tell me, if one of the citizens had entered into a contract with you, stipulating a certain fee while you laid down the condition, each party at his own risk of course, and he demanded the money from you before meeting your condition, saying: 'Pay the fee. I have attempted the deed, I have tried it, I have made an effort,' will you not right away answer this impudent fellow: 'Meet the condition. What business of mine is it that you made an attempt when I contracted with you for the result, not the attempt?' Imagine the law replying to you now in as many words: 'I acknowledge the existence of a contract. I am not altering the conditions. I owe you a reward, but only if you have met the condition: if you have killed the tyrant. The partners in a contract are bound or released by its wording.[27] If I promised a reward for attempted tyrannicide, I shall confer it gladly, but if I promised it to the man who accomplished the deed, how can it be right for you to receive the stipend when I do not receive what I have bargained for?'

In insignificant private deals you will find no one bold enough to demand the profit promised on a certain condition when the condition has not been met, no one stupid enough to pay it if anyone demanded it. And you demand from the state the greatest of all rewards, simply because you tried? Your arguments are nothing but nonsense. I am waiting to hear from you the one proof you ought to furnish. You say: 'I had the intention of doing it, I went up to the citadel, I forced my way past the guards, I drove off the attendants. How insignificant is that which remained to be done! What more do you want?'[28] I want nothing from you but that one deed for which the reward is owed. Have you not yet realized that in this kind of contract the risk is shared, with separate aspects concerning each of the partners: one must pay the price, the other meet the condition? I take upon myself the risk and obligation of paying out the prize-money. You do not regard it as any of your business (and indeed it is none of your business) how straitened are my circumstances, from what source I must scrape together the money I owe you. Similarly, you accept the condition at your own risk, and it is none of my business how difficult or dangerous it is to meet the condition. I leave that whole concern, that whole business, up to you. What would you say if, on fulfilling the condition, I told you that my fields had yielded a poor harvest, that I had lost my income in a shipwreck, that I could extract no money from insolvent debtors, that the sum owed you could not be gotten together without great sacrifice – pray, tell me, would you not say that I was talking nonsense, that none of this concerned you, that I could only satisfy you in one manner: by paying out the money? And no judge will be so unfair as to deny that you are within your rights. Yet you think I have been well satisfied if you come to me with a tale of woe: what great danger you faced, what effort it cost you, how many sleepless nights you passed trying to meet the conditions?

Believe me, the matter admits of too many pitfalls and doubts. It is not feasible for busy lawcourts to ponder another's intent, to consider another's efforts, when each man tends to overestimate his own, and when it is difficult to put an exact value on other men's efforts. To assess a deed, however, is simple. This then lies within the province of a legal decision, by this standard the law usually measures the rest, though it does not refuse at times to consider what is fair and equitable. This is the case in lawsuits based on the traditional formula that 'between gentlemen there must be gentlemanly dealings,'[29] but in contracts that have been drawn up without coercion or fraudulent intention,[30] why should one depart from the letter unless one wanted to break the contract altogether?

What is it that you want? Look around, and if you can find a precedent anywhere, I shall not deny you the prize-money. You have often, I think, been present at Olympic boxing matches, often been a spectator at competitions. Well then, have you ever seen anyone so impudent as to demand the prize on the grounds that he competed strenuously? I think not. And competitions are hardly serious business and certainly organized for pleasure. And you make demands for yourself in this grave and most noble matter, demands which even a very impudent fellow would think shameless to make at those staged events? Tell me, how often have you seen it happen that the man who showed himself the strongest and most competent driver in a race missed the prize by far, whereas the outcome favoured the most sluggish fellow? The former certainly could have pleaded that he dropped the reins, that his horse shied, that a wheel was broken. He may pride himself on being as superior in skills and strength as was Achilles to Thersites,[31] but unless he was the first to reach the finish, he will have no right to demand the prize and can only blame his own bad luck. For the rest, he will not be angry with the superintendent of games, for he entered the race in this spirit, subjecting himself to his conditions, namely, that he would carry off the prize if he was victorious – fortune favouring excellence.[32] Otherwise, if a prize was owed, not only for the result, but also for the attempt, one would need as many crowns as there are competitors in the Olympic Games. Yet in games of that sort, which are organized for the sake of tradition and entertainment, it sometimes happens that prizes are awarded even to losers, not to honour but to console them. But what law, I ask you, ever granted a reward in serious undertakings, in matters as dangerous as tyrannicide, unless a man accomplished the deed and in such a manner that he satisfied all points? How far you are from satisfying all conditions you will hear afterwards, for at present I am dealing only with the question of attempt.

Now the law promises a civic crown[33] to the man who has saved a compatriot in battle. Whoever laid claim to this honour on the grounds that he confronted a hail of weapons and did not escape without numerous injuries? Of course no one demands a civic crown unless he saved a citizen. Whoever demanded the *corona muralis*, the crown for scaling battlements, saying: 'I fought bitterly, gentlemen of the jury, I did everything in my power to scale the battlement, but I was thrown off'? However great his effort, no one will be so shameless as to claim that a *corona muralis* is owed him unless he has in fact scaled the wall. No one will demand the siege crown unless he raised the siege. In fine, no reward is ever claimed except by the one who accomplished the deed promoted by the reward.

The man who brings ashore a ship abandoned during a storm is legally entitled to the goods carried on board ship.[34] What purpose does it serve in such a case to speak of your skill, toil, risk, and enterprise? Assuming that you did everything to save the ship, but abandoned it when the storm got the better of you, will you have the audacity to claim any of the goods on board? And if you do so, can you hope that anyone will let you touch even a hair? I think not.

If anyone has ever been granted an ovation, a vote of thanks, or a triumph because he strained every nerve to obtain a victory, because he fought bravely in battle, and not because he won the victory in the end and eliminated the number of enemies prescribed by the law, you too may take heart and expect to be rewarded for attempted tyrannicide. But if this has never happened in living memory, stop deluding yourself with this novel hope, stop making unprecedented demands for something that is shameless to expect and foolish to grant to the claimant. Do not tell us[35] at what great risk to your life you climbed the walls of the citadel, how bravely you forced your way past the tyrant's bodyguard, fighting off some of them and killing others – a story which, for the most part, you may invent at your pleasure. To obtain the prize for tyrannicide you need say only four words: 'I killed the tyrant.' No matter how much you magnify, aggrandize, and extol your attempt, the prize is owed only to the tyrannicide. Or else, what would you say if on that very day on which you climbed up to the citadel many others had made the same attempt, each confident in his valour, but none successful at killing the tyrant – will they all obtain and share the prize for tyrannicide? After all, they tried! Tell me, what if many citizens had made a concerted effort, but the most sluggish fellow among them succeeded in killing the tyrant (since luck is not always commensurate with virtue) – will not he alone carry off the prize while the others are passed over? And why? Not because he faced greater dangers, but because he accomplished that for which the law decreed a public honour.

At this point you will perhaps start all over again, complaining that you laboured in vain. You will say it is unfair that noble ventures are being deprived of their just recognition if they are not supported by fate's vote.[36] But how can a condition be unfair when no one is forced to accept it unless it is to his liking? The condition proposed may be as unfair as you please – whoever accepts it voluntarily certainly makes it a completely fair business. In the game of dice (if I may be permitted to adduce this example) what can be more unfair than a skilful champion being defeated by an amateur, provided his throw was a lucky one? Yet no one complains that this is unfair, for anyone disapproving of the rules of the game was free not to participate. Similarly, the law publicly and openly states what it would like to see accomplished. What you *can* accomplish is left up to your own estimate. The law desires nothing more than that things may turn out for the best. If you left nothing untried, it was your bad luck that made you fail, and you realize, I suppose, that you have no reason to be disgruntled with the law. Call fate to account, if you so please; you have no case against the law. It promises nothing and it owes nothing, except to the man who has met the condition.

Let us not think, gentlemen of the jury, that our forefathers who made this law acted without having a sound reason when they decided not to set out a reward for attempted tyrannicide.[37] Not only did they take care to avoid attracting those ambiguous and inextricable lawsuits about that sort of attempt, they also realized that an attempt to slay the tyrant could not be made without grave risk to the community. Therefore they foresaw that the state would be destroyed rather than restored by the audacity of adventurers if they set out a prize for attempted tyrannicide. For what is tyranny but a serious and fatal cancer affecting the state? A suitable prize has been set out for the man who would cure it, but he can obtain it only if he produces a remedy that takes immediate effect. Indeed, no one ought to try his hand at curing the ill unless he is a proven expert who, relying on his precautions and his experience, does not allow chance to snatch away the patient's life while he himself is trying to restore his health. What do you say? Do you reckon that in risky situations of this kind an attempt should be encouraged by setting out a reward, or that such an attempt should be discouraged by threatening punishment if a man cannot accomplish what he has set out to do?

Nor does it help you to reason by analogy,[38] as you seemed to do: 'Since the law demands that criminals be punished for simple criminal attempt, it is fair that an attempt at a good deed should count for even more, inasmuch as the law should appear much more disposed to reward excellence than to avenge crime.'[39] But consider how completely off the right track you are in this point. In the first place, you do not realize that the act of tyrannicide is quite unlike any other, for while other attempts enjoin only a personal risk to the agent, tyrannicide engenders such great risk to the community that a rash attempt on a tyrant's life means nothing less than exposing everyone's fortunes through one man's rashness. Secondly, the law does not admit the question of attempt in every form or in every kind of criminal case, but only in a very few, those that deserve loathing for their exceptional cruelty or are the kind of crime that wreaks havoc before the attempt is recognized, for example parricide, poisoning, and treason.

Finally, you do not see that there is no resemblance between invoking punishment and bestowing an honour by law, but that these actions are totally different in their nature and reason.[40] One is the proper function of law, the other a sort of concession of privilege, a kindness, so to speak, on the part of the law. You will come to realize the truth of my words when you consider the many legal injunctions enjoining a penalty for disobedience, the many prohibitions threatening punishment for disregard, and when you consider on the other hand that there are barely one or two cases in which the law invites a specific action by offering a reward. In some cases it would appear harsh and oppressive to induce a man to act by threat of punishment, for example regarding marriage and procreation.[41] In these instances the law naturally deals politely and respectfully with you, adopting the attitude of a father rather than an official, encouraging you by means of a reward to do what you ought to have done voluntarily in any case. Then there are other tasks which any good citizen ought to be willing to undertake, but appear to require more fortitude than the majority can offer and entail greater risk than they would willingly undergo. For example, it seems inhuman to order everyone to show contempt for his life. Therefore the law encourages such deeds by setting out a reward, as if to spur on a man's courage. However, one should not extend these generous provisions beyond the obligations assumed by the law itself. Nor is it surprising if the law is more careful, vigilant, and exact in regard to its proper and natural function than in a matter in which it temporarily adopted a foreign role. To this I may add that a criminal precedent is usually met by a new type of impeachment, and a new situation by a new law or by one derived from a law applying to a similar case. But nothing of this sort happens when someone commits a new kind of praiseworthy deed; no prize is awarded, following a similar decree. Unless there is an existing law expressly setting out a reward for his deed, a man will hardly have grounds for a request, let alone for a claim.

Why would we need a law rewarding citizens wholesale for doing their duty? Whereas it is in the interest of all to let no crime go unpunished, a man cannot do good 'gratuitously.' For what does a grateful citizen not owe to his fatherland?[42] Even if you give your life to your fatherland – is it surprising that you repay what you have received? Just as you deserve punishment if you do not show dutiful respect toward your parents but do not instantly deserve a reward if you do, so you cannot escape punishment if you break the laws but are not immediately entitled to a reward if you have done your duty. For if all citizens acted as they are in duty bound, there would be no need for laws at all. Indeed, they were established, not for the sake of good behaviour but as a consequence of evil practices and, as is truly said in popular speech, have the function of medicine.[43]

Imagine that there were no laws, as in the tales the poets tell of the golden age of Saturn,[44] when each man willingly performed his duty – would you in this case clamour that your good deeds were in vain because no law awarded you a prize? Just as the law does not threaten any but the wicked, so it makes no promise to ideal citizens. And what need is there for a promise when perfect virtue is fully content with itself? To demand what the law has not promised surpasses the height of impudence; to claim arrogantly what the law has promised kindly and generously is the mark of a citizen whose character is doubtful.

What you deserve will be examined shortly. In the mean time let us suppose that you have rendered an extremely useful service for which, however, no reward was owing according to the law. Will you immediately shout that your service brought you no return? Will you call the state to the bar, loudly reproach the people with ingratitude, threaten the jury unless they vote you a reward according to your liking? Or will you rather consider virtue its own sufficiently great reward,[45] enjoy the knowledge that you have done right, and consider it the greatest return for your good deed that, because of your selfless service to others, you are regarded as a man of almost divine benevolence? If you are an excellent citizen, such a reward will certainly suffice you. If you are not content with this reward and desire yet another, fame certainly is the second greatest reward. And fame you have now almost achieved. What price do you put on flying on all men's lips, on being celebrated and praised, having a thousand fingers pointing at you, drawing attention,[46] having all eyes turned upon you? That, I say, is the greatest portion of the reward, for money adds but little weight. You only made an attempt on the tyrant's life; the major portion, in fact the central part, of your deed remained undone – yet you enjoy these benefits, being celebrated like a tyrant-slayer when you have not slain him. I ask you, how small is the portion that is missing from the prize you would have carried off even if you had slain the tyrant? Finally, that very reward appears to me – I had almost said enviable:[47] the fact that you could so many times boast of tyrannicide before the public, that you had an opportunity to demand the most noble prize before a distinguished court, to act out your splendid tragedy before a packed house, with the public looking on. In my opinion, members of the jury, anyone who could make a display of his service has received the reward for his service. You make claims on the state for a gift that came from fate and the gods, and there are perhaps people who impute their freedom to you. And you disdain such great rewards? The real tyrant-slayer would have had to be content with them, had not the law chosen to distinguish attempt from successful execution by a prize. Yet, by Hercules, no prize is more appropriate for the man who attempted to kill the tyrant but did not, than that he should hope to win the prize for tyrannicide but does not. Was this the point in your speech on which you asked us to dwell with you?

Now your attempt is even less deserving of a prize on this account. In the plans of others only luck was missing, in your case, as you admit, the will was lacking. You achieved what you wanted to achieve; what was required you neither did nor wanted to do. But I see that for some time now you are casting around for another line of retreat, for you realize that this argument leaves you no hope of winning the prize. Well then, we shall follow you through all your steps, pursue you as you skip from one point to another, and shall not let you come to a rest anywhere.

'I have not only attempted the killing,' you say, 'I have in fact killed – the son, that is.'[48] And this deed you split into two tyrannicides, first because you removed the son who was worse than a tyrant, and what's more, heir to the tyranny, and secondly because you caused the father's suicide by killing his son. About the first point we shall see later on, but let us now inspect the nature of the second argument. You say you killed the father by virtue of killing the son, by the same token, for you assert that it does not matter how[49] you killed him as long as you accomplished the killing. In fact, you want the deed to appear even more splendid because the tyrant was killed by his own hand, though by your sword.

Such noble words, gentlemen of the jury, may deceive a man who is not sufficiently alert, especially when the claimant parades his story with pomp and colour, calling up before our eyes that valiant youth of flourishing age, so dear to his father, now covered with numerous stab-wounds, and the wretched old father, dead by the same sword, embracing his son, the two men's blood intermingled.[50] A splendid description, but how relevant is it to your case? No one is so blind as not to see, no one so shameless as to deny that this spectacle was of all sights by far the most welcome to the community. When they saw the old tyrant stretched out across the young man's body, corpse upon corpse, they rejoiced at the sight of one man because they were relieved of past calamities, at the sight of the other because they were relieved of future fears.

Of what use was it to exaggerate in your speech this sight, by itself most impressive and welcome to the people? One issue only is to be decided in this court: should the killing of the father, who was indisputably the tyrant, be ascribed to you or to the readiness of fortune and the gods above? How futile and trifling is it to point out that he was killed by your sword! What if the tyrant had been killed by someone who had asked you for the use of your sword? Would you instantly come forward and claim the prize for tyrannicide? Surely not. The law promises a reward to the tyrant-slayer. You stabbed to death a man whose title – whether or not he should be regarded as a tyrant – was debatable, while leaving untouched him about whose title there was no question. If you did so intentionally, you intentionally forfeited the prize. If you did so because of fear, you have much less reason for demanding the prize. Yet you pressed this point with great urgency, wanting to give the impression that you left him untouched intentionally and voluntarily.

But what was your true intention when the power was in your hands and you decided not to free our state from fear completely but to leave untouched the man who would avenge your deed and was the actual and true tyrant? You realized (you say)[51] that the task was accomplished once the son was dead because you knew in advance that under all circumstances the old man would commit suicide at once, using that selfsame sword. Can you see, gentlemen of the jury, through what opening he is trying to make his escape, now that he is caught with a manifest lie? If he had not made up a story about his powers of divination, he could not have extracted himself from this situation.

If you spoke thus in the capacity of an augur, haruspex,[52] or diviner, you would perhaps find some people willing to give credence to your prophecy. But as it is, what can be more impudent, vain, and improbable than to assert that you knew in advance, and for certain, a matter which was likely to have any but this outcome? Or was it by conjecture[53] that you reached the conclusion that it would fall out as it did? But what could conjecture produce other than an expectation or suspicion? Moreover, in so doubtful a situation what sort of madness was it to follow uncertain hope and to neglect certain danger?

Let us hear, I beg you, those certain conjectures by which our soothsayer knew in advance an outcome that came as a surprise to all. 'He was already worn out by age,' you say. 'His strength failed him. He thought he could not maintain the tyranny after the removal of his son. Moreover, he loved his son so tenderly that he did not want to go on living after his death.' Do you realize that your arguments are so completely at variance with the nature of things that everyone will regard them as undone before they are even refuted?[54] Do you or don't you concede power of judgment to the old man? If he lacked judgment, he might have considered as certain what was by no means certain – but then right away you are totally mistaken in your prediction. If on the other hand you think that he had judgment, why did he lack confidence to such an extent? As if a tyrant was sustained exclusively by the physical strength of one man and not much rather by ingenuity, cunning, cleverness, bribing, and cruel repression! Since all of these qualities fit an old man better than a young one, why do you twist your forecast around? Is old age not made wise by experience? Does it not conceal its feelings more deeply? Does it not keep watch more diligently and look out more keenly? Is it not more implacable in anger, more tenacious in remembering injury, and better at making long-range plans? It is by these qualities alone that the tyrant's rule is carried out. Of how little importance is physical strength in a military leader – and how much less so in a tyrant! Why should the death of his son disturb him more than the killing of one of his more valiant bodyguards, when he still had a well fortified citadel, when he still had his wealth, weapons, a vast troop of bodyguards, and a large number of partisans among the citizens, powerful allies who not only sided with the tyrant but even acted like tyrants themselves? I can only hope that we do not have to fear them now – I do not like to predict ill fortune, but let us not smugly disregard them.

Is it likely that the old man who was (as all know) in his strong and vigorous old age clever, bold, ambitious, and certainly not foolish – is it likely that he was thrown into confusion by the single event of his son's death, that he gave up all hope and thought it necessary to seek instant death, especially when the son had not made the father's rule any safer but rather much more unpopular on account of his wantonness, his youthful arrogance, and his audacity, so that it would almost have been expedient for the father to remove the son in order to strengthen the tyranny? For the closer a tyranny approaches the semblance of a just monarchy the less blame it incurs and the safer it is.[55] That young man only aggravated the conditions that tend to be a tyrant's downfall. The safeguards of tyranny, on the other hand, were lodged in the heart of the shrewd old man.

But you say that he loved his son too tenderly to go on living after his death! Are you speaking of a private person, some dear old mother, or of a shrewd, cruel old man, and a tyrant to boot? Why do I bother with counter-arguments in my speech, gentlemen of the jury, when nature itself, when convention, when universal common sense refute him?[56] Whoever heard of a tyrant feeling such affection for his children that he could live with them on agreeable terms, not to speak of wanting to die with them? Believe me, those are the feelings of private citizens. A tyrant does not know what natural bonds, what parental love, and, least of all, what obligation means. He divested himself of all such feelings when he took on the tyranny. He measures everything in terms of profit, intimidation, and coercion. He loves only those whom he fears (if he loves at all, since he hates even the gods) and whom it is not yet expedient to remove, or whose co-operation and assistance he needs to prop up his rule. If he could love anyone at all, surely he would love those similar to himself, godless, violent, grasping criminals, since nothing is more effective in creating friendly feelings than similarity of character.[57] But not even criminals are dear to him unless they are to some extent helpful, so that the tyrant resembles a Stoic, or rather a caricature or parody of a Stoic.[58] For no one ever was a Stoic to the extent of being as devoid of feelings as is the tyrant. The difference between the Stoic and the tyrant is this: the philosopher measures his plans in terms of honour, the tyrant in terms of profit. Or is it possible for a tyrant to feel even a spark of affection for any man when he sins against his native country, which gave him life and sustenance, against the gods on high, the authors of all blessings, so that he oppresses the country with most cruel slavery and despoils the gods' temples, holding their laws in contempt?

But to make some concessions to you, let us allow you to transfer private affections to the tyrant's heart, that is, pour fire into a river[59] – will you convince us that he loved his son so tenderly, so utterly pinned on him all his life's hopes, his pleasures, and strengths that upon his death he thought there was none, not even the smallest incentive left to go on living? Find such a man – not only in this community, but in the whole human race! Not only in this day and age, but in all the history of the world, beginning if you wish with the image created by Prometheus.[60] How many fathers, how many doting mothers have committed suicide on account of their children's death? Grief is natural, but a kind of grief that almost everyone bears in moderation. Ordinary grief satisfies parents in private station, even the most indulgent ones; it satisfies even the most uncontrolled emotions of weak women. Did you, with the eyes of a Lynceus,[61] foresee that only death could do justice to a tyrant's love for his son? Well, even that we shall grant you – a tyrant has surpassed private citizens in his affection for his children, has surpassed all doting mothers in his tender love – yet how could you know which form the father's grief would take, whether it would turn to fury or desperation? The more passionately he loved, the more probable it was that the old man, savage by nature and hostile to the citizens, should greatly desire to survive, if for no other reason than to satisfy a long-standing resentment, sharply provoked and exacerbated upon his son's death, by punishing the citizens. Even if he had been tired of life otherwise, that one reason would surely have kept him alive. What is more bent on revenge than an old man's mind? Are you not aware what uncontrolled fits possess old age, what tides of emotion carry it away, what burning desires consume it when some dreadful and significant disgrace harries it? And what can be more dreadful than the murder of a son as beloved as you say he was? That would certainly provoke and, so to speak, revive whatever cruelty was in him, whatever savagery, hatefulness, bloodthirstiness, and desire for carnage, in short, whatever of the tyrant he had in him. Even rather tame animals are usually driven to fury when they are unjustly deprived of their offspring; and you – the unerring diviner – thought that in a tyrant (whom no animal surpasses in fierceness[62]) we need fear nothing of the sort we see happen in tigers. If you alone were aware that the tyrant was so fond of his son, what could happen other than that through your fault this most savage tiger, infuriated when its cub was snatched away, would pounce on this unfortunate community to rip and tear it in pieces? If, by the extraordinary grace of the gods, this did not come to pass, you deserved much blame for taking it upon yourself to let loose such a savage beast on our lives and fortunes. Now make your choice between these alternatives: either admit the truth, which is that the tyrant had nothing in common with our feelings, or pretend that he felt such love as to surpass the affections of doting mothers. So much is certain: in neither case will your prediction stand up. And if it does not stand up, you have no reason to aspire to praise for a matter that came to pass by fortune's favour and without your planning.

Finally, let us concede even this much, that you knew in advance and knew for certain (evidently because some god informed you, for it could not possibly have happened in any other way) – still, it is just as if you had not foreseen it, since you cannot prove your prescience before the law. Adduce witnesses whom you had told beforehand that it would fall out as it did. Tell us what god, at what hour, announced this to you.

You have no answer. The truth is this. When you saw that the business had ended well, you became a diviner after the fact, as usually happens in life and is expressed in the proverb 'Even a fool is wise after the event.'[63] And to transfer fortune's gift to yourself in your speech, you began to tell us that tragedy of yours and devised arguments to give the impression of having had advance knowledge. But, good gods, what a poor poet you have shown yourself to be, making up such inconsistent and paradoxical stories – of a most savage tyrant departing from life voluntarily because of the devout love he felt for his son, thinking it unsafe to go on living on account of one man's death though everything that makes and maintains a tyranny remained intact, suddenly losing confidence in his affairs and departing for the underworld after the death of the man in whose hands he had placed the defence of the tyranny! Well, I forego my arguments for the moment. We shall believe that all of this is not fiction but fact, even though it contains not a kernel of truth. If in the memory of all mankind you can name one tyrant whose love for his children was so great that he did not much prefer his eunuchs and minions, who was so fond of them that he did not suspect them and keep them under surveillance, who trusted them so completely that he did not place more trust in barbarian thieves and branded slaves,[64] I could give you a long list of tyrants who hated their children so much that they could not bear to see them alive, who feared them so greatly that they would not take a meal together with them, who mistrusted them so completely that they only felt safe after having them removed from their presence. No follower is less useful to a tyrant than his son. He prefers those hirelings from far-off lands: assassins, men on the run, killers, temple-robbers. To their hands he prefers to entrust his life, for they do not have the benefit of a fatherland and enjoy destroying other men's. They excel in barbaric and beastly strength, resembling the unholy giants of old;[65] because of their desires they are easily led to take any kind of risk, and because of their savagery they shrink from no crime. These are servants suitable for a tyrant, these are his trustworthy protectors and by far the surest defenders of tyranny. By removing them one might conceivably give the tyrant a reason for losing confidence in his affairs. For how did the son support his rule? By his age? But a man of maturer years is more useful. By his strength? He was but a single man. By his wisdom? Old age knows more. By the guards he hired? But if he hired them in defiance of his father, the old man should have desired his death; if he hired them on behalf of his father, what trouble was there other than that the guard was reduced by one man? For to whom would the guards defect if not to the man on whose behalf they were kept? The tyrant was therefore going to be safer with his son removed. A violent and insolent son is a cause for concern to a tyrant. The other barbarians are content with pay alone; he is looking for another prize, succession to the tyranny. There is no room for respect once the abominable desire[66] for power has taken hold of a man's heart. Then the laws of nature are disregarded, and a father fears his son, who in turn desires his father's death.[67]

But for some time now you have been longing to say something. Hold on, I know it already: you are urging me to leave nothing unrefuted. If he did not love the son immoderately, if he was not in despair, why did he commit suicide? That is the point which is really and truly surprising. In fact, it happened against everyone's expectations, even yours. But I do not consider it my business to give you an account of the ideas the gods put into his head so that he would inflict injury on himself. I only need to prove that you could not have safely predicted this outcome by any conjecture, however much the tyrant loved his son. Mind you, the reason for his suicide is not all that obscure. Whatever gods were angry with our state had at last been appeased by our long-standing misfortunes. Our prayers, our sacrifices had at last moved them to mercy. The fateful day had come for the wicked old man to suffer just punishment for his manifest crimes in the eyes of gods and men. The avenging Erinyes had come, and the Furies, armed with their firebrands and serpents.[68] It was they who took away his reason, who filled him with vain fears, stunned him, and drove him to voluntary death. He believed anything but that his son's murderer had fled, that he would content himself with one death. This is the one thing you can truly boast of: that you totally deceived the tyrant. He thought that whoever had perpetrated this deed was a man – a man of the kind tyrant-slayers are reputed to be, who disdain danger to their lives and go after the tyrant's person, who do not attempt a deed unless they have given proper thought to a successful method of executing it. Pan,[69] or some other god, raised this idea in the tyrant with new visions of terror. He believed the assassin was after him, felt that his dying day had come, the destiny which no guilty man can avoid.

Why then do you attempt, with specious words, to ascribe to yourself what is owed to the piety of the city and the goodness of the gods? When it was necessary to incur danger, you fled. Now that the business has gone well beyond your hopes, you think it safe to divert to yourself the praise that is due to fortune. But suppose a different result had been obtained. Suppose the tyrant, roused to fury, had seized citizens indiscriminately, subjected them to exquisite tortures, proscribed them, executed them, driven them into exile, and confiscated their property? What would you say then? You would not, I think, allow the blame for these misfortunes to fall on you as their author; you would argue that fortune was to blame. You would say that it should not be imputed to you if by ill luck matters fell out contrary to your plans. But is it not equally unfair that you should wish to transfer all credit to yourself, as if you had been responsible for the result, when with the help of good luck matters fell out contrary to your fears?

The facts themselves declare that you expected nothing less than what did happen. If you had gone up to the citadel with the purpose of killing the son, not the father, one might find it credible that you had conceived some such hope in your heart. But as it is, you fell in with the young man either by chance or because you took fright, and at this point that inspired and prescient mind of yours, which gives out oracles (but only after the event), held you back, though it was necessary to consider flight. At this point, gentlemen of the jury, in this confused situation, he began to deliberate, as if at leisure, whether or not he should consider the old man worthy of dying by his right arm.[70] At this point, finally, he began to divine that the father would lay hands on himself. And to make his impudent story a little more plausible, gentlemen of the jury, he waxed poetical (as he himself boasts),[71] describing what he neither saw nor could have seen, as if he had been a bystander. He told us what thoughts entered the tyrant's mind, what he said, what he did, how he drew his sword.[72] With the same kind of impudence you made up a story about knowing the outcome in advance, telling us what you could not conceive as if you had conceived it.

How much more trustworthy and consistent than this piece of fiction –
your fairy tale, that is – would it have been if you had told us that after killing
the youth you decided to approach the old man with drawn sword, when
suddenly the Homeric Pallas appeared at your back and stayed your course,
pulling you back by your hair,[73] forbidding you to cast a shadow on this
splendid deed[74] by the murder of an old man. She would take care that he
found his death without your doing. Slain by his own hand, but by your
sword, he would add lustre to your glorious deed rather than casting a
shadow upon it. Then from your hiding place you observed him through a
chink or – more appropriate to your dignity – the goddess sheathed you in a
cloud so that you could be present at the tyrant's death, a safe and leisurely
spectator. And you did not depart until you had seen the whole business
accomplished.

Had you told us this story, you might have shown yourself a better
poet, but I suppose you did not have enough time to work out all the details
properly, especially when the desire for profit drew you off to seek the prize
at once. Now the very inconsistency of your story betrays you and declares
you a liar. You went up to the citadel to slay the tyrant and at that time never
anticipated what you want to appear altogether clearer than the sun!
Midway through the enterprise a god restored your sight so that you could
see what would happen.

If you had wanted to give a truthful and credible account, you should
have told us how, like a spy, you went up to the citadel stealthily by night,
creeping into the building secretly – I will not say to take anything, but to see
if you could safely design some venture – and by good luck you encountered
no one. Fortune favoured your enterprise. You came upon the youth alone
and unprotected – for youth is rather careless and thinks little of danger
(besides, the tyranny was now so well established that he had laid aside
most of his fears) – perhaps, also, he was steeped in drink as was his custom,
exhausted after satisfying his excessive desires. And thus, courageously you
killed him, that is, you joined sleep with death, brother with brother, as
Homer says.[75] Then, when the moans of the dying man were heard and the
hinges of a distant door began to creak, you fled, half dead with fear, so that
you had no time to extract your sword from the wound, though in general
neither parricide nor assassin will leave their weapon behind for fear of
being convicted. In the mean time you were hiding out at home, all the while
thinking of flight, casting around in your mind for some distant and remote
hiding place where you could bury yourself and escape the rage of the
exasperated father. As you were already prepared for voluntary exile, news
spread among the people that the city was free, that the tyrant had been
slain together with his son, the others had fled in terror, and the author of

the deed was unknown. Then you suddenly changed your mind in accordance with the new dénouement of the drama, and whereas you had hitherto been anxious for your safety, you were now uplifted by hopes of reward and greed for profit. And before you had given proper thought to the manner in which you could transfer all honour for this unexpected outcome to your own person, you leaped forward, as we have witnessed, and shouted that it was your sword, your deed, and that one prize was not good enough for your bravery.

There was no one who would not have believed you, for your claim was consistent with the natural order of things, confirmed by experience, and accepted in everyone's opinion.[76] But while you tried zealously, though with little skill, to convince us of your courage and efficacy, how much did you relate that was – I will not say completely removed from the truth, but at any rate totally at variance with common sense, custom, and nature! First you told us that the tyrant loved his son with such motherly affection that he refused to go on living without him; that he had been so shaken by fear on account of one man's death that he dared not go on living; that he had placed such wholehearted trust in his son that he had no guards around him; that he was too broken-hearted to be roused to thoughts of revenge upon the savage death of so dear a child; that he was too feeble to be worthy of your strong arm and so completely unarmed that, had you not left him your sword, he would have lacked the means of killing himself. Do you not realize how incongruous your story is – such love in a tyrant, such careless trust in an old man, such fear in one who had been deprived of his son but was still protected by all his other defences, such consternation in a man who had experienced so many dangers, such feebleness in a man enraged? Why was it that you had such contempt for the old man, to the point of considering him unworthy of death by your magnificent arm? Did you consider him unworthy of being slain by you, when this city did not think him unworthy of being feared, when she suffered him to her great distress? We did not think of him as a man to be despised by anyone. Nor did you ever show your contempt – unless perhaps living in wretched fear means showing contempt. You knew that the citadel was well stocked with arms; you knew there were guards, any one of whom would have sufficed to dispatch you if the old man had lacked the strength to do it. You were aware (no one among us was unaware) how much strength the tyrant had left in his old age, partly because of his training, partly because of his fierce nature. Nor did it at that time escape your attention that frigid old age has sometimes been roused[77] by bitter grief to the point where even very strong young men have been unable to resist, when that wonted strength, numbed and chilled, as it were, by old age, was fired up again by some strong emotion. And who is so weak that shame, anger, and deep grief do not lend him strength?

This was why you preferred to kill the son rather than his father: fortune put him into your path unsuspecting, unarmed, and sleeping. In the case of the father you would have had to fight a man who was armed, protected, and enraged at that. This was why you left your sword behind: you thought it unsafe, as you retreated, to tarry even for a moment, and feared, no doubt, that even the lightest burden would slow down your flight. You left your sword behind reluctantly, as it might betray you to the tyrant, but you preferred being betrayed to being apprehended.

Not that I blame you for being afraid. On the contrary, I am surprised that you could remain on your feet, that you could flee when you heard the members of the tyrant's household stir and their arms clank, when you realized that you would have to fight, not with a boy, but with men who were on their guard, armed, and ready, with men who were sober and had been provoked, and last but not least, with the father who was full of rage – not because his son's death moved him so deeply, but because he thought – rightly or wrongly – that he had been the target of your attack, that your hand had killed the son merely by mistake.

Go on, tell me that you expect anyone – I will not say among these jurors, who are the most perceptive of men, but among the common folk – to be so snotty-nosed as not to smell a rat, not to sense and perceive that this whole drama is your invention? And, as is the poets' custom when they are at a loss how to unravel the plot of their tragedy, you artfully introduced Premonition as a sort of goddess,[78] to make this foresight of yours plausible before the jury, for you saw that without this device you could not obtain the prize-money.

'I have supplied the opportunity for the father's death,' he says, 'since I left him a sword as a means of killing himself.'[79] And not only does he consider this a good enough reason for claiming the prize, he even thinks his sword worthy of being consecrated among the gods' weapons and its master of being worshipped like a living god.[80] A simpleton if he really conceived such hopes, an arrogant fellow if he claims what he cannot hope for!

So the tyrant would have lacked a sword if you had not left yours behind? Did you think it necessary to bring arms to the citadel, that is, timber to the forest?[81] Unless by chance that sword of yours was steeped in magical incantations, so that, by itself, it would bring inevitable death! Or do you think it does not matter what kind of opportunity you provided, in what manner, and with what intention? In the first place, you say, you left the sword behind. A tyrant lacks nothing less than a sword.[82] Swords are never absent, either from his bedroom, or from his dining hall, or during sacrifices.

Trembling with fear, you left your sword behind. I admire, by the way, the audacity on your part, the bold front with which you claim the sword as being yours after having given it up for lost. I contend that you were half dead of fright when you left behind the sword, which afterwards you wished you had withdrawn. I say, you left behind a doubtful situation. What if the tyrant had drawn that same sword to slaughter our citizens? What if he had used that same sword to kill young men, chosen from the city's youth, sacrificing them in honour of his dead son? If you are a tyrant-slayer because the tyrant was slain by your sword, the undeserved deaths of all these men would also be blamed on you, by whose sword they died. And if this did not come to pass, it had nothing to do with you. For which way a doubtful situation falls out lies in the hands of the gods. If it turns out well, no thanks are owed to the man who blindly created the situation; if it turns out badly, he stands accused of rashness, for he who creates a dangerous situation is not free of guilt. If things go well, everyone considers it extraordinary; if they go badly, they say it was deserved. But how much more probable was it that the tyrant would use your sword for other purposes than he did!

I know, gentlemen of the jury, that I refute these arguments at greater length than seems necessary, especially since they are such frivolous arguments, but I decided that I should pass over none of his points, leave none of them unexamined, unchallenged, or unrefuted. Therefore I beg you to bear with me and, as you have done so far, listen patiently and attentively to the evidence as I drive him off his firmest stand.

This is the point in which he placed great confidence, this is the point he keenly pursued, saying that the prize was undeniably owed him because he supplied the opportunity for the father's death, either by leaving behind the sword or, if that was not acceptable (for I think that by now he considers this a lost cause), then certainly by killing the son. For, he said, it has been set down by the laws that there shall be no difference between killing with one's own hand and providing the cause of death.[83] And it was only fair, he added, since the laws, in the case of criminal actions, laid charges and exacted punishment for causing death, that they should be even more inclined to consider this point when rewarding good deeds. He said that he remembered this legal clause, adding this Thrasonic touch:[84] 'unless long years of servitude have impaired my memory of the laws.'[85]

You have not forgotten the laws because of their long disuse! Rather, it appears that you have never troubled yourself with inquiring into their meaning, for you are twice mistaken in this case. You fail to consider the manner in which death was caused and the intent of the man who caused it, points that are recorded in the laws. And you fail to understand the difference between charging with a crime and crediting with a service. Tell us, you novel interpreter of the law, do you consider having provided an occasion, in whatever form, by whatever means, a good enough reason for punishment or reward? Does it make no difference at all whether Hector killed Ajax by his own hand or supplied the sword with which he ran himself through later on?[86] But Hector would never have claimed any credit for this himself, though it could seem likely that one enemy supplied another with a sword for this purpose. Then, why do we not summon up all metal workers to punish or reward them whenever citizens are either killed or saved by weapons made in their workshop? In fine, why does not the craftsman who made your sword demand the prize now claimed by you? The tyrant would have obtained a sword, even if you had not supplied yours. You could not have supplied it, had not the craftsman's industry come to your aid.

Tell me, if you had carelessly shot an arrow while hunting and killed the tyrant of the neighbouring city by chance, would you declare that a reward for tyrannicide was owed you?[87] Or would you deserve no part of this honour because you had dispatched your missile without intent to kill and unaware of the consequences? In fact, you should be called into court since (for your part) you killed a citizen with your careless shot. For the fact that it struck a tyrant was none of your doing.

What if you were a merchant and had sold the tyrant a smooth, sweet wine such as Ulysses gave to Polyphemus,[88] and, beguiled by its sweetness, the tyrant gulped it down too greedily, contracted a fever, and as a consequence died. Would you, the merchant, dare to demand a reward for tyrannicide on account of your wine? Who would fail to throw you out together with your claim, taking you for a sot steeped in wine? Yet how much more feeble is the point on which you base the same claim! In the other case one might somehow have guessed or anticipated that an age that is prone to drink would indulge in so tempting a wine rather freely and in uncontrolled fashion, that illness would follow upon this over-indulgence, and death upon illness, especially in the case of an old man – this sort of thing happens frequently. You, however, have caused the tyrant's death in a manner unprecedented in human memory. For who ever laid hands on himself because of a son's death?

Let me examine the matter more closely. Suppose you are the tyrant's cook and know your master's palate well. Physicians forbid him a certain dish which he, however, likes to eat very much. A fatal illness threatens him unless he refrains from it. Of this you are aware, but you make the dish increasingly more tempting by your skill, adding spices and condiments. He keeps eating it and consequently falls ill, as predicted by the physicians. The tyrant dies, the city is free. Will you, the cook, run straight from the kitchen to the Forum and, as you are, dripping with sauce and black with soot, demand the reward for tyrannicide? Will you display your mortar, your pestle, your pots – the weapons, that is, by which you overcame the tyrant? In that case you would not be so impudent, I suppose. Yet your case is much more absurd. For the cook at any rate did not lack the intent to kill and could make a plausible case for having occasioned the death. You did not kill the son so that his father would quit life of his own accord; you supplied him with a suitable reason for doing anything but that!

Listen to the following example, which is as similar to yours as one egg to another, according to the popular saying.[89] What if you had killed the tyrant's mistress, with whom he was passionately and desperately in love, and on coming to know of it, the tyrant cut short his own life. Would you dare aspire to the prize? Would you dare to say that you clearly foresaw that the tyrant would depart from life of his own accord? Although more men have joined their lovers in death than their sons, no one would believe you, no one would award you the prize, all would agree that it had been a dangerous venture of doubtful outcome and would thank fate by whose good will the matter had come to a good end. They would consider you amply rewarded if you got away with a pardon for your deed.

In the first place, then, one ought to distinguish between charging with a misdeed and crediting with a good deed; secondly, one should consider the quality of the occasion supplied; and finally, the intent. And in this manner it will at last become evident what the law owes you. For your argument that the law should be more inclined to award a prize than to inflict punishment may find a place in discussing special privileges, which cannot be cited as precedents, but it is not applicable to common law. While, as I have demonstrated above, the law threatens with punishment anyone doing harm, it provides rewards only for a few beneficial acts. Moreover, in dealing with crimes, it prosecutes and punishes simple attempt; in dealing with good deeds, it always requires a result. And it is neither surprising nor unfair if the law is more thorough in matters for which it was specifically devised and instituted than in matters in which it temporarily assumes a role foreign to it. In both instances, it makes equally sure that the reason supplied is sufficient and that it is a matter of intent rather than mere chance. The difference, however, is this. In good deeds neither adequate reason nor adequate intent satisfies the law unless an adequate result is added to them. As for misdeeds, if you form the intent to do harm, neither result nor reason are matters of consideration. The law evaluates your deed according to your intent, for it reckons that only fate prevented you from committing a crime – would it be right that you should be aided by this fact? In regarding the result, the law considers both the reason and the intent. If it finds that the intent is criminal, it dismisses the question of adequate reason, considering the combination of intent and result sufficient to merit punishment. If, however, to simple intent is added an adequate reason for harm to result, but harm does not ensue, the law connives, so to speak, and does not consider it very relevant to its investigation. If, on the other hand, harm does ensue, the law invokes a penalty for rashness and carelessness even if evil intent cannot be proved, partly because the perpetrator's intent is suspect, partly to deprive criminals of the subterfuge 'I did not mean to do it' – so that men may learn to beware and consider their own risk when acting at the risk of others. Therefore if a man wittingly and knowingly created a situation that is obviously and definitely harmful, the law judges him as if he had done harm with his own hands. For example, if someone has assisted the enemy by supplying him with money and troops, it is just as if he had offered armed resistance himself, for he supplied the means without which no war can be waged. Or if someone has, with evil intentions, put his enemy aboard a ship that can break up so that he will die in the shipwreck; or if he brings him into a chamber with a sagging roof so that he will be crushed on its collapse;[90] or if he replaces the medication by an invalid's bedside with poison, hoping that he will take it and die – even if the patient does not drink of it, the man who put the poison within his reach and acted with evil intent may be accused of poisoning, for it was most likely that matters would turn out according to his scheme. If you take away the intent to harm in this man's case, he will have no dealings with the law. If you take away the intent to harm, but add a grievous result, he will not escape the accusation of negligence unless you plead inculpable ignorance. For instance, if you practise archery in a place not designed for this purpose, on a public highway, for example, or on another man's property, the law does not concern itself with you unless you have killed, wounded, or caused a loss to someone. As for the rest, you do what you do at your own risk. If it has any of the above consequences you find yourself involved with the law. Nor will pleading lack of intent help you, for you are not free from the blame for carelessness.[91] It was obviously up to you to take precautions against a risk that could be anticipated with some certainty.

You see what difference there is between matters which you said were the same.[92] In the first place, what is applicable to punishment is not immediately applicable to reward, and this has its origin, not in the lawgiver's meanness, but partly in the nature of the thing itself, partly in the function of the law. Secondly, the law determines the intent, judges the occasion provided, and takes into consideration the result.

Now go on and plead your case, if you like. Let us examine under what heading you want your deed to be considered. Let us say that you gave the tyrant a definite and necessary reason for dying, but did so unwittingly. In that case you would have no claim to the prize. For can anyone be called an 'unwitting benefactor'? Rewards are given to valiant men, not to those who are merely lucky[93] – a point long settled, I believe, in case you insist hereafter that you killed the son expecting the father to take his own life, a result that not even a soothsayer could have known in advance and that you could not have even suspected. On the contrary, after you created a situation fraught with danger and left it to Fortune's whim, the law does not arraign you, because it turned out well; but if the same business had turned out badly, you would have to suffer punishment for your rashness. Nor would it have helped you to exculpate yourself by pleading ignorance. For what else was to be feared but that the tyrant upon his son's murder should realize that he was the object of a plot and double all the evil measures of tyranny against us?

The point concerning your intent, therefore, is settled. Now for the opportunity that you created. It was not only unsuitable, it was indeed dangerous to the state. Do you want this point proved with the clearest of arguments? Suppose you had killed one of the citizens with malice prepense, and as a result the dead man's father acted as the tyrant did just now. Will you be held on a double or simple charge of murder? A simple charge, I believe. The wife, however, will hold you responsible for her husband's death as well, since by killing the son you had provided the father with a motive for dying. And she will use arguments similar to yours: he loved his son most tenderly and had turned over to him the care for all family affairs; the son had been his father's joy. What's more, the frigid, not to say ridiculous, arguments you used regarding the tyrant she will use convincingly regarding a private citizen and an old man. She will add that you knew all this and had foreseen that he would depart from life on being deprived of a son in whom alone he found all joy of life; that you did not lack the intent to murder the old man but adopted this course so that he would die a more wretched death by his own hand, and you would satisfy your hatred in fuller measure by the misfortune of the wretched father; that you killed the young man for this reason; that you left your sword in the wound for this purpose. Can you see how much more plausible those arguments are in her case than in yours? Yet you will deny that the father's death had anything to do with you and will clear yourself of the suspicion of malice prepense by pointing out the kind of situation created. You will say that this was not a suitable motive for committing suicide, that you could neither have known the result in advance nor seen the risk of this happening because there are few precedents for a father departing from life of his own accord because of a son's death. Otherwise the mother too would have to seek death, for it was common knowledge that mothers loved more passionately and showed less fortitude in distress. You would have no doubts about the helpfulness of this argument in refuting the second charge. And it would no doubt be helpful. But what is valid in clearing you of a criminal charge is even more valid as an argument against giving you credit in the present case. In the former case the argument would free you from the suspicion of malice prepense, since you had not given sufficient and suitable cause for suicide; in the present case, which is based on a much less suitable cause, given the person of the tyrant, you want to create the impression that you not only expected the result but even foresaw it with certainty. In the former case you could not be accused of recklessness, although you provided a motive with intent to harm, yet not a motive sufficient in itself to prompt what happened – on the contrary, the whole business will be imputed to the man himself, and he will suffer punishment under the law, being denied burial because he deprived the state of a citizen without having a sufficient motive.[94] You, however, will be accused of no more than the one murder of the son, even if his mother, daughters, sisters, even if the whole clan had followed the father's example and committed suicide. In the present case you could have been charged, had the matter not turned out well, because one could have anticipated and seen the risk of great danger to the state.

I proceed now to that fourth point of his defence,[95] gentlemen of the jury, which he considered completely safe and irrefutable. From this position I shall rout him so thoroughly that he will not only be unable to hold the fort with his claim to tyrannicide and its glory, but will barely find a hiding place to escape punishment for recklessness and public mischief. Let him come to realize that I am not dealing with him as a personal enemy or busybody (as he alleged), for although I could bring charges against him and demand his punishment, I will be content to keep him from receiving an honour he has not deserved.

He claims that a reward is owed him, if for no other reason, because he killed the son who was already more than a tyrant and the groomed heir to the tyranny; that this was sufficient, even if the gods had not granted that, as a result, the old man cut short his own life. Oh, hopeless impudence! Would you claim a reward even if the tyrant's own Furies had not taken revenge on him? May the gods bring to pass anything but that situation imagined by you. Nevertheless, let us imagine the situation in our speech, if that be safe and permissible, although the mind shrinks at the mere mention of it. Would you claim the reward for tyrannicide with the son slain and the old man surviving? Is it not more likely that you would not be here to lay the claim, or this state to grant it, for you would either have been dispatched by special tortures or languish, exiled, in the remotest corner of Orcas,[96] and we would have to suffer a brutal butcher instead of a tyrant and call down dire curses upon your head – in whatever land you were hiding out – for having cast us into such a tempest of evil by your thoughtlessness, or rather, your rash desire for profit.

'But the son was the real tyrant,' you say. 'The father had nothing left but the empty title.' What do I hear? Was this city sustaining two tyrants then? For no one ever doubted that the father deserved to be called a tyrant. But never before was it said or heard that two tyrants had their seat in one city – a situation more unnatural than two heads on one body. Two queen bees[97] do not suffer each other's presence in one hive. In herds, one bull is forced to yield to the other. Two lions in the same grove do not get along – and a tyrant (although no animal is fiercer than he) will allow his equal in the same city? Do you not see that, of the two, one must either attack the other or else yield to him? Which do you prefer: was the power vested in the father or in the son? If the son obtained the tyranny against the father's will, why do you demand a prize from the state? You have aided the tyrant's interests, not the state's. If he yielded to the father, what else can you call him but a tyrant's governor or follower?

In any case, even you yourself would not dare to take away the title of tyrant from the older man, but to transfer the whole tyranny to the son by some means or other, how much you invented in your speech that was not fact but merely aided your cause! And in devising your story, what complete disregard you showed for propriety of character! For, as I remember, you introduced into your tale an old man mellowed by years who had lost all tyrannical severity on account of his age – like apples that are sour by nature but grow mellow by the passage of time and acquire a new flavour! Next, you introduced a young man carrying on a savage tyranny while the other man was still safe and sound, succeeding his father during his lifetime. A private head of family does not suffer his son to succeed him during his lifetime – and you want us to believe this of a tyrant? A private individual does not allow any of his children to run the household according to his whim and pleasure – and a tyrant, abdicating his power, as it were, has placed the whole business in a young man's hands? No doubt you can see for yourself how frigid these arguments are and how totally against common sense. But what were you to do? If you had not introduced characters of this kind, you could not have devised a dénouement to your tragedy. I ask you, has it ever been heard that a tyrant mellowed with age? When will you stop attributing the characteristics of private individuals and worthy kings to tyrants? Just as the same flame softens wax and hardens clay, age mellows and tempers the majority of men but gradually hardens the tyrant's mind. Just as the progress of time takes the bitterness out of certain kinds of fruit but produces sourness in some wines, so old age fails to take away the tyrant's savage disposition and rather aggravates it. Do you want me to show you the very image of a tyrant's character? Picture a thorn that pricks more sharply the older it is. Picture the hedgehog, whose back is the pricklier the older it is. In ordinary men old age may remove or, at any rate, mitigate some vices, though it aggravates most of them and even generates some new ones. But what effect can old age have on tyrannical minds that are born to be wicked and cruel, trained and instructed in brutality and crime? What effect can it have other than that of increasing their vices – unless perhaps it takes away their sexual appetite?[98] But how small a portion of tyranny is sexual desire! Still, let us assume that the tyrant is more sluggish in satisfying his sexual appetites on account of his age, though also more fastidious. The less able he is to make love, the more inclined he is to use violence. Perhaps fewer young men were castrated for his pleasure, but more distinguished ones. Perhaps fewer young women were brought to him, but more exquisite ones. And why not also a greater number – to overcome the tedium of his old age with choice and variety?

How many witnesses I could produce to prove to you that this is so! The nobler men are, the more gifted the children they have, the greater their fear for them on account of the lecherous old man's desire. Or do you believe that desire declines along with physical strength? On the contrary, in vicious men, old age adds as much desire as it subtracts ability, though in these matters the tyrant's mind is not so much attracted by the thought of enjoying his pleasure as of delighting in our humiliation. While the fire of Venus grows cold in the ageing tyrant, his malice, his cruelty, and his desire to harm boil up and thrive. Finally, that whole host of vices proper to tyrants – greed, rapacity, depravity, shamelessness, irreverence, rage, violence, lack of self-control, suspiciousness, fraudulence, perfidy, cruelty, implacability, criminality, perjury[99] – what need is there to list them all when they are, alas, only too well known to us all – of these, I insist, there is none that is not aggravated by years, for in youth they are sometimes overcome by natural goodness; moreover, some of these vices youth has not yet learned. But in old age the tyrant has totally divested himself, by frequent and continual exercise of crime, of any feeling of shame, kindness, or the better qualities that were naturally inherent in him, and has completely changed into a monstrous beast.[100]

But why prove with arguments that this was the case with that accursed old man, gentlemen of the jury, when his own memory supplies each man with ample evidence?

If the young man showed himself rather overweening, abusing, of course, his father's power, will you right away give him the title of tyrant? In this manner you can easily derive six hundred tyrants from one and the same tyranny. For who is there in the tyrant's household, be he the least important servant, who is not himself almost more ferocious, violent, and criminal than the tyrant?

'The son,' you say, 'was enjoying the fruits of the tyrant's rule. He left nothing to the father except the title.' As if this was not a common characteristic of all tyrannies. By far the smallest part of the profits generally gained from a tyranny reverts to the tyrant himself. Just as it usually happens in robberies, the plunder is divided evenly among all, or rather among those by whose aid it was seized. That band of criminals will not hold together unless their leader, whoever he be, grants them more liberty than he grants even himself, claiming for his person only the title. And towards no one is the tyrant more tolerant than towards his companions in crime, for he realizes of course that his rule is maintained by their aid and service. In the shadow of one man, then, does every hanger-on, every helper, crony, and pimp practise his tyranny upon the people. It would be a ridiculous enterprise, gentlemen of the jury, if I attempted to prove this also by argument. We have seen it, we have experienced it, we know it – unless by chance a few short days have obliterated the memory of such long-lasting misfortunes. Indeed, tyranny would not be such a wretched thing if one had to endure only the brute force of a single man. But how many robbers must be suffered, how many impious scoundrels, how many newcomers from remote and barbarian lands who are more like beasts than men! Nor are those lacking who pretend to have earned the tyrant's favour by their crimes, so that they may be feared on that account by the people. Will you call any one of them a tyrant? And will you claim the prize for tyrannicide for killing any one of them? You will not, I suppose, be so devoid of shame.

'But,' you say, 'the father, weakened by old age, had transferred the whole of the government to his son. Whatever tyrannical crimes were perpetrated in the city were due to the young man's lawlessness.'

But who is so blind as not to see how far removed this argument is from any semblance of truth? Who is so forgetful that he could not refute it on the basis of his own experience? I can name you several followers of the tyrant who were more insolent than his son. Moreover, it is very probable that the old man disapproved of his son's insolence more than of anyone's, either because every tyrant hates all aspirants to tyranny or because he realized that his son's deeds greatly increased the ill will and hatred against him (whereas it is characteristic of clever tyrants to imitate, as far as tyranny will permit, a legitimate monarchy), or because even the worst father takes some offence at his children's vices and prefers to use the services of others rather than those of his own family in perpetrating cruelty. If, then, the son planned robberies, abductions, and crimes of this sort without his father's knowledge, he did not act like a tyrant at all, but like an insolent follower. If he exercised tyranny with his father's approval, on his behalf as it were, which of them should in fairness bear the blame for what happened – the man by whom the deeds were carried out or the man by whose decision and authority they took place? I suppose the answer is clear: of course, the man in whose power it was to prevent these occurrences at will. And what do tyrants not perpetrate through others? They do not personally castrate boys, carry off young girls, execute proscriptions, seize property, despoil temples, lay hands on inheritances, rob the treasury, torment with tortures, kill a man, make armed assaults on villages, or put the torch to houses. They practise this whole tyrannical sport vicariously, through their assistants. Yet the odium attached to the name 'tyrant' falls on one man only, and for killing this one man the law sets out a prize, against this one man it is legal to draw the sword – the others the law reserves for its own judgment.

Men may be given various titles according to the manner in which each benefited the tyrant by his service, but the title of tyrant fits only the one under whose shield, as it were, that whole vile rabble is hiding out. I suppose you have often heard, gentlemen of the jury, the elegant phrases written by wise men: 'Tyrants have not only long, but also numerous hands, numerous and very keen eyes, numerous and very long ears.'[101] A tyrant is indeed a prodigious beast, more of a portent than the Titans Briareus and Enceladus,[102] with a hundred heads, a hundred tongues, a hundred hands and feet. For it seems that the tyrant has as many limbs as he has companions in crime; and just as a body consists of members, so a tyranny is made up of helpers of this kind. And just as that which is called 'body' is nothing but a composite made up of all members, so in a tyranny there is one element that is neither foot, nor hand, nor any other member, but contains them all, yet in such a manner that it can be separated from them. And this element is called 'tyrant.' Go now and exaggerate the young man's insolence and violence as much as you please. Call him prefect of the citadel, call him the tyrant's 'eye,' or if you prefer, his 'right hand,' or if that still does not satisfy you, the very head of the tyrant. But this much is certain: you cannot by any means call him 'tyrant.' For the law considers under this name only the monster by whose power and authority all these members come to life, as it were. That monster alone the law allows to be killed by a valiant citizen. It does not want you to attack some 'eye,' it does not let you cut off some 'head,' lest there come to pass something of the sort that is told by the poets of the Lernean Hydra:[103] two ever more deadly heads sprouting in the place of every one cut off, more and ever keener eyes taking the place of every one poked out, many and ever stronger hands growing for every one cut off. The law makes you master and judge over one man's life only, the life of him who dared to take the name of tyrant and on whose removal the rest of the members will die off as if deprived of their life's breath, or will at any rate be cured.

But why do I use such detailed arguments against you when I can refute you in your own words, catching you in your own noose, as it were?[104] A little while ago you called the young man an important follower of the father – you will not deny that. Elsewhere, in turn, you said that the son had completely taken over the tyranny and yielded to his father only the formal title. How is it fitting to call the same man both a 'follower' and a 'tyrant'? Moreover, if he yielded the title to his father, he did not use it. Legal contracts, however, stand or fall by their wording. The law made a contract with you, using this formula: 'If a man kills the *tyrant*, he may carry off the reward.' Why tell me about the young man's crimes? The law wanted you to kill the beast called tyrant, whatever it may be. You – as you admit yourself – have killed a great follower, not the tyrant. What business do you have with the law, then?

'But,' you say, 'I followed the meaning, not the letter, of the law.[105] I killed him who was the head of the tyranny, the heir apparent of his father's dominion. I gave rise to liberty, I did away with servitude. That is what the law meant, and for the author of this deed it has set out a prize.'

I say that you have killed a follower. I do not care how great a follower he was, how oppressive, how fierce, how wicked. You have merely killed a follower of the tyranny, not its head. Or if he was a head, he was one of many.

But let us grant you all of this according to your fancy. Let us say that the son was the whole substance of the tyranny, that the father had nothing but the empty title of tyrant, like the mythical nymph Echo, who is thought to have been nothing but a disembodied voice.[106] Who permitted you to depart from the letter of the law in such an important matter, especially when the law's words are so lucid that nothing can be clearer, and to adduce before the court that false and home-grown interpretation of yours? I am of the opinion, gentlemen of the jury, that no more ruinous precedent can be introduced into the state than if swindlers customarily depart from the letter of the law and present to the jurors the most favourable interpretation each of them is able to devise in order to disguise his crime.

Can anyone recall a time when it was a practice to question the meaning of the laws unless there was something ambiguous and obscure in their wording, or unless an obviously absurd situation arose from applying the words to an event? In the former case it is generally the response of legal experts and the pronouncement of the jury that is accepted, not any chance comer's fabrications. In the latter case necessity itself compels us to diverge a little from the wording of the law and to observe the fair meaning rather than the letter of the law. You can therefore see two kinds of risks, gentlemen of the jury: one being that we lose sight of the law's intent by being too pedantic in discussing its wording, the other that we overthrow all laws and the respect for court decisions by departing widely from the written precept. The former is by far the lighter risk, since it hardly ever happens that a legislator has expressed his intent in an obscure manner or that some absurd situation arises; the latter is much more dangerous and destructive. For what law could not easily be subverted in future by some clever swindler's arguments made up to escape punishment? And any criminal will be able to escape your judgment unless he is so lacking in imagination that he cannot come up even with a frivolous, insignificant lie. And each man will interpret the law according to his advantage or his heart's desire, substituting a young man for an old one, a follower for a tyrant, murder for tyrannicide, and generally, one thing for another. How will your duty, how will your oath be served, gentlemen of the jury, when you have no secure guidelines to follow in future decisions and will have to consider instead the ambiguous and contradictory theories of litigants? While we must take great care in every case not to depart from the letter of the law except for the gravest of reasons, it is particularly dangerous and even absurd in this case, when nothing can be clearer than the law's words, nothing fairer than its meaning, nothing more destructive than to introduce an interpretation that runs counter to the law. Or do we believe that the author of this law was so inarticulate, so helpless with words that he could not have said, had he meant to, 'Let there be a reward for the man who ends tyranny by whatever means'?[107] For he was certainly aware that, on the whole, a tyranny is usually carried out by followers and deputies, that there are many among them that are more criminal and, in a manner of speaking, more tyrannical and certainly more deserving of punishment than the tyrant himself – except that all crimes of all followers are imputed to the tyrant. Against one man only – against him who is deemed tyrant by his title – were you granted permission to draw your sword. With respect to the others you are not given the same authority; not because the law considers them deserving of life, but because it wants the whole of the tyranny ended by the death of one man, not made harsher by the death of many. It was your duty simply to comply with the law and not to accommodate it to your deed as if its wording was a leaden rule,[108] but to plan your actions in accordance with its instructions.

By this example – the most harmful one can introduce – you would, on account of an arbitrary interpretation of the law, usurp the right of killing at your whim whomsoever you please. In this case, gentlemen of the jury, we must not consider how hateful the man was in the eyes of the state, how deserving of this or any even harsher punishment; no, we must consider over and over again to what unrestrained licence it would lead if this precedent of killing a man contrary to the law were first admitted into the state, then approved by your decision, and finally rewarded by a prize. The right which this man claimed for himself in acting against the tyrant's son another will demand against any one of the wealthy citizens. Any pauper treated with contumely by a rich man will straight away call him a tyrant and go after his life with poison or sword. In the end, if an official displeases a man, if a judge is hateful to him, he will not scruple to do away with him. Then he will consult some sophist or professional slanderer (if he has a rather sluggish mind himself) to defend his deed by bringing before you a novel interpretation of the law. He will say that the legislator had intended nothing else but that citizens of this sort, who were tyrants *de facto* though not by name, should be removed by sword, fire, or poison. And in this manner we should soon come to regret and condemn many times over and in the case of many men the very deed we once joyfully approved in the case of one man. Believe me, it is no slight risk, nor one we should accept blindly – the risk that a private individual, upon having found a pretext, should kill a man who has not been sentenced.

The truth of this will be readily apparent when we consider that there is nothing the law permits with less frequency or more caution. In three cases only, if I remember rightly, does the law allow a man to take another's life without trial: first, the life of an adulterer when he is caught with the avenger's wife,[109] a case in which concessions are made to the husband's uncontrollable and insurmountable grief, but only on condition that he kill both offenders and can prove by suitable arguments that he caught them in the act. Secondly, in repelling force,[110] but only on condition that you show that you could not have escaped death unless you caused death. This act the law interprets in the sense that it constitutes self-defence rather than taking the life of another. In both cases, however, the protagonists are obliged to justify their deed, to give themselves up at once, to accuse themselves of their own accord, so to speak, and not to wait until they are brought before court. Then, if all accounts tally, they are dismissed by the law, but in a manner that makes their deed appear pardonable rather than praiseworthy. Thirdly, and lastly, in the case of tyrannicide, where the law also offers a reward on account of the great risk incurred, but on condition that you kill manfully him whom the law has designated as the victim, denoting him by the title of 'tyrant,' not if you remove a criminal by committing a crime in turn. Nor does the law permit you to extend the licence to kill beyond the person of the single tyrant, except if someone stands up against you so that his death is inevitable in order for you to get at the tyrant. And this deed can be defended on the basis of that second instance, self-defence.

The licence to kill an enemy in battle appears very closely related to the third instance. Yet the law does not leave this matter up to your whim. Unless a man has been publicly declared an enemy, unless you have sworn an oath of allegiance to the general, unless he marched out his troops and ordered the battle sign to be given, it will count as wrong to have killed the enemy. You might say: 'I have killed an enemy, one who committed more than inimical acts. Only the title "enemy" was missing; he acted the enemy in deed.' The law will answer that it was its function to declare him an enemy. Perhaps it will profit from your wrongdoing, but it will exact punishment from you so as not to allow a precedent to steal in.

Is your case any different? The law had pointed out to you one man by name. You are transferring his name to another on your own authority, although it cannot apply to more than one man and ought not to be transferred from the man to whom the law has assigned it, lest you could at one time or another legally call any official, any judge, any citizen you please a 'tyrant.'

And it is not without the gravest of reasons that the law has attached so many restrictions to the licence to take another's life. It took into consideration the fact that nothing more important can be taken from a man than his life. It realized that against a dead man various reasons can easily be construed, and with impunity, since he who lies dead is not about to refute them. It realized how many pretexts each man could find to justify his grief if, after a man has been killed, justifications other than those specified by the law were admitted. In fact, the law even seems reluctant to grant itself the power to deprive a man of life. What clear, what numerous proofs it requires, how much it concedes to the accused, how petty it is in dealing with the prosecutor, whom it does not allow to lay charges except at his own risk, how much time it generously allows to the accused, how much freedom it grants him in rejecting jury members! How far removed do you think is it from the meaning of the law to permit any man to take the life of another because of a private grievance, on his own, home-grown interpretation, or rather perversion, of the law? Nor does it affect this case if you can heap up a mountain of accusations, however true and (I may add) well known the crimes are. You may say: I have killed a parricide, a sacrilegious, incestuous, treacherous man, a spy, a poisoner. The law wants the tyrant to be killed.

'But,' you say, 'this one man was more wicked than a multitude of tyrants, and more fatal to the state.'

The law will answer your long list of crimes succinctly: 'I do not care a whit how wicked was the man who died, I gave you permission to kill one man only, the tyrant. As for the rest, I gave you permission to bring them before the law. If you had brought an accusation against him, he would have been examined, convicted, condemned by me, and subjected to public punishment – and you would have set a salutary example for the whole state. As it is, you have killed him on a personal impulse and have introduced into the community a most pernicious, instead of a salutary, example. You begin the restoration of the laws with an act of violating the laws, that is, you want to cure one ill with another.[111] Do you think I am not aware that there are many in this crowd who are unworthy of life and most deserving of death? But I reserve them for my judgment, not for your hands. We have public hearings, tribunals, juries, prisons, executioners, and torturers. Why do you try to take precedence over me? Why do you seize an official function without having a mandate, acting like a tyrant while wanting to be regarded a tyrant-slayer? After all, why is the tyrant so hateful to me? For no other reason but that he refuses to obey me and tries to put himself above me. Only he will be allowed to brandish the sword whose hands I have ordained. If you had killed the young man because there was no other way to the tyrant's person, I would pardon you for acting out of necessity; but as it is, you have killed one who offered no resistance, who did not come to his father's aid, but implored his help. Content with this one man's death you departed without approaching the tyrant, whom alone I had given you permission to kill. It was my privilege to consider whether or not the young man's death was in the interest of the state, and I would have preferred to display him as an example to all, subjected to special tortures.'

And I am not saying this, gentlemen of the jury, because I am less than pleased at the father being removed together with the son. If only by that same stroke all had been wiped out who welcomed tyranny! But what prevents me from feeling both joy at the goodness of the gods who turned the matter to our advantage, and reluctance at seeing this man's rash deed become a legal precedent if it is approved by your decision?

Nor are we concerned here with avenging the injury done to the young man, but with the violence done to the majesty of the laws. For it is not fair to look favourably on a criminal because the man who was killed in violation of the laws was unpopular. Against whom the crime was committed should not be given as much consideration as the precedent set by the deed. Or else, why would it be any less lawful to attack the tyrant's nephews, minions, young lovers, wives, freemen, and panders? Often it was a wife who counselled the better part of his despotic measures. Sometimes it was a freeman or household slave who instigated the greatest act of cruelty. Why not kill them as well if you have the right to kill a citizen on your personal estimate of his worth? And what if there is anything more harmful than a tyrant? You would not, for all that, have a right to kill that creature. Suppose a man had tried to burn down this whole city – temples, houses, and courts – suppose he had in fact already set fires in several places, but the fire was extinguished by a sudden rainfall. The arsonist's person was known, but he was hiding out and living under cover. Coming upom him by chance, you kill him with your own hand. Will the law approve your deed? Surely not. Yet how much more harmful was that man than a tyrant! The more harmful, the more atrocious it is to destroy the state completely once and for all than it is to plunder it; the more atrocious it is to finish off all citizens by one fire than to rage against the lives of a few. Yet a private individual is granted the power to draw his sword against the tyrant only. As for the arsonist, you have merely the right to indict him. To distort the meaning of the law in this clear case and to cover up your deed by giving it a novel interpretation – what is this but to overturn the authority of the laws and to do by devious means what the tyrant used to do openly and by the use of force?

When a new law is being passed, the people have a right to ponder its rationale and fairness, but when the law has been passed and is sanctioned by long use, it must simply be obeyed. For we must not think that those forefathers of ours – indisputably very wise men – did not have weighty reasons when they ordained that the licence to kill granted to private individuals was limited to the tyrant's person only. In the first place, they thought that they must not open up a loophole giving private men the right to kill indiscriminately. Secondly, they realized that tyranny was a sort of fatal disease of the state,[112] which it was less harmful to endure than to stir up unwisely, and that it could not be removed once and for all except by the death of the tyrant himself. With the removal of the tyrant, who controlled rather than obeyed the laws, there was no more need for private derring-do, especially when the laws had been restored to the government of the state. Indeed, if the tyrant could have been called before the court, the laws would not have surrendered even him to receive justice at your hands.

They also realized that tyranny had a certain similarity to a legitimate monarchy,[113] and that there was only one difference: in a monarchy the people obeyed the king and the king obeyed the law; in a tyranny everything was subject to one man's whim. A king takes into consideration the public welfare; the tyrant his personal welfare. It is therefore in the interest of the citizens publicly to obey the tyrant like a legitimate ruler until a suitable avenger appears who restores the authority of the laws to their original state, and does so (if possible) with the loss of only one life. For in its wisdom, the law generally exercises restraint in dealing with those fatal diseases that have taken hold of the whole state as of a body. Its purpose is to cure the illness by holding up one example rather than by avenging manifest crime, lest in its effort to cure the people it destroy a large part of it. For the same reason it is customary in public uprisings to punish only the instigators themselves and to pardon the rest who were carried away by this tempest. Or rather, one can hardly speak of pardoning in the case of those who kept their peace in the general upheaval of the state. But what plague can be more fatal than a tyranny? What disease spreads more widely through the members of a populace? What part of the city can remain untainted by this vice? I pass over those who are after high office, those who are bound by debts, guilty of crimes, newcomers from barbarian lands (for this whole disgusting lot of men is pleased with tyranny, since there is no other form of government in which there are greater rewards for criminals). But the evil of tyranny implicates even good citizens, as they are either afraid for their possessions or think it right to serve the moment. In this state of things, therefore, the laws, which are only suppressed, not abolished, operate cautiously and circumspectly. They know that this ulcer cannot be irritated without grave risk to the populace but can be cured conveniently by the loss of one head. Therefore they offer a reward to some experienced physician, pointing out what limb they want amputated, what limbs they want spared. The laws pointed out the head – you amputated the right hand. They wanted you to kill the tyrant – you killed the tyrant's bondsman. What prize do you deserve? The prize deserved by a physician who in his ignorance aggravated the illness and brought the whole man into mortal danger; the prize deserved by one who killed a man despite the injunctions of the laws.

Nor do I now accuse you of murder. Perhaps someone else, if it so pleases him, will bring a charge against you. My intent simply was to demonstrate to you that it is monstrous impudence to claim for yourself such a splendid honour, to demand such a splendid prize, when yours is a case in which you could not possibly escape grave punishment if you were dealt with in a more painstaking and exacting manner. Now go ahead and call me meddlesome when I deal with you so generously and civilly, when I could have accused you of a capital crime but content myself with defending the interests of law and state, lest it be defrauded and forced to grant a reward to a man who deserves no favour. Of this I want to convince, not only the jury, to whom I believe it has long ago become evident, but even you yourself; and I am confident that I will be successful if only you could give me your attention for a little while.

Do you want me to proceed as you did, recalling the whole case in summary fashion? Do you want me to investigate how far short your deed fell of satisfying the conditions of the law and how greatly deceived you were when you said it exceeded them by much? The law set three conditions, and in such a manner that it believes punishment is called for, or at any rate no gratitude owed, if any of these conditions is not met. I shall demonstrate that you failed to meet, not just one, but every single one. If I do this, will you be reasonable and give up your claim to the reward, or will you be shameless and persist in it?

Well then, here are the facts. You have no grounds for claiming the reward for tyrannicide unless you have the following three points on your side: intent, method, and result.

Intent covers two aspects: what you hoped for and what you planned to do. For if you had killed the tyrant by mistake, without planning to kill him, a reward would not be owed you any more than if the tyrant's best friend had done the same (for this, too, could happen). Furthermore, you may determine yourself with what plan you went to the citadel: the law will be satisfied that you wanted to kill the tyrant only if you succeeded in doing so. You failed, even though you tell us that it was in your power to kill the tyrant if you had wanted to do it. The law says that it makes no difference whether you came to the citadel without a plan to kill the tyrant or had a plan but suddenly changed your mind.

Now let us consider your hopes. Although the law does not inspect this point scrupulously, all details ought to fit together in the completed act. What if you had killed the tyrant to become tyrant yourself – would you expect a reward or fear punishment? What if you had killed the tyrant to avenge some personal grief, and it was publicly known? Surely you would not dare to ask for a reward? What if robbers had met the tyrant by chance and killed him, would they aspire to this honour? Surely not. What if someone bore a private grudge against the tyrant and had hired you[114] at great expense to give poison to the tyrant and you had administered it, would you, I ask, demand the reward for tyrannicide? Surely not.

I refrain from using hypotheses in the present case. I say nothing against your mode of life, which is so humble that you, otherwise so vainglorious, did not venture to say a word of it. But I have no hesitation to affirm one point: anyone who did not kill the tyrant when he could safely have done so obviously did not want to kill him. Anyone who killed a man whose death was likely to bring utter ruin to the state rather than any benefit either wanted to avenge a private grief, not vindicate the state, or was after private gain at the state's risk, not eager to benefit the state at his own risk. Finally a man who brags so insolently can but seem to be motivated by thirst for glory; one who demands the reward so brazenly can but seem to have pursued his own profit.

Do you not realize therefore how far in this regard you diverge from the whole intent of the law? It wanted the tyrant killed at your risk and for its own sake. And what did you do? Not only did you choose to pass over the tyrant; you agitated him at great risk to the state. And you killed at our grave risk, for your own profit or, perhaps, pleasure, the man whom the law, for its own sake, did not want killed.

Even assuming that you brought to the enterprise a spirit worthy of a tyrannicide, equally disdaining profit and danger to your life, yet it matters a great deal how you attempted to remove the tyrant.

I concede you all points according to your heart's desire, points that no one else would concede you: that you killed the father by killing his son, the man who was tyrant by him who was not. I concede that some Delian informed you in advance so that you could know for certain what the Delian god himself could hardly have divined.[115] I concede that you could have killed the father if you had wanted to, but that this kind of punishment was more to your liking, and that you did in fact end the tyranny, using a novel and unusual method. You see how many concessions I make to you? Yet I shall resist your claim and will not allow you to carry off the prize, because you have not ended the tyranny in a manner approved by the law, but in a manner which does not further public morals and is unworthy of a hero.[116]

Come, what if you had slain the tyrant's infant son in his cradle, and once again that Delian had been present, on whose authority you could know for certain that upon the death of the child the father would take his own life; and this came to pass. Would the state look up to you as a tyrant-slayer or rather execrate you as a cruel and savage man for having vented your rage upon an age that is spared even by the armed host, an age on which even lions would take pity? What then? The state will benefit from your wicked deed, but it will by no means approve your example. What if you had raped the tyrant's wife, whom he loved passionately, and he departed from life, unable to bear the disgrace? Will you demand the praise due a tyrant-slayer or rather fear punishment for rape and adultery? The answer is obvious.

Now let me draw a parallel that comes even closer to your deed. What if you were the tyrant's physician and had killed your patient by giving him poison. Would the state detest you as a poisoner or admire you as a hero? It will rejoice at the tyrant's removal, but will denounce the manner and method by which you accomplished it. What if the tyrant had been on familiar terms with you, and under the guise of friendship you offered him poison at a banquet?[117] Finally, what if you had taken the tyrant's life using magic likenesses and evil spells? Would you expect reward or punishment from the law?

But, however it may be, you did put an end to tyranny. The law rejoices in the result, but it cannot allow so pernicious an example to enter this community, an example by which citizens may become accustomed to avenge one crime by another, to kill a father by killing his son. Do you understand the importance of manner and method in gaining approval for one's deed? When the law gives you permission to do something, it does not give you permission to do it in any way you please. You have the right to kill an adulterer with the sword; you have no right to kill him with poison or magic incantations. And why not? Because using poison at all is setting an unwholesome example, and the law does not allow such practices to make their way into the community for any reason, however creditable. After all, it is not legal to kill even an enemy with poison or evil arts. For at no time does the law approve wicked deeds, and arrows dipped in poison are even forbidden in wars.[118] But if the manner of proceeding is taken into account even in cases where no reward is claimed, how much more relevant would it be in cases where the greatest reward is being sought?

The law decrees a triumph for him who has overcome a certain number of enemies.[119] Suppose someone overcame them, not in battle, but by means of food and drink tainted with poison. Will the citizens calmly watch his triumph or will they rather hate him, and shun and curse him as a poisoner? After all, the manner and method of proceeding are examined even in private actions – how much more readily ought one to do so in public actions, and more particularly regarding this most noble enterprise, one that should be free of any suspicion of crime?

Well now, consider the following case. If you had made a contract with a physician, promising him a fee for delivering you from your illness, and he rid you of the illness by evil spells and incantations rather than by drugs, will you give him his reward, or will you rather bring the man before the court, accusing him of having caused harm by his evil arts? He will protest: 'I have delivered you from your illness. What does it matter to you, by what means? You were looking only for relief from your illness. That is what the reward was promised for.' He will call you ungrateful because you would not even be there to deny him the reward had it not been for his help. You will answer right away that you promised your reward to a physician, not a sorcerer. You will deny that a man who has conferred a benefit by evil means deserves anything but evil in return. Indeed, the man who removed one evil by another can hardly be considered to have conferred a benefit, for this was not removing, but exchanging one evil for another. You will say that your spirit was harmed while your body was being helped, and you will win your case, even before a biased judge.

The law is in the same, or an even better, position. It has a case against you that is more easily won than yours against the physician. For in that case the dispute involved an insignificant private fee, in our case it involves a public award. In that case one man was deceived, in this case it is the law that is being defrauded, and one must take care lest any citizens be wronged thereby. In that case health was restored by a sure and efficient, though suspect and disapproved, method; in this case freedom was not restored, rather the state incurred the utmost danger on account of a lawless, criminal act (for why not call it a criminal act, since it was homicide perpetrated on a citizen in violation of the law?). In fact, your deed is rather like that of a physician who is hired for a fee to effect a cure and administers poison instead of medication, which nevertheless, in a favourable moment, cures the patient of his illness (as not infrequently happens). The convalescent will thank his stars for having survived, but will accuse you of attempted murder in spite of having escaped death. He will not consider it his business whether you administered poison instead of medication because of inexperience, by mistake, or on purpose, for it was your responsibility either not to undertake the business or to bring to the task of healing a reliable character, skill, purpose, diligence, and whatever other qualities are generally sought in an expert craftsman.

However, we shall let you enjoy the concessions we made to you earlier on, agreeing that you certainly killed the tyrant, and in a manner that did not endanger the state. The law will not approve of your deed unless it was far removed, not only from crime, but any semblance of crime, lest the law, which was instituted first and foremost for the benefit of the community to shut out all mischief, be said to owe its restoration to a crime, when it should have owed it to a god or certainly a man very similar to the gods. It will not give its approval, I insist, unless you have killed the true tyrant, whom the law for its part indicated by the title, and killed him in a permitted manner, lest by this loophole a dangerous precedent steal its way into the community. The law will not give its approval unless you have slain the tyrant with your sword rather than by occult and evil arts, with a valiant heart, with your own hand, and openly disdaining any danger to your life. For the law does not only look for one result, the present removal of the tyrant; rather, it wants all men to realize that this community has heroes who are not afraid to act on behalf of their fatherland even at the cost of their own lives and who, by the splendid example of their deed, deter anyone in future from aspiring to the tyranny when they see that our city is not safe enough for tyrants. Indeed, everyone knows that a man who despises danger to his own life is master over another's life.[120] For what escort, what guards, what walls, what citadel, and what arms can defend a tyrant's life against a spirit who believes that the freedom of his fatherland is bought cheap at the price of his own life?

Finally, even if your intent and your method are right, you have not accomplished what was the heart of the whole matter. Far from having killed the tyrant, you aggravated the tyranny, as far as in you was, by killing the tyrant's son. What does it matter if you endangered the state by malice or by ignorance? For nothing is more truly spoken than that popular saying 'Untimely good will differs not from enmity.'[121] Far from having killed the tyrant, you could not even have guessed that as a result he would kill himself. 'But,' you say, 'I have killed the young man, who was more lawless than his father.' What of it? If the law imputes his crimes to the father as well, you have killed an important follower indeed, but not the tyrant. 'But,' you say, 'I have killed the tyrant's heir apparent.' He succeeds to the tyranny who is first at hand and who has more power to seize it. But let it be so; you have certainly removed his successor. In that case you have killed him who was *going to be* tyrant. But that which is *going to be* does not exist yet. The law orders that man removed who *is* tyrant at the time, not the one who in your estimate *will be* tyrant at some time in the future. If a man under contract to deliver a statue delivers an unhewn block, is he considered to have kept his promise? I think not.

Where are they now, the many points that you had in excess of those needed to claim the prize? You can see that you have not satisfied even one of the points that are required without fail. You say: 'I had the intent.' The law gives you credit for intent only on the basis of your deeds. 'I changed my plan afterwards, as circumstances arose.' Then you are owed the same reward as a competitor in the Olympics who abandons the goal halfway through the course, reins in, and turns back to the starting point. But you ventured it. Then you will carry off such praise as is due to an Olympic athlete who exerted himself but was not victorious. But you did kill in the end – a man whom the law did not commit to your judgment and whose death was not in the public interest. But your deed turned out to be to the community's advantage. In that case thanks are owed to the divine spirit who played a role like that Pallas is said to have played in Attica, about whom a proverb is extant, saying that she used to give the ill-planned ventures of the Athenians a good turn.[122] You have not saved, but done away with the laws; it was not you who restored our liberty but some good spirit, a patron of our city, who kindly averted from us the result deserved by your rashness and turned your thoughtless act into an opportunity for restoring our freedom. I am not rendering the people ungrateful towards you; it is you who are at pains to render the people ungrateful towards the gods. Once already you brought danger upon the state, the danger of suffering a twofold instead of a single tyranny. Now you are trying to lure it into danger again, the danger of being cast back into its former slavery or some even graver misfortune by the angry gods.

Why are you intruding upon another's merits with artful pretences? Why are you claiming universal praise in a case from which nothing can rightly devolve on you except punishment for your rash action? If you can prove to the jury and to the state that you had a spirit worthy of a tyrant-slayer, refusing no risk for the sake of the state; if you accomplished your deed, not through some crime, not by setting a ruinous example, but in a lawful manner; if fortune gave your illustrious enterprise prompt issue – if you can prove all three, you may venture to call yourself a tyrant-slayer, you may dare to demand from the state the fairest and almost divine prize. You may dare to cast it into our teeth that the laws have been saved, the community restored, temples, altars, homes, and everyone's fortunes preserved, that boys are safe, maidens untouched, and marriages undefiled; then finally you may speak boldly on the very subject of our debate here in court before the jury. Then you may dare to threaten me because I stood up against you; dare to insinuate that the state is lacking in gratitude if it does not show you due honour; dare to call the jury unfair or corrupt if they do not vote in favour of conferring the award on you.

If, on the other hand, your intended actions were suspect or dangerous, if your deed was against the law and entailed a crime, let your sense of decency prevail. Desist from your outrageous demand for a reward that you have in no way deserved and take steps, if you are wise, to ward off a penalty. This much you may be able to achieve before a fair jury and a people gladdened by the gift of the gods.

Do not think of me as the only one discouraging you from claiming the prize; think of the laws, the state, and the gods as your adversaries in this suit as well. Picture the laws addressing you in these words:[123] 'If you wish to see us truly restored, let our authority prevail first of all in this, your case. You will be more highly praised if you yield to us, obey us, and subject your will to our judgment; if you present your case to the citizens as the first example of our revival; if you show to the community that each man must live, not by the whim of criminals, but by our decrees.'

And on the other side imagine the state using such speech in addressing you: 'If you wish to show yourself a good citizen, do not brand me with the mark of folly, lest it be said thereafter, when the facts become known, that I was drunk with joy when I conferred a reward on a man who was more deserving of punishment. Do not turn the gods against me and rouse their anger once more by this act of ingratitude, after I have barely reconciled them, moved them, and rendered them favourable by lasting vows, numerous sacrifices, numerous prayers, and numerous sufferings. At least, with your permission, let me enjoy their favour.'

If neither the laws nor the state can move you, you ought at least to respect the words of the gods, whom you should imagine dealing with you thus: 'Why do you intrude upon the praise that is our due? Why are you jealous of the honour paid us? Why do you not allow us to be forever well disposed towards this community? Why are you yourself so ungrateful? This community will always owe the restoration of its freedom to me.[124] You owe a twofold debt to our good will, because we have saved the state of which you are a part and because our good will turned your dangerous thoughtlessness, or rather your crime, into an occasion of great happiness. For if we had not been favourable, standing by your side, what would have happened but that you would have perished, and through you the state? If you quite insist on carrying off a reward, consider that we have granted you a sufficiently great reward if, by our intervention, your ill-planned venture turned out well. Consider the laws more grateful than you deserve if they pardon your rash and criminal act out of respect for our approbation. Consider the community to have given you ample praise if it allows your name to be mentioned in the story of their restored freedom. Be content with this portion of honour and desist from your attempt to seize what is our due, appropriating what is our gift to the community and taking away from the laws their authority.'

But I shall make an end, since the water in the clock has run out.[125] It remains for you, gentlemen of the jury, to do your duty and to determine whether you wish to render judgment in favour of the laws, the gods, and the state, or in favour of this vainglorious braggart; whether you wish to impute the city's present happiness to this man's rash and criminal action, in which case it is a happiness often to be cursed and soon perhaps to be taken away from us by the angry gods (let my words not be an evil omen), or to impute it to the gods, to whom everything is indisputably owed, that through their favour it may be preserved, enhanced, and blessed. You must determine whether it is more advantageous to have it said that the laws were cheated in the very first judgment rendered, or to make it clear that the severity of the restored laws and the wisdom of the jurors prevailed against the unjust claims of one man.

COMMENTARY ON OVID'S *NUT-TREE*

In Nucem Ovidii commentarius

translated by

A.G. RIGG

This commentary on Ovid's *Nux* was finished in 1523 and dedicated to John More, only son of Sir Thomas More, with a request that John share the *Nut-tree* ('[whose] fruit is naturally divisible into four parts') with his three sisters and their friend Margaret Giggs. It was published by Froben in 1524 and by several other publishers in the same year. Ovid's authorship of the *Nux* has generally been doubted by modern scholars: the earliest extant manuscript is of the eleventh century. On the other hand, it is clearly a work of antiquity, not a medieval imitation; from a stylistic analysis A.G. Lee concludes that it is either Ovid's or a very good imitation made at the end of the first century AD. L.P. Wilkinson says that it is too short to tell. R.J. Tarrant places the *Nux* under the heading 'Pseudo-Ovid,' but describes it as 'the most accomplished of pseudo-Ovidian poems.' Erasmus had no doubt: in the prefatory letter to John More (Ep 1402, 127 below) he calls it *nimirum Ovidianum* 'very Ovidian' and frequently refers to the author as Ovid, and Erasmus' admiration is not to be ignored.[1]

There are, to my knowledge, no medieval commentaries on the *Nux*;[2] medieval Ovidian commentaries concentrate on the love poetry, on autobiographical problems, and on the difficulties in reconciling the *Metamorphoses* with Christianity and biblical history. Erasmus' treatment is entirely literary. He explicates the text in terms of a legal case, specifically one in which the *status* (the basis of the case) is one of *qualitas*, that is, one in which the facts are agreed and the question is simply one of justice: his principal tool is Quintilian's *Institutio oratoria*. He also cites Pliny frequently, to show how much of the poem's effect consists in the manipulation of natural history. His learning (from sources such as Athenaeus' *Deipnosophists*) is paraded wittily throughout the commentary. Clearly he wished to be judged in the same way that he asked young John More to judge Ovid: 'An outstanding artist always performs consistently, whether he is making a Colossus or a six-inch statuette ... there is greater respect for his artistic skill when he is working in miniature or with cheap material' (127 below). Despite his avowal that this commentary is a sign of his second childhood,[3] he clearly intended it as a demonstration of his learning and skill when working 'in miniature.' The immediate popularity of the commentary shows that his public accepted it in this way.

The translation here is based on the edition by Sir Roger Mynors in ASD I-1. The text is that of Froben (Basel 1524), since, as far as we know, Erasmus never revised his text.[4]

AGR

ERASMUS OF ROTTERDAM TO JOHN MORE, A YOUNG MAN OF GREAT PROMISE,
GREETINGS

My dear friend John, I should not like to appear totally unresponsive to your
gifts and many friendly letters,[1] so I am sending you a nut-tree! Please do not
refuse this small gift – it is really quite elegant and very Ovidian. In any case,
one could hardly regard a whole tree as a *very* tiny gift, or think that
something so eloquent is valueless. You should not be surprised that in
Ovid the nut-tree speaks in Latin; in Lucian there is a very fluent debate
between the vowels,[2] and Homer has the ship *Argo* speaking (and in verse,
too!).[3] So when you read this book, become a Pythagorean for a while and
believe that even trees have a soul;[4] Ovid has simply given the tree a tongue –
or rather, has given it back, for once upon a time the oaks at Dodona used
to speak oracles![5] Although I have had nothing to do with this kind of
pursuit for a long time, it has been a pleasure to recommend to students such
a merry and also learned poem, along with my little commentary. I am well
aware that some people will be quick to shout out the old Greek saying 'The
old man's in his second childhood' and has gone back to his nuts![6] I don't
really think, however, that it is a waste of time for boys (or undignified for
old men) to play with nuts like this; such relaxation helps to restore the
intellect when it has been tired out by serious studies.

But in any case I am not greatly bothered about what other people say. I
should like you, John, to accept the idea that an outstanding artist always
performs consistently, whether he is making a Colossus or a six-inch
statuette, whether it is Jupiter that he is painting or Thersites,[7] whether he is
sculpting in bronze and ordinary stone or in gold and jewels – the only
difference is that there is greater respect for his artistic skill when he is
working in miniature or with cheap material. Ovid's *Medea* has been
praised,[8] but you will see that he is no less Ovid in his *Nux*. In the *Medea* the
content supplied the eloquence, and a good deal of the praise must be
shared with the Greeks, who treated the same story very frequently. In the
Nux, however, anything praiseworthy is due to the poet's own wit.

I'm not the sort of person to paint several walls out of one bucket.[9] On
the other hand, you will be thought a splendid fellow – and I shall seem not
such a disagreeable person – if you would be willing to share this *Nux* (its
fruit is naturally divisible into four parts, even if it's less easy to split the
tree!) with your very charming sisters Margaret, Elizabeth, and Cecily, and
with [Margaret] Giggs,[10] who rejoices in their friendship. They keep on at
me so often with their letters, and with such sound and acute arguments in
such pure Latin, that I have difficulty in persuading my friends that the girls'
letters were composed by their own efforts – though I know it for a fact.

There is no need for me, John, to encourage you to literary studies or to virtue. You yourself have great talent, and you have at home a father who is unequalled in learning and is a perfect exemplar of all honesty and integrity. It would be a great disgrace if you were to fall short of his standards, especially since he abundantly provides what could help to equip you with every kind of accomplishment. You cannot remain unnoticed: you have before you the splendid example of your father's reputation, which you should maintain with great glory – it would be a great shame to disappoint the hope that everyone has in you. Though if you did slacken your efforts, the competition from your sisters would provide an added sharp spur – one would swear, seeing their urbanity, their modesty, their innocence, their openness, and their mutual affection, that they were the three Graces. Their skilful handling of musical instruments of all kinds, the way they flit like little bees through all kinds of writers, both Greek and Latin, here noting something to imitate, and there plucking some fine saying for its moral application, and here learning some elegant little story to tell their friends – anyone who saw them would say that they were the Muses, playing their charming games in the beautiful meadows of Aonia,[11] gathering little flowers and marjoram to make garlands. Certainly their mental dowry is so great that their physical beauty, outstanding though it is, can add little to their merits. Your sisters are running as hard in the race for glory as if they were deliberately planning to leave their brother behind. You will have to study keenly and stretch your sinews all the more for the race if you are to overtake them – they are somewhat bigger than you, as nature brought them into the race earlier. Their rivalry will be with Cornelia, mother of the Gracchi,[12] who brought glory on her sex by both her chastity and her eloquence. Yours is with your father: it would be a fine enough honour to equal him, but he would like nothing more than that you should surpass him. But perhaps we will deal with this subject elsewhere, at a more appropriate time. Now let us turn to the *Nux*.

COMMENTARY ON OVID'S *NUT-TREE*

On the title

I have found prefixed to the poem the title 'An Elegy,' as it comprises a complaint about past injuries and an entreaty against injuries that still threaten it. Both of these elements pertain to the kind of theme (*causa*) known in Greek as δικανικὸν, in Latin judicial or forensic.[1] Consequently, a good part of the treatment of the subject rests in the emotions, especially pity. Pity is aroused partly by an accumulation (*exaggeratio*) of someone's misfortunes and partly by the circumstances of the participants, for pity is accentuated when someone quite undeserving (in fact, someone who has deserved well) suffers unjustly, or conversely when someone inflicts an injury without provocation or repays a good turn by a bad one. If you also want to know the basis (*status*) of the theme, it is certainly one of quality (*qualitas*) or judicial: there is no dispute about the facts; the question is one of right or wrong.[2] There might, however, be some doubt as to whether the nut-tree is the prosecutor or the defendant. On the one hand, it conducts its case as though it were a defendant before the people, but on the other hand it puts the people in the dock for their crimes – not to bring them to punishment but only to protect itself from injury. The sequence of the argument is constantly enlivened by witty allusions to human emotions, as in fables; the more terrible the emotions, the greater the humour when they are applied to a trivial and absurd topic, as in the *Battle of the Frogs and Mice* ascribed to Homer.[3]

The first couplet includes both proposition (*propositio*) and statement of facts (*narratio*):[4]

> *Nux ego iuncta viae, quum sim sine crimine vitae,*
> *A populo saxis praetereunte petor.* (1–2)

> A nut-tree standing by the road, not charged with any crime,
> Yet passers-by assail me with their stones.

According to writers on rhetoric, the proposition summarizes the theme in a few words; the statement expounds it more fully, adding emotional effects and sowing here and there what one might call the seeds of the arguments. The former [the emotional effects] are developed more fully in the peroration, the latter [the details] in the proof. It is a hallowed tradition for poets to begin their poem with a proposition, often combined with an invocation. This is how Homer begins the *Iliad*: 'Sing, goddess, the wrath of Achilles, son of Peleus,' and similarly he begins the *Odyssey*: 'Tell of the man, O Muse, full of guile he was.' The same practice was observed by Hesiod, though less felicitously: not only was he too long-winded where brevity is essential, but he was too obscure in the very passage whose sole purpose is to shed light on what is to follow. He begins one work: 'Muses, from the Pierian slopes ...'[5] and, equally unhappily, he begins the *Theogony*: 'With the Heliconian Muses let us begin our song.' In attempting to rival Hesiod, Virgil surpassed him, particularly in the *Georgics*, and he was at least Homer's equal at this point of the *Aeneid*, where he combined the arguments of both the *Iliad* and the *Odyssey*. Statius' proposition at the beginning of the *Achilleid* was more verbose: 'Great-hearted son of Aeacus, etc.' Lucan began his poem[6] even more pompously, unless he can be excused by the loftiness of his subject-matter – though on an equally lofty theme the cyclic poet offended Horace[7] by beginning his *Trojan War* with the line 'The fate of Priam I shall sing and eke the famous war.' Thus, poets generally invoke a deity out of modesty.

The proposition, however, serves to provide clarity, a particular virtue of expression – and not only at the beginning. There are three principal purposes of the proemium:[8] to win the listener's good will, his capacity for instruction, and his attention; he cannot feel good will or be attentive unless he is being instructed. Clarity of expression is most important for instruction, and must be observed particularly at the very beginning, so that the person who is about to begin can understand clearly what the whole case is about. Obscurity is less of a hindrance in the middle of a speech, since, when most of the parts of the case are understood, one can conjecture one thing from another. The same indulgence might be allowed in the proposition on the grounds that, according to some rhetoricians, the proposition is immediately attached to the statement of facts. Quintilian, however, will not allow any obscurity even in this case: 'Nothing, he says, is worse than to be obscure at that very point whose sole purpose is to avoid obscurity in what follows.'[9] Obscurity, then, is even less permissible at the very beginning of the work. Clarity is especially required in the proposition, the statement of facts, and the proof, as the proper function of these sections is instruction: failure to instruct leads to failure in the rest of the speech.

The proposition summarizes the case, the statement lays out the facts, the proof authenticates the facts by arguments. Just as the first proposition summarizes the whole case, so each individual section (even each argument) is prefaced by its own proposition, to show what has to be proved. Similarly, division (which immediately precedes the argument) consists of as many propositions as the case has sections; if the case consists of one point, only one proposition is set forth. Transitions, which also serve primarily to instruct, consist of a kind of double proposition, briefly recapitulating what has been proved and indicating what remains to be proved. Even in the statement of facts, however, there is a place for transitions; this applies to orators rather than to poets, but it is not uncommon even among poets, particularly when they are instructing the reader. Ovid provides an example of this:

> Their lazy nature gave these tricks to girls, but men derive
>   Their sportive methods from a richer store.[10]

Similarly, Virgil:

> Thus far the tilling of the fields and heaven's starry dome:
>   And now to you, O Bacchus, will I turn my song.[11]

But to return to the specifically poetic proposition, which stands grandly at the head of the work: some authors prefix a title to their work, in order to advise the reader what to expect; similarly the Hebrew prophets generally designed the title as part of their work. In a kind of imitation of this practice, poets begin with a proposition instead of a title. Otherwise, a title that is separate from the work is sometimes omitted by scribes or even altered by over-clever meddlers. This happened to St Jerome, whose work on famous authors had its title altered to *Epitaphia*.[12] Ovid deals with this more successfully than anyone: even his elegies and letters generally have their own title. For the work whose title would have been 'The Book on the Art of Love' Ovid provides this proposition:

> If any man amongst this folk knows not the art of love,
>   Read me – instructed by my songs, love on.[13]

Could any title have covered the content of the succeeding work more clearly? Now take a letter; if a title had to be prefixed, it would be something like 'Paris to Helen, greetings.' How much more effective is Ovid's short proposition:

> To Leda's kin I, Priam's son, submit this toast of health –
>   My health, in turn, depends on you alone.[14]

One of his elegies would be entitled something like 'The Parrot's Epitaph'; this is Ovid's proposition to it:

From shores of eastern Ind to me a parrot came – and died.
   Ye birds, flock round, perform the rites of death![15]

Another of his poems would have required the title 'To His Mistress, Who
Had Destroyed Her Hair through Treatments'; Ovid, playing a part in the
action, writes:

I used to say, 'Don't treat your hair with artificial dyes,'
   And now you have no hair to treat at all![16]

Another would have been called 'Comparison between Love and Military
Service'; this is Ovid's proposition:

All lovers serve; desire commands the battle-camps of love.
   Believe me, friend, that every lover serves.[17]

In some of his letters and elegies the proposition is less explicit, but it is
present in all of them. It is not just in the opening that Ovid strives for clarity;
this most fortunate facility, universally admired in Cicero (and hardly
rivalled successfully by anyone in prose), is exhibited everywhere by Ovid
in poetry. Do not, however, expect to find a proposition in every poem; the
dramatic genre, for example, in which only the actors speak, does not admit
of a proposition. It is appropriate to the exegetical or 'mixed' genre, but is
rare in satire, as satire was the direct successor to Old Comedy. Examples are
not easily found in bucolics, but Virgil has one:

The Muse of Damon and Alphesibaeus, shepherds both,[18]

and similarly Theocritus:

Adonis' death I mourn: the powers of love join in the dirge.[19]

This is because bucolics belong to the 'mixed' genre of poem: Virgil would
not have been able to do this in his 'Tityrus'[20] or Theocritus in his 'Thyrsis.'[21]
Similarly, Horace writes in his *Satires*:

Teiresias, reply to me, who seek one answer more.[22]

Bucolics, like comedies, go under the name of a person instead of a title.
Plato and Lucian[23] (in imitation of Plato) use a double heading for their
dialogues, taking it partly from the person, partly from the content: *Gorgias,
or On Rhetoric, Toxaris, or On Friendship*, for example.

Now, however, I have made my point – that artistic skill consists in summarizing the plot by a proposition that links with what follows and that appears to be part of the argument – and I think it is time to listen to the walnut presenting its case.

> Nux ego iuncta viae, quum sim sine crimine vitae,
>   A populo saxis praetereunte petor.   (1–2)

> A nut-tree standing by the road, not charged with any crime,
>   Yet passers-by assail me with their stones.

No title, even in prose, could have summarized the argument more clearly. Moreover, this proposition, despite its brevity, incorporates many circumstances, which serve both to provide proof and to arouse emotions. '**Nut-tree**': This designates the speaker; there are many kinds of nut, but what follows shows that the speaker is a walnut. '**Standing by the road**': A circumstantial detail, which provided people with the justification for their actions. '**Not charged with any crime**': The second circumstance, magnifying the cruelty of the injury, since even the person responsible for provocation by injury has the right to sue for injury – for example, if someone is provoked by abuse, and then violates the wife of the person by whom he was provoked.[24] '**Assail ... with stones**': Third circumstance: this is the most cruel punishment. *Populo* '**passers-by**': Fourth circumstance: a crime must indeed be terrible that is avenged, not by the due sentence of judges or the official act of the executioner, but by the hands of the people. I do not think that the pun on *viae* and *vitae* was deliberately planned by the author; as often, it just happened.

   Sine crimine '**not charged with any crime**': This phrase is more appropriate than if he had said 'although I am of blameless life.' Since *crimen* 'crime,' 'charge' is more serious than *culpa* 'blame,' the person who has done nothing for which he could be summoned is said to be ἀνέγκλητος 'un-charged' (the word comes from ἐγκαλεῖν 'summon,' whence the noun ἔγκλημα 'summons'). The Latin word *error* 'slip' is in Greek ἁμάρτημα, 'something committed almost by accident.' Latin *error* and Greek ἁμάρτημα do not always imply blame. (Very close to this is Greek σφάλμα, Latin *lapsus* 'slip'). A πλημμέλεια 'false note' [and so 'error'] is made through carelessness and inattention; it comes from πάλιν μέλειν 'sing a second time,' because the error is to be retrieved by care on a later occasion (as the proverb says, second thoughts are best[25]), like μετάνοια 'afterthought' from μετανοεῖν 'think again.' The word *delictum* 'fault' seems to refer to a neglected duty; the Greek ἀμπλάκημα 'fault' is also less serious, so-called because it 'envelops a man' (ἐμπλέκειν). 'Αδίκημα 'wrong' is the generic term, similar to ἀνομία 'illegality,' except that he is said to ἀδικεῖν 'wrong' who injures someone. The Greek αἰτία corresponds most closely to Latin *culpa* 'blame,' which can be applied equally either to a *crimen* (for which one can be summoned at law) or to a less serious wrong (adequately dealt with by a complaint). Thus αἴτιος means 'someone who is blameworthy,' ἀναίτιος means 'someone who is blameless,' and αἰτιοῦν means 'to make a private accusation against.' The word *crimen*, however, seems to come from Greek κρίνω (Latin *cerno*, from which is also derived *dis-crimen*). I need not repeat here Lorenzo Valla's dictum,[26] that he who is charged (*in crimine*) is not necessarily guilty (*in scelere*), just as one must say that someone 'in the dock' is not *ipso facto* guilty. In Latin one can say of charges (what one cannot say of offences) that they may be laid but not committed.[27]

This, then, is the walnut's argument: 'If I had committed a crime worthy of punishment, I should have been summoned at law, and, if convicted, should have been punished according to the laws. Now, although I am innocent, the most cruel punishment is meted out to me – unconvicted and uncondemned! And this is done by passers-by, whose right of way I am not obstructing, as I am only "standing by" the road.' **'Standing by':** That is, adjacent to.

> *Obruere ista solet manifestos poena nocentes,*
> *Publica quum lentam non capit ira moram.*   (3–4)

That overwhelming penalty is right for certain guilt,
For public wrath does not admit delay.

Among the Hebrews stoning was the penalty for blasphemy against God.[28] Roman law did not give the public the right to stone anyone, but, in the case of certain and atrocious crimes, turned a blind eye to the just wrath of the people. Virgil is writing about riot, not legal judgment, when he says, 'And now fly brands and rocks, for rage supplies the arms.'[29] Thus, the people are at fault in two ways: by inflicting a cruel punishment without legal authority, and by doing so against someone innocent. The word 'stoned' (*lapidari*) (like 'hissed off' or 'jeered off') is applied to a book or proposal that is attacked by public abuse. **Nocentes 'harming,'** usually an adjective, means the same as *noxius* 'harmful,' but is here used substantivally with the supporting adjective **manifestos 'clear'**; compare Ovid's '... harming steel and gold more harming yet.'[30] **'Overwhelmed' (obruitur):** Appropriately used of one who is oppressed by force, suddenly, and by a large crowd. **Lentam:** This [adjective, modifying *moram* 'delay,'] implies both flexibility and also slowness and tardiness. *Capit* '**admits**': An elegant substitute for *fert* 'bears.'

Just as this couplet (3–4) is an exaggeration of the proposition (1–2), so the following couplet (5–6) is an exaggeration of this one.

> *Nil ego peccavi, nisi si peccare fatemur*
> *Annua cultori poma referre suo.* (5–6)

> I've done no wrong – unless we grant that wrong consists in this,
> To render to our farmer each year's growth.

Cruelty against the innocent is barbarous; even more barbarous, then, is cruelty against someone who deserves well. The argument is based on definition[31] (Greek ὅρος) and is developed by paradox (Greek ἄτοπον, closely related to ἀδύνατον 'the impossible'). It hypothesizes what is manifestly and self-evidently absurd, so that when this has been rejected the proposition is sure to be proved. In the definition the equivalent term is altered.[32] Sometimes both definitions are set out, for example if one betrays a leader who is urging one to do something contrary to one's own honour and dangerous to the state, and, conversely, if one is loyal to a leader who urges actions that maintain the honour and reputation of a good leader in the eyes of all good men and that benefit the safety of the state – then, I cannot be named 'traitor,' unless it is treachery to benefit both leader and state by loyal advice. If the faithful annual provision of crops to the farmer is a sign of loyalty and good will, then I have done no wrong – unless assistance is a wrong. If this is ridiculous, then I am suffering a conspicuous injustice, in being stoned in return for my good deeds. If I am cultivated in the expectation of my fruit, then why am I being stoned for the same reason? The argument is based on contradictions.

The poet, however, is not serious: his argument is both contrived and ridiculous, for what the walnut calls 'injury' is in fact beneficial to growth. Indeed, if the nuts are knocked off with poles, they grow more abundantly in the following year than if they are plucked, just as (according to Pliny) saffron, flax, fenugreek, and some other plants give more abundant growth because of the 'inflicted injury.'[33] In fact, nowadays some countrymen bind the tree with husks and pound it with sticks in the belief that this makes it more fertile. A different law was once passed about the olive-tree: 'Neither bind nor pound the olive,'[34] since even if the olives are knocked down lightly with a stick, the tree produces fruit only in alternate years because of this injury. Moreover, Pliny (book 16, chapter 28) counts the walnut (like the arbutus and the marisca fig) among trees which are more productive lower down and thus more liable to injuries.[35] In this passage the poet is cleverly alluding incidentally to a moral topic: it is not surprising, he shows, that trees should suffer for their own fertility, since the same thing happens to women.

> At prius arboribus, tunc quum meliora fuerunt
>   Tempora, certamen fertilitatis erat. (7–8)

> But once, in olden days, when better times prevailed, the trees
>   Competed for the crown of bearing fruit.

Trees are here humorously credited with human emotions; the lines are also relevant to human behaviour, for those who attack public morals moan about their own generation and look to the past for examples of good behaviour. Those who compete, the argument runs, are competing for glory. (No one competes except for a prize, and the prize for competitors is particularly glory.) If there is no glory, the competition loses its vitality – and even more so if glory and profit are replaced by shame and loss! He blames the barrenness of wives on their husbands, who value beauty more than fecundity, and similarly blames farmers for the sterility of the trees, since they are cultivated for empty pleasure rather than for utility.

> Tunc domini memores sertis ornare solebant
>   Agricolae fructu praeveniente deos. (9–10)

> Then, mindful of their lord, the farmers used to crown the gods
>   (or, mindful were those lords ...)
>   With wreaths and garlands, as the fruit came forth.

Once every tree was sacred to its god and was believed to be under his protection: the vine belonged to Bacchus, the olive to Minerva, the pine to Cybele, the oak to Jupiter, the poplar to Hercules, the laurel to Apollo, the myrtle to Venus, and other trees in the same way. There is no time here to explain why antiquity dedicated trees, some to one god, some to another, though I am sure that it was for some natural reason. 'Mindful': Used absolutely for 'grateful,' but we are also said to be 'mindful of injury.' *Fructu praeveniente* **'fruit coming in advance':** That is, premature, coming forth before its proper time (unless we should read *proveniente*).[36] The first fruits (Latin *primitiae*, Greek ἀπαρχαί) were consecrated to the gods, to ensure the tree's increased fertility in the following year. The Hebrews used to do the same with their first-born male child,[37] hoping to be rewarded for their piety with abundant progeny in future.

This couplet, however, contains a difficult ambiguity, as it can be interpreted variously: 1/ **the farmers** (that is, the tillers of the land), **mindful of the lord** from whom they rent the land, offer the first fruits of their crops to the gods, as though the workers' piety also benefited the landlord; 2/ taking *domini* and *agricolae* in apposition, we can interpret it as meaning that farmers and lords were once identical, when nobles regarded agriculture as a pursuit suited to their dignity; 3/ taking *agricolae* as genitive, we can interpret it thus: the lords of the land used to honour the gods with the first fruits that had been produced by the farmer's efforts. The lines also serve to magnify the injury done by the stone-throwers, since if fertility is a gift of the gods, injury involves impiety.

> *Saepe tuas igitur Liber miratus es uvas,*
> *Mirata est oleas saepe Minerva suas.*   (11–12)

> Thus often then, O Bacchus, did you marvel at your grapes;
> Her olives often earned Minerva's gasp.

These verses can be interpreted in two ways: 1/ the gods admired premature fruit; 2/ they admired abundant produce. The sense is smoother if we take Bacchus as meaning 'wine' by synecdoche, and Minerva as olive; the transferred usage[38] is, in fact, quite pleasing for its pathos. Virgil writes similarly about a tree that bears grafted branches: 'She marvels at new leaves and fruits that aren't her own.'[39] The sudden change from second to third person is required by the metre, as *es* is short, but the second person apostrophe is in any case quite pleasing.

> *Pomaque laesissent matrem, nisi subdita ramo*
> *Longa laboranti furca tulisset opem.*   (13–14)

> The mother would have suffered from the fruits, had not a fork
> Been placed beneath to aid the branch in toil.

The reason for binding the vine is its weak trunk and its supple branches; the same may also happen to olives. I have often seen apples and pears so laden with the weight of their produce that the whole tree seems to be in labour, and often the branches split. Ovid writes:

> Behold the branches curved beneath the fruit – the tree can scarce
> Support the weight to which she's given birth.[40]

Branches unequal to the weight of their fruit are supported by placing forks beneath them; in fact sometimes trunks and branches growing in the wrong direction are straightened by the application of forks. Horace mentions this: 'Attempt to drive out Nature with a fork, but back she'll come!'[41] **Laboranti 'in toil'**: An apt phrase; to labour means to work; labour involves caring; the sick labour; one labours at a dangerous and difficult task. Truth often labours, but is never overcome. Juvenal writes: 'She alone can aid the moon in labour.'[42] **'The mother would have suffered from the fruits'**: This phrase also serves to increase the pathos. The risk suffered by a pregnant woman in giving birth is to be pitied; since, according to common understanding, particular favour is shown to the fecundity of women who produce many offspring at once, even more pity is felt for women who die from a multiple birth. (For a woman, the birth of quintuplets is a very high number. Dutch chroniclers[43] and even monuments, however, record that one woman, in a single birth, produced 365 live babies, all of which were baptized. There are chronicles to witness it; there is a monument, inscribed with the name; there is even a picture. It was a count of Holland that did it – seigneurs of those days were satisfied with such slight authority! You can see the hill on which he used to have his castle, near to the monastery where the woman is buried. Do we wonder, then, that clever men have been able to persuade an uneducated world to believe in various absurdities, when such stories were credited by simple people in uneducated times? But there is little harm in such matters – similar techniques, however, have spread other beliefs, which have almost extinguished Christianity here.)

> *Quinetiam exemplo pariebat foemina nostro,*
> *Nullaque non illo tempore mater erat.*   (15–16)

> It was, in fact, inspired by me that women bore their young;
> No woman then a mother failed to be.

Examples drawn from dumb animals and inanimate objects carry weight. The she-ass will run through fire to her foal;[44] therefore it is shameful for a mother to neglect her children. Or, heavenly bodies observe the course ordained for them by God; therefore it is shameful for men to disobey divine commands. All trees instinctively perpetuate their species; therefore contrived and voluntary sterility is to be condemned. Contrasting examples are always more effective, such as one taken from a woman and applied to a man, or from a boy to an old man, and vice versa, for the contrast consists not so much in the person as in the thing which is compared to the person. For example, if indulgence in prostitutes is shameful for a young man, it is even more so for an old man. Conversely, if there is no disgrace in an old man's learning what he does not know, there is even less for a boy.

To return to the subject: writers have noticed gender, marriage, and copulation in some trees, to the extent that the female trees remain sterile unless there is a male tree close by; in fact closer observers of natural history assert that the earth produces nothing that lacks sex (see more fully Pliny, book 13, chapter 4).[45] Just as women are rendered infertile sometimes through physical defect and invariably by old age, so are fruit-bearing trees. Almost every defect of the human body is also found in trees; the terminology for the diseases of trees is taken from human pathology – for example hunger, thirst, old age, worms, blight, sickness of the limbs, surfeit, obesity, burning of the eyes [that is, buds], abortion. For the various remedies for these diseases, see Pliny, book 17, chapters 24 and 26.[46] Fruit-bearing trees, however, just like women, do not continually produce every year, even if fertile. **'Woman'**: For 'women,' a pleasing alteration of number.[47]

Among the Hebrews sterility was considered very shameful.[48] In antiquity the production of many offspring was regarded as a fine thing: it was a sign of good fortune to earn the epithet 'well-childed,' and conversely to be called 'childless' was shameful. This is why the poets write about the daughters of Danaus and Belus, and about Priam and Hecuba, and Niobe, and so on; historians commemorate those blessed with copious progeny. In those days the object of matrimony was offspring, but nowadays most people take a wife for pleasure, and a woman who produces many children is called a sow. The ancients used to use drugs to induce fertility, but now, alas, drugs to induce abortions are more well known.

> *At postquam platanis sterilem praebentibus umbram*
>   *Uberior quavis arbore venit honor,*
> *Nos quoque fructiferae (si nux modo ponor in illis)*
>   *Coepimus in patulas luxuriare comas.*   (17–20)

But since the plane-trees, giving sterile shade, were honoured more
  Abundantly than any other tree,
Then we, the fertile trees – if nuts are put among that class –
  Began to spread our branches far and wide.

'Plane-trees': The word *platanus* 'plane-tree' is derived from its breadth, since its branches are spread broad and thick [that is, *praebere* plus *late*], as if to provide shade; some are artificially manipulated and their branches forced apart to produce pleasant shade and to form a kind of hall within the trees themselves in which you could hold a banquet. An oak of this kind can be seen at Basel, under which the emperor Maximilian is said once to have had dinner;[49] a spring has been put there to feed the roots with continual watering. Now, however, they say that it is contracting day by day, as often happens with planes, limes, and turpentine-trees. In antiquity, however, the plane-tree, despite its infertility, was held in such reverence that it was first brought across the Ionian Sea to the island of Diomedes to grace his tomb; from there it passed on to Sicily and was one of the first trees bestowed on Italy, and from there it spread as far as Belgium. People even went so far as to moisten the roots of this tree by pouring in wine, despite the fact that its only use is to provide shade from the sun by the thickness of its foliage in summer, and in winter, by losing its leaves, to admit the sun. Further information on the respect paid to the plane-tree can be found in Pliny, book 12, chapter 1.[50]

Thus, the walnut complains that men, corrupted by luxury, place more value on the infertile plane-tree than on fruit-bearing trees. Offended, as it were, by this insult, fruit-bearing trees began to be less fertile; in order to give greater pleasure they began to squander their sap on the vain display of their leaves rather than, as formerly, on the nourishing of fruit. For some fruit-trees, including the walnut, have wide-spreading branches; the walnut does not, however, mention the fact that its shade is harmful to everything underneath, including its own offspring, as Pliny and Columella relate.[51] Not all fruit-bearing trees produce fruit every year, and even if they do, the harvest varies. Some (including the olive and most acorn-bearing trees) are generally biennial; this sometimes happens with apples and pears. The walnut neatly blames this phenomenon on the attention given to producing leaves, as though the fruit crop suffers if the sap is used up on the leaves. **'Put'** (*ponor*): An elegant variation for 'numbered'; compare Terence, *Phormio*: 'To these, put ten mnas beside.'[52] The use of the word is derived from counting by 'putting' and taking away pebbles, though Donatus thinks that 'drawing up accounts' is named from 'drawing away' the fingers.[53] *Si modo* **'if only,' 'just,' 'now'** may also mean 'if,' 'however.' The word *modo* sometimes means 'a little before,' for example, 'He was just here,' and sometimes, though less frequently, means 'now.' Sometimes it means 'provided that' or 'only,' for example, *velis modo* 'as long as you agree'; thus Terence in the *Phormio* uses *modo non* for 'only not,'[54] like the Greek μονονουχὶ, which could be translated 'all but,' 'almost.' Horace uses *post modo* 'after this.'[55] Further, 'if only [or 'just' or 'now'] I am put among them' avoids envy by its modesty, since in fact, the walnut is pre-eminent among nuts. Indeed, it is thought that the word *iuglans* 'walnut' was originally *diu-glans* because of its excellence: the equivalent of Greek Διὸς βάλανον, Latin *Jovis glandem* 'God's acorn,' and thus, by the loss of the initial letter, *iu-glans*. (Others, however, have preferred to derive it from *iu-vare* 'assist.' For the same reason, they argue, it is called 'basilic,' that is, regal: compare

Macrobius *Saturnalia*, book 3.[56] Pliny does not dissent from this view, but, in order to give the grammarians something to do, I might observe in passing that etymology does not entirely favour this derivation: first, how can a nut properly be called an 'acorn,' particularly a 'Persian acorn'?[57] Second, surely a tree is called 'acorn-bearing' rather than 'acorn'?[58] Third, it is hard to justify derivation from both Greek and Latin roots [that is, Διὸς, *glans*]. Consequently it seems more probable to me that *iu-glans* is derived from *iugulare* 'strangle' and *glans*, that is, 'acorn-throttler,' since there is a natural antipathy between the walnut and the oak: an oak-tree dies if it is next to a walnut (Pliny, book 24, chapter 1).[59]

According to Pliny walnuts were first introduced by kings: thus their chief species is called 'Persian' and 'Basilic.'[60] Macrobius cites the *Moretum* by a certain poet Suevius for the opinion that the walnut, which was first named 'Persian,' is also called a 'mollusc.' The text of the poem reads thus:

> And now the *Persica*, whose name is thus derived:
> The men who once with mighty king to Persia went –
> Great Alexander was his name – with bloody war
> Against the foe they fought. On their return, this tree
> They spread throughout the swollen boundaries of Greece
> And brought a novel kind of fruit to mortal men.
> It's called the 'mollusc nut,' if anyone's in doubt.[61]

On this point Perotti[62] (or whoever compiled his volume), a man of some learning, sharply and disdainfully criticizes Macrobius for not understanding Suevius' poem properly and for thinking that the peach was called a mollusc. The poem [that is, the *Moretum*], of course, is not referring to the peach [*persicus pomus* 'Persian apple'] but to a kind of walnut known as 'Persian'; this nut, the *Moretum* says, is called a 'mollusc' because of the softness (*mollitudinem*) of its shell, which splits open of its own accord – and this is Macrobius' interpretation. Macrobius seems to identify it with the 'Tarentine,' since in the Sabine language *tarentum* means 'soft,' on which Horace puns in the phrase 'and the soft-living Tarentum.'[63]

In size the walnut certainly surpasses every other kind of nut except the pine-cone – and it is far superior to this in its kernel. The walnut, then, seems once to have been especially valued, either because it was imported by kings from distant lands, or because of its religious significance in marriage ceremonies,[64] or because Nature herself seems to have conferred a special distinction on the nut, in that it is protected by a double covering, first of a rounded calyx and then by a woody exterior shell; in addition, the kernel is separated into four compartments by the interposition of a membrane. Finally, the epithet 'basilic' that is applied to the walnut indicates the high status of the tree. Thus, the phrase 'if I am put among them' (*si nux modo ponor in illis*) is *litotes*, verbally making light of something important for the sake of modesty, as it is speaking about itself.

> *Nunc neque continuos nascuntur poma per annos,*
>   *Unaque luesa domum laesaque bacca venit.* (21–2)

But now no longer does our fruit come forth from year to year:
  One nut arrives, and bruised, alas, how bruised!

Here the walnut mentions a double grievance. First, that the trees are productive intermittently and less frequently, as though on the brink of sterility; second, that even that which *is* produced is damaged, as though by divine wrath, by hail, frost, cloud, rain, and heat. Also, in addition to these afflictions, apparently sent from heaven, each tree (like man) has its own peculiar faults and diseases. Remedies have been devised for these also. Pliny lists some trees that bear fruit two and three times a year, but in book 15, chapter 22, under the heading 'extraordinary phenomena,' he says that a man of consular rank told him that he also owned walnuts that produced twice a year.[65] He also lists the trees that produce every other year, including (as we have said) the olive. The walnut, therefore, believes that because of human moral corruption trees, just as women, are not only giving birth more infrequently and stingily but are also producing inferior offspring. As the satirist says: 'And thus the earth brings forth men virtue-less and small.'[66] And how often nowadays do we see births that are either prone to disease or deformed!

> *Nunc uterus vitio est,[67] quae vult formosa videri,*
>   *Raraque in hoc aevo est quae velit esse parens.* (23–4)

The girl who wants to be admired now deprecates her womb;
  She's rare today who wants to bear a child.

Sterility, which sometimes occurs even in fruit-bearing trees, from rot or some other disease, was once regarded as the most serious fault; the poet applies this to women. Nowadays, he says, a woman who wants to please her husband (if there are any) regards her fecundity as a fault and realizes that her appeal for her husband consists more in her beauty than in her fertility, which once upon a time was the principal recommendation in a potential bride. Consequently, wives no longer try to enrich their husbands with numerous offspring but, seeing that physical charm diminishes through frequent parturition, actually induce sterility by drugs. What is worse, they induce abortions in order to avoid ageing through the labour of gestation and the strenuous effort of parturition and, to use the words of Aulus Gellius, to avoid 'the wrinkling of the smoothness of the belly'[68] and the stretching caused by the weight of the pregnancy and the effort of the birth. As with women, so with trees: fecundity hastens the onset of age and sometimes, if it is frequent, even death. As Pliny says, in book 16, chapter 28, 'everything over-fertile grows older quicker';[69] in fact, sometimes they die on the spot, 'when the weather has enticed forth all their fertility,'[70] as happens especially to vines.

Uterus 'womb': Note the careful choice of word; it does not mean simply 'stomach' (the receptacle for food) but refers to a woman's pregnant body. Thus, pregnant women are said to 'carry the womb'; they could not properly be said to 'carry the stomach,' even though *uterus* is sometimes used for *venter*.

> *Certe ego si nunquam peperissem, tutior essem;*
>   *Ista Clytemnestra digna querela fuit.*   (25–6)

> 'Assuredly I'd safer be, if child I'd never born':
>   Thus justly Clytemnestra could complain.

If my argument, the walnut says, is not self-evident in other cases, it is undeniably clear in my own case: I am stoned for no other reason than that I am fertile; therefore, I would be safe if I were sterile. Clytemnestra and I have this complaint, at least, in common, as she was harmed by giving birth in that she was killed by her own son Orestes. The complaint was less justified in her case, however, as she herself had first killed her husband and thus provoked one crime by another; I, on the other hand, have done nothing except give birth. Yet Clytemnestra is thought worthy of pity for having given birth – how much more pitiable, then, am I!

> *Si sciat hoc vitis, nascentes supprimet uvas,*
>   *Orbaque, si sciat hoc, Palladis arbor erit.*   (27–8)

> Once this is known, the vine will cause her nascent grapes to fail;
>   This known, Athene's tree will childless be.

This belongs to the art of practical persuasion, a frequent device in forensic oratory. One might, for example, argue that Catiline should be pardoned on the grounds that even if he deserves punishment, it is not fitting for the glory of Rome's reputation or in the interests of the state. If you are not moved by the injustice of my treatment, the walnut says, at least refrain from harming me out of concern for your own disadvantage. For if the other trees, whose fruit is especially pleasing to you, learned that fertility renders one liable to injury, then they would elect to be sterile. This is a charming poetic fantasy, that news is spread by rumour even among trees. **'Will cause her nascent grapes to fail'**: It is a peculiarity of the vine that when blighted by bad weather (and sometimes by unknown causes) it suppresses its burgeoning grapes; very frequently it grows sterile when it produces its best blossom. **'Athene's tree'**: This tree [that is, the olive] often produces nothing at all, as though on the verge of sterility. The vine **'suppresses'** (*supprimet*) as it always buds and generally blossoms; the olive, however, is **'childless,'** since every other year it usually produces nothing at all, not even budding. A female property is elegantly applied to a tree: 'childless' refers to a woman without children; 'Athene's tree' is planning to be what the goddess herself is, that is, sterile and virgin. Thus the periphrasis [Athene's tree for olive] is not redundant.

> *Hoc in noticiam veniat maloque pyroque:*
> *Destituent sylvas utraque poma suas.* (29–30)

> Let but this truth be recognized by apple and by pear,
> Then both will soon deprive their woods of fruit.

Of all fruits, apples and pears are particularly tasty. **'Woods'**: If the apple and pear become sterile they will be no more than wood. These trees were well-chosen examples since, although most people perhaps could easily go without walnuts, apples and pears are especially pleasing and necessary to mortals. By the word 'woods' people also mean 'timber,' including apple and pear wood, whereas the vine and some other trees are useless for building.

> *Quaeque sibi vario distinguit poma colore,*
> *Audiat haec cerasus: stipes inanis erit.* (31–2)

> The cherry too, whose fruits are all distinct with varied hue,
> If she learns this, her stock will empty be.

The fruit of the cherry is first green, then white, and when ripe it is a glowing red; some are red on one side, white on the other; some are marked by

ON OVID'S *NUT-TREE* LB I 1199B / ASD I-1 159

scattered splotches here and there; some are black. Pliny, book 15, chapter 25 says that Apronian cherries are the reddest, Actian the blackest, and Lusitanians a mixture of reddish black and green.[71] These varieties of cherry are still seen today, but with different names. **'With varied hue'**: This, I think, refers to the grafting of cherry on laurel, which causes the change of flavour and colour. In other fruits also the colour is artificially altered, but in the case of the cherry it is the tree itself that colours the fruit, as though toying with novelty. Also, the cherry's particular charm rests in its colour, which is virginal – for it soon withers!

> *Non equidem invideo; numquid tamen illa feritur*
> *Quae sterilis sola est conspicienda coma?*   (33–4)

> I'm quite devoid of jealousy – but she escapes the stick
> Who, childless, is admired for just her hair.

The walnut modifies its statement, but in such a way as to draw attention to the argument that it is developing. I am not saying all this, the walnut argues, because I am jealous of the fertility of these trees, or the immunity of those, but nevertheless my contention that my fertility is to my disadvantage is supported by the fact that barren trees are not harmed. Since jealousy is a characteristically female vice, the walnut, speaking in the persona of a woman, takes care to deflect any suspicion of this. **'For just her hair'**: A woman's special glory. A tree's foliage is also known as its 'hair' (*coma*).

> *Cernite synceros omnes ex ordine truncos,*
> *Qui modo nil quare percutiantur habent.*   (35–6)

> Behold the trunks that stand in line: not one of them is harmed
> That has no reason why it should be hit.

It bases its argument on neighbouring trees, which were safe from harm because they were barren. **'In line'**: Since trees are laid out beside the road in line at fixed spaces. *Qui modo* **'that'** is the equivalent of *quicunque*, just as *si modo* is the equivalent of *dummodo*.

> *At mihi saeva nocent mutilatis vulnera ramis,*
> *Nudaque decerpto cortice ligna patent.*   (37–8)

> But I, alas, bear cruel wounds, and ravaged are my boughs:
> The bark stripped off, the wood lies bare to see.

Words appropriate to a living body ('**wounds,**' '**ravage**') are cleverly applied to trees; similarly we speak of a tree's 'scars.' A wound that lays bare the bones is deadly. A tree's 'skin' is its bark, under which is its 'flesh'; thus '**wood**' stands for the tree's 'bones.'

> *Non odium facit hoc, sed spes inducta rapinae;*
>   *Sustineant aliae poma, querentur idem.*   (39–40)

> It was not done from hatred but from hope of spoil – the same
>   Complaint will others make, if fruit they bear.

I have not deserved that my assailants should be thought to have acted out of just hatred for me: the sole reason for my suffering is the good that I do. The argument is based on hypothetical events: if others suffer the same as I, then this will prove that I am suffering not for any fault of my own but because of 'hope of spoil.'

> *Sic reus ille fere est, de quo victoria lucro*
>   *Esse potest; inopis vindice facta carent.*
> *Sic timet insidias, qui se scit ferre viator*
>   *Quod timeat; tutum carpit inanis iter.*   (41–4)

> You're almost always guilty if your critic stands to gain;
>   The poor man need not fear a claimant's charge.
> You walk in fear of ambush if your bags are of the kind
>   You fear to lose; the poor man's trip is safe.

The argument is bolstered by two examples. A very loathsome kind of business was once conducted by informers, accusers, and muckrakers, who used to bring accusations against the rich in order to skim off some of the profit from the suit. Those who owned nothing were not liable to this misfortune, as Terence's character Phormio says.[72] The prospect of plunder causes the innocent rich man to be attacked by informers, whereas the humble wayfarer on foot is safe from robbery. Juvenal's line is well known: 'If small the pack you bear …'[73] **Quod timeat 'you fear to lose'** [literally '**which you should fear for**']: Either read *cui* 'for which' instead of *quod*, or take *quod* as 'wherefore,'[74] thus: 'there is no reason why you should fear.'

> *Sic ego sola petor, soli quia causa petendi est;*
>   *Frondibus intactis caetera turba viret.*   (45–6)

Thus I alone am sought, for only I have loot enough;
   The others thrive and grow, their leaves untouched.

Causa petendi 'for I alone have a cause of seeking': The gerund used passively means 'the cause for which I am sought.' In conjecture it is most important to consider 'to whose advantage was it?'[75] **Caetera turba 'the others' [literally 'the other crowd']:** A contemptuous reference to the 'crowd' of non-fruit-bearing trees. For the use of *turba* 'crowd' compare Horace 'we are the multitude.'[76]

> *Nam quod habent frutices aliquando proxima nobis*
>   *Fragmina, quod laeso vimine multa iacent,*
> *Non istis sua facta nocent. Vicinia damno est;*
>   *Excipiunt ictu saxa repulsa meo.*   (47–50)

That other shrubs sometimes have broken branches next to mine
   And many lie collapsed, with broken stays,
Is not their fault; they suffer for their neighbourhood to me
   And catch the stones deflected from my blows.

This removes a possible objection, that fruit trees which border a field are supported by broken branches from barren trees: 'But only,' the walnut argues, 'from trees that stand close to me. They do not suffer this fate because of some crime: they suffer from their proximity to me.' The first couplet does not complete the sentence, a usage occasionally found in Ovid, but it contains a complete grammatical clause (as above in the couplet beginning 'But since the plane-trees ...'[77]); if it did not, this would be a fault in elegiac verse. **Meo ictu 'my blows':** This shows that Lorenzo Valla's rule about the usage of primary and possessive pronouns is not invariable.[78] Otherwise it would have had to read *ictu mei* 'the blow of me,' unless we are to imagine that the stone deflected from the walnut's branch is actually being thrown by it. Compare the phrase *cultori meo* 'my cultivator' above:[79] the walnut is itself being cultivated, it is not doing the cultivating.

> *Idque fide careat, si non quae longius absunt*
>   *Nativum retinent inviolata decus.*   51–2)

This fact would not be credited, if trees that stand afar
   Did not retain their native grace unharmed.

A man is **'not credited'** if he is not trusted; a thing is **'not credited'** if it is not believed. This is a neat introduction to an irrefutable argument: 'Call me a liar, if the facts don't speak for themselves.' 'May I be thought a rogue, you can say I lie in my teeth, if it isn't, etc.' For such phrases provide emphasis, which is often as weighty as a formal proof.

> *Ergo, si sapiant et mentem verba sequantur,*
> *Devoveant umbras proxima quaeque meas.*   (53–4)

> So if they had the wit and words to mirror their intent,
> My neighbours all would curse the shade I cast.

A pleasing pathos is achieved by piling on the misfortune: it was cruel enough to suffer for its fertility – how much more unbearable to incur hatred as well, especially from one's neighbours, by whom one ought to be loved, since propinquity is close to friendship! **Devovere 'curse'**: To curse and invoke the Furies and destruction. This kind of witchcraft holds sway among peasants – hence the laws against tree- and crop-charms.[80] In fact they used to compose spells to curse armies and cities; see Macrobius *Saturnalia*, book 3.[81] **'If they had the wit'**: As though wild trees had less intelligence. If they realized that I was the cause of this misfortune of theirs, they would hate me bitterly; if they could speak, then each of them, the closer they were to me, would powerfully 'curse the shade I cast.' **Devoveant 'would curse'**: Potential subjunctive. The use of the [plural] verb and the [singular] adjective *quaeque* is poetic licence. **'The shade'**: Another allusion to the generally harmful shade of the walnut-tree.

> *Quam miserum est, odium damnis accedere nostris*
> *Meque ream nimiae proximitatis agi!*   (55–6)

> Alas, that I, with all my woes, should suffer hate as well
> And bear the guilt of mere propinquity!

This sentiment acts as an exclamation to round off the proof, for it would have been a general statement if he had said: 'More grievous is sorrow when hatred is joined to misfortune; more lightly is it borne when others share the grief.'

> *Sed puto magna mei est operoso cura colono.*
> *Invenias, dederit quid mihi praeter humum?*
> *Sponte mea facilis contempto nascor in agro,*
> *Parsque loci qua sto, publica paene via est.*   (57–60)

> Perhaps, you say, I give the busy farmer lots of work?
>> But tell me, what, save earth, did he supply?
> An easy birth, with no one's help, I'm born in worthless ground:
>> The part on which I stand is almost public way.

Again, he refutes a possible objection, that 'you deserve to be disliked for causing the farmer so much trouble in looking after you.' Virgil criticizes the vine on this account: '... [the vine] for which no sweated toil's enough: a farmer's work is never done.'[82] **'With no one's help'** (*sponte mea*) [literally 'of my own accord']: That is, the nut is simply buried. It grows better, however, if it is planted flat or crosswise, with its junction implanted in the earth, as Pliny and Palladius instruct.[83] **'I'm born in worthless ground'**: Either because the ground is uncultivated or, as Pliny and Palladius teach,[84] because the walnut thrives in damp, cold, and generally stony places, so that land which is useless for other crops is still good for the production of walnuts.

> *Me sata ne laedam, quoniam sata laedere dicor,*
>> *Imus in extremo margine fundus habet.*   (61–2)

> In case I harm the crops – at least they *say* I harm the crops –
>> The lowest plot, beside the edge, is mine.

However poor the fields, I am assigned the most worthless spot, in the furthest part of the lot and at its outermost edge. This is done 'in case I harm the crops,' since they are convinced that the crops are damaged by my droppings and my shade. Therefore, so that I shouldn't damage anything, I am confined in this spot. **'At least they *say*'**: Cunningly, the walnut neither admits what is evident nor acknowledges what would be prejudicial to its case.

> *Non mihi falx nimias Saturni deputat umbras,*
>> *Duratam renovat non mihi fossor humum.*   (63–4)

> No farmer's pruning-hook cuts back my over-shady growth,
>> No digger turns for me the hardened earth.

Pruning is essential for vines, whenever the buds and tendrils spread too abundantly, but according to Pliny pruning helps to cure the diseases of other trees as well.[85] **'Turns the hardened earth'**: Frequent digging is beneficial to many trees but is essential for the vine. Other trees need irrigation trenches or they will become barren. The walnut needs none of this attention.

> Sole licet siccaque siti peritura laborem,
>> Irriguae dabitur non mihi sulcus aquae.   (65–6)

> Though, parched and dry, I die of thirst and labour in the sun,
>> I'll get no trench of water for my roots.

Some trees need no more than an application of moisture to sprout and mature. Virgil in the *Georgics* gives instructions on how to irrigate a field.[86] Pliny, in book 17, chapter 19, and again in chapter 26, shows what remedies to use to prevent the roots from drying out and withering.[87] Ovid has thus touched on the three principal remedies, pruning, trenching, and irrigation.

> At cum maturas fisso nova cortice rimas
>> Nux agit, ad parteis pertica saeva venit.
> Pertica dat plenis immitia vulnera ramis,
>> Ne possim lapidum verbera sola queri.   (67–70)

> But once the nut is ripe and splits its shell and shows its cracks,
>> The cruel stick draws near to play its part.
> The stick rains savage blows on branches full of fruit, to give
>> Me more to moan about than stinging stones.

In walnuts the splitting of the shell is a sign of ripeness. There is a kind of walnut known as 'Persian' or 'mollusc' which, having a softer covering, splits and reveals its kernel as soon as it is ripe. **Agere rimas 'shows its cracks':** An elegant way of saying 'is split,' on the analogy of *agere radices* 'show forth roots.' **'Draws near, etc':** At the stage of cultivation no one remembered his duty, and no one helped the walnut when it was thirsty or bowed down with leaves, but when it comes to doing damage the stick is ready. The epithet **'cruel'** is a nice touch, as cruelty is a characteristic of men, not of sticks. **'To play its part':** A metaphor from the stage: anyone who does his duty is said to 'play his part.' **'To give me more to moan about':** As if wounding with stones was not enough. I have already mentioned that walnuts are knocked down by poles in order to increase the tree's fertility.[88]

> Poma cadunt mensis non interdicta secundis,
>> Et condit lectas parca colona nuces.   (71–2)

My 'berries' fall. They're not forbidden for the second course,
  And thrifty farm-wives gather them for store.

***Poma* 'berries'**: Note the use of *poma* for 'nuts,' contradicting Lorenzo Valla's note.[89] **'Not forbidden, etc'**: In Athenaeus the question is posed whether walnuts should be served during or after dinner.[90] In both Asia and Greece they are usually served during the meal, because when they are eaten after dinner they inhibit digestion, as they float in the stomach because of their oily quality and also they encourage one to drink while eating them. All nuts, however, share one common fault, that they cause headaches – hence the Greek word[91] κάρυον 'walnut,' and perhaps Latin *nux* 'nut' from *noxa* 'harm.' Almonds are the least harmful. But why should walnuts be excluded from the dessert course, when Pliny (book 16, chapter 6) relates that even in his day the Spanish used to serve nuts for dessert?[92] I too, when I was at Florence,[93] saw chestnuts provided instead of dessert fruit at the home of a very rich man. Almonds, however, as I have said, are the most favoured, followed by filberts. Thus the phrase **'not forbidden'** is used bashfully – the walnut is satisfied to be admitted with the dessert. **'Thrifty farm-wives'**: Walnuts can be preserved for a long time. There are two ways of preserving them: either shell them and bury them in sand, or wrap them in the leaves of their own tree. Fresh walnuts, however, are less harmful to eat, though even old dry nuts become tender if you strip away the outer skin and put them in cold water and let them soften for one night. Almonds that have dried up with age are softened in the same way. **'Farm-wife'**: A countrywoman, of whom Cato writes: 'She should have grapes covered with earth in skins and pots, and nuts of Praeneste covered with earth in a pot.' This is why she is called 'thrifty,' and Cato says she should not be fond of luxury.[94]

Since, however, nuts are more frequently used in games than as a food, the walnut, after these few words on dessert, goes on to talk about games. Playing with nuts was especially the pastime of young boys, and gave rise to the proverb 'to give up one's nuts';[95] see, for example, Persius: 'And everything we do, once nuts are left behind,'[96] and Martial: 'Play on, you say, at nuts; I'll not destroy your nuts.'[97]

> *Has puer aut certo lectas dilaniat ictu*
> *Aut pronas digito bisve semelve petit.*   (73–4)

When gathered up they're torn apart by boys with certain blow
  Or, flat, hit one or twice by finger's aim.

I am quite sure that what Ovid actually wrote was:

Has puer aut certo rectas dilaminat ictu

When standing straight they're split in two by boys with certain blow,

since **dilaminare**[98] means 'split into two layers.' This happens when the joins separate and the nut is split into two halves: a little later[99] the poet refers to the splittable outer casing as a *lamina* 'layer.' Skill in this game consisted in hitting the join with a sure blow. The verb *dilaniare* 'tear apart' – preserved in the Aldine manuscripts – is also against the metre. Second, the word **rectas** **'standing straight'** is contrasted with **pronas 'flat'** [that is, horizontal] in the next line. I think this is our game of splitting very hard apples. The forefinger of the left hand is placed on the base of the apple and the fist of the right hand is brought down sharply on it; success rests on the speed and sharpness of the blow, for if you hit too lightly you bruise your finger and fail to split the apple.

> *Quatuor in nucibus non amplius alea tota est,*
> *Cum sibi suppositis additur una tribus.*   (75–6)

In 'nuts' the hazard rests on only four, no more, when one
  Is added to the three that fell before.

'Hazard' (*alea* **'dice'**): Used wittily to mean 'risk.' When you are losing, the biggest risk is on four nuts, bringing the contest to its most exciting point: if you 'cut' one in addition to the three, you take all four. It is surprising that Julius Pollux,[100] although he has much information on games, makes no mention of 'nuts.' This kind of game was perhaps similar to that of 'bones,' which Horace links with 'nuts' in the second book of his *Satires*: 'You, Aulus, bones and nuts ...,'[101] which shows that the game of 'bones,' like 'nuts,' was popular with boys. Martial also shows that the game with nuts was not unlike dice, for he says in his *Apophoreta*:

> 'Small dice' is merely 'nuts' and seems of no account,
>   But often has it cost a lad his skin,[102]

and similarly in the *Xenia*:

> For me this page is but a game of nuts, a dicing-cup,
>   A sporting throw that brings no loss – or gain![103]

> *Per tabulae clivum labi iubet alter et optat,*
> *Tangat ut e multis quaelibet una suam.*   (77–8)

And down the sloping board another wills one nut to roll
    And from so many touch upon his own.

Another game consists in placing the nuts in a row and rolling one down a sloping board; if it touches the correct nut, the thrower wins.

> *Est etiam, par sit numerus qui dicat an impar,*
>   *Ut divinatas auferat augur opes.*   (79–80)

Another punter calls the fall, an 'even' or an 'odd,'
    To claim, as prophet, wealth correctly guessed.

Horace recalls this game also: 'To play at "even-odd," to ride a hobby-horse.'[104] The pentameter is outstandingly expressed: *auferat* 'claim,' that is, like a victor; **'wealth,'** in schoolboy idiom, as they prize the nut greatly; *divinatas* **'guessed,'** because of the risk of the forecast; **'prophet,'** that is, the one who guesses the fall.

> *Fit quoque de creta, qualem coeleste figuram*
>   *Sydus et in Graecis litera quarta gerit.*
> *Haec ubi distincta est gradibus, qui constitit intus,*
>   *Quot tetigit virga, tot capit inde nuces.*   (81–4)

In chalk they mark out lines conforming to the starry group
    And what in Greek is numbered 'letter four.'
This figure then is marked with grades; one boy stands right inside
    And wins whatever nuts his stick can reach.

This describes a third kind of game. A large triangular figure is made out of chalk in the shape of a Greek capital *delta*. In Egypt the Nile makes the same shape with its course – hence the name, the Nile Delta – and in the sky a similar figure can be seen above the head of Aries. The latter is formed by three stars: two sides are equal, but the third is shorter and has a brighter star at its apex; the Greeks call it Deltoton. Thus, nuts are set out on these marked lines at fixed intervals, here called 'grades'; the boy who stands in the middle takes as many nuts as he touches with the reach of his stick.

> *Vas quoque saepe cavum spacio distante locatur,*
>   *In quod missa levi nux cadit una manu.*   (85–6)

Another game sets up an empty jar some feet away
    And into this a nut is deftly cast.

This game is recalled by Persius: 'and not be cheated by the funnel's narrow neck.'[105] Each boy puts some nuts into a 'whale,' a kind of jar; then, standing at a distance, each of them in turn aims at the neck of the jar. The boy who alone gets his nut in (or who does so most frequently) wins all the nuts.

> *Felix secreto quae nata est arbor in agro*
> *Et soli domino ferre tributa potest:*
> *Non hominum strepitus audit, non illa rotarum,*
> *Non a vicina pulverulenta via est.*
> *Illa suo quaecunque tulit dare dona colono*
> *Et plenos fructus dinumerare potest.*   (87–92)

> Ah, lucky is the tree that grows in some secluded field
> And pays its tribute to its lord alone!
> It hears no din from humankind, it hears no screech of wheels,
> It's not begrimed with dust from nearby road.
> Its produce it can give as gifts to its own husbandman,
> Its harvest it can reckon out in full.

This plea for sympathy is based on a comparison, since the misfortune is made to seem worse by comparison with the good fortune of another. This is why rhetoricians count comparison among the figures of amplification.[106] The walnut shows how many disadvantages it suffers because of its location, one of which is that it cannot pay out all its produce to its lord. **'Pay tribute'**: The walnut is depicted as frugal and faithful to its lord, and its injury is therefore considered all the more cruel. 'Tribute' is owed to one's 'lord,' and a man of good faith takes it hard if he cannot pay what he owes. ***Dona* 'gifts'**: I think the correct reading is *poma* 'apples,' 'fruits.' The word 'tribute' applies to what should be discharged to the lord; it is only for the husbandman that it pays out its 'fruits.' **'Hears no din'**: This is a pleasing fantasy, that trees can hear. **'From nearby road'**: This [that is, proximity] on its own is inconvenient, as lower branches are sometimes sterile because of the dirt and dust.

> *At mihi maturos nunquam licet aedere foetus,*
> *Ante diemque meae percutiuntur opes.*   (93–4)

> But I don't ever get the chance to bring forth ripened births:
> My treasures get knocked down before their day.

This is another example, as mentioned above, of pathos by comparison. The walnut's misfortune, however, is twofold, as it can produce neither 'ripened' nor 'full-term births,' an allusion to still births, a most serious misfortune for women who give birth prematurely. **Ante diemque 'and before the day':** The enclitic *-que* is somewhat awkward in third place, as though *ante diem* were one word, like *propediem*.

> *Lamina mollis adhuc tenero est in lacte quod intra est,*
>   *Nec mala sunt ulli nostra futura bono.*   (95–6)

> The membrane's soft, its centre steeps inside the gentle milk.
>   My losses will accrue to no one's gain.

The injury is crueller that benefits not even the person that inflicts it; the loss is harder that does no one any good. **'The membrane's soft':** The skin hardens as it ripens. Inside the nut there is a kind of membrane to separate the sections of the kernel: this also grows woody when ripe. Hence his earlier use of the word *dilaminat*; see Pliny, book 15, chapter 22.[107] **'Gentle milk':** It is milky juice rather than a kernel, like that found in teasels when their heads are pulled off. **Ulli bono 'to no one's gain':** *Bonum* is used substantively to mean 'advantage'; hence the orators' phrase *cui bono fuerit* 'to whose good was it?' just as *malo esse* 'to be for ill' means 'to be disadvantageous.'

> *Et tamen invenio qui me iaculetur, et ictu*
>   *Praefestinato munus inane petat.*   (97–8)

> And yet there's always someone standing by to shoot, to gain
>   With over-hurried blow a worthless prize.

'Over-hurried': That is, too hasty, premature. Although 'hurry' is intransitive, the poet uses 'hurried' to mean 'accelerated,' and 'over-hurried' to mean 'prematurely hasty.' **Me iaculetur 'to shoot me':** We 'shoot' a stone or any other missile and we also 'shoot' that which we hit; for example Juvenal: 'What mighty ash-trees the centaur shoots,'[108] and Pliny, book 8 (on elephants): 'Some shoot their very tender feet.'[109]

> *Si fiat rapti, fiat mensura relicti,*
>   *Maiorem domini parte, viator, habes.*   (99–100)

> If measure's made of what's been stolen and of what's been left,
>   The passer-by has more than master's share.

Look how the tree heaps up its wrongs on all sides! Here (as with all robbery) she complains that not only is the owner defrauded, but the robber takes the larger share.

> Saepe aliquis, foliis ubi nuda cacumina vidit,
>   Esse putat Boreae triste furentis opus.   (101–2)

The sight of branches' tips bereft of leaves makes some infer
  The work of bleak and raging northern winds.

Another example of exaggeration by comparison. There are four misfortunes that are disastrous to trees: powerful winds, which sometimes break and tear whole trees and sometimes even uproot them; fierce heat; severe cold; and hail. The damage done by passers-by, however, is so great that it is blamed on these natural disasters. **'Branches' tips'**: These parts are particularly vulnerable to the north wind. **'Raging'**: The north wind is the most violent and is said to stir up earthquakes. **'Work'**: Used humorously. People say 'You did this, north wind, this is your work,' whereas the word 'work' properly refers to a house or a statue or something similar that testifies to someone's effort or skill.

> Aestibus hic, hic me spoliatam frigore credit;
>   Est quoque qui crimen grandinis esse putet.   (103–4)

Then this one lays the blame on heat, and this one blames the cold,
  There's one who blames my leaflessness on hail.

Note how he varies the distribution of speakers: first **'some'** [line 101], then **'this one, this one'** (instead of 'another, another'), and finally **'there's one who'** (instead of 'someone').

> At mihi nec grando duris invisa colonis
>   Nec ventus fraudi solve geluve fuit.   (105–6)

But hail, the hardy farmers' foe, was not the source of fraud,
  Nor heat, nor stormy wind, nor freezing cold.

'The hardy farmers': By 'hardy' he means 'able to withstand misfortunes,' and this epithet adds to the injury, that the fruit won by so many labours and by surviving so many discomforts should be destroyed by hail. **'Fraud'**: This sometimes means 'trickery'; in legal language it sometimes stands for 'loss.' The Twelve Tables say, 'Be free of fraud' and 'lest it be my fraud,' that is, 'lest it harm me.'[110] *Fraudare* 'defraud' means not only to deceive but to deprive of one's due comfort: we 'defraud' someone of what is due, but 'frustrate' someone of what is expected.

> *Fructus obest, peperisse nocet, nocet esse feracem;*
>   *Quaeque fuit multis, haec mihi praeda malo est.*
> *Praeda malo, Polydore, fuit tibi; praeda nefandae*
>   *Coniugis Aonium misit in arma virum.*
> *Hesperii regis pomaria tuta fuissent,*
>   *Una sed immensas arbor habebat opes.*   (107–112)

> My fruit brings woe, production hurts, fertility's my bane;
>   For me, as once for many, loot's a curse.
> For Polydorus loot meant woe; the loot of cursed wife
>   Sent Menelaus to the Trojan War;
> The orchards of the western king would not have been despoiled,
>   But untold wealth was hanging on one tree.

The walnut reverts to a topic that it began to discuss earlier, that it is those with something for a plunderer to covet who are particularly liable to injuries. As it warms to its theme, it applies rhetorical figures to lend vehemence to the argument: evenly balanced speech units, repetition of the same word, and what is known as asyndeton, repetition of the same idea. In one line he says the same thing three times: **'My fruit brings woe'**; he repeats it: **'production hurts'**; and repeats it again: **'fertility's my bane'**; and in the next line he repeats it for a fourth time: **'For me, as once, etc.'** **Loot (*praeda*):** He means not what has been taken but what can be taken. This commonplace is developed by means of examples from legends, but the same pattern, of balanced units, repetition of words, and asyndeton, is retained to add vehemence: just as the first line consists of three units without any conjunction ('my fruit brings woe, production harms, fertility's my bane'), [so the next three lines contain] 'loot ... loot ... loot.' ***Praeda malo est* 'loot's a curse':** In Latin the phrase *malo esse* 'be for ill' [dative of purpose] means 'to harm,' just as *bono esse* 'be for good' means 'benefit.' **Polydore:** Direct address [vocative] is used for emotional effect. This is the well-known story of Polymnestor, who 'slaughtered Polydorus and won the gold by force.'[111] **'Cursed wife':** Also well known is the story of Helen: Menelaus went to war to get her back again. **'The western king':** The third story is about the golden apples of the Hesperides [that is, the daughters of Hesperus, 'the western king']. Hercules stole them ahead of any others by putting to sleep the dragon that constantly guarded them.

> *At rubus et sentes tantummodo laedere natae*
>   *Spinaque vindicta caetera tuta sua est.*   (113–4)

The bramble, briar, and other thorns, though only born to hurt,
  Deter assault and so remain secure.

Again, the walnut's case is bolstered by means of comparison: that which is fruitful and harmless is damaged, while the unfruitful and harmful plants go scot-free. *Laedere natae* 'born to hurt': A Greek idiom [that is, participle and infinitive] (πεφυκυῖαι βλάπτειν) rather than Latin, which would use the gerund *natae ad laedendum* 'born for harming.' This transferred sense of 'born (to),' meaning 'is naturally accustomed to' is also used in Greek (πέφυκεν); similarly Latin uses *vulgus amat* 'the people love to' (Greek φιλεῖ) meaning 'are accustomed to,' as Fabius notes in Sallust.[112] This expression [adjective and infinitive] is common in Horace: 'quick to be angry,' 'effective to clean.'[113] 'Other thorns': Referring to the many species of thorns, which include bramble and briar. *Vindicta* 'with deterring vengeance': Because thorns wound anyone who tries to touch them. Now if morals had not been corrupted, it would have been proper that those who harm no one and do as much good as possible should be more 'secure.'

> *Me, quia non noceo, nec aduncis vindicor hamis,*
>   *Missa petunt avida saxa proterva manu.*   (115–6)

Because I do no harm nor take revenge with curving hooks
  With greedy hands they boldly hurl their stones.

'Curving hooks': Some trees, such as the holly and the holm-oak family, have leaves armed with thorns. Juniper has spikes instead of leaves; the leaves of pine, larch, and cedar are prickly; the bramble has a spiny surface. There is also a kind of thorn called 'acanthion' in Greek whose leaves are pointed at the end. Some trees, like the brook-willow, have both branches and trunk protected with prickles.

> *Quid si non aptas solem vitantibus umbras,*
>   *Finditur Icario cum cane terra, darem?*

Quid nisi suffugium nimbos vitantibus essem,
  Non expectata cum venit imber aqua? (117–120)

Suppose I ceased to offer shade to those who flee the sun
  When earth is cracked beneath Icarus' dog?
Suppose I would no longer shelter those who flee the rain
  When unexpected shower starts to fall?

These verses were corrupted in various ways: for *vitantibus* 'those who flee' [117] the manuscripts have *nutantibus* 'those who nod'[114] and, despite the metrical defect, have *suffragium* 'help' for *suffugium* 'shelter.'

Not only, says the walnut, do I provide fruit and do no harm, but I am helpful to the traveller in other ways: he hides beneath my shade when he cannot bear the sun's heat or when a sudden shower catches him out in the open. **'Icarus' dog':** That is, Sirius or Procyon, as it is at the head of the constellation known as the Dog: when the sun is in this sign, it is extremely hot. Legend tells that it was the companion of Icarus and revealed the body of its dead master; for this service it was rewarded with a place in the stars.

Omnia cum faciam, cum praestem sedula cunctis
  Officium, saxis officiosa petor. (121–2)

There's nothing I don't do: with busy care I serve them all.
  My service counts for naught – I'm shied with stones.

Sedula **'with busy care':** That is, according to my abilities. There is a pleasing word-play on *officium-officiosa* **'serve-service.'**

Haec mihi perpessae domini patienda querela est;
  Causabor, quare sit lapidosus ager. (123–4)

And having suffered this, I have to bear my master's moan:
  I'm blamed for all the stones that fill the field.

The walnut's misery is emphasized by the fact that, far from being consoled for all its injuries, it is even cursed by its owner because his field has been made stony by the rocks that have been thrown. Note that *patienda* **'to be endured'** is used in the passive voice, just as *causabor* **'I shall be blamed'** is used for *incusabor* or 'shall be held liable,' in imitation of the Greek αἰτιοῦμαι. Ovid may actually have written *causantis* [to go with *domini*].

Dumque repurgat humum, collectaque saxa remittit,
  Semper habent in me tela parata viae.   (125–6)

He clears the ground, collects the stones, and throws them back again –
  A constant store of missiles lines the road.

Consequently another misfortune is added: the owner, angry at the walnut, throws the stones back on the road, so that the passer-by has no shortage of missiles to throw at the tree. It is a sad remedy that doesn't cure the disease but fosters it.

Ergo invisa aliis uni mihi frigora prosunt:
  Illo me tutam tempore praestat hiems.   (127–8)

And thus the cold that others hate is good for me alone:
  In winter only do I feel secure.

This is a clever allusion to a point we have already mentioned, that walnuts thrive on cool soil. It is here applied to another argument: my misfortune is so great, the tree says, that what other people find tiresome is for me the remedy for an even greater ill, just as gout is good for those who are afraid of paralysis or apoplexy or epilepsy.

Nuda quidem tunc sum, nudam tamen expedit esse,
  Nec spolium de me quod petat hostis habet.   (129–30)

I'm naked then, I grant, but nakedness is much the best,
  For then I have no fruits for foes to cull.

Trees shiver with the cold [*or* abhor the frost] and are ugly when they have lost their leaves, but the walnut prefers these inconveniences to being pelted with stones. Cumulative effect is achieved by the comparison of misfortunes.

At simul induimus nostris sua vellera ramis,
  Saxa novos fructus grandine plura petunt.   (131–2)

But once my branches clothe themselves with fleece, the stones rain down
  More dense than hail to hit my new-grown fruit.

Simul 'once': Here this does not mean 'equally, at the same time,' but is used for 'after' or 'as soon as.' **Vellera** 'fleece': Referring to leaves, a metaphor

taken from sheep, for *vellus* 'fleece' seems to be derived from *vello* 'pluck.'
'More dense than hail': Hyperbole; compare the Greek word χαλαξηδόν
'like hail.'

> Forsitan hic aliquis dicat: 'Quod publica tangunt,
>   Carpere concessum est; hoc via iuris habet.'   (133–4)

> Someone might argue: 'What's adjacent to the public road
>   Is free for plucking – that's the "right of way."'

The basis of the argument is one of quality,[115] in which the justice of the
given act is defended: 'The people have a right over what is public; the road
is public, etc.' He refutes this in three ways. First, that which adjoins a public
route is not *ipso facto* public. Second, not everyone necessarily has a right to
something public or placed in public – standing corn, olive-groves, and
vineyards are adjacent to the public way but cannot be assailed with
impunity. Third, the city gate is public: you can go through it, but you must
not damage it; merchandise is set out in the public market, but it cannot as a
consequence be carried off. Here arises basis A, definition, that is, what does
'public' mean? Secondly, there is basis B, juridical or qualitative, that is,
what is permissible (and what is not permissible) to do to that which is
public. One may *use* it, but not *abuse* it. There are various opinions among
lawyers on these matters – on things sacred, religious, holy, public,
common, things which owe service, the occupancy of vacant property, and
so on. The poet ingeniously alludes to all this.

> Si licet hoc, oleas distringite, laedite messes,
>   Improbe vicinum carpe viator olus.   (135–6)

> If so, snatch olives, trample crops! Base walker, do your worst,
>   And pick the cabbage growing by the road.

He refutes the claim by means of analogy. Olives are spared because they
would be severely damaged if anyone tried to steal them; the damage to
other trees is not as serious. Consequently he uses this as his most powerful
example, since damage to olive-trees is universally condemned.

> Intret et urbanas eadem petulantia portas,
>   Sitque tuis muris, Romule, iuris idem.   (137–8)

> Let equal boorishness invade the gates, and let your walls,
>   O Romulus, be subject to this law.

***Tuis muris* 'to your walls':** An unusual dative, the equivalent of *in tuos muros*. The poet alludes to the fact that the walls of Rome are sacrosanct: Romulus killed his brother Remus for violating them. The apostrophe to Romulus is a pleasing touch.

> *Quilibet argentum prima de fronte tabernae*
>   *Tollat, et ad gemmas quilibet alter eat.*
> *Auferat hic aurum, peregrinos ille lapillos,*
>   *Et quascunque potest tollere, tollat opes.*   (139–42)

> The silver stands outside the stall for anyone to take,
>   And someone else can help themselves to gems.
> Let someone take the foreign stones, another grab the gold –
>   Whatever's not nailed down is free for all.

The multitude of examples reinforces the argument. **'Stalls':** They were in the public market-place, and displayed goods for sale. **'Silver':** This applies to the moneylenders, bankers, and goldsmiths. **'Gems':** This applies to the jewellers. Ovid apparently distinguishes 'gems' (*gemmae*) from 'stones' (*lapillos*); otherwise he would have repeated himself. This point is disputed by Lorenzo Valla in his argument against the lawyers, book 6, chapter 484,[116] but in my opinion he does not explain himself sufficiently. Anyone who has the time can investigate the issue further: I am content just to have drawn attention to it.

> *Sed neque tolluntur nec, dum reget omnia Caesar,*
>   *Incolumis tanto praeside raptor erit.*   (143–4)

> But all of these remain untouched while Caesar rules the world;
>   Beneath his mighty rule no thief goes free.

Ingeniously he takes the chance to flatter Caesar. The argument, however, is based on facts: the theft of public property is *not* lawful, because it is punished by Caesar, whom he calls a protector (*praeside*). The Caesars once possessed the greatest part of the world: their role was to inhibit force and to maintain public justice. Later there arose emperors under whom there was very great freedom to plunder. Octavian[117] (the object, I believe, of Ovid's flattery here) deserved to be counted among the virtuous and just emperors.

> *At non ille deus pacem intra moenia finit;*
>   *Auxilium toto spargit in orbe suum.*   (145–6)

That god does not confine his peace inside the city walls;
  He spreads his help throughout the globe.

Here he deals with an unstated objection, that Caesar forbids theft inside the cities but not on public highways. To call Caesar **'god'** is, of course, fulsome flattery (though he realized that this particular god was not entirely propitious towards him).[118] The term seems less objectionable, however, when one remembers that even now there are people who flatter their princes in this way. I know an Italian astrologer in England who began his preface addressed to the king by saying that he had two gods, one in heaven, the other on earth. **'Help'**: Used emphatically; the power of monarchs should be simply the capacity to be of service – in the words of the proverb, to be a god is to help mortals.[119]

> *Quid tamen hoc prodest, media si luce palamque*
>   *Verberor, et tutae non licet esse nuci?*   (147–8)

But what good's this, if openly, beneath the light of day,
  I suffer blows and nuts can have no peace?

From the digression he returns to the complaint that he has started. The case is amplified by references to time, place, and person. It is an injury to be beaten, especially openly in broad daylight, and, on top of this, on a public road, in contempt of the emperor. ***Non licet esse tutae* 'nuts can have no peace'**: This use of the dative *tutae* instead of the accusative *licet esse tutam* is an elegant variation; either of these is quite common, but the third possibility with the nominative (*licet esse tuta*) is less usual.

> *Ergo nec nidos foliis haerere, nec ullam*
>   *Sedibus in nostris stare videtis avem.*
> *At lapis in ramo sedit quicunque bifurco,*
>   *Haeret, et ut capta victor in arce manet.*   (149–52)

Because of this you'll never see a nest within my leaves;
  No bird will ever use me for its perch.
But any stone that's come to rest within the forking twigs
  Enthroned as victor stays triumphantly.

Not a single argument is allowed to pass unnoticed; here the cruelty of passers-by is inferred from the fact that because of the showers of stones no birds will nest in its branches. In fact, it is more likely that this is the result of the natural bitterness of the leaves and bark, and their strong smell. It is a typical technique of poetry to make some naturally caused event the occasion for a fable, such as saying that God, angry at humanity's sins, has taken up his thunderbolt, when in fact this results from natural causes. The walnut continues to present a conjectural proof based on an accumulation of indications:[120] there is no nest in the tree, but there is a stone lodged there. The following passage belongs to the same order of argument.

> Caetera saepe tamen potuere admissa negari
>   Et crimen vox est inficiata suum;
> Nostra notat fusco digitos iniuria succo,
>   Cortice contactas inficiente manus.   (153–6)

In other crimes the criminals can often bluff it out:
  A bare-faced no denies the culprit's guilt.
But injury that's done to me turns fingers black with juice
  And hands that touch my bark are stained with dye.

Walnut bark is used for staining wool and dying hair, as Pliny[121] says, and will give off its colour when touched. Now blood adhering to the clothes or a sword or the hand is a conjectural indication of murder.[122] Alluding to this he adds:

> Ille cruor meus est; illo maculata cruore
>   Non profectura dextra lavatur aqua.   (157–8)

That blood is mine! That hand is stained with blood that comes from me!
  No water now will ever wash it clean.

Blood can be washed off, but the stain from walnut bark is astonishingly persistent and can hardly be removed by soap or washing-soda.

> O ego, quum longae venerunt taedia vitae,
>   Optavi quoties arida facta mori!   (159–60)

But oh, how many weary hours of long, long life I've had
  And often longed to wither up and die!

The remainder of the poem is taken up with emotional outbursts, though emotion is present in most of the poem. For an account of the longevity of trees, with details of their ages, see Pliny, book 15, final chapter.[123] Ovid's phrase 'weary hours of long, long life' alludes to this longevity. To desire death is a tragic motif, a wish produced in utter desolation. Trees sometimes wither up from old age, but usually from disease or blight.

> *Optavi quoties aut caeco turbine verti*
> *Aut valido missi fulminis igne peti!* (161–2)

> How often have I yearned to feel the whirlwind's blind assault
> Or mighty fiery blast of thunderbolt!

Imprecations are tragic in tone; for example, 'Or may the bolt of mighty Jove despatch me to the shades!'[124] Whirlwinds are produced by the meeting of different winds; they often uproot whole trees completely, or snap them in the middle, or lift them up in the air and put them down somewhere else. He calls the whirlwind **'blind'** because it falls with a mad rush – just as we speak of 'blind love' or 'blind rage.' We often see trees struck by lightning, and sometimes see whole forests ablaze.

> *Atque utinam subitae raperent mea poma procellae,*
> *Vel possem fructus excutere ipsa meos!* (163–4)

> Or would that sudden blasts might blow and snatch away my fruit,
> Or I myself might shake off all my nuts!

Procella **'blasts':** From *procellere* 'strike down'; it is used with reference to both winds and waves. Apples and pears are often blown down by a rather gusty wind, but walnuts are attached to the wood and stick more firmly: they are not easily knocked off, except with a pole. The fruit of other trees generally falls off of its own accord when ripe, as though the tree were shaking it off: the walnut wishes it had the same facility.

> *Sic, ubi detracta est a te tibi causa pericli,*
> *Quod superest tutum, Pontice castor, habes.* (165–6)

> Just as the beaver amputates the part that hunters seek
> And thus preserves the residue intact.

Many writers testify that the beaver, or castor – an amphibious animal that lives both on land and in the water – bites off its testicles when it is endangered by the hunt. It knows that this is the main reason for its being hunted, as its testicles have medicinal properties – hence 'castor oil' (Pliny, book 8, chapter 30).[125] Sestus, however (cited by Pliny, book 32, chapter 3),[126] says that this is not true, as a beaver's testicles are tiny and withdrawn within its loins, and can only be removed by killing it. Ovid also described all this in his book entitled *Halieutica* on the nature and intelligence of fish, cited by Pliny, book 32, chapter 2[127] – I wish I had a copy of this work instead of Oppian.[128] Pythagoras says that trees are alive and possess the spirit of life, albeit sluggish – and so they lack the power to move, like sponges and what they call 'attached animals.'[129] Thus, the walnut laments that when it sees a blow coming it cannot dodge it by moving its body:

> *Quid mihi tunc animi est, cum sumit tela viator*
> *Atque oculis plagae destinat ante locum?*
> *Nec vitare licet moto fera vulnera trunco,*
> *Quem sub humo radix curvaque vincla tenent.*   (167–70)

> What spirit do I have, when passers-by take up their arms
> And with their eyes mark out the target-spot?
> I cannot move my trunk to dodge the threatened savage wounds –
> Its root and grasping rootlets hold it fast.

Nothing arouses the emotions more effectively than presenting the scene before the listener's eyes. *Viator* **'passer-by'**: One who makes a journey, one who summons people before the magistrates or makes announcements on their behalf. He calls the stones **'arms'** and the blows **'wounds'** in order to preserve the metaphor. **'Mark out'**: That is, aim: we 'mark out' something in our mind or with our eyes. It is pitiful to see a wound in advance but to be unable to avoid it.

> *Corpora praebemus plagis, ut saepe sagittis,*
> *Cum populus manicas deposuisse vetat.*   (171–2)

> My body stands exposed to blows, as captives were to spears
> When crowds forbid the loosing of the bonds.

A comparison is used to emphasize the cruelty of the walnut's fate. This refers to a terrible kind of punishment, in which the prisoner is bound and exposed to the crowd's arrows: he sees the arrow aimed at his vital organs, as though at a target, but cannot flinch to avoid the blow. *Manicas* **'bonds'**: Handcuffs, used to bind the prisoner to a stake. Compare Virgil: 'King Priam bids them loose the cuffs, the tightly fitting bonds.'[130] This kind of punishment was provided to satisfy the people's hatred; a kinder method was to shoot at a free man. Just as a prisoner, fastened with handcuffs, cannot avoid arrows, so the walnut, fixed by its roots (which it calls 'bonds'), is compelled passively to await the missile of the passer-by.

> *Utve gravem pavida est ubi tolli vacca securem*
>   *Aut stringi cultros in sua colla videt.*   (173–4)

> Or like the fearful cow that sees the heavy axe upraised
>   Or carving-knives drawn out to slit her throat.

The ox is also tied up for slaughter: when it sees the axe poised at its head it cannot avoid it; when it sees the knives ready at its throat, it cannot pull itself away. Less pity is felt if the victim is killed after having been given the chance of fleeing or defending itself.

> *Saepe meas frondes vento tremuisse putastis,*
>   *Sed metus in nobis causa tremoris erat.*   (175–6)

> You've often seen my leaves astir – 'It's just the wind' you think –
>   But it was fear that caused my leaves to shake.

Great fear induces pallor and trembling. The poet could not attribute pallor to the tree, so he ascribes trembling to it, so that it can claim that what sometimes results from the wind is in fact caused by fear.

> *Si merui videorque nocens, excidite ferro*
>   *Nostraque fumosis urite membra focis;*
> *Si merui videorque nocens, imponite flammae*
>   *Et liceat miserae dedecus esse semel.*   (177–80)

> If I'm at fault and plainly in the wrong, then chop me down
>   And burn my limbs up on your smoky hearths.
> If I'm at fault and plainly in the wrong, then put to flame,
>   And let disgrace befall me only once.

Those who are given up as incurably wicked are, by capital punishment, as it were 'cut off' from the body of citizens. For trees that are abandoned as incurable there are two forms of capital punishment. Either they are chopped down to be used in fireplaces, or, if that is not worth the trouble, they are burned up by the application of flame, so that the remains of the burned-out tree may indicate that it was harmful.[131] The cruelty of the punishment contributes to the emotional effect. Branches are wittily referred to as **'limbs.'** The epithet **'smoky'** (of hearths) contributes not only to the realism but also to the emotional effect: peasant hearths are generally smoky. The pathos is also reinforced by the repetition of 'If I'm at fault, etc.' *Imponite flammae* **'put to flame'**: Perhaps read *imponite flammam* 'put flame to,' meaning that the tree is cut down and then burned up. If this suggestion is not accepted, we must interpret the text as meaning that the tree, having been cut down, is burned in the place where it grew. The passage might perhaps be interpreted as follows: **'burn on smoky hearths,'** that is, suspend over smoke, for it is over smoke that cut wood is usually hardened. Compare Virgil in the *Georgics*: 'And let the smoke infuse the wood suspended over hearths.'[132] **'Disgrace':** It is ignominious to be punished, but it is even worse to have to suffer every day something worse than punishment.

> *Si nec cur urar nec cur excidar habetis,*
>   *Parcite; sic coeptum perficiatis iter.*   (181–2)

> But if you have no cause to see me suffer flame or axe,
>   Please spare this tree! – and blessings on your trip!

If I am guilty, I accept any punishment; if I am innocent, refrain from injuring me. **'And blessings':** He concludes with a binding prayer. A traveller is liable to many perils on his journey: the walnut wishes them a happy trip – provided they refrain from injuring the innocent. May no one harm you in your innocence, just as you show mercy to me – with a hint that if they attack an innocent creature someone may turn up to pay them back in the same coin.

There is an old proverb, my dear More, 'Enough of the oak.'[133] I am afraid that for some time someone may have been murmuring, 'Enough of the walnut.' I will therefore make an end of it – but I must first dispose of one detail. In many cases, tree and fruit are known by the same word: for example, nut, olive (unless you prefer to call the tree *olea* and the fruit *oliva*). In other cases, there are different words: for example, oak and acorn, vine and grape. In most cases the tree is distinguished from the fruit by gender: for example, *cerasus* 'cherry-tree' (feminine), *cerasum* 'cherry' (neuter); *malus* 'apple-tree' (feminine), *malum* 'apple' (neuter). We must now see whether what applies to *nux* 'nut' [that is, signifying both tree and fruit] is true of its species. The tree is called *corylus* 'hazel'; its fruit is the *avellana* 'filbert.' There is a fruit called 'Persian nut'; it has not yet been established whether the tree is also called 'Persian nut.' It certainly seems inappropriate that the tree should be called *iuglans* 'walnut': if the correct etymology of the word *iuglans* is *Jovis glans* 'Jupiter's acorn,' then, since acorn-bearing trees are not known as 'acorns,' the word *iuglans* seems to be appropriate only to the fruit. The authority of ancient writers, however, teaches differently. Pliny (book 24, chapter 1) writes: 'The oak and the olive have such a strong mutual antipathy that each of them dies if it is planted in the other's trench; the oak, however, will die even if planted beside the *iuglans* nut.'[134] There can be no doubt here that by *iuglans* he means the tree. Again, in book 16, chapter 41 he writes: 'The cypress, cedar, ebony, lotus, box, yew, juniper, wild olive, and cultivated olive do not experience rot or old age; of the others, the following are affected very slowly: the larch, oak, cork, chestnut, *iuglans*.'[135] And again, in chapter 19 of the same book: 'Cypresses, *iuglandes*, and chestnuts cannot stand water,'[136] and again in the passage cited above, book 15, chapter 22.[137]

Publius Ovidius Naso *The Elegy on the Nut*
The End

COMMENTARY ON TWO HYMNS OF PRUDENTIUS

Commentarius in duos hymnos Prudentii

translated by

A.G. RIGG

annotated by

A.G. RIGG and ERIKA RUMMEL

The fourth-century Spanish poet Aurelius Prudentius Clemens (348 – after 405) is described by a recent editor as *facile princeps* among the poets of Christian antiquity,[1] and the judgment is fully justified. Apart from his hymns, Prudentius wrote two books *Contra Symmachi orationem*, the *Hamartigenia* (on the origin of sin), the *Dittochaeon* (four-line epitomes of scenes from the Bible), and, his most famous work, the *Psychomachia*.[2] This is a classic personification allegory, depicting the battle of the vices and virtues for the possession of man's soul: it was the principal source for the portrayal of vices and virtues in medieval art and literature.[3] Prudentius wrote two series of hymns, the *Peristephanon* (on Christian martyrs) and the *Cathemerinon* or 'Daily Round,' a series of hymns for the canonical hours, from which Erasmus selected these hymns on the Nativity and Epiphany.[4] Prudentius' hymns did not achieve the liturgical prominence enjoyed by those of, say, Ambrose, though four stanzas of the Epiphany hymn are included in the Roman Breviary for Lauds on 6 January; in the Middle Ages *centos* on specific themes were made from the hymns by extracting lines and stanzas and rearranging them as new hymns.[5] Generally, the textual tradition is literary rather than liturgical; in the introduction to his 1926 edition of Prudentius Bergman cites references to over 280 manuscripts of Prudentius' works.

Prudentius' works quickly found their way into print:[6] Deventer 1492, the Aldine 1501, Basel 1527, Paris 1562, Antwerp 1564, and Hanau 1613. Hymns 11 and 12 are very appropriate as Christmas pieces: 11 celebrates the Nativity (25 December) and 12 the Epiphany (6 January) together with the Slaughter of the Innocents (celebrated on 28 December). Erasmus presented his commentaries on them as a Christmas gift to Margaret Roper, daughter of Sir Thomas More, in 1523. The commentaries are very straightforward, dealing with matters of metre and grammar, the fairly obvious allegorical significations, and the astronomical context of the Epiphany star. Although these commentaries lack the sparkle and erudition of the commentary on the *Nux* sent to the young John More in 1524, editors of Erasmus naturally paired the two pieces as 'commentaries as presents for the More family'; the *Nux* and Prudentius' commentaries are together in all the early editions of Erasmus.

The present translation is based on the edition in LB v (Lyons 1704), but with corrections from the Froben edition (F) of 1524.

AGR

ERASMUS OF ROTTERDAM TO THE VIRTUOUS MAIDEN MARGARET
ROPER, GREETING[1]

I have been put on my mettle so often lately, my dearest Margaret, by letters
from you and your sisters[2] – such sensible, well-written, modest, forthright,
friendly letters – that even if someone were to cut off the headings I should
be able to recognize the 'offspring true-born' of Thomas More.[3] It must not
look as though you had sung your song all the time to a deaf man, and so I
have stolen a brief holiday from the work in which I am buried, and this
Christmas I have put together a small present which I hope will give you
some pleasure.

May there be a blessing on it: William Roper,[4] a man of such high
character, such charm, and such modesty that were he not your husband he
might be taken for your brother, has presented you – or, if you prefer, you
have presented him – with the first fruits of your marriage, and most
promising they are; to put it more accurately, each of you has presented the
other with a baby boy to be smothered in kisses.[5] And here am I, sending
you another boy, who brings more promise than any other: Jesus, born for
the Jews and soon to become the light of the gentiles, who will give the
offspring of your marriage a happy outcome and be the true Apollo of all
your reading,[6] whose praises you will be able to sing to your lyre instead of
nursery rhymes to please your little ones. For he alone is worthy to be
praised continually on the strings and pipe, with songs and every sort of
music-making, but especially with the harmonious utterance of a true
Christian heart.

Nor will he despise the singing of his praises by such a married pair,
whose whole life shows such innocence, such concord, such tranquillity and
simplicity that you could hardly find those under a vow of virginity who
would challenge the comparison. A rare sight, especially in this age of ours;
but I foresee it soon spreading more widely. In your own country you have a
queen who might be the Calliope of your saintly choir,[7] and in Germany too
there are families of no mean station who practise with success the life of
which you have given hitherto such a successful example.[8] Farewell, not
least among the glories of your generation and your native England, and
mind you give my greetings to all the members of your choir.[9]

Basel, Christmas 1524[10]

COMMENTARY ON PRUDENTIUS' HYMN
ON THE NATIVITY
OF THE BOY JESUS

Iambic verse was orginally designed for invective; the short syllable followed by a long syllable expresses the sound of a blow struck and suddenly repeated. (Similarly, the pyrrhic metre imitates the uproar of warriors rushing into battle). Later writers, however, used iambics for any kind of subject, just as they did with elegiacs, which had been originally designed for complaints. Ambrose particularly liked this iambic metre;[1] I have noticed that he generally has a penthemimeral caesura and ends the line with a trisyllable. This arrangement makes the verse run very smoothly, for example, *Dĕŭs crĕātōr* (the *penthemimeris*, or five-syllable unit), followed by the dactyl *ōmnĭŭm*. Similarly *pŏlīqŭe rēctōr / vēstiēns*, and *dĭēm dĕcōrō / lūmĭnĕ*, and *nōctēm sŏpōrīs / grātĭā*. This practice is too common in Ambrose to be accidental. Prudentius frequently observes the same practice, and certainly keeps to it in the first five syllables, for example in line 1 after the penthemimeris *Qŭid ēst quŏd ārctūm* (where the caesura occurs) he adds the dactyl (*cīrcŭlŭm*). Although in iambics the penthemimeral caesura produces a smoother line, poetic licence is not unknown in this metre; in the odd-numbered feet (that is, the first and third) a tribrach (˅˅˅) can be used in place of an iamb (˅−), as it corresponds to an iamb not in the number of syllables but in the measure of time, since a long syllable takes twice the time of a short. (Also note the spondee −−, whose equivalents in time are the dactyl −˅˅ and the anapaest ˅˅−). In the even-numbered feet (second and fourth), however, only an iamb is allowed, except that the second also admits a tribrach; only an iamb or a pyrrhic (˅˅) are allowed in the fourth foot. Ambrose, however, used this licence very sparingly. An anapaest (˅˅−) is elegant in the first foot but not in the third; in either position a dactyl (−˅˅) is rougher. The ancient poets used to compose iambic verse solely from iambs and spondaic verse similarly from pure spondees; later poets, however, introduced the spondee (−−) in order to slow down the tempo of the verse. The alternation of spondees and iambs is considered to be the smoothest form of this metre, and most lines of Ambrose and Prudentius are like this, for example, *Iam lucis orto sidere* or *Iam sol recurrens deserit*.[2]

An exordium that begins with a question ('Why does the sun run back again ... ?') is lively[3] and emotive. This sudden opening suits a poet inspired with the spirit of prophecy, and I am sure that he was inspired when he wrote in this way. Now it is characteristic of a really pious man to interpret everything as an opportunity for piety. Thus, the lengthening of the daytime after the winter solstice, although it happens every year, is adapted by Prudentius as a sign of the boy Jesus already hastening to his beginning. For the days did not lengthen because of the birth of Jesus but because the sun, after entering Capricorn, departs more quickly from the view of people who live outside the tropics and whose horizon is beneath the ecliptic circle – just as, conversely, their days lengthen when the sun enters Cancer. In divine affairs, however, nothing happens by chance; this time of the year was not chosen randomly for the birth of Jesus. Everywhere charity had grown cold;[4] the world lay beneath the darkness of ignorance and the shadow of sins. God had allowed philosophers to fall into error; the higher their opinion of their own wisdom, the greater was their folly. The Pharisees were blinded by their own foolish desires and did not understand the meaning of the spiritual law. Kings and monarchs, whose judgment controlled human affairs, worshipped sticks and stones in place of God; those whom mortals honoured as next to the gods demeaned their majesty before a dumb statue: they offered prayers to things that lacked reason, and sought help from things that could not help themselves. Some races had degenerated so far into insanity as to honour as deities apes, dogs, serpents, cows, and onions.[5] In some races it was considered an act of piety to slaughter one's parents and eat their flesh;[6] in others it was part of their religion to immolate children.[7] This was surely the depths of the night! The light of nature[8] that God first spread for man had been reduced to a narrow point and had almost been extinguished. Also, the lamp of Moses' law, by which God for a second time tried to lighten our darkness, was almost put out by a fleshly understanding [that is, a literal interpretation] through the Pharisees, blind leaders of the blind.[9] So, it was night – and a winter's night.

Now in mystical writings the Lord Jesus is often designated by the word 'light.' Thus, Isaiah: 'The people who sat in the darkness saw a great light, and to those who dwell in the region of the shadow of death a light has arisen.'[10] Also, Zechariah: 'Rising from on high he has visited us, to shine on those who sit in darkness and in the shadow of death.'[11] In fact God himself calls himself 'light of the world.'[12] Christ is in the spiritual world what the sun is in this visible world – whoever lacks him, however learned or clever or eloquent he may be, is blind. In the whole structure of the world there is nothing more wonderful than the sun: it is the source of light; it gives birth to everything and nourishes it, giving it energy and strength; it gives life and growth and joy; it reveals and makes known everything; through it all things get back their own colour and their appearance. The same effect is achieved by the risen truth of the gospel, that is Jesus Christ.

Ignorance of the truth is night; sin is death.[13] Those who live are said to be in the light; when they die they are commonly said to depart beneath the darkness. Now night is the time for sleep, and sleep is an image of death.[14] Thus, at night mortals are, in a way, dead, until the sun rises and arouses them all to life. The physical sun that we see with our bodily eyes never loses its light, whether it is visible or not; we experience night when the sun is removed from us by the interposition of the earth. Similarly, Christ never changes in himself, but rises in the minds of some men (and then there is daylight) but not in the minds of others (and then there is night). Just as the sun is said to set when it is hidden and to be born when it rises, – as Horace says, 'you are born both different and the same'[15] – so Christ's rising is his birth. He is always being born from the Father, like an eternal ray from the everlasting sun. For us, however, he rose in another way when the marvellous machine of this world was established. Again, he often rises in pious minds and sets for those who take a different course. His visible rising was when he came forth as man from the womb of the very chaste Virgin. For she was the mystical gate that looks to the east,[16] from which that unique sun arose, giving light to every man that enters into this world.

Let this suffice as a kind of preface, even if it is not entirely relevant. Now let us attend to our Pindar.[17]

> Quid est quod arctum circulum
>   Sol iam recurrens deserit?
> Christus ne terris nascitur,
>   Qui lucis auget tramitem?   (1–4)

> Why does the sun run back again
>   And leave its narrow course?
> Is Christ now born upon the earth
>   To spread the path of light?

All heavenly bodies are of spherical shape (regarded as the most perfect) and therefore have spherical motion; those closest to the poles are carried round in a narrower orbit. Although the sun's circuit at the winter solstice provides sixteen hours of daylight in some regions and eighteen in others, in our latitude there are only eight hours of day. Thus, he calls it the **'narrow course,'** not because the sun covers less distance but because some people see it for fewer hours, on account of the angle of the ecliptic. The phrase **'run back'** is apt, as though the sun were rushing eagerly to increase the length of the day because of the birth of the child.

> Heu quam fugacem gratiam
>   Festina volvebat dies,

Quam pene subductam facem
  Sensim recisa exstinxerat.   (5–8)

Alas, how fleeting was the grace
  Unrolled by hast'ning day!
The day, by slow degrees curtailed,
  Had almost quenched its torch.

Fugacem means 'fleeing,' **'fleeting,'** though etymology seems to suggest that it comes from *fugare* 'put to flight' rather than *fugere* 'flee.' His description of light as **'grace'** is pleasing, since night brings sadness but the joy of light is unsurpassed. By **'fleeting'** he means 'eager to depart.' There is also a pleasing emphasis in the verb **'unroll.'** 'By slow degrees curtailed': The sun rises or falls in the ecliptic by insensible degrees. The phrase *subducere facem* [literally, 'withdraw the torch'] is used figuratively, as is 'quench the daylight,' but it is also a pleasing piece of poetic imagery: a torch is carried round, [its flame] gradually decreasing until it is completely out. He exaggerates the hardship of the shortness of the day in order to emphasize the 'grace' of its lengthening.

Coelum nitescit laetius,
  Gratatur et gaudet humus.
Scandit gradatim denuo
  Iubar priores lineas.   (9–12)

More cheerfully the sky grows bright,
  The earth in pleasure basks.
Then by degrees the sun's bright ray
  Climbs past its former lines.

In a way the sky has a face: when it is covered with clouds we call it 'sad'; when it is clear we say that it is **'more cheerful'** – this is the meaning of the phrase **'grow bright.'** **'By degrees'**: Astronomers divide the signs through which the sun ascends and descends into 'degrees.' **'Lines'**: A metaphor from the race-track, where the starting-point is marked out by a line; in the same way, astronomers mark out the sky with imaginary lines through which the sun passes in such a way as not to return to us on the same line. By **'former'** he means 'original'; the word *prius* 'before' is sometimes used for *potius* (rather) and *melius* 'better.'

Emerge dulcis pusio
  Quem matris edit castitas,

Parens et expers conjugis,
   Mediator et duplex genus.   (13–16)

Come forth, O sweet and tender child,
   Whom virgin mother bears,
A parent but untouched by spouse,
   A mean, of double kind.

Now, as though eager for the light to rise, the poet uses apostrophe to invite the child to **'come forth'** from its hiding-place in the Virgin's body. **'Sweet'** is an epithet appropriate to sons, as in Horace's 'home and children sweet.'[18] *Pusio* is a diminutive of *puer* 'boy, child,' appropriate to coaxing. *Edit* **'bears'** is used for *parit* 'gives birth to.' *Matris castitas* **'the mother's chastity'** is a poetic way of saying 'the chaste mother.' In the general course of nature a woman cannot conceive or give birth without rupturing the small membrane that distinguishes a virgin from a non-virgin. The Son of God, however, slipped into the Virgin's sacrosanct womb through her ear,[19] without violating any part of her body; at his birth, however, he came out through the part of the body through which other women produce their young. It is not explicitly stated[20] in the Gospels that the birth was accomplished without the opening of the womb or the rupture of the hymen, without birth-pains or the dilation of the part of the body where the birth emerges, or without the usual afterbirths. Nevertheless, it is more likely that this was so, and, in my opinion, it is more pious to believe the traditional account of the most holy and learned Fathers.

The third and fourth lines fit somewhat awkwardly with the preceding couplet, but should be construed as follows. *Castitas* means virginity; she was a **'parent,'** that is a mother, in a non-figurative sense, but also a **'virgin mother,'** that is a mother but **'untouched by spouse.'** The last line, 'A mean, of double kind' must be taken with the first line 'Come forth, O sweet and tender child.' The word *mediator* **'mean'** is not found in Latin writers, but we use it to translate the Greek word μεσίτης, from μεσεῖν, used by the apostles but unknown in Latin. Prudentius combines two marvels in each person: in the mother, fecundity joined with chastity; in the boy, divine and human natures linked by the same hypostatic union. Hence the phrase **'of double kind.'** It was fitting that the one who was to reconcile mankind to God should have a share in both natures, for an intercessor should be familiar with both sides.

Ex ore quamlibet patris
   Sis ortus, et verbo editus:

Tamen paterno in pectore
  Sophia callebas prius. (17–20)

Though from the Father's mouth you sprang
  And by the Word came forth,
Yet first within your Father's breast
  As Wisdom you were wise.

Isaiah says of Christ: 'Who will tell his generation?'[21] apparently referring not only to his divine birth but also to his human descent. Christ's nativity is fourfold. According to the nativity inconceivable to man, he is constantly and endlessly being born from the Father and always has been born, God from God,[22] omnipotent from omnipotent. For the Son of God is to the Father what awareness, or the silent thought of the mind, is to man; he is the eternal thought of an eternal mind. Mind produces thought, and thought, once conceived internally, is a kind of[23] conversation of the mind,[24] by which man speaks to himself. This simile somehow outlines for us that nativity which had no beginning and will have no end: the Son is born from the Father in such a way that the Father's substance is not diminished at all, and the Father produces the Son without being anterior to the Son. However, when the world was founded by the Son, the Father, as it were, spoke the Word and in a kind of way gave birth to the Word for a second time, thus somehow making visible to us that which was invisible. For in created things we can see the wonderful Wisdom of God, the Wisdom which is the Son of God and the Word of God.

'The Father's mouth': God does not have a mouth or any other human limb in the way that anthropomorphists once imagined, basing their belief on the frequent scriptural references to God's limbs – 'Turn not your face from me,'[25] 'Hear my cry with your ears,'[26] 'Did not your hand make all these things?'[27] 'I have found a man according to my heart,'[28] 'The eyes of the Lord are upon the just,'[29] 'He made strength in his arm,'[30] 'The heaven is my seat and the earth a footstool for my feet'[31] – but since the subject here is the Word which is the Son of God, he is said to be 'born' in so far as he is a son, and to be 'set forth' in so far as he is the Word. He is 'born from the heart' and 'set forth from the mouth,' in that the 'heart' and the 'mouth' of God are simply God in his functions of producing and setting forth.

***Quamlibet* 'Though':** Valla correctly teaches that *quamquam* and *quamvis* are used as conjunctions to introduce a sentence of two parts,[32] for example, 'Although (*quamquam*) you are a foreigner, I love you as a Christian,' and 'Although (*quamvis*) you are rich, you don't for that reason have any power over me.' *Quamlibet*, however, operates differently. It does not have its own verb and is simply subjoined to the sentence, but in such a way that the sentence can be analysed in two parts, for example, 'Though rich (*quamlibet divitem*), you're not in his opinion worth a fig.' One could also say *quamvis divitem*, as *quamvis* can be used in either way. Prudentius seems to have missed Valla's note! The usage may perhaps be found elsewhere in approved authors; I have certainly found it in Augustine.

'**And by the Word came forth**': This must not be interpreted as 'the Word was brought forth by the Word,' as though there were two words, one uttering, the other being uttered, as some heretics have imagined; the word **verbum** is used for 'utterance.' For just as a feeling conceived in the mind, at first called διάνοια 'thought,' becomes λόγος 'word' when uttered, so the speech of God was, before the founding of the world, wisdom, always being born from the Father's heart and never leaving it. When this was expressed through the founding of the world, it began, for us, to be speech, through which God spoke to us.

> Tamen paterno in pectore
>   Sophia callebas prius.   (19–20)

Yet first within your Father's breast
  As Wisdom you were wise.

In **sophia** '**wisdom**' the second syllable is long, in accordance with the Greek accentuation, which Prudentius follows elsewhere, shortening the *o* in *idola* and the *i* in *paraclitus*. Metre requires the pronunciation of the double *l* in **callebas** '**were wise.**'

Callebas '**were wise**' is the equivalent of *sapiebas*. The past tense is used not because wisdom precedes nativity in the Son of God, but because before the founding of the world the Word of God lay hidden in the Father's heart as the Father's '**Wisdom.**' In this passage, either Prudentius omits the generation which has no beginning – though he mentions it elsewhere, in his trochaic hymn 'Born from the Father's heart, before the world began,'[33] – or[34] alternatively, the first half of the stanza, beginning at '**you sprang,**' refers to that first continuous birth, and the following phrase, '**And by the Word came forth,**' refers to the founding of the world, to which the adverb '**first**' applies.

> Quae promta coelum, condidit
>   Noctem diemque et caetera.
> Virtute verbi effecta sunt
>   Haec cuncta: nam verbum Deus.   (21–4)

Put forth, this wisdom founded all,
  The sky, the night, the day;
By power of the Word all things
  Were made, for Word is God.

Promta **'put forth'** is the same as *prolata* or *depromta*; you know the text 'Let there be light; and the light was made.'[35] God **'founded'** the world by means of the Word, not in the sense of a tool (as a smith uses an axe for building) – the world was founded by the Son together with the Father. Authority is attributed to the Father, since it is from the Father that the Son and the Holy Spirit come. **'By power of the Word'**: As St Paul says to the Hebrews, 'through which he made the ages.'[36] The word of kings is powerful, but the Word of God is almighty. It is not, therefore, surprising if the Word made the world, for this Word flows from God in such a way as to be God himself. It is expressed from the mouth of the Father without leaving the Father's heart – for in the act of creating the divine nature is not diminished or increased: it is, in short, immutable. Prudentius teaches this in the next stanza.

Sed ordinatis seculis,
  Rerumque digesto statu,
Fundator ipse et artifex
  Permansit in patris sinu.   (25–8)

But when the worlds were organized,
  The state of things arranged,
The founder and artificer
  Stayed in his Father's breast.

Holy Writ frequently uses *secula* **'worlds,'** 'ages' to mean whatever is established in time, and the phrase *ante secula* 'before the ages' to refer to the time before the creation of the world. **'Organized'**: This is an allusion to Chaos, in which all the elements of things were mixed up, as described by Ovid:[37] 'A rude and unformed mass, nothing but sluggish weight, the warring seeds of things not properly put together. All heaped together in the same place.' Similarly in Genesis, light is divided from darkness, waters are divided from waters, the waters are set apart, and dry land emerges; the species of things that grow from the earth and the shapes of living things are distinguished; each thing is assigned its proper function. This is what Prudentius means by **'the state of things arranged.'**

  'Founder and artificer': A 'founder' begins a work, an 'artificer' completes it and runs it, as in Proverbs 8: 'When he suspended the foundations of the earth, I [Wisdom] was with him, arranging everything.'[38] The world had its beginning through the Son; it was arranged by the Son, it is guided by him, it was restored by him, and it will be concluded by him.

Ipse 'The' [in line 27] is the equivalent of *idem* 'the same.' **Digesto** 'arranged' is the equivalent of *distributo*. *Digerere* is not 'concoct' [literally 'cook together,' compare 'digest'] but **'arrange'** everything in its proper place. **Sinum** [literally 'bosom'] is used for 'heart' or **'breast,'** as the bosom is where the heart is located, as in the phrases 'rejoice in one's bosom,' 'pour forth into the bosom.'

> *Donec rotata annalium*
> > *Transvolverentur millia,*
> *Atque ipse peccantem diu*
> > *Dignatus orbem viseret.*   (29–32)

> Till many thousand years were gone,
> > Revolved and turned around,
> When God himself would deign to see
> > The world long steeped in sin.

The first manifestation of Wisdom founded and arranged the world before it came into being. At its second coming it restored the fallen world, namely man, for whose sake everything had been created. The years **'revolved'** because it is by the revolution of celestial spheres that days, months, years, and ages are distinguished. **'Many thousand'**: From the creation of the world to the time of Christ more than 5,199 years are reckoned.[39] **'When God ... in sin'**: Since it was in vain that the law had been given through Moses and that so many prophets had been sent, the Son of God was made man and came in person, as he says in Psalm 39: 'You have not sought a burnt offering even for sin. Then I said, behold, I come,'[40] and again in Isaiah: 'I myself who spoke, behold, I am here.'[41]

> *Nam caeca vis mortalium*
> > *Venerans inanes naenias,*
> *Vel aera vel saxa algida*
> > *Vel ligna credebat Deum.*   (33–6)

> For mortals' blind unseeing mass,
> > Revering empty rites,
> Believed that bronze or ice-cold stones
> > Or wooden logs were God.

By *vis* **'mass,** force' he means 'the multitude,' for not everyone worshipped images. Alternatively, he uses the word *vis* to distinguish human power from God's grace. Once we had fallen through Adam's sin, we did nothing but sin, always declining from bad to worse. By **'empty rites'** he refers to the images that were credited by the ancients with divine mentality, although, despite their human masks, they lacked even human mind. For although we use the word *naenia* to mean any kind of trivial chattering, it is properly a funereal chant, sung vainly to the dead; it is also used to mean 'epitaph.' The worship of images arose from the custom of erecting statues to parents at their death, or to kings or to other human beings who had deserved well of mankind, and then bestowing divine honours on them. In fact at Rome it was the solemn practice to translate dead emperors into gods.[42]

> *Haec dum sequuntur perfidi*
>   *Praedonis in ius venerant:*
> *Et mancipatam fumido*
>   *Vitam barathro immerserant.*   (37–40)

In these beliefs the traitors fell
  Beneath the bandit's sway;
Their life they gave to slavery,
  Submerged in smoky hell.

The Lord of all things is Christ. The devil is a tyrant and a **'bandit,'** who claimed for himself what was not his. He first seduced man to sin; by sin he ruled, and by sin death was introduced into the world.[43] Thus, whoever sins enslaves himself to sin, and whoever is prone to sin passes into the power and jurisdiction of Satan. By this indenture, then, the whole world was vulnerable to the devil's power. They are called **'traitors'** because they defected from God, their king and founder, and turned to dumb images. **'Their life ... hell':** This shows, as I have said, that death invaded the world through sin. The kingdom of God exists through justice, and through justice there is life; by sin the devil is tyrant, and by sin there is death. *Barathron* **'hell'** is a Greek word, meaning a deep, dark place where criminals are imprisoned, or whirlpools that suck up rivers, or oceans. It can be interpreted either as hell, to which even the souls of the pious used to depart at that time, or as eternal death.

> *Stragem sed istam non tulit*
>   *Christus cadentum gentium,*
> *Impune ne forsan sui*
>   *Patris periret fabrica.*   (41–4)

But this defeat of falling men
  Was not allowed by Christ,
For fear his Father's handiwork
  Should perish by default.

Stragem 'defeat' is a military term, from *sterno* 'lay low.' The tyranny of Satan spread far and wide, and he ruled, as it were, with impunity, dragging whole nations down to hell. **'By default':** That is, without challenge or opposition. The world would indeed have been created in vain, if man, for whose sake it was created, perished. Prudentius discloses the reason for God's becoming man.

> *Mortale corpus induit*
>   *Ut excitato corpore*
> *Mortis catenam frangeret,*
>   *Hominemque portaret patri.*   (45–8)

He clothed himself in mortal form
  To rise up from the grave
And break the binding chain of death
  And bring man back to God.

God's design is inscrutable – that is, his motive for allowing man to slide into sin in this way and then for wanting to free him from sin. It was, however, appropriate that man should be redeemed by man, and that death should be removed by death. Christ's death was a factor of his humanity, his resurrection of his divinity. By his death sin was abolished; by his resurrection we were given hope of immortality. **'To bring man back to God':** This alludes to two parables in the Gospels. The first is that of the lost sheep that the shepherd brought back on his shoulders,[44] for Christ, afflicted by our sins, beaten and dying, placed us on his shoulders and restored us to the Father. The second is the parable of the Samaritan, who carried the wounded man on his ass;[45] the ass represents the human form that Christ assumed.

> *Hic ille natalis dies,*
>   *Quo te creator arduus*
> *Animavit et limo induit,*
>   *Sermone carnem glutinans.*   (49–52)

Now is that birthday, when the Lord
  Creator, God on high,

Breathed life into your clay-clad frame,
 Compacting flesh with Word.

Hic ille: There is emphasis on **'that'** birthday because there were, as it were, other birthdays; this particular birthday was the one that joined us to the Father. Prudentius addresses the Son by apostrophe. **'Creator':** The Wisdom of God is said to be 'created' because it was begotten, but here 'creator' could refer to God as creator of the world. **'Breathed life':** Prudentius observes, in opposition to the heretics,[46] that Christ's hypostatic nature consists of three natures: divinity, a human soul, and a mortal body (here called **'clay,'** because our forefather Adam was made of clay, into which God breathed the breath of life). **'Compacting flesh with Word':** By 'Word' he means the Son of God; the term is appropriate to him in accordance with his divine nature. The soul of Christ is a kind of glue between his mortal body and his divine nature.

> *Sentisne virgo nobilis*
> *Matura per fastidia*
> *Pudoris intactum decus*
> *Honore partus crescere?*   (53–6)

O noble maiden, do you feel –
 Despite your timely chore –
Your virgin chastity enhanced
 By honour of the birth?

Again he redirects his address, this time from the Son to the pregnant Virgin. Also, the use of a question heightens the emotional effect. She is **'noble'** because she alone, a virgin, gave birth, and it was God that she bore – though her nobility was also based on a fleshly link, in that she traced her descent from the line of David. ***Matura per fastidia***: By **matura** he means **'timely'**; *fastidium* **'chore'** seems to be derived from *fastus* 'pride' and *taedium* 'boredom.' Whenever *fastidium* refers to the spirit it implies a fault [compare 'tedium'], but Virgil[47] says of a pregnant woman, *Matri longa decem tulerint fastidia menses* 'Ten months brought for the mother long *fastidia.*'

There is no doubt that Mary's womb was swollen; what is uncertain is whether she also felt the weariness of labour – probably not, just as she felt no birth-pains. The 'old Eves' give birth in pain, since they conceive in lustful yearning. The new Eve felt no titillation of desire at the conception, and is therefore rightly believed to have suffered no difficulty in either gestation or birth. **'Your virgin chastity':** Even among pagans virginity has been especially honoured, as it is the human body's special glory and flower. On the other hand, sterility was interpreted as a rebuke for married couples,[48] and by the same token it was a husband's glory to produce an offspring like himself. Mary alone won praise on both accounts, amongst virgins for her chastity, and amongst the married for her fecundity. Many women may have produced more numerously, but none more blessedly. In other women the honour of maternity succeeds that of virginity, just as the fruit succeeds the flower; in Mary the grace of virginity was not harmed but was increased by the excellence of the birth.

> O quanta rerum gaudia
>   Alvus pudicae continet,
> Ex qua novellum seculum
>   Procedit, et lux aurea.   (57–60)

How great the universal joys
  The Virgin's womb contains,
From whom comes forth an era new
  And shines a golden dawn!

Many people think that the prophecy of the Cumaean Sibyl, applied by Virgil to a different purpose in the *Eclogues*, was about Christ. From the fables of poets we learn that under Saturn there was a golden age, when human morals were uncorrupted; this was followed by the silver age, when morals had deteriorated considerably; after that came the iron age, when everything was so corrupt that there were no longer even any traces of the old virtues left.[49] The birth of Jesus, however, renewed everything and brought us back the golden age. These are Virgil's words, based on the Sibyl's decree: 'A mighty line of ages comes anew, / The Virgin now comes back and Saturn's reign, / From heav'n above there comes a lineage new.'[50]

After **'joys'** Prudentius has added the word *rerum* **'universal'** [literally 'of things'] to indicate merriment, as if even the dumb and lifeless things felt pleasure at the birth of Christ. **'An era new':** The old Adam taught his descendants to sin, but the new Adam, Jesus Christ, taught innocence and obedience. St Paul tells us to 'put off the old man,' that is wicked desires, and to 'put on the new,'[51] that is the Lamb, which speaks in Revelations: 'Behold, I will make all things new.'[52] Similarly, it says in Isaiah: 'Father of the future age, prince of peace. But there is no peace for the wicked, saith the Lord.'[53] **'A golden dawn':** This is an allusion to the golden age, though the word 'golden' is in any case appropriate to the sun's brightness: the moon has light, but not of gold; the best of lights he calls 'golden.'

Vagitus ille exordium
  Vernantis orbis protulit
Nam tunc renatus sordidum
  Mundus veternum depulit.   (61–4)

The baby's wails proclaimed the birth
  Of springtime for the world,
For then reborn the world shook off
  Its squalid lassitude.

Vagitus 'wails' is onomatopoeic: a male child, on emerging from its mother's womb, usually utters the first syllable of this word, whereas girls, with their thinner voice, exclaim *Ve*, scarcely an auspicious beginning to a life liable to so many ills.[54] See Pliny, book 7, chapter 1.[55] In Christ, however, the wails heralded the rebirth of the world, for all those who are baptized into Christ are reborn through him, and, setting aside their 'oldness,' that is their former wickedness, are, as it were, born again as infants and long for the soul's milk.[56] **'Springtime for the world':** The year also has its old age: the end of autumn, being dry and cold, corresponds to decrepit senility. Winter cherishes within its womb the moist warm foetus, which the spring produces and brings to adolescence; summer is the adult period of the year. Thus, he writes of the 'springtime for the world,' when it is being reborn. In those parts of the world where Christ was born, however, the winter is much shorter than it is here: in Rome, for example, the earth begins its rejuvenation after 16 January. **'For then reborn':** Although the world itself had not yet been reborn (as Christ had not yet suffered), the one had been born through whom we were all to be reborn. **Veternus 'lassitude'** is a disease common to the old; it induces sleepiness and thirst. Terence[57] describes the senile and feeble eunuch as 'lassitudinous' (*veternosum*). He adds the word **'squalid'** to contrast with the bloom of youth; it is also an allusion to winter, when everything is squalid and sluggish; poets also call winter 'lazy,' because farmers stop work then.

Sparsisse tellurem reor
  Rus omne densis floribus,
Ipsasque arenas syrtium
  Fragrasse nardo et nectare.   (65–8)

The earth, I think, spread flowers thick
  On all the countryside.
The desert's barren rocks smelled sweet
  With nectar and with nard.

The general rejoicing at Christ's birth is not a matter of fable. His conception was heralded by the angel's gentle words, at his birth heavenly music was heard, the shepherds were shown a sudden light, great joy was proclaimed, and the Magi came hurrying at the sign of the shining star. Nevertheless, Prudentius' words here should be interpreted allegorically, like those written by Isaiah: 'The wolf shall dwell with the lamb, and the leopard shall lie down with the kid, and the calf and the lion and the sheep shall stay together. The calf and the bear shall feed together, and their young ones shall rest, and the lion shall eat straw like an ox. And the child shall delight at the breast, at the entry to the asp's den, and the weaned child shall put his hand in at the cave of the serpent.'[58] Similarly, the prophet Joel says: 'The mountain shall drip sweetness and the hills shall flow with milk, and through all the rivers of Juda the waters shall flow, etc,'[59] and Amos says: 'And the mountains shall drip sweetness and all the hills shall be cultivated.'[60] These words are in appearance quite like those of Virgil in the Fourth Eclogue: 'For you, child, the untended earth will offer the first gifts, the straying ivy and rustic nard, a bunch of lilies mixed with sweet bear's-foot. The goats will come home bearing udders swollen with milk, and the cattle will not fear the mighty lions. The very cradle will put forth cheerful flowers for you. The serpent is dead, and the treacherous poisonous herb will perish; everywhere the fragrant balsam of Assyria will bloom,' and the rest of the Sibyl's prophecy as he relates it.[61] Certainly Prudentius is alluding to these words. By **'countryside'** he means uncivilized men who do not blossom with virtues. By **'rocks'** he refers to barbarian nations, which were so cruel and savage, it seemed, that no teaching could teach them gentleness; by Christ they were everywhere made into 'a sweet smell for God,' as St Paul says,[62] and surpass nectar and incense by the fragrance of their piety.

> *Te cuncta nascentem puer*
> *Sensere dura ac barbara.*
> *Victusque saxorum rigor*
> *Obduxit herbam cotibus.*   (69–72)

> Child, all things harsh and barbarous
> Were conscious of your birth:
> The hardness of the rocks gave way
> And covered flints with grass.

The allegory is clear: he is thinking of the Scythians,[63] Goths, and Irish, who were at one time more like stones and rocks than men. This gave rise to the old stories of Amphion, who moved rocks by the sound of his lyre, and of Orpheus, whose cithara caused oak-trees to follow him.[64] Perhaps this (*saxum* 'rock') is the origin of the name of the Saxons.[65] No nation was so removed from humanity or so brutish and wild that it was not softened and tamed by the yoke of Christ: for this was what had been promised through the prophet Hosea,[66] that from a non-people would come the people of God, and in St Paul's words, 'those things that are not would be called as though they were.'[67]

'**Hardness of the rocks':** The word *rigidum* 'hard' applies to something that can be more easily broken than bent; this is why we speak of the 'hardness of rocks' and the 'hardness of winter,' since winter's frost makes everything breakable. There were once people so savage that they could not be tamed by laws or arms or the teachings of the Greeks – only Christ made men out of flints. Certainly this is the meaning of the Lord's threat to the Jews, that God had the power to raise the sons of Abraham from the stones, a threat which he fulfilled.[68] *Obduxit* '**covered':** This is one of those verbs that we can use in two ways with the same meaning, like 'sprinkle' (*adspergo*), for example, 'sprinkle a stain on' or 'sprinkle with a stain,' or 'dress' (*induo*), for example, 'dressed the tunic on him' or 'dressed him in a tunic.' Thus, 'covered grass over the flints' is the same as '**covered flints with grass.'** *Cotibus* '**flints'** is the equivalent of *cautibus*; compare *plostrum* / *plaustrum* 'cart'; Prudentius many have spelled it *cautibus*. Virgil derives a simile for a hard implacable mind from the same word: '... than if the hard flint or Marpesan rock stood in her place.'[69]

> *Iam mella de scopulis fluunt,*
> *Iam stillat ilex arido*
> *Sudans amomum stipite,*
> *Iam sunt myricis balsama.*   (73–6)

> Now honey flows forth from the rocks;
> Now from its arid trunk
> The oak exudes a sweaty nard;
> Now tamarisks yield balm.

This is an expansion of Virgil's 'and the hard oaks will exude honeydew';[70] rocks are usually moistened by the splashing of salt sea-water. The *ilex* '**oak'** is an acorn-bearing tree; poets often use one oak-tree species for another. The '**nard,'** like the wild grape, is both a shrub and the name of its fruit; it is called '**sweaty'** since an ointment is produced from nard in the same way that incense and gums are 'sweated' from their trees. This process is common to many spices: hence, there is a kind of incense known by the Greeks as *stacte* or *stilla* 'drip.' '**Now tamarisks yield balm**': The 'tamarisk' is a kind of low-growing shrub mentioned by Virgil in the Sibyl's prophecy, 'Not all take joy in shrubs or lowly tamarisks,'[71] but among all ointments pride of place goes to 'balm'; see Pliny, book 12.[72]

> *O sancta praesepis tui*
> *Aeterne rex cunabula*
> *Populisque per seclum sacra*
> *Mutis et ipsis credita.*   (77–80)

> Eternal king, how holy is
> Your crib within the stall,
> To people sacred for all time,
> By creatures dumb believed.

He combines here two totally different notions. What is humbler than an animal's '**stall**' or a '**crib**'? Yet what is more sublime than the name '**eternal king**'? In this way, he who summoned up the world planned to produce sublimity from what was humble and despised, and, conversely, to overthrow what was exalted. '**To people sacred for all time**': In the past not all temples were uniformly honoured by all people: each race had its own gods. Then also, times produced variation in religion: Saturn gave way to Jupiter.[73] This cradle which gave us the eternal king, however, is to be honoured by all nations of the world for all time. The worship of an eternal king is itself eternal; the universal king is rightly honoured universally. '**By creatures dumb believed**': From ancient times a picture has come down to us of an ox and an ass at Jesus' manger. This is not, however, expressly stated in the Bible; the event appears to have been inferred from the prophecy of Isaiah, which states: 'The ox knows its owner and the ass knows the manger of its lord, but the people of Israel does not know me, and my people has not understood me.'[74] Prudentius certainly has this in mind: the ox and the ass did not believe anything, but barbarian people, who served demons and their own desire and who lived like beasts, believed in Christ, whereas even today the people of Israel rebel against Christ.

> *Adorat haec brutum pecus*
> *Indocta turba scilicet.*
> *Vis cuius in pastu sita est,*
> *Adorat excors natio.*   (81–4)

Brute beasts pay homage at the crib,
  That is, the untaught crowd;
They worship here, that heartless tribe,
  Whose might resides in food.

The word **'crowd'** is used contemptuously, in contrast with Israel, God's own special chosen people. They were **'untaught'** because they were ignorant of the most important thing of all, God, whereas the Jews alone, through the law, knew the one God. This is why Christ sat on an ass,[75] which prefigured the gentiles. They are called **'brute beasts'** because they had no understanding, and **'untaught'** because of their ignorance of the law. Their **'might resides in food'** because of their lust and desire, which they obeyed like brutish animals who were made by nature 'prone and obedient to their stomach.'[76] They were **'heartless'** because they did not have what David desires when he says, 'Create in me a pure thought, O Lord';[77] this is why sinners are told to 'return to the heart.'

> Sed cum fideli spiritu
>   Concurrat ad praesepia
> Pagana gens et quadrupes
>   Sapiatque quod brutum fuit,
> Negat patrum prosapia
>   Perosa praesentem Deum
> Credas venenis ebriam
>   Furiisve lymphatam rapi.   (85–92)

But though the pagans and the beasts
  With spirit full of faith
Together to the manger run,
  Though what was dumb learns sense,
The heirs of patriarchs deny
  And hate the present God.
You'd think them drunk on poisoned draughts,
  By Furies' rage bedrenched.

In elegiac couplets the sentence is usually completed by the pentameter; similarly, in iambic dimeters it is completed by the fourth line. The rule is not, however, invariable: here the syntax is left incomplete, but in such a way that the first four lines complement the main clause. The sense is this: although the shepherds flock together at Jesus' cradle, together with the Magi, the Scythians, Arabs, and Indians, a pagan race that brought nothing but simple faith, as it had no law or religion or good deeds (by **'pagan'** he means 'rustic,' estranged from the sacred, and by **'beasts'** he implies the brutish desires which they had previously obeyed), nevertheless the Jews, from whose race Christ came, deny and hate his presence, although they had awaited him for so many ages, crying, 'Come, O Lord, and free us; come, do not delay; release the sins of your people Israel!'[78]

'You'd think,' that is 'you could believe,' the potential use of the subjunctive. **'Poisoned draughts,'** that is, madness-inducing drugs. **'Bedrenched'** (lymphatam) is what fanatics are said to be; they are excited by a madness induced by some kind of spirit. *Lympha* means 'water.' It was once believed that if anyone saw a nymph in a fountain he was driven mad by the Furies.[79] Also, there are springs whose taste produces madness.

> *Quid prona per scelus ruis?*
> *Agnosce, si quidquam tibi*
> *Mentis resedit integrae,*
> *Ducem tuorum principum.*   (93–6)

Why do you headlong rush in sin?
  Accept – if of your minds
There still remains a healthy part –
  The leader of your chiefs.

This is an apostrophe to the Jews. The word **'accept'** means to recognize and embrace that which we already know. The prophets and typological figures of the Old Testament had depicted Christ; such a one as was promised has now arrived, and yet the Jews are unwilling to accept him. *Resedit* **'remains,'** that is, 'is left'; *integrae* [literally 'whole'], that is, **'healthy.'** *Ducem tuorum principum* **'The leader of your chiefs':** Prudentius may have written *principem*, meaning that the 'leader' was the first and foremost 'chief' [thus: 'accept the leader as the chief of your chiefs']. Moses, Jesus Nave, and David were 'chiefs,' but Christ was the chief of them all. He led Moses out of Egypt and escorted him through the desert, accompanied by a rock, and as St Paul says, 'the rock was Christ.'[80] He breathed on Samuel and the prophets, and he inspired David. Although the word 'Christ' [literally 'anointed'] refers to his human nature, nevertheless, because of the uniqueness of the hypostatic union, what is peculiar to divine nature is also predicated of him as a man, and vice versa.

> *Hunc quem latebra et obstetrix*
> *Virgoque foeta et cunulae,*

Et imbecilla infantia
  Regem dederunt gentibus,
Peccator intueberis
  Celsum coruscis nubibus
Deiectus ipse, et irritis
  Plangens reatum mentibus.   (97–104)

Him, whom a hiding-place, a nurse,
  A pregnant maid, a crib,
And weak and feeble infancy
  Produced as king for man,
O sinner, you will yet behold
  On high with flashing clouds,
Yourself downcast, with useless tears,[81]
  Lamenting your misdeeds.

For a second time the sentence continues after the fourth line. Prudentius depicts two advents of Jesus, the first when he came humbly as the saviour of all mankind, the second when he will come sublimely, as judge of the living and the dead. Those who here despised him for his humility will there be in awe of his sublimity. ***Hunc* 'Him':** That is, *eundem* 'the same,' as he will come as the same person, in visible form. **'Hiding-place':** He was born in an obscure little town, in the humblest quarters of an inn. An ***obstetrix* 'nurse'** [literally 'midwife'] is a despised kind of woman. **'A pregnant maid'** is an event beyond belief; a ***cunula* 'crib'** is a manger. **'Weak and feeble infancy'** is the most despised period of life of all. Nevertheless, all these despised and rejected things produced a **'king for man'**: it was God's plan that the eternal kingdom should arise from such humble beginnings.

    You [a Jew] are called a **'sinner'** because you would not be a believer. **'You will ... behold':** They will look on him whom they pierced.[82] At his resurrection he showed himself only to his disciples; on the last day he will show himself to everyone. **'On high with flashing clouds':** This is what he himself promised in the gospel: 'Henceforth you will see the Son of Man coming in clouds with the majesty of the Father.'[83] **'Flashing':** Just as lightning bursts in one part of the sky and scatters in every direction, so God will be revealed in a flash. **'Yourself downcast':** On that day roles will be reversed: he and his companions, with whom on earth he was the lowest of the low, will be on high, and those who here seemed to be exalted will be cast down lowest. **'With useless tears':** Repentance will then be too late: each will reap as he has sowed.

Cum vasta signum buccina
  Terris cremandis miserit,
Et scissus axis cardinem
  Mundi ruentis solverit,
Insignis ipse et praeminens
  Meritis rependet congrua,
His lucis usum perpetis,
  Illis gehennam et tartarum.   (105–12)

When trumpet vast gives forth its sound
  For earth to be consumed,
And shattered axis breaks the hinge
  That held the falling world,
In glory he, preeminent,
  Will pay to each his due –
To these eternal light to see,
  To those the fires of hell.

'**Trumpet vast**' is a splendid phrase, as there is nowhere that it will not be heard. As St Paul says, 'For the trumpet shall sound.'[84] '**For earth to be consumed**': Just as the world was once purified by flood, so it will then be purified by fire. The pagan poets had a vision of something like this, from the prophecies of the Sibyl, to which Lactantius has many references, but the same account is given by Peter, Second Epistle, chapter 3: 'The heavens which are now, and the earth, have been set aside by the same word, reserved for fire on the day of the judgment and destruction of the wicked,' and, a little later: 'The day of the Lord will come like a thief: the heavens will pass in a mighty rush, and the elements will be dissolved in heat; the earth and all its works that are on it will be burned up, etc'[85] – I need do no more than point out the passage to which the poet has alluded. '**The shattered axis**': Each heavenly body's orbit revolves round its own pole, just as the whole universe rotates on its axis.

Iudaea tunc fulmen crucis
  Experta qui sit senties,
Quem, te furoris praesule,
  Mors hausit, et mors reddidit.   (113–16)

You Jews will feel the cross's blast
  And find out who it is
Whom Death, led by your insane rage,
  First took, and then set free.

I have restored this stanza, which was corrupted by an ignoramus: it originally had *quae* for *qui* and *quae* for *quem*. This is the meaning: O unbelieving nation of Jews, who were unwilling to recognize Christ at his first coming, but called out 'Crucify, crucify, we have no king but Caesar,'[86] when you see the triumphant sign of the cross on high, blinding the eyes of the wicked like a thunderflash, then you will recognize who and what that man is, long despised and treated with scorn, whom Death swallowed up, **'led by your insane rage'** – that is, when you were the author of his death and drove Pilate against his will to the wicked deed – and whom Death **'set free,'** just as the whale swallowed Jonah and spewed him up again on the third day.

A SHORT COMMENTARY
ON PRUDENTIUS' HYMN
ON JESUS' EPIPHANY

Christ, who came to save everyone, caught each nation by means of the things in which they took pleasure and in which they trusted. He enticed the Jews by miracles; the Magi were enthusiastic astrologers, and so he attracted them by the sign of the star that shone with its own peculiar light. To the Greeks he sent Paul, as he was an able orator and well suited to take issue with philosophers. He came in humble form in order to bring us to the love of heavenly things; he ascended into heaven so that after being reawakened by him to the new life we would no longer be bound by a love of humble things but would give our attention to following where our chief had led the way. And so,

> Quicumque Christum quaeritis,
>   Oculos in altum tollite
> Illis licebit visere
>   Signum perennis gloriae.   (1–4)

> Whoever of you seeks for Christ,
>   Raise up your eyes on high:
> They'll[1] be allowed to see a sign
>   Of glory without end.

For the Magi the star was a guide to Christ, but for us it represents him. In a column of cloud and fire he led the way and brought the sons of Israel out of Egypt; for us he was a guiding light, calling us back from the darkness of sin and opening our way to the homeland of eternal light. He came down to us to lead us to heaven. If the Magi had not looked upwards, they would not have seen the star; if we do not raise the eyes of our hearts to heaven, we shall not find Christ. Those who scour the earth for veins of gold or silver, those whose attention is fixed on their desks or their dinner-plates, or those who pile up estates on estates do not see this star, as their eyes are glued to the ground. **Visere 'see'** properly means 'go to see,' but is sometimes used simply for *videre* 'see.' **'A sign of glory without end'**: Only the glory of Jesus is everlasting; otherwise, 'all flesh is grass, and all its glory is like the flower of the grass;'[2] therefore, 'let him who glories glory in the Lord.'[3] The star was

a sign of the one who is the light of the world.[4] A star is a shining body, so
Christ put on human flesh in order to become visible to us.

> Haec stella, quae solis rotam
> > Vincit decore et lumine,
> Venisse terris nuntiat
> > Cum carne terrestri Deum.   (5–8)

> This star whose beauty and whose light
> > Outshines the solar orb
> Proclaims that God has come to earth
> > In earthly flesh enclosed.

Here Prudentius explains his use of the word 'sign.' **'Whose beauty ... solar
orb':** It is unlikely that the star was bigger than the sun, but it surpassed it in
brilliance. By its light the sun blinds and dazzles those who look at it, but
Christ tempered the light of his divinity (which was beyond human
comprehension) by clothing it in the familiar form of a human body, so that
we could look at it. Therefore Prudentius adds the words **'God ... in earthly
flesh enclosed.'** For since God saw that men could only love what they could
see, he made himself visible to us so that he could be loved, at least in this
way. As he wanted men to have complete trust in men, he gave them one
man, so that when they had lost faith in other men they would transfer all
their trust to this one man who would never let anyone down, since he was
also God.

> Non illa servit noctibus
> > Secuta lunam menstruam,
> Sed sola coelum possidens
> > Cursum dierum temperat.   (9–12)

> This star's no servant of the nights,
> > The monthly moon's esquire;
> Alone it rules the skies and guides
> > The circuit of the days.

At the beginning of the world the sun was set up to rule over the day, but the
moon was to provide some comfort of light in the darkness of night – not
because the moon does not sometimes shine by day, but then it is obscured
by the brightness of the sun, like the other stars. The latter do not follow the

moon, but shine even when the moon is shining. In fact they are bigger than the moon; they seem smaller because of their greater distance from the position of an observer, as the moon's orbit is closest to the earth. He calls the moon **'monthly'** because it completes its course in the ecliptic within thirty days; the sun completes it in a year, and some others are even slower. The moon's light is borrowed from the sun: when it is closest to it, it appears non-existent; as it gradually moves away from the sun its brightness increases, until it is in complete opposition to it and shines with its full circle; later, as it approaches the sun, it wanes. In mystical writings the moon typifies human affairs, in which there is much darkness and no stability: 'The fool,' says the wise man, 'changes like the moon.'[5] The sun, however, stands for Christ, who is the Wisdom of the Father, and not subject to any changes or alternation. The suffix -ly in 'month-ly' (*menstruum*) is like that in year-ly or dai-ly (*annuum, diurnum*).

'Alone it rules the skies': The star appeared on its own. By **'skies'** (*coelum*) he means the air, as it is not believed that the star was one of the fixed stars or of those called 'wanderers' [planets] or that it was fixed in any sphere: it was newly created in order that its path through the air would lead the Magi to that eternal star Jesus Christ; Prudentius' words are certainly appropriate to Christ. **'The circuit of the days'**: Historically, the star did not shine continually before the Magi but only when it was needed; allegorically, Christ is the star which alone possesses heaven, the leader and author of all divine truth. He is the 'day of souls' which never sets. Balaam made this prophecy on the subject: 'A star will arise from Jacob.'[6]

> *Arctoa quamvis sidera*
> * In se retortis motibus*
> *Obire nolint, attamen*
> * Plerumque sub nimbis latent.*   (13–16)

> Although the northern arctic stars
>   Turn back upon themselves
> And never set, their normal course
>   Is hidden by the clouds.

Within the coils of the Serpent there are two stars called by the Greeks 'Arctoi,' that is, 'She-bears'; they are so close to the north pole (which is therefore known as the 'arctic') that we never see them set. Virgil refers to them in the *Georgics*: 'The Arctoi, fearing a wetting in the waters of the ocean,'[7] and Ovid writes: 'The Greater and the Lesser Bear, one rules the Greeks, the other the ships of Sidonia, and both stay dry.'[8] Ovid calls them 'dry' because they are not submerged – not that any star is ever really submerged, but when they set they appear to us to sink in the ocean. **'Turn back upon themselves':** Their orbit round the pole occupies very little space, and they quickly seem to return to their starting-point. They do not set, but they are generally invisible, as they are covered by clouds. Christ, however, does not set and cannot be hidden by any darkness; allegorically this is what Prudentius is saying.

> Hoc sidus aeternum manet,
>   Haec stella numquam mergitur,
> Nec nubis occursu abdita
>   Obumbrat obductam facem.   (17–20)

This constellation always shines,
    This star is never sunk.
It never hides behind the clouds
    Or covers up its beam.

A **'constellation'** consists of many stars, like the Bear or Taurus; a **'star'** is singular. Thus, Prudentius is either misusing the word 'constellation,' a common poetic licence, or is using it to refer to Christ together with his 'members' [of the church].

> Tristis cometa intercidat
>   Et si quod astrum Sirio
> Fervet vapore, iam Dei
>   Sub luce destructum cadat.   (21–4)

Let gloomy comet pass away,
    And if some star should burn
With Dog-star's vapour, let it fall
    Beneath the light of God.

In addition to the seven principal stars known in Greek as 'planets' ('wanderers' in Latin) and the countless fixed stars in the eighth sphere, there also frequently appear new kinds of stars that herald some major good fortune or disaster for mankind. These are known in Greek as 'comets' and in Latin as 'hairy stars,' as Pliny says 'bristling with bloody locks and with a shaggy head like hair.'[9] There are also the 'bearded,' the 'speared,' the 'horned,' the 'lamps,' and many others, whose shapes are indicated by the names they are given. They are discussed by Pliny, book 2, chapter 25,[10]

among others. There is debate as to whether they are permanent or are
generated suddenly when moisture acquires the force of fire and afterwards
die away, since they are not always seen in their orbits but often appear in
our atmosphere, like the Castors[11] seen sitting on ships' masts, or like
fire-balls and arrow-meteors. Some people think that our souls have some
affinity with the stars, and that each person has his own private star which is
born and dies at the same time as himself.[12] However this may be, the star of
the Epiphany was probably newly created and not fixed in any orbit, but was
guided by an angel through the air to show the way to the Magi.

'Let gloomy comet': This must be interpreted allegorically, for comets
have often appeared since Christ's birth, but after the appearance of this star
of gospel truth there is no need for anyone to fear Satan's pestilential stars.
Whether comets portend war or famine or plague, there is no danger for
those who follow the leadership of the star that is Jesus Christ.

'And if some star': There are some constellations whose rise or fall is
harmful to human affairs, like Orion, Hyades, and the Pleiades, which bring
bad weather. At the rising of the Dog-star the sun's heat becomes very
intense, the seas boil, wine is agitated in the cellars, marshes swirl, plagues
fester, and throughout all this time dogs turn savage. The Dog-star is called
Sirius because of the brightness of its flame, though the compiler of
Etymologies of Greek Words gives so many opinions that I cannot be bothered
to relate them.[13] Figuratively, however, Sirius is Satan's star, as he inclines
men's minds to mad passions and wars and discord. When Christ arose he
put out these stars and shone as a guide for our minds.

Sirio vapore 'Dog-star's vapour': The use of the noun form *Sirio*
instead of an adjective is (like using *Italos mores* for *Italicos*) quite elegant. A
'vapour' is a warm exhalation.

> *En Persici ex orbis sinu*
> *Sol unde solvit januam,*
> *Cernunt periti interpretes*
> *Regale vexillum Magi.*   (25–8)

> Behold! From Persia's distant land,
> The gateway of the sun,
> The Magi, skilled interpreters,
> Discern the royal sign.

The origin of the Magi is uncertain, except that we read that they came from
the East: Persis is to the east of Palestine, where Jerusalem is located. They
were 'skilled interpreters,' because as soon as they saw the star they

interpreted it as the birth of a king, saying 'Where is he who is born king of the Jews?'[14] Further, **'Magi'** is the Persian word for Greek 'philosophers'; the study of astrology is the oldest kind of philosophy.

> *Quod ut refulsit, caeteri*
>   *Cessere signorum globi,*
> *Nec pulcher ausus est suam*
>   *Conferre flammam lucifer.*(29–32)

> When this blazed forth, the other globes
>   That shine above gave way:
> The Morning Star, though fair, dared not
>   Compare its flame to this.

Lucifer, the Morning Star, is the same as Venus; it is the most benevolent and most brilliant star, for it sometimes appears in the daytime and is the only star to cast a shadow on earth. There is no glory – whether you compare the prophets and patriarchs, the angels, or anything magnificent on earth – that is not dim by comparison with Christ. He calls the stars **'globes'** because they have a spherical shape, even if they seem to us uneven in their rays because of their immense distance from us.

> *Quis iste tantus, inquiunt,*
>   *Regnator astris imperans,*
> *Quem sic tremunt coelestia,*
>   *Cui lux et aethra inserviunt.*   (33–6)

> Who is that mighty lord, they ask,
>   That gives command to stars,
> Whom heavenly bodies hold in awe,
>   Whom light and ether serve?

Prudentius describes the star as Christ because of the star's symbolism. He **'gives command to stars'** because they fall and are dimmed. **'Hold in awe'**: That is, 'revere.' **'Light and ether'**: The ether is the purer part of the heavens. The heavens themselves also have their own light.

> *Illustre quiddam cernimus,*
>   *Quod nesciat finem pati,*
> *Sublime celsum interminum,*
>   *Antiquius coelo et chao.*   (37–40)

It's something wondrous that we see,
   To which there is no end,
Sublime, on high, and without bound,
   Before both sky and void.

No human empire has ever been or will be everlasting. This star signified a king who had no beginning and will have no end; consequently, the Magi perceived his divine nature, for according to theologians nothing lacks both beginning and end except God alone. **'Before both sky and void'**: Before the creation of the world there was **'void' (*chaos*)**, so there is nothing older than this.

> Hic ille rex est gentium,
>   Populique rex Iudaici,
> Promissus Abrahae patri
>   Eiusque in aevum semini.   (41–4)

Here is that king of nations wide,
   The king of Judah's tribe,
Once promised to old Abraham
   And to his seed always.

Prudentius abandons direct speech by the Magi which he has been using and resumes the narration himself. **'King of nations … king of Judah's tribe'**: The Jews call him the God of Abraham, Isaac, and Jacob, but the gospel teaches us that he is the king of all peoples, for Abraham is the father of all believers; whatever was promised to him is available for his posterity. The people of Judah are those who profess the name of Jesus and whose mind is 'circumcised' from earthly appetites.

> Aequanda non stellis sua
>   Cognovit olim germina
> Primus sator credentium
>   Nati immolator unici.   (45–8)

He knew his seed would be beyond
   The number of the stars;
He sacrificed his only Son
   And first sowed seeds of faith.

This touches on the story told in Genesis 22. After Abraham had prepared himself to sacrifice his only son Isaac, God said to him: 'I have sworn by myself, saith the Lord, because you have done this thing and did not spare your only-begotten son on my account, I will bless you and multiply your seed like the stars of the sky.'[15]

> *Iam flos subit Davidicus*
>   *Radice Iessaea editus,*
> *Sceptrique per virgam virens*
>   *Rerum cacumen occupat.*   (49–52)

Now comes the flower of David's line,
    Produced from Jesse's root,
And, thriving on the sceptre's staff,
    Attains the topmost rank.

This refers to the prophecy in Isaiah 11: 'A staff will come out of the root of Jesse, and the flower will ascend from the root.'[16] Allegorically, this means that from David son of Jesse came forth Christ. A **'staff'** is what kings carry; its **'thriving'** indicates a long-lasting kingdom, and its **'flower'** symbolizes its outstanding eminence. The kingdom of the gospel was born from humble beginnings, but grew by the uprightness of truth and occupied the whole world. In the same prophecy follow the words 'and the staff of his mouth will strike the earth,'[17] alluding to the staff of the truth of the gospel. He uses **subit 'comes up'** for 'emerges': compare Virgil's *subjicit* 'throws up' for 'throws on high.'[18]

> *Exin sequuntur perciti*
>   *Fixis in altum vultibus,*
> *Qua stella sulcum traxerat*
>   *Claramque signabat viam.*   (53–6)

And then, aroused, they followed on,
    Their gazes fixed on high,
Along the star-traced furrow, marked
    To show the shining way.

'And then': That is, after the appearance of the star. They were **'aroused,'** burning with a desire to see the boy: the star was a sign, but their spirits had been inspired by a kind of hidden power. **'Furrow'**: Poets describe a ship 'tracing a furrow' through the sea;[19] similarly, the star seems to plough a furrow through the air.

Sed verticem pueri supra
  Signum pependit imminens,
Pronaque summissum face
  Caput sacratum prodidit.   (57–60)

But once above the young child's head
  The sign, suspended, paused;
It bowed its flame in humble wise,
  Revealed the sacred head.

It **'bowed its flame'** in adoration. **'The sacred head':** That is, the boy; this is synecdoche, as when we say 'dear heart' or 'sweetheart,'[20] referring to the whole person.

Videre quod postquam Magi
  Eoa promunt munera,
Stratique votis offerunt
  Thus myrrham et aurum regium.   (61–4)

And when the Magi witnessed this,
  They held out Eastern gifts:
In worship prone they offered scent
  And myrrh and royal gold.

Quod **'this':** Understand 'head.'[21] The gifts are **'Eastern'** (*Eoa*), that is, oriental, either because the East is rich in such goods or because the Magi came from the East.

Agnosce clara insignia
  Virtutis ac regni tui,
Puero cui trinam pater
  Praedestinavit indolem.
Regem Deumque annunciant
  Thesaurus, et fragrans odor
Thuris Sabei, et myrrheus
  Pulvis sepulcrum praedocet.   (65–72)

Perceive the emblems of your power
  And of your realm, O child;
Your father preordained for you
  A threefold heritage.

The gold and Saba's frankincense
  Proclaim you king and God;
The powder of the myrrh foretells
  The sepulchre of death.

An apostrophe to the child. In the text *puero* 'to the boy, to the child' should be emended to *puer* 'O child';[22] someone wrote *o* above the line to indicate the vocative, and a scribe incorporated it into the word. **'A threefold heritage':** In his hypostasy Christ had three substances or natures: his divine nature, his human soul, and his human body. Prudentius here, however, makes a different point, that there were three, as it were, 'personae' in Christ: of God, of a king, and of man, that is, of a priest. Insofar as he was a man, he suffered death, that is, he sacrificed himself for the sins of men. This aspect of Christ is symbolized by myrrh, as it used to be the duty of priests to burn incense and to smear the bodies of the dead with myrrh to prevent them from putrefying. He was king, for he himself said: 'All power has been given to me in heaven and on earth';[23] this was shown by the gold. He was God, in that he performed miracles and brought himself back to life; this was prefigured by frankincense, which is consecrated to divinity.

  Hoc est sepulcrum, quod (Deus
    Dum corpus extingui sinit,
  Atque id sepultum suscitat)
    Mortis refregit carcerem.   (73–6)

This is the sepulchre where[24] God
  Allowed his corpse to die,
And raised it up from burial
  And broke the chains of death.

Prudentius explains the significance of the sepulchre. The grave is to lifeless corpses what hell is to the souls of the dead. As a man, Christ died and was buried; as God, he came to life again, although the tomb was closed. Similarly, his soul descended to hell, like that of a man, but being joined to the divine nature it returned from hell and freed the souls that were imprisoned there.

  O sola magnarum urbium
    Maior Bethleem, cui contigit
  Ducem salutis coelitus
    Incorporatum gignere.   (77–80)

O Bethlehem, of cities great
   Still greater, you alone
By chance brought forth salvation's prince
   From heaven clothed in flesh.

This is an apostrophe to Bethlehem, Christ's birthplace, but also an allusion
to the prophecy in Micah 5: 'And you Bethlehem of Ephrathah are small
among the thousands of Juda.'[25] He calls Bethlehem **'great still greater'**
because it was greatest among the great. **'From heaven clothed in flesh'**:
This does not mean that Christ's body came from heaven, but that he was
conceived by heavenly assistance without male seed.

> *Altrice te summo patri*
>   *Haeres creatur unicus,*
> *Homo ex tonantis spiritu,*
>   *Idemque sub membris Deus.*   (81–4)

To God the Father, by your care,
   Was born his only heir:
A man from the Almighty's breath,
   Beneath the flesh, a god.

This alludes to the prophecy in the psalm: 'The Lord said to me, You are my
son, today I have begotten you. Ask of me, and I will give you peoples, your
inheritance, etc.'[26] **'A man from the Almighty's breath'**: He was man,
conceived from the Holy Spirit; he was God, but in a human body. Thus, in
one person the highest was joined to the lowest.

> *Hunc et prophetis testibus*
>   *Iisdemque signatoribus,*
> *Testator et sator iubet*
>   *Adire regnum et cernere.*   (85–8)

The prophets testify and sign
   To Christ as rightful heir;
His sire, God, as testator bids
   Him come and claim his realm.

This develops the theme of the 'only heir.' His **'sire'** (*sator*, literally 'sower')
was God the Father; he was also the **testator**, because he appointed the Son
as his heir – this is why it is called the New and everlasting Testament. In the

making of a testament, witnesses and lawyers are provided in order to make it more valid. The witnesses to this promise are the prophets, and they are, as it were, signatories to the divine Testament, for – if I may put it this way – God was not free to rescind his testament once it had been issued by the prophets. All that remained, therefore, for this legally made promise to be put into effect was for the designated heir to be summoned to enter into his inheritance. This was done when the Lord Jesus was born, for he was sent to claim the kingdom for the Father with whom he shared it. The phrase *et cernere* **'and claim'** is, I think, used for *decernere*, for the tyrant Satan had to be ousted.[27]

> *Regnum quod ambit omnia*
> *Diva et marina et terrea*
> *A solis ortu ad exitum*
> *Et tartara et coelum supra.*   (89–92)

> His kingdom's bounds embrace the world,
> The sky, the sea, the earth,
> From farthest east to farthest west,
> And hell and heaven above.

The **'kingdom'** embraces not 'the things that are of this world,' circumscribed by narrow limits, but everything. *Diva* **'The sky':** That is, *coelestia* 'heavenly things'; the phrase *sub dio* 'in the open air' means 'beneath heaven,' and I suspect that Prudentius actually wrote *dia* here. **'Hell'** is beneath the earth; **'above the heavens'** are the angels. Such is the extent of the kingdom.

> *Audit tyrannus anxius*
> *Adesse regum principem,*
> *Qui nomen Israel regat*
> *Teneatque David regiam.*   (93–6)

> The anxious tyrant hears the news:
> The king of kings is come
> To rule the name of Israel
> And hold King David's throne.

The **'king'** was Christ, and the **'tyrant'** was Satan, who makes war on Christ through Herod; he heard the news from the Magi, after summoning his scribes. **'Anxious':** You read in the gospel that King Herod was 'disturbed.'[28]

Exclamat amens nuntio,
  Successor instat, pellimur.
Ferrum satelles corripe,
  Perfunde cunas sanguine.
Mas omnis infans occidat,
  Scrutare nutricum sinus,
Interque materna ubera
  Ensem cruentet pusio.   (97–104)

He's frantic at the news and cries:
  'A rival – we're deposed!
Attendant, grab your sword of steel,
  Let cradles flow with blood!
Let every infant male child die!
  Search in the nurse's lap
And still between its mother's breasts
  Each boy must stain the sword!

'News':[29] The thing that had been announced. **'A rival,'** that is, Christ, is threatening, because he had been born. **'We're deposed':** But this was a different kind of kingdom from what Herod supposed, as in the words of the fine hymn sung by the church choir: 'O Herod, wicked enemy, / Why do you fear Christ's birth? / He does not claim mere mortal things, / Who gives us heaven's realms.'[30] Herod's cruelty is universally abominated, but all those who are devoted to wealth or worldly honours are guilty of similar cruelty towards the innocent, whenever some danger threatens the loss of what they hold dear.

Suspecta per Bethleem mihi
  Puerperarum est omnium
Fraus, ne qua furtim subtrahat
  Prolem virilis indolis.   (105–8)

'In Bethlehem I fear the tricks
  Of every mother new,
Lest one by stealth should hide away
  Her male child out of sight.'

The metre requires that **ne qua** 'lest one' must be for *ne aliqua puerpera* 'lest some recent mother'; otherwise, *ne qua* could have been interpreted as *ne quā viā* 'lest in any way.'

Transfigit ergo carnifex
  Mucrone districto furens,
Effusa nuper corpora,
  Animasque rimatur novas.   (109–12)

The butcher therefore draws his sword
  And, raging, drives it through
The just delivered infant limbs,
  And searches out new lives.

Effusa nuper 'just delivered': That is, recently born. The **'lives'** are **'new'**
since they have been created by 'pouring in.'[31] The butcher **'searches out'** to
find a place to thrust the deadly wound.

Locum minutis artubus
  Vix interemptor invenit,
Quo plaga descendat patens,
  Iuguloque major pugio est.   (113–16)

The killer scarce can find a place
  Within the tiny limbs
On which the open blow can fall –
  The dagger dwarfs the throat!

He handles the pathos with remarkable skill. **'The dagger dwarfs the throat':**
A dagger is a shorter kind of small sword, but is still bigger than the child's
throat. This is an 'exclamation within the narrative.'[32]

O barbarum spectaculum!
  Illisa cervix cautibus,
Spargit cerebrum lacteum,
  Oculosque per vulnus vomit.   (117–20)

O cruel, savage spectacle –
  The neck crushed on the rocks,
The milk-white brain splashed far and wide,
  The eyes spewed through the wound!

In order to build up the atrocity of the slaughter, he places before our eyes
the various kinds of death. **'The eyes spewed through the wound':** The eyes
are pushed out and jump forward. The **'brain'** is **'milk-white'** because it has
not yet been marred by phlegm or by otherwise diseased humours.

Aut in profundum palpitans
   Mersatur infans gurgitem,
Cui subter arctis faucibus
   Singultit unda et halitus.   (121–4)

Or here a shuddering babe is drowned
   Below the water's depths
And underneath, with narrowed throat,
   Inhaling water, chokes.

An infant's body is tender and used to being cossetted by warmth, and so it **'shudders'** at the feel of cold water. **'Inhaling water chokes':** Boys often choke from weeping; here the icy water and the blocked breathing produce convulsions.

Salvete flores martyrum
   Quos lucis ipso in limine
Christi insecutor sustulit,
   Ceu turbo nascentes rosas.   (125–8)

Hail to the blooms of martyrdom
   Whom, at the gate of dawn
Christ's enemy destroyed, as wind
   Kills roses in the bud.

The **'bloom'** is the beginning and prospect of fruit to follow; thus, boyhood is the blossom-time of life. The Innocents were succeeded by the richest fruits of adult martyrs. This kind of apostrophe is appropriate to the conclusion of poems of praise.

Vos prima Christi victima
   Grex immolatorum tener,
Aram ante ipsam simplices
   Palma et coronis luditis.   (129–32)

O, Christ's first victims, tender flock
   Of sacrificial lambs,
Before the altar, innocent,
   You play with palms and crowns.

To be a **'victim of Christ'** is to offer up one's flesh and its desires, which rebel against the spirit, as St Paul writes in Romans, chapter 12: 'Present your bodies as a living, holy sacrifice, pleasing to God, and your reasonable worship.'[33] The outstanding sacrifice, however, is to give up one's whole body for the glory of Christ, as St Paul says in the Second Letter to Timothy, chapter 4: 'I am now ripe for plucking, and the time of my departing is at hand.'[34] *Aram ante ipsam* **'Before the altar'**: For *ipsam* I suspect that we should read *cuius*.[35] **'With palm and crowns'**: The palm was an emblem of victory; victors were also awarded crowns. Note how he observes the diction appropriate to the character: **'play'** is a boyish activity. They **'play'** before the altar on which they were sacrificed, but they **'play with palm and crowns'**; they were removed from life before they knew that they were alive.

> *Quid proficit tantum nefas?*
>   *Quid crimen Herodem iuvat?*
> *Unus tot inter funera*
>   *Impune Christus tollitur.*   (133–6)

> What was the use of such a wrong?
>   Did Herod gain from crime?
> Alone amid so many dead
>   Christ disappeared unharmed.

Human vigilance is of no avail against the plans of God. Herod did everything possible to avoid Christ's escape – and Christ alone escaped.

> *Inter coaevi sanguinis*
>   *Fluenta solus integer*
> *Ferrum, quod orbabat nurus,*
>   *Partus fefellit virginis.*   (137–40)

> In torrents of coeval blood
>   The Virgin's child alone
> Intact escaped the steel by which
>   Young mothers were bereaved

The phrase **'torrents of blood'** is ponderous, but **'coeval blood,'** that of infants of the same age, is felicitous. *Orbabat nurus* **'mothers ... bereaved'**: He uses *nurus* [literally 'daughters-in-law'] to mean 'brides'; *orbare* is to deprive of children or of something very dear in some other respect. Also poetic is the use of **'steel'** for 'sword.'

> *Sic stulta Pharaonis mali*
>   *Edicta quondam fugerat*

Christi figuram praeferens
  Moses praeceptor civium.   (141–4)

Thus wicked Pharaoh's foolish rules
  Were long ago escaped
By Moses, saviour of his folk,
  The antetype of Christ.

The Old Testament story is linked with that of the gospel. Pharaoh, king of Egypt, saw that the Hebrew people were increasing and so ordered every male child to be exposed; Moses was exposed on the Nile, but by God's will he was saved without the king's knowledge.[36] Prudentius compares Pharaoh with Herod, Jesus with Moses. Jesus freed the prisoners who had been held under the tyranny of the devil, and made them citizens of the heavenly Jerusalem; Moses led his people out of Egypt. **Receptorem:** **'Saviour'** [literally 'receiver'].

Cautum et statutum iusserat,
  Quo non liceret matribus,
Cum pondus alvi absolverent,
  Puerile pignus tollere.   (145–8)

Decreed and fixed, the order said[38]
  That mothers weren't allowed,
When once they'd freed their womb of weight,
  To raise their young boy-child.

'When once they'd freed their womb of weight': That is, on producing the birth. That which is completed or released is said to be **'freed.'** The word **puerile 'boy-child'** is from *puer* 'boy,' as he means a male child. *Tollere* is used to mean **'raise,'** 'educate,' or 'remove.'[39]

Mens obstetricis sedulae
  Pie in tyrannum contumax
Ad spem potentis gloriae
  Furata servat parvulum.   (149–52)

The pious midwife's stubborn mind
  Resists the tyrant's will:
In hope of glory unconfined
  She steals and saves the child.

This story is told of Moses' mother in Exodus, chapter 2. She did this **'in hope of glory,'** as the child's nature portended something special.

> Quem mox sacerdotem sibi
>   Adsumpsit orbis conditor,
> Per quem notatam saxeis
>   Legem tabellis traderet.   (153–6)

Then God, the founder of the world,
   Chose Moses as the priest
To whom he would transmit the law
   Inscribed on slabs of stone.

Moses was a leader; Christ also was a leader. Christ was a priest, and Moses instituted the priesthood. Moses brought down the law inscribed on tablets of stone. Christ is the author of the law of the gospel, written by the Holy Spirit on the hearts[40] of the faithful.

> Licet ne Christum noscere
>   Tantisper exemplum viri?
> Dux ille caeso Aegyptio
>   Absolvit Israel iugo.   (157–60)

And surely Christ can be discerned
   In such[41] a leader's deed,
Who, killing an Egyptian, raised
   The yoke from Israel?

The comparison is made explicit. Moses was destined to be leader of his people; when he saw an Egyptian unjustly mistreating a Hebrew, he killed the tormentor and freed the Hebrew. What was here done for one person was later done for the whole people, when a way was opened through the Red Sea and Pharaoh and his army perished in it.

> At nos subactos jugiter
>   Erroris imperio gravi
> Dux noster hoste saucio
>   Mortis tenebris liberat.   (161–4)

We were forever slaves beneath
   The harsh commands of sin;

Our leader dealt the foe a wound
　　And freed us from death's shades.

For Hebrews the word 'Egyptian' means 'darkness,'[42] and so in mystical writing it stands for a life subject to vice and sin. To be a slave to vice is a real servitude and by far the most wretched. We were freed from it by our leader Jesus, not by an act of law but by grace: by the light of faith he dispelled the darkness of sin.

> *Hic expiatam fluctibus*
> 　*Plebem marino in transitu*
> *Repurgat undis dulcibus*
> 　*Lucis columnam praeferens.*   (165–8)

He cleansed the people in the waves
　　When passing through the sea;
In waters sweet they're purified,
　　A beam of light their guide.

Baptism[43] is symbolized by the Red Sea, which saves the Hebrews by the blood of Jesus Christ and sets them free, drowning Pharaoh and all his army. The Egyptian armies are the sins and wicked desires. In the night the Hebrews were led by a pillar of fire: when we awaken to piety, the truth of the gospel shines before us.

> *Hic praeliante exercitu,*
> 　*Passis in altum brachiis*
> *Sublimis Amalech premit*
> 　*Crucis quod instar tunc fuit.*   (169–72)

As Moses' army goes to war,
　　He spreads his arms on high;
Sublime he conquers Amalech
　　And represents the cross.

Prudentius adduces the story in Exodus 17: Moses stood on the top of a hill and raised his hands on high, and in the mean time the Hebrews who were fighting Amalek were victorious.[44] On the cross Christ stretched out his hands for us, and our enemy Satan was defeated.

> *Hic, nempe, Iesus verior,*
> 　*Qui longa post dispendia*

Victor suis tribulibus
   Promissa solvit iugera.   (173–6)

The truer Jesus was the one
   Who, after long delays,
As victor gave to all his tribe
   The promised tracts of land.

Jesus Nave drove out the inhabitants and led the Israelites into the promised land.[45] He was unquestionably a figure of our Jesus, who conquered Satan and leads his people into the kingdom of heaven. **'After long delays'**: Although it is not very far from Egypt to Syria, the Israelites, through various misfortunes, wandered in the desert for forty years. **'To all his tribe'**: Christ's brothers are those who are joined to him by faith.

Qui ter quaternis denique
   Refluentis amnis alveo,
Fundavit et fixit petris
   Apostolorum stemmata.   (177–80)

The stream flowed back and in its bed
   He then put thrice four rocks;
On these he founded and secured
   The apostolic lines.

The story told in Joshua 3 and 4 is adapted to the allegory. When the Israelites crossed the Jordan on foot, the lower part of the river flowed away and left the bed of the stream dry; the upper part heaped itself up into a high ridge. Joshua ordered one man to be chosen from each tribe; they were to go into the Jordan again, and from the middle of the river bed they were each to pick out a very hard stone; he had these set up to commemorate the event.[46] These men are interpreted as the twelve apostles through whom Christ established his church, as you can read in Revelations, chapter 21: 'And the wall of the city had twelve foundations, and on them were inscribed the names of the twelve apostles and the Lamb.'[47] **'Thrice four'**: Twelve. **'Flowed back'**: As the psalm says, 'The Jordan has turned backwards.'[48] By **'lines'** (*stemmata*) he refers to 'monuments.'

Iure ergo, se Iudae ducem
   Vidisse, testantur Magi,
Cum facta priscorum ducum
   Christi figuram finxerint.   (181–4)

The Magi, therefore, rightly swear
   That they saw Judah's prince,
For all the deeds of ancient chiefs
   Were prototypes of Christ.

Jesus was born of the tribe Judah, as the prophet says: 'For from you will come forth a leader to rule my people Israel.'[49] They **'swear that they saw'** because they said, 'Where is he who is born king of the Jews?'[50] **'For all the deeds':** They said, 'We have seen his star'; they had seen Jesus in a sign, just as the Jews had seen him in symbolic riddles and in the oracles of the prophets, before he was born. This is why Prudentius says, 'For all the deeds of ancient chiefs / Were prototypes of Christ'; this is what he has just shown in his accounts of Moses and Joshua. By *finxerint* 'were prototypes of' [literally 'made up,' 'feigned (the figure of)'] he means symbolized.

> *Hic rex piorum iudicum*
>   *Rexere qui Iacob genus,*
> *Dominaeque rex ecclesiae*
>   *Templi novelli ac pristini.*   (185–8)

Of pious judges he was king –
   They guided Jacob's line –
And king also of Lady Church,
   Of temple old and new.

Christ was born in the midst of the world in order to embrace both times, time past and time to come. He was king of the synagogue; he is now king of the church. He was king of the patriarchs, the kings, and the judges of Israel; the same Jesus Christ is also king of those that come after. **'Lady Church'** is so called because the whole world is obedient to her. By **'new temple'** he means the church, that is the temple of the Spirit; by **'old temple'** he means the temple of Solomon, which was a figure of the church. The same Christ ruled over both, but in different ways: to the Hebrews he was designated, but to Christians he was made manifest; to the former he was sketched in figures, to the latter he was openly declared; to them he was promised, but to these he was granted. The Hebrews were saved because they believed that he would come; we are saved because we believe that he has come.

> *Hunc posteri Effraym colunt,*
>   *Hunc sancta Manassae domus:*
> *Omnesque suscipiunt tribus*
>   *Bis sena fratrum semina.*   (189–92)

The followers of Ephraim,
  Manassees' holy house,
All tribes, the seeds of brothers twelve,
  All honour him as king.

Christ is adored not only by that part of Judea in which he was born, but also by all the tribes, twelve in number, who got their names from the twelve patriarchs, the sons of Jacob.

Quin et propago degener
  Ritum secuta inconditum,
Quaecumque dirum fervidis
  Baal caminis coxerat:
Fumosa avorum numina
  Saxum, metallum, stipitem,
Rasum, dolatum, sectile
  In Christi honorem deserit.   (193–200)

And even progeny that erred
  And followed unsound rites,
Whoever moulded cruel Baal
  Within a flaming forge,
Ancestral smoky images
  Of metal, stone, or wood
Cut out by file or saw or adze,
  Abjured,[51] and followed Christ.

The true Jews are those who trace their descent from Abraham, Isaac, Jacob, and the twelve patriarchs, for they worship one God. By **'progeny that erred'** he means those who traced their descent from Agar, Moab, and Ammon, from whom originated the gentiles who worshipped many gods. **'And those who moulded cruel Baal / Within a flaming forge':** The Scriptures frequently mention Baal, who was once worshipped by wicked men; an altar of Baal, together with a grove, was demolished by Gideon,[52] who built a new altar. Since there were various nations that worshipped images, he says **'whoever moulded cruel Baal,'** that is, a detestable image, 'in their **flaming forges**.' He calls the **'ancestral images' 'smoky'** either because of their age or because of the smithies' workshops. **'Of metal, stone, or wood':** This refers to the three materials from which their gods were made: bronze, stone, and wood. Similarly, there are three ways of working them: metal is rubbed with a file, stone is cut with a saw, and wood is shaped by an adze.

Gaudete quidquid gentium est,
  Iudaea, Roma, et Graecia,
Aegypte, Thrax, Persa, et Scytha,
  Rex unus omnes possidet.   (201–4)

Rejoice, whichever race you are,
  Judea, Rome, or Greece,
Or Persia, Scythia, Egypt, Thrace –
  One king alone rules all.

The poet invites all nations of the world to praise Jesus, king of all, through whom alone we are all called back to life.

Laudate vestrum principem
  Omnes beati ac perditi,
Vivi, imbecilli, ac mortui,
  Iam nemo posthac mortuus.   (205–8)

All people now, come praise your prince,
  The blessed and the lost,
The live, the sick, the dead also –
  For henceforth none are dead.

Those who prosper are called **'blessed'**; the **'lost'** are those who are afflicted by various ills – but often the afflicted are more blessed than the blessed. In either case, both should praise their prince Jesus: the blessed, because they enjoy their prosperity through his kindness; the afflicted, because through his mercy they are amended and purified lest they perish for ever. **'The live, the sick'**: 'Whether we die or live,' says St Paul, 'we are the Lord's.'[53] Let him who lives and thrives praise his prince, who gives him life so that it may be made better. Let him who is sick praise his king, who sends diseases for our own good. Let him who dies praise his prince, since he is being transferred to a happier life. But that way which will lead straight to eternal life should no longer be called 'death,' now that Jesus has opened the kingdom of heaven. For those who die in Christ do not die but merely sleep,[54] in bodies that will awake at the voice of the angel.

TRANSLATIONS FROM GALEN

Ex Galeno versa

EXHORTATION
TO STUDY THE LIBERAL ARTS,
ESPECIALLY MEDICINE

THE BEST KIND OF TEACHING

THE PROPER PHYSICIAN

*Exhortatio ad bonas artes,
praesertim medicinae*

De optimo docendi genere

Qualem oporteat esse medicum

translated and annotated by
ERIKA RUMMEL

In the spring of 1526 Erasmus published Latin versions of three essays by Galen,[1] basing his translation on the Greek text of the Aldine edition of 1525. He dedicated the work to his physician-friend Jan Antonin of Košice[2] and expressed the hope that it would 'kindle in young men a desire to study medicine.'[3] This purpose is well served by two of the essays, the *Exhortation* and *The Proper Physician*, both of which deal with career ambitions, professional ethics, and goals in education – suitable topics and congenial to Erasmus' own views. The third treatise, however, is a less obvious choice. *The Best Kind of Teaching* is concerned with epistemological questions that have little or no relevance either to Erasmus' interests or to his stated purpose in publishing these translations. Moreover, while none of the essays is entirely free of textual problems, the Greek text of *The Best Kind of Teaching* contains a number of serious corruptions that obliged Erasmus to improvise or to reproduce an obscure text.[4] The fact that the treatise was included in the publication despite its drawbacks suggests that editorial considerations prevailed over literary preferences.

Galen, the author of the treatises, was a celebrated Greek physician of the second century AD. He was born in Pergamon, studied in Alexandria, and later settled in Rome, where he became personal physician to the emperor Marcus Aurelius. Aggressive rivals threatened him with assassination, however, and he was forced eventually to leave Rome and to return to his native country. Galen's medical and philosophical treatises enjoyed great popularity in the Renaissance. A Latin version of Galen's collected works first appeared in Venice (Pincio de Caneto) in 1490; another with new translations was published by the Venetian printer L. Giunta in 1540–1. It was followed shortly afterwards by Froben's *Galeni opera omnia* (Basel 1542), which contained Erasmus' translations.[5]

Erasmus' versions of the three Galen pieces had already been published separately by Froben (Basel, May 1526) and been reprinted by Bade (Paris, June 1526). They had also appeared in Cratander's selection of Galen's works published in Basel in March 1529. The Basel *Erasmi opera omnia* of 1538–40 contained a corrected version, which was reproduced in the Leiden edition of 1703–6 (LB I 1045–64). A modern critical edition can be found in the Amsterdam *Opera omnia*.[6]

The essays selected by Erasmus belong to the epideictic genre. In the *Exhortation* Galen encourages young men to study the liberal arts. He draws an elaborate comparison between men who rely on the flighty goddess Luck and those who follow Mercury, the patron of arts. Examining various goals in life, Galen shows that wealth, nobility, and beauty rank far below the supreme good of learning and knowledge. He supports this view with a reference to the dual nature of man: just as the soul is superior to the body, so its cultivation must take precedence over physical concerns. The argument continues with a tirade against professional athletes and their preoccupation with physical exercises that are not only detrimental to their health and looks but also lack a practical purpose. The treatise concludes with an exhortation to cultivate the mind and to adopt a profession worthy of a gentleman, preferably that of a physician.

The Best Kind of Teaching is directed against Favorinus, a representative of the Academic school of philosophy, which denied the possibility of certain knowledge and advocated *epoche*, suspension of judgment. Galen condemns this view as absurd and self-defeating, arguing that any discussion is futile if man's faculty of judgment is called in question. Drawing a comparison between the tools of craftsmen and the philosophers' methods of investigation, he insists that reliable criteria of judgment can be established. The treatise ends with a rejection of scepticism and a mocking reference to the inconsistency of Favorinus, who denies the possibility of knowledge, yet allows his students to pass judgment on scientific matters.

In *The Proper Physician* Galen criticizes those who profess to admire Hippocrates and yet ignore his recommendations. True followers of Hippocrates must combine industry with integrity, practise the art of reasoning, and study the sciences – in other words, master the three disciplines of philosophy: ethics, logic, and physics. It follows that the physician who practises his art according to Hippocrates' principles is by definition also a philosopher.

Erasmus' task of translating Galen was complicated by the poor quality of the text available to him at the time.[7] He dwelt on this difficulty in several letters to friends, complaining that the Aldine edition was so full of errors that his work was not confined to translating, but required a great deal of editing and textual criticism as well.[8] Some passages in *The Best Kind of Teaching* that taxed Erasmus' skills remain a challenge to philologists today, but in many instances Erasmus was successful in his emendations and, as far as can be ascertained by retranslating, anticipated a number of corrections now generally adopted by modern editors.[9]

When Erasmus published his first translations of classical authors, he explained that as a neophyte he 'preferred to err in seeming to keep too close rather than be too free,' but even in his earliest translations he considered it his duty 'to weigh the meaning, not to count the words.'[10] The Galen pieces belong to a late period in Erasmus' life and represent the work of a veteran translator whose credentials have been established in the scholarly world. His mature work is characterized by purity of language, *copia*, and a certain degree of freedom, which give the translation a peculiarly Erasmian stamp.

Concern for purity of language prompted Erasmus to avoid literal translations that smacked of the Greek original. Not only did he keep his version free of Grecisms, he gave it an authentic touch of Latin rhetoric by introducing superlatives,[11] heaping up parallel expressions,[12] and generally modifying Greek phrases to suit Latin idiom.[13]

Erasmus' versatile treatment of Greek words that lack a Latin equivalent deserves particular attention. In some cases he retained technical terms, such as *dolichon, in diaulo,* or *homeomere,* but added explanatory phrases: 'a course of twenty-three furlongs,' 'a course of two furlongs, back and forth,' 'which means "of similar parts." ' [14] In other cases he paraphrased the Greek word, rendering φιλάνθρωπος 'loving mankind' as *familiaris et amica humano genere* 'a friend and patron to mankind'; ὁμοίοι τοῖς μορμολυκείοις 'like hobgoblins' as *ad terrorem arte factae imagines* 'artfully made horror-masks'; and βάναυσος 'menial' with a certain flair as *sedentarius* (a rare word, literally 'sitting').[15] In a few cases he used Latinized versions of Greek terms, but usually on good authority. Words like *nothus* 'bastard,' *basis* 'base,' and *oeconomus* 'steward' had all been introduced into Latin in antiquity.[16]

Although Erasmus' translation is not unduly free, he is fond of *copia* and often renders one Greek expression by two Latin phrases. For instance, he translates λόγος 'fame' as *nomen aut ... dignitatem* 'fame or ... honour,' ἠμελημένον 'neglected' as *neglectum et incuratum* 'neglected and uncared for,' ἀθροίζειν 'collect' as *colligunt et coacervunt* 'collect and store up.'[17] The tendency to be more expansive than the Greek original is also pronounced in the following expressions: 'What harvest do they reap other than...' for a succinct τί ἄλλ' ἤ 'what else but...'; 'one who engages in the teaching profession' for the simple Greek term διδάσκαλος 'teacher.'[18] This practice might be interpreted as the mark of a scrupulous translator who wishes to give the fullest possible meaning of an expression, but the verbiage seems to evidence the translator's wealth of expression rather than his punctiliousness. Of course, Erasmus' delight in *copia* and variation adds an element of Ciceronian rhetoric to the translation. As Erasmus himself noted: 'It is characteristic of Cicero to reinforce a single idea by using two words meaning the same or nearly the same thing.'[19]

In the examples cited so far Erasmus' expressions show more flourish than the Greek original but are at any rate faithful to its meaning. In other cases he goes so far as to introduce a difference nuance – without, however, changing the general tenor of the passage. For example, he renders a neutral expression, ἐπιστάς 'approaching' in the sense of 'addressing,' by the more definite *insultans* 'scoffing' or translates ἐπιχειρίζειν 'adducing arguments' more forcefully as *obicere* 'casting into one's teeth.'[20] Elsewhere he implies that philosophy is the product of human effort rather than a divine gift, an idea which is not implicit in the Greek.[21]

In a few instances Erasmus diverges considerably from his original. Most of these cases must be explained as errors and are discussed in the notes.[22] Other divergences from the Greek text are editorial in nature and include material that a modern translator might relegate to the footnotes: explanations or, in the case of Greek technical terms, translations. Occasionally such additions appear superfluous or at any rate addressed to a simple-minded audience. For instance, when using the Latinized Greek term *tessara* 'cube,' Erasmus explains that this figure is 'supported on all sides by its four corners'; elsewhere Galen lists carpentry tools and Erasmus adds their uses; in another case Galen relates the reversals of fortune experienced by famous men but Erasmus feels obliged to be more explicit, explaining that these men are now in a 'very different position.'[23]

In these cases the Latin translation seems unnecessarily long-winded, but such minor flaws cannot obscure Erasmus' superb linguistic skills. On the whole, he produced a most spirited translation and was highly successful in recapturing the rhetorical style of Galen's treatises. And this is what recommended the publication to his readers. Galen had been translated before,[24] but never in such pure and elegant language. Erasmus' predecessors had made accessible to readers of Latin the content of Galen's essays – Erasmus enabled them to appreciate their form as well. He presented Galen's speeches in full regalia, adorned with the rhetorical splendour appropriate to their genre. In spite of the stylistic merits of Erasmus' translation, however, classical scholars today will share with him the sentiment expressed in a letter to Lord Mountjoy: 'If only the knowledge of Greek literature were so widely diffused that the tedious task of translating could deservedly be censured as superfluous.'[25]

ER

ERASMUS OF ROTTERDAM TO THE EXCELLENT PHYSICIAN JAN ANTONIN OF KOŠICE,[1] greetings

Dearest Antonin, I learn from a letter of the most distinguished Johann Henckel[2] that I cannot hope for your return.[3] Although I shall miss your company, it is a great comfort to know that you are detained in your native country by the highest favours and most generous rewards of princes. Moreover, I understand that you have married a woman excelling no less in moral principles than in appearance, who will not grant you leave but keeps you tied with pleasant fetters.[4] It remains for us to keep in touch as best we can.

Galen's work has been published in its entirety speaking to us in its own language, and I am sending you the first fruits of my translation, undertaken to kindle in young men a desire to study medicine. The task was more troublesome than you would believe. I shall not plead my case: if you will take the trouble to compare my text with the Greek original[5] you will realize at once that translating it was the lesser of my labours.

Your pearl will never allow me to forget your endearing frankness and your sincere character. I quite understand the significance of the chaplain's[6] Sebastian:[7] it means that Erasmus is exposed to the darts of slanderers. The most noble Krzysztof,[8] count of Cracow, has also presented me with bountiful gifts,[9] not unworthy of a king either to give or to receive. I shall write back to each of my benefactors individually unless perhaps this short publication reaches their part of the world more speedily than a letter of mine.

Farewell, dear Antonin, and greetings also to your sweet wife: may you live a long and happy life together.

Basel, 28 April 1526

AN EXHORTATION
TO STUDY THE LIBERAL ARTS,
ESPECIALLY MEDICINE

Are so-called senseless creatures completely devoid of reason? That remains an open question. Animals may not share with us the kind of reason associated with language, called 'enuntiative,' but they do possess the kind of reason associated with the soul,[1] called 'emotive.'[2] All living beings share in this quality to some extent. Of course man is greatly superior to the other creatures in reasoning. The proof is obvious: he alone tackles a wide range of arts and has the knowledge to acquire whatever skill he wishes. Hardly any of the other creatures have a share in the arts. The few exceptions are animals that have acquired their skills by nature rather than through instruction,[3] and even they possess no art that man does not practise. He has imitated the spiders in the art of weaving, the bees in the art of modelling (which is called 'plastic'[4]), and he is not unskilled in swimming, although he is a creature of the land.

Nor is man without divine arts. He imitates the medical art of Aesculapius (which he shares with Apollo) and in addition all the other skills that Apollo has, namely archery, music, and prophesy.[5] Man also knows the arts peculiar to each of the Muses and is ignorant neither of geometry nor of astronomy. Indeed, he contemplates 'both what is beneath the earth and what is above the skies,' as Pindar says.[6] And finally, he has provided for himself, by his own industry,[7] the highest of all goods: philosophy. Thus, even though the other creatures are not devoid of reason, man alone is called rational because he is pre-eminently so.

Is it not most shameful, then, that we neglect the only thing we have in common with the gods, that we interest ourselves in other matters, scorn the arts, and abandon ourselves to Fortune? To draw our attention to her troublesome nature men of old represented Fortune in paintings as well as sculptures as a woman.[8] And although this in itself was indicative of Fortune's folly, they were not content with it, but also placed in her hands a rudder, under her feet a base in the shape of a ball, and, furthermore, deprived her of eyes – all, no doubt, to show her unreliability.

Imagine[9] a man on board a ship tossed about violently by storms, indeed dangerously close to being overwhelmed by wind and waves and plunged into the deep: would he not be out of his mind to entrust the helm to a blind navigator under such circumstances? The same reasoning applies to life, in my opinion. In fact, more serious disasters occur in many houses than befall ships at sea, and he is a poor judge who entrusts himself to a blind and unstable goddess when he is surrounded and beset on all sides by great troubles.[10] Fortune is so senseless, so out of her mind, that she frequently passes over good men who deserved her attention and heaps riches on unworthy men. And even in this she is not constant but soon takes back her gifts as rashly as she has bestowed them.

A large crowd of uneducated men follow this goddess, who never remains in one position because the base on which she stands[11] is unstable and drives her hither and thither, carries her along[12] the edge of cliffs and sometimes even into the sea, where all her followers perish alike. She alone escapes unharmed and unscathed, laughing at them in their misery. In vain they implore her help – she does not benefit them any more.[13] Such are the ways of Fortune!

Now in turn consider Mercury, the lord of reason[14] and father of all arts. How different, how contrary to Fortune's image is the shape in which those men of old depicted him in paintings and statues:[15] a graceful young man whose beauty is not at all affected or augmented by cunning adornments, but shines forth, illuminated by a vigorous mind. The god's countenance is cheerful, his glance spirited, and the base on which he stands is of all shapes the most solid and least moveable: a cube supported on all sides by its four corners.[16] Sometimes even the god himself is represented by this figure.[17] And you may see his worshippers equally cheerful, just like the god whom they follow, never complaining about their patron as the followers of Fortune are wont to do. Nor do the acolytes of Mercury desert him or part from the god, but forever follow him and benefit from his forethought.

By contrast one may observe the followers of Fortune: sluggish and slow to learn the sciences, always eagerly led on by hope, flying with a flighty goddess, some rather close to her, others quite far away, a few hanging on to her hand. Among them you can see those two famous men, Croesus[18] of Lydia and Polycrates[19] of Samos, and perhaps you will marvel at their power: the river Pactolus running with gold for Croesus,[20] and the fish of the sea being purveyors to Polycrates.[21] In the company of these men you will also find Cyrus,[22] Priam,[23] and Dionysius.[24] A little while later, however, you will notice the same men in very different positions:[25] Polycrates nailed to the cross, Croesus subdued by Cyrus, Cyrus in turn deposed by others, Priam bound, and Dionysius in Corinth. And if you contemplate those who from a distance pursue yet never capture Fortune as she runs, you will certainly detest this retinue, for among them you will find a great many demagogues,[26] harlots and fornicators, traitors and murderers, grave-robbers and bandits, indeed many who did not spare even the gods, but despoiled their temples.

In the other circle all are honourable professional men, who do not run, shout, or jostle. The god is in their midst and his followers around him, each man in his station, none deserting the rank assigned him by the god. Some are very close to him and surround him in set order: geometricians, arithmeticians, philosophers, physicians, astronomers, and grammarians. These are followed by a second circle of painters, sculptors, writers, carpenters, architects, and stonemasons. Thereafter comes a third class comprising the representatives of the remaining arts, each arranged in order, but in such a way that all face their common god and equally obey his commands. Here, too, you will notice a numerous throng of people keeping close to the god. Next, you will perceive a fourth class, selected and standing apart from the rest, quite unlike those who accompany Fortune. For Mercury is not inclined to judge a man's merit by his career, ancestry, or possessions: he honours those who live a life of virtue and excel in the arts, those who follow his commands and practise their arts lawfully. Such men he cherishes and ranks above the others, keeping them his close associates forever. If you knew the members of this circle you would no doubt admire if not worship them.

In this class are Socrates, Homer, Hippocrates, Plato, and their devotees, whom we think worthy of the same honours as the gods because they are the ministers and servants of a god. Yet, even among the others no one has ever been neglected by Mercury. He not only cares for those who are in his presence but even stands by those who are out at sea, and he does not desert them in disaster.

Thus it once happened to Aristippus on a sea voyage that he was shipwrecked and cast onto the shore of Syracuse.[27] As soon as he saw geometric lines in the sand, he began to take heart, for he reckoned he had come to Greeks and to knowledgeable men, not to barbarians. Afterwards he entered a gymnasium in Syracuse and spoke these verses:

Who will now receive with scanty gifts
The exiled Oedipus wandering day by day?[28]

Upon this some people came forward and, learning who he was, forthwith provided him with all he needed. Later on, when some men who were about to sail to his native Cyrene inquired if he wanted to send any message to his people, he said: 'Tell them to acquire for themselves such possessions as will float to the surface together with their shipwrecked owner.'[29]

But many wretched people measure everything in terms of wealth, and if they meet with disaster they prop up their gold and silver, tie it around their bodies, and lose their lives together with their possessions. They cannot even reflect on their own preferences: after all, they themselves

favour among the senseless creatures chiefly those that are distinguished by
their skills. For instance, they prefer to other animals horses trained for
warfare and dogs skilled in the hunt. They even have their slaves instructed
in the arts and often spend a great deal of money on them while they neglect
themselves. Now, does it not seem shameful if a slave is valued at ten
thousand drachmas while his master is not worth even one drachma? One
drachma, did I say? No one would take him into his service[30] if he came free
of charge! Have not such people in the end made themselves the meanest of
all, since they alone have learned no art? They instruct senseless creatures
and train them in skills, they consider worthless a slave who is unproductive
and unskilled in any of the arts, they take care of their fields and the rest of
their possessions to make each of them as good and valuable as possible –
they neglect only themselves! They do not even know whether or not they
have a soul and are quite obviously no better off than the most despicable
slaves. Therefore one may scoff at such a man and rightly address him with
words of this kind: 'My dear man, your household is prospering. All your
slaves, horses, dogs, fields, and other possessions are in good order, but
you yourself are not properly cared for!'

This sentiment is splendidly expressed by Demosthenes and Diogenes.[31] One called wealthy uneducated men 'sheep loaded with golden
fleece'; the other said that they were 'like fig-trees standing on the edge of a
cliff – their fruit being eaten by crows and jackdaws, not by men.' Like the
fruit of these trees, the wealth of rich but ignorant people is of no use to good
men, but wasted on flatterers. And when nothing is left and the flatterers by
chance[32] meet the men whom they have depleted, they pass them by,
pretending not to know them. A man of wit once likened the rich to wells,
for once they have run dry, the people who used to draw water from them
lift up their garments and urinate into them. And it seems only fair that rich
men who are admirable for nothing but their wealth should suffer a similar
fate. Once they have lost their money they must also do without the honours
enjoyed on account of their wealth. What else can men expect who possess
no inherent good but forever depend on external goods and on circumstances which are of Fortune's giving?

Of the same calibre are men who vaunt the nobility of their family and
are smug and arrogant because of it. They too lack good qualities of their
own and therefore resort to the images of their forefathers without realizing
that the nobility of birth in which they take pride is like the official currency
of individual cities – valid indeed among those who have issued it, but no
better than counterfeit among others:

Ancestry did not raise you up on high.
– Nor was I raised to shame my ancestry.[33]

Plato says: 'A splendid treasure are the virtues of our fathers.'[34] But it is nobler to be able to answer with Sthenelos:[35] 'But we by far surpass our fathers and grandfathers.' For there is only one advantage in high birth: adducing the example of family members kindles a desire for imitating them. If, however, we should turn out to be inferior to our ancestors' excellence, they will rightly be pained (if indeed the dead have feelings), but we ourselves are disgraced in proportion to the glory of our family. Inexperienced men who are of obscure origin can use to their advantage the fact that most people do not know what kind of men they are. But what about those whom the glory and fame of their ancestors does not allow to take cover? What harvest do they reap[36] from their noble birth other than that their misfortune is made more obvious?

Indeed men who do not live up to their noble birth are more despised than those of obscure origin.[37] If therefore a foolish man trumpets the glory of his ancestors, he declares in effect that his shortcomings are less deserving of pardon. For we do not scrutinize or appraise common men by the same criteria as those of noble birth. If common men are endowed with even a modicum of virtue, we commend and accept them, attributing any deficiencies to their low birth. Those, however, who offer nothing worthy of the images of their forefathers we do not admire even if they surpass all other men. Therefore a sensible man should turn to the practice of some art, so that if he is noble, it will make him appear worthy of his ancestors, and if he is not, it will enable him to bring glory to his family himself. Let him follow the example of the famous Themistocles of old, who said, when he was reviled for being a bastard:[38] 'At least I'll be the founder of my own race: my race will start with me, but yours will end with you!' Nor did a barbarian origin prevent the Scythian Anacharsis from being admired and numbered among the wise.[39] When someone taunted him for being a barbarian by descent, and a Scythian at that, he said: 'My country is a shame to me; you are a shame to yours.' A fine retort to a man who had nothing to recommend him and who took pride only in his place of birth. If you consider human affairs with greater attention and concentration[40] you will find that men did not become famous because of their cities, but on the contrary, cities were made famous by their native sons, good men who excelled in the arts.

What honour would Stagira have achieved if it had not been for Aristotle? Or Soli, if not for Aratus[41] and Chrysippus?[42] And whence did Athens, long ago, derive its fame? Not from its fertile land, for its fields bore a scanty harvest, but from those who were born there, many of whom grew up to be excellent men and shared a considerable portion of their fame with their country. You will recognize the truth of this assertion if you consider the fate of Hyperbolus and Cleon,[43] for whom the fame of Athens did nothing other than to make their misdeeds more notorious.

'Once men used the expression "Boeotian swine,"' Pindar says, and repeating the same idea, 'we have escaped the reproach "Boeotian swine."'[44] In both instances Pindar expresses the hope that his poetry could erase the stigma of ignorance adhering to nearly all of his people.

One may rightly praise the Athenian lawgiver who forbade a father to demand the right of sustenance from a son whom he had taught no art.[45] Since all art was practised[46] at a time in life when the body seemed to be most beautiful, many men neglected their minds because their looks were admirable. Afterwards, too late and in vain, they moan and say: 'Ruin to beauty that has ruined me!'[47] Then they recall Solon's instruction: 'First of all consider how a man's life ends.'[48] Next, they blame old age when they ought to blame themselves. And they praise Euripides, who says: 'To have beauty in excess is no advantage.'[49]

It is therefore better to commend those who have judged the beauty of youth to be like the flower of spring,[50] a temporary pleasure, and also to praise Sappho's words: 'For he who is beautiful is so only while he is beheld, but whoever is good, will at once also be beautiful.'[51] Moreover we must obey Solon, who offers the same advice:[52] 'Then comes grievous[53] old age, threatening like a storm,' and lacking not only footgear and clothing, but also a comfortable home and numerous other things. Against this time one ought to prepare like a good helmsman, far in advance, as if against an oncoming[54] storm, for it is a pitiful saying: 'The foolish man is wise after the fact.'[55]

Of what use is a young man's beauty if it is not refined by an art? In warfare perhaps? Homer's words are a fitting answer here: 'Why not carry on with conjugal pleasures?' Or else: 'Go home and attend to your business!' Indeed, 'Nireus, most handsome of men, had come to Troy but proved a weakling.'[56] Therefore Homer mentions him but once, in the catalogue of ships, and for no other reason, in my opinion, than to declare how useless men of good looks are when they have, apart from this, nothing that contributes to advantage in life.

Some wretched fellow may have the impudence to say that beauty helps to acquire wealth, but usually it is an art that provides an honourable and lasting income worthy of a gentleman, whereas gains from physical beauty are always shameful and infamous. Therefore a young man contemplating his appearance in a mirror[57] ought to remember the old rule: if he sees a handsome face he must take care to have a like mind and consider it very strange indeed if in a shapely body lives a crippled mind. On the other hand, if he sees that he is unfortunate in his appearance, he must show all the more care to refine his mind, so that he can say with Homer:

This man's less fortunate in appearance, but
The god has graced his form with elegant speech
His hearers, charmed, behold his face with joy.
He speaks the truth with pleasant decency,
Surpassing in the council all the rest,
And in the streets is gazed on as a god.[58]

From my words it is obvious to any but the most benighted that one must not rely either on high birth or wealth or beauty and thus neglect the study of an art. And these admonitions might suffice, but perhaps I had better add Diogenes' words, as a fair refrain.[59]

When he was feasted in the house of a man who kept all his possessions prudently arranged and in good order but had shown no care at all for his mind, Diogenes cleared his throat as if to spit out, then looked around and, as he could find no place to spit out, aimed straight at the master of the house himself. When the man angrily demanded to know the reason for this behaviour, Diogenes answered that he could see nothing in the whole house so filthy and neglected as the man himself. All the walls had been decorated with exquisite paintings, the floor had been inlaid with precious stones in symmetrical design depicting gods, all the vessels were clean and shiny, even the blankets and couches were beautifully crafted and artfully designed – only the master seemed neglected and uncared-for. And all men (Diogenes said) are in the habit of spitting out in the ugliest spot around.[60] Take heed, then, young man, lest you too deserve to be spat at, even if you think that you have everything beautifully arranged. Rarely can you combine all gifts and be at once noble, rich, and beautiful. And even if a man should succeed in combining all these goods, it would nevertheless be absurd that you[61] alone among all your resources should deserve to be spat at.

Go on, then, my young listeners, strive to learn an art. Do not be misled or deceived by those who would instruct you in base or useless professions. You realize that any profession that has no practical purpose is no profession at all. Throwing dice, walking the tightrope, turning cartwheels, not to mention[62] the works of the Athenian Myrmeciades and the Spartan Callicrates:[63] nothing of this sort deserves the name 'art.' This much, I am sure, you can see for yourselves. I am apprehensive only about athletic exercises,[64] for they hold the promise of strength, win glory among the common people, are publicly honoured among the elders with generous presents every day, and are considered as worthy as the most outstanding arts.[65] Such recognition may deceive a young man and lead him to prefer athletic exercises to any other art. It is therefore better to be put on guard, better to have considered the matter in advance, for every man is easily deceived concerning those matters about which he has not taken forethought.

Consider this, young men: the human race shares qualities with the gods as well as with brute animals; with the gods the use of reason, with animals, mortality. It is preferable, therefore, to turn our minds to the better part of our common nature and to aim at learning and knowledge. If we achieve this goal we shall possess the highest of goods; if we fail, at least we need not blush for having been rendered lower than the most useless beasts. If someone engages in athletic exercises, however, and does not succeed in his endeavours, he stands disgraced. And even if he is extremely successful, he cannot hope to surpass brute animals. For who is stronger than a lion or an elephant? Who is faster than a hare? Who indeed does not realize that the gods themselves are praised for nothing other than their arts? Even men of excellence are deemed worthy of divine honours, not because they have done well in a race or have thrown the discus expertly or wrestled skillfully in the palaestra, but because they devised arts.[66]

In fact Aesculapius and Bacchus (whether they were men once or gods from the beginning) earned the highest honours, one because he showed us the art of healing, the other because he taught us the art of cultivating vines. But if you do not want to put your faith in me, let the authority of the Pythian god admonish you,[67] for he is the one who pronounced Socrates the wisest of all men,[68] he is the one who addressed Lycurgus, greeting him in this manner:

> Lycurgus, to my well-stored temple you have come,
> Of Jove and all Olympic gods a favourite son,
> Lycurgus, do I call you god or man, I ask?
> A god, I think you are, deserving reverence.[69]

And the same god also seems to have shown extraordinary honour to the dead Archilochus, for when his murderer wished to enter his temple, he forbade it, saying: 'The famous poet you have slain. Keep out!'[70]

Now tell me, what athletes have been honoured with such address? You cannot answer, for you have nothing to say, unless perhaps you reject my witness as untrustworthy! For I suspect something of this nature when in your speech you resort to the testimony of common people, pitting their praises against my argument. And yet, if you suffered from a disease, you would certainly not entrust yourself to the common people, but choose from a select few and only the most experienced physicians. Nor would you, on board ship, entrust yourself to any one of the passengers, but of course only to the helmsman. Even in the most trivial matters you consult an expert: if you build, you have recourse to a carpenter; if you need boots, you rely on a cobbler. But in matters of utmost importance you assume the power of judgment yourself, rejecting the authority of those who know more than you – the experts, I mean, for I say nothing of the gods. Listen to Euripides and what he thinks of athletes:

> Innumerable ills spread throughout Greece
> And yet the athletes' race is worse than all.
> They do not take good counsel for their house,
> Although they should – and how indeed can one
> Who serves his throat and stomach like a slave,
> Provide the means wherewith to live at home?
> And yet he cannot go without, or rest
> Content with Fortune's scanty offerings –
> For never trained in honourable ways,
> Shameless, they quickly turn to shameless arts.[71]

Listen once more to Euripides' words, if you please, and you will realize that all their pursuits are worthless:

> What wrestler or what man in foot-race swift,
> Or else, what man who throws the discus well,
> Or strikes the jaw of his opponent straight,
> Has won his victory for the fatherland?[72]

If you wish to hear even more explicit words than these, listen:

> Or will they fight against the enemy,
> The discus in their hands? When shields are used
> Will they, fleet-footed, drive the host away?
> I think not: all their skills will come to naught
> When close at hand the sword begins to flash.[73]

Assuming we do not want to listen to Euripides and other authors of his kind and grant the right of judgment only to philosophers – so be it. The philosophers' verdict is unanimous; they condemn athletics with one voice. Not even among the physicians can anyone be found who approves of it. Take first of all Hippocrates' dictum: 'The condition of athletes is contrary to nature; a healthy state[74] is better.'[75] The same advice has been given by all the best physicians after Hippocrates' time.

I personally would prefer not to let my judgment depend on witnesses, for I consider this a rhetorical device unworthy of a man who values truth itself. Some people, however, resort to a large number of witnesses[76] and from this practice derive vain glory, neglecting to examine the nature of training by itself, apart from external evidence. Their practice compels me to follow suit and to bring witnesses against them, so that they may realize the inferiority of their arguments even in this point.

It may not be untimely to relate Phryne's story in this context.[77] Once she attended a banquet where a game was being played in which the guests took turns giving each other any order they liked. Since Phryne had noticed that some of the women present had their faces made up with mascara, powder, and rouge, she had water brought in and soon gave instructions that all should dip their hands in the water, touch their face once, and then wipe it immediately with a cloth. She herself was the first to do so. Now, all the other women's faces were so full of blemishes that they looked like artfully made horror masks.[78] Phryne herself, however, appeared more beautiful than ever, for she alone did not use any beauty aids, but kept her natural appearance. She had no need for evil arts to commend her beauty. Just as true beauty is ascertained when it is on its own, stripped of all external attributes, so also one ought to examine athletic exercises on their own merits to determine if they bring any advantage either to the community in public life or to athletes in their private life.

Now qualities that are good by nature are of various kinds, namely spiritual, physical, and external. All other goods can be arranged under these headings. Anyone can see that men who pursue athletic exercises never attain to spiritual goods, not even in their sleep, since they do not know whether or not they possess a soul, let alone realize that it has a share in reason. Athletes keep adding to the strength of their flesh and blood, but keep their souls steeped in mire,[79] so that they cannot know anything with certainty and remain just as dull as the souls of brute animals.

Perhaps athletes will protest and say that their exercises contribute something to the good of the body. But can they claim good health, which is the body's most precious possession? Not at all. On the contrary, you will find none with a more precarious physical condition, if we can believe Hippocrates, who said: 'The extreme physical health which these men seek is dangerous.'[80] And here is another of Hippocrates' correct observations praised by everyone: 'Healthy training means not to be cloyed with food, but to be nimble in all respects.'[81] But athletes do the opposite: they work out in excess and they take food in excess. In short they defy the venerable Hippocrates' words as if seized by Corybantic madness.[82] He showed what kind of life helps to preserve good health: 'Work, food, drink, sleep, sex – all in moderation.'[83] But every day athletes train more strenuously than is good for them, indulge in food, sometimes even forcing themselves to eat, and extend their feasting into the middle of the night, so that one may rightly turn Homer's words against them:

> The others, gods and men, lay fast asleep
> Throughout the night; sweet Dream relaxed their limbs,
> But sleepless were the wretched athletes all.[84]

They show a lack of moderation not only in eating and exercising, but also in their sleeping habits, for when the rest of the people who live in a natural manner come home from work and are ready for dinner, athletes just get out of bed. Their life resembles that of pigs, except that pigs do not exert themselves beyond measure or force themselves to eat. But athletes suffer that and more: sometimes the stain of oleander leaves marks their backs![85] And let us add another dictum by the venerable Hippocrates: 'To fill or empty the body, to make it hot or cold, vehemently and suddenly, or to disturb it in any other way, is dangerous.' 'For,' he says, 'whatever is extreme is hostile to nature.'[86] Athletes, however, listen neither to these nor to other words wisely spoken by Hippocrates. They transgress his rules – in fact, they indulge in everything that is at odds with his precepts.

In my opinion, therefore, athletics contributes nothing to good health. On the contrary: it attracts diseases, for this is my interpretation of Hippocrates' saying that 'the athlete's condition is unnatural; a healthy state is better.'[87]

Hippocrates plainly states that exercises are contrary to nature. In fact, he refuses to call the athletes' condition a 'state' [habitudo], depriving them of the very term of honour that all the ancients used to apply to those who were truly in good health. For a 'state' is a stable and lasting condition, while the top condition of an athlete's body is precarious and easily changed into the opposite. Having reached a peak it does not admit improvement, and since it cannot remain in the same state, it can only deteriorate. Athletes reach this point when they are in training, but when they stop exercising they are in a much worse condition. A few die shortly after retiring, others live longer, but even so fail to reach old age. And if they do so occasionally, they are not unlike the Homeric Litae,[88] 'lame, wrinkled, blind' and deprived of sight.

Just as the parts of a wall that have been pounded by missiles collapse under any stress and cannot bear tremors or any other strong impact, so the bodies of athletes, ruined and weakened by the blows and wounds received during training, are injured easily at the first insignificant occasion. Moreover, their eyes are often hollow[89] and, as they have no resistance left, filled with fluid. Their teeth, loosened by frequent blows and deprived of their function as time goes by, fall out easily. As for the rest, their joints are too weak to withstand any kind of external force, since they have been frequently twisted. And whatever has once been broken or bruised is easily dislodged again. Therefore, as far as good health is concerned, it is obvious that no group of people is more pitiful than athletes. One could therefore rightly say that 'athlete' is a suitable name for them,[90] for either *athlios* 'hapless' is derived from 'athlete' or both words are derived from *athliotes* 'misery,' sharing common ground.[91]

So much for good health, the highest physical good. Now let us go on to the other advantages. How do athletes fare as far as beauty is concerned? Not only do athletic exercises contribute nothing to beauty, on the contrary, many athletes were perfectly proportioned until trainers took up their care and changed their physical appearance for the worse, fattening them and stuffing them with meat and blood. They even caused some athletes' features to become absolutely repulsive and distorted, especially those instructed in the pancratium or in boxing matches. And when these athletes finally have their bones broken, their limbs twisted, and their eyes gouged out, then, I think, the result of their art, their 'beauty,' is made manifest. So much for their success in achieving beauty while they are healthy! But when they retire, the rest of the body's organs are ruined as well, and all its limbs, as I have said, are twisted so that they look quite deformed.

But perhaps athletes claim nothing of this sort and aspire only to strength. For I know exactly what they are about to say: 'This, of all things, is of great concern to the public.'[92] What strength, for God's sake? And of what use? In agriculture perhaps? A fine job they can do of digging and mowing or whatever else pertains to agriculture! You may say: 'Perhaps their strength is effective in warfare.' Let me quote Euripides once more, who sings their praises thus:

> Or will they fight against the enemy
> The discus in their hands? When shields are used
> Will they, fleet-footed, drive the host away?
> I think not: all their skills will come to naught
> When close at hand the sword begins to flash.[93]

You may say: 'Their strength lies in enduring heat and cold.' Oh yes, indeed! They are the very image of Hercules, clothed as they are in the same skin both in winter and in summer, unshod at all times and sleeping in the open air, lying on the ground! In these matters they are weaker than new-born babies.[94]

In what area then will they give us an example of their strength? Why should they be pleased with themselves and hold up their heads?[95] Surely not just because they can defeat amateurs in the palaestra or in the stadium: cobblers, builders, and architects.[96] Perhaps they think it is a commendable practice to roll in the dust all day. If that is a cause for pride, let us sing the praises of quails and partridges, for they spend all day covered in mud.

By Jove, they say the famous Milo of Croton[97] once took upon his shoulders one of the sacrificed steers and carried it around the stadium. Oh, singular folly of men! Do you not realize that shortly before, when the steer was alive, it carried that same body and with much less effort than Milo, for it could have run while carrying it? And yet the steer's mind was of no account and neither was Milo's. The circumstances of the man's death show how little sense he had. For once when he saw a young man splitting wood [lengthwise][98] by inserting wedges, he laughed at him, shoved him aside, and daringly split the wood using no other means than his bare hands. He gathered all his strength in the first thrust and soon held apart the sections of the tree. In the mean time the wedges had fallen out, but he could not split the remaining part of the tree. For a long time he strained, until he was exhausted. Then, when the halves of the trunk snapped together, he was unable to get his hands free. They were caught and crushed, an injury which caused his pitiful death.[99]

What good was it to have carried the dead steer in the stadium? It did not protect Milo against injury. And would he have been able to save the Greeks[100] at a time when they were waging war against the barbarians? Would the strength of Milo, which he manifested in carrying a steer, have been more effective than the wisdom of Themistocles, the man who first rightly judged and understood the meaning of the oracle and then conducted the war successfully?[101] 'For one prudent counsel overcomes many hands, but ignorance in arms is worse than any evil.'[102]

I think it is obvious by now that athletic exercises bring no advantage to everyday life. Moreover, you will realize that athletes are worthless even in their chosen field when you hear the following story, set out by a witty man in a long poem.[103] The story goes like this:

Let us assume that by the will of Jove all creatures lived together in agreement and that the herald at Olympia called to the contest not only men but also gave permission to all animals to assemble in the same stadium. If this came true, in my opinion no man would win a crown. For in the *dolichon*, a race over twenty-three furlongs, the horse [he says] will win by far; and in the shorter run, which covers no more than one furlong, the hare will carry the day. In the *diaulum*,[104] in which the race back and forth covers two furlongs, the wild goat will get first prize, and no man will be of any account.[105]

Oh, how trifling are your exercises, athletes (or rather 'wretched men')! Indeed, not even a descendant of Hercules could be stronger than an elephant or a lion. And in a boxing competition I think a steer will carry the crown. The donkey (so the story goes) will be victorious if it has a mind to compete in kicking. And in the record of the various events it will be entered that once an ass defeated man in the pancratium: 'In the twenty-first Olympics, Brayer carried the day.'

This story shows in a charming manner that the strength of athletes is not a quality to be cultivated by human beings. But if athletes cannot claim pre-eminence over animals even in strength, which of the other goods will they claim for themselves?

Someone may want to number physical pleasure among the goods, but athletes do not experience pleasure either during exercising or after they have stopped exercising, for while they are in training they labour miserably, not only because of their exercises, but also because they are driven to gluttony. And when they finally have won their discharge from the profession, they are lame and crippled in almost every one of the body's limbs.

Perhaps they take pride in the fact that they collect and store up more wealth than the others. But one may observe them all bound by debts. Never will you find an athlete who is richer by a penny than a rich man's steward, either at the time when they practise athletics, or after they have been discharged. Besides, the fact that one makes money from one's profession is not noble in itself. It is nobler to seek an art that will 'float to the surface with its master after the ship is wrecked.'[106] And this is achieved neither by men who look after the affairs of the rich nor by tax-collectors or merchants, and yet these are the men who profit most from their art. If their money is gone, however, their business is gone as well, because they need some working capital for their transactions, and if they lack it, they cannot renew their former business activities, for no one gives them a loan without collateral or mortgages.

If someone wishes to provide himself with a safe and honourable means of gaining wealth he must practise an art that will last him a lifetime. Now there are two principal categories into which occupations can be divided: some are intellectual, and these are noble and honourable; others on the contrary involve physical labour (they are called sedentary and manual), and these are looked down upon. Thus it would be better to learn any one of the first kind, for physical skills often desert a craftsman when he is burdened with old age. In the first category are medicine, rhetoric, music,

geometry and arithmetic, dialectic, astronomy, grammar, and jurispru-
dence. Add to these, if you like, the crafts of sculpturing and painting, for
although these consist of manual work, their practice does not demand
youthful strength. Young men therefore ought to choose one of these arts, if
they are not entirely dull-witted, and they ought to choose among these arts
the best, which is in my opinion the art of medicine. To demonstrate this will
be our next task.

THE BEST KIND OF TEACHING

In Favorinus' opinion,[1] the best kind of teaching is the one that prepares us to argue 'on both sides,' [εἰς ἑκάτερα]. This is the term used by Academic philosophers[2] in accordance with their practice of advocating opposites. The older generation of philosophers therefore considered this doctrine to lead to *epoche*.[3] They used this term to denote 'suspended judgment, lack of determination,'[4] that is, passing no judgment, making no definite pronouncement on anything.

More recent philosophers however – Favorinus is not the only one – sometimes carry *epoche* to the point where they claim that nothing can be grasped by the intellect, not even the existence of the sun. Or else they advance judgment to the point where they allow their pupils to decide on scientific matters before they have studied them.[5] This is what Favorinus says in his book about the nature of Academic philosophy, entitled *Plutarch*.[6] He reiterates this view in his book *To Epictetus*,[7] in which he introduces as partners in discussion Epictetus and Onesimus, Plutarch's servant. In his next work, *To Alcibiades*,[8] he praises other Academic philosophers who practise reasoning on both sides, maintaining conflicting and opposite propositions but allowing their students to choose whichever argument they consider more truthful. In the *Alcibiades* Favorinus expresses the opinion that nothing can be known with certainty; in the *Plutarch*, on the other hand, he seems to concede the possibility of certain knowledge.

It is better to use the term 'knowable' and to abandon the Stoic term 'apprehensible'[9] which some people use.[10] I am amazed (heaven be my witness!) that Favorinus, who normally follows Attic usage in all his terms, continually employs 'apprehensible,' 'apprehension,' and 'apprehensive impression' and describes their opposites (that is, the lack of these qualities) as 'non-apprehensive impression' or even uses the term 'non-apprehensibility.' He is so fond of this terminology that he has written three books, each entitled 'About Apprehensive Impression' (one *To Adrian*, another *To Dryso*, and a third *To Aristarchus*). And in all three books he argues vigorously trying to show that there can be no apprehensive impression.[11]

In my opinion 'apprehensible' and 'apprehend' are equivalent to 'knowable' and 'to know for certain,' and 'apprehension' corresponds to 'apprehensive impression.'[12]

Now sometimes it only seems to us that we see, hear, or perceive things somehow (for example, in dreams or attacks of madness[13]); at other times it is not only our imagination, but we actually see or perceive things somehow. This type of perception is within the realm of certain knowledge and is accepted by everyone except the Academics and the Pyrrhonists.[14] Dream images and mental delusions, however, are generally regarded as false. If the Academics and Pyrrhonists admit that this is the case, let them delete from their books their statement: 'In the judgment of things, the sane man is no more trustworthy than the insane, the healthy no more than the sick, the waking no more than the sleeping.'[15]

If one group of people is no more capable of knowledge than their counterparts, the criteria of truth are indeed in a state of confusion. Neither the Academic teacher himself nor his pupil will be able to pass judgment on the conflicting arguments offered on either side. Indeed, there would be no need at all for such teachers. We ourselves could read the various discussions by authors of different schools. We ourselves could understand them as well as any Academic philosopher, and if anything remained obscure in these authors, the Stoic teachers could expound Chrysippus more reliably,[16] the Peripatetic teachers Theophrastus[17] and Aristotle and so forth, so that the Academic teacher would have nothing left to teach, at least according to Favorinus' argument.

Those philosophers of old denied that man has an innate power of judgment by which he can compare all[18] things and make exact distinctions between them. Consequently they held that one should not make definite pronouncements and should in all cases suspend judgment.

But if they concede us physicians[19] any sensory experience, as is proper, we need no longer practise arguments on both sides. Our requirements[20] are different: repetition is needed, for craftsmen do not instantly[21] convey their art to their disciples, they demand something else: scrutiny of what is handed down,[22] a 'reckoning,'[23] as many people call it. This entails supervising their apprentices, watching out for mistakes, and having the faulty parts (and only the faulty parts!) corrected. Trainers of young boys follow a similar method when they correct mistakes in wrestling. So do teachers of grammar, rhetoric, geometry, and music. They do not weaken or destroy their pupils' faith in natural criteria; on the contrary, they urge their trainees on until they no longer make mistakes in their individual tasks. They certainly do not introduce suspended judgment!

Suspending judgment and thereby refusing to accept either evidence or sense perception is the same [24] as rejecting what is considered certain knowledge by others. Carneades,[25] for instance, refuses to accept even the most evident and generally acknowledged principle: if A has dimension C and B has dimension C, then A and B have the same dimensions.[26] The arguments by which Carneades attempts to destroy this maxim and many other conclusions that are obvious and generally accepted as true are extant to the present day, written down and collected by his disciples. Yet no

solutions have been offered by them or by any other Academic philosopher
after Carneades. This in itself shows that all his arguments are sophisms and
we, dear students, are to find the answers to them! A sorry business indeed.
And no less sorry are the works of the men who wrote these sophisms down
without indicating their nature.

I wish I could ask Favorinus personally if he wants me to believe all
these arguments or if he wants me to examine whether they are true or not.
Surely he would at least permit me to examine them. Then I would put the
question to him in general terms. Do we have a natural ability to distinguish
between truth and falsehood, or is there an art or science of recognizing
each? If we have a natural ability, why do we disagree and give out different
opinions on the same matters? If correct judgment depends on some art or
science, it should have been learned first of all. Then the teachers in charge
of the schools should have trained their students in various ways by
exhibiting many examples, just as those are trained who learn wrestling,
shoemaking, building houses or ships, composing speeches, reading, and
writing – in sum, any activity that follows the rules of an art.

If any Academic philosopher has defined the meaning of 'proof' and of
'sophism,' and has established a mode of distinguishing between the two or
a method of practising them, Favorinus [is right in] admitting[27] the
judgment of students who are versed in arguments on both sides, except
that this is superfluous – [if] indeed an Academic philosopher taught all we
mentioned and we had teachers who taught their own doctrines.[28] But if
none of them write anything about the difference between sophism and
proof, if none of them trained anyone, they seem to act like a carpenter
directing his apprentices to measure, plane, draw lines and circles but failing
to provide them with tools: an ell for measuring, an adze for planing, a rule
for drawing lines, and a compass for drawing circles.[29]

Perhaps someone will say that such matters are irrelevant to philosophical doctrine.[30] Well then, do not pretend to have knowledge, do not
make any pronouncement, and do not abandon the decrees of the older
Academy, who taught suspension of judgment. And do not preen yourself
on your teachings while you act like a grammarian who practises the rules
laid down by prior generations. It is clear to anyone who reflects upon this
matter that there is nothing sound in such doctrines. They are mere stuff and
nonsense, unworthy of a professional teacher.[31]

What hope is left then? What source of true knowledge remains?
Anyone who lacks the ability to distinguish between true and false has no
hope of knowledge. Try only to teach the sophists that we have no natural
power of judgment. Then perhaps someone wanting us to wallow hopeless-
ly in logical speculation will be impudent enough (he says) to concede us a

sense and an intellect by which we can clearly discern the truth.[32] But anyone who would take away all hope [as such a person does] is prating in vain. It is therefore clear that Favorinus turned everything upside-down in his embarassment, for he agreed with the older Academics and Pyrrhonists that nothing could be known,[33] yet pretended to allow his students to pass judgment, a privilege that the older philosophers did not grant even to themselves.

I think I have clearly shown that the kind of doctrine advocated by Favorinus, his kind of instruction for students aspiring to an art, is not only inferior to other teachings, but does not even deserve the name 'doctrine.'

And now let us examine which of the other doctrines can lay claim to excellence, starting anew from the same principles. It is obvious to us that a natural power of judgment exists,[34] although the sophists try to discredit it. After all, the compass draws a circle, the ell measures length, and the scales measure weight. All these tools were made by man himself, directed by his natural faculties and powers of judgment, which are the best and clearest criteria we have. This must be our starting point.

The mind itself declares that we can either trust or question our faculty of judgment, but that we cannot pass judgment on this faculty by anything else. How could it be that the faculty by which we judge everything else should itself be judged by another? Tell me, are you willing or not to believe your eyesight and your tongue's taste when they declare that one object is an apple, another a fig? I shall give you a free hand if you wish to engage in a discussion with me. But if you do not trust your senses, you are preposterous and I want nothing more to do with you.[35]

Let us assume that you do not believe your senses and have no hope of learning anything from me (for that is how I started out[36]). Next, let us assume the opposite: that you believe and hope to learn judgment from me. My position is this: I pass judgment on perceptible phenomena on the basis of what is clearly evident to my senses; I judge conceptual matters on the basis of what is clearly understood by my mind.

Based on our natural powers of judgment, instruments are devised in all the arts and technical criteria are established by which men can make their own devices or judge those of others. And correspondingly, I shall teach you the instruments and criteria of judgment in general so that you may either prepare your own true arguments or judge those proffered by others. And this is all you need.

If something is obvious to the senses or to the mind, there is no need for further inquiry. If this is not the case, knowledge must be derived from another source. But I offer to provide you with means of investigation corresponding to the tools devised in the arts; also, criteria like those of the craftsmen by which you can verify your findings. And when you have learned that, I shall train you with many examples so that you can quickly and precisely find what you are looking for and judge the material accurately. And you will no longer need a book or another doctrine to discover the truth, but will soon be able to recognize when others mention anything pertaining to your research. Indeed, anyone who knows the right method[37] needs no other doctrine to refute those who are in error, and anyone who has learned the correct method of proof can at the same time also tell what methods are wrong.[38]

As for Favorinus, he seems to act like someone who tells you that you[39] are blind but are still able to determine which of us is dirtier or cleaner, without considering that one must have sight to judge such matters. And as far as judgment is concerned, it makes no difference whether you are quite blind, or can see but do not trust your vision. The same applies to mental judgments, for example, the argument 'if A and B are like C, then A, B, and C are alike.'[40]

No one allows asses to sit in judgment because they are completely devoid of intellect, and the same goes for people who have no mind they can trust. It makes no difference whether you completely lack powers of judgment or lack trust in them; in either case your judgment of matters under consideration will not be dependable.[41] It is ridiculous of Favorinus to allow his students to pass judgment when he creates uncertainty about the criteria of judgment.

If nothing is evident to our intellect and nothing clear by itself, there can be no certain judgment of things. But let us assume that there are reliable physical or intellectual means of judgment (such as the eye and, corresponding to it, the mind), but that not all people have equally keen faculties. If this is the case, it is only proper that the man who has the keener vision lead the man whose sight is weaker to the object of contemplation. By the same token those whose mind can clearly perceive its object should guide the man who is least discerning in the contemplation of it. And this is the teacher's responsibility, as Plato says[42] (and I agree with him).

I have written about this matter in more detail in my treatise *On Proof*[43] because such a doctrine is conducive to certain knowledge. I have also explained how one can best prove what can be proved, starting with the basic elements and first-beginnings in each case. The admirable Favorinus, on the other hand, has written a whole book to show that one cannot even apprehend the sun. Then he would have us forget this assertion and listen to his disputing on both sides and his concession that something can be known for certain after all, the judgment and choice of which he leaves up to his students.

THE PROPER PHYSICIAN

Most athletes would like to become Olympic victors, but never bother to undertake the training necessary to achieve their goal. A great many physicians have adopted the same attitude: they praise Hippocrates and place him above all physicians, but have no genuine desire to become like him themselves. Some, for instance, say that astronomy and its necessary prerequisite, geometry, are of considerable importance to medicine,[1] yet they themselves not only are unwilling to study either of these sciences, they even find fault with those who venture to do so. Another,[2] in turn demands[3] exact knowledge of the body's nature,[4] asserting that this is the basis of all medical science. But such is their interest in these matters that they are not only ignorant of the nature, tissue, conformation, and size of each individual organ and its connection with adjoining parts – they do not even know its position!

Now Hippocrates declared that medical error in directing treatment stems from the fact that we do not know how to distinguish between diseases by species and genus. He therefore prescribes for us training in logical reasoning.[5] The physicians of our time, however, far from having been trained in logic, condemn others for studying it, as if they were engaging in useless pursuits.

Hippocrates also said that it takes much effort and careful preparation to recognize in advance[6] what diseases have previously affected a patient, are affecting him at the time, and will affect him in future. They, however, care little about this aspect of medicine. If anyone predicts haemorrhaging or sweating, they call him a charlatan whose claims lack credibility. They barely tolerate any other predictions that are put forward, yet they themselves are hardly ever able to decide on a diet for the impending climax of a disease, although Hippocrates says that the patient's diet should be controlled in these circumstances.[7]

So what is left of Hippocrates' doctrine? In what point do they imitate the man? Certainly not in clarity of exposition, which is one of the fields in which Hippocrates excelled.[8] On the contrary: one may observe many of them making two errors in one expression, which is indeed difficult to understand.

I have therefore decided to investigate this matter. Why is it that everybody admires Hippocrates but refuses to read his books or at any rate fails to understand their meaning? And why, if someone has acquired an understanding, does he not put Hippocrates' theory into practice, why does he refuse to consolidate what he has learned and to introduce it into his routine? Surely [the aspirant to excellence] realizes that everything will turn out to his heart's content only if he has both determination and ability.[9] If either of these prerequisites is lacking, he must fall short of his objective. Athletes are a case in point: if they fail to achieve their desired goal, it is either because of physical shortcomings or because of negligence in their training. Indeed, if a man's physical condition is fit for victory and his training perfect, what could prevent him from carrying off a crown[10] in the races?

Do the physicians of our time miss out on both counts, then? Do they bring neither ability nor sufficient and adequate determination to the practice of their art, or do they possess one, but lack the other? I think it is preposterous to say that not a single person can be found in our time who has the natural disposition[11] to learn an art that is such a friend and patron to mankind. After all, the world is no different now than it was before. Neither has the order of seasons been altered, nor the sun's course been reversed, nor have any of the other stars or planets been changed.

Why is it then that our age has no sculptors of Phidias' calibre[12] or painters like Apelles[13] or physicians like Hippocrates? One plausible explanation is that the education received nowadays is unsatisfactory, another that wealth is valued more highly than excellence. And yet, we have no slight advantage over past generations whom we have succeeded in time: we have received the arts from them in a highly advanced state. The teaching of Hippocrates, developed over a long period of time, can now be learned with utmost ease in a few years. And once we have mastered that, we can spend the remainder of our life discovering what still needs to be discovered. But a man who considers wealth more important than excellence and who has learned his profession, not with a view of benefiting mankind, but for the purpose of becoming rich, cannot possibly obtain the degree of perfection proper to medicine. Indeed, others will become rich before we can perfect our science. It is therefore quite impossible to do both: satisfy our desire for money and practise such a difficult art. A man who is too keenly inclined towards one goal must needs neglect the other.

Can we, then, discover among our contemporaries a man who only desires enough money to satisfy his bodily needs? Does a man exist who is able, not only to express in words, but also to show in his actual practices that, according to nature, ultimate wealth consists of nothing more than absence of hunger, thirst and cold? If such a man exists, surely he will despise both Artaxerxes[14] and Perdiccas.[15] He will not even deign to look upon Perdiccas' face, though he will treat the ailing Artaxerxes when he calls upon the art of Hippocrates. A permanent life at court he will disdain, however, and rather heal the poor in Cranon and Thasos[16] or treat the sick in other small towns. Indeed, Cos[17] and its citizens he will leave to Polybus[18] and many others of his disciples, while he himself will travel through all of Greece, for he has an obligation to write about the characteristics of places.[19]

In order to test by experience what he has learned in theory, he must see with his own eyes all communities, facing north, south, east, and west. He must see communities situated in plains, on an elevation or on a shore,[20] and exposed to water; those with an abundance[21] of water from springs and rainfalls or with a supply from rivers and lakes. And he will not neglect to find out if a community makes use of water that is very cold or hot, rich in minerals or tonic, and other things of this sort. He will visit communities overlooking great rivers, situated on lakeshores, close to mountains, or by the sea. And he will contemplate all the rest about which Hippocrates himself has taught us.

To become such a one, a man must not only neglect money matters, but also be extremely energetic and industrious. Now a heavy drinker cannot be energetic and industrious, nor can one who stuffs himself with food or eagerly pursues Venus – in short anyone who is a slave to his sex and his stomach. It is therefore the man who loves temperance and truth no less who is found to be the true physician.

Moreover, he must learn and practise the art of reasoning to find out the number of diseases in general, their classification by genus and species, and the methods of treating each of them. The art of reasoning also teaches him about the nature of the body:[22] the substance consisting of primary elements, which are all interconnected with each other and mutually dependent; and the substance consisting of secondary elements, namely those that can be perceived, called *homeomere*[23] (which means 'of similar parts'); and in addition the third substance consisting of functional parts. Besides, logic also teaches him how each of the substances mentioned benefits the living being and how they work. And he must not take these matters for granted, but ought to be certain and convinced by proof. This too is a part of logical training.

In what respect, then, does the physician who practises Hippocrates' art as it deserves fall short of being a philosopher?[24] If it is fitting for a man to be trained in logic so as to understand the nature of the body, the difference between various diseases and the methods of curing them, and if, to pursue these practices with dedication, a man must despise money matters and observe temperance, he will indeed know all aspects of philosophy: logic, physics and ethics, as they are termed.

And one need not fear that a man who despises money and practises temperance will do anything irresponsible. Whatever the crime committed, a criminal acts either beguiled by greed or deceived by desire. It follows that he who is free of greed and desire also possesses the remaining virtues, for they are all interdependent. It is impossible to cultivate any one of them and not acquire the rest as well, because they follow each other as if roped together.

If physicians need philosophy, both to recognize the first-beginnings of their art and to practise the subsequent steps, it is obvious that whoever is a physician is also a philosopher in the full sense. For I consider it unnecessary to show that physicians need philosophy to make proper use of their art, since we generally see that men who are bent on making money and use their profession for purposes other than those for which it was conceived are not physicians, but poisoners.

Surely, then, you will no longer quibble about words and engage in useless arguments, contending that a physician must indeed be temperate and modest, that he must despise money and be just, but that it is not necessary for him to be a philosopher or to know the nature of bodies, the activities of organs, the function of parts, the difference between diseases, and the methods of treatment; and since you admit that he is versed in logical reasoning or in practice,[25] are you not ashamed to quibble? Enough![26] At present it is better not to behave[27] like jackdaws or crows, and argue about words –let us rather attend to the truth of the matter. No one can become an expert without learning and practising, not even a weaver or a cobbler. Therefore you will not claim that a man can instantly become just, temperate, and skilled in giving proofs. Nor can he instantly excel in the knowledge of nature without having taken a teacher or having trained himself – it would be absurd to make such a claim. The previous argument, however, is worthy only of a man who disputes about words, not facts. We true followers of Hippocrates must practise the kind of philosophy described before.[28] And once we have done so, nothing can prevent us from becoming like him, and I dare say, superior to him, since we may learn thoroughly what he has correctly recorded, and then go on to discover by our own enterprise what still remains to be discovered.

THE TONGUE

Lingua

translated and annotated by

ELAINE FANTHAM

Erasmus was already ill at ease in Basel and beginning to consider alternative places of residence when he turned to composing the *Lingua* in 1525. We cannot tell when he first conceived the work, but his preface marks its completion in July of that year.[1] It was a bad year for him, and its trials are reflected in the relative sombreness of the work itself. Towards the beginning of February he suffered an appalling attack of gallstones, which he describes to Pirckheimer as all but fatal.[2] Around him the peasants' uprising was spreading into southern Germany, and in his most pessimistic letters he sees Europe as on the edge of barbarism.[3]

If he felt persecuted on all sides, it was not without justification. While the pope and emperor remained well disposed,[4] he suffered from the resentment of the Swiss reformers that he would not join them, and twice in this year wrote to the town council of Basel justifying his quietism and advising them to show respect for the authority of the church, even while they deviated from its practice.[5] He had been considerably embarrassed by Oecolampadius' attempt to claim him as a supporter and reveals his basic anxiety in a reproachful letter. Oecolampadius is seen as undoing by his untimely praise[6] all Erasmus' achievement in proving his loyalty to the church by *De libero arbitrio* in 1524.

In this atmosphere of increasing suspicion and acrimony Erasmus had not only to intervene on behalf of innocent friends and scholars,[7] but also to defend himself against various forms of misrepresentation and slander. It is this context which explains the brooding dominance of *calumnia* at the centre of the *Lingua*, and the bitterness of his allusions to both mendicant friars and established theologians.[8] The most serious confrontation was with Noël Béda, formerly of the Collège de Montaigu, and now syndic of the faculty of theology of Paris, who examined Erasmus' *Paraphrases* for evidence of theological error. Béda circulated his findings and had them printed by Josse Bade late in May 1526. His correspondence with Erasmus maintains a surface courtesy,[9] but Erasmus clearly resented the source of this criticism as much as its thinly veiled accusation of heresy. To make things worse, the faculty condemned Louis de Berquin's French translations of four works of Erasmus, the *Encomium matrimonii*, the *Inquisitio de fide*, *De esu carnium*, and the *Querela pacis*.[10]

The bitterness of Erasmus' feelings is evident in his statement to Béda that he might easily have been driven by the persecution of the academic theologians to join the Lutherans, and if he had done so things would have come to such a pass that no one would any longer heed any theologians.[11]

Encouraged by the attitude of the Sorbonne a Carthusian, Pierre Cousturier (Petrus Sutor), had composed and printed an attack on Erasmus. July saw the completion of Erasmus' reply: *Apologia adversus debacchationes*

Petri Sutoris in three books, dedicated to Jean de Selve,[12] *premier président* of the Bordeaux parliament, who was also chief negotiator for the ransoming of Erasmus' patron, King Francis, from the emperor. As always, Erasmus found effective allies in the governing class of the laity, who recognized his power for reconciliation.

Another letter of this month reflects Erasmus' ironic contempt for the oblique attacks of the Louvain theologians. Silenced by an injunction of Pope Adrian vi in 1522, they had returned after his death to their attacks both on the Collegium Trilingue and on Erasmus himself. A Dominican named Vincentius Theoderici[13] had issued under the pseudonym of Taxander a pamphlet accusing Erasmus of heresy and distortion of the Scriptures. In Ep 1582 Erasmus was led to recall the earlier attack of Latomus (Jacques Masson) on the study of the Scriptures in Greek and Hebrew, in which Erasmus was not named but, as he claimed, quoted anonymously and condemned.[14]

Thus he found himself attacked by the men who should represent the church he was defending, and accused of cowardice by the reformers whom his loyalty and moderation forbade him to join. But although Erasmus may have been provoked to the composition of the *Lingua* by his recent experiences of slander and *odium theologicum*, he was writing in a long tradition that could be said to have bridged the gap between the age of Jerome and Augustine and the revival of pagan learning. A recent article by Mark Johnston has surveyed the treatment of speech in precept literature, in scriptural exegesis from the patristic period, and in monastic rules from the seventh to the fourteenth century.[15] Thus the *Scintillarum liber* (*Book of Sparks*) of Defensor in the seventh century gathers biblical and patristic precepts on the *vitia linguae* (sins of the tongue) under similar headings and in very much the same order as the *Lingua*: loquacity, vainglory, swearing, lying, detraction, and idle talk.[16] Taio of Saragossa's *Sententiarum libri v* (*Five Books of Aphorisms*) recognize loquacity, perverse talk, whispering, and lying.[17] The work *De copia verborum* (*On the Source of Language*) attributed to Seneca draws on excerpts from Seneca's letters to Lucilius but also on Martin of Braga's *Formula vitae honestae* (*Rule for a Virtuous Life*).[18]

Johnston quotes from sermon literature St Valerianus' sermons on the wantonness of the mouth and on idle speech, which cover 'loquacity, harsh words, taciturnity, foul words, boasting, evil talk, falsehood, lying, slander, detraction, joking, and theatre.'[19] Both Bede in his explication of the Epistle of James, chapter 3[20] and Hrabanus Maurus commenting on *Ecclesiasticus*[21] list the sins of speech. The lists grow more extensive in later works such as St Bernard's sermon on the threefold control of hand, tongue, and heart.[22]

Monastic rules seem to have opposed all these sins of the tongue to the silence proper to the cloister. Johnston discusses Abbot Smaragdus' ninth-century commentary on the Rule of St Benedict[23] and singles out from the twelfth century two substantial treatments: Philip of Harveng's *De institutione clericorum* (*On the Training of Clerics*), which has an extended allegorical exposition of monastic silence,[24] and Hugh of St Victor's *De institutione novitiorum* (*On the Training of Novices*), of which a third is concerned with speech, associating rhetorical defects of speech and delivery with moral corruption.[25]

The thirteenth century saw the systematic classification of vices of the tongue as a separate category subordinated to or added to the seven capital sins. In his *Summa de vitiis et virtutibus* Peraldus adds the offence of the tongue as an eighth sin after envy and anger.[26] In contrast Laurentius Gallus divides *gula* (gluttony) into gluttony proper and the sins of the tongue in his *Somme le Roy* (*Compendium for the King*).[27] Etienne de Bourbon's *Tractatus de diversis materiis praedicabilibus* (*Treatise on Various Materials for Preaching*) opens the account of the sins by the threefold division into sins of thought, tongue, and senses which we met in St Bernard;[28] we might compare Vincent of Beauvais' *Speculum doctrinale* (*Mirror of Doctrine*) and *Speculum naturale* (*Mirror of Nature*); the former follows the treatment of *luxuria* with a section on vices of the tongue; the latter observes the same tripartite division between sins of the heart, mouth, and senses.[29]

Most important is the concern of St Thomas Aquinas with the evil done by sins of the tongue. In book 2 of the *Summa theologiae* he divides these sins into two groups: defamation, detraction, whispering, ridicule, and cursing offend by destroying the bond between individual men;[30] lying, deception, hypocrisy, boasting, false modesty, flattery, and quarrelling destroy the bonds between the individual and society in general.[31] Just as Cicero declared that eloquence founded society by persuading men into co-operation,[32] so St Thomas treats language as the foundation of human organization in the community. This positive aspect of speech, in both its pagan and its Christian celebration from Cicero and St Augustine through to his own time, has influenced the last quarter of Erasmus' diatribe, the use of speech for man's salvation, in the service and for the greater glory of God.

One country alone appeared untouched by liturgical or theological conflict, and it is to the representatives of this land, Poland, that Erasmus turns, dedicating his work 'on the use and abuse of the tongue' to Krzysztof Szydłowiecki, castellan of Cracow and chancellor of the realm, through the intermediary of his young protégé Jan (II) Łaski, nephew of the archbishop of Cracow.[33] Letters to and from other Polish friends report the enthusiasm for Erasmus in Poland: Jan Łaski's brother Hieronim confirms to Erasmus that Szydłowiecki was delighted with the *Lingua*, and we have an admiring letter from the poet Andrzej Krzycki (Critius) associating himself proudly with previous local editions of Erasmus' works.[34] The *Lingua* was to be published at Cracow by Vietor in the following year.

The first edition by Froben in August 1525 was quickly repeated in February and July 1526. According to Vander Haeghen the *Lingua* was also published by Stephanus at Paris in 1525, but Schalk records only the later Stephanus edition of 1529. (In view of Berquin's execution, it is not surprising that there is no record of any French translations of the *Lingua*). The year 1526 saw editions not only by Froben in Basel and Vietor in Cracow but also by Hillen in Antwerp[35] (he put out another edition in 1537) and an unnamed publisher in Hagenau. The *Lingua* was also published separately by Hittorp at Cologne in 1530 and 1539 and by Gryphius at Lyon in 1538, before inclusion in the Basel *Erasmi opera* of 1540.

The only external evidence for Erasmus' own correction of the *Lingua* is a letter of October 1525 written to Pierre Barbier (Ep 1621), asking him incidentally to correct an error of 200,000 ducats into 200,000 talents on the last sheet of folio *n*, on the recto, near the bottom of the page.[36] This was left unchanged in the printing of February 1526, but corrected, along with some minor changes in the preface, in the modified edition of August that year.

Between 1540 and the Leiden edition of 1703–6 (LB IV 656–754) the *Lingua* was republished by Froben at Basel in 1547, at Coburg in 1623 and 1624, and at Leiden in 1629 and 1649.

The appeal of the *Lingua* seems to have been uneven. There are no English editions, nor are translations into English recorded in Devereux's check-list for the sixteenth and seventeenth centuries; to my knowledge no English translation has appeared prior to my own. But the work was quickly translated into Spanish, since Schalk lists two Spanish versions published at Valencia in 1531 and two more in quick succession from Toledo.[37] Interest in Erasmus had been fostered by the work of the University of Alcalá on the Polyglot Bible, which gave Spanish scholars the background for their study of Erasmus' New Testament and his edition of St Jerome. Vives too had a great part in spreading appreciation of Erasmus in Spain, despite the relative indifference of Erasmus to Vives' own scholarship.[38] Marcel Bataillon has investigated the authorship of the first anonymous translation and noted the influence of *Lingua* on the academic admirers of Erasmus' Latin rhetoric. The five editions published between 1541 and 1551 are attributed by Schalk to the enthusiasm for emulating Erasmus' style, *lengua elegante y estile divino*, to quote the prefatory poem of the 1531 translation.[39]

The *Lingua* was repeatedly translated into Flemish between 1534 and 1634, generally under the title *Lingua, dat is de Tonge*. But Schalk also reports a German translation of 1541 made by a naturalized citizen of Basel, Basilius Johannes Herold, and dedicated to the margrave of Baden. The subtitle given is '... und wirdt darin angezeigt was die Zunge sei, wie sie das und das Böst Glied sei, auch ihren stant thun und lassen, was je Böss daraus entstanden. Auch was guts davon kommen sei, wider alle Klapperer and Schwetzer, die irer Zungen Knecht seindt / ... and herein is shown what the tongue is, how it is the most wicked organ of man, also as to the evil that constantly arises from leaving it uncontrolled. Also the good which derives from it, against all chatterers and drivellers who are slaves to their tongues.' The translator has divided the work into twenty-eight chapters and permitted himself some reorganization to bring together contradictory arguments.

The *Lingua* was intended to be a source of pleasure as well as edification, though perhaps it has little more in common with Erasmus' other, more famous ethical diatribe, the *Moria*, than its direction to the general and secular reader. The work is in the rhetorical tradition, blending the analytical approach of ancient essays on the nature of a given phenomenon with the epideictic techniques of invective and encomium that ultimately go back to Isocrates and the sophists. Traditionally the scholar writing on a theme would discuss the origin, nature, cause, and purpose of the subject, whether the purpose be that of a human inventor or of a providential creator. It was rhetorical practice to enumerate and amplify the powers of the subject, stressing the inseparability of its power to do good and evil.

Though Erasmus makes his starting point the physical function of the organ, the *Lingua* coincides in many of its positive claims with the praise of *logos*, which denotes in Greek both thought and speech and was singled out by the early sophists like Gorgias as the distinctive gift of man.[40] The two aspects of *logos* must be translated separately in Latin, but the praises which rightly belong to *ratio* (logical thought) are freely given to *oratio* (speech) by Cicero in *De inventione* and *De oratore* on the grounds that thought in man is ineffective without persuasive speech.[41] But the pagan rhetorical tradition naturally inclined to glorify rather than condemn the power of speech, and Erasmus' work, almost three-quarters of which deals with the misuse of speech from folly, intemperance, or malice, draws on other sources as well: anecdotes from satire and comedy, moral essays (giving pride of place to Plutarch's essay on the evils of talkativeness), Senecan dialogues, and collections of sayings. The latter are used by Plutarch and other Greek sources to illustrate the wit and wisdom of either a famous man or a community (such as the Spartans) and thus do not prescribe to Erasmus the moral applications which he gives to them. He has adapted principles both of pagan prudence and of Christian charity to draw from this material lessons that gradually rise from the practical to the moral and spiritual levels.

But instead of a single sequence passing from the abuse of the tongue to its services, Erasmus follows the first short sequence by a second one four times longer. In the first cycle (starting at 269 / ASD IV 245:254), the section which I have headed 'Undisciplined use of the tongue: talkativeness' is followed (at 285 / 261:802) by a shorter unit which I have headed 'The benefits of silence and of careful use of the tongue.' But when Erasmus begins the second cycle (293 / 268:1078), his discussion of the abuse of the tongue extends over more than 70 pages. I have divided this for convenience of reference between Erasmus' treatment of folly and indiscretion, headed 'The evils of an undisciplined tongue' (from 293 / 268:1078 to 318 / 289:1840), and his discussion of the malicious and slanderous tongue, headed 'The evils of a vicious tongue' (which extends to 367 / 332:3418). In comparison, what Erasmus has to say on 'The usefulness of a good tongue and remedies against an evil tongue' (367 / 332:3418 to 402 / ASD 362:4530) still gives as much attention to the evils of the tongue as its remedies. The final positive and hortatory section on 'Christian use of the tongue' is shortest of all, occupying only 10 pages (from 402 / ASD 362:4530 to 412 / 370:4838).

Erasmus' own recent experiences led him to a preponderant concern with deliberate malice, and the central section of the *Lingua* voices his personal grievances against friars and theologians (naturally left unnamed) and his sensitivity to charges of intellectual dishonesty and heresy.[42] This sense of grievance creates an imbalance in the work, leaving relatively short Erasmus' development of positive recommendations to Christians to use their speech to restrain malice, to reconcile, to turn away wrath, and at its highest to serve them as apostles, like Paul, to spread the word of Christ. In this connection we may note that Erasmus introduces the key concept of Christian charity four times in the central section denouncing calumny, where charity towards God and one's neighbour defines his requirements of the Christian, whether layman, priest, or monk; this section ends with the Pauline injunction to 'bless them that curse you; bless and curse not.'[43] But when Erasmus returns to the teaching of St Paul after a digression on pagan principles of restraint, though he repeats the same injunction, his exhortation to his readers to adopt Christian standards of kindness and even to imitate the speech of Christ himself never refers again to charity. This is all the more extraordinary as his final invocation of 'the tongue of angels'[44] can only recall Paul's famous outcry: 'Though I speak with the tongues of men and of angels, and have not charity, I am become as sounding brass or a tinkling cymbal.'[45] This remarkable omission of the most important moral concept is not only strange in itself, but when seen in contrast with the prominence of charity in the earlier section suggests a discontinuity between

Erasmus' composition of the diatribe against calumny and the final climactic invocation – a discontinuity that has not been healed by any revision. It is perhaps most easily explained if the section on calumny, with its stress on charity, was inserted after Erasmus reached the end of his original composition, and reflects his reaction to the provocation of Béda, Taxander, and other contemporary 'Pharisees.'[46]

Erasmus has used different sources for different sections of the work, which may have been composed at intervals. Though it is bound together by thematic imagery, like that of the serpent's venom, healed by the Psylli in God's service,[47] there are repetitions that are not thematic or deliberately resumptive, but sheer oversights[48]; there are also abrupt connections, and isolated passages of close adaptation from individual sources, such as the book of Sirach,[49] Pliny on poison and antidote,[50] Plutarch's *Apophthegmata*, (which Erasmus himself later paraphrased and expanded),[51] and even of his own *Adagia*.[52]

Erasmus would have done well to abridge or at least tighten the argument of the *Lingua* and make the direction of his thought apparent by headings. I have taken the liberty of inserting these to help the reader move forward without too much distraction from anecdote.

The discouraging effect of the *Lingua* is perhaps largely due to the disproportion between its extensive parade of human error and its too brief proposals for the beneficial use of speech. But this was in part because Erasmus had already formed the ambition of writing a larger and more comprehensive study of the art of preaching, a counterpart of the fourth book of Augustine's *De doctrina christiana* on harnessing rhetoric in the service of God. It is above all the anticipation of this later work (begun by 1523 and barely finished at his death)[53] which enabled Erasmus to follow his discursive diatribe against the misuse of speech with so economical a section of recommendations, giving the weight of his attention to remedial speech designed to counteract human folly in a social context and leaving to the last brief exhortation the prophet and preacher's use of the tongue of angels.

Apart from careless transcription of Greek ligatures and many typographical errors in the Latin text,[54] ASD differs minimally from the Leiden edition; a few divergences have been noted in the annotations.

Quotations from the Vulgate (not from Erasmus' own text of the Bible) have been rendered by the slightly archaic English of the Douai Bible, itself based on the Vulgate; the translations from Greek and Roman poetry into verse are my own. Erasmus quotes poetry for its content, not its literary beauty, and I have aimed to represent this while adhering as closely as possible to the form and tone of the original.[55]

EF

TO THE ILLUSTRIOUS KRZYSZTOF SZYDŁOWIECKI, PALATINE AND PREFECT OF
CRAKOW, CHANCELLOR OF THE KINGDOM OF POLAND, FROM ERASMUS OF
ROTTERDAM, GREETING[1]

Distinguished sir, distinguished for more than the glory of your line, the life
of mankind is beset on all sides by so many great misfortunes that when
Homer compared our lot with that of all the different kinds of living
creatures, he concluded that 'there is no creature more miserable than
man.'[2] Silenus judged it best never to have been born, or, once born, to
perish at the earliest possible time.[3] Pliny thought that no greater or more
generous gift was given by the gods to man than shortness of life,[4] and that
no one was denied the power to end that life, if he so decided. In Lucian,
Pythagoras, whose soul is supposed to have changed its abode repeatedly
and to have entered into the bodies of creatures of every kind, men and
women, bipeds and quadrupeds, admits that he lived a much happier life as
a frog than as a king.[5] All this may sound absurd, but it would not be far from
the truth, if that heavenly teacher of wisdom had not convinced us that
everlasting happiness is laid up for those who have placed all their hopes of
bliss, from stem to stern,[6] as it were, in him. So powerful is this hope that
even in the greatest misfortunes it preserves and sustains the joy which
belongs to a soul at peace with itself, especially since it always has that
wonderful and miraculous talisman that turns all the gall of this life into
honey.

Since man, being composed of body and soul, is troubled by two kinds
of affliction, wise men have always sought to know whether the ailments of
the body or those of the soul are worse, and the answer they have given is
that ailments of the soul have more terrible consequences. Yet common
opinion is far from agreeing with this view. There are few indeed who do not
think it worse to suffer from dropsy than from avarice. Similarly it is
considered a greater blessing to have a splendid physique than a mind
enriched with fine learning and noble qualities. We cannot be surprised that
men who put the body before the soul also make inverted judgments about
what is good and what is bad. Antiquity counted some three hundred
varieties of disease besides accidents and deformities; to this number new
and previously unknown diseases have been added,[7] and continue to be
added every day in a sort of guerrilla war against the science of medicine.
But who could count the ailments of the soul? I wish it were only in number
that they surpassed the ills of the body, but, alas, they have the advantage in
many other respects as well. For in the first place it is the better part of us
which they harm. Then physical illnesses only make men sick, but diseases
of the soul make us evil and wretched as well, because they come from
within ourselves. Again, there are some physical illnesses which do not

entail acute pain, like consumption. But would you say that the physical pain of dropsy or fever surpasses the mental torment caused by the craving for money, or rampant lust, or jealousy, or envy? Moreover, illnesses of the body often bring relief to the troubles of the mind, whereas moral failings are generally accompanied by physical problems too. We are more apprehensive about physical ailments that are not only disagreeable but carry a stigma as well; but all moral ailments act like this: for not only do they rob the mind of its calm, but they bring shame to the sufferer.

Doctors think that there is no type of illness more dreadful than that which robs the patient of his capacity to understand his trouble. The sufferer from gout who keeps complaining of his troubles and has the doctor called in is easier to cure than the lunatic or the lethargic.[8] One of these thinks he is sane, the other assaults the doctor who wants to help him.[9] Almost all sicknesses of the mind are like this – the worse the illness is, the less will the sufferer accept the doctor's help. These ailments, too, differ among themselves. It is far easier to heal self-indulgence, lust, extravagance, and all the less complicated mental illnesses – if I may call them that – than to cure ambition, envy, selfishness, and hypocrisy. You will see many people who could never be charged with fornication or drunkeness but who are totally immersed in self-love and measure everything by this yardstick. If someone opposes them, there is no type of revenge they will not resort to, and their abominable desires are covered up with a mask of fine-sounding names. Nothing is more destructive or more difficult to cure than this type of man.

The mind can pass judgment on the ailments of the body, but this is impossible in the case of illnesses of the mind, because we are damaged in the very part which enables us to judge. What remedy then could you apply to help the man who calls his insatiable acquisitiveness 'taking thought for the future' or his envy 'a passion for honour,' or who gives the name of 'prudence' to blind self-love and covers up a compulsive scurrility with the label of 'frankness'? We might add that the man whose feet are crippled with gout is still sound in eye and ear, but a single moral ailment corrupts the whole mind. Again, a man troubled with the stone is free of other diseases.[10] But there is no moral sickness which does not bring with it a whole regiment of vices.

Furthermore, if we should estimate the seriousness of a disease by the danger of infection, then, if we believe Pliny, old men are immune from the plague; nor does the plague spread at random, but arises in the south and generally travels westward.[11] Some illnesses do not affect children, and others pass over the female sex; some, such as eczema, attack the ruling class and spare the common people.[12] Some diseases affect only particular ages, or even districts. Leprosy[13] and *gemursa*[14] quickly died out when they crossed over into Italy. England did not experience the deadly sweating-sickness until thirty years ago,[15] and it is a scourge which does not generally pass beyond the limits of the island. All these diseases have their particular territory and their particular seasons and tend to attack certain persons and even certain parts of the body. But plagues of the mind spare neither rank nor sex nor age and are restrained by no boundaries, but sweep the earth with unimaginable speed. Nor do they yield place to one another in turn, as plague and quinsy and whooping cough break out one at a time. But each moral weakness is responsible for another, like the links in a chain; and once they have set in, it is not easy to be rid of them.

Suppose someone asked which disease of the body should be accorded the first place. In my opinion the prize will fall easily to that disease of unknown origin which has stalked every region of the earth for many years now, though there is no settled convention about its name. Most men call it the French, but some the Spanish pox.[16] Is there any plague which has traversed the various regions of Europe, Asia, and Africa with equal speed? Does any penetrate more deeply into our veins and organs, or persist more doggedly or defy more stubbornly the skill and treatment of the doctors? Is any disease more contagious or responsible for more cruel torments? Psoriasis is not harmful except for the disfigurement of the skin, and it admits of cure.[17] Eczema covers first the face and then the rest of the body with an ugly scaling rash, but there is no pain and no risk to life, although it is true there is no cure except one that is worse than death.[18] But this scourge brings in its train all the terrifying aspects of other illnesses: disfigurement, pain, infection, the risk of losing one's life, and a treatment that is both difficult and extremely unpleasant; and no matter how successfully it is controlled, it suddenly breaks out again, like gout.

Finally, if anyone were to consider diseases of the mind and ask which had the greatest power to harm, I would not hesitate to give this unrewarding award, this prize which no one prizes, to the affliction of an unbridled tongue. This plague is neither new nor simple in nature, but includes all the diseases of the mind. No generation has ever been so sound in morals that it did not complain of this affliction. Some fevers and plagues never die out, but erupt from time to time like a flood and rage more violently than before, and over a wider region, threatening the human race with annihilation. In the same way we can now see how this deadly sickness of a malicious tongue has infected the whole world with its awful venom, pervading the courts of princes, the homes of commoners, theological schools, monastic brotherhoods, colleges of priests, regiments of soldiers, and the cottages of peasants. So great is the force of the onslaught that it threatens the total ruin and destruction of the liberal arts, good morals, civic harmony, and the authority of the leaders of the church and the princes of the realm alike.

When the scourge of which I spoke a moment ago first began to spread, our initial reactions were torpid, and even now we are not awake to the danger of infection, although sufferers from leprosy, a less serious illness, are isolated from human contact. But faced with an even greater threat to human society, we have done nothing so far to control the reckless frenzy of men's tongues, and we are still doing nothing. Meanwhile the sickness grows worse each day and is passing beyond cure. There are some who, like incompetent doctors, have merely aggravated the disease by their ill-advised treatment. Bishops who combined Christian prudence and knowledge of the gospel with an attitude of moderation should have made this matter their special province. We can see what has been achieved so far by branding, mutilation, and imprisonment.[19] As for my own contribution, although I do not possess the authority, learning, and wisdom which the gravity of the malady requires, in my distress over the general calamity which has befallen the Christian world I am offering such palliatives as I can. If the disease cannot be eradicated completely, it is my hope that by these means it may at least be weakened.

I have heard from the honourable Jan Łaski[20] that there is still much of that old-fashioned morality among your people – I might say in poetic terms that Astraea, in her flight from the world, seems to have left her last footprints in your land.[21] I understand that it is enjoying great prosperity, thanks to the wise government of that virtuous and watchful ruler, Archbishop Jan Łaski, who in our decadent age is reviving the example of the bishops of old. I find these reports easier to believe, having experienced in my informant an honesty and self-discipline such as I have rarely met before in any other man. If, as I think, this general scourge of a malicious tongue has not yet reached your own dear Poland, then I thought I might celebrate your good fortune with this composition; but if some trace of the infection has spread to you, my gift will serve as an antidote.

It was the Jan Łaski whom I mentioned a moment ago who encouraged me to publish this work under the auspices of your name. He has never ceased to speak most enthusiastically about your great natural gifts and outstanding qualities. As a result I too have been filled with admiration for your merits, and feel I must congratulate both you and the whole kingdom of Poland upon your excellence as a minister of affairs. The person who inspired this dedication is quite young in years, but he is mature in character and old in judgment. He is too shrewd a witness to be deceived; and claims which are advanced with such persistence and enthusiasm cannot be invention. Indeed if you will be kind enough to accept a poor creature like myself into your circle, I shall count myself fortunate to have you as friend or patron. I feel no embarrassment about this request, for the friendship of such men as you has always seemed to me the greatest factor in human happiness. Yet it is not for ourselves that we seek the favour of princes, but for the cause of piety and learning, which are now everywhere endangered by the factious feuding of certain individuals and would collapse altogether if they were not propped up by the authority and loyalty of men like you. I would cut a sorry figure indeed if I were still seeking offices and benefactions for myself, when I am so soon to leave this life. Such gifts are mere burdens; they weigh a man down when he is preparing his soul to take flight, and cannot follow him when he is gone. If I have been of any help to the humanities or to the Christian faith by my studies, or by the good men whom my exhortations have aroused, then this will be my prize, and I shall gladly take it with me as provision for the journey.

But I have kept you too long from the *Lingua* itself. I fear there are places where a discriminating man like yourself might hope to see a clearer arrangement. But the material is of immense variety, and in trying to touch on every aspect and to combine the sacred with the profane, I have found it difficult to avoid confusion, all the more so since I had no leisure to polish all the material which I have brought together. Farewell.

Basel, 14 August 1525

THE TONGUE

[The tongue: its nature and capacity]

I beg you all to listen with such care and attention as you generally give to good advice on important and weighty matters, for my speech concerns you all, and I have to tell of no mere donkey's shadow,[1] as they put it, but of those things which are most vital for the happiness or ruin of human life.[2] Now let each of you consider this question thoughtfully. Imagine that one of you brought an instant poison, strong enough to inflict sudden death on contact, and had it sealed in a phial so that he could not throw it away. He might be careless enough in other matters, but surely he would take the greatest precautions in case by accident or negligence it caused death either to the possessor or to others whom he loved, like his wife and children. How carefully he would put away that container, how scrupulously he would prevent anything seeping out, or any poisonous vapours, and ensure that no one touched it inadvertently. Suppose instead that someone was carrying about a drug which was a ready cure for all sicknesses, which could restore youth or avert imminent death. Would he not be most anxious in case any fraction of this valuable substance was wasted, when its careful use could bring such great benefit to its possessor and everyone with whom he chose to share it? I doubt that anyone would be so indifferent as to be casual in these circumstances.

Then how is it that men are so careless of their tongue – more indeed than of any other possession? For we carry around with it both deadly poison and a life-giving remedy. In human society nothing is more destructive than an evil tongue, and yet nothing is more healing if a man use it rightly. The ancient philosophers realized this and declared it to posterity; they could not know the true philosophy of Christ, but by their human reasoning they discovered much that is of great value, helping us to live both happily and honourably. In the early days when wisdom had not yet been taught fluency by the services of Plato, Carneades, and Chrysippus,[3] it was expressed in pithy sayings like oracles, or even by actions, like mute symbols. Amasis, king of Egypt, once sent a sacrificial beast to his friend Pittacus, renowned among the seven wise men of Greece, and asked him to return the parts of the carcass which he thought worst and best of all. He was sure his friend would send him two very different parts. But he cut out the tongue, and sent it to the king to show that no part of man was finer than a good tongue or more harmful than a wicked one.[4] I add 'of man' because the tongue is neither the best nor the worst part of other living creatures. So let everyone think over this problem. Suppose someone had a box like the legendary box of Pandora but containing a greater mass of evil, namely, afflictions fatal to all men's bodies and ruin as widespread and more terrible for their minds. Suppose also that it contained as many blessings as troubles, so that the risk lay entirely in misuse, if it was opened at the wrong time or with insufficient control. Surely then he would take great pains to learn how to use this dangerous treasure, particularly if there was danger of an infection that would afflict this steward and storekeeper worst of all. An evil tongue quite often benefits the men it seeks to hurt, but inevitably hurts its possessor, perhaps with material loss, which is quite common, but in any case with the far more serious loss of decency and sanity. Now if anyone owned such a container, he would be free to hurl it into the sea, so that it would neither harm nor help any living person, but we have to keep the treasury of our tongue with us, whether we like it or not. So we must be even more scrupulous to ensure that by care and restraint our tongues cause us the least possible harm and extend the greatest possible advantage to all men.

It is virtually a fact of nature that things which produce the greatest benefit can also cause the worst destruction. For instance, nothing is more beneficial or even essential than the heavenly bodies, but what disasters arise for men when they are in a dangerous conjunction! It is air which enables us to breathe, but what a slaughter of creatures tainted air will cause! Take rivers and seas: they supply abundant nourishment and resources, and greatly ease our travels and dealings in life. But when they are swollen by storm or flood they bring immense loss and danger. What gives greater service than fire? On the other hand, what causes a more dreadful hazard? Even the earth, mother and nurse of us all, produces earthquakes, fissures, landslides, and noxious emissions of vapour. And no land gives birth to more poisons than the soil most fertile in crops and medicinal herbs, such as Africa, according to popular belief.[5] The honeys of Attica are renowned above all others, but the same region produces the most poisonous honey. We might compare the verdict on the men of Attica, that they are either conspicuously good or conspicuously wicked, with the nature of Attic honey; that old saying is universally true, that where there's honey there's gall, where there's good soil, there are weeds.[6] Formerly men thought no medicine more useful than hellebore, but if it is taken in the wrong dosage, it means certain death. Is anything more poisonous than the viper? Yet we derive healing theriac from its venom.[7] Fortune has met the reproaches of all races of men since time immemorial, because she carries aloft to success on her unstable wheel whomever she fancies and sweeps others down to disaster.[8] But so does the human tongue. The men of old assigned to every person two attendant spirits,[9] one of whom brought blessings and the other misfortune. I do not know whether this is true, but it is absolute truth that both spirits are present on the tongue of each and every man.

Wise men have remarked on the same thing which Plato noticed in men of the most talented, I might say heroic, natures, that they would bring their community either great good or great harm.[10] When Themistocles was a boy his tutor realized this and predicted that he would be nothing ordinary, but either an immense blessing or a dire evil to his country.[11] Alcibiades, Julius Caesar, Alexander the Great, and quite a few others were men of a similar disposition. When the return of Caesar[12] caused panic in the entire body of the senate, everyone turned to Cato of Utica, hoping that he would offer help, since he had been the first to prophesy the coming disaster. Cato proposed that in this crisis the affairs of the nation should be entrusted to Pompey, with the rider that Pompey should ensure that the constitution suffer no harm, because he himself was convinced that great evils were usually averted by the men who had originally provoked them. Kings too are usually either bad men who cause the world great suffering or good men who bring the world great good. Now the evils that descend on us from stars or forces of nature cannot be completely averted, but human effort can ensure that their harm is reduced.[13] We have derived medicines from the most poisonous of creatures;[14] we tame wild animals and monstrous beasts; we can make land which was rough with brambles and overgrown with poisonous weeds productive and adapted to the needs of men. This is how we train colts, converting their natural spirit and mettle into a docility responsive to our needs. By training we can take the proud, unbending spirit of young men, with its potential destructiveness, and convert it to good citizenship. Why then can we not achieve the same success in taming the force of the tongue?

Now no one can make proper use of anything without understanding its nature and capacity, just as in other circumstances most people learn to distinguish between healthy and harmful things only by trial and error, at great cost to themselves. I would not like this to be your experience in dealing with the tongue, and so I will first reveal to you what terrible scourges in life are inflicted by an ill-governed tongue, and then describe the great benefits to us if it is given play only as God intended when he bestowed it upon us. Finally I will offer a sort of manual or method of controlling this part of our body.

I would address myself especially to women, who commonly are reproached on this score, if I did not see all around me so many foul-tongued men that women appear subdued and restrained in comparison. Hence it seems fair that I should claim equal attention from all in this crucial matter, which does indeed concern us all.

First, then, Nature herself seems in many respects to have indicated to man by the shape of his body what is fitting for him.[15] For example by setting him upright and facing heaven she taught him to despise the humble and transitory things towards which she lowered the gaze of other creatures, showing him that he should seek higher things, immune from change. Again, in making man's body soft and hairless she reminds us that we are born for harmony and good will amongst ourselves, not for war, like the beasts she has armed with different kinds of weapons. When she chose to set our reason in the brain, the very citadel of our body, she surely indicated to us that all our desires must be subordinate to reason. Nature created the tongue in such a way that the observant man can understand her intention. She wanted us to remember that no part of our body was more destructive if misused, and none more beneficial if care and control were applied. The forethought of Nature gave its proper place to each part of the body according to its dignity or the convenience of its use. While she gave the mind its abode in the citadel of the brain, our heart was given place in the chest-cavity, that is, above the diaphragm and beneath the left breast; the lung, attached to the rear of the spine, overhangs it like bellows, and alternately taking in and expelling breath sustains the heart, which is refreshed with this slight coolness. Now the heart is all muscle, and woven as it were of threads of sinew, with two hollows or cavities or recesses, the hidden containers of breath and blood. The lung is light and porous like a sponge, divided into two lobes like a cow's hoof, so as to be more receptive of the breath, giving it out and taking it in alternately. The stomach is immediately beneath the chest-cavity; on its right is the liver, and next to the liver the gall-bladder. On the left is the spleen. The small intestine is attached to the base of the stomach and is called *ieiunum* or the 'starveling' because it keeps none of the food it takes in, sending it straight through to another intestine, which is narrower but twisted in many tight coils. Next to this at an angle is another intestine, which they call *caecum*, the blind gut, and its lowest part, through which the coarser remains of food are excreted, is called *rectum* or the bowel. Urine on the other hand flows from the kidneys through whitish tubes called ureters into the bladder. The part of the body which performs sexual intercourse has been allocated the position below the belly, as it were in bottom place.[16]

As for the tongue, Nature gave it a central position as spokesman of the heart and mind,[17] clearly setting its place beneath the brain, but not far from the heart, keeping the organs of all the perceptions – eyes, ears, and nostrils – above but near at hand. Taste is the special sense of the tongue, although some scholars, including Aristotle,[18] have claimed it as a kind of touch. It is beyond dispute, however, that taste cannot occur without contact; whether some unique distinction separates taste from other forms of touch is not really relevant to our theme. At any rate the sense of touch diffused over all parts of the body is so acute in the tongue that there is scarcely any part of the body more sensitive. The base of the tongue is attached to the chest-cavity, home of the heart. We need not investigate here whether the seat of the human mind is in the brain or the heart, because their relationship is so close that if one is damaged the other instantly fails. Hence when the forethought of Nature granted the tongue its place in the highest part of the body, she made quite clear to us the importance of this organ. Again, when she chose to set it in the region between brain and heart, as interpreter of the human mind, surely she made it obvious that the tongue must not be in conflict with the heart but must obey reason, beneath which it is placed, and should not break into speech until the neighbouring senses have been consulted, especially sight and hearing, which have primacy among the perceptions. Yet it is much more important to consult the inner perceptions of the soul, intelligence (or reason) as well as memory; both of these have their place and workshop in the brain. This should make it clear enough how absurdly men act when they let loose their tongues in speech before they have listened or looked or weighed in their minds the nature of what they intend to say or the character of their audience; for the services of this organ should come last of all.

Now as Nature did not give us this feature for a single use, but intended it as an organ first of taking in food and drink, and second of sound, and third of articulating speech, we should pause to consider what a small and shapeless part of the body, like a raw lump of flesh, she has adapted to this versatile service. First she made it fleshy, with a network of veins and membranes; plump, perhaps, but still light and easily rolled in all directions; a little rough on the upper surface, especially along the central ridge where it is closely joined to the palate – although it is less rough in man even here than in most animals. The under surface however is quite smooth, and to ensure its flexibility there is constant moisture, so that this moist and slippery organ seems virtually to float in a moist and slippery region. At the base, where it is broadest and takes on the texture of the adjacent flesh, two tubes converge, separated by the thinnest of barriers. The Greeks call the outer tube *arteria trachea* 'windpipe,' and it conveys breath to and from the lungs in turn. The second tube, further on, called *stomachus* 'gullet' by some, is softer and conveys food to the stomach. Over the junction of these passages a little fleshy protuberance overhangs, called by the Greeks *epiglottis* 'overtongue' from its position. Its function is to seal the voice-passage, so that food and drink can be transmitted to the stomach without harm. When it moves into the other position it opens a passage for the breath.[19] The tongue has its own peculiar moisture; unless this combines with food and contact follows between tongue and palate, there is no taste. Now although this ability is diffused all over the tongue, it is believed to be keenest at the rear, and this is why some of the Greeks have called it *geusis* 'the taster.' The tongue distinguishes what is rough and smooth or hot and cold by the ordinary sense of touch shared with other parts of the body, but with such refinement that not even the finest hair mixed with food would pass unnoticed. Then there are countless differences of flavour, which it distinguishes by its special kind of touch. Think of the many flavours of wine. It recognizes them all and distinguishes between them at first taste. Need I mention here the countless nuances of flavour in fish, flesh, fowl, cereals, herbs, and spices? The flexibility of the tongue is designed for taking in food; it can expand, contract, lower, rise, flatten, and spread itself out at will, and while in other animals it tends to be narrow and elongated so as to serve as hands for some species, like cattle grazing and dogs lapping drink, a man's tongue is shorter, but also broader to shape sounds. This is why birds that can mimic human voices generally have a proportionately broader tongue than the rest.[20] Even the shape of the tongue facilitates uttering sounds; so fish, with a tongue quite different from land-creatures, are completely mute. The part of our tongue which touches the front teeth and protrudes is more pointed. The Greeks called this *proglottis* 'the foretongue.' In the formation of articulate sounds,[21] the palate and teeth also co-operate with the tongue, as it is applied against the teeth in various positions, sometimes held apart, sometimes closed. The lips too contribute, whether compressed, parted, or pouting. Even the jaw, with its own muscles and those of the throat, serves the tongue, so that the voice comes out fuller, more sharp, or more blunted in tone, more wheedling, or more severe. Now Nature gave each creature its special cry, but man and only man can mimic the sounds of them all with the plectrum of his tongue, doing it so exactly that if you only overheard the mimic you would think a child was crying, a pig grunting, a horse whinnying, a wife nagging her husband, or the cuckoo competing against the nightingale.[22]

Just count up the varieties of letters, syllables, and words, the pauses, clashes, and hisses peculiar to each of the languages. That single plectrum forms all those varied noises and produces them in the many languages of different nations. Tradition has it that Mithridates knew twenty-two languages well enough to pronounce the law for each man without an interpreter.[23] If a barbarian preoccupied with the administration of a kingdom could do this, what could an Athenian have achieved with leisure simply for developing his speech? It was no mere accident that the old riddle called man 'first four-footed, then two-footed, then three-footed, flying over all the earth, and speaking in the tongues of all creatures.'[24] There are certain harmonies, rhythms, and modes of music which can calm or arouse different human emotions by some secret force. Although musicians achieve this by means of different instruments, the plectrum of the tongue unaided produces the pitch and timbre of them all. For war it becomes a trumpet or bugle, but can call a retreat at will; it is a flute for festivity, a lyre for sensual enjoyment, and yet can utter a funeral dirge if it chooses. Why are we amazed at the remora,[25] which, despite its tiny body, can bring to a standstill a ship in full sail, when we feel no surprise that the tongue, which is not much bigger than this fish, can summon or recall so many thousands of men wherever it chooses, and can arouse or lull them and provoke not just a war between states, but a continental war of Africa, Asia, and Europe.

Well now, what is more successful or powerful than this organ? But then, what can be more destructive? Nature has given it such a constitution that whenever the situation brooks no delay but calls for ready speech, the tongue is instantly available. This happened when Croesus' son saved his father and held in suspense the sword brandished over his head.[26] Just as Nature intended the tongue to be a governor of human life, ready for its responsibility, she carefully warned it not to indulge in a wild and wanton flow of words bringing ruin instead of advantage, destruction instead of assistance, and poison instead of cure. That is why she gave us two eyes, two ears, two nostrils, but only one tongue, and contrived a man's ears so that they were always open, whether he willed it or not, and could not be blocked or turned away, although, as we see, many creatures have this power. So the facts cry out what James taught in the Epistle: 'Let every man be swift to hear, but slow to speak.'[27] Again, Nature covered the eyes with nothing but a frail membrane, suited only for sleep, but buried the tongue virtually in a dungeon, and bound it by many bonds – above, near the back of the palate, again on either side at the opening of the throat, and finally with cables stretching down into the chest-cavity. It is tied underneath to the lower jaw right up to the rampart of the teeth. This part is called *hypoglottis* 'undertongue' by the Greeks, and is so tightly attached that some men need surgery to enable them to speak clearly.[28] In fact Varro thinks the word *lingua* 'tongue' comes from *ligare* 'to bind.'[29] Then Nature sets in its path the double rampart and barrier of the thirty-two teeth. Homer implies a great deal when he speaks of 'the rampart of the teeth,'[30] since the tongue can be disciplined by a bite or wound of the teeth if it disobeys reason. Nature even sets in the front rank the teeth more fitted to wound, which the Greeks call *tomeis* 'incisors' for that reason. It is quite common for men moving their tongue carelessly as they eat to realize from the pain of biting it that this organ should not be casually employed. Nature also set in its path the double doors of the lips, to show, I suppose, that we have a valuable treasure in the tongue, since she has hidden it away so thoroughly, but also showing the great danger of using it carelessly or out of season; hence although it is held down by many cables, she has enclosed it within a double palisade, to prevent that unbridled licence which is not a matter of uttering words, but of blurting out whatever comes into one's head.

[*Undisciplined use of the tongue: talkativeness*]

Perhaps no failing has ever been more loathed even by the pagans;[1] certainly Cato the Censor held it as a great reproach against M. Caelius, calling it a disease, not a failing, for he said that when it took hold of a man, it maddened him as surely with the insatiable lust for chatter as a sleeping-sickness possessed a man with the craving for drinking and sleeping. He declares that the power of this sickness is so uncontrollable that the sufferer not only indulges his failing at every opportunity, but if there is no one ready to listen will deliberately hire and assemble a crowd whose ears he can weary with empty garrulity, like travelling quacks in the market-place who set up their stalls and entice the public with crazy promises. Admittedly someone hears them as they throw out incredible boasts with their babbling tongues, but no one heeds them, because their speech convinces no one. What happens is that men with no business of their own hear their phrases, but there is no one in the whole crowd who would choose to entrust himself to them if he were sick, despite their promises of miraculous cures. Cato holds it against this fellow Caelius that he can as easily speak or keep silent: 'He can be hired for a crust either to keep quiet or speak out,' he says, showing that nothing is more disgraceful for anyone than to hold his tongue cheap and sell it, either to speak or to be silent when the situation calls for speech. The Greeks rather neatly called men of this kind 'belly-talkers.'[2]

Of course no one will feel surprised that a real old Roman like Cato, not debauched by an indulgence of Greek-style training, was offended by silly chattering, but consider M. Tullius Cicero: he devoted his entire life to the pursuit of eloquence, and his boast 'Let triumphal laurels yield to the power of the tongue'[3] is notorious, but he preferred sense without eloquence to senseless fluency and thought nothing more demented than the hollow ring of even the best and richest diction, if it had no thought behind it. Men who talk like this do not seem to know that they are talking, but, like the description of raving prophets, they utter mindless sound,[4] neither considering what to say nor understanding their own utterance. Their words are not produced but spill out, and so it often happens that just as they do not think first what they are going to say, they cannot even remember afterwards what they did say. Quite often indeed they will brazenly deny that they made any of these irresponsible remarks. When Homer represented Thersites as the worst and lowest fellow of all who came to the siege of Troy,[5] he described nothing so exactly as his wild, haphazard, clumsy speech, full of shouting and frenzy. This is how the poem reports it:

> 'Thersites alone started brawling, a man of speech without measure,
> Who had in his head all disordered a welter of words in abundance,
> All vain.'

The proverb too says that measure is best in all things,[6] and lack of measure is nowhere more tasteless or dangerous than in speech; that is why Homer calls Thersites 'of speech without measure' and says not that he spoke but that he 'brawled.' He knew how to talk, but in quantity, not to the point, and would pour out his words without choice or sequence, so the poet calls them disordered. Because the ill-timed verbosity of such giving tongue is without effect and simply obstructive, he adds the comment 'all vain.' But it is often the case that the most stupid talkers shout most offensively, so the poet has not passed over this fault but says 'shouting shrilly.' Next he adds: 'But shouting from a distance, he jeered Agamemnon with insult.'[7] Cicero is supposed to have made a neat criticism of this failing – he said that orators who couldn't handle their arguments resorted to shouting like cripples mounting on horseback.[8] Our poet here calls Thersites' delivery flouting and jibing, not speech, and makes it clear that Thersites was particularly hostile to Achilles and Ulysses because each of them was supposed to be skilled in speaking and vigorous in action. There is no need to tell you about Ulysses. But Achilles' heroic deeds have cast his success at oratory into the shade, so I will call Homer to witness. He speaks in these terms in the first book of the *Iliad* about Phoenix, tutor of the young Achilles:

> ... all these things did he teach him;
> He made him a speaker of tales no less than a doer of deeds.'[9]

Homer makes the eloquence of Nestor, Ulysses, and Menelaus very different from Thersites' verbosity, though they won approval by distinct merits of style.[10] He allots to Nestor 'speech flowing sweeter than honey from his venerable lips'; to Ulysses he gives rich and passionate speech, but makes him ponder long before he begins to speak, and adds that 'he brought forth a mighty voice from his breast.' He credits Menelaus with eloquent brevity and phrasing that never wanders from the point, but in contrast he gives Thersites bitter language, hurled at random without choice of content or diction, so that his tongue anticipates his thought; lastly he calls him a crazy shouter who grates men's ears with his meaningless din of words.

Pleasant speech, shrewd and serious, flowing when the occasion demands it but brief and concise when necessary, can win a man great distinction if it is adapted to the subject, circumstances, and persons involved. Instead, Thersites is beaten with Agamemnon's staff and bursts into tears, making the whole army laugh, because he never learned to speak, and was only taught to keep quiet at his own cost. The story confirms the words of Euripides: 'Of mouths unbridled and lawless folly doom is the outcome.'[11] He could not have conveyed more vividly a loose and rambling tongue, thoughtlessly blurting out anything without giving firm consideration to what is appropriate and useful and what is not, than by calling the mouth of such a chatterer 'unbridled' and his lack of thought 'lawless.' A horse uncontrolled by the bridle often drags himself and his rider into some ravine or bog, involving him in his own ruin. The tongue is the same; unless it is disciplined by right reasoning it brings ruin not only to the credulous listeners, but most often of all to the rambling speaker himself. We might compare the tongue left to its own whims with a field of good but neglected soil, and the crops it produces. For personally, I believe that *telos* in this verse of Euripides does not mean 'end,' as scholars thought until now, but 'product,' 'outcome.' Each part of the body has its function, and rightly used brings considerable advantage, but put to bad use, it will cost the man who misuses it some loss – for instance a man who sees things askew will stumble and incur either a bruise on the shin or a running sore on his brow. In this way control of the tongue brings the greatest distinction and profit, but ruin is the natural product of misuse. Financial expense is probably a trivial loss, whereas loss of reputation is the worst blow imaginable, just because it is an especially valuable possession. Throwing away one's life however is a still heavier loss than this; once lost, no human skill can recover it, whereas a financial loss is easily made up, and even reputation can be restored somehow despite the difficulty. But worst of all is to destroy our soul, that is, to lose everlasting bliss and gain instead eternal death.

Given that all these evils come to us chiefly from an unrestrained tongue, surely the man who neglects this organ, with its beneficial and destructive potential, is his own worst enemy. Now since loss of reputation is generally, and perversely, rated less seriously than loss of money, I will deal with this issue first. Some faults of character incur hostility or ill will, like arrogance or bullying; others meet with contempt, like self-indulgence and lust, sloth and stupidity; but no fault makes a man so cheap and despised, and at the same time such an object of loathing, as loose and wearisome verbosity. As proof take the many nicknames used by the ancients, the witticisms and proverbs and anecdotes in which they criticized men addicted to this failing, who had learned how to speak but could not keep quiet. Eupolis, for instance, said they did not talk but chatter, and described one such as 'greatest of chatterers, incapable of speech.'[12] That is how the poet discriminated between chattering and speaking, as Sallust distinguished loquacity from eloquence when he spoke of a man 'with loquacity enough but little sense.'[13] Eloquence is never found without sense, and equally loquacity is always combined with stupidity. There is a famous line of Epicharmus, too, in which he criticized a man who was a terrible chatterer, with no ability in speaking but unable to keep quiet because of his affliction of the tongue; his words are: 'No expert as a speaker, but unable to keep quiet.'[14] The poet Aristophanes once portrayed a tiresomely talkative man with a host of vivid epithets coined for the purpose:

> A coarse country loud-mouthed fellow,
> His mouth unbridled, unwatered, unlatched –
> He can't be out-talked, this prater of boastful nonsense.[15]

Shame can control men when reason fails to keep them from stupid chattering. That is why Aristophanes mentioned boorishness, calling the man 'coarse country fellow'; then, since people like that repeat all their statements with a lot of shouting, and give way to no one because confidence always consorts with ignorance, he called him loud-mouthed. Then he labelled the unbridled licence of the tongue, and that sort of addiction to chattering, and finally that indiscretion which keeps nothing secret – with three well-chosen words: 'unbridled, unwatered, unlatched.' The first of these is taken from horses without a bridle, the next from neat wine, the third from buildings without an outer door; indeed the Greeks have for the last vice a similar idiom: 'open-tongued-ness,' 'open-mouthing.' They call overflowing and gushing speech 'overwordiness,' a fault we can detect and forgive even in the writings of scholarly men. Now Aristophanes used the word 'overchattering' expressly to indicate a man who chattered away excessively, so that you could guess he was insupportable on two counts, because he blurted out nonsense, a failing of women and children, or rather of madmen, and because he did even this to excess. The third word[16] is a sophisticated compound of three words, of *kompos*, meaning 'arrogance or boasting,' of *phakelos* 'a bundle or heap,' and *rheo* which means 'flow'; hence *rhema* and *rhesis* 'flow of words' to suggest indiscriminate speech flowing at random and full of arrogance. The Greeks call this kind of fellow other insulting names; for while they name experts in speaking *rhetores* 'orators' and *logioi* 'men of words,' they call those men talkative nuisances, chatterers, bletherers, and gossips. Latin speakers label them with equally insulting names – tongue-users, talk-merchants, gossippers, wordy-fellows, empty-mouths, nonsensical blethering fellows, and bellowers – and they are not said to talk, but to babble, gossip, blether, chatter, burble, nag, heckle, bore, bluster, croak, bellow, bark, boom, grunt, caw, clatter, or rattle.

The talkativeness of the sophists was not unedifying, but deeply resented by the men of their day. Just think how many proverbs have made fun of this sickness, borrowing metaphors from every kind of object or creature whose noise is tiresome to the ears. This is the origin of phrases like more talkative than a pigeon (or a magpie, a gull, a starling), more heckling than a goose, more shrilling than a cicada, more sounding than a reef or surf, more babbling than a psaltery.[17] As for the chatterer himself, we call him Archytas' rattle because he doesn't know how to stop, or the windgong of Dodona, a piper like Arrhabius, a word-spewer, a Daulian rook, Tellenicus' echo, or just a bath-attendant.[18] The man who blurts out every secret entrusted to him they call a leaking pitcher. As for the disease, it was clever of the Greeks to call it 'drunkenness without wine,'[19] because some men are always tipsy with the lust for talking, in the way most people are likely to blurt out secrets when hot with wine – the longer they talk, the more nonsense they let slip.

Even the Gospels mention the reproach of *battologia*, though it came from a secular story about the shepherd Battus.[20] Mercury was leading away stolen cattle and gave Battus a cow to keep the theft quiet. He swore he would keep absolute silence, but when Mercury came back with a change of voice and appearance and offered him a cow if he informed on the theft, he instantly said they were 'near to the mountains, near to the mountains they were.' The story goes that Mercury laughed and mimicking Battus' mannerism of speech said: 'Traitor, it's me you're betraying, betraying my crime to myself.' Then he turned the fellow with the faithless tongue into a kind of stone, called *index* 'an informer' by Latin speakers, which is used by goldsmiths to test gold, as the poet adds wittily at this point: 'Little the boulder deserves it, but suffers the age-old disgrace.'

Just as bath-attendants have long suffered a bad name for their compulsive gossiping, barbers have this reputation now; idle and talkative men gather in their places of work, and infect them with the same faults. Indeed a story was invented to fit this circumstance. You must often have heard of Midas' ears: the king covered them with purple turbans, but couldn't deceive the royal barber. Now the fellow dared not tell the secret for fear of his master, but couldn't keep it quiet because of his weak character, so he went away to a deserted piece of land and buried the words he could not suppress in a hole in the ground: 'King Midas has asses' ears.' Then he piled back the earth, covered the hole so that the words could not leak out among men, and went off feeling relieved. Later a bed of reeds grew on the spot, and spread abroad the words buried beneath the ground, so that nothing was more notorious than the saying 'King Midas has asses' ears.'[21] We are free to laugh at the story, so long as we realize the moral and take it to heart. We see so many people today like that barber; tell them a secret and they go into labour as if they would burst unless they pass on what they have heard, blurting it out to someone else. They look for another like themselves, demand eternal secrecy with many oaths, and then drop their burden; he in turn looks for someone else, who looks for another, until the whole country knows within a few days what was entrusted to one man. 'At times the crowd discerns the truth; at other times they blunder.'[22] But it has to be a flagrant and manifest disease totally detestable to our natural feelings for the ignorant crowd to determine on destroying it with all those jeers and proverbs and insults and tales – more than it ever used to scourge theft or adultery or sexual abuse. If the voting pebble of any single man in the crowd has little weight, the unanimity of so many nations and generations can hardly be considered a triviality. This is not just a vote of the people, but a divine pronouncement of nature. It would really be tedious however if I went on to report all the witticisms and sayings with which wise and important men have denounced this disease of a wanton tongue.

Of all the styles of oratory,[23] the Attic style is most praised because it is furthest removed from an empty clamour of phrases. But the Spartans, whose honesty has been praised beyond that of other Greek states in all other affairs, held empty chatter in special abomination. These were men vigorous in action but sparing of talk, so that they did not admit any professional training in speech, because professional craft is close to craftiness; they thought that speech should come from the heart of good men, not from their art. In Rome too, honour came late to teachers of rhetoric, and the dispute continued long whether ability in speaking depended on training or good sense and whether the rules of these rhetoricians, which were subsequently transmitted to them by the Greeks, were helpful or harmful to good speaking. At any rate many in Cicero's day were dissatisfied with the model he had presented as a likeness of the perfect orator; it certainly failed to meet the approval of Brutus,[24] with his high principles. In Athens too, although the city was nurse and mother of all the refined arts, there was great distaste for the reputation of the sophists who taught rhetoric at that period – though it was a rhetoric more for display than the treatment of serious matters. This argument is not intended to condemn an art that even Aristotle, that great and earnest philosopher, did not hesitate to present in detail; merely to make us realize how silly verbosity revolts everyone's natural taste, since even rhetoric, the noblest of arts, acquired a bad reputation with most people because of its association with such verbiage.

But to return to the Spartans;[25] they so detested talkativeness that they would not let Ctesiphon remain in the community because this eloquent man claimed to be able to talk all day long on any prescribed topic;[26] they argued that the function of a good orator was to match his speech to the subject-matter. He should not be too brief for the situation, nor yet too long-winded. In fact it was just a theatrical trick when some men with more fluency than eloquence said they could both shrink the mightiest topics into a small compass and exalt absolute trivialities into a vast theme by their language. According to the teachers of rhetoric the most damaging failing in an orator is this excessive accumulation of words. What can you hope to achieve before a juror weary of listening or too confused by your welter to grasp your meaning? Cleomenes deserved commendation when the Samian envoy tried to persuade him to wage war on Polycrates in an extremely wordy speech.[27] His reply was: 'I can't recall what you said at the beginning, so that I failed to understand the middle section; as for the last section, I disagree.' There is a similar story about another Cleomenes, the son of Cleombrotus. Someone made an unnecessarily long speech, which irritated him, so that he interrupted: 'How long will you go on composing mighty introductions to these petty issues?' A speech surely should match the issue you are presenting. Aristotle made a witty criticism on this disease. The story has it that someone had spoken to him at great length, and then added, as a sort of apology for his verbosity, 'But I am talking nonsense, and to a philosopher like you!' 'Not to me,' said Aristotle, 'I didn't take any notice of a word you said.'[28] The philosopher could not have said anything more critical, or more cutting, to that chattermonger. I like the remark of King Archelaus, too; when a too talkative barber put the towel around his neck and asked him how he would like his shave, he said, 'In silence.'[29]

The Spartans were not alone in appreciating brevity, although laconic speech took its name from them;[30] Phocion, for instance – a most high-minded Athenian[31] – was walking in the market-place with an air of preoccupation, when one of his friends said, 'You look thoughtful, Phocion.' He replied, 'You're quite right: I am considering whether I can prune or discard any of the speech I am going to make to the Athenian people.' Incidentally this was a marvellous criticism of other men's attitudes. They anxiously rehearse their speeches to make them as full as possible, which seems to me as silly as hosts who are anxious to make a dinner-party as long as possible, instead of aiming at elegance and comfort. A man of equal sense and honesty put this into a nutshell. Leosthenes had made a speech to incite the Athenians to war by a host of lavish promises; our friend commented that it was like cypresses: they might be noble and lofty, but they bore no fruit. The Spartans particularly worshipped Heracles,[32] no doubt because he symbolized success in action rather than words. So when some rhetorician wanted to recite to Antalcidas, the Spartan commander, a eulogy of Heracles that he had most zealously composed, he thought he would receive warm thanks, but Antalcidas refused to listen to him. 'Heracles?' he said, 'Who's attacking him?' It was his firm opinion that one should reject any speech that was not concerned with essentials. So if we are dealing with an audience hostile to men of distinction, we may sometimes need to make a speech; but to waste speeches on praising a man whom no one criticizes is as absurd as defending a client whom no one is prosecuting. A man like Antalcidas would have been totally intolerant of a mob-orator ranting and raving with wanton tongue against the characters of good men, since he did not even tolerate the encomium of his own patron, because he thought it superfluous. The story told of Agis, son of Archidamus, is appropriate here too.[33] When the envoy from Abdera had just ended a most long-winded speech, and asked him what he should report to his people, Agis commented, 'Tell them I listened to you patiently for as long as you wasted time in talking.' He shattered the envoy of the Perinthians with a similar witticism: this fellow had indulged in a long-winded speech, and asked what reply he was to give to the Perinthians. He answered, 'Why, tell them you could hardly make yourself come to the end of your speech, and I could barely make myself keep silence.' Now surely the lack of restraint of this chattering tongue forestalled all the usefulness that might have come from that embassy. Those solemn orations[34] which torment rather than honour modern princes are just the same; they are compelled to hear their own praises – sometimes quite insincere – suffering embarrassment or boredom so as not to waste the orator's three months or so spent embellishing the speech. Once a fellow praised a certain sophist to Agesilaus[35] as a superb craftsman, who could develop trivial matters on a vast scale. Agesilaus retorted, 'I wouldn't call a man a good cobbler if he fitted a huge shoe onto a dainty foot.' That shows how much shrewd and serious men are distressed by empty fluency of the tongue.

Men generally fall into this fault if they use the instruction of dialecticians and rhetoricians and the training methods of the declaimers to arm their tongue with words, and fail to fill their breasts with moral reasoning. So Agasicles' retort deserves its fame.[36] When someone said he was surprised that Agasicles did not employ Philophanes the sophist as a teacher of oratory he replied: 'The right thing would be for me to learn only from the man I can call father.' What had this shrewd man learned from his forefathers? Not sophistries and syllogisms or figures of speech and devices for developing a theme, but models of gallant and honourable leadership. We can be sure he detested silly womanish chattering if he declined to study oratory, an intrinsically useful subject, from a famous expert. Supposing he had encountered a ranter like the fellow Horace portrays in the *Satires* who clings so hard he cannot be thrown off, and interrupts, talking incessantly about random matters, so as to be beyond endurance.[37] Horace says, 'The sweat trickled down to my heels as he chattered away, finding praise for the streets and the city.' In the end he thought his day of reckoning had come, because he was at the mercy of this dreadful chattering fellow, and really held it to be Apollo's divine intervention that saved him, when the other fellow's opponent at law appeared and hauled the assassin off to court.

So, as God has given us speech for this one purpose, to make the relations of men more pleasant, chattering makes the very gift which is naturally sweetest when properly employed into a source of misery in life.

We can see that Nature has always been most concerned to create harmony amongst all creatures, however they might seem to be opposed. She has provided pleasure, like a bait,[38] to foster this harmony; this is how she has made attractive to us the desire to beget children and to nurse and rear them. This is how she has produced friendships between old people, between young people, and between members of both groups. We even cherish wolf- and lion-cubs as long as they give us pleasure. The disease of chattering ruins this beguilement of Nature in the finest of all our activities. In just this way, wine, Nature's special concession for dispelling gloom and enlivening human spirits, has through our fault been turned into a source of quarrelling and murder; in fact nothing causes more trouble than this liquid, which was bestowed as a cure for troubles. Who does not shudder at a lunatic? Yet I do not think it any more pleasant to keep company with a drunk – is there anything more like a lunatic than an angry man and a drunkard? In fact each condition is so close to insanity that both anger and drunkenness alike can turn into permanent lunacy. Even at other times, philosophers think there is no difference between anger and madness, except that anger is a short-lived frenzy;[39] for when the bile simmers down, health of mind returns, and when wine has been digested, sobriety is restored. Now nothing is more like drunkenness than talkativeness,[40] so that common folk say about this sort of thing, 'He's getting drunk on his own talk.' Clearly this is why silly chatter is worse than drunkenness, because it is freely induced by our own fault, whereas men are often compelled to drink, and quite often tipsiness can come upon men unawares, if they are inexperienced, for instance; sometimes wine overwhelms a drinker more violently than he expected. That is why the young man in Terence complains he has been fooled: 'The wine I drank has got the better of me,' he says, 'and yet when I was reclining at table I thought I was nice and sober.'[41] So words blurted out in men's cups are usually blamed on Bacchus' violence and put down to the wine. King Pyrrhus of Epirus forgave his soldiers their outspokenness on the occasion when one of them said, 'We'd have killed you, your Majesty, if the bottle hadn't run out.'[42] Yet drunkenness does not make every man loose-tongued; it strikes some dumb and more prone to sleep than to chatter, so that the words of the proverb, that what was hidden in the sober man's breast floats out on his tongue when he's drunk,[43] are not entirely true.

But if anyone brings on this tipsy tongue through his own fault, what excuse can be given, or what grounds for exoneration? And yet the fact is that the chatterer talks more tipsily when sober than any drunk who is not naturally prone to this failing. Drunkenness induced by wine has some advantages, which even earned it the praise of Plato:[44] it dispels foolish bashfulness, soothes melancholy of the soul, arouses sloth of spirit, breaks harmful silence, and exposes some faults which were best revealed in this way, so that they can be cured in the general gaiety, without serious offence. In short, while among the Lapiths and other savage tribes war often arises from drinking, strong friendship has grown up between many men from their drinking companionship.[45] But what advantage can be drawn from silly talkativeness? In fact, if we believe the philosophers, inebriation is not outright drunkenness unless it entails a loose tongue. For they declare as a definition that drunkenness is nothing but silliness brought on by excessive indulgence in wine: hence they do not completely condemn inebriation if it keeps quiet, but it is the addition of stupid talkativeness which converts tipsiness into drunkenness. In common use men who get merry with wine are called 'well warmed,' not drunk, unless their tongue begins to wander.

This silliness is less harmful because it wears off with the wine and is no trouble except when men are in their cups, when no serious business is carried on. Contrast the chatterer. At any and every time and place he is a pest with his kind of drunkenness: he butts in at gatherings, at meetings, in the courts, in the streets, in private homes, on shipboard, in vehicles, at parties; he doubles our distress in time of trouble, and in happy times like a cloud or storm his appearance makes everything downcast. On a journey he makes one more dizzy than the jolts of the road; on shipboard he inflicts boredom worse than seasickness. When we travel on foot a pleasant companion is as good as a carriage, but a chatterer is like a heavy pack, even when we have transport.

At drinking-parties, when all men approve talking and listening in turn, he brings us boredom instead of pleasure; thanks to him we can neither listen to the lute, nor watch the play, nor hear and answer other men's conversation. At the theatre he wearies his neighbour to death, in court he ruins good cases, either by boring the juror to death as he pours out endless random phrases or because men like him are unconvincing even when they tell the truth. In serious discussion he wastes time. He forces his way into the house with his unwanted greeting, he accosts us at street corners, escorts us, follows us and dogs us, clinging closer than pitch itself, all the time muttering something in our ears. At times of sickness he sits day and night by the invalid, a worse affliction than their disease itself – indeed sometimes he will hasten the death of those who might otherwise have survived. He disturbs the leisure of those at rest and hampers busy men from completing their business. Even in the heat of war and danger, when circumstances require instant assistance, he simply chatters on with idle tales. Sometimes he will actually tell stories to an audience of sleepers because he cannot bear silence. Men accept reproof given in moderate quantities, but with a chatterer even his praise is more wearisome than another man's abuse. It has been noticed that men possessed by this sickness, after spending all day pestering those awake around them, keep on talking even in their sleep, often blurting out what they should have kept quiet. Although it is universally agreed that silence is proper in a bedroom, as a place set aside for rest, the talkative man will even bore his bedfellow to death with his stories, driving off sweet sleep as it steals over our eyelids, or breaking into the sleep that possesses us, so that he does not even allow the night, bringer of rest to all creatures, to pass in peace – that time when, according to Virgil's description,

> Now weary bodies savour gentle sleep
> Throughout the world, the woods and savage seas
> Are stilled, and planets roll on their mid course.
> Silent each field, the cattle, vivid birds
> That dwell by lovely lakes or bushy heath;
> Composed in sleep and silence of the night
> They soothe their cares, and hearts relaxed from toil.[46]

Neither the nightingale nor the starling nor any other kind of bird is so chattering and noisy that it does not keep silence at night. The gossiping cicada is only heard after the mists of dawn have been dispelled by the sun, and falls silent towards evening. Frogs prolong their chatter to a later hour, but night enjoins silence even on them. But our chatterbox does not let even

that part of night be still which is called 'stillness'[47] because of the deep
silence of all creatures. Nor does he think it ill-timed for his chatter, although
it is called 'dead of night,' being unfit for any business but suited only to
repose. No place or time obtains the boon of repose from his unbridled
tongue. Admittedly the chatterbox does not always go scot-free: when he
cannot keep quiet under the barber's razor, he gets a wound, or chattering
incessantly while he eats, he will choke on food that has slipped down his
windpipe. Martial makes fun of a man called Matho, who declaimed when
he had a high fever and earned a reputation not for eloquence but for
madness. There is a Phrygian too whom he mocks for preferring to go blind
rather than to drink more sparingly.[48] But the lust for chattering can even
cause death at times, when a man convalescing from a wound or abscess,
under doctor's orders to keep rest and silence for a few days, can't keep
himself from storytelling and brings on his own doom instead of the
recovery promised by his physician.

   The cauldrons of Dodona only ring when struck, and although they
prolong the ringing each time they are disturbed, they do finally come to an
end of it.[49] That vociferous arcade which men call the seven-voiced,[50] as I
reported, falls quiet after the seventh echo; but the chatterer begins his din
without provocation, and if he is offered even three words as an excuse for
speaking, will set no limit or end to his chattering. The famous piper
Arrhabius had to be paid more highly to stop playing than his original fee.[51]
But the fellow who has once reached intoxication with his own talk cannot
be paid to stop at any price. If we believe Horace, the dreadful tribe of both
singers and poets has this failing, that

>   Among their friends
> When asked they can't be coaxed to give a song,
> But uninvited, never reach an end.

   With or without invitation the chatterer starts up a song that has no
end. According to the poets the house of *Fama* 'Rumour' only rings out
when touched by the sound of gossip.[52] The chatterbox produces a vast
mass of stories like a spider from its own secretions. Frogs croak at fixed
times of the day; geese do not always clamour; the swallow does not pester
us with its garrulity at all seasons, nor the cuckoo in every month. Moisture
gathering in the sky buries the cicadas in deep silence, and even the
nightingale, exhausted by song, comes to an end; the chatterer wearies at
any and every place and time, 'a leech unwilling to release the skin without
his fill of blood.'[53] Insatiable, the chatterer never lets go until he has slain the
victim who falls into his clutch.

If someone distressed us by his excessive silence, this would not seem very surprising, since speech was granted to give sweetness to human intercourse. But when a man inflicts distress with the very talent granted to us to avert distress, his fault simply turns honey into bitter gall, no less. The girl who wears Venus' girdle[54] and yet is loathed by all for her sluttish behaviour must be exceptionally unattractive. In the same way a man must have been born under the curse of all the Muses to earn all men's loathing by his speech, a gift granted by the gods to men to win them love and good will. This failing is accursed beyond all others, because the miser or lecher or social climber at least has the enjoyment of his desires. The chatterbox strives to be a source of pleasure and makes himself an object of universal loathing; he longs to be listened to, but no one is less able to find an audience.

Moreover, since inquisitiveness comes with talkativeness, such men suffer this second curse, that they are thirsty to know all, but no one trusts them with a word. For men discussing private business will adjourn their debate and flee if they catch sight of the chatterer in the distance; or if he happens to come upon them, you would say Mercury had stepped in, or the wolf in the tale,[55] so sudden is the silence. So that wolf slinks off slavering with hunger, as the saying goes, or if he is shameless and begins to talk away, the gathering of friends scatters – just as sailors, if they see the north wind blowing off a cliff, anticipate a buffeting storm and seasickness and make for a haven before the storm sets in – presently when the chatterbox opens his mouth to speak, they steal away each in a different direction before he can embark on his interminable monologue. Also, if they get a hint from some source of the talker's approach, the council is instantly dismissed, and just as camp must be struck instantly when the enemy is reported, so each man looks round for a place of refuge. If there is no chance of escape, for instance if they are in the same ship or carriage or attending the same dinner-party, no one who knows the man will willingly sit near him. Indeed no one will freely buy a house if the neighbour is an excessive talker, or a farmstead suffering the same ill fame – so true is Hesiod's comment, 'A bad neighbour is a blight.'[56] That is why Themistocles, wanting to make the piece of land he had for sale more attractive, told the auctioneer to add to its other assets that it had a good neighbour.[57] The man who has a talkative and indiscreet neighbour has the worst neighbours of all.

Now if excessive and ill-timed indulgence in talking is such a plague, even if it is limited to silly, idle tales, who will endure men who add to the boredom of talkativeness boasting to outdo a Thraso,[58] slanderers, informers, and liars, or men who blurt out secrets and shout comments that are a menace even to those compelled to hear them. But of this more anon. At the moment we are dealing only with the failing that we find at times even in otherwise good and decent men – for the error of the talkative man in conversation is sometimes committed by scholars out of their excessive enthusiasm for writing or lecturing. Martial has given us a neat portrait of someone like this: I think it is worthwhile quoting the whole poem, since it is very stylish.[59] This is how it goes:

No one's really pleased to meet you,
Crowds run from you and you know it.
There's an empty space all round you,
People shun a full-time poet.
It's a very dangerous failing,
Ligurinus – not more dreaded
Is the frenzied whelpless tigress
Or the sun-scorched arrow-headed
Viper lurking in the desert
Or the scorpion unrelenting.
Let me ask you, what brave hero
Would endure such endless ranting?
You declaim when we are standing,
You declaim when we are sitting,
You declaim when we are running,
You declaim when we are shitting.
If I run into the baths, then
I can't swim for your recital.
If I'm late for a club dinner
You detain me with the title
Of your latest, or attack me
When I'm sitting at a banquet.
If I fell asleep exhausted
You would rouse me from my blanket.
Do you want to get the picture
Of the harm that you have done?
You're the only honest fellow
Whom his best friends fear and shun.

It is naturally beneficial to read out work you have toiled over, but from excess and importunity a recitalist may barely be able to scrape together an audience by pressing invitations on people or even hiring them, for all that Persius says, 'He knows how to reward a recalcitrant friend with a cloak or a hot dish of tripe.'[60] That is how Pliny portrays Regulus.[61] Horace too in *Ars*

poetica describes a fellow whom the jury would rather honour with the cedar
book-chest in advance than hear in recital.[62] Whenever a plague like this
threatens, nothing is more valuable than one's feet, 'since one's only hope of
safety lies in flight,' as Archilochus wrote.[63] Philoxenus preferred to return
to the stone quarries than to listen to Dionysius' poetry.[64] Horace too wishes
he could be throttled rather than listen to the chatterbox reach his grand
finale: 'Give me the *coup de grace*.'[65] So we often have to hear the same works
repeated, either because there is not always a supply of new subject-matter,
or because this mighty talker has forgotten what he said to whom. 'Didn't I
ever tell you about the Rhodian fellow?' 'I've heard it over a thousand times,
but do go on.'[66]

Men say fine tales are best told twice or three times,[67] yet hearing, the
most fastidious of the senses, can hardly bear even this. So who could
endure a fellow constantly dinning the same trivialities into busy ears and
burdening them with a tedious patchwork of tales? If you repeatedly reread
the same speeches by Cicero, you would feel the monotony. A speech of
Lysias which had given intense pleasure at the first reading began after a
second or third time round to seem stiff and insipid to the man for whom he
wrote it (although men swear this style had every gift of Venus and the
Graces). His witty retort to this objection was, 'But will you deliver it more
than once to the jury?'[68] Only Homer seems to have escaped causing surfeit
through the marvellous variety of his stories, although perhaps not
everywhere, since Virgil pruned back many passages; indeed Homer does
not escape monotony in some places where the reader is forced to hear the
same message from the giver and messenger, a rare occurrence in Virgil.[69]
The Spartans so appreciated economy of words that Anaxandridas reproached a man for telling the ephors what was true and helpful, but in too
much detail: 'My friend,' he said, 'you are making untimely speech of a
timely matter.'[70] We can gather from this how much harm is caused by
uncontrolled talkativeness on silly topics, and how much boredom it causes
to good and sensible men, if an otherwise helpful speech was reproached
simply for being a bit long-winded. In general it is recognized as true that
wherever there's too little sense there's too much tongue.

Nature gave birds the power to chatter and mimic other creatures'
speech; she didn't do the same for bulls and lions. Consider children, old
people, and women: their tongue is less controlled because their mental
powers are weaker. No one would have tolerated Cicero's fluency and
fertility of speech if he had not been so brilliant – indeed even he was called
an Asianist.[71] Yet those who admired his speech and intellect did not dare to
trust his strength of character when circumstances demanded a firm and
courageous man. Demosthenes is considerably more compressed in speech

than Marcus Tullius,[72] yet the Greek orator's integrity has not won as much admiration as his eloquence. Both Catos had unsurpassable strength of spirit, and we read that both caused amazement by encompassing a great deal of meaning in a few words.[73] So I assume from the occasion when Cato the Elder spoke to the Athenians: they were particularly amazed because the interpreter (for he was speaking through an interpreter) could scarcely render by long roundabout phrases what Cato had said in a few words of Latin; this convinced them all that Greek speech came from the lips, but Roman from the heart. For a man who has arrived at a sound judgment of what is right and has made a firm decision about right behaviour needs no verbal rags and tags to unfold his judgment and intention. Nobody speaks more verbosely than men who either don't understand what they are talking about or have not thought very carefully about the subject, as if they only began to work out what to say when they were already speaking. Similarly no men explain an issue in fewer words than those who have the most precise grasp of the principles of speaking. The speakers who best know and understand the issues on which the whole case depends and the arguments best adapted to prove it find it easy to discard what is superfluous and express the essentials. If a man adds sense combined with honesty to his training, he will easily escape the failing of talkativeness. Cato the Younger, called Uticensis, was like this: he moved men's hearts by the weight of his opinions rather than the abundance of his language, and 'never leaped forth to speak' unless the situation demanded his speech.[74] Another such, but among the Athenians, was Phocion, whom we have mentioned elsewhere.[75] This is the style of all the speakers whom the men of old admired for honesty and sense. Their speech is like gold coinage, little in weight and size but of great value, whereas the talk of chatterboxes loads the ears of the listener with a crowd of useless words, like a man weighed down with iron obols or brass coins that add little to the total sum.

So talkativeness is most distressing to those whose approval it would be most glorious to win for our speaking. Aristotle once was wearied by a man's silly talking. The fellow said, as if he had reached the conclusion of a splendid case, 'Isn't that amazing, Aristotle?' He answered, 'What you said isn't amazing, but it's really amazing that anyone with a pair of feet can hear you through.'[76] For talkativeness causes another kind of boredom: it neither lets the listener keep quiet nor offers a chance to reply, but demands that you keep making encouraging comment, as if applauding or begging the fellow to go on. 'My, that's wonderful!' 'What happened next?' 'Quite, quite.' 'What's that you say?' I know someone, monstrous grand with a cardinal's hat but still more talkative than a city wag, who after telling each trivial tale utters that 'ho ho ho ho' from Aristophanes' comedy[77] with extraordinary vulgarity, as if he were claiming applause from his hearers and virtually applauding himself. If someone is telling a good tale, he doesn't demand applause until he says the farewell line. The gossip never says farewell, but keeps bidding us applaud the silliest nonsense. Not content with one anecdote, he spins one out of another like splicing flaxen thread. To such imitators of Ligurinus we too will be able to say, 'Do you want to get the picture of the harm you're doing?'[78] You are polluting speech, the sweetest of all pleasures; you're wearing out your tongue – the most useful and beneficial of organs – to no avail, and losing all the great profits that accrue from controlled use of the tongue, squandering your most valuable treasure of all. Keep the water jar at the door,[79] as they say, since water is the cheapest drink. On the other hand precious possessions are kept behind more than one lock, and no one entrusts a treasure to a private home with unbarred doors or, I suppose, their money to a purse that will not shut, yet you carry this invaluable treasure around and walk about with your mouth wide open. Nothing is easier than silence, but you are indulging in a practice that will ruin your fame and fortune. You are a pest to everyone, but above all to the sanest men among us. No one trusts you even when you are telling the truth. You offer yourself for others to laugh and look down their noses at. You are cutting yourself off from human society just as though you were guilty of parricide. Who wouldn't prefer to associate with a criminal, but a discreet one, rather than a talking fool, however blameless in other respects? You get no benefit from your affliction and torture others with boredom.

It is really a worse fate to be mocked than loathed. As Juvenal says: 'Poverty has no more cruel sting than making us absurd.'[80] For a man reaches the peak of misfortune when he is so afflicted that he deserves no kindness or compassion, but suffers mockery into the bargain. You surely know this from experience. Yet I rather think that we are wasting our time trying to cure a chatterer by the use of speech; he can't keep quiet to take his medicine, like patients who vomit back their dose before they have swallowed it all down. That man Stertinius in Horace who tried to cure Damasippus with philosophical utterances first got him to listen and settle his toga around him.[81] So though many faults are more criminal, I doubt if any is more incurable than talkativeness.

[*The benefits of silence and of careful use of the tongue*]

Let us consider, then, the benefits and esteem conferred either by silence or by a careful and restricted use of our tongue. Admittedly one can err at times in this direction too, for there are occasions when it would have been better to speak than keep silent. Many have incurred the reproach of putting tongues up for sale, but others have been shamed by selling their silence – men on whose tongues an ox is said to sit, as they said Demosthenes was suffering from a silver quinsy[1] – it has now become notorious from proverbs that Amyclae was destroyed by silence.[2] But I think there are very few men who can't truly say with Simonides (Valerius Maximus gives the credit for this reply to Xenocrates): 'He often regretted his words, but never his silence.'[3] In fact any harm done by silence can be mended by speaking, but 'a word dispatched flies off beyond recall.'[4]

As the proverbs all declare, the mean is best – as in all matters, so especially in speech. But when men deviate from the mean, the one who tends to extravagance is more tolerantly treated than the one who tends to niggardliness, whereas the man who is over-silent is less offensive than the unrestrained talker. The former failing is both safer and more honourable; at least nothing can be more sublime than shrewd brevity of speech. That is why someone made the significant comment that we take men as our instructors in speech, but the gods to teach us silence. Oracles are seldom vouchsafed, and encompassed in very few words, and for this very reason have great authority and are regarded as utterances of the gods. The sayings of the wise men of the past are very like this, for instance the many attributed to Pythagoras, to Socrates, and to other wise men. For what is more marvellous than the judgments of men of distinction? What abundance of ideas there was in such unrefined language! The age of the ancients contented itself with few laws, and these recalled the brevity of oracles, for example the laws of Solon for the Athenians, of Lycurgus for the Spartans. Twelve tables were enough for the Romans to cover every circumstance, and one formal rule, that 'amongst men there should be honest dealings,' was adequate to bar fraud in all civil contracts.[5] Plato called kings the children of the gods,[6] and the ruler was the living embodiment of the law; hence disciplined speech, powerful with weight of meaning, like divine oracles and ancient laws, is best suited to kings.

The other liberal arts[7] have also degenerated from their original simplicity, just like the morals of society. They have grown more fluent and less authentic; the loquacity of the declamatory schools has ruined eloquence. Again, what is more elaborate than present-day music,[8] mimicking the chatter of many birds with such a large number of vocal parts. What would the Spartan ephor Emerepes say now?[9] He was the man who cut away two of the nine strings from the lyre of Phrynis the musician with his axe, telling him not to ruin the art of music. Supposing he heard one and the same instrument imitating trumpets, horns, bugles, recorders descant, tenor, and alto, thunder, and the voices of men and birds in our houses of

God? The standard of our music reflects that of our fashion in clothing and furnishings and architecture. The original simplicity has vanished, and elaborate caprices grow daily more common. As long as men's way of life was unspoiled, their speech too was sparing, as a man can easily detect by comparing ancient writers with more recent ones, Hippocrates, for example, against Galen, Socrates against Chrysippus.[10] Now all philosophy has degenerated into a loquacity that outdoes the sophists and has lost its reputation for wisdom and come into contempt, disregarded except by untalented minds. I need not mention our laws, with their boundless verbosity. So if it is pleasure we seek from speech, the incessant talker destroys it – if we believe what Juvenal wrote: 'Restraint in use increases pleasure's charms.'[11] This is why kings barely know the delight derived from jewels, rich clothing, food, and wine, because they are constantly surrounded by them. If any chance reduces them to the point of hunger and thirst, then they will acknowledge that they realize the pleasures of which they have been cheated all their lives; for water is sweeter to a man desperate with thirst than any honeyed wine, and even acorns would be sweeter than honey cakes. In the same way the speech of men who talk seldom and in few words is all the sweeter.

But if we are concerned with profit, there is no profit in a speech unheard. Yet this is the consequence of chattering, that no one either can or will listen, and if the speaker is heard, he has no effect because he is not trusted. No one trusts a man who waxes eloquent not from conviction but from addiction, not to mention that a reputation for stupidity always attaches itself to the fault of talkativeness; hence the popular saying that empty pitchers make most noise.[12] While silence may not always be the outcome of good sense, it is still an indication of seriousness and good judgment. That was a witty comment which someone made to a silent fellow at a dinner-party: 'If you are wise, you are acting foolishly, but if you are foolish, your silence is wise.' Again, someone remarked about another man: 'If he had kept quiet he could have passed for a philosopher.' For nothing is less tolerant of silence than stupidity. So when Demaratus, king of Sparta, was silent at a gathering, he was asked whether he kept quiet out of stupidity or for lack of conversation. 'Hardly the former,' he said. 'A fool can't keep quiet.' The story told of Bias is very similar. He was silent at a banquet, and reproached for it by some chatterbox, as if he were ignorant and lacking taste. He replied, 'Not at all. What real fool can keep quiet in his cups?' He certainly turned the insult of stupidity effectively against the man who misjudged him. There is also a smart repartee made by Zeno. A prominent man at Athens was planning to entertain envoys of the king and knew that they liked learned conversation. To make the banquet more agreeable he had some philosophers invited. While these men were discoursing amongst themselves, each as it were bringing his own contribution to the feast, Zeno alone said nothing. The envoys were amazed. They accosted him courteously and drank his health, asking, 'What shall we tell the king about you, Zeno?' He answered, 'just tell him there is one old fellow at Athens who knows how to keep quiet at a dinner-party.'[13] He stressed the uniqueness of his persistent silence by making three points: that he was old, since that period of life is usually prone to the fault of loquacity; that it was a drinking-party, when wine and the sight of men chattering provoke a man to talk; and finally that this happened at Athens, the most talkative city of all. Archidamidas too spoke neatly in defence of Hecataeus the rhetorician, when someone held it against him that he had been invited to their party and said nothing. 'You don't seem to realize,' he said, 'that it is a part of the technique of oratory to know the right time to speak.'[14] For well-timed silence is a product of the same art as well-timed speech – we might compare Alcibiades' claim in the *Symposium* of Plato that well-calculated flight required as much skill in war as effective fighting.[15] Singers who blunder during the rests that separate the vocal parts display their ignorance of music and suggest that they are not even singing their parts with artistic understanding. So a man with the discretion to choose silence reveals himself each time he speaks as having chosen speech. For speech is only productive if it does not spill out, but is measured and dispensed. Physiologists tell us that men suffering from what doctors call gonorrhoea, whose semen runs without control, are generally sterile. So is the speech of those who talk from addiction and cannot be silent even if they wish. Another observation has been made by experts, that children who begin to talk rather late eventually develop a stronger tongue, whereas those who learn to speak precociously have a weaker instrument. In the same way plants that shoot up suddenly are less healthy, and timber that grows fast to a great height is less hard and firm. Horace was rather silent by nature,[16] but he still speaks to us. Filistus, a wordy and unscrupulous creature, used to insult Virgil. When he reached such a pitch of effrontery as to call Virgil inarticulate in front of Augustus, the poet, a most modest man who always endured him with great patience, told the ranter to be quiet; for, he said, when he chose he would speak forth with a trumpet that would be heard far and wide. Then turning to Augustus he said, 'Caesar, if this fellow knew the right time for speech, he would seldom speak.' For you must always keep quiet unless silence would harm you or speech would benefit others. The witless Pero is silent now,[17] so is Carbilius; Petilius is silent, Avitus is silent, and all the Virgil-beaters;[18] only Maro himself still speaks. Their ephemeral talkativeness has faded away, but the tongue of Maro will never be unheard.

Talk that contains a great concentration of meaning in a few words is like a
dry seed, tiny and insignificant to look at; you bury it in the earth, and it
sends forth a magnificent tree. Even in men who seek fame by their fluency
of speech, only brief and pithy sayings, called *epiphonemata* 'after-comments'
because they are voiced in comment on the finished tale or completed
argument, provoke applause and shouts of approval from the crowd. In
archery contests it is not the man who discharges most arrows but the man
who hits the bull's-eye with a single shot who wins the praise. In the works
of philosophers there are short statements or conclusions which are called
axiomata 'required beliefs' because of their worth.[19]

Again, those men have not been without authority who preferred to
signify their recommendations by actions, like silent symbols, rather than by
language. When there was a riot, and Heraclitus was asked by his fellow
citizens to advocate reconciliation in the assembly, he mounted the platform
and filled a cup with cold water; then he mixed in flour with his finger, drank
it, and departed, indicating by his action that civil disturbances usually arise
from luxury and greed for unnecessary things.[20] It followed that harmony
was easily reached among men who would be content with a few modest
necessities. Scylarus, the Scythian king, used a similar device to show his
sons (they say he left eighty of them) the merits of co-operation. When he
was near death he had a bundle of javelins brought, and told the healthy
young men that anyone who could do it should break up the bundle just as it
was bound up. When each one had tried and given up the attempt in
exhaustion and despair, he himself drew out the javelins from the bundle
one by one and broke them without difficulty. Even with the most
prolonged speech he could not have persuaded the young men more
effectively that their power would be invincible if they maintained the bond
of brotherly harmony, whereas if they were separated from each other by
quarrelling, they could very easily be overcome. Again, how could Sertorius
ever have persuaded the rude and savage rabble of Lusitanians not to risk
the chances of war in a wholesale battle with the Roman forces by any
speech, however carefully rehearsed, as successfully as he did by a simple
demonstration?[21] He displayed two horses, one very strong, the other weak.
By the latter he stood a youth of superlative strength and by the other a
feeble old man, and he ordered each to pull out the tail of the horse to which
he was assigned. While the young man clutched the whole tail and wore
himself out in the attempt, the old man, by gradually pulling the hairs out,
easily stripped away the whole tail. Lycurgus too displayed to the people
two hunting dogs, one bred from pedigree hounds but brought up in
idleness, the other a mongrel but trained by hunting. Then the prey was let
out of the cage and at the same time food was thrown down for them. The

thoroughbred, reflecting his conditioning rather than his heredity, ran to the food, but the other disregarded the food as he had been trained and leaped on the prey.[22] Could he have convinced the common people more thoroughly by any argument of the importance of proper training? Tarquin used a similar trick to communicate with his son Sextus Tarquinius.[23] Sextus had sent a messenger to ask what he should do with Gabii, now it was in his power; Tarquin gave no answer but led the messenger, whom he did not trust, into the garden and as if absent-mindedly struck off the heads of the tallest poppies with the stick he was carrying while the messenger stood by. On his return the man reported what he had seen, and the shrewd young man guessed his father's meaning, that he should eliminate the leading men of Gabii by exile or beheading. Someone asked Cleanthes the difference between dialectic and rhetoric. In reply he showed them a fist, and then unclenched the same hand and stretched it out.[24] How many long-winded phrases would another have needed to explain this? No one could have expressed it more completely.

The Spartans won special glory for this meaningful brevity in their sayings, as we began to explain earlier. When Archidamus heard that the Eleans wanted to come to the aid of the Arcadians, he wrote nothing else in his letter except 'Archidamus to the Eleans; neutrality is a fine thing.'[25] But there is an even more Laconic tale:[26] when Philip asked the Spartans whether they would admit him within their frontiers or not, they wrote nothing else on the parchment but one syllable in large capitals: NO. When Philip sent them a letter full of threats, in particular, 'If I invade Spartan territory I will utterly destroy you,' they answered with one word: IF ($\alpha\ddot{\iota}\kappa\alpha$) – the reply would have been even shorter if they had used the general Greek form $\varepsilon\dot{\iota}$, which is found as a dedication in the temple of Apollo and has tested the ingenuity of many scholars. When the king threatened dire measures, they merely replied, 'Dionysius has retired to Corinth,' hinting that he should take care in case, while he was busy invading other men's territory, he was exiled from his own – for this happened to Dionysius, who was reduced from an autocrat to a schoolteacher. The Spartans sent a one-man delegation to King Demetrius, and when he protested indignantly, inquiring why they had only sent one envoy, their representative replied calmly 'one to one.'[27] When Menecrates, known as Jupiter, wrote to Agesilaus and retained his boastful title in the greeting, beginning 'Menecrates Jupiter bids Agesilaus hail,' Agesilaus wrote back thus: 'King Agesilaus bids Menecrates recover'[28] – that is, his sanity. By changing one little word he reproached him with madness for laying claim to the name of Jupiter, although he was a mere man, and perhaps worse than most. Even in wars and mortal perils, short words have always been more powerful than the most fluent speech. The soldiers of Tarentum whom we mentioned earlier would have died when they were reported for treasonous abuse of King Pyrrhus in their cups, if one of them hadn't put their case in a nutshell. 'If the bottle hadn't run out, we'd even have killed you, your Majesty.'[29] Or take the commander who spoke to his soldiers when they were about to join battle: 'Groom yourselves well,' he said, 'since you will be dining with the queen of the dead.'[30] With this short phrase, he roused the spirits of them all to deeds of valour more effectively than if he had tried to do so with a long and well-rehearsed speech. Simple naked truth has inborn vitality and its own goads to action, which make it more effective than a torrent of language. Just so, an expert wrestler throws a man faster and with less effort than another who lacks technique, however sturdy and violent in his attack. When Croesus, king of Lydia, was taken prisoner by King Cyrus of Persia and saw the victorious army rushing hither and thither through the city, he asked Cyrus what the soldiers were doing in such disorder. 'Why,' said Cyrus, 'what all victors do to the vanquished; they are plundering your city.' Croesus answered, 'No, Sire, *your* city. Nothing here is mine any longer.'[31] This brief answer with its home truth provoked the king to stop the sack which was under way and forbid the carrying off of what had been looted.

The Theban general Epaminondas was once indicted with his colleagues on a capital charge because he had held command over Boeotia for four months against constitutional law. He persuaded his colleagues to divert the charge onto himself, on the grounds that he had compelled them. Then he himself presented the case to the jury complete in a few words. He said he had no words more convincing than deeds, and he thought it was fair that if they declared he was to be executed, they should write the charge on a column so that it would be known to all the Greeks: 'That the Thebans had been coerced by Epaminondas into ravaging Laconia, a state unharmed for 500 years, and pacifying Messenia, a state harassed by continuous strife for 230 years, into reconciling the faction-ridden Arcadians with one another, and restoring freedom to the Greeks.' (These were the achievements of Epaminondas during the period when he kept command contrary to the law.) This brief plea was so effective that the jury did not even take a vote but arose and adjourned with scornful laughter, because they thought it so outrageous that a court should consider condemning a man who had served his country so well.[32]

They tell a very similar story about Scipio Africanus.[33] When the tribunes Petilius and Quintus prosecuted him before the popular assembly and loaded him with many serious charges, he said, 'Citizens, this is the anniversary of the day when I defeated Hannibal and the Carthaginians: I am going up to the Capitol wearing my festal garland to make a sacrifice. Let those who want to pass a verdict upon me, do so.' With this remark he set out for the Capitol, and the whole people escorted him, deserting the prosecutors – so by not pleading he made his plea more successfully.

Here is another argument advanced by those who have left us manuals of rhetoric: that charges which cannot be extenuated by argument should be disposed of by a short jest.[34] Cicero was reproached with accepting money for defending his client, and it was alleged that he was buying a town house with that money. He retorted, 'I will admit the charge, if I buy the house.' When he had purchased the house and was confronted with the exposure of his insincerity, he passed it off with a witticism. 'Don't you know,' he said 'that a shrewd householder conceals his intention to buy?'

Some men have such moral strength that they impress the hearers by a nod or a mere look. After Seianus was dragged to his death, many risked condemnation by the Emperor Tiberius. Others excused themselves by different ploys and pretexts, but Crispinus openly admitted that he had supported Seianus: 'Of course I supported him,' he said, 'when I saw you yourself put so much trust in him.'[35] His plain short-spoken truth persuaded the emperor as no lengthy and carefully composed speech could have done. When Themistocles told the Athenians that he had a fine proposal, but one which could not safely be exposed to the crowd, the assembly authorized him to confide it to Aristides and decide its acceptance or rejection on his word alone. (This was the scheme to burn the Greek federal fleet.) When this was done Aristides declared to the people, 'I have never heard a more profitable scheme than that of Themistocles, nor anything more outrageous.'[36] With this economy of language the plan of a consummate statesman was rejected.

They say that a pirate was once brought before Alexander the Great, who asked him what right he claimed to make the seas dangerous for others. 'They call me a pirate,' he said, 'because I do it in one little ship; you do it with an immense fleet, and are known as a king.'[37] Now it was a pirate speaking, and a king listening, but the truth convinced him with these few words. Pompey the Great intended to kill all the Mamertines because they had supported Marius. Sthenius, the leader of their community, went to him and freely admitted that all their actions had been on his authority. 'I persuaded your enemies and compelled your friends to join Marius' party,' he said. Pompey admired the man's sheer courage, for putting his fellow citizens' safety before his own, and made him his friend, forgiving the Mamertines their disloyalty as a favour to Sthenius.[38] If plain unadorned truth had so much weight with a party leader, what would it not achieve with honest impartial men?

This kind of courage has been found even in women. When Testha, the

sister of the tyrant Dionysius, was accused by her brother of being an
accessory to the flight of her husband Polyxenus and not informing on him,
she answered her brother's reproaches simply and bravely. 'Do you think I
am such a vile and contemptible woman that I would have guessed my
husband was intending flight and not followed him as his companion in
exile for ever?'[39] This not only put an end to all suspicion of her guilt, but
won her praise as a chaste and virtuous wife. When he was very old and
greatly respected in public life, Aemilius Scaurus was accused of treason
before the Roman people by a fellow called Varius of much less public
repute. He presented his case in a few words. 'Varius of Sucro says that
Aemilius Scaurus betrayed the state. Aemilius Scaurus denies it. Which of
us do you believe?' After this statement he was acquitted by the vote of the
whole people and even with the agreement of the tribune.[40] Iphicrates, the
famous commander, was similarly prosecuted before the Athenian assembly for treason, and asked his accuser Aristophontes, 'Would you have
betrayed the state if someone had paid you?' When Aristophontes said he
would not, Iphicrates retorted, 'So you wouldn't have done it, but you
assume I did?' This brief defence secured his acquittal of the charge.[41] The
Greeks believed Demosthenes was their greatest orator but Phocion the
most effective speaker, simply, I believe, because Phocion said little, but it
was true and to the point, whereas Demosthenes would make many
pretences to win favour with the people. That is why Demosthenes feared
only Phocion, although he despised all the other orators. Now when
Phocion got up to speak, he used to whisper to his friends, 'Here comes my
little axe': of course his effective and vigorous brevity easily cut through
artificial syllogisms, so he called it his axe.[42] Nor is it unjustified that men
commonly say that great talkers are great liars, since, as the tragic poet has it,
'simple is the tale of truth.'[43] But there is such a quantity of this kind of
illustration in our writers that it seems superfluous to want to enumerate
them.

[The evils of an undisciplined tongue]

I believe we have said enough to make clear how silence or brevity of speech
befits great men, and how much more weight and authority accrues to a
short and pithy saying than to the limitless talkativeness of chatterers, even
if it has no fault beyond excessive fluency of speech. Nowadays this
affliction has brought with it a great host of evils: an insatiate lust for chatter
about nonsense, about other men's business, about irrelevancies that
concern neither the speaker nor the listeners; or dangerous slips of the

tongue most difficult for the incessant talker to avoid; or indiscretion in blurting out secrets, mostly at the risk of the speaker, but often of those in front of whom they are revealed; or vanity, the usual companion of talkativeness; or damaging another's reputation by informing and spreading slander. For lack of control over the tongue gradually progresses to these evils, even if it is originally nothing more than the childish failing of chattering, more deserving of laughter than loathing.

The first merit of speech is that it should be appropriate, taking into account the case, circumstances, place, and people involved.[1] How can a man keep to these principles if he cannot keep quiet – a man who does not speak by conscious choice, but blurts out words compulsively? Gaiety of speech and sensible and timely jesting contribute a great deal to the pleasantness of human intercourse, and a controlled frankness of speaking among friends is most welcome; but when it is displayed out of place it often leads to serious trouble. For we must not sport at random with wisecracks, nor may we call figs figs and call a spade a spade on all occasions.[2] That was a lucky retort of the young man who was asked whether his mother often came to Caesar's court (for he resembled Octavius in his facial features): 'No,' he said, 'Mother never attended, but Father often did.'[3] This was possible with Augustus, who had a reasonable character and greatly delighted in gay and witty sayings. He would not have got away with it before Caligula or Nero. When a prisoner was taken before King Antiochus, his guards bade him keep cheerful, for he would enjoy the king's clemency once he came before his eyes. He replied, 'You are telling me I have no hope,' referring to the fact that the king had one eye. This joke, splendid in itself but inopportune, caused the man's death, for the king was offended by the remark and had him crucified.[4] A jester met a cruel return from the emperor Hadrian, when he greeted him garlanded with parsley and was removed from the gathering by the emperor's command. He flattered him from a distance with these words: 'You have achieved all, and conquered all; now be deemed a god.'[5] This flattery would have earned a reward from another, but it was unwelcome to the superstitious emperor. But your chatterbox would rather lose a friend than a witticism; he prefers to pay the heaviest penalties for a trivial thing rather than fail to indulge his compulsion.

Once as Alexander's father, Philip, was presiding over an auction, one of the men who were being sold as prisoners of war called out, 'Spare me, Philip, I am a friend of your father.' When Philip answered, 'In what way?' or 'How is that, my good man?' he said, 'I'll tell you, if I can speak with you more privately.' Brought before the king he said privately, 'Pull down your cloak; the way you are now sitting is not decent.' The king was delighted by the man's timely warning, and said, 'It is my wish that this man be freed, for I had not realized that he was so well disposed and friendly to me.'[6] It was also good advice that Aristotle gave to his nephew Callisthenes when he set out to join Alexander the Great, that he should talk little to the king or talk agreeably to him. But Callisthenes, forgetful of this warning, brought ruin upon his own head.[7] I would think, too, that the advice given by Parysatis, mother of Cyrus and Artaxerxes, was not just the product of a woman's caution. She used to warn them that whoever intended to approach the king should soften his frankness with words of the finest delicacy.[8] For when circumstances require that a king should be criticized, the bitterness of the truth must be diluted with great sweetness of language.

In this matter, indeed, it is not enough to consider a man's age or dignity, but we must also take the time and place into account. Even Plato, that great philosopher, was unsuccessful in his frankness to Dionysius, tyrant of Sicily, and so was Dion.[9] Yet that old woman succeeded when she repeatedly importuned King Philip to hear her case. When he replied wearily that he had no time for it, she said to him, 'Then you should not go on being king.' Stung by her comment, Philip heard her case.[10] They tell a similar anecdote about the emperor Hadrian, who, for all his many virtues, almost outweighed them with his faults.[11] Diogenes once found his way into the Macedonian camp. When he was brought before Philip and the king cried out, 'Spy!' he said, 'You have guessed rightly. For I came here to find out whether you were really as insane as the gossip has it, since you could enjoy your own kingdom in peace, but instead you prefer to provoke the Greeks, even risking your life.'[12] But not everyone could have risked what Diogenes said, and you would not easily find men who reproduce the moderation and democratic tolerance of Philip. On the contrary; it is not even really safe to provoke men of ordinary rank by witticisms.

For it often happens that the man aiming to set his teeth in a chewable morsel breaks them on a hard surface,[13] and a slanderer hears worse abuse in reply. It is most foolish of all to provoke with comments and criticisms men with the power to slit your nostrils in return.[14] Thus when Polyxenus, who instructed in dialectic, said in the fashion of dialecticians to Dionysius the Younger, 'I will refute you,' the other retorted, 'With argument, perhaps, but I will convict you with facts.'[15] Similarly, when the Argives abused Cleomenes, son of Anaxandridas, as a sacrilegious oathbreaker, he said, 'You have the power to use foul words, but I can retaliate with foul deeds.'[16] The abuse of the Old Comedy was controlled by law when its sporting humour turned into savagery, and the Cynics were popularly compared to dogs just for this reason, that they condemned human vices, and quite rightly, but without respect for persons, occasions, or circumstances.[17]

Now although no other type of man is more loathed than those who wear out all men's ears with the din of their random questions, still that fellow is far more hateful to everyone who has a leaky tongue instead of open ears; he examines all men's secrets most inquisitively and yet can't keep anything to himself, even at risk to the survival not only of others, but also himself, although he could have kept quiet without any trouble were it not for his awful disease. Hence those men have earned the greatest acclamation from mankind who have kept their pledge of silence better than the others. What feat is more renowned than that of Papyrius Praetextatus, who could not be cajoled or threatened by his mother into blurting out the subject of the discussion in the senate? When she was preparing the birch for him, he tricked his mother with an improvised story; but she instantly spread the tale among the crowd and stirred up a ridiculous uproar making her indiscretion notorious. The boy was honoured for his restraint.[18]

In his essay 'On Chattering'[19] Plutarch tells quite a charming story of a similar episode. At Rome there was a debate over a serious and secret issue for several days in the senate. When people had formed different suspicions about the topic, a woman who was decent and honest enough in other respects but with a woman's faults began to pester her husband with coaxing and wheedling to confide the secret business to her: she would keep silent; she promised her secrecy with tears and on oath, invoking dreadful curses upon herself; and she added the usual complaints that her husband did not trust his own wife. So the Roman, to prove the silly woman's folly, pretended to be won over by his wife's supplications and said, 'I had resolved to keep quiet, but I surrender. So listen, but only if you will keep silence. There has been a dreadful omen announced by the priests – a quail was seen in flight with a golden helmet on its head, bearing a lance – and the senate is deliberating about this, because the augurs are uncertain whether this portent means good or evil. But take care you tell no one.' After this explanation he went to the Forum. But the woman, like one entering labour, got hold of the first servant-girl who came her way and began to beat her breast and tear her hair in front of her, shouting out, 'Oh dear, my poor husband, my poor country, what disaster is hanging over us?' so as to provoke the maid into asking what was the trouble. So she asked the question, and the wife reported the whole affair in detail and added the usual postscript of all gossips: 'Take care no one hears this from you, but don't say a word.' Soon the maid, just like her mistress, picked on one of her fellow slaves and told her the story of the quail. She in turn told her lover, who happened to be on hand, and so shortly the story, rebounded from one to another, reached the Forum. Indeed it travelled so fast that it overtook its inventor, for one of his acquaintances met him and said, 'Have you only just come from home to the Forum?' 'Yes, just now.' 'Then you haven't heard anything yet?' 'No, but is there some special news?' 'Yes,' he said. 'A quail has been seen flying with a golden lance and helmet, and the senate is being convened to discuss it.' Then he laughed and said, 'Splendid, dear wife! You certainly made sure that the secret I confided to you reached the Forum before me.' So he quickly went to the leading statesmen and revealed the story, freeing the community and the senate from unjustified panic. Then he returned home and scolded his wife: 'So, my lady, you've ruined me. The senate has found out that this secret was spread abroad from our household, so I must pay the penalty for your wagging tongue and go into exile.' She was really distraught, and at first denied it, then said, 'Didn't you hear this in the company of three hundred others?' 'You fool,' he said, 'What three hundred are you talking about? When you had worn me down with tears and requests to tell you the secret, I invented everything I told you on the spot, in order to test how much you could control your tongue.'

He acted shrewdly in testing his wife's reliability without great risk, just as men who want to discover whether new jars leak pour in water, not wine or oil, so that the experiment is cheap. If Fulvius had used the same care, he would not have driven himself and his wife alike to ruin. He was a personal friend of the emperor Augustus. He heard the emperor, weary with old age, groaning over his derelict and childless family, because his two grandsons had been borne to an untimely death, and Postumus, who survived them, had been driven into exile by slander, so that he was forced to adopt his wife's son as his successor in power. Family affection was now moving him to consider the recall of his grandson. Fulvius returned home and repeated to his wife what he had heard, and presently she reported it to Livia, who protested violently to the emperor, saying, 'If you have been thinking of such a plan for so long, why don't you recall your grandson? Why do you put me into an invidious position with your successors to imperial power?' The next day, Fulvius, unaware of these events, came as usual to the emperor and said 'Hail!' to him. The emperor in reply said not 'Hail!' but 'Recover!' that is, 'recover your senses,' as if reproaching him with madness, not wishing for his health. Since Fulvius realized what this form of greeting meant, he went straight home and said to his wife, 'The emperor has discovered that the secret which he knew I shared has been divulged, and through my fault. So I have resolved to kill myself.' And his wife replied, 'Quite rightly, for you either failed to realize the indiscretion of the wife who has lived with you for so many years, or, if you realized it, you took no precautions. But although you are responsible for the offence, I will take the lead in dying' – and she instantly snatched his sword and stabbed herself.[20]

Fulvius paid a dreadful penalty for disregarding the proverb 'Never trust a purse or a woman' and the famous maxim 'Tell no man what you do not wish repeated,' not to mention the claim – if we trust in proverbs – 'You can't trust a woman even when she is dead.'[21] But I wish the danger lay only in women. That saying of Epicharmus 'Keep sober and remember to trust no one' is always relevant,[22] even if the female sex is more notorious for this affliction. The elder Cato used to say to his friends that at every stage in life he regretted three things: first if he trusted a secret to a woman, second if he had ever travelled by ship where he might have proceeded on foot, and third, if he carelessly allowed any day to slip past without benefit.[23] Cato was a lucky man, since nowadays most people are tormented by regret because they risked trusting some secret to their closest friends and forgot the shrewd advice of Chilon, 'Treat your friend as though he may one day be your enemy.'[24] Cicero disapproves of this recommendation, but he did not find it safe even to trust his brother.[25] For there are friends who, even without disloyalty, lack judgment or firmness of purpose, so that their natural failing defeats their intention, like the slave Parmeno who appears in Terence's *Hecyra* – not a bad fellow in other respects, except that he longed to know everything and could not keep quiet what he found out, so that when he swore he would not spread the secret which he was asked about, he was told by the girl, 'Don't be silly, Parmeno, you know you are far more eager to tell me the secret than I am to hear the answer to my question.' Indeed he admits his own failing, but none the less, bargains for her silence: 'If you promise me you will keep it quiet.'[26]

There is no man alive so still of tongue or cautious of mind that doesn't have at least one person to whom he dares entrust everything that is trusted to himself; and this man has another, who has another, and so as soon as we depart from the singular, the affair is quickly broadcast to the biggest crowd. For whatever is one is single and undivided and does not exceed its limits – hence its name unit (*monad*). But even a pair (*dyad*) is the beginning of an unlimited series of distinctions. Shortly, when you have doubled one with another, the consequence is an unlimited quantity. So as long as a secret stays with the one who was the first and only man to know it, it is really a secret. But once it has extended itself to a second person it turns into common gossip, for now it is no longer in your power to recall the secret that is in flight[27] or to confine what flits from one place to another at whim. this is why Homer regularly calls words 'pinioned,' that is, winged or flying.[28] An arrow too has its feathers; the man who holds it can keep it still, but once he has shot it he cannot recall it from stirring its swift wings and flying around in all directions. But a missile when discharged does not spread its effect, but at its most destructive kills only one or two; in contrast once a remark has been let out when it should have been kept quiet, it brings whole districts to the utmost ruin. Again, a bird set free strays without becoming more than one, but talk seethes and multiplies and grows, 'gathering power as it moves,' as Virgil says.[29] When a ship has once left harbour and trusted itself to the high sea, if it drops anchor, it can at least be restrained somehow, and a return to harbour is open to it; on the contrary there is no means either to confine the gossip you have confided to another or to recall it whence it came. Again, a missile once discharged does not fall back on the man who hurled it but carries destruction to others; a remark let fly brings to no man more certain destruction than to the man who discharged it.

Since this is so, how can a man have the nerve to reproach others with indiscretion when he has not observed discretion himself? Would we be justified in saying to this protester, 'Why are you accusing me shamelessly? If the secret you trusted to me should not have come out, why did you pass it on to me? Or did you think someone else would be more loyal to you than you were to yourself? If I did anything wrong, I only copied your wrong.' What is more stupid than to take refuge in another man's loyalty when you have dishonoured your own? But you will say, 'I committed a secret to a friend.' Yet you knew that this friend also had friends. And first you should have acted as a friend to yourself. If the man to whom you are trusting the secret is like you, then you have brought the risk on yourself, but if he is superior, that is, if he keeps quiet what has been trusted to you, you are more fortunate than you deserve, since you have found someone more loyal to you than you are to your own self. Indeed he does not even owe you the duty of silence, since you trust your secret to him compulsively rather than by considered choice. According to Epicharmus' maxim we owe no thanks to a prodigal, who makes presents not from generosity but compulsively;[30] in the same way we owe no duty of silence to the man who himself was the first to break the bond of silence.

Many years ago I was dining with a man as shrewd as he was learned, who was then acting as representative of his king in our country. A Dominican who was performing the business of the Roman pontiff joined us, and requested a secret interview; they moved aside. The Dominican said that what he wanted to pass on was secret, but he would not convey it unless the other swore he would keep silent. But he refused to swear over a matter which he had no desire to know. 'If you don't trust me,' he said, 'don't inform me; but if you do, what is the need for an oath? Even if it bound me, so long as it was advantageous for my sovereign to know what you had confided to me, I would not keep it from him.' For honest men do not undertake oaths on such terms,[31] which require that they break their pledge to their sovereign in order to keep an oath to a third party. 'Indeed,' he said,

'I owe a pledge to my lord on more than one count; first as a subject, and second as his representative. If your secret is such that it can be kept without disloyalty or the guilt of failing in my duty, I guarantee my silence, but I do not swear it, because I am not wont to swear lightly, and I am a man able to keep silence; otherwise, keep your sacred mystery to yourself.' Convinced by this speech, the fellow passed on a triviality of no concern either to the sovereign or his representative. In fact it has often befallen me that I was gravely and repeatedly urged, requested, begged, and adjured by someone who had entrusted a secret to me not to tell anyone, especially a particular person; then I heard the same information from many people, and from the very men whom I had been explicitly forbidden to inform. Amazed and wondering how they had found this out, I pretended not to believe it, and asked who was their source for this story. They declared and even swore that they had heard it from the same fellow who had confided it to me.

Now in trivial matters this indiscretion may be a joke. But this example should remind us not to trust anything to another which could cause our ruin if it became generally known. For the sufferer from this affliction would blunder at even greater cost to you if he had the chance. Both extremes are seen as a fault: to trust absolutely no one is the attitude of a tyrant; to trust men at random, an act of stupidity and frivolity. Yet as I said before, it is better to swerve in the direction where the danger is less and the possibility remains of making good the error. At least men who are aware of their proneness to this affliction should hold aloof from deliberations of state and the business and intimate arrangements of monarchs, lest when they cannot keep to themselves what should have been suppressed their blunder brings ruin not only on themselves but on many others, and they meet the fate of vipers – who, it is said, themselves suffer death in labour, split open by their emerging young, and bring forth creatures that will inflict harm on others[32] – or share the fate of the man holding a wolf by the ears[33] or children carrying snakes in their arms: since they can't keep hold of the creatures, they themselves are killed and bring danger upon their companions. Hieron, who held the tyranny at Syracuse after Gelon, said that men who were outspoken in his presence were not any trouble to him, only those who revealed others' confidential talk to him. He used to say that the latter even harmed those to whom they betrayed others' secrets, because we hate not only the men who reveal what we want kept secret, but even those who have heard what we don't want them to hear. For this reason, he reckoned that more resentment was stirred up against him among his subjects by those who furtively informed on other men's secrets than by those who assailed him with outspoken comments.[34]

But it is a greater hazard for us to receive a confidence from the powerful than to report it to them. King Lysimachus loved the wit of Philippides the comic playwright and kept him among his intimate friends, honouring him with all kinds of favour, Once when the king said to him, 'Which of my affairs shall I confide to you, Philippides?' he replied neatly, 'Anything you like, Sire, except a secret!'[35]

In warfare, just as secrecy is most essential to obtain victory, so indiscretion often brings on appalling disasters. Scholars praise the saying of Caecilius Metellus when one of his young officers asked him what was his plan of campaign, and he replied earnestly, 'If I knew this tunic was privy to my battle plan, I would strip it off instantly and hurl it into the fire.'[36] King Antigonus, who was called the Great, told his son, who had asked when he would join battle, 'What's the matter? Are you afraid you'll be the only man to miss the bugle-call?' Perhaps he could have safely trusted a comment to the man whom he intended to trust with his kingdom, but he wanted to train the young man in the importance of silence to a military command. Eumenes even added deception to his silence. When he had been secretly informed that Craterus was coming against him with his front line, he told none of his subordinates, but pretended that it was Neoptolemus approaching, for the soldiers despised him as a cowardly commander, but they respected the valour and authority of Craterus. So when battle was joined, the troops did not realize the commander was Craterus until they had killed him without knowing.[37] So great was the victory won by their commander's discretion. Now Eumenes' cleverness was a marvel to them all, since the very outcome persuaded them that no one should resent this trick. Indeed if anyone had intended to complain, it was better to be reproached for caution and lack of trust, once the victory was won, than to suffer defeat and deserve condemnation for his inability to keep a secret. There is no kind of soldier less fit for warfare than chatterers. For they either provoke the enemy with ill-timed abuse and, as they say, congratulations before the victory,[38] or they betray the plans of action and put the enemy on the alert, aiding him with a favour when they intended to do him harm. The result is that they unwittingly either obstruct victory or increase its cost in bloodshed. Agathocles rose from being a potter's son to be king of Sicily, a fact which he was so far from denying that he used to mix ordinary earthenware with the gold and jewel-encrusted with this argument: 'I used to make pots like this' (and he would show the earthenware), 'now, because of my energy and courage, I live as I do.' When he was besieging the city of Syracuse, some fellows hurled abuse at him from the walls: 'Potter, when will you pay your soldiers' wages?' He smiled and replied, 'When I've taken that city of yours.' Such insults only inflamed the enemy to fight more fiercely.

Now Agathocles himself bore with this insolence with restraint,

content to answer insult with insult; for when the city had fallen, and the
men who had hurled abuse from the walls were put up for sale, he said, 'If
you provoke me again with abuse, I will complain to your masters.'[39] But
such insolence would have angered Nero or Hannibal to the point of
destroying the entire city. Indeed this almost happened to the state of
Athens. Sulla was not particularly hostile to it beforehand, but he was so
enraged by the silly abuse which men were hurling at him from the walls
that he almost came to the point of utterly destroying the most prosperous
state in all Greece.[40] So the commander Memnon, who fought for Darius
against Alexander, was rightly praised when he struck with his lance one of
his mercenaries who was hurling coarse insults at Alexander and said, 'I pay
you to fight against Alexander, not to abuse him.'[41] Or, as the chattering
cook was told in Plautus, 'We hired your hands and not your tongue.'[42]
Those who fight with the tongue have been lashed with many insults; in
Virgil Drances is asked:

> Or will you always fight
> With windy tongue and with those coward's feet –
> Is this your Mars?[43]

and in the same writer, the saucy Rutuli are told,

> The Trojans twice defeated send the Rutuli
> Their answer thus.[44]

For generally shame is a more powerful spur than praise. Consider
Epaminondas, in other respects a mild man; he tolerated with great
forbearance Ctesippus, the son of his dearly loved Chabrias, in memory of
his departed friend, although the youth fell far short of his father's
character. But once at least his tolerance was exhausted by the boy's tasteless
chatter. For when he was preoccupied with an expedition, the boy was
wearying him with silly remarks, questioning him, advising him, even
setting him right in some matters, and acting as though he were the
general's colleague, until finally in anger he said, 'Chabrias, Chabrias, I am
paying a terrible price for our friendship, in bearing with your son.'[45] That
great man, who had borne with long-suffering the folly and self-indulgence
of the boy in other circumstances, really could not endure his talkativeness
in matters of war, divining from this very fault that he would be useless for
military purposes, since he kept his tongue busy where there was more need
for hands and ears.

The same sort of loose talk among the soldiers enraged that glorious
commander. When the troops were fussing around him offering different

advice he said, 'I can see many generals here, but few soldiers.'[46] He saw
that men who had shown themselves so energetic in counselling would be
useless in battle. I don't like to leave aside a story about Phocion. Polyeuctus
was making a long-winded speech to the Athenians about taking up the war
against Philip. When Phocion saw him sweating and panting as he spoke,
and gulping down water to revive his flagging breath (for the speaker was
fat and middle-aged), Phocion said, 'Is it really right, Athenians, for us to
heed this fellow when he urges us to war? What could he do in battle,
weighed down with a helmet and cuirass, when he is in such difficulties just
speaking about war that he risks panting to death?'[47]

The historians tell a splendid story about the younger Scipio. When
Carthage was being besieged a young man offered a cake moulded in the
shape of the city, which he called 'Carthage,' to be torn apart by the party
guests; he was using it as a token to jest about the destruction of the city. But
the general demoted him from his place in the cavalry, and when he asked
why he was deprived of his mount, Scipio replied, 'Because you sacked
Carthage before me.'[48] Now indeed it is almost the regular practice when
rulers are at war with one another to incite them each in turn with
denunciations, caricatures, slogans, and playlets reminiscent of the abuse of
the Old Comedy. We have watched the savage war between Pope Julius II
and King Louis XII of France,[49] in which nothing else so inflamed each
against the other as reports on each side of some too freely uttered comment.
For the king, enjoying a soldier's outspokenness, called him a drunkard – a
name no one at Rome could fail to know was true. Provoked, the pope
replied that he had indeed been drunk to invite the French into Italy – he
wished he could get drunk once more and drive the whole lot out again, and
from then on he would stay sober. The tempers of both leaders became so
inflamed by this sort of remark that the entire world was shattered by this
old men's quarrel. About the same time, when Henry VIII of England had
taken up the defence of the pope against the French, some comedies
performed in this style at Paris aroused the tempers of the English even
more to hasten on the war, and renewed the old resentment, which had
grown milder with the lapse of time. And the Nervii or, as we now call them,
the people of Hainault, were hardly very lucky when some wits among them
aimed some mocking abuse at Emperor Maximilian on his passage through.[50]

We were staying in England at the time when an Italian with a most
elegant but misplaced wit came as envoy on behalf of Julius to incite the king
to war with the French.[51] When he had finished the customary speech in the
privy council, he was answered on behalf of the king that the king was very
anxious to defend the dignity of the pope, but that the realm of Britain had
from long peace lost the habit of warfare; thus, since this would entail
conflict with a most powerful king, his request could not be granted

immediately, but a lapse of time would be needed for the preparation of such a conflict. He replied, more thoughtlessly than with evil intent – since there was no need to add any comment – that he had said exactly the same thing to Julius. Hearing this remark quickly provoked suspicion among the lords that although acting as the pope's envoy he rather favoured the Frenchman. When he was subsequently watched and found in conversation with the French envoy at night-time, he was led away to prison and stripped of all his possessions; indeed he would not even have escaped with his life if he had come into Julius' hands. Furthermore this slip of the tongue caused the king – who might perhaps have reconciled the quarrellers by delaying the affair – to hurry on the outbreak of war.

Of all crimes none is regarded as more wicked or loathsome than treason. Yet this offence has won for many men great success as well as dishonour. For Euthycrates erected a magnificent mansion from the timber acquired from Macedon; Philocrates acquired a great quantity of gold and lost his ill-gotten gains by worse indulgence in vice;[52] the king gave estates to Euphorbus and Philagrus, his agents in the betrayal of Eretria.[53] There are an enormous number of others for whom treason won, if not good reputation, at least a goodly fortune. But the chatterbox does just this without thanks or reward. By his talkativeness he alerts the enemy and incites him; he betrays his country, his children, his wife, and himself, at the same time earning as much detestation from the enemy as from his fellows, because he acts as he does not from calculation but from compulsion. For if a man is led by calculation to commit an offence, and we offer him advantages or parade the hazards before him, he can be either deterred from his intention or maintained in the path of duty. But in the case of the chatterbox, you can count on nothing to justify any man's trust in him. And yet, in Homer, when Ajax is wildly abusive, Nestor does not resent it, because he compensated for his weakness of tongue by his valour in successful combat.[54] But the man who suffers the natural fault of talkativeness impedes the valour of others, and for himself is so lacking in valour that no one is less fitted to any honourable activity. Hence Homer, the greatest of poets, makes those he presents to us as men of distinction firm keepers of silence. Ulysses, challenged in so many ways, persevered in concealing his true identity; even sitting beside his own wife he is moved neither by the sight of her he has yearned for for so long nor by her tears to reveal who he is before the right time, but

> He pitied in his heart his dear wife's grieving,
> Yet were his eyes as dry as horn or iron,
> Beneath their lids unblinking.[55]

Homer portrays Telemachus his son like this too, and Penelope, and even the old nurse whose chatter could be excused on the grounds of either her sex or her age, for he says, 'Yet outwardly was she like flint or iron.'[56] Even in the midst of his wanderings Ulysses generally conceals his identity. With the Cyclops he calls himself Noman, and meeting Pallas Athene in disguise, he conceals by a lying story who he is.[57] The poet gives the same perseverance in silence to his comrades, who preferred being eaten alive to blurting out anything that had to be kept silent.[58] And Virgil portrays Aeneas as the same kind of man – 'feigning the look of hope, he buries deep his pain.'[59] When battle must be fought at close quarters, the barbarians in Homer rush into the fight with a great shouting;[60] the Greeks await the enemy onset, silent and breathing fierceness. If there is any urgent danger, silence makes us safer and more terrifying to the enemy. And if any good fortune occurs, boasting calls down Nemesis; silence keeps and increases what has been won. Even in the campaigns of Cupid, if we believe Ovid, 'The silent man's secure, but boys who call / The lasses names, are riding for a fall.'[61]

At war Socrates used to direct his eyes in all directions and kept them unblinking and alert, but kept his tongue tied down.[62] He did his debating at parties, where there was no danger. If men are looking for a chance to settle a quarrel, silence is best, so that peace may come more easily when resentments are not inflamed by talking. If they are determined to destroy the enemy, however, talkativeness alerts the enemy to protect himself and will not let a surprise attack remain concealed. Even nowadays, most men when they hear two fellows raving at each other with violent shouting say that the situation is safe from the risk of bloodshed; obviously common sense has convinced them that mighty talkers are not mighty fighters.

Geese suffer from a bad reputation for chattering and are said by Virgil to 'raise a din'; yet whenever they migrate from Cilicia and are about to fly over the Taurus range, which is thronged with eagles, they block their windpipes with a gulp of sand and carry a pebble in their mouths, and so fly over silently by night. When they are half way over the mountain they drop the stone, and when they are finally safe they regurgitate the sand from their windpipes.[63] Although Plutarch transfers this story (which Pliny tells about cranes) to geese, at least cranes too are winter migrants, just as storks migrate in summer. So it would be shameful if cranes or geese, both of which for some reason suffer a bad reputation for stupidity (geese among the British, cranes among the French) had more sense than human beings. Men who go courting win their sweethearts faster if they know how to keep quiet. Men who have a pretty wife keep her more safely if they keep silent. For if the crow could eat silently, he would have more food 'and a great deal less quarrel and blame.'[64] The Spartan leader Antalcidas was urged by the priest when he was being initiated into the mysteries of Samothrace to confess to him, as was the custom, the most wicked thing he had done in his life. (It is clear that those impious priests invented this practice to put into their power the men whom they had admitted into their criminal rites, so that they could not easily reject what they had embarked upon and make public the secret ritual out of distaste for the vileness of these outrages.) Antalcidas replied, 'Why should I? For if I have done anything of the kind, the gods themselves know about it.' Admittedly some sources relate this story of Lysander, who was consulting the oracle in Samothrace. The priest ordered him, as if it were a matter of religious obligation, to tell him what was the most vile thing he had done in his life, and he asked, 'Am I supposed to admit this at your demand or that of the gods? When the priest replied, 'At the gods' demand,' he retorted, 'Then you be off from here, and I will tell them if they ask me.'[65] Not even under the influence of this pagan worship could this shrewd man be persuaded to reveal any secret to the representative of the gods. It is obvious from this story that even among the pagans of old the confession of hidden offences was part of religion, and perhaps the custom has come down from them by which the Franciscans nowadays demand that any man whom they admit to the rites of their order should lay bare his entire past life. The men of old aimed at brevity and thought the shame of the one worst offence was sufficient to put in their power the men they were initiating into their filthy rites.

Although it cannot be recorded among the models of excellence, it is certainly a most fitting commendation of silence to recall the story about a certain Spartan boy. He was concealing a live fox which his comrades had stolen (for the youth of Sparta were allowed to steal on certain days), and it savagely tore the boy's abdomen right through to his bowels, but he endured it until the men seeking the fox went away. But when the other boys said it would have been better to reveal the fox than to suffer such injury himself, he said, 'No, truly, it is better to die in torment than to betray a theft out of cowardice and fear of death.'[66] What would they say to this, those important men of high standing who blurt out whatever is trusted to them at the risk of their life and reputation? It was the custom among the Spartans, based on Lycurgus' code, that the eldest person should stand at the door and say to each man entering to share the public dinners, as he pointed to the doorway, 'No word passes out through this doorway.'[67] Horace too reports this among the rules of the dinner-party:

> 'Let there be none among true friends
> To spread their talk abroad ...'[68]

And Martial quite wittily says that he hates a good memory in a drinking companion.[69] I don't know whether Gyges' shameless deed can be said to have turned out well: he obtained a kingdom for himself by a cruel outrage. At any rate it was King Candaules' lack of control over his wagging tongue which deprived him of his empire and his life, for he had babbled about his wife's beauty to his courtier – if we put any faith in Herodotus.[70] The Spartans would not tolerate praise of their wives by guests, because the wives should have been known only to their husbands[71] – so it is much less proper for husbands to boast about their wives' beauty to others. But men also treat their wives with even less decency if they quote at parties and in casual conversations with strangers all the sport they share with their wife in bed or bedroom. If it is disgraceful to make known what men say in their cups, how much more disgraceful it is to be unable to keep to oneself acts of which only the nuptial couch should be a witness!

Some men blunder into making cheap jests when they are aiming to be witty. Now what could be more disgraceful than a bishop or monk playing the jester? Indeed I only wish there were fewer of these. I do not consider it safe to entrust the secrets of the confessional to men like these,[72] for how could a man keep others' sins secret when any victim of this disease cannot even keep his own sins to himself? Or how can he show concern for risk to another when he would rather put himself in danger than keep quiet?

At this point the subject occurs to me of malicious informers, whom I will deal with presently. One of these will produce the slander that I don't approve of confession. You slanderer, I am not comdemning confession, but I am giving this reminder so that no one need regret his confession (which is a correct act in itself) – unless perhaps a man who advises a patient in a dangerous state not to consult a bad doctor is condemning the practice of medicine. And since the subject of doctors has arisen, I will mention in passing that Hippocrates imposed by his oath an absolute silence on doctors, which proves how true it is that a man with a loose tongue cannot even be a good doctor. Yet if a doctor made a disease public knowledge, it would merely embarrass the sufferer, whereas if a priest is a gossip, he will put many men even in danger of their lives. Many people think it is less hardship to be ill than to suffer a doctor who talks too much. There are even some whom no one likes to invite to a party because they are doctors to excess and out of season, with nothing on their lips except paralyses, apoplexies, epilepsies; they discuss the whole anatomical system while men are enjoying a drink, and so turn the most lavish hospitality into a matter for disgust. How anxiously the wise Jew warns that wine should not be given to kings: 'O Samuel do not, I say, do not give wine to kings.' What is the risk if they drink it? 'Because there is no secret where drunkenness reigns.'[73] So the man who cannot keep a secret is not fit to administer a kingdom either. Herod in his cups gave the head of John the Baptist to a cheap dancing girl. His tongue had sworn rashly when it was out of control from drinking.[74] Many rulers drop remarks while drinking which bring destruction to great numbers of men. Plutarch reports that among the Egyptians it was forbidden for priests to drink wine.[75] But now we see most of them drunk when baptizing babies, drunk when hearing confession, and it is the least of their sins if they fall asleep and fail to hear what is said, except that even so they sometimes betray what they have heard. Not so many years ago an event occurred that I am going to describe to you. A man had started his confession to a priest like this. When he realized that the man was in a deep sleep, he got up and went away, breaking off his account. When he had gone another came and, as the priest fell asleep again, the man confessing awoke him and said, 'You aren't listening to what I say!' The priest, bewildered with sleep and thinking this was the same man who had begun to confess earlier said, 'No, I am listening hard. You said you had broken your neighbour's strong-box; go on and tell me the rest.' He had remembered this as a conspicuous point from the first man's confession, although he was nodding and half asleep. But the man confessing was enraged, saying that he had never been a smasher of strong-boxes. By this accident the second man discovered the secret of the first, so each of them left, hampered and embarrassed by the tipsiness of one priest.

Men are right to praise the maxim of Publius the mime-writer: 'He who quarrels with a drunkard talks to empty air.'[76] But the man who trusts his secrets to a drunkard is acting even more foolishly. For he is not just wasting his efforts, but putting himself and others in danger. For in truth he is making a poor guess if he believes the priest will be silent who is seen every day treating himself to wine and blurting out in conversation what it was in his own interest to keep quiet. Someone may suggest that he plays the fool in foolish matters but is restrained in matters sacred. Let someone else believe that at his own expense – but don't believe it yourself. It was a good rule imposed by our forefathers that no one should celebrate a mass except before breaking his fast, but apparently it would have been more worth while if they had laid it down that no one should teach the gospel or hear a confession except when sober.[77]

Victims of epilepsy do not fall where they would like but wherever the fit takes them, even if they are standing on the brink of an abyss. In the same way victims of this disease of the tongue lapse as much in important matters as in trivial ones if a seizure takes them – and it can be aroused by the slightest cause in men like this. Even in matters of life and death they betray themselves like the shrew-mouse[78] and under no external compulsion bring ruin upon their heads. The murderers of the poet Ibycus met a fate which has even become a proverb. For while he was being killed in the wilderness, he called the cranes flying overhead to witness the crime. A long time after, when the men who had done this crime were sitting in the theatre and some cranes flew overhead, they burst into laughter and whispered to each other, 'There are the cranes, the avengers of Ibycus.' This comment was heard by the men sitting nearby, and since Ibycus had now been missing for a long time, suspicion arose, and the story was reported to the magistrates. They were thrown into prison and presently, betrayed not by the evidence of the cranes but by their own wild tongues, they paid the proper penalty.[79]

The ancients used to say that men who had committed murder or some other abominable crime were persecuted by the dread avenging goddesses. But for those men their uncontrolled tongue played the role of the Furies.[80]

The story I will tell happened in England, in the house in London where I was then living. A thief had crawled into the house over the roof-tiles to hunt for loot, but his hunt ended badly, for the noise betrayed the man and there was an alarm, with even the neighbours rushing to aid. When he saw the disturbance, he mingled with the crowd like one of those tracking the thief, and so went unnoticed. When they thought the thief had got away they stopped hunting. Now since the thief had tried in vain to get out through the windows when the neighbours made it difficult, he decided to leave by the doorway, believing he would escape notice there as he had done during the hue and cry. And so he would have, if he had not had a tongue as hard to keep still as his thieving hands. By the door he met several men talking about the thief. So our fellow cursed the thief, because of whom, he said, he had lost his cap. Now the cap had been lost as he fled, and picked up with the idea that the thief might be detected later on its evidence. So suspicion was created by his remark. He was seized, confessed the crime, and was hanged.

There is a story like this reported by Plutarch. The Spartans had a bronze shrine of Pallas, which they called the *Chalcioicos*. Some temple-robbers plundered the shrine, and an empty wine-flask was found in the middle of the temple. When the people had gathered there, most of them were arguing about the reason for the flask. Then one of the bystanders said, 'I will tell you, if you like, what I suspect about this flask.[81] I think that when the temple-robbers planned this crime they drank aconite' (though what Plutarch reports about the aconite other writers say is peculiar to hemlock, the effect of which is weakened by a quantity of wine[82] – for I believe aconite is a poison without antidote) 'and brought the wine with them, so that if they succeeded and were able to escape detection, they could drink up the wine and dilute the effect of the poison so as to leave unharmed, but if they failed, having a ready means of painless death, they could escape the tortures of an interrogation.' Since he told them this not so much like a man guessing, but as if he was sure of his facts, different people began to challenge the fellow: 'Hey, who *are* you?' 'Who knows you in our city?' 'How could you know all that so precisely?' Need I say more? The poor wretch was caught and confessed his act of robbery. Now perhaps someone will attribute this piece of indiscretion to the avenging deity, and I do not object to this, so long as we agree that the deity chose to use the man's own fault to secure revenge.

There was less real criminal intent in the story that I will tell next, yet the penalty was no less awful. King Seleucus, nicknamed Callimachus, had suffered a defeat against the Galatians. After destroying and discarding his diadem, he was fleeing with three or four companions on horseback over trackless country until, faint with weariness and hunger, he was forced to take refuge in a private house. Having found its master, he asked for bread and water, but the owner provided with the greatest affability not only this but everything his country household possessed. Meanwhile he had looked at the king and recognized him and was delighted that fate had brought him to his own house in particular. If he had been able to keep his delight to himself he would have won some lavish reward for his hospitality, but when he had escorted the king as far as the road, so as to leave no homage unpaid, he said as he turned to depart, 'Hail, King Seleucus.' The king stretched out his right hand as if to return his salute and drew the man to him to kiss him, but at the same time nodded to one of his companions to behead him with his sword – and he did just that.[83] But it would be unending to review all the instances of talkativeness by which so many kingdoms and nations and states have been utterly overthrown, as both the histories of the ancient world tell us and we see happen every day.

Sulla was about to abandon his siege of Athens, because he was pressed on one side by Mithridates, who had occupied the province of Asia, and on the other by Marius' party, which had again taken possession of Rome. But while some old fellows were gossiping in a barber's shop they had said among other things that the Heptachalcis was unguarded, and so there was a risk that the city might be taken from that approach. Spies who happened to be there reported to Sulla what they had heard in the barber's shop. So he quickly gathered his forces and at dead of night led his soldiers through that quarter to the city, and was within an inch of destroying it utterly – at any rate he filled it with blood and slaughter until the Ceramicus overflowed with blood.[84] This was the great disaster caused by an inopportune remark, whereas if it had been said privily to a magistrate, it would have deserved a great reward.

Often private loss brings with it public disaster, so deadly is a wanton tongue. Rome, or rather the whole world, had long groaned in pain under the tyranny of Nero. Only one night was left to pass before everything was ready and the tyrant could be slain, and the state would have become free, if the man who had undertaken to kill Nero had had as still a tongue as his heart was brave. For when he saw a man being led into the amphitheatre to fight before Nero, and the fellow was lamenting his fate, our assassin, moved by ill-timed pity, whispered into his ear, 'My good friend, pray to the gods that this day may pass. For I know full well that you will thank me tomorrow.' The man being escorted reported to Nero the suspicion he had formed from this remark, putting his own safety before consideration for the good of his informant or the community, especially as he was unsure how the conspiracy would turn out. So forthwith his comforter was carried off helpless and subjected to torture by fire and the lash. For a long while under torture he denied what he had voluntarily blurted out under no external compulsion, until torture extracted a confession of the truth. The poor fool had by the same act caused his own doom and delayed the restoration of freedom to his country.[85]

The conspirators to kill Julius Caesar kept M. Tullius Cicero – though he was a good man, as they said, and hated tyranny – from participation in the conspiracy from mistrust not of his heart but of his tongue.[86] Indeed I only wish he had crushed Antony by armed violence with as much success as he showed courage in challenging him in speech. But the philosopher Zeno bit out his own tongue and spat it in the tyrant's face, to make sure that he would not ultimately yield to torture and betray the secret of the conspiracy.[87] And the honour paid to the woman Leaena for her marvellous example of silence was certainly well earned. She was a courtesan and a friend of Harmodius and Aristogeiton, and a party to the conspiracy: indeed she shared with them as far as a woman may the hope that it would succeed, since she had drunk of their common loving-cup and was an accessory to their mysteries as if she had been initiated by the same rites. When they failed, however, and had been punished with death, she was summoned for interrogation but could not be driven by any tortures to betray the other accomplices in the conspiracy. The Athenians, in admiration for the woman's extraordinary endurance, erected to her a bronze lioness without a tongue, and dedicated it at the gateway to the citadel, so that the lion would display the courage of her unyielding spirit, while the fact that it had no tongue meant the assurance of her silence.[88] But the Roman people was not so appreciative, although a model of silence is no less marvellous in a slave than in a woman. The orator M. Antonius was being prosecuted for incest, so his accusers demanded his slave for interrogation, because he was said to have carried the lantern for his master when he went to his incestuous assignation. The slave, still a beardless boy, was standing by and saw that this would entail his own torture. But when they came home, and he saw his master desperately anxious about this, he deliberately urged him to hand him over to the judges for torture, swearing that no word would pass his lips to harm his master's case, and he kept his pledge with marvellous endurance under every kind of most brutal tortures.[89] But when C. Plotius Plancus was being sought by the enemy with murderous intent, and the slaves after long torture faithfully denied that they knew where their master was hiding, he came out of his own accord, preferring to die rather than let such faithful slaves be tortured any longer on his account. He could not have paid more honour to the silence of his household.

Or consider the remark of King Agesilaus of Sparta. When a criminal endured with obstinate silence through the torture, he said, 'What perseverance of spirit he shows in an evil cause.'[90] For he admired the man's strength of purpose and control over his tongue, and regretted that such extraordinary courage was being wasted in a dishonourable situation, since it would have won the greatest glory if it had been applied in the right context. When conversation in a barber's shop turned to the subject of abolishing Dionysius' tyranny, which some men called iron and invincible, the barber laughing in an ill-timed joke said, 'How can he be invincible, when I regularly put my razor to his throat?' This comment was reported to Dionysius, and the barber was crucified.[91] Indeed many people drag themselves down to destruction from eagerness to announce new tidings. Take the awful defeat which the Athenians suffered in Sicily. A barber heard of it from the slave of a man who had escaped from the disaster, and quickly left his shop, as if afraid someone would snatch the glory of the first report from him, and hurried into town as fast as he could and filled the whole state with the rumour. When a panic arose and the people gathered, first of all they asked for the originator of this rumour, and the barber was dragged forward and ordered to reveal the source of the story, whose name he did not even know. Immediately the wretch was tied to the wheel for torture as if he had invented this most dreadful rumour. Meanwhile men came bringing definite news of the defeat, and everyone was going home to weep over his own miseries, leaving the barber still bound. At length, when he was released by the torturer towards nightfall, he asked even then whether he had heard anything about the fate of Nicias, and how he had been killed, for Nicias was the commander of the army. His failing was so compulsive that even then he preferred to hear about other men's misfortunes, rather than bewail his own suffering, or take care that nothing similar should happen again.[92]

Now it happens that just as men who have drunk offensive and stinking potions are inclined to vomit even at the sight of the cups from which they have drunk, so we loathe those who report particularly sad news. But why bother to seek examples of this affliction from old histories, when the whole life of mankind is everywhere full of such cases? Men suffer from the same kind of disease when they delight in forecasting future woes, so as to seem like prophets or astrologers or wizards. They often prefer to lose their life rather than their chance of a prediction. Admittedly Henry VII of England preferred to make fun of a prophet like this, rather than eliminate him.[93] The fellow had prophesied from the stars that the king would die that year. The matter was reported to the king, who summoned the man in courteous terms, concealing what he had found out. Among other questions the king asked him whether anything could be predicted with certainty from the stars, and he said yes. Was he expert in his skill? He agreed, hoping he would receive even greater honour from the king. Then the king said to him, 'Tell me where you will be this Christmas' (for the birthday of our Lord was approaching), and the man was in trouble. When the king continued to press him, and he admitted he could not predict this, the king said, 'Well then, I am more expert than you, for I know that you will be in the Tower' (that is what they call the fortress which towers over London, in which men are kept whom they wish to have in safe custody), and at the same time he nodded to have the man led away. When his enthusiasm for prophecy had sufficiently cooled in that prison he was released with a laugh. But truly it is better to abstain from this kind of prophecy, because there is a risk that you will not always benefit from a king of such moderation. I count in this category men who give advice at the wrong time and call down hazards on themselves and others.

Perillus,[94] the inventor of the bronze bull, had congratulated himself that he would enjoy the gratitude of the tyrant Phalaris, but he found out to his cost the truth of what Hesiod wrote, which is now a proverbial saying: 'Evil designs often most evil cause / To their designers.'[95] Let me recall a story which I heard in Paris when I was living there – I am not sure if it is true, but it is certainly likely. There is the mouth of a sewer that men show in the Corn Market, unless I am mistaken, in which a man had himself buried when he repented too late of a bad piece of advice. He had noticed that the king was grim and harassed – the reason for his distress was a shortage of revenues. To help the king, he persuaded him to demand one or two coppers each from the sale of the small produce which peasants bring into town, although only for a two-year period. When it became evident that a considerable quantity of money was raised in the busy city, that is, to quote Hesiod, a vast pile had grown from many little sums,[96] the tax was not cancelled once it had already begun to be paid. It is dangerous for a dog to taste blood pudding.[97] Instead many levies were invented on this precedent. When the original adviser saw that he did not have the same power to argue against taxation that he had wielded in advocating it, to punish himself for his ill-advised advice, and at the same time to warn others against stumbling over the same block, he laid it down in his will that he should be buried in that sewer, because all the refuse flowed into it from the market, where indeed the continuation of this levy persists to this very day.

The examples we have given so far of faults of the tongue are generally such that they tend more to stupidity or, if anyone judges more unfavourably, to madness than to outright evil intent. So if these bring such ruin to the affairs of mortal men, what are we to think of men who with deliberate wickedness never cease to aim and discharge that most accursed weapon, the tongue, to bring about the private and public ruin of the human race – men who deliberately spread false prophecies so as to bring nations and monarchs into mutual conflict by foretelling what they wish to happen by predicting the victory or defeat of now this leader now that, men who report false news on purpose to drag their chosen victims to destruction, who trap and ruin the innocent with lying tales, who turn the heads of rulers with vile flattery, who throw human affairs into confusion by their cunning policies, who perjure, who slander, who by whispering campaigns and secret information destroy friendships, alliances, and marriages, who stir up revolutions, who enrage the heart of a brother with abuse, who teach false doctrine, who vomit forth blasphemies against God and all his saints, until it seems trivial that they are no more sparing of the world's greatest leaders than, as men say, of wolves? Look around at all the murderous tragedies of this world; you will discover that the source of all evils is usually an evil tongue. I wish this plague held sway only in the courts of princes and not above all among men who wish to seem mainstays of the Christian way of life and who expect to be treated as models of Christian religion and honour. I do not want this discourse to become long-winded, so I will say nothing of flatterers – although nothing can be more accursed than this tribe of two-footed creatures – partly because I have written against them copiously elsewhere, partly because those who will can inform themselves from Plutarch's most elegant essay, which I have translated into Latin.[98] But a few words may be said about evil insincerity. Only God perceives what lurks in the heart of man.[99] But the tongue was given to men so that by its agency as messenger one man might know the mind and intention of another. So it is fitting that the copy should match the original, as mirrors honestly reflect the image of the object before them. For lying tales, as they are called, are used only to raise laughter. For this reason the Son of God, who came to earth so that we might know God's will through him, wished to be called the

Word of God, and likewise wished to be called Truth, because it is most shameful for the tongue to be at variance with the heart.

But now even among Christians, O everlasting God, how rare is honesty of speech? How many men are there who have become so accustomed to lying that they do not even know they lie? In comedies this is treated as a feature of the slave character, but in our way of life it is scarcely thought improper in priests and monks, and when it occurs in our leaders is even given the name of policy. I need not mention at this point those whose whole life is nothing but a lie. For they do not only lie in their speech, always keeping on their lips religion, the church, and Christ, the faith and the gospel, but even in their feigned countenance, their portentous apparel, their diets, titles, and ceremonies, they lie before the whole world, bringing great damage to the religion which they dishonestly profess. Such were those Greek philosophers, who offered the promise of a rare kind of wisdom with their beard and cloak, always keeping on their lips virtue, honourable behaviour, and frankness, although most of them were steeped in more than common faults and were the slaves of their bellies and their vanity. Such, too, were the Pharisees among the Jews, pursuing a reputation for righteousness with the common and ignorant folk by the grimness of their countenance, their broad phylacteries, and other devices. Since both groups carried the name of virtue on their tongues, both groups have the same reputation – that is, if we can believe the story of the leader, more gallant than fluent, who heard the philosophers in the Academy disputing about the correct way to live, and when their dissertation was at an end, was asked what he thought of them. 'It only remains,' he said, 'for you to put into practice what you are preaching.'[100] He meant that throughout their lives they had done nothing about virtue except discuss it. Now what was Christ's reply to the Pharisee? 'Thou hast answered rightly; now do this that thou mayest live.'[101] I only wish that among Christians we did not have men who surpassed the pretences of the philosophers and the self-seeking hypocrisy of the Pharisees. The shades have passed,[102] the light has come, and pretence does not suit the children of light. Is there anyone against whom Christ, the Truth, has shown more wrath than against hypocrites? Or what profession was once more dishonoured than that of actors?[103] The laws of pagan nations disqualified from office those who had performed a play in a theatre, and yet this most accursed tribe of actors usurps all the offices of the world while practising its art of pretence everywhere, in marriage, in the alliances of princes, in the courts of kings and emperors.

In comedy the character who was asked, 'Aren't you ashamed of your insincerity?' was hissed offstage when he answered, 'No, so long as it's profitable' – for it is a pimp who answers, and the insult which soon follows,

'You midden,' wins applause.[104] But in real life, how many are there who outstrip Dorio in insincerity, so long as it is profitable, and yet bear the character of Plato or the Catos? A man who is born male and puts on female clothing is punished by law,[105] and yet it is a daily sport to play the buffoon, the trickster, the fraud, and the arch-thief beneath a philosopher's clothing or holy vestments. What tricks do they not play! I blush and cannot bring myself to enumerate the rest of their offences. In the other men's case a deceitful garment is made a criminal charge, even if they have otherwise committed no offence; for these, the disguise of their costume is a defence in every kind of outrage. If once a lie is admitted, trust is inevitably destroyed, and when trust is gone, all human association is destroyed. For who would be willing to deal with a man who is not ashamed of lying? Or who could love the fellow who says nothing sincerely? The common saying 'Show me a liar and I'll show you a thief' is justified. This evil would be less serious if the dishonesty of liars did not prevent men from trusting even those who tell the truth as well as the liars themselves, whose repeated falsehoods have rightly destroyed their credit. Of course there is no pity for the beggar whom no one helps up when his leg is broken because he so often deceived those who ran up to him when he feigned a broken leg;[106] but this extends to others who speak sincerely. Just so creditors repeatedly disappointed by debtors in bad faith even deny a loan of money to others who are unlike them. Yet those who offend from a natural failing and an addiction to lying are less wicked than those who lie from deliberate evil intent. For there really are people who scatter prophecies on purpose, so as to stir up revolution and involve monarchs in dire warfare with each other. There is no shortage of men who invent portents, dreams, and visions for this very purpose. This is almost a sport with monks. Others bury those they hate several times over in each year,[107] to torment their friends if only for a short time, with the sad report. In fact it has now become a regular practice to publish slanderous pamphlets under false names, even usurping for this purpose the name of the man they wish to harm. The laws now turn a blind eye to these abominable crimes.

But it is better to dismiss these cases in order to have more time to follow up what is more germane to our present purpose. I will only add that men need not be ashamed of a lie if they feel no shame at having Satan as their parent, whom the divine Scripture declares to be the source of falsehood; let men despise a truthful tongue, and call it foolish if they will, who do not desire to be members of Christ. I am coming to the subject of forswearers, although for Christians all lying speech is forswearing according to the gospel[108] – indeed in Christians all evil living is forswearing. And surely the holy commitment of taking an oath was invented so that one's neighbour might not be deceived by lying, so that a magistrate or prince might not be elected by fraud, so that public office might not be used dishonestly, so that witnesses might not speak except on their honour, so that prosecutors and counsel might not act improperly, and judges might not give an improper verdict.

Now pray open up the annals of men of old: when will you find an oath so highly esteemed as it now is among Christians, and where will you find more oathbreakers?

There is never an end of swearing. The prince swears when he is crowned, so do magistrates, so does the people; the whole business is done with great ritual. Scrutinize the clauses to be sworn, and you will see the oath is no less absurd than that sworn by men embarking on the profession of the seven liberal arts, or law, or theology. The men who enter on public office are sworn in, and then exercise that office as if they had sworn to forswear themselves. How often do the emperors swear before they receive the holy crown? How often are treaties of princes made on oath and then violated by breaking that oath? Those who are ordained in holy orders swear again and again before the bishop. The papal notaries swear, and so do what are called suffragan bishops. How often do monks swear before their abbots? Scrutinize their actions and you will find everything full of perjuries. At the same time, the oath is not being sworn by the stone Jupiter[109] or Hercules, but by the cross of Christ, by the holy Gospels of the Lord, by our spiritual salvation and, as if this were not enough, the holy bread, the most reverend of all symbols, is broken and distributed. But it is the tongue that breaks all these bonds. We are amazed in the case of Peter, that he three times denied the Lord,[110] whom he loved only with a human feeling, since he had not yet his divine spirit, nor had he seen him resurrected, or ascending into heaven – and yet it seems a sport for us to perjure ourselves, as if perjury in God's name were anything less than denying him. And yet even today those who perjure unsuccessfully are removed from the jury bench and from office. But if you were to scrutinize the lives of some important men, what a great host of false oaths you will find! Indeed nowadays it is treated as worse than perjury when someone puts on a black robe instead of an ash-grey one, or instead of a linen tunic, wears one of wool.[111] For they call it apostasy, which was once the worst charge against those who had denied Christ's name and deserted to the worship of pagan gods. But now that all the life of mankind passes as if the sacrament of baptism were a joke, no one recognizes an act of perjury; no one is ashamed of such an impious apostasy. Here I am not championing those who thoughtlessly abandon an honourable mode of life, but pointing to the inverted values of the common herd.

[*The evils of a vicious tongue*]

I come now to the venoms of the tongue;[1] no viper, no aconite contains more instant death. Even by the laws of the pagans men are condemned for bewitching a crop from other men's fields or invoking a pest upon them;[2] but think how much more harmful is the tongue that by its impious words abolishes piety, that drives away decency by foul language and unleashes a lust for shameful pleasures, that whispers counsels of cruelty and avarice to the prince instead of mercy, and pollutes with deadly poison the public source from which all men must draw? Witches are burned to death for doing violence to men's minds or harm to their bodies with poisonous herbs, for calling up ghosts, for sacrificing to pagan gods with magic rites, for using the evil eye, even if not one of these practices takes place without the services of the tongue, as Virgil bears witness:

> When stepmothers
> Have cruelly dosed men's cups and brewed up herbs
> And words of incantation full of harm.

Or again he says:

> With foxglove fronds
> Circle the brow, lest evil tongue should harm our poet.[3]

And yet no one wonders when harmful tongues constantly perpetrate all these offences in the life of mankind – the practice has become so customary. Is any evil eye more wicked than the corrupt training of youths and girls? When a man teaches impiety, hasn't he mixed aconite in the cup? When he taints innocent youth with obscene talk, isn't he pouring in an incurable poison? It is true that certain remedies have been recorded against the wiles of evildoers, but what remedy could you find against the poison of an evil tongue? There are spells to bewitch a serpent, but there is no kind of spell to control a slanderer's tongue.

Now Nature, being closer to a cruel stepmother than to a mother, has allocated to each poison its own kind of destruction and indulged herself in a cruel variety and abundance, but to the tongue alone she has attributed every destructive power. When an evil tongue has persuaded a man through thirst for possessions to the point of cheating his brothers and robbing temples, to acts of murder and poisoning, hasn't it done more harm than any dipsas-snake, whose bite leads to an insatiable thirst for drink, even to the point where a man will cut open his own veins?[4] The centipede is a tiny little animal, but so powerful is its poison that whoever it has stung rots away so completely that even his bones disappear.[5] But surely a poisonous tongue that drips into another man's heart the poison of envy, by which he utterly rots away, body and soul, has instilled a more instant poison than that of the centipede, although this is awarded the prize among all varieties of serpent, because while the others take away life, this creature alone does not even leave a corpse? Consider. Surely the tongue that plants the venom of ambition into the soul with its corrupting talk or the flattering tongue that so turns a man's head that he seems to himself to rival the gods and swells up with vain pride has caused more harm than any scorpion, whose bite leads to a monstrous swelling of the body.[6] When a mere man claims divine honours and sets himself up against all that is called or worshipped as God, is he not worse swollen with dire poison than if he had been bitten by a scorpion's tooth? – whose venom does indeed make the victim's body swell beyond human size, but not up to the size of an elephant. But the spirit of a man puffed up with conceit swells right up to the height of God himself, who is beyond measure or imagining. Alexander the Great had his bad counsellors,[7] who took the already frenzied man and incited him further to war, promising something like lordship over the whole earth, constantly, as it were, applying fresh kindling: 'This land still remains for you to conquer,' 'This nation shows you disrespect.' Meanwhile the wretched youth, who was soon to die, threw everything into confusion with murder and bloodshed, not even sparing his dearest friends, because he could not endure being disregarded by any man. Surely he had drunk a worse poison from their wicked tongues than those bitten by the haemor-rhois, the snake that gets this name from the Greeks because the man it has stung sweats pure blood all over his body.[8]

Again, a harmful tongue that distracts a man from correcting his life for the better, that bewitches him into carelessness, that urges him to live in luxury without concern for the future, that says, 'Let us eat and drink, for tomorrow we die,'[9] or 'God has no concern what men do,' or 'Our concern is pointless, since God, whether we will or not, will do with us whatever he has once resolved' – a tongue, I say, that has instilled a deadly sloth into a man's heart with words such as these has surely inflicted a wound more deadly than an asp's sting, which leads to a profound sleep bringing death without consciousness of pain?[10] Just so do men who live in luxury count their days as a blessing and descend in a moment to the nether world. Come now, consider an informer's tongue, which ensures the outlawing of an innocent man by a powerful but foolish prince, so that the victim, like one struck by lightning, perishes before he has felt the blow. Would you say it did less harm than the snake that is called dart, because it hurls itself like an arrow and passes through a man's temples so swiftly in its trajectory that death comes not a moment behind the wound?[11] The basilisk is harmful both by its gaze and its bite; indeed its venom is so instant that if you do not immediately cut off the limb, there is no hope of life.[12] Doesn't the jealous man have the effect of the evil eye, since he is consumed with envy at his brother's good fortune, which should give him as much pleasure as his own? Surely he adds a kind of sting more harmful than the poisonous glance in criticizing and slandering perfectly correct behaviour, distorting by a malicious interpretation honest words, wielding heresy as a charge, where there was a praiseworthy act of piety, insinuating treason where there was an honest and beneficial proposal deserving approval. O innocent basilisk, when it is compared with tongues such as these!

The venom of the basilisk is immediate and swift, flying instantly along the barb into the right hand of whoever has touched it; that of the fish called *narcos*[13] is even more immediate. When it is hooked, it sends the venom through the steel, through the long line, through the knots of the rod into the hand of the fisherman holding it. But an evil tongue transmits its poison further, for its speech creeps like a cancer and does not make an end until it has spread over a great part of the world. It infects the husband through the wife, the parents through the pupil, through one magistrate it infects the others, until the effect of the poison has penetrated into the courts of princes, and thence into the entire world. Meanwhile these *narci* among men, sluggish with idleness and safe only because of their poison, feast on the unfortunate without punishment; indeed nothing suits them so well as the fact that women lack all sense, the crowd is dazed, the rulers are demented. They say that among serpents no venom is more incurable than that of the asp, just as among herbs they give the prize for harmfulness to aconite, which shares with the asp its power to kill by sleep. Yet no poison is so utterly destructive that the energy of man has not discovered an antidote. For Varro reports that it is an effective cure for the man stung by an asp to drink his own urine.[14] And the effect of aconite is diluted by rue and sea-holly distilled in goose-gravy,[15] not to mention other antidotes of doctors, of which there is an infinite number.

There are many varieties of things by which we drive off and keep away poisonous creatures, like fumigation[16] with the herb ebulum, also with galbanum and with the tamarisk, which is a sterile kind of fruit-tree.[17] The smell and smoke of the *costus* tree and the *panaces*, centaury, sulphurwort, *thapsia*, hellebore, and larchwood have the same effect. The ash has so much power against serpents that not only will its juice when drunk or applied to the wound help those harmed by poison but no serpent will even approach the shadows of this tree at morning or evening, however far they may be cast. And if you shut in a serpent so that it can escape only into the fire or towards the ash tree, it will prefer to go into the fire. Pliny reports this as though he had established it by experiment.[18] The charred antler of a stag has the same effect.[19] Indeed this animal itself, which is naturally hostile to serpents, can draw them out of caverns with its breath and kill them. Hence we read that whole armies were safe although surrounded by poison. For nature has given a special power to the race of Psylli by which they are not only immune themselves to all poisons, but can even heal others bitten by snakes with their spells and saliva, and by sucking draw out the poisons from the actual ulcers and spit them out again without any harm to themselves.[20]

But a poisonous tongue defeats all human skills. Amongst all the scourges of life, none is more dreadful in my opinion than the affliction caused by a rabid dog's bite.[21] For the asp's bite kills with sleep, the gentlest kind of death, and harms no one by further contact, since they report that the flesh of a creature killed in this way is harmless. But a dog's bite, besides causing a cruel death and a mind destroyed by madness, even spreads to many people in its cruel contagion. Yet men have countered this evil too with a great number of antidotes – only the tongue has a poison beyond cure. A quantity of wine weakens the effect of drinking hemlock;[22] some poisons bear their antidote with them:[23] a scorpion applied to the wound it has caused reabsorbs its own poison, and a man bitten by the Spanish fly will obtain relief if he pulls off its wings and lays them on the wound. Men tell the same story about the hairs of a mad dog. If only pills were made of the pounded tongues of slanderers, so that they might aid by this cure those whom they harmed by their poison!

There are areas in which absolutely nothing poisonous lives; indeed you do not find any particular poison in every kind of place. But to what corner of the world will you flee where you will be safe from an evil tongue, which contains in itself every kind of poison? It is recorded in the histories that some men were so protected by antidotes against poisons that they could not be harmed by any variety;[24] only the tongue contains an invincible evil. Here you may add that poisonous creatures do not casually harm anyone unless they are provoked, that is, when they are trodden underfoot. But a harmful tongue offers its poison unprovoked and harms no one more seriously than its benefactors. Intimacy and simple trust offer a handle to do harm; this is how the scorpion embraces[25] before it drives home the sting of its tail. Again, not every poison is a poison to all. Serpents provide a harmless food for storks,[26] and a fatal poison to man; but the poison of the human tongue is deadly to all. Indeed certain creatures are harmless in certain regions. For pythons are only harmful in Africa; elsewhere they are mild and harmless;[27] the peach when transplanted in Italy ceases to contain poison.[28] Again, snakes generally are torpid and harmless in the chill of night; some waters are harmful if drunk by night, but by day they are drunk without harm. But an evil tongue carries its poison mixed and ready in every place and at every time. Now among poisons those are especially feared which attract by their deceitful appearance, for instance in the case of rowan-berries the most beautiful are poisonous,[29] and some springs are deadly to drink although they flow pure and clear. There is a kind of honey too which is sweeter than all the rest but contains poison.[30] There are creatures all the more dangerous because they change colour, like the chameleon.[31] Others are not only poisonous, but supreme in speed. But what is more beguiling than a poisonous tongue? Does it not transform itself into every kind of creature in turn? What is more flexible? Now from vipers and aconite there are derived many remedies against the most serious diseases,[32] so that nature seems to compensate abundantly for their evil. But an evil tongue is nothing else but venom. Poisons are milder in this respect, that a scorpion does not attack a scorpion, and a viper is harmless to a viper. Only man has a poison against man. And do we still shudder at poisonous frogs[33] and field snakes, while we embrace man, more harmful than all these creatures? Do we instantly amputate a limb bitten by the basilisk,[34] and not shun the embrace of a slanderer? Who is so mad as to nourish a viper in his bosom? Yet we sometimes cherish even in our beds creatures more harmful than vipers. If Pythagoras forbade us to shelter a swallow under our roof, although this bird is ignorant of poison, just because its great chatter makes it disturbing,[35] surely we shall exclude a poisonous man from our company? We shudder at a scorpion, which only strikes at the incautious and whose poison is not always deadly – in fact it can be safely killed by a mere blow of our fist after the sting and when applied to the wound has the same healing effect as Achilles' spear in the myth;[36] but an evil tongue has something in common with those possessed by the devil who by their wicked magic send evil on whom they choose but cannot remove what they have unleashed. For the poison spreads even against the will of the man who set it in motion, and the world is so designed by nature that it is most easy to do harm but most difficult to heal it. There are many tools to overthrow the life of mortals – stones, swords, arrows, artillery, ambushes, wars, sorcery, poisoning, attacks by wild beasts and poisonous creatures, plagues, earthquakes, thunderbolts, flooding, and other innumerable calamities – from all of which together less destruction arises to the human race than the tongue causes unaided, since we also owe to the tongue a large part of those evils which I have just mentioned. No kind of disaster brings a worse flood of destruction than war; but there would be no war between mortals if there were no evil tongues to supply causes for war.

How many thousands of men does slander ruin every day?[37] How many does flattery destroy? How many does the wheedling tongue ruin with evil suggestions? How many does the harmful tongue ruin with the evil eye of envy? How many does the slanderous tongue harm, how many the tongue violent with darts of abuse? Go back to the records of the ancients, read again all the tragedies there are, whatever cruel or tragic deeds have been done by tyrants, and you will find the beginning came from an evil tongue. That little flabby organ contains so many evils unless an honest spirit is there to rule and control it.

At this someone will perhaps interrupt my discourse, not without justification, and say, 'You just go on abusing a harmful tongue, but we are waiting to hear the cure.' We will provide that too, in the right place. Indeed in the case of diseases of the spirit a good part of the medicine is to know thoroughly the extent of the evil. If I succeed in establishing that even from the Holy Scriptures, I shall try to show you the cures as well. But I seem to have discussed the disease of chattering sufficiently at this point. I will only add this in passing, that no one has condemned the vice of talkativeness more briefly or more effectively than our Lord in the gospel, when he said that we must render account of every idle word at the day of judgment.[38] Now what is an idle word? All stories, all jokes that in no way contribute to our eternal salvation. What, then, will they say on the day of judgment who spend all day long chattering of the most trivial trifles, wasting the leisure and work time of both themselves and others? As I said, foolishness and insincerity are accompaniments of talkativeness. Now as God speaks most seldom and most briefly, so he speaks a truth both absolute and powerful. God the Father spoke once and gave birth to his eternal Word. He spoke again and with his almighty word created the entire fabric of the universe.[39] And again he spoke through his prophets, by whom he entrusted to us his Holy Writ, concealing the immense treasure of divine wisdom beneath a few simple words. Finally he sent his Son, that is the Word clothed in flesh, and brought forth his concentrated word over this earth, compressing everything, as it were, into one epilogue. He combined the pledge of silence with brevity of speech, adding to both qualities the highest and most powerful truth. What manifests his pledge of silence? The fact that once the record of death is obliterated, there is then no mention of past offences. What proves his succinctness of speech? The fact that he has encompassed the law and the prophets in two words: trust and love. The infinite talkativeness, so to speak, of forms and rituals has been eliminated, since the body and gospel light itself has shone forth. What shows us his truth? The fact that whatever had been promised for so many centuries he fulfilled through his Son.

In the book of Job, Elihu speaks thus: 'I am full of matter to speak of and the spirit of my bowels straiteneth me; behold my belly is as new wine which wanteth vent, which bursteth the new vessels. I will speak and take breath a little.'[40] You are listening to a talkative man unable to endure silence. But God, as the same book says, 'speaketh once, and repeateth not the self-same thing a second time.'[41] This is how that wise man Sirach restrains the tongue eager to chatter: 'Be not hasty in thy tongue and remiss in thy works.'[42] How well he castigated the common ways of men, who are most vigorous with their tongues, but lazy in their actions. Now Solomon gives us the same advice; he says: 'He that setteth bounds to his words is knowing and wise, and the man of understanding is of precious spirit.'[43] How wisely he has associated economy of speech with prudence, and a mind capable of silence with learning. A little later he adds: 'He that answereth before he heareth showeth himself to be a fool and worthy of confusion.'[44] The wise Ecclesiastes knows a time for speech and again he knows a time for silence.[45] Amos the prophet realizes this too; he says: 'Therefore the prudent shall keep silence at this time, for it is an evil time.'[46] Moreover since chattering about sacred matters is most dangerous, Zechariah rightly warns us: 'Let all flesh be silent in the presence of the Lord, for he is risen up out of his holy habitation.'[47] And Psalm 64 gives the same instruction according to the Hebrew version: 'Silent praise shall be given to thee, O God in Zion, and vows shall be offered in thy name.'[48] Again how neatly Sirach portrays for us a wineskin bursting with new wine: 'At the hearing of a word the fool is in travail, as a woman groaning in the bringing forth.'[49] Likewise the man who cannot even keep his own secrets is reprimanded, or rather instructed: 'Tell not thy mind to friend or foe, and if there be a sin with thee disclose it not. For he will hearken to thee and will watch thee. Hast thou heard a word against thy neighbour? Let it die within thee, trusting that it will not burst thee.'[50] And somewhere further on he says: 'There is a lying rebuke in the anger of an injurious man, and there is a judgment that is not allowed to be good, and there is one that holdeth his peace,'[51] and again in the same place: 'There is one that holdeth his peace that is found wise, and there is another that is hateful, that is bold in speech. There is one that holdeth his peace because he knoweth not what to say, and there is another that holdeth his peace, knowing the proper time. A wise man will hold his peace till he see opportunity, but a babbler and a fool will regard no time. He that useth many words shall hurt his own soul.'[52] And presently he adds: 'The slipping of a false tongue is as one that falleth on the pavement,'[53] and again: 'A parable coming out of a fool's mouth shall be rejected; for he doth not speak of it in due season.'[54] If a good opinion spoken out of its proper time shall be rejected, what should we say of those who exhaust the ears of all men with silly talkativeness? Solomon says similarly: 'As if a thorn should grow in the hand of the drunkard, so is a parable in the mouth of fools.'[55]

Now the sayings even of the Greeks teach us that silence is the only adornment of a good woman, and our authority Sirach has spoken about this too; he says: 'Such is a wise and silent woman, and there is nothing so much worth as a well-instructed soul.'[56] What befits a woman is also fitting to a young man in the presence of his elders. He says: 'Hear in silence, and for thy reverence good grace shall come to thee. Young man, scarcely speak in thy own cause. If thou be asked twice, let thy answer be short.'[57] Indeed Solomon says of the indiscreet fool: 'He that walketh deceitfully revealeth secrets, but he that is faithful concealeth the thing committed to him by his friend.'[58] Sirach teaches us to beware of such a man, saying: 'Affect to speak with him as an equal and believe not his many words. For by much talk he will sift thee and smiling will examine thee concerning thy secrets.'[59] Horace too warns us: 'Flee from the questioner, for such men chatter,'[60] and Sirach warns us again: 'A man wise in words shall make himself beloved, but the graces of fools shall be poured out.'[61] And another time he says: 'The heart of the fool is like a broken vessel and no wisdom at all shall it hold.'[62] You learn that the chatterer not only is a fool, but cannot be taught wisdom.

Now hear how chattering is wearisome. He says: 'The talking of a fool is like a burden in the way. But in the lips of the wise grace shall be found.'[63] And presently he says: 'The lips of the unwise will be telling foolish things, but the words of the wise shall be weighed in a balance.'[64] Indeed a pagan made the same comment: 'As is a man, so is his speech.'[65] And according to Isaiah the fool will speak foolish things.[66] Again Sirach says of the indiscreet tongue: 'The heart of fools is in their mouths, and the mouth of wise men is in their hearts.'[67] What does this mean, to carry one's heart on one's tongue? It is to pour out speech before you think what should be said. What does it mean to have your tongue in your heart? That is to avoid speaking, except of things you have thought over and weighed up. And another time he says: 'Let not thy mouth become accustomed to indiscreet speech; for therein is the word of sin.'[68] And the saying of Solomon agrees with this: 'In the multitude of words there shall not want sin, but he that refraineth his lips is most wise.'[69] And somewhere later he adds: 'He that keepeth his mouth, keepeth his soul, but he that hath no guard on his speech shall meet with evils.'[70]

We have often spoken of the talkativeness of barbers. Now let us listen to Sirach: he says it is difficult for a merchant to be delivered from carelessness and an innkeeper shall not be excused from the sins of his lips.[71] Now listen to Ecclesiastes: 'The words of the mouth of a wise man are a grace, but the lips of a fool shall throw him headlong. The beginning of his words is folly and the end of his talk is a mischievous error.'[72] I will not recall here in how many places Paul attacks vanity of speech[73] and how sternly he checks the uncontrolled tongue of women.[74] And yet these faults are thought to be the least serious failings of the tongue – mere foolish chattering, and indiscretion with confidences. They certainly should be treated as serious, when the sacred Scripture condemns them in so many places, of which we have selected only a few. For, as I said, folly is inseparably bound up with these faults.

As in sacred matters God the Father begets from himself his Son, so in us our mind is the source of our thoughts and speech; and as the Son proceeds from the Father, so in us speech proceeds from our mind. The Son is called the likeness of the Father, so like indeed that whoever knows either of them knows both persons. So in us, speech is the reflection of the mind; hence the famous saying of Socrates: 'Speak, so that I may see you.'[75] A young man of handsome appearance had been brought before him so that he could judge the man's character by looking at him. But Socrates did not see the young man while he remained silent, because the mind shines forth less from a man's face than from his speech. Doctors infer the symptoms of sickness not only from a man's appearance but also from his tongue. Surely the most reliable symptoms of a sick or healthy mind are in the tongue, which is the appearance of the mind.

Women, poor things, are mocked for painting their face, but men would be even more of a laughing-stock if they repeatedly took on a different stage mask and came into the city square now as old men, now as young, at times ruddy-faced, at others pale, sometimes fat, and sometimes thin. Yet men are just like this when their speech is at variance with their mind. And no one is shocked by this type of actor; nobody drives them off the stage. If, as the proverb goes, likeness begets love,[76] and difference brings loathing, nothing is more loathsome to God than a lie, since he is truth itself. Accordingly a lying tongue is steeped in Satan's poison, and damnation springs from it, just as salvation springs from truth. As Solomon says, 'a deceitful tongue loveth not truth, and a slippery mouth worketh ruin.'[77] Truth is the light, and lying is darkness. Whoever is removed from truth shudders at the light. Moreover the habit of lying will make you lie often and unintentionally, not without great risk; clearly this is why he added 'and a slippery mouth worketh ruin.'

Now you might find some men so inured to lying that they believe themselves to be telling the truth even when they lie most shamelessly. For in other faults also the evil of habituation is that once the addiction has almost become part of our nature from habit we do not notice our affliction and begin to offend openly and heedlessly. Hence comes ruin not only for liars but also for others to or about whom they lie. It is a dangerous sickness when anyone is provoked to silly talk by a restless tongue, but far more

dangerous when someone is led to talk silly nonsense by a shameless delight
in lying itself. Hence Solomon or it maybe some other wise Hebrew prays to
escape two exceptionally grave evils, on the grounds that he would indeed
be lucky to achieve their avoidance before his death – these are falseness and
lavishness of tongue, their opposite, or poverty. He says: 'Remove from me
falseness and lying words.' Indeed he only dreads the first of these evils
because it leads to lying. This is how the passage runs: 'Give me neither
beggary nor riches. Give me only the necessaries of life, lest perhaps being
filled I should be tempted to deny God, and say, "Who is the Lord?" or being
compelled by poverty, I should steal and forswear the name of my God.'[78]
Now there is no more accursed kind of lie than to deny God, as the Stoics
declare, and the Peripatetics are largely in agreement with them;[79] but it is
even more accursed to acknowledge God but deny that he cares for the
affairs of men, or at least is indulgent to their faults. But surely this is what
anyone seems to be affirming who dares to forswear in God's name.

Now riches are generally of ill repute, simply from our experience of
the world, because they teach men to neglect God, as we see especially if we
look at the lives of some of the monarchs of this world whom the common
herd treat almost as gods. But how can men face themselves if they bring
beggary upon their heads, and not only cast away their property, if they
have any, but even bind themselves to idle beggary, although Paul himself
earned his support by work during the night, and told those who shirked
labour and were seeking to live at another's expense to earn by the work of
their hands not only enough for themselves to live on without being a
burden on others, but also the means of sustaining others burdened by
need.[80] And yet we must not conceal the fact that a sufficiency of income
depends more on the attitude of its owner than the scale of his resources.
That was the nature of Paul, the chosen vessel of Christ, celebrated in all
men's writings; but this chosen servant of Christ, praised by the most
praiseworthy of men, has found no emulator. Christ was the true shepherd
and Paul his true emulator, as he himself does not hesitate to say: 'Be ye
followers of me, as I also am of Christ.'[81] So God cannot but hate apostles
who lie and are most unlike Paul, since he is truthful in each and every way.
For if those who benefit men by lying are offensive to him, surely those men
are far more offensive to him who by their lying cause ruin to body and soul,
and by falsehood bring into the power of Satan those whom Jesus Christ, the
eternal Truth, has set free from Satan's falsehood? For he did not stand firm
in the truth, but from the beginning was a liar and the father of lies.[82]

Nor does this scourge come alone, but brings with it the ruin of all
virtues and releases a sewer full of every crime. The Lord himself makes this
known, speaking through the mouth of Hosea and threatening vengeance

upon the people of Israel: 'There is no truth,' he says, 'and there is no mercy and there is no knowledge of God in the land; cursing, lying and killing, and theft and adultery have overflowed, and blood hath touched blood: and the earth will mourn for this.'[83] Notice the stages of destruction he marks: where there is no truth, there is no compassion. For the truth of philosophers and Pharisees has arrogance instead of pity. Where there is lying, that is hypocrisy, no matter how human disciplines thrive there is no knowledge of God, that is, the wisdom that according to the teaching of James springs from on high,[84] ignorant of strife and bitterness, but chaste, peace-loving, modest, easy to deal with, full of compassion and good works, in no way wavering, and free from all pretence. There can be no knowledge of false things, but neither does anyone have knowledge of God, unless he believes in the sacred Scriptures; yet no one either understands or believes these unless the heavenly spirit has breathed upon him. Without the Scriptures, slander overflows through the spirit of Satan so long as we attack the failings of our neighbours with insults and abuse when we should have healed them with gentle and brotherly warnings.

From this level the world descends to the lie, a far more accursed thing, as we bring our neighbour into danger by false accusations. From slander the world rushes on to murder, theft, and adultery. How many does slander deprive of life? How many men does treacherous informing strip of their ancestral property? And theft arises from lying, bringing murder with it. What is left? Adultery. It is a most grievous sin to defile another man's wife, but more grievous still to defile your neighbour's reputation. If someone kills a man with the sword, he is depriving only one man of life, and one destined to die in any case; but someone who drains another's possessions into the prince's treasury is cutting the throats of many by that act of theft – his wife, children, and household, whom he is reducing to starvation and the noose. But the violation of another man's reputation seems to be more wicked than any of these. A good man is destroyed under the name of a traitor or heretic. We know of men that were murdered in prison, and by extraordinary trickery the common people were persuaded that they had committed suicide, and the legacy of this disgrace was handed down to their wives and children. O what a dire flood falsehood has poured out upon us, mingling bloodshed with more bloodshed and sowing one impiety from the seed of another! This is the ruin that entangles all those who depart from the whole truth of divine Scripture. They brawl, whereas Paul beseeches us. They act through pretences and feign true piety with rituals, and to preserve their own domination they do not even abstain from murder. For the man who teaches false beliefs is also a murderer offering poison disguised as an antidote, and in claiming the glory of God for themselves, men commit a sacrilegious theft, seducing from the Lord the simple souls whom Christ has betrothed to himself, and they inflict a most wicked act of adultery in handing them over to Satan to be perverted and corrupted. For this meaning also is offered to us by the allegory of the prophet's speech.

Clearly this is that act of adultery which God so often abominates in the books of the prophets, reproaching an ungrateful people with his generosity and thrusting before their eyes the great dignity from which it has cast itself down into such a depth of shame. Jeremiah too combines lying with adultery in his argument, and he saw 'in the prophets of Jerusalem the likeness of adulterers and the way of lying.' Where is the lying? 'They say to them that blaspheme me, "Ye shall have peace." And to everyone that walketh in the perverseness of his own heart, they have said, "no evil shall come upon thee."'[85] Where now is the adultery? Whenever a people corrupted by the false doctrines of those who sell and adulterate the Holy Scripture departs from its God of salvation and withdraws from association in the church. Oh what a wretched and lamentable separation! The Lord of the gospel disdains this adulterer, who turns away from the truth and clings to falsity. For he was the bridegroom, and sought for a simple, chaste betrothed, faithful and without stain or disfigurement. 'O you corrupt and adulterous tribe,' he cries out, 'how long shall I be with you? How long shall I suffer you?'[86] The Jewish nation seems to be like this even today: it does not recognize the bridegroom, but has destroyed by murder him whom it rejected by lying. Nor does it stop furtively stealing his flock, which he ransomed with his own blood, nor does it cease to attack with blasphemies in its synagogues the Lord at whose name all that there is in heaven and earth and hell bends the knee in homage.[87] How Paul curses and abominates this separation among those whom he had led away from the yoke of the devil and betrothed to Christ. He says: 'I have espoused you to one husband, so that I may present you as a chaste virgin to Christ. But I fear lest as the serpent seduced Eve by his subtlety, so your minds should be corrupted and fall from the simplicity that is in Christ.'[88] Nor does he conceal the source from which he fears this adultery – that is, from nothing but corrupt doctrine. For, he declares, such false apostles are 'deceitful workmen, transforming themselves into the apostles of Christ.'[89] Nor is it surprising, since Satan himself has transformed himself into an angel of light.[90] Then who was the first author of adultery? That cunning serpent who tricked Eve with guile, abusing her virgin simplicity, and who through Eve corrupted her husband into joining bloodshed with bloodshed. How did he trick her? With a falsehood: 'You shall not die the death ... and you shall be as gods.'[91] He himself had deserted the truth, lying to himself: 'I shall be like the most high,' and soon he fell and envied those who still stood. So that he might seem truthful, he made God out to be a liar, for God had said 'For in what day thou shalt eat of this tree, thou shalt die the death.'[92] How great a slaughter, what a mass of murdering did this destructive lie pour out upon the world! But we will touch on this matter at length when we come to the slanderous tongue.

So it happens that whenever God is provoked by the impiety of man to prepare his vengeance, he makes use most of all of the lying tongue as an instrument. For just as in Homer when Jupiter resolves to afflict the Greeks with a great disaster, he sends a destructive dream to Agamemnon to give him the hope of capturing Troy,[93] so in the Books of Kings, a lying spirit is sent by the Lord to be on the lips of prophets and thrust the king into the disaster that his impiety had deserved.[94]

Moreover I am seriously afraid that God, estranged from us by our sins, may often send such a spirit into the mouths of our prelates and theologians, so that they may by their perverted interpretations compel even the sacred Scripture to lie, turning it aside, not for the correction of princes or of the people, but for their own advantage. Hence comes that slaughter of souls, that piteous plague of impious doctrines, which the holy Job called architects of lies, and cultivators of perverted doctrines;[95] hence come the conflagrations of strife. Now no kind of falsehood is more ruinous than one drawn from the divinely inspired Scripture, which is the source and canon of eternal truth. From this, however, we have woven patchwork cloaks of lying falsehoods.

It seems that this spirit has been absorbed by fortune-tellers, vocal tricksters, soothsayers, diviners, augurs and astrologers, who by their hollow promises repeatedly arouse foolish princes and the trusting populace to political disturbance, to the great harm of the human race. Indeed, so that they can be more effective in their ruinous deceptions based on the stars and scrutiny of men's palms they promise victories to some men, a happy marriage and good health to others, to others again the highest honours, and to others the wealth of Midas. Surely these are the men of whom Jeremiah wrote: 'They have taught their tongue to speak lies, they have laboured to commit iniquity.'[96] So lying is a skill with them, and this evil skill is aided and developed by their yet more evil practice.

At this moment I will say nothing of the sophists who cheat the unsuspecting with verbal conjuring, for my argument is driving me on. Nor will I raise that notorious and confusing question, whether it is in any situation permitted for a Christian to lie. But I dare to declare that whereas it is often good sense to keep the truth unspoken or concealed, those who have once absorbed the spirit of truth and given its name to him who is truth should abstain from every kind of falsehood. Whoever knowingly lies is

close to forswearing; but whoever knowingly forswears is close to blasphemy, which is now the worst degree of impiety.[97] So that we might not come
to this hazard the Lord Jesus utterly forbade us to swear either by heaven or
earth or by any man's person.[98] But now an oath is required for any
business, however casual, and men perjure themselves just as casually.

Among the pagans men who swore by the pagan gods or by the stone
Jupiter were branded with dishonour;[99] among Christians it is almost a game
to perjure oneself in God's name, so much that most men feel no shame at
their sacrilegious practice, which prevents them putting ten words together
without interposing an oath, not invoking the goose,[100] but the death and
wounds of Christ, the belly and shoes of God, and other phrases which a
devout spirit shudders even to mention. Would they be afraid to perjure
themselves if any advantage invited them, when they daily swear oaths
without any need or hope of advantage? The sacrilegious statement 'My
tongue swore, but my mind remains unsworn'[101] is hissed even in the
theatres of the heathen. Why is it not driven out of Christian men's lives?
The false-swearing procurer with the tongue to pay off all his creditors is a
laughing-stock in Plautus' plays; why are men who behave like that
procurer esteemed among Christians? Once the oath by Venus was invoked
in a game;[102] now almost every solemn oath is treated as a game, like the
prince swearing to his people, or students undertaking the pursuit of the
seven liberal arts in colleges who swear most illiberally, since they act from
habit rather than conviction. Just as it is very hard to avoid a slip of the
tongue when overfond of talking, so it is likely that a regular oathtaker will
hardly escape perjury.

The ancients observed a scrupulous custom that boys who wanted to
swear by Hercules were not allowed to do so under cover but were told to go
out in the open, so that they would learn through this delay to swear more
sparingly and more cautiously. At any rate that is how wise men have
explained this public practice. Some add that Hercules himself was most
scrupulous and modest in swearing, so that he only swore once in his whole
life, and then only to Phyleus son of Augeas. They say that the Pythian
priestess recommended this form of oath to the Spartans, so that it would be
passed on to later generations, and added that it would be better still if they
committed themselves without taking oaths.[103] As for us, we swear by
Christ even before his altar, not merely by Hercules in any building.

The Romans believed it was a religious violation for the priest of Jupiter
to swear.[104] They offer various reasons for this scruple: either that both the
body and mind of a priest should be inviolate, and an oath is a form of
torture; or that it is absurd not to trust in the affairs of men the man to whom
the affairs of God are entrusted; or because the customary ending for an oath

is the curse 'I doom myself and my whole house if I knowingly have deceived.' Moreover since every imprecation is grim and to be averted, it is improper for a priest of Jupiter, who does not usually invoke evil even on others. So that well-known priestess at Athens deserved her praises; for when the common people demanded that she should curse Alcibiades, she said she had taken on the priesthood to pray for good things for all men, and not to pray for evil to befall any man.[105] Some authorities gave an additional reason for the practice, that since a perjurer is loathed as an impious man by any deity, and any man who swears is close to the hazard of perjury, then if any impious man or one who has offended the gods offers vows on behalf of the state, he would be more likely to call down the anger of the deities than obtain their favour.

At this point perhaps someone will interrupt: 'What have the customs and examples of the pagans to do with us?' The answer is that the Lord Jesus is accustomed to make use of these examples as the most effective to shatter the hard-heartedness of his own race, thrusting upon them the Canaanite woman and centurions, publicans, and sinners, the queen of Sheba, Nineveh, and the people of Tyre and Sidon. It would indeed be most shameful for Christians to be deaf to the voice of their God and Lord, since he so strictly desired us to avoid all swearing in case we should in some circumstance lapse into perjury, while pagans have shunned taking oaths either by the prompting of their nature or by superstition rather than real religious scruple. Or perhaps we think that someone sanctified by the blood of Christ could be less sacred than the priest of Jupiter was to the Romans of old? Yet the first commandment is to acknowledge God, and that one God is common to all, creator and ruler of all things, on whose goodness depends all our hope of salvation. And the next after this is that we shall not abuse his sacred name to deceive our neighbour. For God is not mocked.[106] Only God is truthful and thus he can safely swear by himself, since his will is unchangeable and he has it in his power to fulfil whatever he has promised. On the contrary every mortal is a liar, since his mind changes from hour to hour, and if his mind does not change, it is still often beyond our power to fulfil what we have undertaken. Then surely the man who takes an oath lays himself open to the risk of perjury? Accordingly the Lord bids us limit our speech to the words 'yea yea, no no.' But the apostle James does not consider even this quite safe, but warns us to add, whenever we promise we will do something, 'if we live and the Lord wills it.'[107]

Indeed even if these limitations are not made explicit, they should be understood in all the speech of Christian men. How far from this scruple over promises is the tongue of those who do not fear to say, 'I will heal you despite God and the devil alike.'[108] There, you are shuddering at this open blasphemy – then do not accept thoughtless use of the oath, from which blasphemy springs. If you loathe the fruit as deadly, cut away the root. To the Greeks *blasphemia* has the same sense that abuse or insult has to the Romans. There is a type of parasite or buffoon which is feared by honest men for its abusive tongue. If only the act itself was as abominable to men as the name of parasite and buffoon is loathed. But such is the strength of this addiction that they do not even abstain from attack on those who have the power, if they wish, to slit your nostrils with their sword.[109]

There are degrees and varieties of this disease, and it advances gradually from lesser instances to what is the most serious of all. For at first we allow ourselves to vent our mad temper on servants or maids. Soon we use the same petulance against our wife and children, or friends, and from this habit our tongue becomes ready to utter any abuse against anyone at all, as Horace said of the buffoon.[110] Gaining boldness from such beginnings, the tongue is wielded against princes and priests, and finally it does not control the words that will return in the form of a slit throat, although the wise man Ecclesiastes gives good advice: 'Detract not the king, no not in thy thought, and speak not evil of the rich men in thy private chamber, because even the birds of the air will carry thy voice, and he that hath wings will tell what thou hast said.'[111] The heart too has its tongue, that is, thought, by which a man speaks to himself. If he wishes to be safe, let him especially control this tongue, lest by some chance the evil saying born in his heart is spread by anger or wine or provocation and rises to his tongue, and returns as a cut throat. In Jeremiah the Lord is angry with those who kept hurling abuse at the mountains of Israel. He says: 'I have heard all your insults which you spoke about the mountains of Israel, saying, 'The desert places have been given to us to consume, and you have risen against me with your mouth and have belittled me." I have heard your words.'[112] Israel, that is the church, has its mountains and this world too has its mountains, and the contempt for low things raises up the worldly mountains beyond everything that is called or worshipped as God. For these are the abominable mountains of Gilboa upon which neither the dew nor rain of heavenly grace descends.[113] Again there are mountains and hills which, grown eager in the hope of promised salvation, rejoice like rams, and are excited like the lambs of sheep,[114] praising the Lord in the heavens, and not knowing how to abuse any man, but returning blessings for curses.[115] So as often as you hear men puffed up with Plato, Aristotle, and Averroes call Moses a wizard, the prophets mere dreamers, and the apostles ignorant yokels, recognize the voice of these impious mountains spewing forth blasphemies against the mountains of Israel. For whatever is said against those who have been inspired by Christ's spirit is said against Christ himself. Or, as Paul says: 'Do you seek a proof that Christ speaks in me?'[116] And for that reason he adds, in the words of the prophet, 'and you have risen up against me with your mouth.' Finally, whoever dares to despise the authority of the Holy Scripture, from which the truth shines forth as if from the highest mountain and from which the thunderbolts of the holy oracles break forth for us, is himself an accursed mountain, and abuses the mountains of Israel, and by that act abuses God, who dwells in such mountains as these. There is another covert kind of blasphemy, which is to twist the Holy Scripture by a cunning interpretation to suit your own desires when you dare not impugn its authority. We must not refuse forgiveness to the man who blunders from simple error in expounding the Holy Scriptures, but whoever does this from cunning malice and malicious cunning is not free of the charge of blasphemy.

To differ in some point from the holy Doctors of the church, whose authority the agreement of the church reveres, as it holds their memory sacred, is as far from being culpable as it would be impious if anyone wished to put their authority level with the canonical tomes; but to wantonly insult Chrysostom, Augustine, and Jerome is not far from blasphemy. In the same way, to feel modest doubts about human ordinances is as far from impiety as it would be impious to equate human ordinances with the teachings of God; but to mock and spit upon and curse all ordinances of all men at one's personal whim does not, as I see it, differ at all from blasphemy.[117] I think we should make the same judgment about the decrees of the councils, especially if the agreement of all people professing Christ has been accorded them. Now if it was safe to abuse the princes of this world, it would still not be pious, since the Lord forbade this too. 'What is from God has been laid down, and all power over nations is from God.'[118] If this order is disrupted, what can follow except universal confusion? The Lord declared in Exodus: 'Thou shalt not speak ill of the gods, and the prince of thy people thou shalt not curse.'[119] And Paul acknowledges this principle in the Acts of the Apostles,[120] so that no one may claim it has been abolished by the gospel: he even bids a Christian wife to obey her pagan husband, as long as he does not initiate a divorce,[121] and bids a Christian slave to obey an idolatrous master;[122] he orders all men to be subordinate to their superiors, not only to good and gentle ones, but even to those harsh and ill-tempered; he ordains that the tribute and the land tax should be paid to public officials, and due honour be given them.[123] He begs them to offer vows to God for kings and representatives, so that under them there may be a calm state of peace. But surely he who gives such teaching and advice will not approve a wanton tongue, which does not heal the powerful but enrages them to a more savage tyranny. And if God wishes Christians to behave so towards their idolatrous officials, what will he say about us if we wantonly rage with abuse and disloyal protests against Christian princes and even priests? For if they are good, they deserve honour, not insults; if they are poor they need help to succeed; if indeed they are bad, but can be set right, they should be corrected by restrained warnings and private, gentle encouragement; but if they are unbearable or beyond hope, they must either be tolerated until God hears the cries of his people and finds his own way to punish them, or their lack of self-control must be restrained by the agreement of citizen and senate. In any case we should take care that the cures are not worse than the disease, and the tyranny does not turn to anarchy and rioting – just as if a lethargy driven off by drugs were to turn into a frenzy, or gout or pain in the loins turn into apoplexy. In the mean time even bad princes should receive their due of honour, or else the people will acquire the habit of showing disrespect for good ones too.

Moreover it is not Christian to retaliate against evil with evil, even if God sometimes uses the impious to punish each other, using a bad wedge to split a bad knot.[124] Even Peter, the elder of the apostolic senate, passionately condemns in his second letter those who despise men endowed with public authority and who do not fear to assail with abuse men prominent in public standing.[125] Nor does Jude disagree with Peter – indeed he imitates him so closely not only in opinions but also in the texture of his style that he seems a second Peter. He too is angry with those who reject their masters to suit their whim and heap abuse on those who hold public office.[126] For such men do not hate princes and officials because they are impious, but because they prevent any man at all doing what he chooses. It is not without reason that they carry a sword. Thus the untrained multitude suffers the experience of over-mettled horses, who when they have shaken off their rider hurl themselves into a ditch or a pit. It is dangerous to entrust absolute power to one man, and the common people do nothing except riot. So it is most fair, just as the elements control and temper each other with their balance, to have the power of kings, the respect due to priests, the authority of councils, senates, and leading cities, and the agreement of the people, tempering and balancing each other in due turn so that the state turns neither to rebellion nor to tyranny. For the one evil tends to be born from the other, that is, as tyranny turns to anarchy and the suppression of anarchy begets tyranny.

So he who abuses the power that God has ordained is abusing God, exactly as he who offends the emperor's governor offends the emperor himself. I would say further that whoever abuses a Christian is abusing Christ, for as he is seen and cherished in his members, so he is injured and humiliated in his members. He who curses a priest for no other reason than that he is a priest, he who rejects a bishop for no other reason than that he is a bishop, he who despises a Christian for no other reason than that he is a Christian, surely he is openly humiliating Christ? So from these disguised blasphemies he advances to the worst degree of blasphemy. For the source of all things is one and the same. For just as those who have enslaved themselves to the lusts of the flesh loathe princes and officials because, thanks to them, men cannot do as they choose without fear of punishment, so the impious loathe God because he is the inescapable avenger of evil deeds. Hence, so as to indulge their vile desires at whatever cost, they either deny that there is any God, or invent a different god for themselves, or say that the gods are not concerned with the affairs of men but that everything is moved by either fate or chance. Do you want to hear the blasphemy of the Stoics[127] or of Averroes? Listen to what the psalm declares: 'The fool hath said in his heart: "There is no God."' Now look at the source of blasphemy: 'All men are become abominable in their desires and there is none that doth good, no not one.'[128] They convince themselves of a lie, indulging their vices, to which they futilely promise impunity; but wickedness lies to itself, and those who deny that God is just are no less sinful than those who deny that God exists. For he would not be just if he neither gave to the pious their reward nor took his revenge upon the impious. There is anger against such men in Malachi: 'You have said: "He laboureth in vain that serveth God, and what profit is it that we have kept his ordinances, and that we have walked sorrowful before the Lord of Hosts? Wherefore now we call the proud people happy, for they that work wickedness are built up, and they have tempted God, and are preserved?"'[129] Now let us hear that blasphemy which is most accursed of all, when the people of Israel, recoiling from the laws of God, made for itself a molten calf and hailed it: 'These are thy gods, O Israel, that have brought thee out of the land of Egypt.'[130]

What could have been a greater blasphemy against God than to place him who excels in power, greatness, wisdom, and goodness all the conceptions of men and angels after a dumb creature? But it is even more outrageous that they set him behind its dead likeness. The heathen would rather worship evil spirits than the true God, because he abominates all foulness, whereas they look kindly on vices and cherish corrupt desires and are not offended when they are represented in entertainments and tales with such bad character as no man would wish to find in his son or wife, or his servant either.[131] Such gods suit them because under them, as the heathen think, it is possible to wench and commit adultery and cheat and thieve and set up a tyranny or stir up a revolution as Jupiter is said to have done when he ousted and gelded his father and seized power,[132] and just as the rest of the gods raised a mutiny and drove out Jupiter and his supporters. Perhaps you would not easily find this kind of blasphemy

among Christians now, though it is monstrous even that it should be found
at all. For it is certainly found, and not all the severity of the laws can heal or
discipline this frenzy of the tongue.

But there is another variety of blasphemy, somewhat more veiled but
not much less destructive, practised whenever the people in adoring its
rulers bestows divine honours upon them and the rulers gladly embrace this
degree of honour. So at times it happens that a prince has flatterers and
mockers instead of citizens and counsellors, while the people have crazed
tyrants instead of princes – and on both sides God is assailed with
blasphemy.

There is yet another kind of blasphemy, which is not much more veiled
either, but which is so widespread that it is not considered a blasphemy. If it
is blasphemy for a man to say to an image of Jupiter, 'Save me,' is it not
blasphemy for a miser to say to his money-chest stuffed with coins, 'Save
me, or else I am ruined'? If the man blasphemes who thanks Jupiter with
incense for his safety and wealth and kingdom, then is he not a blasphemer
who credits all his happiness to money obtained by fair means or foul – a
man who fights on its behalf much more obstinately than any man ever
fought for his hearths and shrines, and who cries out when it is lost that he is
doomed, and takes refuge in the noose?

It would seem shameless for me to say this, if Paul had hesitated in his
letter to the Ephesians to call avarice idolatry,[133] that is, the worship of
images, for it makes no difference whether you name an impious act in
Greek or Latin, except that among Latin speakers the Greek name idolatry is
even more scandalous than their natural word. Paul also indicates when
writing to the Philippians that there are some who treat their bellies as their
god.[134] And the Lord himself opposes mammon to God in the gospel,[135] as if
mammon were another god, to whom those who value money more than
God sacrifice and enslave themselves. Again, writing to the Corinthians
Paul affirms that not only the belly and mammon are a god to some men, but
they have many other gods. He says: 'Although there be those that are called
gods either in heaven or on earth (for there be gods many and lords many);
yet to us there is but one God and Father, of whom are all things and we unto
him; and one Lord Jesus Christ by whom are all things, and we by him.'[136]

So whatever you put before God's teachings, this you make your lord
and master. The fornicator has Venus as his deity, the man enslaved to
luxury and gluttony has Comus as his god, the drunkard worships Bacchus
as his god. He does not sacrifice sheep to them, but makes himself their
sheep and sacrifices himself. He does not burn incense before them, but
kindles the fragrance of his foul repute, most welcome to the devils that
instigate such foul practices. He who glories in foul deeds sings hymns to his

god full of blasphemy against the true God. I call on you then, Christians, if you shudder whenever you hear or read the blasphemies of the impious against God, keep in mind that the life of all who are enslaved to gluttony, lust, envy, and ambition, who are slaves to riches, is filled with blasphemy. Now blasphemy is a much greater insult precisely because it comes from those who profess the name of the true God, as the Lord protests in the book of Ezekiel. He declares that because of the impious life of his people, which professes the name of God in its words but denies him by its deeds, his own name is defiled among the heathen when men say: 'That is the people of God.'[137] Truly how unfitting it is when men daily say to God: 'Thy name be glorified,'[138] and by their impious lives defile the holy name of the Lord.

Now there is no difference between the abusive tongue and the tongue as flatterer or vituperator or slanderer, except the difference between the cut-throat who attacks openly with a sword and the man who murders by treachery or poison.[139] Shimei shouts in his rage against David: 'Come out, come out, thou man of blood and thou man of Belial';[140] clearly this is the madness of the tongue about which Hosea writes: 'Their princes shall fall by the sword, for the rage of their tongue.'[141] What could be more cruel than this tongue, which assails with brutal abuse a man besieged with disasters, as if someone wantonly pelted with stones a fallen man whom he should have raised up? Such were Job's comforters, who instead of offering consolations for his sorrows redoubled his anguish by their reproaches. And his wife's tongue is by no means the least of evils: 'Dost thou still continue in thy simplicity? Bless God and die.'[142] Nor did the holy Tobit burst into tears until he was flailed by his wife's tongue: 'Clearly your hope has been made foolish, and your acts of mercy have just revealed themselves.'[143] Even our Lord himself, most cruelly pierced upon the cross by staves and thorns, was pierced more cruelly still by abuse. 'Let him come down now from the cross: Vah, thou that destroyest the temple of God.[144] For He said ' "I am the Son of God" – let him now deliver him if he will have him.'[145] What darts dipped in any dreadful poison could be more grievous than the darts of a wanton tongue? Hence it is a rare kind of happiness that is promised to the holy Job: 'Thou shalt be hidden from the scourge of the tongue, and thou shalt not fear calamity when it cometh.'[146]

Paul is eager that a bishop above all should be remote from this vice when he says: 'I do not want a striker,'[147] that is, *plektes* in Greek. For a violent tongue has brought sudden death to many without any wound to the body. There are even men who wield their tongues against their brother with the purpose of killing him. I count in this category men who stir up quarrels on any trivial pretext and brew tragic dramas about mere goat's wool.[148] The shepherds of Gerar quarrel with the shepherds of Isaac: 'It is our water,'[149] and for this reason the name Calumny was given to the well.[150] How full of wells like this is the Christian life of our time? What contract is there, what act of possession, what will, what priesthood, what public or private benefaction, without quarrels and law suits springing from it? A quarrelsome tongue pollutes the pleasantness of all companionship. As the wise man says: 'It is better to sit in a corner of the housetop than with a brawling woman and in a common house.'[151] And he says elsewhere: 'A foolish son is the grief of his father and a wrangling wife is like a roof continually dropping through.'[152] Not everyone suffers the presence of a quarrelsome wife, but we must take care that we nowhere experience that quarrelsome ill temper which allows nothing to remain agreeable – what the Greeks call *dyscolia* 'surliness' or *micrologia* 'pettiness,' since it is difficult to deal with such men because they quarrel offensively about the most trivial matters. Indeed this is the difference between contentiousness and abusiveness, that contentiousness sometimes is disguised: it often acts surreptitiously and, if it is forced into the open, puts on the appearance of justice, making a charge, be it false or true, moved by the desire to harm if it can, even by a false accusation. An abusive man does not always press a specific charge, but often some family scandal, or the misfortunes of his ancestors, or a physical blemish, which the sufferer did not bring upon himself and could not set right if he would – as when they call a bastard child a bastard, or a one-eyed man one-eyed, or an old-fashioned fellow old-fashioned.

The backbiter is different from the contentious man because he wields his tongue either secretly or in a man's absence, more like a serpent than a lion, but a flatterer is more destructive than either, for his embrace suffocates and kills with poison brewed with honey, just as if a man blended aconite with Falernian wine. It is an abominable evil, and yet scarcely any other is more welcome in human life. The abuser often benefits his enemies by indicating what should be set right. The hostility of the contentious man, who leaves nothing uncriticized, makes us more careful in carrying on our affairs and sometimes even adds light to our reputation, which it is trying to darken. The backbiter is the same, acknowledging his inferiority to the man he criticizes by this very fact, that he operates stealthily in whispers, and does not dare to join in open combat. But the flatterer turns the fool into a madman and the madman into one beyond cure. That is why Solomon declares that a flatterer deserves public abomination. He says: 'They that say to the wicked man, "Thou art just" shall be cursed by the people, and the tribes shall abhor them.'[153] And the Lord cries out through Isaiah's lips also: 'O my people, those who call thee blessed, themselves lead thee astray and destroy the path of thy steps.'[154] Again, Solomon warns them: 'If sinners shall entice thee, consent not to them.'[155] And again elsewhere: 'The words of a talebearer are as it were simple, but they reach to the innermost parts of the belly; when he shall speak low, trust him not, because there are seven mischiefs in his heart.'[156] As Ecclesiastes says: 'It is better to be rebuked by a wise man than to be deceived by the flattery of fools.'[157]

The siren has, it truly has, most beguiling songs, but they entice into bitter destruction. Hence the words of the wise man Sirach; he says: 'He that speaketh sophistically is hateful; he shall be destitute of everything.'[158] The holy psalmist prays to keep this plague most harmful to kings far from himself: 'The just man shall correct me in mercy and shall reprove me, but let not the oil of the sinner fatten my head.'[159] And Ezekiel the prophet curses this tribe of men, who say to the people 'Peace' and there is no peace, who daub a wall without mortar, who sew cushions under every elbow and make pillows for the heads of persons of every age to catch their souls![160] If flattery were not the greatest evil, David would not abominate it with such anxiety: 'Lord free my soul from unjust lips and from a guileful tongue.' And to make known how difficult is the remedy of this evil, the prophet of the Lord cries out, hearing God say: 'What could be given or set before thee against a guileful tongue.'[161] Indeed no other remedy offers itself, except that we send against it the sharp arrows of the Almighty, that is, the word of God, which is sharper than a two-edged sword, cleaving so far as to separate breath and soul, and the coals of desolation, so that by knowing from these our own unhappiness, we may cease to be pleased with ourselves because of the false praises of flatterers and, having grown desolate from mistrust of our own resources, may through God's compassion regain breath and life. For such are the arrows of the all-powerful Scripture; they kill, but give life to those they have killed. Such are the coals of repentance; they blacken a man and cast him down, but when they have again grown hot, they bring solid and enduring joy.

But let us dismiss the subject of flattery, and move on to contentiousness, if we first say a little in passing about the tongue as agent of treachery and the tongue as a source of ruinous counsels. Such was the tongue of Joab, which killed Ammon with the pretext of a soothing address;[162] such was the tongue of Delilah, who betrayed Samson;[163] such was that of Judas, 'Hail, Rabbi.'[164] You have a model of ruinous advice in the books of Kings, with Jonadab, who showed Ammon how he might take his own sister, whom he foully desired, and from this came a grievous flood of evils.[165] Who does not curse the impious Jezebel, who drove the king to make an impious decision by her advice?[166] And did not the advice of young men deprive Rehoboam of a great part of his ancestral kingdom?[167] Moreover, there is good sense in the Greek proverb that says an evil counsel is worst for the man who gives it.[168] This is shown by those who intended to bring Daniel to ruin, by guileful advice to King Darius, but were themselves thrown into the cistern and torn apart by lions.[169] Compare also what the wise Sirach says: 'A mischievous counsel shall be rolled back upon the author, and he shall not know from whence it cometh to him.' And he warns us elsewhere to preserve our soul from evil counsels.[170] So there is mortal danger from a bad counsellor, unless you fortify yourself against him with a rampart. We shall talk in a little while of the right methods for achieving this.

Now let us consider what a great scourge of human life is the slanderous tongue, that is, the truly devilish tongue. For what the Latin speakers call *calumnia* 'slander,' the Greeks call *diabole*,[171] and from this above all that common enemy of the human race derives his name – the same who is called Satan by the Hebrews, which in our tongue means 'the adversary.' Our God is called the God of peace, since through his Son he won back the world to himself, wiping out the record of sin by which we were held liable to the penalty of death; and Christ is called by the prophet the counsellor of peace.[172] Satan is always opposed to him, since he was the first to sow enmity between God and man, accusing God himself of lying before man: 'You shall not die, but you shall be as gods.'[173] Nor does he cease even now to tear apart the grace that has been restored by Jesus, slandering us before God. Christ has wiped away our true guilt, giving his justice to us, but the devil is eager to burden even devout men with false accusations, as he slandered Job: 'See if he bless thee not to thy face.'[174] Surely he is inciting that holy man to the offence of blasphemy? Christ has taken our impiety upon himself, but the devil tries to impose his own impiety upon us. Christ appeals to his Father on behalf of our offences, so that we may be saved; the devil appeals to ensure our damnation. He does not always achieve this by his own actions, but he has tools almost more evil than himself.

You will say, 'What are these?' The tongues that inform against the innocent – indeed, they are not tongues but swords dipped in venom. He says: 'Their tongue is a sharp sword and the venom of asps is beneath their lips.'[175] And for this reason scholars who have made a pursuit of gathering the sayings of wise men report a witty comment of Thearidas, the Spartan commander, who was asked whether his sword was sharp enough (for he was sharpening it). 'Sharper than slander itself,' he said.[176] How many has this sword slaughtered in the past, how many does it slay even now? You have heard it in the Psalms: 'Their tongue is a sharp sword';[177] and in Jeremiah men who use their tongue as a sword say: 'Come and let us strike him with the tongue.'[178] Now we see that the tongue has the shape of a sword, but the colour is fire. Indeed an evil tongue will cut both ways, wounding both by slash and thrust, and dipped in poison besides and as James says 'being set on fire by hell.'[179] I will pass over instances that occurred under men like Nero, Caligula, and Claudius, Sulla and Marius, Dionysius and Hiero,[180] and that are at times reported under Christian princes also. They are too many to be enumerated and too infamous to need enumeration. And I prefer to report the evidence supplied by the Holy Scriptures.

Holy Joseph, you felt the poison of this sword: in return for your loyalty to your master and your abstinence from your master's wife, you earned prison and the risk of death. 'The Hebrew servant came to me to abuse me, and when he heard my voice he left the garment that I held and got out of the house.'[181] Need I recall you, Susanna, model of chastity and piety? You would have died from the slander of the old men if the Lord had not rescued you from the swords of impious tongues through the aid of Daniel.[182] O cruel point of the tongue. What can any real sword do to match this, even if deadly steel is made more deadly by poison? It takes away life, but cannot take away reputation. Slander, cunning in doing harm, can do a great deal more, for it brings death with disgrace. The same Joseph was attacked earlier by the slanders of his brothers, who had laid charges against him to his father on an evil accusation. Or so the translation of the Septuagint records,[183] and in my opinion this symbol is more fitted to Christ, whom the Jews accused with many charges before the chief priest and the governor. Nor is it likely that Joseph, when he was still a boy, informed on his brothers before his father, since when at a later time they had treated him most badly he did not accuse them, but saved them.[184] Even the context of the language here supports my interpretation, for what follows is: 'Now Israel loved Joseph above all his sons, because he had him in his old age.'[185] So the slanders of his brothers achieved nothing, because his father loved him above all the others. Finally Chrysostom in translating follows this interpretation which I have proposed.[186] Nor does Jerome mention in his *Liber hebraicarum quaestionum in Genesim* that this passage was corrected, although he examines and thoroughly opens out other more trifling points.[187] Those who have changed the passage seem to have objected because they thought this awful accusation did not become Joseph's innocence, and they would have been justified in their objection if there had been no mention of the brothers' envy and their false charge. Otherwise they should have objected even more, because our Lord, who was far more innocent than Joseph, was accused of blasphemy. The devil's tongue contrived this destruction, but God turned others' malice into good for his own people, since the slander of his brothers provoked even more strongly Jacob's tenderness for Joseph, and the queen's accusation offered an opportunity for Joseph to be promoted to greater honours by the king.[188]

So too Joab informed before King David against Abner, who had served the king well, and yet he did not convince the king, though he convinced himself into treacherously killing an innocent man.[189] What should I say of Jezebel, who in order to ease her husband's grief forged a letter in the name of King Ahab, and sealed it with the king's seal ring, and sent it to the nobles and fellow citizens of Naboth. This was the purport of the letter: 'Proclaim a fast, and make Naboth sit among the chiefs of the people, and suborn two men, sons of Belial, against him, and let them bear false witness that he hath blasphemed[190] God and the king; and then carry him out and stone him.'[191] What should amaze us most in this tale, the boldness of that wicked woman, or the impious compliance of the leaders and people in obeying such a letter, or the king's stupidity in trusting his ring to his wife? David found the same obedience in his commanders when he ordered Uriah to be killed.[192] If only our princes did not have their own henchmen only too eager for deeds like this! A king of England is notorious for the murder of a most excellent archbishop;[193] when he heard that all those who possessed and occupied the property and estate of the church had been committed to anathema by the holy Thomas, the archbishop of Canterbury, he was violently angry that a bishop dared to play a bishop's part. 'This general excommunication includes me too,' he said, 'since I occupy some of the houses and revenues of the bishops.' And he added, 'That priest would not dare to act thus if I had the sort of servants I should.' At this cry of his, three of his nobles set off for Canterbury and murdered that holy man most cruelly. When a king openly gives impious instructions, whoever obeys him is a traitor, while the man who rebels and resists is a true friend. For what must be considered is not what will please a man in anger, but what will continue to please him. The men who gave Alexander the Great his spear when he was raging with drink and anger so that he killed his friend Clytus [Cleitus] were traitors to him, for a late and futile remorse soon followed his hot deed.[194] What honour he would have paid to his noble friends if they had bravely disarmed him until his sanity of mind was restored! Those who attended the king at that time should either have refused him arms when he was disturbed in mind or not have snatched the weapons from him when he was preparing to exact punishment on himself. We must indeed obey kings, but only while they are behaving like kings. As it is we act absurdly, humouring their desires when it is absolutely wrong, but not heeding them when they give good commands. This kind of obedience achieves nothing except to give us tyrants instead of kings. The lot of kings itself contains enough scope for cruelty, even if no kind person intervenes to add oil to the furnace.[195] Sulla adopted the name 'the Successful' because he felt he had achieved many great successes.[196] But amongst all his successes he used to take most pleasure in two facts: first that he had Metellus the Pious as his friend, and second that he had not destroyed Athens, but had spared the most celebrated city in all Greece. And yet there is no doubt that many men at the time of his anger urged him to do this, and if he had trusted their words, they would have been as offensive to Sulla once Athens was overthrown as he was subsequently pleased with himself for having saved the city.

We have combined our treatment of the traitor, the flatterer, and the evil counsellor, because these are related vices. A man is commonly called a traitor if he defends the people's rights and resists a king's desires. But the man who betrays a prince to a tyrant, although he is a double traitor, is considered a good and loyal fellow. If princes really hated traitors, they ought to rage most violently of all against flatterers and deceitful counsellors. When Pompey the Great was fleeing from Caesar's power and, making for Egypt, was nearing Pelusium, there was a debate among the counsellors of the king, who was still a boy, whether Pompey should be received or barred. Opinions were in conflict, and for lack of better men a Chian called Theodotus was invited to the council. He had been allotted to the boy-king as his teacher of rhetoric. So when he was asked his opinion he proposed that Pompey should neither be received in the kingdom nor barred, but received in order to be killed, and he added to his wicked proposal the caddish saying that dead men don't bite. He won the day. So that great man, who had emerged unharmed from so many dangers, perished because of the tongue of one miserable Greek.[197] But the advice, as the old proverb has it, went most badly for those counsellors. For when Caesar entered Egypt he inflicted a horrible punishment on those responsible for Pompey's death. Theodotus was an exile for some time, but when he finally came into Brutus' hands, he paid the penalty for his wicked proposal.[198] For advice must not be diluted to suit the immediate whims of princes, but their whims must be turned aside towards those actions which are intrinsically right. Shameful propositions are pleasing for a while, while the passion lasts, but the outcome of actions makes us long grieve for what delighted us for a brief time and curse those who were responsible for our undertaking an evil enterprise. For rulers are only men, and since they are distracted with all kinds of business and may sometimes be inexperienced as well, many issues pass them by.

In this a good and faithful counsellor, simply speaking man to man, can be like a god, as they say. When Mark Antony was governing the province of Asia, he indulged his caprices and was led by flattering courtiers to squander a vast amount of money; as a result he deprived many individuals of their property, contrary to the law, and burdened the province with intolerable taxation. So when he was about to demand a second levy on the harvest from the Asians, an act which would undoubtedly have led to his overthrow, it was opportune that Hybreas stood by, to give loyal advice in the interests of both the Asians and Antony himself. 'Demand the tithe twice in the same year,' he said, 'if you can ensure that we have two summers and a double autumn within that year.' Then, when he had shown Antony that the Asians had paid out two hundred thousand talents to him already, he added, 'If this vast sum of money has not been delivered to you, see that you reclaim it from the men who have extorted it from us. But on the other hand if all this sum of gold was delivered to you and spent, there is no hope of recalling it.' Frank as it was, the truth of this speech was powerful enough to change Antony's mind, and he abandoned the demand for a second tithe.[199] As I said above, the advice of the young men was disastrous for Rehoboam, son of Solomon,[200] and in Homer Agamemnon asks nothing else for success but ten men like Nestor.[201] The advice of slaves saved Naaman the Syrian, for he was about to leave in resentment and would have doubled his curse of leprosy by his impious muttering; instead he was called back by slaves more wise than their master, and was healed.[202]

But we must return to calumny, which prefers to attack the innocent.[203] That is how Socrates and Phocion were destroyed, how Aristides was driven out by ostracism, and how Epaminondas and Scipio were in danger of disgrace. By why mention these? That is how Christ, the source of all innocence, was destroyed. He was pierced by so many daggers of the Pharisees and false witnesses, indeed of the whole nation: 'Away with him, crucify him.'[204] What charges did calumny not wield against him? Those who destroy a man with weapons are called cut-throats; but if they kill with the sword of the tongue, although they are not called cut-throats they are more wicked than all the cut-throats in the world. 'Come,' they said, 'let us strike him with the tongue.'[205] What does an assassin take away, except the life of the body? It is far more cruel to steal good repute than mere life. And this was the intention of the Jewish calumniator, that Jesus' glorious name should be utterly abolished. God, however, turned aside the impious assaults of calumny. The Lord returned to life, having regained his immortal body in return for the mortal body, and that name was given to him which surpasses all names whether in heaven or on earth.[206] We owe this blessed outcome to the almighty goodness of God, and yet the malice of a slanderous tongue is not more worthy of pardon if it does not achieve its intention, since it left no evil unattempted.

Through Christ, the calumny of the wicked will result in blessing for all who suffer calumny in Christ's name. The charge of blasphemy was aimed against Stephen; he was condemned and died – say, rather, he was saved.[207]

Is there anything more glorious or beloved than his name? Paul was called 'destroyer of the law' and 'a leader of cut-throats,'[208] and calumny triumphed at that time. Is there anything now more sacred than his name? Both witchcraft and infanticide were made accusations against those early Christians – but what did calumny achieve? It brought disgrace upon itself and glory upon the name of Christian. Calumny drove St Chrysostom into exile, even attempting to have his name obliterated from the catalogue of bishops.[209] Who is there now more famous than he? Was there any vile trick that a slanderous tongue did not attempt against the most holy Jerome? His prefaces and defences bear witness to this.[210] But whose memory is now more glorious? And (if we may with propriety add pagan illustrations here) Homer had his Zoilus, Virgil his Pero, Horace his Maevius, Ovid his Ibis – yet even the names of these men would not survive now if they had not been transmitted to latter days by the services of those they belittled.[211] Herostratus won himself a name among the Ephesians for burning the temple of Diana;[212] in the same way Hyperbolus became notorious among the Athenians for his hyperbolic slander.[213] He devoted his time only to tracking down the faults of individuals and making them public, supplying much raw material for sneers and jibes to the writers of Old Comedy. It was he who secretly plotted the ostracism of Alcibiades. This was a kind of condemnation in which the voting-sherds submitted in the assembly decided the exile of leading men who had brought upon themselves the resentment of the common people by their power, wealth, and authority. Alcibiades discovered the attempts of Hyperbolus, and reconciled himself with Nicias, the leader of the opposite faction; the result was that the ostracism rebounded on the head of its originator. And later the Athenian people regretted this action, for from that time the authority of this procedure was undermined because it had resulted in the condemnation of a low and worthless man with no source of power except a slander, a man who had deserved severe punishment, whereas until then ostracism had usually mitigated the resentment of the crowd by exiling men of distinction from the state.

We ourselves witnessed an affair very like this, but we will withhold the names of those involved. At Rome I was on familiar terms with a man who used evil methods to speed his path to offices and wealth, showing envy to all who surpassed him. He unsealed everyone's letters, even those sent from kings, so as to base his plots upon them. But his chief aim was to cause conflict between two archbishops who were most respected in their own country, because he knew that in other respects they were not much in agreement. One of them sensed the man's guiles (for he was at Rome at that time, and was subsequently elected to the college of cardinals). This is how he was avenged on Hyperbolus. He reconciled himself with the other archbishop to act against the other fellow, and he showed him a way by which they could take revenge on the fellow, if he would support the pretence. A diploma was deliberately sent in the name of a prince, which offered the man the rank of bishop in Ireland – for they knew he was desperately thirsty for this honour and was stirring up all these plots for its sake. Blind with desire, he failed to realize the diploma was a trick and sought its confirmation from Pope Julius. Having paid his contribution he obtained his request, at no cost to the pope. Soon he had taken the tonsure, shaved his pate to the earlobes, and put on the linen garment. Need I say more? He went out in public completely the bishop. Meanwhile the devisers of this trick kept quiet. Then, when it was known to every man in Rome that he was acting as a bishop, and he had already written to all his friends about it and received congratulatory letters in reply, a man was hired to reveal the trick at a crowded party. This man asked him where his bishopric was. He gave out the title of the see. Then he was asked whether he was sure that the see was vacant. He said yes. Then he was asked how he knew that the man whom he intended to succeed was dead. He told many stout lies about this. Finally, when the exchange was developing into a quarrel, the accomplice laid bare the mysterious secret in a few words: 'The bishop whose see you are claiming is fit and well; make inquiries and you will find it so.' Soon the gossip was spread all over this most talkative of cities. What was Hyperbolus the bishop unbishoped to do about it? He stayed at home all day long, for he was ashamed to wear the robes which he had put on prematurely – but again was ashamed to return to his former attire and admit he had been deceived. So he only came out at night, and in a few days he went into a decline from sheer mortification.

Among the pagans no other name was more accursed than that of informers, spies, and double-crossers. M. Tullius Cicero, greatest of orators, was censured for his excessive concern with joking – Cato even said of him 'Ye gods, what an amusing consul we have!'[214] – but at the same time his honesty was praised because, although he was king in the courts, he devoted all his marvellous eloquence to defending the prosecuted. For he attacked no defendant with the sole exception of Verres,[215] and this accusation was less an accusation than a defence of the provinces which Verres had afflicted. It caused some loss of lustre to Cato the Elder's glory that he so often prosecuted and was prosecuted in return.[216] Aemilius Paulus let no accusation pass his lips against his repudiated wife, but simply held out a fine new shoe and pointed out that only he felt where the shoe chafed.[217] Caesar showed in the courts the same restraint which Aemilius exercised in conversation with his friends, for when he was called as a witness to say something against the wife he had divorced, he declared he knew nothing;[218] calumny seemed to these great men such low and ungentlemanly behaviour that they were not even willing to disclose true charges against the women they had excluded from their household. Indeed the laws of the pagans and not just the Mosaic law demanded the penalty of retaliation for the slanderer. The man who prefers a false charge against his neighbour is more wicked than a lying witness, for the former is responsible for hiring the other. Yet in Deuteronomy God ordains that a witness found guilty of slander should suffer the same penalty that would have been inflicted on his victim if he had been condemned: 'Thou shalt not pity him, but shalt require life for life, eye for eye, tooth for tooth, hand for hand, foot for foot.'[219]

From what source did this evil of Satan creep into the life of man? It is less amazing if a slanderer is found among the pagans, who worshipped spirits instead of God. Nor is it all that amazing in the case of the Jewish people, who have always been tormented by envy, the mother of slander. But there is really cause to wonder from what source it has flooded into the life of Christians, until the most loathsome of all faults has through familiarity almost ceased to seem a fault.

Perhaps someone will suggest the courts of princes as an excuse, since by their unique nature they attract this kind of plague to themselves, just as men say the north-east wind brings clouds.[220] But should we not lament with every kind of weeping that this devilish scourge is so rampant among scholars, so rampant among priests, and so prevalent among monks? For what wild beast would you find in the whole world that bites and tears and savages its own kind with such frenzy? Who can be safe nowadays from the tongues of informers? No mercy is shown to benefactors, or to age, which even enemies spare in open warfare; no mercy is shown to the rank of princes, or bishops, or the supreme papal authority. And, as if this devilish tongue were too ineffectual, we find defamatory caricatures in addition; scandalous pamphlets are disseminated, and this abominable livelihood supports many printers. The man who picked up a painted clog is torn limb from limb as an instigator of rebellion. But is there anything left unsaid by the pictures which are spread at random nowadays? Once upon a time, the man who disclosed his name and published a scandalous pamphlet ran the risk of prosecution; now men amuse themselves at random with anonymous pamphlets, or those with false ascriptions[221] – these enable them to keep risk away from themselves while spattering innocent men with disgrace. When they are caught, what excuse do they offer? 'I hunt for my livelihood wherever I can,' they say. 'I must support my household. If you are willing to support it, I will stop what I am doing.' But who would listen to a thief or robber who conducted his defence in this way? Yet thieving is not immune. So an offence which is even more wicked than thieving should have been far less immune, unless a man holds his reputation cheaper than his money. If on the other hand they are more concerned with security than honour, let them prostitute their wives and learn to snore with sleepless nose among their cups.[222] For that is legally secure, at any rate. As it is, the laws themselves are asleep as regards this outrageous offence, and any man may without fear of punishment vent his temper against the life and repute of any other.[223]

Now indeed calumny is common practice: to call one's neighbour a heretic or leader of heretics, a schismatic, and a debaser of the faith. And the men who do this most are those who boast that they are dead to the worldly life, proclaiming themselves in the number of those to whom Christ gave these teachings: 'Love your enemies; do good to them that hate you; and pray for them that persecute and calumniate you, that you may be the children of your Father, who is in heaven.'[224] Good God, how far they are from this rule, when they slander the undeserving or even attack their benefactors with harmful tongues! When will such men return blessings instead of abuse, since in return for beneficial advice they thrust a charge of heresy in men's faces? Such are the weapons dipped in hellish poison borne by those poor in spirit who carry with them neither wallet nor staff.[225] They have no artillery, but, in the words of Jeremiah, 'their tongue is a piercing arrow' and 'they bend their tongue as a bow for lies.'[226] They do not carry around poison in a casket, though some do even this, but, in the words of the psalmist, they carry around a mouth 'full of cursing and of bitterness and of deceit.' They carry around a tongue under which are 'labour and sorrow.' They lie 'in ambush with the rich in private places that they may kill the innocent.'[227] By what guiles does this kind of man insinuate himself into the court of princes? What poisons do some fellows let drop into their ears? Furthermore they disguise a more than devilish malice with the pretext of religion, and when othey are tormented with the zeal of envy and hatred, they say, 'The zeal of thy house consumes me.'[228] Surely this is what follows in the psalm: 'They sit in ambush with the rich in private places that they may kill the innocent. Their eyes are upon the poor man; they lie in wait in secret like a lion in his den. They lie in ambush that they may catch the poor man, to catch the poor whilst they draw him to them. In their net they will bring him down.'[229] O you fishers of men![230] The apostles used to fish for evil men to win their salvation, but these fish for good men to encompass their ruin. They use their slanderous tongue like a net, with which they pull in whom they choose, and then they overcome by any kind of false information those whom they have pulled in. They appoint themselves judges, prosecutors, and witnesses.

Now if the calumny is too blatant to be concealed, they invoke the loathsome nature of the charge and the privileged claim of religion. Instead, the more outrageous the charge, the more severely we should punish the man who alleges it falsely. And I suppose it is fair that an innocent man should suffer the extreme penalty to ensure that no one holds hostile opinions of a Franciscan or Dominican cowl.[231] Why don't they ensure by their own behaviour that no one judges or speaks of them unfavourably? Let them try to be what they wish to seem. This is a quick way for them to acquire the highest standing in all men's judgment. But just to perpetrate whatever they choose and force mankind not to see what they see or not to know what they know and to praise what deserves abomination is surely worse than the act of a tyrant. And these men think they deserve to be supported and revered by the world in idleness – if only they were merely idle! These are the men who sell their good deeds, by whose pure prayers the fire of divine wrath is quenched. Let no one, I beg, turn to the abuse of good men the saying rightly applied to the wicked, that they should either be avoided or set right. And yet we see everywhere nowadays such a flood of evils that we can almost take upon ourselves that utterance of the psalm: 'They are all gone aside, they are become unprofitable together; there is none that does good, no, not one. Their throat is an open sepulchre: with their tongues they acted deceitfully; the poison of asps is under their lips. Their mouth is full of cursing and bitterness: their feet are swift to shed blood.'[232]

If the Turk is to be driven from the necks of the people, these holy men claim that they have neither soldiers nor money;[233] then they adduce their religious obligation to peacefulness and declare that monks should keep as far as possible from shedding blood. But to slay their brother with slander or pierce their neighbour with a stab of the tongue is seen as violating no obligation – the very point which the psalm makes: 'There they have trembled for fear where there was no fear.'[234] If a Franciscan's shoe is solid leather, an offence has been committed; if his tongue commits murder, it is a religious obligation. We detest double-dealing tricksters who lay a charge of theft or provoke a suit for damages from which they win themselves a considerable profit, and yet we do not detest those who falsely lay a charge of heresy to destroy all prospects, life together with good repute, for their victim. They do not bear the arms of a soldier, though there are certainly some who hide their daggers beneath their holy robes, but their effrontery is as good as an armoury. Solomon says a man that beareth false witness against his neighbour is 'like a dart and a sword and a sharp arrow.'[235]

Let them deceive men as much as they wish with the pretence of righteousness, they will not escape divine vengeance, even if they take refuge in the bosom of Dominic or Francis.

Solomon says: 'A man that doth violence to the blood of a person, if he flee even to the pit, no man will stay him.'[236] Some men have altars, tombs, temples, or statues of emperors to shelter them from the fury of the laws, but there is no refuge for the slanderer from divine wrath. The ancients used to say that murderers were harried by dread avenging goddesses;[237] these men too will not lack their Furies. They will come face to face with the avenging goddesses sooner than they expect. The wise Ecclesiastes laments over this evil also in human life. He says: 'I saw all the calumnies' that are done under the sun, and the tears of those who suffer calumny, and they have no comforter, and there is strength in the hands of those slandering them, and they have no comforter. And I praised the dead rather than the living, and I judged him happier than them both that is not yet born nor hath seen the evils that are done under the sun.'[238]

Is there, then, any evil more fearful than death? Yet the wise man declares that the tongue of a slanderer is such an evil. Then where are those who detest parricide and treat slander as a sport? What Ecclesiastes declared, Ecclesiasticus corroborates: 'Of three things my heart hath been afraid, and at the fourth my face hath trembled. The accusation of a city, and the gathering together of the people, and a false calumny; all are more grievous than death.'[239] In Hosea, the Lord threatens death, which may cause division between brothers: 'O death, I will be thy death; O hell, I will be thy bite.'[240] Nothing is more united than the love of brothers, no partnership is closer than that of body and soul, no knot of affection is tighter than that of marriage. All these bonds, the bitterness of death destroys. Yet it sends us into a more blessed life, while slander is more harmful because it aims at more cruel sufferings than death without compensating for its damages by any advantage. We bear death more calmly because it is shared by all on equal terms, because it is a product of necessity not choice, because however bitter in its nature it makes no man wicked. But there is nothing among all evils that slander does not cause on some occasion. It would be tedious to enumerate every instance. Let everyone direct his eyes around him over private homes and colleges and monasteries and princely courts and cities and kingdoms, and he will quickly learn how great a plague the slanderous tongue spreads everywhere.

If I were to combine flattery with slander I should seem perhaps to present such a team as if someone should yoke a serpent to an ape. Yet such disparate qualities are bound together. For as kings who want to harm one man must flatter many and must enslave themselves to many even of the vilest creatures in their desire to reduce one man to slavery, so when the slanderer is devising a false slander against one person he must wheedle many with false praises. In the same way, in order to get the better of the stag, the horse accepted a rider on his back and a bridle in his mouth.[241] Again, in committing the fault of backbiting how shamelessly we forgive ourselves; we even flatter ourselves and seem witty to ourselves, as we nibble away the reputation of our neighbour. God, who forbade theft in Leviticus, in the same passage prohibited slander and backbiting: 'You shall not lie; neither shall any man deceive his neighbour. Thou shalt not be a detractor, nor a whisperer among the people. Thou shalt not stand against the blood of thy neighbour.'[242] Solomon, indeed, shows us what a loathsome evil is backbiting: 'The thought of a fool is sin, and the detractor is the abomination of men.'[243] He who thinks ill of his neighbour but keeps control of his tongue is not actually without sin, but is guilty only in the sight of God. But the man who wields his poisonous tongue at random against his absent neighbour is an object of cursing and abomination even among honest men, because everyone fears for himself the scorpion's venom and hates a man addicted to this failing, even if he speaks the truth. For since he acts compulsively and not from rational choice, he would also tell lies, if it came into his head. How rare is the man against whom no true accusations could be made! But suppose someone is remote from every fault, even so, honest men fear false disgrace. And granted one can take precautions against the assault of an abusive tongue, how do you protect yourself against the whisperer? He attacks a man stealthily, lying in wait; he is pleasant and friendly to your face, and if you make a protest, he swears he never said the words he spoke out in front of many different people. But the men who add trickery to their addiction, with preliminary words of praise and good will when they injure with a disguised bite – these are even more of a scourge. 'He is a good man and a friend of my father's, so I congratulate him on his good luck in being acquitted in that case.' 'He is a most learned man, but I wish his honesty matched his learning.' 'He is my friend, but truth is dearer still.'[244] This is the inky vomit of the squid. This is sheer corroding rust.

Now there are men led by a tongue out of control or otherwise aroused by the circumstances of conversation to blurt out facts that spread a smear on their neighbour, although they have no ill will. It is these others who are real cut-throats, concealing a murderous weapon; these are the real scorpions, who embrace before they plant their sting – they are more vicious than any poisoner, when they smear over their deadly poison with honey. And yet it is those men who feel a religious scruple against the study of rhetoric who are particularly skilled in such arts. Indeed men who condemn all liberal disciplines and allow no other study except the Old and New Testament do not hold aloof from this art. For since the backbiter is seen to be motivated by hatred, he usually does not carry conviction. So they have discovered the art of concealing their hatred and imposing conviction so that they can injure more effectively.

This fault is usually seen as most common in women, but now it has even spread to men and crept into the courts of princes, the schools of the learned, the colleges of priests, and the brotherhoods of monks.[245] Indeed I do not think there has been any age in which this scourge has ruled more widely than it now does through the whole Christian community. St Augustine is said to have attached this couplet to his table:

> He who delights to hurt an absent friend
> Should know his welcome here is at an end.[246]

Indeed it has been the practice before now to post this rule even in public inns, and anyone who embarked upon a backbiting tale was shouted down by the rest of the drinkers. And if this happened at the parties of rulers, it was the law for the staff-bearer, whom the French now call a herald, to turn over the bread set on the table or tear the tablecloth and declare the conversation unworthy of a prince's table. But what else do we hear nowadays at all dinners except 'He is worse than a heretic,' 'He is conspiring with Luther,' 'He knows nothing of theology,' or 'Although he is thought to be a decent man, he once committed such and such a crime,' 'He is the child of shameful parents,' 'He has dishonoured his family,' 'He has gone bankrupt.' It is with this kind of entertainment that laymen, priests, and monks now season their dinners. How ill matched are the scenes of this drama! The table is sanctified by the invocation of God. The meal is inaugurated with a reading from the Scriptures. Then men turn to backbiting gossip, then again they say grace. After that they return to their interrupted backbiting. And the men who pass their time in these tales are those whom God has forbidden to let any idle word fall from their lips. It would be horribly offensive to vomit over the table. But who covers the table more offensively with vomit than the man who pours out the bile, the abomination, and the contagious pus of his spirit at a dinner-party? And no one offends more shamelessly in this respect than those who more than anyone should have seasoned other men's foolish talk with words full of salvation. How have these so-called theologians, men who gloat in this title because they talk of the affairs of God, dared to become masters in the art of malice?

It is not the class which I am attacking; rather I am amazed that men are found in this lofty class who so ill match their own class. Men who call themselves preachers instead of the Holy Scriptures preach of others men's offences, or rather false charges against them. Men who are called observant brothers surely should observe discipline over their tongue, for if it is loose and unbridled, all their religious observances are hollow. The effect of their brotherhoods is that the pus of one tongue spreads at the greatest speed to them all. What some single Franciscan said in his cups is spread by the couriers (whom they are nowhere without) around the entire order within a month. They not only exploit dinners and the respect of the table for this evil purpose; they also carp at their neighbour even in sacred readings, in sermons preaching the gospel, and in the secrecy of the confession. And the common people learn the devilish art from the very source from which they were expected to learn the discipline of the gospel. Young lads are sent by their parents to the public schools to learn the liberal arts, and instead they learn from their teachers the most illiberal art of all, that is, of backbiting their neighbour. Indeed it is an art most easily learned and most hard to unlearn. They even pollute the hymns in which they praise God with this hellish poison. 'Let us pray to God,' they say, 'to deliver such and such from the heresy of Luther.'[247] No, they even distort the sacred writings to serve their slander, they degrade the gospel, they degrade the canticle of Mary to serve their poisonous and lying backbiting.[248] Yet this is the religion of some who declare that the church could not stand firm if it were not supported by their piety. These are those celibates who are supposed to turn to compassion for the world the divine vengeance as it brandishes its avenging sword. And all the time they flatter themselves marvellously, saying, 'Curses against those that deserve them are blessings, and not curses.' But they base this estimate of desert on the most trifling details. Perhaps someone has spoken with too little reverence of this or that Franciscan. Although so many scandals are detected daily even by the common people, bringing some measure of shame to them – or at least great distress to us – they immediately treat this as a just reason why this man should be dishonoured throughout the whole world by six thousand Franciscan tongues.

I had resolved not to say anything about myself, but I will recall one episode of which I have absolute proof – although it is a case more deserving of ridicule than loathing. A certain Franciscan had read my paraphrase on St John the Evangelist; he gave it all his approval. Then he reached the appendix, which I added for one reason only, to fill the empty page. This too met his approval until he reached the tag end, where I reproach some people, and indeed warn everyone, that if they wish to depart this life in good faith, they must not plant the anchor of their hope in unworthy matters. While I am discussing this I add these words: 'as if a man about to die were to think himself safe if he is buried clad in a Franciscan or Dominican habit.' At that point my admirer suddenly turned carper and condemned everything, even the work he had previously approved. Not content with this, he egged on his brothers to ordain by a senatorial decree that no Franciscan should read Erasmus' books.[249] If I had said 'in a Dominican habit' and left out the word 'Franciscan,' I should have been a Christian in his eyes. But now I have been turned into a heretic by that one little word. Yet the warning I give incidentally in that passage is what they themselves should be teaching to the people in their popular sermons, if they only desired to be what they want to be thought. For they will not achieve this by cursing but by living purely and with holiness, so that they may be a sweet fragrance to the Lord in every place. 'Well,' they say, 'it is in our interest that the common people should think well of our order.' But it is even more in our interest that the crowd should think favourably of the order of the priesthood, which Christ himself unquestionably founded. And again it is in our interest that priests who live impiously and who teach impiety should either be warned and set right or exposed, so that they do not lead astray the unsuspecting. Yet those fellows have the habit of venting their temper against this order 'from the wagon,'[250] as they say, sparing neither abbots nor bishops, nor even the pope of Rome, whenever it seems convenient to them. Good men do not take offence if criticism is made of the bad. Bad men, but those susceptible of cure, will judge that they have been warned, not assaulted, when no man's name is published. As for the incurable, their viciousness should be exposed, to prevent them deceiving the innocent with the feigned appearance of righteousness. Why do they declaim from their pulpits against every kind of man? Obviously – they will say – to ensure the correction of vices. So do they not really want the vices of their own brothers to be put right, since they object to being found guilty?

Kings bear tolerantly advice and even open criticism given in published writings provided that there is no disloyal abuse, and yet a Franciscan who professes the meekness of the gospel, once stung by an odd word, resorts to extreme measures, and in return for a slight insult, if indeed it is an insult, will aim a charge of heresy. If anyone diminishes the majesty of the cowl he is stabbed by the points of so many tongues. Or is it in the interest of the common people to believe that no one is damned who is buried in a Franciscan habit? It does indeed serve the interests of the Franciscans themselves, who live – and even indulge themselves – at the public expense. But where all this time is that apostolic charity that they profess, which seeks not what is its own, but what belongs to Jesus Christ?[251] The generosity of the people will not fail them if they live well. And if it fails them, they have the refuge that Paul the apostle not only indicated in his words, but embodied by his deeds. The great apostle did not hesitate to sew skins in labour by night;[252] yet among so many thousand, of whom a large part live in idleness, is there no one who will stoop to earn his living by the work of his hands if necessity presses hard? Now who compelled them to cast away their own possessions so that they might live from those of others? Do they set more value on the petty constitutions of men than on the teaching of Paul? See now how unfair this is: if you do a kindness to any one of them, you will have thanks only from one, but if you injure any individual, the whole order will be roused against you. And this is no less unfair, that in return for a trivial jest against the cowl, they aim at me more than capital charges. I beg for a second and third time, that no one will think these words are said in abuse of good men. We love piety, under whatever cloak and name. And those remarks are not aimed particularly against them, but against all those who need this remedy. In fact I say such things for my own benefit, I act as my own adviser, so that I can unlearn the habit of backbiting along with you inasmuch as I am liable – for who is not sometimes liable? If I am not liable, then I say it to make me wary in case I ever fall into that pit.

There is also another disguised form of backbiting, which is conveyed by aposiopesis, or innuendo. 'He has heaped up false accusations against me; if I revealed the truth ... but I prefer to recall only what is worthy of me.' 'They think highly of him, but if they knew what I know – I will say no more.' 'And far be it from me to repeat without shame what he was not ashamed to do.' Men who are otherwise utterly without culture possess all the tricks of the rhetoricians in this respect.[253] What is absurd is the inconsistency: while they never stop vomiting the pus of their spirit, they swear to individuals that they have said thus, or will say it, to no one else, and they demand from each other an oath of silence, though they themselves do not even keep the pledge of the confession, which they consider as part of the sacrament, as a religious obligation.[254] They call what is mere gossip the seal of secrecy, and the pledge of secrecy is useful only for their impunity and a guarantee of their trickery. Ecclesiastes says: 'If a serpent bite in silence, he is nothing better that backbiteth secretly.'[255] Sometimes they even abuse good men for a wicked purpose, especially if they know someone of indiscreet tongue to spread rumour. In front of such fellows they privately lament the life of this or that man, so that they seem anxious not to backbite but to offer healing. The other fellow, not realizing the disguise of this trickery, which he takes at its face value, convinces others, and they again convince others. So an innocent man is slandered by the pretence of a wicked tongue and the ears of the listeners are polluted in passing, as the plague spreads from man to man. If it is an outrage to attack one's neighbour when there is no compulsion to spit out true charges, how much more disgraceful is it to assert as a certainty what one does not know?

But it is most disgraceful of all to invent charges out of malice with which to cut your neighbour's throat, because it is forbidden to do so with the sword.

Charity interprets even bad deeds kindly; the whisperer degrades even good words and deeds. And the whisperer is all the more wicked than the false accuser. When the charge is openly brandished, if the victim of the calumny is made aware of guilt, he is warned to set himself right, and although he is warned in an adverse way by an adversary, it is pleasant to receive a kindness from any quarter at the time when we need it. Clearly it is better to receive it from an enemy, because the recipient is free from the burden of repaying thanks.

On the other hand the stealthy backbiter strives with all his might to ensure that everyone knows the other man's shame, and only the one man who stood to gain by knowing is left in ignorance.

Among murderers the fellow who openly attacks his man with a sword is less loathsome, because he acts at some risk to himself as well; in the same way the false accuser is less abominable, because he attacks another at some risk that the retaliation will fall back upon himself. If you wanted to deal with a backbiter, when will you catch the originator of the false information, which has barely reached your ears at the hundredth remove, especially when the man who first said it spoke to one man, having bound him to silence and uttered the prefatory 'speak kindly'? They will all be free to deny it. But supposing it is not possible to deny the whole charge, they will deny[256] that they said it in the form that was reported and invent a new version of the speech. And here the notorious elusiveness of human memory generally favours the lie. Now why should they feel embarrassment in denying what they said privately to one man, or to a few at a dinner-party, when they constantly deny what they have preached in public lectures, or even in sermons? Yet no one does this with less risk than those who use cowls as a shield. They dart here and there over the whole world and are at home wherever they travel. They not only have the company of brothers in the same way of life but they even have houses and women loaded with sins, supporters of their order, whom they entice and hunt down for this purpose. So whenever they choose to vent their temper conspicuously from a pulpit at someone, they hire a buffoon ready for any dirty deed; the opportunity to preach is granted to the cowl and not to the man himself – that is the level to which the Christian religion has sunk. So this fellow blurts out everything, proper or improper, to complete his wicked tale. The fact that he holds his ground is due to the place and to the moderation of the people. Yet the sanctity of the place does not save those who have committed a crime in that place itself, just as a murderer is not safe in a sacred place if that is where he killed his man. Raise the question with the trickster – but he will have moved on elsewhere already, or at least you are told he has moved on.[257] Raise the question with the prior, and he will reply, 'He does not belong to this college, and I did not guess that he would say such things.' But suppose you have caught the originator of the calumny, how will you drag him to court? They are exempted by countless diplomas from secular judges and bishops, some are even exempt from the law of their own order. So you must seek out the provincial, or the vicar, or the general, as they call them. Each of these shifts the responsibility on to the other, since each favours his own cowl, even if they cannot justify the deed. O secular religion! O you pillars of the church! O you salt of the earth! I repeat, these criticisms are not made against all – for I will have to repeat this often. But amongst these, why do those who are good only mutter about these offences? Why do they not either throw out or discipline such men? But the bad ones are the majority, and it is the worse amongst them who conduct their affairs. So we must weigh up the question whether it is in our interest, for the sake of a few good but downtrodden men, to support such hosts of bad fellows, who even exploit the piety and good repute of those decent men for their own evil intentions. What could be conceived more improper? In their ash-grey habits they profess the simplicity of the gospel, and they bear on their tongue the cunning of the devil.

The basilisk is an object of fear to all other poisonous creatures. So too even courtiers fear the guiles of Franciscans, and even princes fear them, although they are unarmed and would be harmless, except that they bear their tongue with them. They display themselves in a white habit and yet they carry about the ink of the squid or cuttlefish on their tongues. Others declare themselves by their dark habits of mourning to be dead to the world; they may well be dead to brotherly charity, but they are alive for slander and backbiting. They will sell their abstinences, but they will not abstain in the mean time from lies and abuse.[258] Their belly rumbles from hunger, but their tongue is tipsy. They abstain from consuming flesh, but at the same time do not hesitate to gnaw the flesh of their neighbour.[259] They restrain their teeth from biting on animals, but they plunge a serpent's fang into their neighbour. They spare cows and sheep, and do not spare their brother, for whom Christ died. O what a Pharisaical and irrational religion! It is a religious violation to tend the sick on the Sabbath, but no violation to devise the death of an innocent man through slander on the same Sabbath. To what end do you boast to me of your belly filled with pulse and fish, while you wield a man-eating tongue? You do not bite chicken, but you will bite your brother? You do not injure a sheep, but you injure your neighbour? You do not devour the flesh of cattle, but you devour the flesh of your brother? For whoever backbites against his brother bites him, yes he really bites him, he wounds him, and he devours him. Compare what Paul writes to the Galatians: 'But if you bite and eat one another; take heed that you be not consumed, one by another.'[260] What benefit is it to shun flesh, if you are entirely flesh? 'By their fruits,' Christ says, 'ye shall know them.'[261] Yet backbiting almost claims pride of place among the works of the flesh. For nothing is more opposed to the charity of the spirit than envy of one's brother, hatred, backbiting, and defaming. What is the purpose of profess-ing Christ in your words when in deed you play the devil's role? You shudder at the name of the devil, and mark a cross on your brow, and yet you are the very thing that you abominate. And perhaps there is a place here for the words of the wise Jew: 'while the ungodly curseth the devil, he curseth his own soul.'[262] You obey a man who instructs you not to dine, and you do not obey God when he forbids you so often from backbiting. For every time he instructs you to love your neighbour, he is forbidding you to backbite.

What is gained when you enclose yourself in a narrow cell, if you dart through the whole world with venomous tongue and insinuating pam-phlets? You boast of the psalms and hymns that you sing to God, but use that same tongue to sing a chant most dear to the devil, denigrating your neighbour; you use the same tongue to call formal blessing upon the Lord and for cursing the members of God. You observe the silence that a man has prescribed, but the man prescribed it so that you might unlearn the habit of backbiting. He prescribed an abstinence from speech not so that you might wallow more gluttonously in silly chatter, but so that you would grow accustomed to talking more moderately and cautiously even about honour-able matters. You laugh, and you condemn the abstinence of those who, having brought on a crazy desire for food by starving themselves, then eat and drink with too little control. But your abstinence of the tongue is just the same.

Here someone will ask, 'What, then? Do you condemn the way of life, isolation, abstinence, and obedience of monks?' No indeed, I praise it as a method of rearing the weaker brethren while they are advancing towards a greater perfection. But I condemn their superstition, or rather hypocrisy – for they are as unscrupulous in the matters of real piety as they are scrupulous in outward behaviour – I repeat, I condemn those who exploit clauses devised for training the childhood of the feeble as pretexts for their own evil natures. A man abstains with piety, if he is learning through abstinence to control not only his other organs but also his tongue. A man obeys human instructions with piety if he learns through this to obey divine law. He will wear a clean white habit to good effect if he lets himself be reminded by it to show clean and fair behaviour. He sings hymns to God with piety if this practice accustoms him not to wield a slanderous tongue against his neighbour, but to bless God in the person of that neighbour and to bless the neighbour for God's sake. He buries himself in his cell to good effect if solitude teaches him to turn the thoughts of his heart from the din of this world to simplicity of heart. He is right to observe the silence enjoined by men if he learns through this never to unleash his tongue unless either necessity compels him, or some great advantage to his neighbour provokes it.[263]

Just as no one commands properly unless he has first learned to obey commands, so no one speaks properly unless he has first learned to be silent. For the saying may be true among orators, that from speaking comes the ability to speak well.[264] But among devout men the opposite is true: it is from silence that the ability to speak well comes. However, as is the heart, so is the tongue – if indeed speech does proceed from the heart. So the men who have a heart endowed with chastity, modesty, and charity towards God and their neighbour, breathe forth, as if from a vase of fragrant flowers, that pleasant and wholesome odour of chaste and benevolent speech. On the other side, whenever those who have a heart full of hatred, envy, arrogance, and ill will, open their mouth they emit a foul and infectious breath. As the psalmist says, 'Their throat is an open sepulchre: with their tongues they acted deceitfully: the poison of asps is under their lips.'[265] So those who with rituals, customs, and ceremonies profess absolute piety but have a wanton and slanderous tongue are simply whited but gaping sepulchres. You block your nostrils at the smells of a sewer or a tomb, and yet you do not block your ears against the far more contagious effluences of a backbiter. No one chooses to take his seat near a bog or a public sewer, in case he should contract some physical plague from the proximity, and yet you choose to keep company with a backbiter. No one chooses to listen to men at close quarters if they breathe out foul breath from rotting organs, because doctors will declare that the infection of rotten breath is harmful to bystanders, and yet you think yourself safe in constant company with a slanderer!

There is a kind of slander where we lay the blame for our own fault upon others. Adam had learned this from the devil: 'The woman whom thou gavest me … led me astray.' And the woman said: 'The serpent deceived me.'[266] Rather that is how we backbite God, and thrust the causes of our woes upon the best of all craftsmen. Yes, he had given you a woman, but so that you would be her guide to achieve piety, not her companion in impiety. He had formed the serpent, not so that you would trust in him more than in God but so that you would admire the craftsman's skill in making every kind of creature. That Pharisee in the gospel carped at the tax collector and other mortals even in his prayers and thanks, and he is backbiting before God: 'I am not as the rest of men, extortioners, unjust, adulterers, nor such as this publican.'[267] Our Pharisees imitate this kind of behaviour, but more wickedly still. For the Pharisee sins only through arrogance, but they pray with the malice of Phormio himself:[268] 'Let us pray,' they say, 'for all who do good to us, so that God may save them from the heresy of such and such. And we must also pray that as God converted Paul, so he may convert to a sounder mind all who love Greek scholarship, from which heresies are born.' And at that these jesters in cowls seem even witty in their own eyes. And they feel no shame to approach the Lord's table often with this kind of behaviour, and to touch the sacred body of our Lord with rotten tongues. But I suppose they convince themselves that those against whom they say such things deserve it. Their hatred persuades them of this, because it is blind and lacks judgment. That is how robbers flatter themselves too: 'This abbot has more than enough and misuses what he has in loose living; he deserves to be stripped.' So we can often hear some monks telling us as they speak from a cart or a platform, 'We are only human.' Sometimes muttering and backbiting arise among them – 'This fault is not as serious as some men think. It is a human failing.' They speak in this way so as to persuade the people that no worse fault can found among them than common backbiting – if only they spoke the truth! But when men so exaggerate the blunders of others, how can they dare to excuse their own evil? Let them bring their knapsacks around to the front[269] if they want to be thought truly religious: let Christian charity excuse and mitigate the evil of its neighbour, but let them be unyielding censors of their own faults.

How disloyally they vent their temper on priests with concubines, and command on this topic all the forms of amplification the rhetoricians teach, and feel no hesitation in declaring before the people that a woman who sleeps with a priest commits a more grievous sin than if she were to copulate with a brute creature. I am not inventing this. That statement has been heard in public sermons. But when it comes to their own outrages, which are too blatant to leave room for denial, what was an impiety beyond expiation in others becomes a human failing, a weakness of human nature, an error to be forgiven in the light of so many other services, to be suppressed for the honour of the order. When a creditor has been cheated, or a hired man, when a deposit has been embezzled or a will tampered with, they adduce the favour due to religion and answer that God must not be cheated of his portion. When they have administered poison or falsely laid a capital charge, they adduce the zeal of the Lord, and anyone who shows too little favour for these pillars who support the tottering church[270] on their shoulders is banned as an enemy of the church. They even have secret doctrines, which they only communicate to those initiated in the same mysteries. Among these is the belief that it is right and good to eliminate secretly by poison anyone who is aiming at the ruin of the church, and further that it is the undoubted ruin of the church if anything is subtracted from their perquisites or authority. But Paul exonerates[271] idolatry among the gentiles, along with that whole hydra's nest of abominable offences, adducing the ignorance of those times from which God somehow concealed such knowledge. Peter excuses the impious act of the Jews whereby they condemned the Lord of Glory and set him on a cross, recognizing what had happened as due to ignorance.[272] Since Paul could not excuse the persistent malice[273] of the Jews he understated it, calling it a local and temporary blindness, so that they would be tolerated by others until they recovered their senses. But see how he sends thunder and lightning against the men of his own class. When is he not raging against false apostles? He calls them slaves of their belly, enemies of the cross, dogs, and deceitful workmen. If Paul the apostle is right to shout denunciation of false apostles,[274] so that the simple folk among the Christians would not be deceived by their guile, then sincere monks should not rage more savagely with their tongue against anything than against false monks, and on this point they should take more account of public honour than of private gluttony.

But let us avoid a further digression from the faults of the tongue, slandering and backbiting. The man who has impaired another man's property is strangled with a noose, and yet the backbiter who with malice aforethought and every kind of slander and blatant lies vents his temper against his neighbour's repute, perhaps also indulging in scandalous and anonymous pamphlets in order that the poison may spread, is allowed to approach the Lord's table like one free from corruption and praised as embodying the zeal of the Lord. Yet the man who steals reputation steals a more valuable object than money. Once the thief used to pay fourfold restitution,[275] so it was in one's interest to be robbed. But what restitution will a slanderous and abusive tongue offer? Or with what reparation will it make good the wounds inflicted?

Now it is impious to sadden a brother's heart by wicked deeds, such as by inflicting damage, or by assault, but men of a generous and noble mind are more distressed by abuse than mistreatment, and are sooner reconciled to those who have pilfered their cash-box or inflicted a wound on the body than by those who have spread a stain over their reputation. No one tolerates the pollution of a wife or daughter by adultery, but it is more serious to have polluted a reputation. The laws rage against those who have administered poison, but the backbiter offers a more harmful venom. The poisoner and calumniator have the same intent – each is aiming at destruction – but a slanderous tongue kills more often than poison. For poison is often adapted to serve as a remedy. Now granted poison does kill, it kills only the man to whom it is given, whereas the venom of the tongue seeps abroad, infecting a very great number, and the originator has no more power to control the course of this evil as it spreads far and wide than those who have contaminated a public water supply. Those with no other activity in life than to spread their venom on all decent men let themselves be beguiled by this deadly offence without noticing how severely this disease is condemned by distinguished men whose piety has been made known to us by the witness of the Holy Scriptures. David says: 'Incline not my heart to evil words: to make excuses in sins.'[276] If we want to seem truly devout, let us hear Solomon offering salutary advice: 'Remove from thee a forward mouth, and let detracting lips be far from thee.'[277] And let us not flatter ourselves and believe our life is pleasing to God, who is the God of peace and charity, if we have a tongue that destroys brotherly charity and devises hatred and ill will. Solomon says: 'Six things there are which the Lord hateth, and the seventh his soul detesteth: haughty eyes, a lying tongue, hands that shed innocent blood, a heart that deviseth wicked plots, feet that are swift to run into mischief, a deceitful witness that uttereth lies, and him that soweth discord among brethren.'[278]

Do you see how he has linked the backbiter with murderers and mentioned him last of all, as if he were the most wicked of all offenders? There are vices, such as extravagance, and splendour and luxury in banquets, that make us loathsome to God, although they earn good will among men. But backbiting is loathed even by wicked men. The sage Sirach, no less great among the wise men of the Jews than Thales among the Greeks,[279] teaches us this; he says: 'The talebearer shall defile his own soul, and shall be hated by all, and he that shall abide with him shall be hateful. The silent and wise man shall be honoured.'[280] Admittedly this passage is interpreted differently in the Greek text: 'The talebearer defiles his own soul, and shall be hated among his neighbours.' There is an old Greek proverb, 'A bad neighbour is a plague.'[281] But the man who has a whisperer near him has the worst kind of neighbour. For, as the same wise man says elsewhere, 'A whisperer and a man of two tongues is accursed, for he disturbs many who are keeping their peace.'[282] Agesilaus, king of Sparta, used to say that if he happened to hear a man praising or blaming anyone, he believed the character of the speaker should be scrutinized as carefully as that of those he appraised.[283] For clearly the man who praises wicked persons or wicked deeds is proclaiming himself a fool or equally wicked. Conversely, the man who abuses good men or good deeds not only reveals the merit of those he mentions but also makes known his own character.

But the backbiter must be loathed by all sensible men, since everyone fears for himself, thinking, 'You would say the same about me if I were not here.' Antigonus made use of a certain man's treachery to betray the enemy, and when his friends were amazed that he gave no thanks for actions that he had desired, he answered, 'Traitors are only dear to me while they serve me; once they have served, they are loathsome.'[284] So too Octavius Caesar uttered a similar remark against a Thracian called Rhumitalcus, that he liked a betrayal, but utterly loathed a betrayer. When the girl Tarpeia betrayed the Tarpeian citadel, having demanded as her reward what the Sabines wore on their left arms, Titus Tatius their leader crushed the girl to death by hurling both bracelets and shields upon her – perhaps this action was quite in keeping with the ancient customs of those days. At least it is unlikely that any sensible man sincerely feels good will to a traitor. But just as men who require the gall or venom of animals for remedies find pleasure in them while they are needed but loathe and shudder at them when the need is over, so nobody feels affection for a traitor except while he exploits the man's vice. When he has obtained what he desired through the man's agency, he loathes and abominates the criminal and dares not trust him, being well aware of his treachery against those to whom he should most of all have kept faith. I think this is how all honest men feel about calumniators and backbiters; for no one really supports them, except either the complete fool or the arrant knave.

One of Solon's laws was especially praised by men of good judgment. He forbade anyone to hurl abuse against the dead, believing it an act of piety to treat as sacred those who had departed from this common life and an act of justice to refrain from harming those who had passed away; finally he thought it was humane and civilized to put an end to feuds at some time and not to allow quarrels to perpetuate themselves without limit.[285] For this reason it seemed abominable even to the pagans to denigrate the dead and fight with phantoms.

But nowadays does a backbiting tongue spare any man? It does not spare sex, or age, or kin, or comradeship, or service, or rank. Among us young men denigrate old, to whom they should have paid respect; we do not spare maidens and wives; we snarl abuse at brothers and cousins; we speak ill of those who have served us well; we grumble against our officers and princes and bishops. If a pagan denigrated a Christian, we would have to tolerate it, but Paul is most indignant that this scourge should arise among Christians. For this is what he writes to the Corinthians: 'For I fear lest perhaps when I come, I shall not find you such as I would, and that I shall be found by you such as you would not. Lest perhaps contentions, envyings, animosities, dissensions, detractions, whisperings, swellings, seditions be

among you. Lest again, when I come, God humble me among you.'[286] You
see what company backbiting keeps; you see that he does not ignore this evil
as vulgar and trivial. Obeying the order of God, Paul does not want
Christians to curse idolators, but instead to return blessings for curses. For
this is what he writes to the Romans: 'Bless them that persecute you; bless
and curse not.'[287] But what would you say, Paul, if you saw Christians now
suffering at the hands of Christians, colleagues suffering from colleagues,
theologians from theologians, priests from priests, monks from monks, in
short the dead suffering from the living, all snarled at, savaged, and torn
apart with the madness of a rabid dog? If we have grown deaf to the laws of
Christ, if we despise the warnings of so great an apostle, at least let us hear
the laws of Solon. He forbade us to abuse the dead and those absent. If
anyone uttered any insult against another in a holy place, in court, before an
official, or in an assembly of the people gathered for public contests, he
forced him to pay three drachmas to the man he had insulted and two to the
public treasury. What place or time is so sacred to us that we feel a scruple at
heaping up abuse against our neighbour?

   Once it was a religious offence to drag a guilty man away from the
altars. Now before the very altars we assault our neighbour with the weapon
of our tongue. O ambivalent organ, from which such a great plague of life
can spring up for men, and yet from it such benefits could flow, if anyone
directed it as they should! As our wise man says, 'A wicked word shall
change the heart, out of which four manner of things arise, good and evil,
life and death, and the tongue is continually the ruler of them.'[288] For the
tongue exercises equal domination whether you wish to save or destroy. But
he wrote this saying in imitation of Solomon, who wrote: 'Death and life are
in the power of the tongue; they that love it shall eat the fruits thereof.'[289]
The evil tongue is a whole world of evils, but conversely, 'best among men is
the treasure of the tongue / a sparing tongue, most dear when it keeps
measure.'[290] The tongue is Ate, strife personified, if it lacks a pilot. It is a
horn of plenty, if you use it well. It is Eris, rouser of quarrels, but the same
tongue is Grace, who wins good will. It is Erinys, the bringer of all evils, but
it likewise calms all things. It is the venom of the asp if it acts with ill will, but
a universal antidote if good intentions control it.[291] It is the source of wars
and civil strife, but it is also parent to peace and concord. It overthrows
city-states and kingdoms, but it also founds and establishes them. Finally it
is the deviser of death, but equally the bestower of life. As Solomon says:
'The mouth of the just is a vein of life.'[292] And Paul had good reason to
delight in the comic verse 'Thus evil converse spoils good character,'[293] but
he would not have condemned this verse either: 'Speech can be medicine to
the sick at heart.'[294]

Anger is a violent disease of the spirit, but 'a soft speech turneth away anger.'[295] The tongue of Nabal had provoked the spirit of David to a monstrous deed, but the tongue of Abigail quenched the fire that had been kindled. Nor did David conceal how much he owed to this woman's tongue. He said: 'Blessed be the Lord God of Israel, who sent thee this day to meet me, and blessed be thy speech, and blessed be thou, who has kept me today from coming to blood and revenging me with my own hand.'[296] Why should I mention to you here the Greek proverb 'O my tongue, where are you going? Are you about to destroy a city, and raise it up again?'[297] What is more glorious than, having constructed a city, to bring into the partnership of laws and walls and religion and fortunes men who live like wild beasts, and to turn them from enemies into citizens? Just because this is achieved most of all by a peaceful tongue, the ancients have invented the story that cities were founded by Mercury.[298] But the tongue destroys whatever it has set up if it turns itself to causing harm. So let each man say to his tongue, whenever it is swept into speech or tickled into calumny, backbiting, and obscenity, 'O my tongue, where are you going? Are you preparing to do good or harm?'

But why do I search out these quotations from the records of the pagans, when St James has depicted the ambivalent power of the tongue so vividly and so fluently? First let us learn from him how much benefit is brought by control of the tongue. He says: 'If any man offend not in word, the same is a perfect man. For he can even direct his whole body with a bridle. Now if we set a bridle in the mouth of horses, to ensure their obedience to us, we can turn their whole body around. And see how mighty ships that are driven by a great wind are turned round by a small tiller, wherever the will of the steersman has chosen.'[299] Take an experienced sailor away from the rudder, and all who are conveyed in the ship will be at risk. Withdraw reason from control of the tongue, and the whole house or city is endangered. Take the bridle from the horse's mouth, and both horse and rider are in danger. Let the tongue follow its lusts, and it brings ruin to all.

Now hear what downfall an evil tongue brings to all affairs. 'Even so the tongue is indeed a little member, and boasteth great things,' says the apostle. 'Behold how small a fire kindleth a great wood, and the tongue is a fire, a world of iniquity. The tongue is placed among our members, which defileth the whole body, and setteth on fire the wheel of our nativity, being set on fire by hell. For every kind of beasts and of birds and of serpents are tamed, and hath been tamed by mankind: but the tongue of man no man can tame. It is a restless evil, full of deadly poison. With the tongue we praise our God and Father, and with the same we abuse men who have been made in the image and likeness of God. From the same mouth proceedeth blessing and cursing. My brethren, these things ought not to be so. Doth a fountain send through the same passage sweet and bitter water? Can the fig tree, my brethren, bear grapes, or the vine figs? So neither can the salt water yield sweet.'[300] And yet we think ourselves splendidly scrupulous with our Pharisaical pretences, while we carry with us the fire of hell in our tongues, when we say one thing seated and another standing, and when we constantly turn our tongue into more forms than any polypus can take on. Whence comes this inconsistency? Because we do not have a simple heart. Nor is it surprising that men who have more than one heart are also double-tongued: 'With a double heart have they spoken,' says the psalmist.[301] But you could say that some men nowadays are not double-tongued but a hundred-tongued; men should have as great a number of hearts, while instead they have no heart. Whoever has received baptism has professed his religion, so let every Christian listen, but especially those who are proud in the profession of a special form of religion. He says: 'If anyone believe himself religious, yet does not curb his tongue, but leads his heart astray, then this man's religion is hollow.'[302]

When Anacharsis had dined with Solon, he was found sleeping in this position: his right hand was on his lips, and his left on his genitals,[303] clearly showing by this action that the tongue and the genitals were the two most rebellious organs, but that the tongue had to be curbed with more care than the genitals. This was the behaviour of a Scythian philosopher, a heathen and a barbarian, and it was approved by the pagan philosophers, and yet we think ourselves more than philosophers if we differ only in our clothing from mountebanks, jesters, and sycophants. There is much more that could be said against an evil tongue, but there is a risk that I may receive an answer like Diogenes when he trampled on Plato's cushion. When he commented, 'I am trampling upon Plato's pride,' Plato replied, 'So you are, but with another pride of your own.'[304] So someone may say to me, 'Yes, you are venting your temper against the abusive tongue, but with another kind of abuse.' For I confess that in persecuting evils there must be a limit, except that there is no limit to this evil, especially in these times.

[*The usefulness of a good tongue and remedies against an evil tongue*]

So now I shall demonstrate the usefulness of a good tongue, and at the same time offer remedies against an evil tongue, although a large part of this promise has already been fulfilled if I have made sufficiently clear what a deadly thing is an evil tongue. If I have convinced you how great is the reward from a good tongue, and how great the ruin from an evil one, I think you will freely listen with attention as I report the means of achieving this advantage and avoiding such a mass of evils. So just as doctors first take care to protect the body from diseases before helping it to thrive, and if disease has taken hold, they are more concerned to empty it out by draining away the noxious humours than to provide a diet that renews vitality, we too will first try to show by what means we can avoid the infection of evil spreading to us from elsewhere and, if it does spread, how it can be driven off and the habit discarded.

Now there is a twofold danger, one from infection, the other from the damage caused by the evil that an evil tongue brings to those whom it assaults. For just as a man who lives constantly with stammerers himself learns to stammer, and one who keeps constant company with the blear-eyed is infected by the ailment himself, and, if we believe the proverb,[1] the lame man's neighbour himself learns to limp, so a man who shares intimacy with talkative and abusive fellows becomes like them. For no other fault is more quickly transmitted to another man than this. But the routine of healing will also have to be twofold, for we must not only ensure that we cure the disease that we ourselves have contracted, but also if possible, that of others. If this seems beyond hope, then flight will be the safest course[2] – a remedy which is recommended in this and other places because it is most effective in all circumstances. So in order to make this precept the start of our curative method, whenever we notice a man of tipsy tongue or one compulsively addicted to backbiting and virulence, if it seems an established and incurable evil, we should withdraw ourselves at the first opportunity from his company, just as we flee from a man who is disfigured by leprosy or has contracted plague.

For first of all the man who associates with such fellows only does so at the risk of his good repute, since everyone is normally judged to be like the companions he keeps. And quite often men are involved in danger when they have heard someone revealing what it would have been safer to keep unspoken. Often those in the habit of listening to chatterers and idle talkers are even tainted with the affliction. For the vice that originally offended them first grows sweet and becomes a pleasure because of man's innate envy and his inquisitiveness to know another's misfortunes. In this respect, if we are truly Christian we should listen to the apostle Paul, who gives salutary advice to the Corinthians and through them to us all, saying: 'If any man that is called a brother be a fornicator or covetous or a server of idols, or a railer or a drunkard or an extortioner; with such a one [do] not so much as to eat.'[3]

Now, consider, I beg you, how great a scourge is evil talking, since according to Paul, the great spokesman of peace and mutual good will, it destroys even the common enjoyment of the table among Christians, whereas Paul does not wish a Christian wife to be divorced from an idolatrous husband, or a Christian slave to leave an impious master.[4] Then we must mark also the catalogue in which he has listed an abusive tongue among brigands and idolaters. Perhaps indeed there would be less risk from an idolatrous companion than from an abusive one. We must also note this point, that he combines the railer and the drunkard with the same connective, either because arrogance of speech arises from tipsiness, or because lack of control over one's speech is a kind of tipsiness, as we said before. Paul does not forbid a wife who has professed Christ to take food with a pagan husband, nor on that account does he forbid her to unite with him in their common bed,[5] yet he does not want a Christian to share a common table with a Christian who is also a railer.

The man who does not shun the fire is thought crazy; does then a man who maintains intimacy with slanderers seem sane? When a fire has broken out even the gouty and the lame find speed for flight. Yet we have learned from St James[6] that an evil tongue is not a tongue but a fire, from which a conflagration develops, not for one house alone but for vast kingdoms; so do we cherish this fire in our breasts, and not think of flight? Solomon says: 'The wicked man diggeth evil; and in his lips is a burning fire.' The perverse man stirs up lawsuits, and the wordy man comes between princes.'[7] Yet meanwhile he is called candid and witty, although he is usually an arsonist. If ever a serpent's hiss strikes your ears, how swiftly you flee. And yet do you hear the hissing of a poisonous tongue without concern? The epigrams of the ancients report that a certain man had been bound to his pallet by the chains of gout for many years, but when a viper creeping up entwined his shin in its coils, he suddenly forgot his old disease and leaped up and never again felt the illness, so great was his fear of venom. Yet do we live unconcerned with a man of loose and virulent tongue? But the psalmist teaches us that no poison is more immediate; he says: 'The poison of asps is under their lips.'[8] And the canticle in Deuteronomy speaks no more gently: 'Their grapes are grapes of gall, and their clusters most bitter. Their wine is the gall of dragons, and the venom of asps, which is incurable.'[9]

If someone offered you a measure of wine blended with dragons' gall or the venom of asps, would you not shudder? But it is a more deadly poison that is offered you by the denigrator, the abuser, the informer, or the flatterer, yet we drink it in with greedy ears. There are caverns that breath out deadly miasma. We run from those with even our nostrils blocked, and yet we greedily gape at the words of the slanderer who breathes a more instant poison upon us. There are bogs that breathe out mephitic vapour, deadly even to the birds who fly over them,[10] but the poison breathed out by

the cavern of the slanderous mouth is more deadly. You have heard that
'their throat is an open sepulchre';[11] nor does Solomon disagree: 'The mouth
of a strange woman is a deep pit, he whom the Lord is angry with shall fall
into it.'[12] He repeats this opinion in the next chapter: 'For a harlot is a deep
ditch: and a strange woman is a narrow pit.'[13] A harlot is a pit, which never
says, 'It is enough'; it is this you would call the greatest danger to men. She
also has thieving hands, and a belly that consumes vast estates, but she has
no organ more deadly than her tongue. With this she wheedles, with this
she rouses up the lover's spirit, with this she stirs up quarrels and slaughter.
She sows feuds between husband and wife, between son and parents. O
plague-ridden cavern! Into this falls the man with whom the Lord is angry.

With whom then is the Lord angry? Surely with those who listen more
to the feigned wheedling of a stinking harlot than to the commands of God,
who heed more quickly the woman enticing them to destruction than their
parents calling them to honourable purposes. If you see any man with an
uncontrolled tongue, think of him as a harlot. Step back from this pit, lest, as
the Scripture warns elsewhere, loving danger, you should perish in it.[14]
With what anxiety we shake off a scorpion if ever it crawls on us, before its
clasp inflicts the sting; and yet, in Ezekiel's words, do you live with
scorpions[15] and freely embrace a venomous creature? In Malta Paul shook
on to the fire at once a viper that had crawled out and was clinging to his
hand,[16] so he felt no harm; but you cherish and embrace a man dripping the
venom of heresy, slow to act, until you swell up utterly and are consumed,
and collapse with an injury grown incurable. The army of Cato, retreating
through the Libyan desert, found remedies against the local creatures, since
it could not avoid them.[17] Shall we then sleep unconcerned among so many
poisons? Indeed no part of Africa has more deadly creatures than the whole
of mortal life, wherever you flee to. We walk to the moment of death in this
great and dreadful wilderness, in which there are serpents whose breath
burns, scorpions and dipsas snakes, and to make them more dreadful, there
is no water. Who can be safe from these great evils unless he has God as his
guide, who has drawn forth a holy spring from the hardest rock? If we are
true Israelites, that is, if we are obedient to God's commands, and place all
our trust in him, no kind of poison shall harm us. For God promises this in
Psalm 90: 'Thou shalt walk upon the asp and the basilisk, and thou shalt
trample underfoot the lion and dragon. Because he hoped in me I will
deliver him, I will protect him because he hath known my name.'[18]

What the psalm promises, Christ himself, who spoke in the psalm,
confirms: 'And these signs shall follow them that believe: in my name they
shall cast out devils. They shall speak with new tongues. They shall take up
serpents, and if they shall drink any deadly thing, it shall not hurt them.'[19]

Whoever has not departed from the commands of God has removed himself from the poisons of tongues. Our flesh is the harlot, which never ceases to pester us towards destructive pleasures, wheedling, flattering, intimidating, terrifying, in short leaving no stone unturned. So when we have escaped all evil tongues, this last hazard will be there for us to shun. The flesh has its own tongue, the spirit has a tongue utterly different. The flesh speaks in an old tongue, the spirit has a new tongue, but utterly different from it. If you listen to the tongue of the spirit, you have escaped from the tongue of the flesh. If the tongue of your flesh shouts its demands from a distance, it does so without risk of harm. Hear the advice of the wise man, showing us what must be shunned and what pursued: 'My son, attend to my wisdom and incline thy ear to my prudence, that thou mayst keep thoughts and thy lips may preserve instruction. Mind not the deceit of a woman. For the lips of a harlot are like a honeycomb dropping, and her throat is smoother than oil. But her end is bitter as wormwood and her tongue sharp as a two-edged sword. Her feet go down into death; and her steps go in as far as hell. They walk not by the path of life: her steps are wandering and unaccountable. Now therefore my son hear me, and depart not from the words of my mouth. Remove thy way far from her and come not nigh the doors of her house.'[20]

Here I will not hesitate to blend in something from the fables which is in harmony with Holy Scripture. The ancients thought there were certain satyrs in the forests, half men and half goats, but witty in any case. They say that one of these, compelled by the rigour of the winter, took himself off to a countryman's cottage. He was welcomed by the hearth, and as this kind of creature is very inquisitive, he noticed his host breathing on his hands. He asked why the man was doing this. He replied, 'So as to warm my hands.' When they had reclined at table, the host again breathed, this time on a too-hot helping of barley porridge. The satyr was amazed and asked why he was doing that. He replied, 'To cool my barley porridge, which is too hot.' Then the satyr said, 'What is this then? Can you blow hot and cold from the same mouth? I don't fancy setting up house with such a creature.' He got up and returned to his wilderness, preferring to suffer cold there rather than be warmed in the house of such a host.[21] To make it seem less strange that this surprised the satyr, I must say that this has tormented the intellects of philosophers; how can it happen that when breath is first released from an open mouth it makes things warm, yet when the mouth is pursed and breath is blown from compressed lips, it cools? This instructive joke in the fable should at least warn us to abstain from contact with the double-tongued fellows 'who say good is evil and evil good, setting down darkness as light and light as dark, setting the bitter down as sweet, and the sweet as bitter.'[22] Janus masks are laughed at in popular comedies because they show one face in front and another very different one behind,[23] but speech is the face of the soul. Now what is more extraordinary than that this should be so varied? In Solomon the two-tongued mouth is abominated by the divine wisdom.[24] Ecclesiasticus too abominates the two-tongued, judging this charge more shameful than theft. He says: 'Confusion and repentance is upon a thief and an evil mark of disgrace upon the double-tongued.'[25] Nor will Paul tolerate the double-tongued among the servants of bishops.[26] Now it is almost inevitable that a man moving in a crowd should fall sometimes among the talkative wielders of tongues; so we see that highly esteemed men left cities and emigrated into immense deserts, believing innocence would be safer among wild beasts than among men.

But if you cannot avoid associating with many people, including the talkative, there is a twofold anxiety: first, that you should heal a man's failing, if possible; if not, that you yourself should not be harmed. The wisest of men did not speak lightly when they said no one could be harmed except by himself. So the first requirement in councils that contain a number of vicious and talkative men is that men of pious thought should claim priority in speaking, so that the undisciplined fellow gets no pretext for chattering of matters best left unmentioned. A reading from the Scriptures can be used to exclude stupid and unrewarding tales, or we may use a problem quoted from the books of scholars, provided it does not lead to contention. If the gossiper begins to pile up his stories without shame, he must be curbed by a rebuke or cut short by a witty comment. M. Tullius Cicero once scored off most wittily a man who attacked Cato the Younger for drinking all night: 'Ah,' he said, 'but you can't add that he plays dice all day long too.'[27] For when Cato had given the whole day to affairs of state, it was sometimes his practice to prolong a dinner with his friends late into the night, since he often had no chance of leisure with them by day. But the slanderer picks on the bad element, and even perverts it by suppressing the element of good. On another occasion, when some gossiping fellow was asking a question to which he knew the answer, a Spartan, realizing his addiction, carefully gave him an untrue answer. But when the questioner retorted, 'You're lying,' he replied, 'So aren't you an extraordinary fool to ask what you already knew?'[28]

Again, in England, when one of the nobles at a dinner was retailing gossip at the expense of a very wealthy abbot and listing the varieties of food and number of courses served at his table, the king pretended to be amazed at the abbot's gluttony, so the other man deliberately exaggerated everything to increase the king's enjoyment of this story, which he thought very amusing; in fact he added considerably, as tends to happen, to the facts. So when it was time to interrupt this windbag the king asked him, 'Was the abbot a giant, or a cyclops?' He replied that he was of normal size. 'Then I suppose he has an immense belly?' He admitted that in this respect the abbot did not much exceed other men. 'Well then,' said the king, 'where does he put away all that food? Your story doesn't seem plausible to me.' At this the ranter, checking himself, said, 'He doesn't eat all these things by himself, Sire; he has many guests and a huge household.' 'Faugh,' said the king. 'Then what is new in your story, if a man who supports many dependants has many dishes? In fact anything you have said against the abbot you could have said against me.' In this way the king chastened the stupid chatter of his foolish dinner-guest. If this is not possible, or if you think it will be futile, take care you don't nourish and develop the man's lack of control by your reply. For that is how things end in rabid fury,[29] whether you approve of what is said, or reject it. Some men encourage a fellow talking nonsense by their nodding and smiling, although they stay silent. He would stop a lot sooner if you listened with a grim expression to anything that should not have been said, or if you listen as though you are not listening, and presently, when there is a pause, you bring up another subject, which will put an end to the one badly begun. Although it is not courteous to interrupt the speech of a man talking sense, it is decent to break off stories that are bringing distress to the spirits of the listeners. I knew a man once who fooled a dangerously talkative fellow by a shrewd piece of trickery. While this other man had been saying much that it was not really safe even to overhear, our friend all the time was concentrating with a thoughtful air on the volume that he usually carried with him, perhaps for just this purpose; so when he was asked his opinion of what the fellow had said, he answered as if he had been roused from a very deep sleep, 'You will forgive me, I'm sure, but I didn't hear a single word of all that was said; for all this time I was completely preoccupied with Bruges' – for he was on a mission to this place as his prince's representative.[30]

Indeed when one story succeeds another, and gossiping bestrides the world, with kettledrums reverberating one after another, can we expect anything from the tongue except crazy drunkenness? If you murmur assentingly 'Quite so,' 'That's right,' 'Fine,' 'Splendid,' 'What's that I hear?' 'What are you saying?' and suchlike phrases, the man will go on chattering; if you relate a similar story, he will utter two in return; if you resist, a battle will brew up. So silly gossiping must be kept out either by wholesome conversation or by readings; or it must be checked by rebuke, or reproved by the severity of your expression, or cut short by introducing better topics; or if all else fails, at least it must be put to shame by your silence and directing your ears elsewhere. If you are not even permitted silence, but are compelled to make some sort of reply, the best thing will be to say something quite unconnected[31] so as to give the impression either of paying no attention or of misunderstanding what is said. For no one really enjoys telling a long tale to a deaf man.[32] On quite a few occasions it will be worth while feigning sleep, if no other means of escape offers itself.

Now men greatly provoke an abusive tongue when they encourage someone to drink during conversation. For this is outright pouring of oil on the furnace.[33] In Lucian, Aristaenetus came off badly when he ordered a huge bowlful of unmixed wine to be offered to the Cynic Alcidamas. He thought that once the man was busy drinking he would stop pestering his fellow guests. But after the brief silence that the wine had gained, there followed a mighty uproar.[34] This is just like trying to put out a fire by throwing on logs; they would put out the flame for the time being, but soon it would get the upper hand and create an even greater blaze that would engulf everything all round it. So if we are in authority over anybody, such as our own children or pupils or wives or servants, we must conscientiously correct their affliction of the tongue, by scolding or warning or training. Now the common people usually punish their children with a beating for breaking open a storage jar, but overlook it when they spill out random chattering. They punish theft, but let a lie go unpunished. So we must be taught from our earliest days what an unbecoming and destructive thing is an unbridled tongue. Some men punish a lie, but treat talkativeness in their dependants with a smile; yet talkativeness is the beginning of insincerity, insincerity of forswearing, and forswearing of blasphemy. We usually find our children and slaves much as we formed them by our training. Consider Cato the Censor: he used to buy up many prisoners of war, but only young ones, so that it would be easier to mould them to his ways. He trained them never to enter another man's house, except on his command or that of his wife. If they were asked what Cato was doing, they were accustomed to say simply that they did not know.[35]

If your friends are prone to this affliction, it would be more gentlemanly to heal them by a private reproof. Or if it seems unlikely they will accept the remedy of reproof, it will help if you punish your son or servant severely in front of them, either with a scolding or even a beating, for their misuse of their tongue. In this way boys marked out as future rulers, whom it is perhaps neither safe nor helpful to scold or beat, learn from seeing others beaten or scolded what they themselves deserve for committing the same offence for which the others were punished. This ruse will also enable you to spare the embarrassment of a friend whom you hesitate to rebuke; he can be casually invited to the reading of a work in which lack of control over one's tongue is severely censured. However, in the case of pupils, children, wives, and servants, we must above all avoid the risk of them learning from us what we punish in them. Our rebuke will lack weight if we teach by our own behaviour what we abominate in others. In the comedy Chremes is told, 'Does it seem so outrageous to you that your grown-up son has a girl-friend, when you have two wives? Do you feel no shame? How do you dare scold him? Answer me.'[36] And in another play Clitipho ignores his father's warning because he has heard him in his cups boasting of the same deeds in his youth from which he discourages his son when sober. 'When he's had a little bit to drink, what exploits of his own he tells me! But now he says, "Draw from others the experience which will be useful to you." '[37] In Plautus the old man Demaenetus is reclining besides his son's girl-friend. How improper it is for him to say, 'A young man should be modest, Argyrippus.'[38] A solemn and grave warning indeed, when it comes from an old man who was behaving so immodestly in front of his son's own eyes! Admittedly this example presented by Plautus is rather too ungentlemanly even for a comedy. Yet we see in the life of Christians what we do not tolerate in a play. What silly and obscene tales quite a few teachers and parents pour out in front of their pupils and children! The satirist was justified in his advice:

> A child deserves respect; if you intend
> Some shoddy deed, honour his youth, my friend.[39]

Indeed if ever you are tempted to trifle with your tongue, honour a child's youthful innocence and send anyone of tender years off on some errand; even then it is safest of all always to be what you wish to seem to your dependants. How little men consider the chastity of their virgin daughters when they blurt out immodest tales in their presence! It is reported among the extraordinary achievements of Cato the Elder that he also personally instructed and trained his own children, since he did not really trust any tutor. He shunned uttering an obscene word in front of them, just as if he was talking to the vestal virgins. This was the man who as censor expelled Manlius from the senate because he embraced his wife (she was frightened by the sound of thunder) at dinner in front of his daughter.[40] The wise man Sirach would not allow a father to look upon his daughters without severity in his expression, so delicate and vulnerable a thing is virginity. He says: 'Hast thou daughters? Have a care of their body, and shew not thy countenance gay towards them.'[41]

It was once the custom among the Romans that fathers-in-law did not enter the bath with their sons-in-law.[42] But now we enter the bath with our wives and sisters, as if we were eager to prostitute them, and while our children look on, we will say and do anything with our wives, not to mention our favourites, whom men even invite to the family couch, the witness of our marital bliss. And yet they are surprised later that their children are not chaste, although they have brought them up in this way from their tender youth.

By nature the class of servants and of women are chatterers. How will you dare to demand control over their tongue from these people if they constantly see you blurting out every kind of nonsense? And then we wonder that our servants lack obedience when we give them good instruction, but cheerfully use them not only as witnesses but as accomplices in our follies. So we must punish them not only if they betray a secret or lie or slander or revile another's reputation or say something coarse; we must punish them even if they waste time in idle nonsense or if they reply without being addressed or if, when several have been asked, the youngest jumps in ahead with his answer or is in too much a of hurry to reply, without having understood properly what his questioner meant, so that he soon gets the proverbial retort, 'It was a spade I asked for.'[43] We should punish him even if he replies rather thoughtlessly or in more detail than the circumstances required. It would not be amiss to repeat Plutarch's tale about Piso at this point. He could not stand his slaves' talkativeness, probably because of his short temper, so he told them never to speak unless he himself asked them to, and not to answer anything beyond what they were asked. Then as it happened he invited Clodius to a dinner-party in his honour, and he had provided entertainment worthy of such an important man. When the time for dinner came, and the rest of the guests were assembled, only Clodius, for whose sake he had invited others, was still to come. So he repeatedly sent out his slave secretary to see whether Clodius was coming. Then when night was falling, and there was no hope that Clodius would come, Piso at last turned to his slave and said, 'Didn't you invite Clodius?' 'Yes I invited him,' he replied. 'Then why hasn't he come?' 'Because he declined the invitation.' 'Why didn't you tell me that straight away?' The slave replied, 'Because you didn't ask me.'[44] It is a comic mistake, but the slave's self-control deserves praise. Yet I do not think that it is easy to find the sort of man who errs on the side of silence.

We will enjoy much easier relations, then, with our friends, wives, children, servants, and pupils, if we train them by these methods to practise economy of speech. We will ensure it more easily if we ourselves are free from the affliction when we try to heal other men's sicknesses. And for some time now, the moment has been clamouring for us to say something on this topic. The disease of the loose tongue is either naturally born in man, or comes from habit, or else again corrupt associations and the habit of chattering reinforces the weakness of nature. For doctors think that it is also relevant to the art of healing to explore the cause and origin of the disease. It is very important to distinguish whether a cold has arisen from a hot or cold moisture and when fever has arisen from excessive indulgence in drink or from infection of the blood. Some diseases are as it were inborn, inherited from parents, like paralysis in some men, or epilepsy, or toothache. Again different nations are more prone to different ailments. In the same way the Greek is more talkative than the Roman, and nowadays the Frenchman is more talkative than the German. And among the Greek communities, the Athenian is more talkative than the Spartan and the Asian more talkative than either. Now each sex and age has special ailments. Women are more inclined to the affliction of talkativeness than men (consider this as a general statement) and young men and old alike are more talkative than men in the prime of life, whether this arises from a deficiency in reasoning or because nature compensates in readiness of speech for what is withheld in strength of the body. 'Spare us please, so that you have strength to argue with her,' Nausistrata is told in the comedy.[45] And Homer makes Nestor rather talkative, just as we hear Cato the Elder was. These tendencies apply to man in general. But if you look around for the reasons why this affliction occurs in an unnatural degree, you would find it usually springs from such causes as idleness, association with those infected, inquisitiveness, thoughtlessness, stupidity, and an undisciplined way of life. This is why barbers have always suffered from a bad reputation for talkativeness, as I said before, because men who have nothing to do at home sit idly in their shops.[46] So because they hear sailors boasting of their shipwrecks and the soldier boasting of his victories and others chattering on and on about other nonsense, from sheer infection, as it were, they themselves become chatterers, although they are not themselves idle. This also happens to bath-attendants, drivers, sailors, and innkeepers, for travellers love to pass away the time in stories, because they have nothing else to do. The same argument will have served to explain the process of infection.

Now I think we have made it quite clear above, that curiosity is the very nurse of talkativeness, although each nourishes the other. Further, if it were not clear from other sources, it is obvious from the parties of common people how much a full belly and tipsiness contribute to looseness of the tongue, for these dinners are in the beginning calm and quiet, but what an uproar of shouting they sometimes come to in the end! You would say it was the crash of breakers on the seashore. In Plautus there is a comment by some women, 'When we're loaded up, we're lavish with our talk,'[47] but this is a weakness men have in common with women, except that we outdo them, acting among ourselves like Suffenus,[48] but playing the part of Cato for them.

Now there are some even more specialized reasons for this failing. There are certain topics about which one man or another delights to talk with a special enthusiasm: as the proverb puts it, the recall of bad experiences is pleasant,[49] provided they are the kind which are not associated with shame. For old soldiers who have experienced warfare in many campaigns love to boast about their battles to others. Sailors love to recall their hazards, and men who have been to many remote places love to describe what they saw or suffered there. In the same way, the memory of what brought us pleasure, so long as the pleasure is associated with honour, is something we love to revive by retelling. For example, it is usually a pleasure to women to recall how their husbands first fell in love with them, and what gifts and endearments they used to woo them. In fact whenever anything matters greatly, whether it is pleasant or distressing, we love to talk about it. The proverb says that where a man feels pain, there he keeps his hand.[50] But it is just as true that wherever something gives us pain or pleasure, there each man finds his tongue. If he dearly loves anyone, he is glad to recall him; on the other hand if he feels strong anger or hatred, he can hardly keep quiet on the subject of his torment.

In addition, those who have put a lot of effort into any art and surpass others in it like to introduce discussion of the topics on which they believe they can earn admiration from others. We see experts in medicine acting in this way, and astrologers, alchemists, and students of history. Someone will say, 'What is the point of bringing up these many examples?' Simply so that we may recognize all the circumstances of this behaviour and more easily avoid the hazard of intemperance.

First of all we will easily avoid the silly trifling of our tongues if we are always concentrating on some serious and respectable enterprise, especially when the storm has driven us into a gathering of gossipers. In a coach or on shipboard it is possible to read something from the good authors, and nothing prevents you doing the same thing if you are forced to wait around in barbers' shops and public baths. Even in the senate, Cato did not stop reading until the senators were assembled.[51] Pliny used to listen to a reader both in the baths and at dinners.[52] Socrates deeply resented it when the harmony of a discussion was broken into by singers, for he preferred to hear men talking about justice and self-control, rather than playing Phrygian and Lydian tunes.[53] Yet I believe the men of old devised music on purpose to exclude unsuitable conversation from dinner-parties, just as I observe quite a few people invite jesters. Gaius Caesar used to dictate letters even on horseback, to two and sometimes three secretaries at a time.[54] The Theban commander Epaminondas once heard that one of his officers had died of disease in camp; he said he was amazed that the man had time to fall ill on campaign.[55] Someone might with more justice express amazement that men distracted by many important affairs have time to listen to silly stories.

Although courtiers and monks differ in their entire way of life, they generally are matched in their loose control of the tongue, simply for this reason: both groups live in equal idleness. The same thing has become a habit in countries where the custom is established for those in wealthy circumstances to support many idle servants for the sake of prestige – I only wish this plague was confined to the English. Contrast the behaviour of the emperor Heliogabalus, who used to give certain instructions to his freedmen and slaves that were superficially amusing; for instance that they should summon all the men affected with hernia to the baths, or invite to a dinner eight bald men, eight one-eyed men, eight sufferers from gout, eight deaf men, eight conspicuously dark and eight conspicuously tall men, eight extraordinarily fat men, eight men with big noses, as if representing the Greek proverb 'eight of everything,'[56] and he would offer a reward and commission these retainers to bring him each a thousand pounds of spiders' webs – indeed they say that ten thousand pounds were actually collected. When men expressed wonder why he did it, he answered that the greatness of Rome could be inferred from evidence like this.[57] But at least he thought it better for the slaves and freedmen of his court to be kept busy even by such nonsense rather than be led by idleness to act like courtiers of other emperors, laying information, slandering, selling whiffs of gossip. It was Heliogabalus also who established a senate of women on the Quirinal Hill, which he called his little-senate, where senatorial decrees were passed on the authority of Symiamira [sic] Augusta[58] – absurdities about the laws governing ladies, such as who it was right should go where in what clothing, which ladies should give way to whom, who should approach to kiss whom, who should be conveyed in a trap, on a pack horse, or on an ass, who should ride in a mule cart, who in an ox cart, who in a chair, who might have ornaments of bone or ivory or silver, and who might have gold or jewels on her footwear. He wanted his mother to be kept busy with the married ladies every day by this kind of triviality so that they should not disturb public and sovereign business, as women do who live in idleness.

Alcibiades cheated the slanders of the common people by a similar device. For there was no limit or end to the abuses of the common people, so he bought for seventy minae a dog of extraordinary size, cut off its tail, and set it loose in the community. When it wandered around at random, and everyone knew it was Alcibiades' dog, it aroused preposterous stories from everyone, since this behaviour seemed stupid and fatuous to everyone. At length when his friends privately reproached him about this and reported the stories that were being spread about him, Alcibiades laughed and said,

'Obviously things have gone as I planned. For I did this just to divert the gossip of the Athenians to this kind of talk, so that they would be busy and stop saying worse things about me.'[59] I admit it is an advantage to turn men from more serious evils to trivial ones, but for us the issue is rather to call men back from shameful to honourable behaviour, or at least to behaviour not associated with disgrace: in this way I usually pass on to my servants something to copy out or investigate, not for my own benefit, but to stop them being spoiled by idleness. Now William, the archbishop of Canterbury,[60] possesses this gift among his other talents. As an exceptional patron of scholarship he cannot endure ever to be idle himself or that any of his dependants should grow lazy with idleness. If only all sovereigns or at any rate bishops or masters and mistresses of households imitated his example! For what is there to wonder at if we see so many idle gossipers among priests of our present day? When they have mumbled their statutory prayers to an end (if indeed they even fulfil this obligation), since they neither perform manual labour nor are attracted by study of Holy Scripture, they soon move off to the market, the eating houses, and their little drinking sessions, and from these they go off to the arcades, where they feed their itchy tongues with gossiping tales and prying eyes. So what would you expect from men used to this life except absolute drivel? And all this time where is that priest described to us by Malachi: 'The law of truth was in his mouth, and iniquity was not found in his lips: he walked with me in peace and in equity, and turned many away from iniquity. For the lips of the priest shall keep knowledge, and they shall seek the law at his mouth, because he is an angel of the Lord of Hosts.'[61] Where is the salt of the earth, with which the folly of the people ought to have been seasoned?[62] Instead of salt, we carry with us venom on our tongues. So we see many who are well suited by what follows in the same prophet: 'But you have departed out of the way, and have caused many to stumble at the law. You have made void the covenants of Levi, saith the Lord of Hosts. Therefore have I also made you contemptible and base before all people, as you have not kept my ways and have accepted persons in the law.'[63]

These words are said here not to add confidence to those who are now condemning and attacking good priests and bad alike, but to urge everyone to a life worthy of the priesthood. Public good will will follow a change in your way of life. They say that when St Bernard expressed abomination of the simony prevailing in the Roman papal court, Pope Eugenius[64] gave this reply: 'When you have eradicated grumbling from the monasteries, I will eradicate simony from my court.' Yet it will not be difficult to eliminate an evil tongue from the monasteries if they take delight in silence, if they avoid self-indulgence and tipsiness, if they are possessed by love of the Holy

Scriptures, if they shun idleness, if by turns of praying, reading, and writing, and even toiling with their hands they beguile the boredom of idleness. For what is more wretched than those monks who waste away from boredom unless they beguile the time with drinking bouts, hunting, cards, dice, and scandalous stories, when all the daylight is too short for true monks? So those who realize that they are naturally inclined to looseness of tongue or have contracted a touch of this ailment somewhere, somehow, should devote themselves to honourable activities, which actually become agreeable when you are accustomed to them. The next thing will be either to live by themselves or with those whose companionship will help them unlearn this vice of their nature or conditioning, and to avoid intimacy with gossipers as far as in them lies. As the preacher Ecclesiasticus says: 'Who will pity an enchanter struck by a serpent, or any that come near wild beasts? So it is with him that keepeth company with a wicked man, and is involved in his sins.'[65] To help you avoid this, nature has added some signs by which you may recognize looseness of tongue, such as hesitation of the instrument itself, stammering which repeats the same syllables or words,[66] stuttering, or lisping, and a conspicuously pursed-up mouth. Although these symptoms are not absolutely reliable, they frequently reveal the faults of nature, silliness, gossiping, and shallowness. If only the afflictions of the tongue were limited to those who are made suspect by these symptoms! Wherever we have detected this evil the company of such men must be shunned.

Doctors recommend that men who want to protect their physical health should live among those of sound body, vigorous, young, and cheerful men, and avoid the company of those whose wretched constitution makes them thin, pale, fretful, moody, or feverish, or inclined to epileptic fits. We should be much more conscientious in taking care to improve ourselves by intimacy with good men, and ensure that we do not bring on an infection of the disease by constant companionship with evil men. For evils of the mind are transferred much more swiftly than those of the body.[67] So just as a man is safer from epileptic seizures if he prevents fainting and dizziness by taking drugs, so there will be less risk from the disease of the tongue if they avoid the kindred and corresponding evil, so to speak, of curiosity. This itself generally arises from idleness, so that you would not be unfair in saying that chattering was sister to curiosity, since each has idleness for a father, and stupidity for both mother and wet nurse. What could be more stupid than to act like Morychus as he was described by the ancients, neglecting his own affairs to peer at those of others,[68] just like Ollus and Afer jeered at by Martial;[69] or what could be sillier than to chatter about other men's business, with no advantage to yourself, but at great cost and serious risk to property, reputation, and life itself, all the time boring your listeners, without any benefit to them. But since Plutarch wrote a neat essay on this topic,[70] we will omit it for the sake of brevity.

Thoughtlessness is very like stupidity. For the stupid man is deceived by bad judgment; the thoughtless man blunders in not paying attention when circumstances require it. It is a mark of stupidity when (as we often notice with amusement) the same thing happens in speech as in singing or dancing, that the man who has least skill is first to begin the song or dance. We will avoid stupidity if, first, before we leap up to speak we steep our mind, the source of speech, in the understanding of the truth and in honourable beliefs and if, second, we never unleash our tongue for speech without allowing a brief delay. This will offer us two advantages: the first, that we do not answer what we have not understood, the second that we do not blurt out our speech and say something that causes us immediate embarrassment. Although this delay is suitable to every age, it is particularly appropriate to youth. For what Seneca says, that delay benefits nothing but anger,[71] is not entirely true. Even in warfare Fabius' delaying was beneficial,[72] and in my judgment the saying 'What's well done is fast enough'[73] is never out of place. Why, taking advice is itself a kind of delaying, which we are told to practise, not so as to do what is needed quickly, but to do it in good time. Otherwise it often happens, as Plato says, that he who began too fast will finish too late.[74] This kind of caution should be applied more in talking than in action, because in speaking a slip is very easy, but there is still danger involved. When we see someone tackling a job that is hot to handle, as they say,[75] we warn him ahead of time: 'Watch what you are doing.' Indeed we say it to ourselves whenever we feel our tongues itching: 'Weigh up what you are saying.' So whenever a phrase rushes to our tongue, before we unlock the barrier of our teeth for it let us think to ourselves, 'What is this remark which is so driving on our tongue and trying to burst out by force?' Or, 'Where will my tongue come aground now? What advantage will there be if I say it, or inconvenience if I keep it quiet?' We should not drop a remark the way we drop a burden. The man who drops a pack is unburdened, but he who drops a remark is weighed down even more. So we must never indulge in speech unless it is either necessary to us or seems likely to afford some profit or honourable pleasure to the listeners, so that it performs in human intercourse the same function as salt in food; this is usually mixed in sparingly and only when it is needed, otherwise it gives no pleasure but spoils the dishes. But if the words hovering on the tongue will not be useful to the speaker, or essential to the listeners, or bring any pleasure or sweetness to others, what is the point of uttering them?

If you are planning a journey, you think to yourself, 'What is the advantage if I go there?' If you see no advantage from the journey, even if there is no disadvantage, you change your mind and say, 'Why should I do that without purpose and to no effect?' And yet these words 'without purpose' and 'to no effect' are not so appropriate to conducting business as they are to uttering statements. For, as we said earlier, since such serious evils arise from this trifling cause, we must consider even more scrupulously whether it is more useful to keep silent or to speak out. I have seen men who would cough, belch, and gulp from sheer habit. According to the wise men of old, human concern is most powerful, even absolute, in deciding every enterprise. If then men are able, even with some difficulty, to dispel and overcome coughing or gulping arising from natural causes, it will not be all that troublesome for us to unlearn this wild looseness of the tongue. At the beginning it seems impossible, but after a month of practice it will be very easy; what has been reinforced by habit soon becomes natural to us. It will perhaps be a point of courtesy to be first in greeting others, but generally in a group of several, whoever speaks first without the claims of seniority or office is betraying his own lack of restraint. Hence this trimeter of Sophocles has been justly praised by men deserving praise themselves: 'Counsel and coursing differ in their goal,'[76] that is, 'Advice and racing do not have the same end.' For anyone who gets the lead in a race is praised and wins the prize, while we laugh at the slower man, but in deliberation the opposite is often the case. For if the first speaker has expressed adequately all that is needed for the discussion in hand, the man asked to speak after him should not either disagree or add superfluous comment just in order to get part of the credit, like the three consultants in Terence, of whom one says the legal decision can be reversed, the next denies it, and the third thinks they should make further deliberations.[77] I wish that we had to laugh at this self-seeking only in comedies. Instead this pest is found even in the deliberations of princes, and happens daily among doctors, of whom scarcely a single one will approve unreservedly a drug prescribed by another, or if he is more decent, he will add further medicaments to what is already excessive so as not to seem incompetent – but really he will get honour enough if he simply praises and confirms a good decision, and he will profit by a reputation as an honest and unpretentious man. For some men are so grudging or greedy for honours that they cannot bear the voters to support another man's proposal, and they waste time quibbling rather than endorse a good decision for which they were not responsible themselves.

    If anything really has been omitted from the replies of earlier speakers, then we can inform them without offence of anything that has escaped their notice or explain without ill will what was left out; since this is never out of place, the man who speaks last often earns the most credit. But whenever a man answers before his companion has finished speaking, this provokes laughter in comedy and even more often in real life. So you will be well advised to leave a moment to your questioner after he has already finished speaking, in case he wishes to add to or correct what he has said. Meanwhile he too is weighing up what or how he should reply. Again, men are often a source of amusement when their haste in replying leads them to give the wrong kind of answer because they don't understand the issue before them. This is merely absurd in men who are inclined to deafness or ignorant of the language, but in others it often entails some risk. In the gospel, our Lord sometimes answered the unspoken thoughts of the Pharisees before they could reveal their intentions. Such swiftness is right in those inspired by the Holy Spirit, but we should learn the intention of the speaker before we answer, if we want to answer properly. Now it is not only lacking in courtesy but downright rude when a question is addressed to one person and another anticipates his reply. Not only is he apparently claiming too much for himself, he is actually insulting towards the other man, as if he judged him unfit to answer the question. For when someone does this, isn't it as though he were saying 'What is the point of asking him? He doesn't know anything' or 'Why ask anyone else, when I am here?' If the person who has been asked gives an ill-informed reply, he should be pardoned for replying as best he could when invited to do so, but surely the usurper who has displaced the person addressed deserves our derision if he gives an unsatisfactory reply. Even if he gives a complete answer to the question, men will think him discourteous and tactless. When Themistocles was young and thrust himself forward repeatedly as speaker, even though he had good proposals to make, Eurybiades said to him, 'O Themistocles, in races men who start before time are usually thrashed.'[78] At dinners too it is disgraceful not to wait for your turn. I was once amazed at the conceit of a certain Franciscan. He had read nothing except Scotus. Some question or other was being discussed amongst the scholars at the table of the archbishop of Canterbury. When he noticed this, but was too far away to hear what was under discussion, he leaped up and shouted, 'What's that, what's that you are discussing?' – with the same kind of expression as if he were saying, 'You will waste your time unless I resolve the problem' (and yet there were some learned bishops among them), 'for any difficulty there is I can disentangle, since there is nothing I don't know.' This matches the arrogance of those men who set up their teacher's chair and announce that they will answer immediately every question from whatever source.[79]

But perhaps it is a small hazard simply to bring laughter on one's head. I knew an envoy of a great prince who was taken to prison on suspicion that he was devising some plot contrary to his instructions. This had happened at night. The next day, when the king discovered what had happened, he sent two of the leading men to indicate that this was not done by the king's command, but that his servants had been confused about the offender's identity. They had scarcely made the opening statement that they had come by the king's command, when he broke into their speech and begged humbly and like a suppliant that the king would treat him mercifully. Now they were intending to send the man away free with the king's pardon, but guessing from his pitiable and abject speech that he knew his own guilt, they kept back their instructions and returned to the prince, reporting what had happened. So the poor fellow was brought to his ultimate downfall. It cost him so dearly that he had forgotten the teachings of St James the apostle: 'Let every man be swift to hear, but slow to speak.'[80] He should have kept his tongue still until they had come to the end of their instructions and then answered calmly that he knew both his own innocence and the justice of the king too well to believe that this had been done at the king's command and that the servants' action had not been aimed at him but at the fellow whom they thought they were arresting. Then he would have escaped that disaster in the first place. What is more he would even have increased his former influence with the king, whether the arrest had really been without the king's knowledge or the king had entertained some suspicion but decided to be content with that penalty, as a means of warning the man not to indulge in meetings by night with the enemy's ambassador.

So it is likely that the custom that we see nowadays too in the disputations of the Sorbonne either originated with shrewd men or was introduced of necessity. There, no one may interrupt the dispute between questioner and answerer unless he has been appointed for this purpose. And when there is a silence, the man who takes over does not raise a question without first requesting the indulgence and consent of all present. When he has put his question, the man brought forward to answer does not give any reply except to repeat the question set, once and then twice; in the mean time the questioner may change, correct, and add whatever he wishes. This delay for modification and repetition is sometimes boring to the listeners, but provides an essential remedy against the uproar and confusion of speakers. When the argument has become heated, the assembly of those sitting or standing around sets a limit to his speech so that there may be a chance for others also to speak. I admit that in this way the man most deserving of a hearing is sometimes ordered to be silent, but it is better that some points are not heard than that nothing should be heard. Now this remedy is particularly appropriate to the French nation, since, although it is most cultured, it not only has great fluency of tongue, but a certain tendency to heat and passion in dispute. But in general, whoever is speaking speaks in vain if he is not given trust and attention. But he can win both responses for himself by arousing men's expectation with an expression of hesitation – a device recommended by those who have written in detail about rhetoric.[81] Whoever opens in this way clears himself from suspicion of pretence because he seems to be thinking out on the spot what he ought to say, not to have brought with him a contrived piece as a means of deception. In deliberations, above all, we think a man is going to make some weighty and extraordinary statement if he first goes over what he is to say. So those who teach us that the essence of art is to conceal art affect this hesitation as a pretence so as to make their listeners more attentive and trusting. This is how Homer presents Ulysses.[82]

So we will need to weigh up not only the question itself, but also the motive behind it. For we do not always ask questions because we need an answer, but sometimes we entice our more bashful friends into taking their turn in conversation by these amiable little inquiries. In this the man who anticipates another's chance to reply and draws to himself a mind or ears directed towards another acts no more courteously than if he came in front of a man wishing to be greeted with a kiss and took the kiss himself, or if he turned towards himself the gaze of someone directing his eyes upon another. When Octavius asked the young boy who was said to resemble him in features whether his mother had at any time been in the emperor's court, he might have been given a guileless answer, although his question was not free of guile. Then the joke would have been ruined. But when the boy guessed the double meaning from the expression of his questioner, he answered that his mother had never been to court, but his father had often attended it, thus turning the witticism against Caesar's female relations and earning some credit for his wit.[83] In our time also, there are many who provoke men's talkativeness by artificial questions, so that they can enjoy a laugh.

Once a certain Dominican was master of ceremonies at a dinner of businessmen and men were deliberately invited to provoke this ready and conceited man by their questions. He answered all of them without hesitation; indeed he took them seriously. At length among the questions that were relevant to their business someone inserted this: 'If a man had contracted to supply two canisters of sheep's milk, would he be acting rightly if he supplied two canisters of hen's milk instead?' Without hesitation the Dominican made this distinction. 'If hen's milk is more useful to the man receiving it than sheep's milk, then the man who supplied it has filled his contract.' General laughter ensued.

This restraint will be more courteous if the man asked makes his ignorance grounds for excuse and in turn offers the role of answerer to others on the grounds that they are more suited to solving the problem of the inquiry, as men do when the cup is passed to them, and in courtesy they offer it to the very man who is extending it, and after accepting it pass it on to others as if they were more worthy of honour. And at the same time a man should not feel shame to confess honestly that he has no advice ready which he thinks worth hearing; he can say that he will consult his books, weigh up the matter, and report anything that comes to his knowledge. This kind of modesty often wins more praise than if you were to give a good reply. So sensible men do not give approval to those who too eagerly seek glory from ready speech rather than speaking well. Indeed no one has been so averse to extemporary speaking as those who have transmitted skill in speaking to others. They say that Demosthenes was usually in the habit of speaking from a written text, so much so that he could not even be incited by the demands of the assembly to rise and speak without preparation.[84] As far as I know, it is recorded that M. Tullius Cicero did this only once: but this was on the occasion when he was to plead a case before the Board of a Hundred on a fixed day. He gave his slave Eros his freedom simply because he had announced that the hearing was postponed to the next day.[85] He was the most admired and experienced artist in speaking, a man who could have outdone the careful preparations of all other men even by an unprepared speech, but he felt this great anxiety in case he should say anything improperly through a lack of care. Clearly it was prudence that made these orators slow and hesitant about speaking, while it is ignorance that begets our conceit. So Sirach the Hebrew gives us a grave warning, when he says what we began to quote elsewhere: 'Listen in silence and thou wilt gain fair thanks for thy respectfulness. Young man, speak but a little in thine own case, when it shall be needful: if thou art asked twice, let thy reply have an opening. In many matters act as one ignorant, and hear in silence and inquiry. Claim not to speak in the midst of great men, and do not speak much when old men are present.'[86] Our wise man dislikes a speech without a formal opening.[87] But some men's speech is even more foolish, having neither head nor feet. Men speak like this when they answer stupidly and yet can make no end of speaking. It would have been enough to answer the question, as Socrates learns from Euthydemus in Plato.[88] For instance, if someone is asked, 'Is your father at home?' it is enough to answer, 'No he is not.' For if the questioner wants to know more, he will add, 'Then, where shall I meet him?' But if you want to give a more obliging answer to an acquaintance, it is enough to say, 'He hasn't returned from the senate yet.' It would be superfluous, and a case of silly talkativeness, if someone when asked whether his father was at home said that he had set out secretly three days ago on the order of the senate to go to the emperor, and told the whole narrative of the mission. Indeed it is difficult to judge who acts more foolishly, the man who offers a mortar to the neighbour asking for the loan of a serving dish, or who thrusts his whole array of equipment on a person who only asked for a funnel.

Men who take a question about any matter as an exercise-ground for their chattering and go into the matter more deeply than is required make the same kind of mistake. Horace criticizes the man who begins his Trojan War from the double-yolked egg,[89] but men blunder even more seriously when they answer 'matters bearing neither on earth nor heaven,'[90] the one milking a he-goat while the other holds a sieve beneath it, to quote Demonactes.[91] They are so in love with the adage 'It is shameful to stay silent.'[92] In lawsuits, the loquacity of a witness often ruins the defendant, either because he answers more fully than he should, accidentally blurting out harmful information, or because it is very difficult when talking to excess to be consistent and to remember what you have said, since this is the main cause for evidence being discredited.

We have already spoken more than once about lack of restraint in eating. So let us come to more special cases, where the general recommendation seems right that no one can control his tongue until he has accustomed his emotions to obey his reason. We see that men of excessive bile often have the experience that when they have resolved either to keep silence or reply most moderately, anger arises like a hurricane and breaks away the helm, sweeping their tongue into every kind of abuse. Uncontrollable joy does the same thing, or uncontrollable grief, fear, or hope. Now the man who by careful practice has accustomed his spirit neither to admire nor loathe nor fear nor hope for anything too strongly will control his tongue by the same process of controlling his spirit. Just as it is futile to advise a lunatic 'Walk like this, straighten your clothes, and control your features like this' until you have first driven out his bile by drugs and brought about a different physical condition, so you will warn to no effect a man dominated by ambition, anger, pride, greed, lust, jealousy, love, and hatred, a man tormented by hope or fear, the special tyrants of human life. It will be useless to say 'Speak in this way, control your tongue thus' unless you first persuade him to curb the rebellious passions of his spirit with the bridle of reason.

We must exercise particular care in those matters where we feel ourselves especially prone to stumble, and so it will be most helpful if each man follows the Pythian oracle and learns to know himself.[93] Socrates' patience was justly praised by all, because, contrary to nature, he had so mastered and tamed all his passions by much constraint and habituation that he seemed utterly without passion. From endurance of spirit he had secured for himself an equal endurance of body against all hardships, however great. Philosophers don't deny that it is far more difficult to bear thirst than hunger, although each is extremely hard to bear. But Socrates used to drive away thirst by this training. After he had exercised his body in the ancient fashion for the sake of his health, at that time when drink is most desired, he did not allow himself to drink until the first jug had already been poured out for others – not that he feared any risk if he drank with the others, but to teach his irrational appetite to wait for the command of reason. In the same way he had hardened his body to an incredible endurance of sleeplessness, guard-duty, heat, cold, and exertion.[94] A man who has so successfully kept his desires under his mastery will also be able to control an itching tongue. If he can command himself to abstain completely from drinking when he is desperately thirsty, he will easily control himself from drinking too much. In the same way, when the chance of speaking arises and a man feels his tongue as it were thirsting to pour out in a discussion which he enjoys, he may be able to command himself to remain quite silent until necessity or usefulness demands speech. Such a man will easily control himself, so that when he begins to speak he does not glut himself and become drunk with silly chattering. Such control in speech should not be derived from the mood of the speaker, but from the listeners. This will succeed if you consider not what it is pleasant for you to say, but what it pleases or benefits others to hear. If a sailor or soldier does not stop talking nonsense about his dangers and victories until he himself is satisfied with recalling them, his saga will outlast any Iliad. But if he considers what interest these have for his listeners, he will conclude that it is better to send them away still gaping and in suspense, rather than suffering nausea and ready to puke with over-indulgence. At the end of comedies it is customary to add, 'Farewell, and give us applause.' That is how they end, so as to send the spectator away still hungry. But instead of applause at the story of silly chatterers, men generally offer a yawn, and instead of praise the comment is, 'Ho there, stop!' So whoever controls himself when he is longing to talk on the themes that his natural inclinations lead him to dwell upon will easily restrain himself on other topics.

The philosopher Athenodorus asked to be released by Augustus because of the increasing burden of age, and as he was about to leave, he gave him this advice, that Augustus should not do or say anything in anger until he had recited the Greek alphabet in sequence, as if there was some remedy in this against anger – but really the philosopher was showing him that he should impose a period of delay. Caesar was delighted by this saying and embraced him saying, 'I still need you,' and kept him by himself for another year, so that he should learn silence from Athenodorus as his teacher.[95] Why don't we too give as much pause to the tongue in its eagerness to burst into speech as will enable us to run through the sum of the alphabet? When old Laches in the comedy is about to speak to the courtesan Bacchis, this is how he addresses himself: 'I must make sure that I do not obtain fewer concessions than I could because of my anger, and that I do not do anything extreme which it would be better later on to have left undone.'[96] The old man was convinced that Bacchis was standing in the way of Pamphilus permitting the recall of his wife. If this had been true, he would have had just grounds for resentment. But if he had given way to his inclination in his mood at that time, the story would not have had a happy ending. As it was, he protested in courteous terms, and received a courteous reply: he recognized his misunderstanding, obtained the favour he desired, and the entire confusion of the comedy was resolved by a happy turn of events.

If laymen do this in comedies, how should priests and Christian monks behave in preaching, and especially in publishing books? What Pallas Athene does for Achilles in Homer,[97] reason should provide for us. And yet that Homeric Pallas only holds him back from fighting, quite content if he limits his resentment to verbal abuse, whereas our Pallas Athene does not allow us even to vent our passion against a man in abuse, even if we do keep our hands clean. No, if we want to heed the spirit of Christ, whenever he plucks at our ears, we must return blessings for curses.[98] Anger is an uncontrollable emotion, but pleasure too contains great possibilities of intoxication. It is sweet for a lover to chatter endlessly about his love, but others who are free from love do not feel the same desire. Because of the incontrollable passion which possesses them, lovers do not merely think all men care what they are doing, they even address inanimate things as if they had feeling, like the young man in Plautus who addresses pleas to the bolts and doorway;[99] so lovers exchange unending tales with the couch that is witness to their bliss, with the lamp that beholds them, and with violets and girdles and rings sent by their mistresses or destined for them.[100] Similarly the shepherds in Bucolic narratives fancy that their emotions are the concern of the flocks and mountains and woods and streams.[101] It is sweet to vent one's anger against an enemy with the tongue, but this kind of tale is unwelcome and tedious to men who neither love nor hate them and perhaps do not even know them. I know a man who had just begun to learn Greek, and because he dearly loved it, he greeted in Greek anyone he could find and talked at him at length in Greek even if the other man knew no Greek. He had such a great desire to show if off. But at the same time he was an absurd nuisance even to those who knew Greek, because their Latin was far more fluent. Plutarch tells the story of a man who happened to have read two or three books of Ephorus, and bored every living creature by summarizing what he had read, and prevented any party from being enjoyable by constantly repeating the battle of Leuctra to the point of general nausea. As a result the popular jest gave him the name of Epaminondas, because he prated about the achievements of that leader more boastfully than Epaminondas himself, who had achieved them.[102] Those men are prone to a similar vice who return home fresh from the universities having won a degree and a laurel in some branch of learning. But this craze to show off, which time itself eases and sets right in due course, would have been better controlled by the exercise of reason. When men anticipate a flood, they fortify the dykes more carefully where the onslaught of the river is more violent; we in the same way should apply the restraint of reason more carefully wherever any pleasure entices us more strongly to speaking. Socrates used to say he did not like drink or food which beguiled men to eat and drink without hunger and thirst – foods like honeyed wine, spiced wine, sweet cakes, and Athenian sweetmeats – because they entailed a special risk of gluttony.[103]

So we must protect ourselves above all from the topics of conversation whose sweetness seizes us and carries us away too far. You will be well advised to weigh up all the circumstances before you loosen the bolts of your tongue; as you prepare to speak think who you are, what sort of theme you intend to discuss, what kind of men will be your audience, and what the time or place requires. Finally consider what good or evil may arise from your words, whether to yourself or others. There will be motives among these considerations to restrain your itch to speak or convince you to keep silence. You should also try out the categories from which according to the rules of rhetoricians we derive the arguments of the persuasive form of oratory: whether it is right, honourable, or fitting, whether it is expedient, safe, pleasant, easy, or necessary.[104] Examination of these points will produce caution in our speech.

Hence, we read, as we have mentioned in passing, that the most eloquent men were barely willing to rise and speak and were nervous at the opening of their speech. Obviously in this respect too prudence begets timidity, whereas ignorance gives rise to confidence. Pericles was said to speak thunder and lightning because of men's amazement at his eloquence; but when he was about to mount the platform, he used to pray to the gods that he should let no word fall accidentally which was not conducive to his proposal.[105] Among the Romans too it was customary for the magistrate about to speak before the assembly to pray in a few lines that the gods would let his words be beneficial and fortunate to the state.[106] Now propriety sometimes is modified by the nature of the place, time, and persons involved: but indiscretion, backbiting, abuse, and obscenity are never anything but improper. Admittedly some faults are more tolerable in certain men than in others. For obscenity – what the Greeks call talking of shameful things – does not suit any man, but it is more loathsome in an old man than a young one, in a priest than in a soldier; again, it is more acceptable in front of youths than in front of men, to your own children than to the children of other men. Let each reader paint himself an eloquent picture, intensifying the imagined evil by all possible circumstances. What is more detestable than that white-haired old men, almost falling into decay, should practise with their tongues shameful things that their bodily weakness has long since prevented them from indulging? Paralysis has taken control of their hands and gout of their feet, their loins are ruptured, their quavering head wobbles, their mind wanders – only their tongue is wanton with dirty tales. Imagine the expressions of the diners and their thoughts as we watched this happening – for we have seen it more than once. And imagine the comments about the man after his departure.

I will tell of something I myself witnessed in Italy – but discreetly, to avoid harming or bringing suspicion on any man. I was in company with three Greeks, one of whom was a monk, another reasonably well educated, and the third a boy of about thirteen. The monk had absent-mindedly let the lunch hour go past. So we saw to it that some food was brought to him. He was happy with two eggs, and did not let more dishes be served; he also drank most sparingly. He had always seemed to me a good and moderate man, by no means indifferent to the Holy Scriptures, although he knew no language except the vernacular Greek. But his grooming was so cheap, so rough and shabby that I believe Hilarion himself would have been better clad.[107] Thus far all his characteristics befitted a monk. But the dessert served at this dinner was out of keeping, for when the food had been taken away they reverted to exchanging stories. The scholar produced a book written in Greek, which recorded miracles. Now they say that it is the custom among the Greeks for the priest to read at the end of the mass to the people if a miracle has occurred anywhere. A pupil of Satan had imitated such a text so that the prefatory formula was the same as that which the priest used to arouse the attention of the people, and again had the same blessing which the people used to sing as thanks and glory to God after they had heard the miracle. But in between there were obscenities such as no harlot among us would dare to speak out even in the public baths. When these were read aloud, the monk began to be fantastically amused, as if it were a marvellously witty tale; he began to get excited, to break into chuckles, and after each item of obscenities he kept chanting the customary blessing. The boy was seated between them, although decent stories might have been more fitting to his youth. Personally I found the monk more lacking in proper training than a decent nature. Clearly men tend to be formed this way by learning nothing except rituals. Then the meat dishes were presented, and this was a day on which it was the rule to eat other foods. The monk refused with great scruple, and indeed he would not have let them change his clothes for him – yet in this behaviour, a matter for real religious scruple, he was so indifferent to religion. At least respect for the lad should have called the man away from such obscene jokes. Paul did not decree the use of a hair shirt or a mean garment.[108] But he decreed chastity of the tongue in more than one place, for instance in Ephesians: 'Let no evil speech proceed from your mouth, but that which is good, to the edification of faith, that it may administer grace to the hearers,' and again in the next chapters: 'But fornication and all uncleanness or covetousness, let it not so much as be named among you, as becometh saints: or obscenity or foolish talking or scurrility which is to no purpose; but rather giving of thanks.'[109] He abominates insincerity, saying: 'Wherefore putting away lying, speak ye the truth, every man with his neighbour, for we are members one of another.'[110] How anxiously he discourages Timothy from senseless words, which he calls 'empty sounds.' How angrily he abominates men who talk of senseless and fruitless matters, whom he calls 'vain speakers.' And when he writes to Timothy, he will not tolerate idle and inquisitive widows who wander through other men's houses saying what should be kept silent;[111] he expresses loathing, when he writes to the same Timothy, for useless disputes which beget strife in the guise of scholarship, calling them by the meaningful name of 'battle of words.'[112]

Now indiscretion, abuse, and backbiting, besides being unworthy of a Christian, are often neither useful nor safe. Perhaps they contain some stimulus to pleasure, but it is dishonourable, bringing with it a great dividend of pain. You have blurted out what should have been kept quiet, then soon remorse follows, and unending anxiety in case the secret which you entrusted to another's ears when you were carried away by the intoxication of chattering cannot be recalled, and men will in turn blurt it out to another, until the secret seeps through to those whom it is most unsafe to have alienated. Just so, the short-lived pleasure of slander is repaid with great and unending pain as, like the proverb, 'when you have said what you choose, you will be forced to hear what you don't choose to'[113] and, as Hesiod wrote, 'when you have said evil things, you will hear worse of yourself.'[114] So let the man who is ready to attack another examine himself to see whether he is free of every charge. Now it will be most disgraceful if the false accuser is found to be guilty of the same charge that he has laid against another man, as if in an exchange of abuse a one-eyed man called another 'One-Eye.' But it will be even more disgraceful if the man who has accused another of common theft has himself committed a sacrilege, or if a man polluted by incest contrives an accusation against another involving a mere whore. Surely this is to see the mote in your brother's eye while you bear a beam in your own eye.[115] Surely we are bound to become less rash in talking ill of others if once the knapsacks are turned around, and the one on our back is brought forward on to our breast.[116] In this way the fear of evil will be able to control the man whom consideration for the good does not restrain from slander, and awareness of one's own risk will drive off the itching of the tongue, as nail drives out nail.[117]

It will also be useful to go over in one's mind the instances of so many men whose lack of control over their tongues cost them dearly, especially if any disadvantages have arisen to ourselves from this. So first let everyone say to himself, 'This one slip of the tongue caused me such a disaster – I will not risk stumbling again over the same stone.' It is also helpful if when each man demands an account of the past day from himself, he brings into the reckoning his offences in words no less carefully than offences in deed. If he discovers that he has let anything slip out that it would have been better to keep to himself, he should beat himself with the Homeric lash: 'What word escaped the barrier of your teeth?'[118] By this discipline we will easily develop a kind of thrift and sobriety in speaking and a caution blended with good judgment. The wise preacher Ecclesiastes also suggests another palliative so that we would not be easily moved by the abuse of other men, that when we are assailed by abuse, we should re-examine how we ourselves have quite often abused others. This will ensure that we bear more moderately the insult inflicted on us, and if we expect to be forgiven ourselves it will be only fair to forgive others. These are the words of Ecclesiastes: 'But do not apply thy heart to all words that the impious speak, lest perhaps thou hear thy servant reviling thee. For thy conscience knoweth that thou hast often spoken evil of others.'[119] We must deliberately ignore some men's abuses, so that we hear without hearing. Otherwise, if we hunt out with our ears whatever each man is saying about us, we will often be distressed by the conversation of our servants.

I have described how we should cure other men's rudeness of speech and ourselves be on guard against the affliction, or how we must set right the ailment once it is contracted. Now the course of my argument urges me to indicate briefly how we can be least hurt by the venom or indiscretion of other men's tongues. In this respect there is no better cure than this. Each man should direct his whole life so well that the abuser's tongue has no just and proper charge to aim against him. Admittedly there is also false accusation, which does not hesitate to assail the innocent, but it can scarcely ever create an upset over nothing; either it exaggerates what was minimal, or it distorts what was straightforward in itself but appeared in some way wicked. The spider turns whatever it sucks up into poison, but it does not crawl on every kind of plant. For it does not touch wormwood, and there are some woods that it always avoids. No false accusation was ever made against Aristides, because his purity of life was so great.[120] So if any evil gossip arises against an innocent man, it quickly withers, since it has no root to give it nourishment, and having been born from nothing, it melts away to nothing; sometimes it is even transformed to increase the glory of the man wrongly suspected. The apostle Paul, well aware of the evil intent of false informers, warns us to keep far not only from all evil, but even from all appearance of evil. He admits that an idol and an offering to idols are without religious significance, yet in view of men's impious suspicions he bids us abstain from the meat offered to idols if anyone among those at table warns us that it is sacrificial meat.[121] He admits it is lawful for an altar-server to live on sacrificial meat, and yet he did not use this privilege among the Corinthians, because it was not in the interest of the gospel. Julius Caesar repudiated his wife Pompeia because there was gossip that she had been seduced by Clodius. Afterwards, when Clodius was prosecuted for incest, and Caesar was summoned and told to give his evidence, he denied that he had suspected any such thing in his wife's case. Then when the accuser had added the question, 'So why did you repudiate her?' he said, 'Because the wife of Caesar should be free of even malicious gossip and false charges.'[122] Caesar spoke impressively, but he would have earned more praise if he had maintained in his own life what he demanded from his wife.

We, however, must manfully maintain what he did not: like Paul, enduring all things[123] sooner than give any offence to the gospel, that is, the profession of Christianity. Paul required a bishop to be innocent of any charge, so strongly indeed that he thought a man unworthy of that office, unless he were approved even by evidence of those outside the church.[124] For that is what he calls those who have not yet embraced the profession of the gospel. And we have no reason to fear false accusation if we offer to Christ a sound conscience, as the apostle Peter explains admirably in his first letter: 'And who is he that can hurt you, if you be zealous of good? But if also you suffer anything for justice's sake, blessed are ye. And be not afraid of their fear; and be not troubled. But sanctify the Lord Christ in your hearts, being ready always to satisfy everyone that asketh you a reason of that hope which is in you. But with modesty and fear, having a good conscience; that, whereas they speak evil of you, they may be ashamed who falsely accuse your good conversation in Christ. For it is better doing well (if such be the will of God) than doing ill.'[125]

But since it is exceedingly difficult to ensure a life so free from guilt on all sides that a false accuser will find nothing either to backbite or distort, we must discover how we may come to suffer as little harm as possible from a slanderous tongue. First, it is helpful if when we are clear in our own conscience we are not distressed by insults, and do not retaliate against abuse by returning it but either fall silent or satisfy the accuser with calm speech. In this way the quarrel will settle down if no one provokes by retaliation. Otherwise the alternating sequence of insults will always increase and become worse until it finally turns to open fury. And no humble Christian, even if he is utterly free of guilt, should resent experiencing what the Lord of all suffered for us: when he was assailed with insults, he did not reply with insults; when he suffered though innocent, he did not threaten, but surrendered the vengeance entirely to his Father, who judges justly. Indeed it is a mark of exceptional love that he prayed for his crucifiers, and those who jeered at him and reviled him. Stephen was the first of all to renew this example,[126] and then the great Paul after him. He says: 'We are reviled and we bless, we are persecuted and we suffer it. We are blasphemed and we entreat.'[127] He taught what he performed, and performed what he taught. He says: 'Bless them that persecute you; bless, and curse not.'[128] He goes on: 'If it be possible, as much as is in you, have peace with all men. Revenge not yourselves, my dearly beloved, but give place unto wrath.'[129] And let us not be influenced by that line of Ovid: 'The unfair penalty must claim our grief.'[130] No, rather 'the penalty deserved must claim our grief.' When Phocion, the noblest man among the Athenians, was about to drink the poison, and his wife, weeping like a woman, said, 'Dear husband, and you die innocent!' he said, 'What, woman, would you prefer me to die guilty?' And when he was asked what death-bed instructions he gave to his sons, he said that they should not be moved by memory of this deed to any hostile act against the Athenian people.[131] Again, when Aristides was going into exile, condemned by the ostracism, and his friends asked what return he wished on the ungrateful Athenian people for expelling a most upright man who had served the state well, he said, 'I wish them such unending good fortune that they never again think of Aristides.'[132] When Socrates was destroyed by a false charge, it is said that he never uttered any savage curse on Anytus and Meletus, but joking, after his fashion, he threw on to the ground the sediment in the cup after he had drunk the poison, and said he offered this toast to Anytus and Meletus.[133] Once when he was struck by some fellow, and a man expressed amazement that he endured the insult in silence, he said, 'What can I do?' The other replied, 'Drag him to court.' At this Socrates laughed. 'What use is that? If a donkey kicked me, should I call him to court?'[134]

Some men make abuse seem worse to themselves, interpreting everything in the worst way. How much more sensible it would be to belittle the insult: 'He spoke in the immediate heat of excitement,' 'He was under the influence of drink, not speaking from conviction,' 'He was provoked to this by others,' 'He did not know the facts,' 'He was not attacking me, but the man he thought I was.' There are so many examples of pagans who endured the abuse of men with the greatest restraint, yet we, who call ourselves Christians, return such blasphemies and brutalities in reply to a minor insult, even a mere phrase which lacked respect! Cleomenes king of Sparta thought it enough to punish with a witticism an abusive fellow who constantly savaged him with insults in front of everyone. 'Do you abuse everyone so,' he said, 'just to make sure we get no turn to talk about your ill nature?'[135] Orontes once spoke rather harshly and arrogantly to King Demaratus. When he had left, one of the king's friends said, 'Orontes should not have treated you so rudely.' 'Oh no,' said the king, 'he did me no injury.'[136] Indeed it is men who speak with flattery to win our good will who harm us, not those who speak harshly out of hostility. Leotychidas, the son of Ariston, showed the same control. When someone reported to him that Demaratus' sons were talking indecently about him, he said contemptuously, 'That doesn't surprise me, by the gods; none of them could ever speak decently.'[137] He was a sensible man and attributed the insult against himself to their weakness of character. For no one is angry with a pig for grunting, or a dog for barking, or a goose for raising a din, or a camel for rumbling. A similar situation arose with Lysander: when some man was raving with abuse against him, he took no offence, and said, 'Come on, stranger, attack me often and hard, in case you leave anything out, if this helps you to relieve your mind of the evil humours that seem to fill it.'[138] It is as much a mark of self-control not to be upset by abuse as it is not to be excited by praise. Pleistarchus, the son of Leonidas, treated it as a novelty when he was praised by an abusive fellow: 'I'm quite surprised,' he said, 'unless someone persuaded him that I was dead; he certainly couldn't bring him to praise any man living.'[139] Some writers report that Pericles had an arrogant nature, yet he showed control beyond his nature when he employed caution in deliberation. An ignorant man with an unruly tongue was raving against him with insulting remarks, but Pericles did not say a word, and without reacting went into the Portico; towards evening he left it to go back home. The abusive fellow followed him on his way, becoming more and more enraged, because he was being ignored. At length, when they reached the door, and it was night, Pericles ordered one of the slaves to take a torch and escort the man home.[140] If it is right to avenge abuse, this is the most splendid form of revenge.

Pericles' action was more courteous, but Plato showed no less lofty a spirit when Dionysius was about to send him away. He had not always treated him decently, and so he is supposed to have said, 'Plato, when you go back to your friends and companions in scholarship, you will tell them a lot of things to my discredit.' Plato, smiling, said, 'No, your Majesty, my friends cannot possibly take enough leisure from their studies to have time to think of you.'[141] There was a famous remark of Albert, king of Poland – brother of the monarch who now governs that kingdom with God's blessing and by his recent triumph over the Turks has greatly added to its wealth and stability. It was a proof of his truly royal and lofty spirit that when he was informed of a man who abused him in front of everyone, he was moved to no anger, but said 'I would rather one man abuse me before everyone, than everyone should abuse me before him.' And the reply of Antisthenes the Cynic reflects the same magnanimity. Men told him that Plato was speaking insultingly of him, and he replied, 'It is the fate of a ruler to be badly spoken of for treating men well.'[142] Plutarch transfers this remark to Alexander the Great,[143] for nothing is so like a supreme monarch as a Cynic philosopher. Volumnius and Sacculio, a mime and a straight actor, did not even refrain from abusing the commander Brutus when they were prisoners in his camp. But although Brutus was frequently disturbed with requests to control their wanton tongues, he took no notice. At length, when they would not stop abusing him and Casca was pressing him earnestly for action, he allowed his friends to take what measures they thought right against them.[144]

This one occasion offers us a double lesson: first that the reward of an unbridled tongue is disaster, and second that high-minded men should disregard the abuse of those who speak ill of them not from conviction but from addiction. And we should not bear them with less patience than we show in bearing with those who abuse us in fever or a fit of insanity. Perhaps it would not have been appropriate here to mention the Lindian sacrifice, either because the story is mere legend, or because the event, if it really occurred, shows more the savagery of a soldier and barbarian than the magnanimity of a noble spirit. When Hercules was starving and came upon a Lindian peasant ploughing with a yoke of oxen, he asked him to give him one ox to appease his hunger. For this stout man was not hungry for onions or pulse or eggs, but for whole oxen. When the countryman declined on the grounds that all his income and his household depended on this pair of oxen, Hercules, rightly angry, took both oxen from him and slew and ate them. Meantime the old countryman was shouting a lot of insults at Hercules, since he could do nothing else; but he was so indifferent to them that he said he had never enjoyed abuse so much, since the countryman was acting as a jester for him.[145] If you compare this example to those I mentioned earlier, it is certainly barbaric and only fit for a soldier, but if you compare it with the outrages our soldiers commit daily among the peasants, it may seem a piece of extraordinary courtesy, for soldiers now are not content to appease their howling hunger with food but devour all the finest things they can find anywhere, and destroy or burn what they can neither eat nor take away, to make sure it can be no use to anyone. Meanwhile the poor peasants not only cannot retaliate for their distress with insults, but they suffer outrages in the raping of their wives and daughters and are forced to act as suppliants and offer thanks because the soldiers have been willing to let them escape with their lives. We may call the action of Hercules (a man who had served mankind well, as is recorded) brutal and barbaric, although he was driven by hunger, but we must first show how it can seem right for Christian soldiers to behave like this on their way to war or returning from it when they are hired, or sometimes not yet hired. They even commit such offences when they are not goaded by hunger but merely provoked by lack of discipline to commit such offences, and not even against enemies but against their own side. Yet when these men return home they are treated as respectable, and any past misdemeanours are blamed on the war, though in all other cases the laws are savage in their punishments against brigands, thieves, arsonists, and raiders.

But let us return to our theme, that is, how we can continue to suffer the least harm from other men's abuse. It is wiser, however, to turn even the weaknesses of slanderers to our own advantage. They remind us of what should be put right, they show us what failings we must beware of, and in general they shatter our lethargy and indifference. King Philip of Macedon was bombarded by the leading Athenian politicians with a mass of abuse. He said he was most grateful to them, because through them he was being improved from day to day in both his speech and his actions, while, as he put it, 'I strive to show up their folly and error by my words and deeds.'[146] When his friends urged him to banish an abusive man, he said, 'No, I shan't,' and to answer their surprise at his decision, 'or else he will travel around and speak badly of me to a larger audience.'[147] When Smicythus informed him that Nicanor constantly spoke badly of him and his friends were urging him to summon the fellow and punish him, he said, 'No, Nicanor is not the worst of the Macedonians. So we must consider whether we have done him any wrong.' So since he noticed that Nicanor was suffering from poverty, he ordered a bounty to be given to him immediately, as if he had forgotten his obligation in overlooking a hard-working man. After this when Smicythus reported that Nicanor was now a different man, and talking about Philip everywhere in complimentary language, he said, 'There now: you see, it depends on us whether men speak of us ill or well.'[148] Someone once reported to Telecrus, a leading man in Sparta, that his father was abusing him. He replied, 'He would never have said such things without good reason.' This man's brother complained that although he was born of the same parents, he was not equally respected by his fellow citizens. His answer was 'That is because you do not know how to accept injustices as calmly as I do.'[149]

We read that this kind of self-control was shown by Tiberius Caesar to an exceptional degree. When it was reported to him what a great number of insults the common people were hurling at him, he refused to seek revenge, but answered that in a free state both the mind and the tongue should be free. Again, when the senate voted that it should set up a commission to judge these matters so that men's wanton abuse should be checked, he answered that he was too busy to have time for attention to such business, for if he once adopted procedures to deal with such things, there would never be any leisure to handle other business.[150] When a certain Greek growing hot in conversation told the emperor Claudius, 'You are both a fool and an old fool,' Claudius pretended not to notice the insult.[151] Vespasian had a similar reputation for leniency. I will repeat one or two instances. A certain Cynic who had been shouting rude abuse against him subsequently happened to meet him, and did not bother either to get up or to greet the emperor, but continued to utter some bark of protest. Vespasian was content to call him a dog. When Salvius was pleading for a rich defendant, he dared to say, 'What difference does it make to Caesar if Hipparchus (for this was the defendant's name) has a hundred million sesterces?' This remark was reported to the emperor, since it really attacked him by a disguised libel, as if the emperor were making trouble for Hipparchus with a false allegation so that the man's wealth would be added to his personal treasury on his condemnation. Now Vespasian knew very well the advocate's motive for saying this, but he still praised him, converting into a proof of his own integrity what the man had uttered to create ill will against him.[152] A pagan who knew nothing of Christ and had not read the gospel, a man with the power to take revenge if he chose, behaved like this. Shall we after professing the philosophy of Christ scarcely bring ourselves to tolerate a friendly and gentle reminder, even distorting what has been said in an open and friendly manner? There was a lawsuit between a senator and a man from the class of knights about a dispute. Then the emperor declared that it was wrong to speak ill of a senator, but to do so in return for ill-speaking was lawful and within a citizen's rights.[153] By this verdict he relieved the man from the lower class, and discouraged the more powerful from relying on their authority and influence and provoking a lesser man with insults, unless they were willing to hear the same insults in return. But our Lord Jesus Christ does not even grant us the right to speak ill in return. When some fellow splashed Archelaus with water and his friends urged him to seek revenge, he said, 'It was not me he splashed, but the man he took me for.'[154] But when some general remark is made in order to warn us, we take it up as a personal insult. Human reasoning has led some philosophers, and human sense has persuaded many princes, but neither the teaching of heaven nor so many examples given by Christ, the source of our faith, lead us to this point of enlightenment. It will help us too, when a crazy slanderous tongue raves against us though we are innocent, if we talk to ourselves like this: Supposing God wanted me to be punished through this fellow for the flattering praises I so dangerously swallowed, and the glory I eagerly drank in, when I should have spurned it? So let us say like David: 'Let him curse, in case the Lord may be appeased and pity me.'[155] It would be too long to handle the topic of when and how one should answer such abusive fellows. We read that he who neglects his repute is cruel, and 'Reply to the fool according to his foolishness.'[156] And our Lord was silent in answer to certain abuses, while he replied carefully to other instances. He heard the name 'Samaritan' and pretended not to; he heard them say, 'Thou hast power over devils' and he scrupulously refuted the false charge.[157] There are sources of shame which it is not in our power to put right, such as being born among the Scythians or of a shameful family or poor; these things are better eased by silence, except that we may derive this advantage from the fault of an abusive man, that when we are reminded by his abuse, we wipe away the stain of fortune with good deeds and the distinction of our good qualities. But if it is a vice that we are reproached with, and one incurred by our own fault, let us turn the ill will of this enemy into the service of a friend. We assume it is true that the reproaches of an enemy have a sharper spur to the correction of our life than the modest reminder of a friend. But if the accusation is false, we will be well advised to look around and make sure that we never gave him scope for a false charge. Soon we will prune away the features from which we realize this evil has come into being, and we will be more cautious in other matters. Finally, a man gives an adequate reply when he shows by his words and deeds before all men that the insult does not fit him. The result is that the shame rebounds on the slanderer. And anyone who takes all precautions to deserve no abusive comment is surely taking care of his reputation.

There is however a time and place that demands speech, when our own discredit is bound up with danger to many people. If Christ had endured in silence the insult that he was casting out devils with the help of Beelzebub,[158] the salvation of all men would have been at risk. Paul the apostle also is vigorous in protecting his own authority against false apostles, because it affected the interests of all men. A bishop falsely slandered with the shame of a loathsome charge should not keep quiet, in case his people should take the example for adoption or despise the bishop's doctrinal faith. But there is a difference between warding off a charge and making countercharges oneself. There is a time when it is fitting to answer the fool according to his folly, lest he imagine himself to be wise. And there is a time to avoid answering according to his folly, 'lest thou be máde like him.'[159] When the Pharisees tried to trap him, the Lord replied, 'The baptism of John, whence was it? From heaven or from men?'[160] and they were caught by their own cunning. He gave a similar reply about the paying of tribute to Caesar,[161] and healing a man on the Sabbath.[162] He did not give answer to fools according to their folly when he was called 'son of a carpenter,' and 'drinker of wine.'[163] Paul answered that fool the magician Elymas according to his folly: 'O full of all guile and of all deceit, child of the devil, enemy of all justice, thou ceasest not to pervert the right ways of the Lord. And now behold, the hand of the Lord is upon thee; and thou shalt be blind, not seeing the sun for a time.'[164] Peter too answered Ananias according to his folly.[165] That happened rarely among the apostles, for they were able to say, 'Or have ye agreed together to tempt the spirit of the Lord dwelling within me?'[166] But to us miserable men silence is more fitting, or a short and restrained answer, unless circumstances force us to another choice.

We have shown how we should heal the disease of another's tongue and demonstrated how we may either escape or put an end to our own affliction; we have pointed to an antidote against the venom of an evil tongue attacking us; what is left but to exhort all Christians to the pursuit of a Christian tongue? Amongst the signs that would be associated with those who believe in Christ, this is mentioned by name: 'They shall speak with new tongues,'[167] and what we said above is added: 'And they shall take up serpents.'[168]

[Christian use of the tongue]

So far I have spoken to the general crowd of readers, but now let pagans keep far off – I speak as a Christian calling Christians. If we are what we call ourselves, we acknowledge the promises of our leader. When he was about to ascend to heaven, he strengthened the spirits of his followers with these last words: 'He that believeth and is baptized, shall be saved, and these signs shall follow them that believe: in my name they shall cast out devils, they shall speak with new tongues. They shall take up serpents, and if they shall drink any deadly thing, it shall not hurt them. They shall lay their hands upon the sick, and they shall recover.'[1] And this power was transferred to those first heralds of the gospel, so that what was visible remained for a

time, but what was spiritual remained for ever in them all. The gentiles too
had their baptisms by which they believed themselves purified, and their
professions; they killed and were killed for their shrines and altars and
hearths. They also had their special initiations, and each observed carefully
the rituals and procedure of his own cult. Those initiated to Bacchus knew
their own mysteries, and those initiated to Ceres or Cybele knew the secrets
of their own cult. They had their own kind of inspiration, their own
exorcisms, and their new tongues which they had never learned before,
which happens beyond all doubt to those in mad frenzy, and which doctors
think arises from the onslaught of illness without any miracles. They had
Marsian charmers against snakes, and they had the Psylli, who not only
handled venom but even sucked venom from others without harm to
themselves – their birth gave them this ability.[2] They had incantations and
utterances, they had temples of Apollo and Aesculapius, and they had rings
for cures against diseases. All these things should be most perfect in us
unless either the Lord deceived us or we are boasting of a false title. Now if I
asked whether you believed in the gospel, there is none of you who would
not instantly reply, 'I believe,' and if I asked whether he were baptized he
would say, 'Of course.' Now I also hear a recurring profession, and, as I see
it, above and beyond the common profession, that many men are specially
initiated not to Bacchus or Ceres or Osiris or Isis but to highly respectable
saints like Dominic, Francis, Benedict, Bernard, Augustine, Bruno, and
Bridget.[3] Yet at the same time the profession of Christ is common to all, and
if nothing were added to it, it would be sufficient to require the signs. So let
us require them in turn from ourselves. Where are the signs of our faith?
Whoever truly believes and is baptized is born from heaven, not as a
Marsian or a Psyllian, but as a man from heaven. But where is our power to
remove venom? The disciples removed poisons from the gentiles, but we
ourselves mix poison for both gentiles and Christians. We wage war, we kill,
with both daggers and poisons. Is this not like unleashing serpents?
Everything is full of venom and poisonous creatures, but where are the
Psylli of the gospel, who drive away serpents with the incantations of a
learned tongue, or suck the poison from men's inner beings with the
application of brotherly consolation and admonition? Everything everywhere is full of mad frenzy – unless perhaps we think those who are
inflamed with envy, hatred, anger, ambition, and avarice, who shatter the
world with demented upheavals and throw everything into confusion with
fire, plunder, and slaughter, are still not driven by the spirit of Satan – but
where are the exorcists of the gospel? I see those who are succeeding to the
place of the apostles, but where are those who in the name of Jesus strike
down devils? Has the strength of the Holy Spirit died out? Has the vigour of

the almighty name perished? Is the power of faith weakened? Then how is it that impious spirits are so powerful and unpunished? How great is the power of afflictions over a Christian people! How great is the number of those succumbing to deadly sicknesses! But where are those healing hands which drive off disease by the holy touch? Where is the new tongue, to fulfil all these promises which we have named? It strikes down devils, it takes up serpents, it restores to health those it has touched. The Romans, led by false apostles into Judaism, drank in poison. Is there any kind of incantation which Paul did not apply then? The Galatians were sick, for among them too false apostles had tainted Paul's doctrine of salvation with a blending of poisons. What did that miraculous champion 'the Psyllian' not do to draw the deadly virus out of their souls? Now he probes gently, now he scolds and reproaches, now he teaches and convinces. 'I wish I were only among you and could change my voice, since I am confounded in you,' he says.[4] Men who use the magic arts usually need to touch the place where the pain is. So Paul, like a wise magician, wants to be there to change his voice, obviously to suit the range of people and the affliction. A letter could not do this. But with what concern he handles the ulcers of the Corinthians, so as to heal them, how he stoops always to the extraction of the poison, shunning no act, however humble, provided he can draw out the poison!

I have shown you one magician, one Marsian, one Psyllian. There are still men alive today, especially among the Italians, who claim Paul as their ancestor.[5] They come to the aid of those wounded by creatures or arrows with certain prayers and magic remedies. But where are Paul's real descendants, who can cure men's souls with holy incantations? We see the baptism of all men, and hear their profession of faith, yet the power of the baptism itself cannot be seen, nor can faith itself be heard; they are only inferred from signs. Nor is it idle if it is concealed, but it puts forth its power. The surest proofs lie in the tongue. So if we have really put on Christ, if we have really cast off at our baptism the old man with his deeds and put on a new one, who is created according to God,[6] how is it that there is still the old tongue in us – I mean that indiscreet chattering, headlong lying, bitter quarrelling, abusive, slanderous, reviling, immodest, forswearing, beguiling, impious, and blaspheming tongue? If we have really drunk in the spirit of Christ, or if we are truly members of Christ, since the spirit has knowledge of the voice, why is there no sound from us of the sober, sparing, modest, decent, careful, truthful, mild, peaceable, kindly, honest tongue, able to beseech, console, exhort, confess, and give thanks? We have read of various tongues in the Holy Scriptures: the tongue of a serpent and the devil, the tongue of dogs, the tongues of men and of angels, the tongues of earth and heaven, the tongue of little children, and the tongue of God. Whoever lies, forswears, cheats, or teaches impiety, or urges unjust behaviour, or sows discord among his brethren, whoever competes, quarrels, or accuses, speaks with the tongue of the devil. If we have truly renounced the devil and dedicated ourselves to Christ, why can the tongue of the serpent still be heard in us? If we are truly sons of God, why is the tongue of men still heard in us? Who is of the earth is earthy and speaks of the earth. The apostles were still such when they said, 'Lord when shall the kingdom of Israel come?'[7] But now they are made heavenly, and now the heavens tell the glory of God.[8] The psalmist mentions the tongue of the dog.[9] Those were dogs who cried out: 'Away, away; crucify him, crucify him.'[10] Those were dogs who barked at him as he hung from the cross: 'Vah, he who destroyest the temple of God.'[11] Those were dogs who cried out: 'There is no hope of salvation, except ye be circumcised according to the law of Moses.'[12] Yet there are also the good dogs who keep watch before the house of the Lord, who have a healing tongue, and lick the ulcers of the poor man Lazarus.[13] And there are dogs who are guardians of the flock, who are silent in the face of wolves, but display their voice and teeth against the sheep. These are most harmful dogs, who do not allow the voice of the gospel to be heard.

The Jews are reproached because they had an uncircumcised heart;[14] if only there were not men among the Christian who had an uncircumcised tongue! The man who talks of nothing except building and farming and putting children out to hire speaks with the tongue of men, and reveals himself to be thus far nothing except a man. But he who speaks among those who are perfected, uttering wisdom concealed in a mystery, this man perhaps speaks with the tongues of angels. For this is how Paul writes to the Corinthians: 'If I speak with the tongues of men and of angels,'[15] yet he too when he was utterly misled in adhering to Judaism and was fighting for the ancestral law, refusing to acknowledge that Christ put an end to this law, spoke with the tongue of a little child: 'When I was a child, I spoke as a child, I thought as a child.'[16] Admittedly there is also a different kind of child from those who are children in ill will; these are complete adults in perception, and God has completed the achievement of his glory out of their mouth. And there is also the tongue of God. For so you may read in the prophets: The mouth of the Lord has spoken.[17] And in Job we read: 'And I wish that God would speak with thee, and would open his lips to thee, that he might show thee the secrets of wisdom.'[18] Before this tongue every tongue of men and of angels falls silent. For that which is foolish in relation to God is wiser than men. This was the tongue, I believe, which Paul heard when he was swept up into a third heaven,[19] but the human tongue could not utter its secret nature. God has diluted, however, the sublimity of the heavenly tongue, and has spoken in a more modest form to us through his Son Jesus

Christ, so that by listening to him and imitating him we may reach eternal salvation. Christian, I beg you, mark the nature of Christ's tongue, he who is your Lord. Did he tell silly tales? Did he boast of his own merits? Did he inform on any man? Did he kill any man? Did he deceive any man? His disciples heard this tongue and they said: 'Lord to whom shall we go? Thou hast the words of eternal life.'[20] He preached the glory of the Lord, he taught those who were gone astray, he rebuked those deserting, he urged on those hanging back, he consoled the afflicted, he gave his blessing to children, he healed the sick, he put impious devils to rout, he purified lepers, he stilled tempests, he awakened the dead, he gave forgiveness of sins, he prayed for the impious that they might be restored to their senses, he gave thanks to the Father. He did not keep his tongue to return insults, yet he was eloquent to intercede with his Father for those who brought about his death.

Why do we not imitate this tongue with all our might? This is a modest tongue, a healing tongue, mild and reconciling all things that are in heaven and earth. But no one can imitate the tongue of Christ unless he has drunk deeply of Christ's spirit. For the apostles did not begin to speak with new tongues until they had received the spirit from heaven. When the disciples said, 'Lord dost thou wish us to bid fire come from heaven and destroy this city?'[21] they spoke with the tongues of men. Again, when the apostles disputed amongst themselves who would be the greater in the kingdom of heaven,[22] they were speaking with a human tongue. When they asked the Lord as he was ascending to heaven, 'Lord wilt thou be present at this time, and when wilt thou restore the kingdom to Israel?'[23] they still were speaking with a human tongue. But when they had received the tongues of fire, what did they speak of? Not of archbishoprics, or high offices, or estates, or wives, or buildings. Of what then? They spoke the wondrous deeds of the Lord, and they began to speak with divers tongues, but with one accord, for they had one heart and one spirit, because one spirit had filled them all.[24]

But today we see the schools of the philosophers disputing with so many opinions, and all Christians battling to the death with so many conflicting dogmas. Are we not repeating the construction of the tower of Babel? What harmony can exist among those carried away by vanity, when no man yields to another? Paul knew this well when he wrote to the Philippians: 'If there be therefore any consolation in Christ, if any comfort of charity, if any society of the spirit, if any bowels of commiseration, fulfil ye my joy, that you be of one mind, having the same charity, being of one accord, agreeing in sentiment. Let nothing be done through contention neither by vainglory.'[25] What then is the cause of such a confusion of tongues and minds among us, if it is not arrogance? Why do we not adhere to one stock, since we are tendrils of the same vine, and are one with ourselves, just as we are joined to Christ? Why do we not listen to Christ speaking to us on the lips of Paul: 'God is faithful; by whom you are called unto the fellowship of his Son Jesus Christ our Lord. Now I beseech you, brethren, by the name of our Lord Jesus Christ, that you all speak the same thing and that there be no schism among you; but that you be perfect in the same mind and in the same judgment.'[26] If one limb is torn from another, where is the body? If the body is severed from the head, where is the life of the body? Clearly this is what Paul means when he says we are called into the community of the Son of God, because we have been grafted by faith on to his body, that is, the church, but the name, *ecclesia*, church, means an assembly, not a separation of parts.[27] So since we cannot attach ourselves to the head unless we agree amongst ourselves and are bound together by mutual charity, he says for this reason, 'Be ye perfect,' that is, a whole body, neither mutilated nor shattered, but solid and strengthened in Christ, by the bond of his spirit.

Paul is distressed because these voices of discord were heard among the Corinthians: 'I am indeed of Paul, and I of Apollo, and I of Cephas, and I of Christ.'[28] What would he say if he were to hear the confused tongues of men in this century: 'I am a Transalpine[29] theologian,' 'I a Cisalpine theologian,' 'I am a Scotist,' 'I am a Thomist,' 'I am a follower of Ockham,' 'I am a realist theologian,' 'I, a nominalist,' 'I belong to the Paris school,' 'I belong to the Cologne school,' 'I am a Lutheran,' 'I am a follower of Karlstadt,' 'I am a theologian of the gospel,' 'I of the pope.' I am ashamed to repeat the other claims. 'O house, how thou art scattered,' 'O city, how thou art divided in thyself.' 'O body, where now is that blessed unity, outside which whoever dwells, dwells not in Christ?'[30] Why do we not cease to pile up this tower of Babel, this tower of pride and strife, and begin to restore Jerusalem and the fallen temple of the Lord? From where shall some Ezra arise for us to reduce this confusion of tongues to the Jewish tongue, that is, a tongue declaring the truth of the gospel? For Ezra had seen the Jews taking in wedlock women of the tribe of Azotus, and of Ammon and of Moab, and their children, being impure, since they were of mixed descent, spoke in a mixed tongue, half in Hebrew and half in the tongue of Azotus.[31] If the Christian people is really one, why does it not know its own tongue; why does it pollute the tongue of the gospel with a foreign tongue? It is the wives who are to blame, the foreign-born wives whom the church does not know. We have married as many barbaric wives as the number of sects to which we have bound ourselves. These overthrew even Solomon,[32] so let no man be confident who has dealings with foreigners.

So what remedy is there to help us change our tongue? Let us return to the opening of the gospel. It says: 'Do penance, for the kingdom of heaven is at hand.'[33] Let each man acknowledge his own sins, let him turn his life around for the better, and the Lord will be merciful to us, though his anger rightly rages against us. From the sole of the foot to the crown of our head there is no health in us. The priest is like his people, and magistrates and officials are like the princes. All of them seek what is their own, not what belongs to Christ Jesus. The pupils are like their teacher, the children are like their father, and the household is like its head. We all attack each other's lives and teachings, while no one takes pains to correct his own offences. In the case of other men, we accuse even what is right, but in ourselves we forgive each and every thing.

Therefore let the beginning of this renewal of harmony proceed from a tongue that confesses all. Let us cease to be the children of the old Adam and Eve, who laid the blame for their sins he upon his wife and she upon the serpent. Let us cease to be the children of Cain, who concealed his murder of kin. Let us now find no pleasure in the example of Ananias and Sapphira, so that we lie to the Holy Spirit;[34] instead let us confess to God what does not escape his knowledge, even if we do not confess it. Let this be the first act of all lips. Let us imitate the tongue of David, which appeased the anger of the Lord and in some way moved him to repeal his decision.[35] Let us implore the mercy of the Lord with Isaiah, saying: 'We shall roar all of us like bears, and shall lament as mournful doves. We have awaited judgment, and there was no judgment, we have awaited salvation, and it has been taken far from us. Our iniquities have been redoubled in thy presence, and our sins have answered us, because our crimes are with us, and we have come to know our own iniquities, to sin and lie against the Lord, and we have turned away so that we might not go behind the back of our Lord so as to speak false accusation, and we have conceived trespasses, and have spoken the words of falsehood from our heart,'[36] and all the rest that follows at this point. Let us take lamentation upon ourselves, as Jeremiah urges, and let us pray with him: 'O Lord, remember me.'[37] Or again let us say with Daniel: 'I beseech Thee, O Lord God, great and terrible.'[38]

None of us should be loath to implore the mercy of the Lord with the same words which the most holy prophets used to implore him. There will never be an end of warfare if we try to get the better of other men's ill will by using our own, if we add error to error, if we defend basely what was basely undertaken, and if we obstinately support what was said without due thought. Let our princes be true princes; let our bishops, priests, monks, and theologians be in truth what they are called; let the sheep of Christ be sheep in truth; Let the man who has offended with his tongue correct by speaking well the sin he committed by speaking evil, imitating the model of the blessed Job, who said: 'What can I answer, who have spoken inconsiderately? I will lay my hand upon my mouth. I have said one thing which I would gladly not have said, and another to which I shall add nothing more.'[39] One proud man demands humility from another and one proud man opposes another, one covetous man robs another, and one heretic calls another such, heretic, and there is no limit to fighting, plundering, and quarrelling. Let this tower be destroyed, and the confusion of minds and tongues will be at an end. When everything is everywhere thrown into confusion, they ask what counsel can we take? Whom should we listen to, if not Peter, the founder of our church? 'Be ye humbled therefore' he says, 'under the mighty hand of God, that he may exalt you in the time of visitation; casting all your care upon him, for he hath care of us.'[40] The man who refuses to bow himself before God is immensely proud. If the dignity of princes and bishops does not allow them to bow themselves before man, yet they should not be loath to make themselves humble in the sight of God, to whose power they are subject, whether they will or not. Only in this way will they be truly great. Let the people also obey the divine ordinances and be submissive to every creature for God's sake. In that way it will be truly free, if it is enslaved to no sin. Let us shun excess of talking, in which sin cannot be avoided, since the Lord condemns stammering even in prayer.[41] Let us love silence, learning over a long time what we may teach, being swift to hear and slow to speak. Let us not release the instrument of our tongue in superfluous talking, but remember that according to the declaration of the Lord, we shall render an account of any idle word at the day of judgment,[42] and listen to Paul as he constantly warns us, so that we avoid vain talk,[43] that is, all speech which does not pertain to the task of eternal salvation. Let us leave the fools to talk foolishly, and make it our goal that men can say of us that the mouth of the just man will ponder on wisdom, and his tongue shall speak judgment,[44] and, following the teaching of Paul, let our speech be always grace seasoned with salt, that we may know how we should answer every man.[45] Let no evil speech proceed from our mouth,[46] but let the tongue be at one with the heart. If we love truth, let lying be far from our mouth.

If, heeding Paul, we think and ponder 'whatsoever things are true, whatsoever modest, whatsoever just, whatsoever holy, whatsoever lovely, whatsover of good fame, if there be any virtue, if any praise of discipline,'[47] then our tongue also will speak of the same things. You will say, 'What reward will there be then, O apostle?' Listen earnestly and the God of peace shall be with you.[48] If our heart loves Jesus, let our conversation be about Jesus, and he will deign to be in our midst. Instead of cheap jests, let good conversation be heard, which conduces to the edification of the faith, that it may administer grace to the hearers. Let all bitterness and anger and indignation and clamour and blasphemy be put away from us, with all malice.[49] Let fornication and filth and covetousness not be named among us, but rather thanksgiving, because divine pity has set us free from these evils. Let drunkenness, mother of witless talkativeness, be far from us, but let our cheerfulness and joy be born from the Holy Spirit, so that we may be filled with it, and talk whenever we assemble, in psalms, hymns, and spiritual chants, singing and playing to the Lord in our hearts, and always thanking him on behalf of all men, in the name of our Lord Jesus Christ, God and Father.[50]

Instead of the venom of slander, let our tongue offer brotherly rebuke, instead of insults, consolation, instead of curses, prayers to God, instead of denigration, a mild and honest reproof, instead of a hotbed of conflicts, conciliatory speech, instead of the poison of ulceration, sound doctrine, instead of muttering, psalms and hymns, instead of quarrelling, spiritual chants, instead of silly tales, the speech of knowledge, instead of accusation against our neighbour, the confession of our own evils, instead of the most bitter persecution of other mens' failures, the desire to give healing. How carefully we cherish a weak member, how devotedly we offer treatment to an infected or wounded limb, how skilfully we reset a dislocated joint in place! How reluctantly, and with what objections, we resort to desperate cures, employing amputation or cautery! Finally, when every method has been tried in vain, with what grief we amputate what there is no hope of healing! Why do we not show the same charity and gentleness in healing our neighbour? How bitterly we denounce human failures! Yet at the same time, we show such indulgence, even shamelessness, in cosseting our own sores but contempt in reproving others. In contrast, we make great protestations if anyone in turn reproaches us, however mildly, for our error. It is only too true that we lack that pure charity in rebuking our brother which neither suspects nor thinks of evil, so that in our desire to hurt we even pervert what was rightly said, as we try to be clever at the expense of other men's books, and secure the glory of scholarship for ourselves from other men's repute. We have disguised the envy and hatred in which we are steeped, and the self-seeking and arrogance with which we are puffed up, under the name of zeal. So we vent our malice against other men's vices as if we did not hate them, but envy them. I admit it is the role of bishops to expose sinners, but there should be such restraint in the exposure that the man convicted realizes he is being handled by a doctor, not a butcher. This is how Paul beseeches Timothy to preach the word of the gospel: 'Be instant in season, out of season, reprove, entreat, rebuke.[51] But he gives these recommendations to a man who was already filling the role of an unofficial bishop, against whom no accusation could be laid. And he did not say simply

'reprove ... rebuke,' but he set in the first place 'preach the word.' The first
duty is to teach; then between 'reprove' and 'rebuke' he put down 'entreat,'
and not content with this, he added 'in all patience and doctrine.' But when
our neighbour is led astray we only coerce him and do not condescend to
teach him. When shall we recall our brother from error, if he sees he is
dealing with enemies? Blind with hatred we make an impetuous judgment,
and we do not at the same time correct our own obvious failures in case there
should be any diminution of our authority. Yet somehow it is by this kind of
behaviour that the authority of theologians is most weakened. We bark
abuse at all strangers, condemning whatever we do not understand. So let
us pray the Lord to pour his spirit over the bishops and teachers of the
church, and give them a learned tongue, such as Isaiah congratulates
himself upon: 'The Lord hath given me a learned tongue, that I should know
how to uphold by word him that is weary.'[52] Clearly this is the tongue of a
good shepherd, which knows how to bind up what is broken, to make firm
what is frail, a tongue that is not wont to shout, but powerful, not quenching
smoking hemp, nor shattering a broken reed,[53] just as the words of Jeremiah
bestow upon those men a mouth that will deign to cleanse by its contact and
to order by its words, and say to each one of them: 'Behold I have given my
words in thy mouth. Lo I have set thee this day over the nations, and over
kingdoms, to root up, and to pull down, and to waste, and to destroy, and
to build, and to plant.'[54]

What a mass of evil equipment a man bears with him who bears an evil
tongue, a sword dipped in venom, a dagger, an arrow, an incantation, an
evil eye, aconite and whatever other kind of deadly poison there is
anywhere. But when a priest has a tongue worthy of himself, what tools he
bears in this one member. He has a remedy against all the diseases of the
mind, an instant antidote against all poisons, a sword of the spirit, with
which to cut down all harmful things. This is what Isaiah says: 'And he hath
made my mouth like a sharp sword.'[55] He has an arrow with which to
wound and sting men into remorse and repentance for their former life. And
this also follows in Isaiah: 'and hath made me as a chosen arrow.'[56] He has a
trumpet with which to arouse those deeply sleeping into wakefulness and
sobriety, to arouse the dead to life. He has a rod and sceptre with which to
command kings and kingdoms, he has a hoe, with which to pluck out
harmful passions and impious beliefs from the breasts of men; he has a
crowbar with which to undermine every foundation rearing up against the
church of God, he has a harrow with which to destroy root and branch and
scatter every young crop which has not come from God, he has a
ploughshare with which to prepare the cleansed fallow for the sowing of the

gospel, he has a mason's trowel, with which to rebuild what is destroyed, and a mattock with which to plant the tender new shoots.

Let us pray that our bishops may have a tongue as powerful and successful as this; let us pray to give our princes, magistrates, and people a heart that can be taught and molded, a heart of flesh, with ears and wings, yet not without tongue – with ears so that the people will gladly heed their shepherds calling them to a better life, with wings to follow them eagerly as they advance with vigour on the way of the gospel; and they must have a tongue so that with it the ignorant folk may answer the blessing of the bishops with a loud 'Amen.'

In this way, if we all turn ourselves with honest hearts towards God, he will become well disposed and in turn drive away from us this piteous storm, and when calm weather is restored we shall all alike rejoice in the Lord. The progress of our speech has brought us to the tongue of angels,[57] which is that of priests and bishops. We will investigate the nature of this gift of God in the books on the method of preaching, which we are now beginning, with the aid of the same Almighty God, to whom is due all glory for ever and ever.

Notes

Works cited frequently in this volume are referred to in the notes in abbreviated form only. A list of the abbreviations and full bibliographical information are given in Works Frequently Cited (pages 520–1). In these volumes references to the correspondence are to the English translation of the letters in CWE, where these have already been published, or to the Latin edition of Allen. Since Allen's numbering of the letters has been adopted in CWE, letters are cited by epistle number and, where applicable, line number (for example Ep 66; Ep 373:5–6). In references to letters not yet published in CWE 'Allen' will be inserted before the letter and line numbers (for example, Allen Ep 1814:23).

References to the works translated in this volume refer to page numbers.

Introduction

ix

1 *Ciceronianus* CWE 28 441
2 *De conscribendis epistolis* CWE 25 27, 43

x

3 CWE 24 303:17–19; cf 679:15.

xi

4 See 31 below.

xii

5 Cf ASD IV-1 321:10–11.
6 ASD IV-1 337:599, 352:3; cf 281:562, 273:256.

xiii

7 ASD IV-1 368:767; cf Eph 5:19.
8 Ie, derivatives of the main classical branches of oratory: protreptic and forensic, then rooted in real political and judicial situations, and epideictic, an aspect of which is eulogy
9 Cf *De doctrina christiana* 5.4.

10 Reedijk no 15:18–19
11 Ep 49:109–11; CWE 23 97:20–21

xiv
12 *Paraclesis* Holborn 139:3–4
13 CWE 28 447
14 Ep 1341A:259–60
15 It is derived from Roman funeral *laudationes*. The first *laudatio* of a woman was pronounced by Julius Caesar for his aunt Julia, around 70 BC.
16 LB VIII 553D, 554A
17 LB VIII 554E, 556C

xv
18 LB I 70F, 68F, 69B
19 Erasmus' speech is of course an example of forensic oratory as practised in the schoolroom. Such exercises are known to us from Greek rhetorical writers like Libanius as well as from Seneca the Elder and Pseudo-Quintilian. Cf D. Russell *Greek Declamations* (Cambridge 1983) on the genre, and on the topic of tyrannicides, 19, 22f, 45ff, 123ff.

xvi
20 Ep 1341A:507–8, 552–3, 575 / CWE 24 694, 695, 696

xvii
21 Cf *De ratione studii* CWE 24 666:14–15, 669:1–3.
22 Cf Ep 1341A:241–4, where he expresses satisfaction that the knowledge of Greek was now so widespread that his translations were no longer in demand; cf Ep 456:255–63 and LB VI ***2v: 'I have no doubt that the time will come – and has perhaps already dawned – when these works will seem for the most part superfluous.'

xviii
23 R. Bainton *Erasmus of Christendom* (New York 1969) 32
24 Ep 753:5–6
25 Ep 999:115–17

xix
26 Ibidem lines 273–8

xx
27 Allen Ep 1572:66–9

Erasmus and the Greek Classics

xxi
1 Ep 1341A:42–3; cf Allen I 592–3 and Ep 1110:1–10. Erasmus' progress in Greek has been traced by H. Dibbelt 'Erasmus' griechische Studien' *Gymnasium*

57 (1950) Heft 1, 55–71; his career as translator and editor of classical Greek texts has been sketched by M.M. Philipps 'Erasmus and the Classics' in *Erasmus* ed T.A. Dorey (London 1970). For a synoptic view see E. Rummel *Erasmus as a Translator of the Classics* (Toronto 1985).

2 *Compendium vitae* CWE 4 404:26–30
3 On Erasmus' early education, see ibidem 404:35–54; on Winckel 405:54n; for Erasmus' judgment of Winckel see Ep 447:86–94.
4 Just how much Erasmus owed to Hegius is a matter of dispute. Erasmus himself paid tribute to his preceptor in the *Adagia* (i iv 39), acknowledging that he had learned from him the rudiments of Greek. On the other hand he repeatedly emphasized that he was self-taught and, on one occasion, declared that he 'owed very little indeed to Hegius' (*Spongia* LB x 1666A, in the context of establishing his impartiality in praising Hegius). In fact, it may be argued that Hegius' influence could not have been significant, because the year of his arrival at Deventer (1483) coincided with Erasmus' departure from the school. Moreover, Erasmus himself attested that he heard Hegius only 'on the high days when he lectured to the whole school' (*Compendium vitae* CWE 4 405:46), but it is clear that he thought these occasions memorable. We have evidence that he remained in touch with Hegius after leaving Deventer (cf Ep 28:11–20) and that he was linked with Hegius by contemporaries (Jacobus Faber dedicated his edition of Hegius' poems to Erasmus; cf Ep 174). We may therefore conclude that Hegius, though exerting little practical influence, nevertheless played the role of the Socratic midwife in fostering Erasmus' interest in the Greek language.
5 Ep 149:18–19; cf Ep 1341A:223.
6 Cf *Compendium vitae* CWE 4 405–7:55–105.

xxii

7 Ep 447:118–120, and cf 410–16.
8 Cf Ep 39:125–7, 148–9.
9 Cf Allen I 592. But in a letter written in 1489 Erasmus mentions that he headed an ode with Cornelius' name written in Greek (Ep 23:118); Greek words also occur in Ep 26 (composed in 1489).
10 Ep 66:17 (*leucophaeus* means 'grey'), Allen Ep 93:85–6; Greek also occurs in Epp 64, 83, 89, 105, 108, 113.
11 Cf Epp 67–8, 121–2.
12 Cf Ep 531:452–5.
13 Ep 118:20–3

xxiii

14 Epp 124:72 ('I have turned my entire attention to Greek'), 138:49–52
15 Ep 124:72–4
16 Cf Ep 138:46–7; cf Ep 123:25–7 and next note. On Hermonymus, see CEBR II 185–6.
17 Allen Ep 194:22 (*Graeculus*)
18 Ep 129:77–80; cf *Antibarbari* CWE 23 32:22.
19 Ep 157:46–50, and cf Ep 172:17–18; at the same time he also encouraged Jacob de Voecht in his Greek studies; cf Ep 159:54–8.

20 Cf Ep 160:5–13, addressed to Bensrott, but we know of no further developments. Cf Ep 245:37–40, addressed to Andrea Ammonio: 'I am quite delighted that you are Lucianizing, and when I get back to London ... we will pursue Greek studies together.' For Erasmus' co-operation with More see pages 74–6 and n75 below.

21 Ep 172:13–15; cf n14 above and Ep 189:15.

22 See xxxiii below.

23 Ep 203:3–4; see Erasmus' grateful acknowledgment of the help received in *Adagia* II i 1 (LB II 405 B–C).

xxiv

24 Cf Ep 225 introduction.

25 Ep 193:22–3; cf Ep 188:52–3 on Euripides: '[I was] attracted by the more than honeyed sweetness of this poet's style.'

26 Ep 131:5–6

27 Epp 129:78, 337:679

28 *De ratione studii* CWE 24 669:25–7; cf Ep 149:22–4: 'For whereas we Latins have but a few small streams, a few muddy pools, the Greeks possess crystal-clear springs and rivers that run with gold.'

29 Ep 1341A:260, and cf Allen Ep 1572:65ff; on Xenophon see Allen Ep 2273:25f; on Lucian, Ep 193:64–6 (said of the cock in *Gallus*).

30 Ep 138:52–4

xxv

31 Ep 188:5–6, to justify his translations of Euripides; see also Ep 138:52–4.

32 Cf Ep 181:36–40.

33 Ep 149:24–30

34 Ep 164:51–3

35 Ep 181:99–104

36 Ep 182:136–9, 219–222

xxvi

37 Ep 337:637–9

38 Ep 1062:68–72

39 Allen Ep 2468:77–9

40 Ep 188:26–8; this is the prefatory epistle to Euripides' *Hecuba*.

41 Ep 177:114–17; cf Cicero *De optimo genere dicendi* 14.

42 Ep 188:64–6, 71–4; cf *Ciceronianus* CWE 28 390–1.

43 Ep 188:58–63

xxvii

44 See xxx and n72 below.

45 Ep 208:24–5

46 Cf Epp 187:20–1, 428:56, Allen Ep 1479:155–6

47 LB I 553A, 549B, 551B (all from Libanius' *Legatio Menelai*). For a more detailed appreciation of his Libanius translations see Rummel *Erasmus as a Translator* 22–6.

48 ASD I-1 411:42 (from Lucian's *Icaromenippus*); LB IV 614F, 611D, 614C (from

Isocrates' *Ad Nicoclem*); cf δυσείκαστα / *coniectu difficilia*, ἀτέκμαρτα / *nullis notis deprehendi possent* (from Lucian's *Icaromenippus* ASD I-1 411:32). For the stylistic qualities of Erasmus' translations from Lucian and Isocrates see Rummel *Erasmus as Translator* (xxi n1 above) 58–69, 105–8.

49 LB I 551B (from Erasmus' Libanius translation); cf 222 below.
50 See 222 below.
51 See 223 below.

xxviii

52 See 222 below; LB I 553B; LB IV 645C–D.
53 This is a point frequently made by Erasmus in his *Annotationes*, eg LB VI 601B–C, 560E, 5F, 40E, 62D. Cf M. O'Rourke Boyle, *Erasmus on Language and Method in Theology* (Toronto 1977), especially 4–11; E. Rummel *Erasmus' 'Annotations' on the New Testament* (Toronto 1986), especially 96–7.
54 Cf Epp 208:16–20, 209:28–35.
55 Ep 198:8–9; Erasmus here denies (line 7) that convenience was a consideration, but see Ep 208:17–18, where he expressed the hope 'that scholars would take my difficulties into account and pardon me for this.' Cf also Ep 209:33–5 where similar views are expressed.
56 For examples of these characteristics see W.O. Schmitt 'Erasmus als Euripidesübersetzer' *Übersetzungsprobleme antiker Tragoedien* (Berlin 1969), especially 139–44, and J.H. Waszink 'Einige Betrachtungen über die Euripidesübersetzungen des Erasmus und ihre historische Situation' *Antike und Abendland* 17 (1971) 70–90.
57 Ep 188:77–8
58 Allen Ep 177:2 (*periculum facere, progymnasmata*); Allen I 8:35 (*iecimus transferendi aleam*)

xxix

59 The dedicatory epistle is Ep 177; for the reward see Ep 178:7–9.
60 Cf Ep 177:6–7. Erasmus' edition is the *editio princeps*, and the manuscript used by him has not been identified; see R.A.B. Mynors in his introduction to the text in ASD I-1 177.
61 Ep 177:72–3, 110–13
62 Cf Allen Ep 177 introduction.
63 Ep 1341A:121–64; the dedicatory epistles are Epp 188, 208; Ep 198 is a preface addressed to the reader.
64 See xxiii and n20 above.
65 Ep 188:22; cf Ep 1341A:122–4
66 Allen Ep 1341A:133–4
67 Cf Epp 188:46–50; Ep 1341A:124–8.

xxx

68 Epp 208:8–9, 188:33
69 Ep 208:27–31
70 Ep 209:33
71 Cf Epp 188:40, 209:11–16 and 13n, 15n.
72 See J.H. Waszink in his introduction to the text in ASD I-1 208–9.

73 Cf Ep 187 introduction.

74 Allen I 7:1ff; cf Ep 1341A:206–7.

75 Allen I 8:7f; cf Ep 1341A:236–7. For the 'contest of wits' between Erasmus and More see Ep 191:5–22; cf C.R. Thompson's preface to More's translations of Lucian in Yale CWM III xvii–xli; 72 below.

76 For the various editions and their contents see Christoper Robinson's introduction to the text in ASD I-1 370–2; for a more general account see M. Delcourt 'Erasme traducteur de Lucien' in *Hommages à Marcel Renard* Collection Latomus 101 (1969) 303–11.

xxxi

77 Ep 193:32–55

78 Cf Epp 199:9–12, 550:7–12.

79 Ep 205:40

80 Ep 261:5–6

81 Work on Plutarch is first mentioned in Ep 264:27–8; on the publication of Plutarch translations see the introductions to Epp 268, 284, 651, and Allen 1572; cf A.J. Koster's introduction to the text in ASD IV-2 103–116.

82 Allen Ep 1572:61ff; cf Ep 1341A:260–3. Erasmus voices similar complaints about the Galen text; see xxxii and n91 below.

xxxii

83 Allen Ep 1572:52–8

84 Ibidem lines 65–6

85 Allen Ep 1663:28–9: 'I thought this book would furnish you with an antidote, lest your modesty should lapse into insecurity.' Ep 272:48–50: '… a remarkable technique, making it a simple task to discriminate between a sincere, true friend and the impostor who poses as such.'

86 Erasmus' use of Plutarch's *Moralia* in the *Parabolae* is indexed in CWE 24 725–6; for Plutarch as a source of the *Apophthegmata* cf Allen Ep 2431:42–67.

87 On Erasmus' judgment of Isocrates' merits see O. Herding 'Isokrates, Erasmus und die *Institutio Principis Christiani*' in *Dauer und Wandel der Geschichte* (Münster 1966).

88 Ep 393:70–3: '… for he was a sophist, instructing some petty king, or rather tyrant, and both were pagans; I am a theologian addressing a renowned and upright prince, Christians both of us.'

89 Allen Ep 2273:25–6; on the earlier, abandoned attempt, ibidem, lines 10–13.

90 In 1500 Erasmus composed an *Encomium medicinae*; see 31 below. On Erasmus' translation of Galen see L. Elaut 'Erasme traducteur de Galien' *Bibliothèque d'Humanisme et Renaissance* 20-1 (1958) 36–44.

xxxiii

91 For this complaint see the dedicatory letter Allen Ep 1698:11–13; cf Allen Epp 1707:3, 1713:30.

92 Cf Ep 677 (the preface to *Ad Demonicum*), Allen Epp 2432 (the preface to Aristotle), 2695 (the preface to Demosthenes), 2760 (the preface to Ptolemy). The Ptolemy is an *editio princeps*, the extent of Erasmus' involvement in which is disputed; cf Allen's introduction to Ep 2760.

93 Ep 1341A:240–4

Erasmus and the Latin Classics

xxxiv

1 Ep 20. On Terence's presence among the prose authors see Reedijk 98.
2 Ep 31:96–9

xxxv

3 Eg Epp 26:63, 31:83, 44:22, 92:14, 104:45
4 Eg Epp 3:11, 17:13, 47:80–1, 49:75–6, 80:22
5 Ep 2584; see xlix below.
6 See CWE 23 xxxvi, xlv–xlvi; CWE 25 xv–xvi, xx–xxii.
7 Allen Ep 1390:103–10
8 Epp 38 (Hermans' letter to the tutor of Philip of Burgundy), 152:20–3, 40–1 (dedicatory letter to edition of 1501)
9 Ep 20:97–8; cf Ep 27:48–54. Cf Erasmus' recommendations in *De ratione studii* CWE 24 669 of the authors whom the young student should read: 'Among Latin writers, who is more valuable as a standard of language than Terence? He is pure, concise, and closest to everyday speech, and then by the very nature of the subject matter is also congenial to the young ... second place will go to Virgil, then third to Horace, fourth to Cicero, and fifth to Caesar.' He also considers additional reading from selected plays of Plautus and from Sallust. Note that he regards the *Georgics* (no doubt because of its morality of toil and suffering) as Virgil's greatest work (Ep 1334:129).
10 On Erasmus' love of Horace and adoption of his attitude to life, see Eckard Schäfer 'Erasmus und Horaz' *Antike und Abendland* 16 (1970) 54–67.
11 For Erasmus' early ambitions as a poet see Reedijk 42–52.
12 Ep 19:5–7
13 See Reedijk 143–6 and Ferguson *Opuscula* 9, who believes all the poems of the *Silva* belong to the years 1488–9.

xxxvi

14 Ep 19:24–8
15 Ep 20:63–4
16 Ep 441:373–87. Ferguson (*Opuscula* 10) notes that in the *Catalogus lucubrationum* (Allen I 6:7–8 / Ep 1341A:174–6) Erasmus deprecates this secular ambition of his youth.
17 *Antibarbari* CWE 23 44 / LB X 1705E–F / ASD I-1 69
18 Ibidem 60 / LB X 1712F / ASD I-1 83

xxxvii

19 Lorenzo Valla is a key figure in Erasmus' secular and sacred studies. His *Elegantiae*, published in 1471, are a guide to good Latin style in the form of a list of key words and idioms exemplifying their use. Erasmus made an epitome of the *Elegantiae* (ASD I-iv 206–332) and in two letters to Gerard (Epp 23, 26) praises Valla as the reviver of good Latin, defending his com-

mand of style and his personal integrity against the criticisms of Poggio. He recommends the study of Valla to form the schoolboy's Latin in *De ratione studii* (CWE 24 670) and includes a brief encomium of him in *De copia* (CWE 24 616). More important was Valla's influence on Erasmus' critical approach to the Vulgate text of the New Testament. Valla's original notes, which used Greek texts of the New Testament as a basis for correction of the Latin version, were edited from his manuscript and published by Erasmus with Bade in 1505. The preface (Ep 182, to Christopher Fisher) is a vindication of Valla's scientific approach, which was to become his own throughout the five editions of the New Testament.

20 On his list of compatriots see Reedijk 52. Erasmus takes in two generations of scholarship, but the Italians he cites – Aeneas Silvius, Filelfo, Guarino, Poggio, Gasparino – were undoubtedly better known than the local writers. See also his advocacy of Baptista Mantuanus and Campano as poets in Epp 47:86, 49:111–20, 61:152–4.
21 On the publication of this volume by Reyner Snoy in 1513 see Reedijk 90; Ferguson *Opuscula* 11.
22 Ep 47; cf Propertius *Elegies* 3.1 and Horace *Epistles* 1.19, 2.2.
23 Reedijk nos 4–7; on Erasmus' increasing mastery of verse see Reedijk 114–17.
24 Ep 51:16–17
25 Ep 141:46–9
26 Ep 126:135–48
27 Ep 138:41–65; cf Ep 139:50–5.

xxxviii
28 Epp 152, 1013
29 Ep 1390; see xliii below.
30 The *Lucubrationes* included, along with selected early poems, the *Oratio de virtute amplectenda* and the *Concio de puero Iesu* translated in this volume.
31 See xxviii–xxxii above.
32 Cf Ep 296:161–9 to Servatius Rogerus, an assessment of his own scholarly achievements to date.
33 Ie the prose philosophical works; his edition of the tragedies had already been sent for publication.

xxxix
34 Ep 292:4–5
35 Ep 421:99–100
36 Ep 298:20
37 Ep 263:2–21

xl
38 Ep 1341A:440–1. Erasmus discusses his work on the Latin authors ibidem lines 422–77.
39 He attributes the *Controversiae* to the philosopher in eg the dedicatory letter of the *Lucubrationes* Ep 325:104 and in *De copia* (CWE 24 299:3n).
40 Cf the letters from Rhenanus and Nesen, Epp 328 and 329; on the reception of

the book in England see Ep 388:193–4 (from More) and 389:50–2 (from Ammonio).
41 Cf Ep 1341A:463–6, Ep 1479:89 (to Haio Herman in 1524). Erasmus criticizes the earlier edition of Fortunatus, but when he came to prepare his second edition he used both Fortunatus' printed text and the text of Agricola, annotated in his own hand, which he had borrowed from Herman (Cf Allen Ep 2091:104–14).

xli
42 Ep 704; cf the negotiations recorded in Epp 606, 612, 633, 693.
43 Cf Ep 1341A:568–70.
44 The dedicatory letter to Frederick and George of Saxony is Ep 586; on the value of the texts see lines 52–76. For Albert of Brandenburg see CEBR I 185–7.
45 Valerius Maximus is the only *historiographus* named in *De ratione studii* (CWE 24 676:28). My comments on Erasmus' attitude to history are based on the full study of Peter Bietenholz, *History and Biography in the Works of Erasmus* (Geneva 1966).
46 LB V 369f / ASD V-3 101, discussed by Bietenholz 13–14, 24, 27

xlii
47 This is Laurentianus Mediceus 68.1. On this codex and the early editions see Goodyear *The Annals of Tacitus I–VII* (Cambridge 1972) 36. Goodyear sees the first Froben text of 1519 as little improvement on the *editio princeps* of Bérault, but praises the second Froben edition of 1533 as a considerable advance.
48 His report of Seneca's political career and death in Allen Ep 2901:523–51 depends on *Annals* 13.11.2, 13.14.5, and 14.53–6 and 63. For echoes of the *Dialogus* in *Ciceronianus* see nn77 and 79 below. The actual comment on Tacitus as a stylist in *Ciceronianus* CWE 28 409 / LB I 1006C / ASD I-2 657 is strangely brief and ambiguous: 'After that I don't dare to offer Tacitus [ie as a Ciceronian] ... nor would it be any use.'
49 See Ep 919, the commendatory letter, especially lines 30–1, 14–15, 58–60, 1–2, 62–6. Livy 33.17–49 and 40.37–59 could now be included among the previously known books.
50 Cf Epp 26:58, 45:110, 63:44.
51 Ep 2435. The manuscript is now classified as Palat. Vindob. Phil. Lat. Gr., or Vindobonensis Latinus 15; for an evaluation see P. Jal *Livius, Histoire Romaine* XXXI Collection Budé (Paris 1971) lxxxiii–v. It and the two Froben editions of 1531 and 1535 are the basis of the modern text of these books.

xliii
52 Ep 2686 to Bonifacius Amerbach
53 Allen Ep 1013 introduction
54 ASD I-3 251–2:620–33 / Thompson 65–6

xliv
55 Ep 1390:1–18, 40–8 (to Johann von Vlatten, provost of St Martins at Kranenburg, who was also the dedicatee of the *Ciceronianus*)

56 Cf Epp 152, 1013. There is even some repetition of rhetorical form; cf eg Ep 1390:50–1 ('I do not know how others are affected, but when I ...') with the same turn of phrase at Ep 1013:48–9.
57 Ep 1390:96–7
58 Ibidem lines 103–4
59 Ibidem lines 123, 133
60 The *Commentarius in duos hymnos Prudentii* was published with the *In Nucem Ovidii commentarius* (Basel: Froben 1525); the dedicatory letters are Ep 1404 and Ep 1402.
61 CWE 24 673. Erasmus is dealing here with *copia rerum*, as opposed to *copia verborum*. This is as near as medieval education came to the modern school syllabus of elementary geography, history, and natural science; such things were not taught in school, but read by the adult. Aristotle is cited here, along with his pupil Theophrastus, as a naturalist and zoologist; both were then authorities in fields for which we no longer consult them.
62 Ep 139:82–3
63 About scorpions, for example; see *Parabolae* CWE 23 234, 261.

xlv
64 Allen Ep 1544 introduction, 113n
65 'Mundum docet Plinius'; cf Allen Ep 1544:90–3. The previous sentence shows that *mundus* is Pliny's subject-matter rather than his audience. In praising Pliny's industry during a life dedicated to public service Erasmus is merely echoing Pliny's own nephew (*Epistles* 3.5 end).
66 Ep 1544:19–35 (Pliny as a source of distinction to the reader), 60–6 (the carelessness of printers), 99–113 (conservative editors), 113–15 (*codex vetustissimus*)
67 The description of the work as a treasure-house comes from Pliny's own quotation of Domitius Piso in *Naturalis historia* preface 17; Pliny adds: 'By perusing about two thousand volumes we have collected in thirty-six volumes twenty thousand noteworthy facts obtained from a hundred authors that we have explored.'
68 Erasmus even derives the separate thesis of his prefatory letter to Krzysztof Szydłowiecki (Ep 1593) from an essay of Plutarch comparing the diseases of the mind and body, *Animine an corporis affectiones sint peiores* 'Whether the Affections of the Soul are Worse than those of the Body' (*Moralia* 500B–502A).

xlvi
69 One chapter on talkativeness (*Noctes Atticae* 1.15) is assimilated and its anecdotes redistributed over the first quarter of the *Lingua*.
70 The notes to my translation clearly indicate Erasmus' reliance on classical authors. And having pursued his comments to their source, I do not think it unfair to add that much of the lore has clearly been taken over without any attempt at verification.
71 Ep 1522 to Henry Stromer, alluding to Horace *Epistles* 1.1.4–5; cf 1.19 end.
72 *Cicero und der Humanismus* (Zürich 1946); see especially 119–25 on the *Ciceronianus*.
73 LB I 998D, 999E / ASD I-2 645, 647 / CWE 28 394, 396: 'We dare not profess paganism openly, so we camouflage it with the name of Ciceronian.'

xlvii

74 Christian eloquence and Christian values: LB I 992E, 994F / ASD I-2 637 639 / CWE 28 383, 387; Cicero himself, if he lived now, would be Christian: LB I 1019C / ASD I-2 698 / CWE 28 436

75 LB I 986A / ASD 626 / CWE 28 369

76 Propriety: LB I 992C / ASD I-2 637 CWE 28 383; knowledge and sincerity: LB I 994E, 1002D–E, 1026B / ASD I-2 640, 651, 709:21–2 / CWE 28 387, 402, 448

77 LB I 981A–C / ASD I-2 618 / CWE 28 359–60; the criticisms are based on Quintilian 12.10 and perhaps Tacitus *Dialogus de oratoribus* 18–19. See n79 below.

78 Eg LB I 1001F / ASD I-2 650 / CWE 28 400, based on *De oratore* 3

79 LB I 992D / ASD I-2 636 / CWE 28 383. Erasmus' phrasing recalls Tacitus *Dialogus de oratoribus* 20: 'Quis nunc feret oratorem de infirmitate valetudinis suae praefantem ... quis quinque in Verrem libros exspectabit?'

80 LB I 989D–990E / ASD I-2 632–4 / CWE 28 377: 'I mean that his virtues, because they are great, approximate to faults.'

81 Cicero's receptivity to others' speech and thought: LB I 1002C / ASD I-2 652 / CWE 28 402; Cicero's innovations of language: LB I 996D / ASD I-2 642–3 / CWE 28 390–1

82 LB I 1022D / ASD I-2 704:28: '... spirans imago tui pectoris.' He adds (CWE 28 442): 'That will make your speech live, breathe, move, influence, carry away; it will make it express you wholly.'

83 Translated with an introduction by Maurice Pope in CWE 26 348–62 (introduction), 365–475 (translation)

84 Ep 1804 to Thomas More

85 On Erasmus' work in editing Seneca see the detailed study by W. Trillitzsch 'Erasmus und Seneca' *Philologus* 105 (1965) 271–93.

xlviii

86 Allen Ep 2091

87 See especially lines 258–340, moving from comment on his style to criticism of his life-style. Quintilian dominates, and his hostile evaluation in the tenth book (10.1.125–31) is quoted seven times, together with other comments drawn from 7.1.41 and 4.3.2.

88 Lines 507–513

89 Lines 456–66; Erasmus goes on to criticize Seneca with an understanding that sprang from knowledge of his own similar weaknesses as a writer: 'He does not always state his thesis and list its arguments, and if he has done so, he does not follow his own outline but digresses at every opportunity to resume later at a new starting point; he seldom uses formal transitions, which are a most helpful practice in teaching; often he begins to list his arguments towards the end of the work; at times he forgets himself and repeats the same point. This shows that he either contracted this failing from impromptu declaiming or, as is more likely, approached writing without preparation, composing less by calculated design than by sheer innate enthusiasm' (lines 466–74).

xlix

90 Allen Ep 2465:168–237 (1531, to Agostino Steuco)

91 Allen Ep 2584, dated December 1531; on the utility of Terence, see lines
   70–88; on the value of practising verse, lines 100–5.

ORATION ON THE PURSUIT OF VIRTUE /
ORATIO DE VIRTUTE AMPLECTENDA

3

1 See Ep 179 (the dedicatory epistle for the *Panegyricus*) and Ep 180 for a defence of formal panegyrics.
2 Reading *assentandi* for LB's *assentanti*
3 Borrowed from Lucretius 1.936–42 and 4.11–17
4 Cf Quintilian 1.3.7.
5 A maxim displayed on the temple of Apollo at Delphi
6 A youth who fell into a pool of water in which he was admiring his own
  reflection; Ovid *Metamorphoses* 3.339–510

4

7 See Diogenes Laertius 2.33, and cf 6 below. This admonition also appears in
  Galen's *Exhortatio ad bonas artes*, which Erasmus translated; see 225 below.
8 Philip the Good
9 See introductory note.
10 Philip the Fair, duke of Burgundy and archduke of Austria. He was the son of
   the Hapsburg emperor Maximilian I and Mary of Burgundy (d 1482), the
   granddaughter of Philip the Good.
11 Solomon; cf Wisd 8:19.

5

12 In one Greek myth the creator of the human race. See Apollodorus *Library*
   1.7.1 and the note on that passage of J.G. Frazer in the Loeb Classical
   Library edition.
13 Erasmus refers to Seneca's discussion at *Epistulae morales* 66.1–4 of *Aeneid*
   5.344.
14 Here and below Erasmus refers to the myth of the charioteer at *Phaedrus*
   246A–257A. Cf n20.
15 Ie a source; see *Iliad* 14.201 and 302.
16 Erasmus quotes and translates the Greek phrase, which is not an exact quotation from Homer.
17 *Iliad* 2.217–219
18 Erasmus actually uses the cognomen Maro.
19 Cf *Aeneid* 4.141–2 (Aeneas), 5.570 (Iulus), 5.294–5, 9.433 (Euryalus).
20 See n14 above.

6

21 Erasmus refers in a general way to the pseudo-Aristotelian *Physiognomica*,
   especially ch 2 and 3; cf *Prior Analytics* 2.27.
22 See *Sermones* 2.2.79. Erasmus actually uses the cognomen Flaccus.
23 See Plato *Symposium* 221E–222A.

24 Erasmus gives the Greek of a proverb used by Lucian to refer to the disappointment of hopes aroused by deceptive appearances (*Zeuxis* 2.840; *Timon* 41.153; *Hermotimus* 71.813; *Philopseudes* 32.58). See *Adagia* I ix 30.
25 See Epictetus *Enchiridion*, especially ch 3.

7
26 An adaptation of Virgil *Eclogues* 7.48; cf Ovid *Fasti* 1.152, 3.328.
27 *Aeneid* 6.130
28 A variant reading is 'most pious.'
29 Dicaearchus and Theophrastus were Peripatetic philosophers; see Cicero *Ad Atticum* 2.16.3. Erasmus gives the Greek for 'practical' and 'theoretical' lives.
30 See *Republic* 7, the myth of the cave, especially 514A–521B.
31 *Republic* 7; also 539C

8
32 Includes broad literary culture as well as music in the modern sense. Plato's account of the ideal primary education is at *Republic* 2.376E–3.412B.
33 Anthony of Burgundy; see introductory note.
34 Named after the winged horse captured and tamed by the hero Bellerophon, who rode the steed into battle
35 Erasmus gives the Greek of a Homeric phrase: *Iliad* 18.353, 23.169; cf *Adagia* I ii 37.
36 See, for example, *Trinumnus* 988.

9
37 See introductory note and CEBR I 100–1; he was tutor to Adolph by 1498 and until his death, sometime between autumn 1501 (Ep 166) and May 1502 (Ep 170).
38 See *Iliad* 9.432ff. The quotation (in Greek) is from 11.442–3. This example is often used by Cicero, eg, at *De Oratore* 3.57.
39 Horace *Epistles* 2.1.128
40 This general theme is developed at length by Erasmus in *De pueris instituendis*. That some ages are too old for education is a view he held in that work (CWE 26 319). Seneca (*Epistulae morales* 76) and Epicurus (at Diogenes Laertius 10.122) say that no age is too old for learning.
41 *Adagia* I i 8
42 See *Odyssey* 10.302–6.
43 A magic herb given to Odysseus
44 A witch who turned men into beasts; see *Odyssey* 10.135–9 and 210–40.
45 Horace *Sermones* 2.2.26
46 Cf *Adagia* II vii 10.

10
47 The king of Macedon 359–336 BC. For the anecdote, cf Plutarch *Alexander* 7 and Erasmus *Apophthegamata* 4.22.
48 Cf Horace *Odes* 1.12.7–12.

49 Cf Horace *Odes* 1.24.16–18.
50 The Muses
51 Hippocrene, the fountain of the Muses on Mt Helicon; see Hesiod *Theogony* 1–115. For the phrase 'vales of Helicon' cf Ovid *Amores* 1.1.15.
52 See n57 below.
53 A reminiscence of Horace *Odes* 3.4.4
54 *Iliad* 1.247–52, but see n57 below.

11

55 A sacred spring near Apollo's oracle at Delphi
56 Also the patron of oratory
57 From 'Lastly, you read too of the goddess Peitho' (10) Erasmus has been exploiting the rhetorical works of Cicero. *Brutus* 58 contains the reference to Nestor, and *Brutus* 59 is the source of this tribute to persuasion. Cicero gives a quotation from a lost work of Ennius, who honoured the orator Cethegus in lines modelled on Eupolis' similar praise of Pericles. But Erasmus also drew on *De oratore* 2.187 for the epithet 'who sways the heart'; it occurs there in a quotation from a lost play of Pacuvius. The translation *suadela* for the Greek *Peitho* (Persuasion) comes from Horace (*Epistles* 1.6.38), not Cicero.
58 Ep 61, written in the name of Heinrich Northoff but actually composed by Erasmus himself as an epistolary model, praises Erasmus in very similar terms (cf lines 131–2)! Parnassus is the mountain on whose slopes Delphi is located.
59 All early Latin poets and dramatists of relatively humble origins

12

60 Epithets of the Roman god Jupiter
61 Special potted plants, quick to grow and quick to die, used at Athens to celebrate the festival of the vegetation and fertility god Adonis; another reminiscence of Plato's *Phaedrus* (276B). Cf *Adagia* I i 4.
62 Wife of the Titan Epimetheus, who was given a box containing gifts from all the gods
63 Amalthea, a nymph whose goat had a horn filled with various fruits and flowing with milk and honey (or nectar and ambrosia); cf Ovid *Fasti* 5.115–28.
64 See Ep 93:93n.
65 *Odyssey* 1.301–2, 3.199–200

13

66 *Odyssey* 3.300, 7.277, 15.482
67 *Odyssey* 11.10, 12.152
68 See Ep 93:113n. The prayers are given at LB V 1210E–1216B ('Precatio Erasmi Roterodami ad Virginis filium Iesum'), 1227D–1234C ('Paean Virgini Matri dicendus, compositus in gratiam Dominae Veriensis per Desiderium Erasmum Roterodamum'), and 1233D–1240A ('Obsecratio ad Virginem Matrem Mariam, in rebus adversis, per Desiderium Erasmum Roterodamum').

FUNERAL ORATION / *ORATIO FUNEBRIS*

Introductory note

16

1 The source for this information on Berta is Reedijk 159–61. See also Berta Heyen and Margareta Heyen in CEBR II 189–90.
2 For a fuller discussion of Erasmus' use of Jerome and other sources see Inwood 'Erasmus' use of Historical *Exempla*' *Erasmus in English* 12 (1983) 10–13.

Funeral Oration

17

1 This description of his difficulties is a close imitation of Jerome *Letters* 60.1 and 108.32.
2 A quotation from Virgil *Aeneid* 2.120–1; Erasmus has *recurrit* for Virgil's *cucurrit*.
3 Ps 30:11 (RSV 31:10), Ps 17:5 (RSV 18:4), Ps 87:18–19 (RSV 88:17–18); the Vulgate has the masculine for 'friend' and 'beloved' where Erasmus uses the feminine.

18

4 Persius *Satires* 1.47 (the Latin says 'horn,' not 'stone'); *Adagia* I vii 44
5 A paraphrase of *Aeneid* 4.366–7
6 Erasmus wrote 'something from our own literature.' The quotation is from Job 6:12.

19

7 A reminiscence of Horace *Odes* 1.3.8
8 An imitation of Jerome *Letters* 60.15
9 Job 16:12. Erasmus adapts the Vulgate text to the singular.
10 Cf Jerome *Letters* 60.1.
11 *Letters* 60, 108

20

12 Juvenal *Satires* 3.30
13 This refers to pseudo-Cicero *Rhetorica ad Herennium* 3.13; cf *De oratore* 2.44. Cf Jerome *Letters* 60.8.
14 Ezek 18:4, quoted by Jerome *Letters* 60.8. Erasmus follows Jerome quite closely in this paragraph.
15 Erasmus borrows from Jerome (*Letters* 108.15) the proverb which also appears at Phaedrus *Fables* 1.3, Babrius 72 and Horace *Epistles* 1.3.18–20.

21

16 For the images see J.W. Smit *Studies in the Language and Style of Columba the*

Younger (Amsterdam: Hakkert 1971) 172–89 and Hugo Rahner *Symbole der Kirche* (Salzburg: Müller 1964) 272–303.

17 *Aeneid* 2.369 with one word changed, a line also used by Jerome *Letters* 60.16. Cf *Adagia* III vi 91.

18 The conventional hazards of legendary sea voyages, based on the *Odyssey* and the *Aeneid*. See Rahner (n16 above) 239–71. All these hazards are also mentioned in *De contemptu* ASD V-1 42:66ff / CWE 66 137.

19 Mary is the type of tranquil obedience and piety; Martha represents one who is troubled by active service to God; Luke 10:38–42 (cf John 11:20).

20 For this description of and excuse for Berta's marriage, compare the very similar Ep 145:164–76 addressed to Anna van Borssele, describing Anna's reasons for marrying.

21 Cf Phil 3:19.

22

22 1 Cor 7:29, with minor differences in wording from the Vulgate

23 Col 3:18; cf Eph 5:22–4 and 1 Pet 3:1.

24 An adaptation of Eph 5.33

25 Quoted from Juvenal *Satires* 6.268–9

26 The phrasing is inspired by Sallust *Catilina* 20.4.

27 1 Cor 7:39; the Vulgate has 'law' for the first occurrence of 'husband.'

23

28 An echo of 1 John 3:17 and Col 3:12

24

29 The main order of Franciscan monks; informally recognized by Innocent III in 1209, they were formally recognized by Honorius III in 1223 and granted the right to preach and hear confession in any place.

30 Judgment Day

31 A paraphrase of Matt 25:35–40; cf Matt 10:42.

32 St Elizabeth of Hungary (1207–31). Born into the royal house, she was happily married and bore three children. After her husband's early death she intensified her charitable activities and worked, as a Franciscan tertiary, for the relief of the sick, the poor, and the elderly.

33 On the proper reward for almsgiving and the proper way to dispense charity, see Matthew 6:1–6.

34 One of the Furies in Greek myth

35 The Brigittines were an order of monks and nuns (also called the *Ordo Sancti Salvatoris*) founded by St Bridget (Birgitta) of Sweden c 1363 and recognized by Urban V in 1370. Monks and nuns lived in the same cloister – the only order to do so. The order existed throughout northern Europe, and Bridget was a particularly popular saint among women. Erasmus also refers to St Bridget in Ep 447:102.

25

36 An imitation of Jerome *Letters* 108.20

37 We do not know to what misfortunes Erasmus is referring beyond
   Margareta's death, an account of which follows.
38 On Margareta see Reedijk 159. There are striking parallels between this anecdote and the one related in *De contemptu* CWE 66 168–9 about a Margaret
   whose entry into a convent is lamented by her family.
39 *Aeneid* 4.331

26
40 This is a pastiche from *Aeneid* 1.208–9 (with a change of gender) and 4.474–6;
   the final two lines ('I become worried …') are by Erasmus himself and echo
   Aeneid 1.197 and 4.394.
41 Job 1:21, with a trivial change in one word from the Vulgate text
42 The following list of historical *exempla* is a very close borrowing from Jerome
   Letters 60.5, who is citing from Cicero's lost *Consolatio*.
43 LB has a misprint here, 'Paris.'

27
44 Prov 31:10.
45 On widows as maidens cf Ep 145:164–76. But perhaps LB *virgo* should be
   corrected to *virago*, which is used in just this sense for a manlike woman at
   Panegyricus ASD IV-1 42:539.

28
46 A paraphrase of Mark 14:38
47 A close paraphrase of 1 Cor 10:13
48 See n35 above. Her feast fell on 9 October.
49 Ie, a scornful laugh; Juvenal *Satires* 10.28–53, especially 34
50 Cf John 14:28; Erasmus wrote 'homeland' for the Vulgate's 'father.' The
   change is deliberate.
51 Luke 23:28 with a change of gender; 'yourselves' is feminine in Luke.

29
52 From the *Salve regina*
53 For 'darkness' Erasmus wrote 'Cedar,' as does the Vulgate at Ps 119:5–6 (RSV
   120:5–6); Jerome (at *Letters* 108.1) renders the Hebrew word thus when he
   quotes the same biblical text.
54 Ps 47:9 (RSV 48:8), quoted by Jerome at *Letters* 60.7, 108.22
55 A paraphrase of Ps 136 (RSV 137):1–4
56 Here follow two poetic epitaphs, the first in dactylic hexameters, the second
   in anapaestic dimeters (or paroemiacs). For textual details, see Reedijk
   159–61, nos 12–13.
57 An echo of *Aeneid* 6.661

30
58 A Mediterranean wild strawberry
59 LB reads *agat*, the MS *agit*.
60 The Latin has Orcus, a Roman god of the underworld. This phrase is an echo
   of Horace *Odes* 2.14.6–7 and *Epistles* 2.2.178–9.

61 Prudentius *Cathemerinon* 10.120
62 An echo of *Aeneid* 11.212
63 LB reads *quîs*; the metre demands *quibus*.
64 Cf Prudentius *Cathemerinon* 10.37–40 and 137–140.

ORATION IN PRAISE OF THE ART OF MEDICINE /
DECLAMATIO IN LAUDEM ARTIS MEDICAE

Introductory note

32
1 CWE 24 665–91
2 See Curtius 64–105.
3 *Rhetorica ad Herennium* ed H. Caplan (Cambridge, Mass 1964)
4 *Rhetorica ad Herennium* 173–195
5 Allen I 38ff / Ep 1341A:500–639 / CWE 24 694–7.
6 Ep 268:21–3
7 1543. An English translation is available in the *Transactions of the Royal Society of Medicine* (June 1932).
8 Cf Erasmus' remark in *De ratione studii* CWE 24 673:2.

33
9 ASD I-4 153–54 (Amsterdam 1973)
10 Ep 1381
11 Published in 1533
12 Ep 1341A:666–7
13 Allen Ep 95:11n

34
14 Epp 87–9
15 Ep 637
16 Ep 771 introduction
17 See the introduction to Domański's edition in ASD I-4 158–9.

Dedicatory letter

35
1 This dedicatory letter is Ep 799. Henry Afinius of Lier was chief physician of Antwerp. Erasmus dedicated the *Encomium medicinae* to him in gratitude for a gift of silver cups. See Allen Epp 799 introduction and Ep 638:5–6; see also CEBR I 12. Like many of the humanists, Erasmus was, in Johnson's phrase, 'compelled by want to attendance and solicitation' (*The Rambler* no 108). Charges of corruption are inherent in such a situation; witness the charge laid against his friend Thomas More of accepting a 'fair great gilt cup for a bribe'; see William Roper and Nicholas Harpsfield *Lives of Saint Thomas More* ed E.E. Reynolds (London 1963) 30–1.

2 The *Encomium medicinae* was, of course, not delivered by Erasmus himself, but, most probably, by his friend Ghisbert, physician of St Omer; see J. Domański in ASD I-4 147–9. In essence, the art of rhetoric consisted in the presentation of a convincing case stated within the limits of well-recognized conventional terms. Much of this convention will strike the reader of *Encomium medicinae* as strained and artificial; but what is important for an evaluation of the thought is the essential requirement that it should not in itself have rung false to Erasmus' audience. See Curtius 64–105. The encomium was a branch of epideictic oratory; see *Rhetorica ad Herennium* trans H. Caplan (London 1964), especially li–lviii and 173–225.
3 In 1499. See Domański in ASD I-4 147.
4 For the long gap in time between composition and publication, see the introductory note.

Oration in Praise of the Art of Medicine

36
1 *Infantia*; for Erasmus' use of this word in the sense of incompetent oratory see CWE 24 681:16n.
2 In antiquity, eulogies of arts and sciences commonly appeared as a topos in a didactic work on the subject concerned. Cicero has a eulogy of eloquence in *De inventione*, Varro (*Res rusticae* 3.1.1–8) one of agriculture.
3 *Adagia* III i 49
4 Both terms are drawn from the rhetorical handbooks. See *Rhetorica ad Herennium* 3.11.3; Cicero *De oratore* 2.82.334. Erasmus may also have in mind the *rationes necessariae* or 'convincing arguments' of medieval dialectic, by which the Christian, meditating upon the nature of medicine, could come to see its 'necessity,' given the nature and purpose of God as presented in Christian teaching. See D. Knowles *The Evolution of Medieval Thought* (London 1965) 93–115.
5 For the battle of the arts, see *The Battle of the Seven Arts ... by Henri d'Andeli* ed L.J. Paetow (Berkeley 1914). The rivalry between the various faculties, which was particularly acute in the case of medicine and law, was expressed in the opening lectures delivered every year by each professor in praise of his own subject. See E. Garin *La disputa delle arti nel quattrocento* (Florence 1947); P.O. Kristeller 'Humanism and Scholasticism in the Italian Renaissance' in *Renaissance Thought* (New York 1961) 92–119; L. Thorndike 'Medicine versus Law at Florence' in his *Science and Thought in the Fifteenth Century* (New York 1929) 24–58.
6 *Adagia* I v 52
7 *De copia* 437:7–11, 507: 9–15. Cf Quintilian 8.4.1ff.
8 *Adagia* I iii 88. Erasmus is not simply referring to inflated and simple literary styles but is concerned with underlying moral issues as well; cf CWE 24 686:17n.

37
9 The same idea occurs in Italian treatises on medicine. See Poggio Bracciolini, cited in Garin *La disputa delle arti* (n5 above) 16, 21; Nicoletto Vernia ibidem 115.

10 *Naturalis historia* 25.2

11 In Pliny 7.123, the passage which Erasmus has in mind, the reference is to Hippocrates, not Asclepiades.

12 There were three basic attitudes open to Christian civilization in addressing pagan authors: complete rejection, the attitude of the anchorites of the Egyptian desert; the acceptance of those secular sciences necessary for the study of Scripture, the approach of Jerome in the west and Origen in the east; full incorporation of pagan culture into Christian civilization, when the pagan gods were felt to have become innocuous. Erasmus shares the last standpoint, with the proviso that the moral content of much of pagan literature is for him potentially dangerous to the Christian. See CWE 24 663.

13 Cf Epp 124:18, 132:36.

14 *Naturalis historia* 26.9

15 Christendom first recovered ancient astronomy and astrology from the Arabs. Astrology was regarded as merely applied astronomy, the conjunction of the heavenly bodies at the moment of birth having certain relevance to the individual's medical history. The explicit determinism of astrology made it seem incompatible with Christian doctrine. On the other hand, the Star of Bethlehem gave scriptural respectability to planetary influence upon human destiny. See T.S. Kuhn *Copernican Revolution: Planetary Astronomy in the Development of Western Thought* (New York 1959), especially ch 4.

16 Cf Pliny *Naturalis historia* 25.3.

38

17 The corpus of medieval and Renaissance medicine basically comprised the works of Hippocrates and Galen, together with their Arabic and Jewish commentators.

18 Cf Ep 132:20–3.

19 *Adagia* IV ix 2

20 Cf Ep 132:19–20, Allen Ep 1809:1–2.

21 Cf *Adagia* I i 69.

22 Pliny *Naturalis historia* 29.1. Tyndareus was king of Sparta and father of Castor, Pollux, and Helen of Troy.

23 The Latin form of Asclepius, Greek god of medicine

24 Pliny *Naturalis historia* 7.124, 26.15

25 Pliny *Naturalis historia* 25.14

26 Erasmus writes *halis* but in Pliny the word is *balis*. The plant is unidentified.

27 Cf Pliny *Naturalis historia* 25.14, where the location is Arabia, not Africa.

28 Cf Ep 132:19–23.

29 *Naturalis historia* 7.173–6

39

30 Erasmus may have in mind the Hippocratic belief (*Mul* 1.1) that the blood in the female is hotter than in the male. For the physiological connection between heat and fatigue, cf Hippocrates *Morb* 4.45, 3.99.

31 *Adagia* I i 69. See also Cicero *Pro Ligario* 12.38; Pliny *Naturalis historia* 2.18.

32 *Adagia* I i 69

33 Cf Pliny *Naturalis historia* 29.17.

34 See Allen Ep 1381:195.
35 *Adagia* II vi 37
36 Evidently the elixir of life of the alchemists, a concept based on a mixture of
   Greek and Oriental ideas. The alchemist was concerned with the problem
   of change, the removal of one property of matter and its replacement with
   another. It was closely related to the Aristotelian distinction between matter
   and form and the basis of individuation. Given its intellectual assumption,
   alchemy was theoretically quite feasible. For Erasmus' scepticism towards
   its claims, however, see Ep 225:12–16.
37 Cf *Rhetorica ad Herennium* 2.27.44 and Cicero *De inventione* 1.1.94.
38 The idea of the body as the tomb of the soul derives from Socrates and Plato.
   Cf *De conscribendis epistolis* CWE 25 32.
39 Cf Allen Ep 1381:189.
40 For further development of the comparison between theologian and physician see Allen Ep 1759:1.

41
40 Similar sentiments are expressed in *De praeparatione ad mortem* LB V 1311F.
42 Cf *Adagia* III i 100.
43 The teaching of the Gospels was specific about spiritual survival, but impre-
   cise about its nature. In the thirteenth century, handbooks for the laity
   were produced, such as *La Lumiere as Lais*, in which it was stated that the
   blessed would experience beauties of all five senses. Erasmus would have
   been aware of this tradition, and it may have some relevance to the importance he attaches to the physician as protector of the body, both body and
   soul being necessary to the blessed in the afterlife.
44 According to the ancients, there are four principal humours in the body:
   phlegm, blood, choler, and black bile. As one of these predominates it
   determines the temper of the mind and body; hence, sanguine, choleric,
   phlegmatic, and melancholic humours. The configuration of the planets at
   the time of birth was also believed to determine the humour of a man.
   Hence Erasmus' reference to 'ill-starred.' See R. and M. Wittkower *Born under
   Saturn* (London 1963).
45 Cf *Enchiridion* LB V 15A / CWE 66 45 and *De libero arbitrio* LB IX 1264A.
46 Erasmus here employs the Greek terms. Cf Plato *Timaeus* 74D; Aristotle
   Historia animalium 7.2 (589b).
47 Cf Plato *Phaedrus* 246A, 253C. See E.R. Dodds *The Greeks and the Irrational*
   (Berkeley 1951). Erasmus employs the same image in *Enchiridion* LB V 15A /
   CWE 66 45.
48 Cf Plato *Republic* 533D; Cicero *Orator* 29, 101.
49 Cf *Enchiridion* LB V 21B–D, 42B–43A / CWE 66 54–5, 90–1.
50 Cf Plato *Republic* 4.431A, 442C, 443D. For the meaning of 'philosophy' in
   Erasmus, see J. Domański's *Gloses concernant la conception érasmienne de la
   philosophie* (Warsaw 1969).

41
51 The dignity of man is a topos of Renaissance literature. The most famous
   example of it is the *Oration on the Dignity of Man* by Giovanni Pico della

Mirandola (1486). See *The Renaissance Philosophy of Man* ed E. Cassirer, P.O. Kristeller, and J.H. Randall jr (Chicago 1948) 215–54.

52 Cf Allen Ep 1381:56–7.

53 For an account of the emperor's madness, see Suetonius *Caligula* 50.

54 Cf Allen Ep 1381:45–7.

55 Cf Pliny *Naturalis historia* 29.5.

56 Sir 38:1–3. See too Allen Ep 1381:400.

57 Erasmus was troubled by the circumstances of his own birth, and had been granted papal dispensation from the disabilities of illegitimacy. See Ep 517:8–11.

42

58 A Greek philosopher born in Samos c 580 BC. His followers practised asceticism, particularly in the matter of food. See Pliny *Naturalis historia* 24.156–8, 25.13; Diogenes Laertius 8.19, 8.44; CWE 23 68–9; CWE 24 423.

59 Stoic philosopher of the third century BC. His longevity is referred to in Lucian's *Longaevi*, which Erasmus translated; cf ASD I–1 626:16.

60 On his longevity, cf Diogenes Laertius 3.2, 45, 85.

61 A third-century BC Roman politician, Cato was strongly opposed to the introduction of Greek culture to Rome and sought a return to the primitive simplicity of an agricultural state. Cf Pliny *Naturalis historia* 25.4, 29.15 and CWE 23 51, 84.

62 One of the elder Pliny's sources on botany. Cf Pliny *Naturalis historia* 25.9.

63 Cf Allen Ep 1334:32. The source for this belief would appear to be Hilary of Poitiers *De trinitate* 10.23.

64 2 Cor 12:9

65 Erasmus expresses similar views in his *Annotationes in Novum Testamentum* LB VI 793E–794C.

66 1 Cor 12:9

43

67 See R.W. Southern *Western Society and the Church in the Middle Ages* (Harmondsworth 1970) 136–40.

68 Cf *Liber sextus decretalium Bonifacii* VIII tit v.

69 Cf *Sermones* 278.4–5.

70 Cf Augustine *Letters* 153.

71 Cf Allen Ep 1381:128–36, where Christ is equated with the physician when he drove out evil spirits and restored the dead to life. For the earliest pictorial representation of Christ as Asclepius healing the sick see *Age of Spirituality: Late Antique and Early Christian Art, Third to Seventh Century* ed K. Weitzmann (New York 1977), 414–16. For the intellectual background see D.P. Walker *Spiritual and Demonic Magic from Ficino to Campanella* (London 1958).

72 The ironic tone of this passage is at variance with the serious treatment of the theme, and has led L. Elaut to suggest that the *Encomium medicinae* is a sequel to the *Moriae encomium*; cf his 'Erasme, traducteur de Galien' *Bibliothèque d'Humanisme et Renaissance* 20 (1958). It should, however, be remembered that *iocatio*, or facetious conversational tone, was a rhetorical device that could

properly be introduced into the most solemn discourse. See *Rhetorica ad Herennium* 3.23, 3.25.

73 Cf Pliny *Naturalis historia* 30.1.

74 In the *Moria* Erasmus asserted that the men of the golden age had been guided by instinct and nature, *naturae ductu instinctuque* (cf CWE 27 108). See H. Levin *The Myth of the Golden Age in the Renaissance* (New York 1969).

44

75 Cf *De concordia* LB V 504E. For the *prisca theologia*, that is, the assumption of a pagan tradition of religious truth which derived from Moses, see D.P. Walker 'The Prisca Theologia in France' *Journal of the Warburg and Courtauld Institutes* 17 (1954) 204.

76 Cf Pliny *Naturalis historia* 25.12.

77 Cf Pliny *Naturalis historia* 7.107, 25.11. See too *Adagia* III ix 23.

78 A fabulous herb endowed with magic properties. Cf Homer *Odyssey* 10.287–92, 302–5; Pliny *Naturalis historia* 25–6.

79 Cf Homer *Odyssey* 4.220–6; Pliny *Naturalis historia* 25.12.

80 For these physicians see Homer *Iliad* 2.732, 4.200, 11.506. Cf Pliny *Naturalis historia* 25.29.

81 Cf Homer *Iliad* 5.401, 899–904.

82 Homer *Iliad* 11.514–15

83 A formulation of Galen rather than of Homer; cf ASD I-1 11–17. Elsewhere in Erasmus medicine is afforded a less exalted status, cf *Moria* CWE 27 108; *Institutio christiani matrimonii* LB V 661D–E.

84 Cf Pliny *Naturalis historia* 25.13.

85 Aristotle's successor as head of the Peripatetic school of philosophy (c 371–287 BC). Among his extant works are the *Historia plantarum* 'Inquiry into Plants' and the *De causis plantarum* 'Growth of Plants.' See Diogenes Laertius 5.44.

86 According to Quintilian, Varro (116–27 BC) was the most learned of the Romans. His treatise *Disciplinarum libri ix* on the liberal arts was subsequently used by Martianus Capella in his *De nuptiis Mercurii et Philologiae*, a work of great importance in the Renaissance. Book 8 of Varro's treatise deals with medicine.

87 Mithridates VI, king of Pontus in the first century BC. He capitalized upon the hatred felt in Asia for Rome, and was supported by some of the Greek states. He was eventually defeated by Lucullus and Pompey. Cf Pliny *Naturalis historia* 7.88, 25.6–7.

88 Cf Pliny *Naturalis historia* 25.6. Mithridates had fortified himself by antidotes against poison so strongly that he could not poison himself.

45

89 Cf Pliny *Naturalis historia* 25.7.

90 On the relation of Christ to the liberal arts cf *Antibarbari* CWE 23 90:10–12.

91 Cf Allen Ep 1381:128 and *Exomologesis* LB V 150C.

92 Matt 9:11–12; Luke 5:30–31

93 Cf Luke 10:3–4. The identification of Christ as the Samaritan is taken from Jerome. Cf *Translatio Homiliarum Origenis in Lucam* PL 26 292–4.

94 Cf John 9:6; Mark 8:23.

95 Cf Matt 10:1, 8; Mark 6:13; Luke 9:1–2.

96 1 Tim 5:23

97 Tob 6:5–9. See J. Gamberoni *Die Auslegung des Buches Tobias in der griechisch-lateinischen Kirche ... bis 1600* (Munich 1969).

98 Cf Ep 82:25–6. But see *Adagia* III iii 1: *Sileni Alcibiadis*, where the supreme good is seen as spiritual. Cf M.M. Phillips *The Adages of Erasmus* (Cambridge 1964) 269–96.

99 Cf Jerome *Adversus Jovinianum* 1.36 PL 23 272A.

100 Cf Pliny *Naturalis historia* 29.17–19.

101 Cf Ovid *Ex Ponto* 3.2.37–100.

102 Cf Livy *Ab urbe condita* 6.24.9.

46

103 Cf *Adagia* I i 2 (CWE 32 45:394), where the source is given as *Rhetorica ad Herennium* 4.48.61.

104 The story occurs in Pliny *Naturalis historia* 10.75.

105 The Latin means to walk on the outside of a person, as a mark of respect. Cf Juvenal *Satires* 3.131.

106 On the addition of this paragraph to the text in 1529, see J. Domański's introduction in ASD I-4 158–9.

107 See Plato *Gorgias* 451E; Aristotle *Rhetoric* 1394b11.

108 Cf Plato *Republic* 410C–411E.

109 Cf Allen Ep 1523:3–4. The classical source is Plutarch *Moralia* 515C.

110 Cf Plato *Republic* 458B–461E.

111 For sumptuary laws in Rome see Macrobius *Saturnalia* 3.17, 3.13.

47

112 See Suetonius *Caesar* 44.

113 Cf Pliny *Naturalis historia* 7.124; Curtius Rufus 9.5.25.

114 Cf Pliny *Naturalis historia* 29.7.

115 *Adagia* I vi 74. See also Ep 132:64.

116 Cf Ovid *Tristia* 3.10.4–6, 4.1.93–4. For Erasmus' identification of Sarmatia with Poland see Allen Ep 1393:18–25.

117 The point being, of course, that English law is based primarily on case law, not the Roman law prevailing in most of Europe. In writing of John More, a judge of the king's bench, Erasmus implies that the study of English law was not regarded as a proper part of education in his day. See Ep 999:155–7.

118 *Adagia* I vii 33

119 Cf Pliny *Naturalis historia* 29.20–3.

120 On those arts which belong to the education of a 'free' man, the liberal arts, see P.O. Kristeller, 'The modern system of the arts' in *Renaissance Thought* II (New York 1965) 163–227.

48

121 Cf Pliny *Naturalis historia* 29.14, quoting Cato.

122 Cato is associated by some scholars with the expulsions of Greek philosophers and rhetoricians from Rome in 161 BC (cf Suetonius *On Rhetoricians* 1) and

advised the expulsion of the philosophic delegation from Athens in 155 BC.
See A.E. Astin *Cato the Censor* (Oxford 1978) ch 8.
123 See Cato *De re rustica* 106–108.
124 Cf Pliny *Naturalis historia* 29.18.
125 Cf Allen Ep 2145:16–17.
126 Legend relates that Stesichorus (c 640–555 BC) was struck with blindness for
having censured Helen in one of his poems, and that his sight was restored
after he had written his *Palinodia* or recantation, in which it was not Helen,
but her phantom, that accompanied Paris to Troy. Cf Ep 26:40–3.
127 Erasmus uses the Greek word taken from Aristophanes *Plutus* 706.
128 Cf Ep 1334:10ff. The classical source is probably Diogenes Laertius 6.3.

49
129 Cf Pliny *Naturalis historia* 29.21. The necessary distinction between the institution and its professors is characteristic of Erasmus' thought. See R. Pfeiffer
Humanitas Erasmiana (Leipzig 1931).
130 Cf *Adagia* I vii 9, where the proverb is explained as meaning that many
pass themselves off for what they are not. Erasmus quotes the Greek in his
text.
131 For the Hippocratic oath cf *Ratio* LB V 76B.
132 Cf Pliny *Naturalis historia* 29.3.
133 *Adagia* II i 12

A HOMILY ON THE CHILD JESUS /
CONCIO DE PUERO IESU

Introductory note

52
1 Ep 106 introduction
2 See K.K. Chatterjee *In Praise of Learning* (New Delhi 1974) 85–92.
3 Quoted by J.H. Lupton *A Life of Dean Colet* (London 1887) 279 and Chatterjee
104
4 See Ep 218 introduction.
5 See Ep 260 and CWE 24 280–1.
6 CWE 24 662
7 Reedijk no 85
8 Reedijk no 94

53
9 Reedijk no 86
10 See J.H. Rieger 'Erasmus, Colet and the Schoolboy Jesus' *Studies in the Renaissance* 9 (1962) 187–94.
11 Cf Mark 16:15: 'Go into the world and preach the gospel to every creature.'
12 See H. Caplan 'Classical Rhetoric and the Medieval Theory of Preaching'
Classical Philology 28 (1933) 73–96; J.W. Blench *Preaching in England in the Late
Fifteenth and Sixteenth Centuries* (Oxford 1964) 71–3.

54

13 Ep 1110:25–33
14 *De doctrina christiana* 4.2 PL 34 90
15 See Reedijk 292; Epp 219, 222.
16 See 52 above.
17 Epp 302, 305
18 Ep 305: 145–53

55

19 By Diego de Alcocer; see the facsimile edition with an important introduction by E. Asensio (Madrid 1969).
20 A transcription of this work, known in only one copy, now in the British Library, was produced by J.H. Lupton ('A Sermon on the Child Jesus,' London 1901), and part of it is reprinted in *Thought and Culture in the English Renaissance* ed E.M. Nugent (Cambridge 1956) 343–8.
21 Thus the edition edited by Samuel Bentley (London 1816)

A homily on the child Jesus

56

1 Cf Ps 8:3; Matt 21:16.
2 Cf John 6:69.
3 Cf Heb 4:12.
4 Cf John 7:38.
5 Matt 11:15
6 Phil 4:13

57

7 *1511* and other editions before the revision made in 1514 have 'my speech expounding his praises as yet knows no limits, but it must make limits for itself.'
8 The LB reading, *dulci Iesu* 'sweet Jesus,' is an error for *duci Iesu* 'our commander Jesus,' the reading of all earlier texts.
9 Unlike the other parts of the speech, this section is not marked off in the text, but there is a clear division between the preceding introductory material and what follows.
10 Cf Heb 1:3; Ambrose *Hymns* 7.1 PL 16 1222
11 John 1:9
12 Cf Matt 28:18.

58

13 Examples of such events are found in Matt 8:23–7; John 2:1–11; Matt 8:1–15 (etc); Matt 28:4; Matt 8:28–33 (etc); Matt 27:45, 51; Matt 27:51; John 11:1–44; Luke 7:36–50 (etc).
14 Cf the Nicene and Apostles' creeds.
15 Cf 1 Cor 1:25.
16 Matt 17:5

17 Cf Matt 10:28.
18 See the narratives of Christ's birth in Matt 2 and Luke 2:1–39.
19 Erasmus may be thinking of the medieval story (*Acta sanctorum* 28 August, 357–9) of St Augustine, who when walking by the seashore saw a child emptying water out of the sea with a shell. On being told by Augustine that this was pointless, the child replied by comparing the saint's attempt to contain the mystery of the Trinity in his treatise on that subject.

59
20 John the Baptist; see Mark 1–7 and Luke 3:16.
21 Cf James 2:19.
22 Cf Eph 1:4.
23 The editions printed before the text was revised for Schürer in 1514 here place a third clause, preceding the other two: 'supplied us with all the faculties of our senses.'
24 In the *Exultet*, the pronouncement (of seventh-century origin) which follows the blessing of the paschal candle in the liturgy of Holy Saturday
25 A patristic commonplace (eg Athanasius *De incarnatione* 54.3), but no doubt most familiar from the prayer said in the mass since early times at the mixing of the water and wine
26 Cf 1 Cor 15:53–4, 2 Cor 5:4.

60
27 A reminiscence of the words introducing the Lord's Prayer in the mass
28 John 14:6
29 1 Pet 1:19
30 Cf perhaps Venantius Fortunatus *Hymns* 2.6.9–12.
31 A liturgical phrase used in connection with the Ascension

61
32 *Adagia* I iv 30
33 Classical examples of loyal companions who saved their friends from death
34 Pliny *Naturalis historia* 37.59, a statement often repeated in later writers
35 The source is Pliny's *Naturalis historia*; see 10.18, 8.56, 8.59–60 (*panthera* is identified with *pardus* at 8.63), 9.59–60 and 8.61. Similar comparisons are used in *Expostulatio Iesu cum homine suapte culpa pereunte* 47–56 (Reedijk no 85), a poem printed with the *Concio* in all the early editions.
36 For example, Isa 7:14, 9:16; the classical terminology may suggest that Erasmus has also in mind Virgil's fourth ('Messianic') eclogue.
37 Luke 1:39–44
38 Cf Matt 2:16.
39 Matt 21:15

62
40 Matt 19:13–14; Mark 10:13–14; Luke 18:15–17
41 Matt 18:2–3
42 Matt 18:6; Mark 9:41; Luke 17:2
43 Matt 18:10

44 Matt 18:2–3
45 John 3:3
46 1 Pet 2:2
47 Gal 4:19
48 1 Cor 3:1–2
49 Cf 1 Tim 4:12
50 This sentence and the following are marked by untranslatable word-play in Latin: 'non in annis ... sed in animis, non in temporibus sed moribus ... qui mento levi ... mente sunt hirsuta ...'
51 The text of 1511 here continued: 'In the gospel we hear of children who mocked Jesus as he carried his cross; for their sake he told their mothers to weep, saying of them: "If they do this when the wood is green, what will they do when it is dry?"' Erasmus no doubt omitted this sentence in the revision because he had come to another interpretation of Luke 23:31. The context does indeed mention women, but no mocking children are said to be present, and a more natural explanation of Christ's words is that by the 'green wood' he refers to his own innocence; this is the gloss later given by Erasmus in his paraphrase on Luke (1523) LB VII 461D–E.
52 A common medieval and Renaissance topos; see Curtius 98–101.
53 1 Pet 2:1. In the unrevised text this quotation took a different form, presenting *rationabiles* for *rationabile*. This form could be rendered 'like newborn babes, possessed of reason, long for milk without guile.' For Schürer's text, Erasmus corrected the passage in accordance with the Greek and with the better manuscripts of the Vulgate. The change to the more accurate version, however, makes the point of what follows less cogent.

63
54 1 Cor 14:20
55 Eg Mark 16:5
56 The statement probably derives from Apuleius *Apology* 42–4, where children are said to be particularly apt for magical purposes. In the following sentence Erasmus may also have had in mind Cyprian *Letters* 16.4, where a comparison seems to be drawn between magical arts and the action of the Holy Spirit.
57 Shown by his part in securing Susanna's acquittal in Dan 13:45–62 (Vulg; in AV and RSV, the apocryphal book of Susanna)
58 3 Kings (RSV 1 Kings) 3.5–14
59 In the 'burning fiery furnace' (Dan 3:23–5). At Dan 1:4 they are called children, and the deuterocanonical 3:24–90 is known as the Song of the Three Holy Children, although in the surrounding context the three are 'men.'
60 1 Kings (RSV 1 Sam) 3:2–14
61 In the case of the first three saints Erasmus may be thinking simply of the holiness which according to medieval narratives manifested itself at an early stage in childhood. The references to female saints seems more specific: Agnes, who was martyred at a very young age, placed special emphasis on her marriage to Christ (Jacopo da Voragine *Golden Legend* ch 24), and the Golden Legend also relates that the young Cecilia was constantly engaged in 'divine colloquies' (ch 164).

64

62 Cf Horace *Epistles* 1.2.69–70.

63 Luke 2:40

64 Prov 22:15

65

65 Rev 21:5

66 Cf Isa 29:14; 1 Cor 1:19.

67 Matt 11:25; Luke 10:21

68 Duns Scotus (d 1308), one of the most famous of the nominalist philosophers, is picked as a typical example of the irrelevance of scholastic philosophy to true devotion and the following of Christ's teaching.

69 Luke 2:41–51

70 Cf Luke 2:46.

71 Eph 4:13

72 Luke 2:51

66

73 Luke 2:52

74 *Sermo* 115.4.4 PL 38 657

75 Cf Phil 3:13.

76 Socrates' supposed ignorance is the basis on which most of the discussion in Plato's dialogues rests; he is made to expound the method in *Theaetetus* 150B–151D.

77 In Greek

78 1.3.3. Both here and in the following reference he is called Fabius.

67

79 At 11.2.41 Quintilian actually says, 'As many things as possible should be learned ...'

80 John 17:3

81 Matt 11:29–30

82 Cf *Works and Days* 291–2: '... rough at first, but as it goes on it becomes easy, despite being tough.'

83 Similar proverbs are known in Latin and French, but I have not found this form anywhere else other than in Erasmus himself (*Enarratio in Psalmum 22* ASD V-2 378:693). The whip is unique to this version, and may suggest a reference to the whipping contests held in honour of Artemis Orthia at Sparta; cf Xenophon, *Constitution of the Lacedaemonians* 2.9 and Tertullian *Ad martyres* 4.7 PL 1 626. The identity of the sage remains obscure.

84 Cf Rev 20:4.

68

85 Cf James 4:14.

86 Wisd 5:7

87 The whole passage which follows is strongly reminiscent of the similar treatment of the theme in *De contemptu mundi* ASD V-1 62 / CWE 66 155.

88 Matt 19:29

69

89 Cf Virgil *Aeneid* 2.798.

90 This description of the perfect Christian bears a strong resemblance (at least at first) to that of the Stoic sage; see for instance Cicero *Academica* 2.136; Horace *Epistles* . 1.1.106–7.

91 Cf 2 Cor 1:12.

92 Cf Matt 10:30; Luke 12:7.

93 Cf *De contemptu mundi* ASD V-1 76:989ff / CWE 66 167 and *Moria* LB IV 503C–504A / ASD IV-3 192–3:248ff / CWE 27 152 (the latter written in 1509 and revised for publication in 1511, the same year as the *Concio*). See M.A. Screech *Ecstasy and the Praise of Folly* (London: Duckworth 1980), especially 173–9.

94 Cf Isa 64:4; 1 Cor 2:9. The passage is also cited in this context in *Moria* (see preceding note).

95 Ps 91:13 (RSV 92:12)

70

96 Cf Eph 4:13.

THE TYRANNICIDE, ERASMUS' REPLY TO
LUCIAN'S DECLAMATION / *TYRANNICIDA,
DECLAMATIONI LUCIANICAE RESPONDENS*

Introductory note

72

1 *Luciani ... compluria opuscula ... ab Erasmo Roterodamo et Thoma Moro inter-pretibus optimis in Latinorum linguam traducta* (Paris: Bade 1506), containing twenty-eight translations by Erasmus and four by More, as well as a declamation by each man in reply to Lucian's *Tyrannicida*. The Latin texts are in ASD I-1 379–627 (ed Christopher Robinson) and in Yale CWM III-1 (ed C.R. Thompson). For a history of the text see Robinson's introduction 374–7, Thompson's more detailed account in his introduction lv–lxvii, and E. Rummel *Erasmus as a Translator of the Classics* (Toronto 1985) 49–69.

2 The *editio princeps* appeared in Florence (de Alopa 1496), but Erasmus and More are more likely to have used the Aldine edition published in Venice in 1503.

3 In *De ratione studii* CWE 24 669:4–6 he names Lucian among those 'whose diction, apart from its refinement, will also entice learners by a certain charm of subject-matter.'

4 Epp 192:15, 197:8–9, 199:9–10, 293:23

5 Ep 1341A:240–1

6 Cf Robinson's introduction 365.

7 The text of Erasmus' composition is in ASD I-1 516–51. Parts of the speech are translated by Charles R. Rayment in 'The *Tyrannicida* of Erasmus: Translated Excerpts with Introduction and Commentary' *Speech Monographs* 26 (1959) 233–47. Both Erasmus' and More's declamations are discussed and put

into their historical context by C.R. Thompson in the introduction to his
commentary in the Yale CWM III-1 149–55.
8 Seneca the Elder *Controversiae* 2 preface 4; Quintilian 2.10.1–12. Seneca
wrote two collections of model speeches, the *Controversiae* and *Suasoriae*.
A similar corpus of *declamationes* has come down to us under the name of
Quintilian. Tacitus, specifically mentioning the topic of tyrannicide, calls
such subjects 'remote from real life ... presented in bombastic style' (*Dialogus
de oratore* 35; cf Isocrates *Helen* 1–13 for a similar condemnation of contrived and paradoxical themes). For a summary of criticism in Roman literature see S.F. Bonner *Roman Declamation* (Liverpool 1949) 71–83.
9 Ep 191:28–33

73
10 *Dialogus de oratore* 35; Juvenal *Satires* 7.150ff: 'Or do you teach rhetoric? Oh,
Vettius, what an iron heart must you have when your crowded class slays
cruel tyrants ...' On the historical background, the legislation concerning
tyrranicide, and its reflection in literature see H. Friedel *Der Tyrannenmord in
Gesetzgebung und Volksmeinung der Griechen* (Stuttgart 1937).
11 Cicero *De inventione* 1.14.19; Quintilian 4 preface 6

74
12 Eg the purpose of laws (11–12, 22–5), the issue of the meaning vs the letter of
the law (69–73), the circumstances under which homicide was legal (74–5)

75
13 Yale CWM III-1 152; cf Epp 191:5–6, 999:277–9, 1341A n45.
14 More ibidem 97:6–9; cf 80 below.
15 More ibidem 99:24–7; cf 78 below.
16 More ibidem 101:11–12; cf 106 below.
17 More ibidem 103:2–4; cf 95 below.
18 More ibidem 102:12 (*unus est cuius ... umbra freti*); cf 108 below (*sub unius
umbra* ASD I-1 539:30).

76
19 More ibidem 109:7ff, 123:15ff; cf 95 below.
20 More ibidem 121:32–4; cf 105 below.
21 More ibidem 121:18–19; cf 99 below.
22 More ibidem 119:30–121:6; cf 97 below.
23 Quintilian 2.6.2, 5; cf 7.1.4.
24 Ep 914:61–2, 28–30

The Tyrannicide, Erasmus' Reply to Lucian's Declamation

77
1 Cf Cicero's advice on how to gain the jurors' good will in the exordium: '... if
it is shown in what honourable esteem they are held' (*De inventione* 1.16.22).
2 These are key words describing the purpose of the exordium, which,

according to classical theory, was to render the audience 'well-disposed, attentive, and receptive' (Quintilian 4.1.5; *De inventione* 1.15.20). In medieval handbooks the exordium was therefore aptly called *captatio benevolentiae*, 'attraction of good will.'

3 In Lucian's *Tyrannicida* 4 the claimant alleges that his adversary acted 'because of his grief over the dead men, and in the endeavour to avenge them upon the man who caused their death.' According to Cicero (*De inventione* 1.16.22), one of the purposes of the exordium is to 'weaken the effect of charges that have been preferred.'

4 Quintilian 4.1.7 recommends emphasizing this motive. Cf 81 and n17 below, where the same device is employed.

78

5 Quintilian 4.1.20 recommends playing on the fears of the jurors or audience. The devise is also used at 92 and 121 below.

6 Discrediting the opponent's character was a favourite topos of *exordia*, cf *Rhetorica ad Herennium* 1.5.8. The same device is employed below, eg 79 (braggart), 91 (liar), 96 (coward).

7 Cf *Tyrannicida* 3: 'It was my thought, therefore, that I should get for this a still more generous gift from you and should receive rewards to match the number of the slain.' Quintilian 4.1.54 considers the drawing of material from the opponent's speech a clever device, since it gives the speech a spontaneous note. For its use see eg 82, 83, and n47 below.

79

8 Cf *Tyrannicida* 1: 'I have come to claim but one prize for both.'

9 A braggart soldier in Terence' *Eunuchus*

10 Cf *Tyrannicida* 19: 'Would you not have enshrined the sword among your hallowed treasures? Would you not have worshipped it along with the gods?'

11 That he favoured tyranny; see 77 above.

80

12 The figure of apostrophe, or turning from the jurors to address the opponent, was used to good effect in the exordium by Cicero and Demosthenes; cf Quintilian 4.1.63–9.

13 Cf Horace *Ars poetica* 282–4 on Attic comedy: 'Its freedom sank into excess and a violence deserving to be checked by law. The law was obeyed ... the right to injure being withdrawn.'

14 *Adagia* II vii 90: *Fulgur ex pelui*

15 Cf *De inventione* 2.5.19: 'No one can be convinced that a deed has been done unless some motive is given why it was done.'

16 *Ethos* was a significant aspect of a speech, for 'the excellence of the speaker's character will make his pleading all the more convincing' (Quintilian 6.2.18).

81

17 Cf 77 and n4 above. The further claim that he was pleading on behalf of the gods was an effective device to gain the audience's attention. Cf *De*

inventione 1.16.23: 'We shall make our audience attentive if we show ... that the [arguments] concern the immortal gods or the general interest of the state'; cf *Rhetorica ad Herennium* 1.4.7.

18 Cf *Tyrannicida* 3.

19 To assert this is a means of retaining the audience's attention: 'We shall also find it a useful device for wakening the attention of our audience to create the impression that we shall not keep them long and intend to stick closely to the point' (Quintilian 4.1.34).

20 Here starts the second part of the oration. Tradition prescribed a *narratio* or statement of facts, but Erasmus had no need to outline the situation, as this had already been done by his opponent, and the audience was now sufficiently instructed. He therefore turned immediately to the preliminaries of the main section, proof, putting forth a proposition ('For the question is not how wretched is tyranny or desirable liberty. Your investigation ... concerns another matter'). Cf Quintilian 4.4.1: 'After the statement of facts some place the proposition, which they regard as forming a part of a forensic speech.'

82

21 Here follows the traditional *divisio*, outlining the speaker's steps in proving his point. Cf Quintilian 4.5.22: Division will 'greatly add to the lucidity and grace of our speech. For it not only makes our arguments clearer by isolating the points from the crowd in which they would otherwise be lost and placing them before the eye of the judge, but relieves his attention by assigning a definite limit to certain parts of our speech.'

22 Echoing *Tyrannicida* 22: 'How many punishments were there in all this, how many wounds, how many deaths, how many tyrannicides, how many rewards?'

23 Cf Propertius 2.10.6: *In magnis et voluisse sat est* 'In great matters will also is sufficient.'

24 Reminiscent of Persius *Satires* 5.27

25 Judges in the underworld

83

26 Recalls the formula of the Athenian citizen's oath: '... to kill the tyrant if it be in my power' (quoted by Andocides *De mysteriis* 97).

84

27 This is one of the three main 'issues' (*constitutiones*): fact, wording, and quality of action. The *constitutio legitima* or *definitiva* deals with the letter of a text (cf Cicero *De inventione* 2.16.52ff; *Rhetorica ad Herennium* 1.11.19ff).

28 *Tyrannicida* 10

85

29 Ie bona fide transactions; the formula is quoted by Cicero *De officiis* 3.15.61.

30 Cicero ibidem uses the phrase *dolo malo*; the legal formula is *nec vi nec clam* 'neither by force nor by secrecy' (*Digest* 41.1.22).

31 Achilles was the champion of the Greeks; Thersites, synonymous with

ugliness, was given to mocking and jeering. He was killed by the enraged
Achilles with one blow of his fist.

32 Cf *Adagia* I ii 45: *Fortes Fortuna adiuvat*, which follows Terence *Phormio* 203; the
proverb is found in another form in Virgil *Aeneid* 10.284.

33 This and the following honours are described by Livy *Ab urbe condita* 6.20.7,
23.18, 7.37.2.

86

34 A case of this sort is discussed by Cicero in *De inventione* 2.50.153 and in
Rhetorica ad Herennium 1.11.19.

35 As he did in *Tyrannicida* 14: 'I wanted it, willed it, undertook it, essayed it.'

36 A similar argument is advanced by Seneca *Controversiae* 3.6, also dealing with
a disputed case of tyrannicide: *Saepe honorata virtus est et ubi eam fefellit
exitus* 'valour is always honoured, even when it is denied success.' Seneca's
Controversia is an outline of arguments for and against a claimant who, on
being caught in an act of adultery with the tyrant's wife, killed the husband in
self-defence. For other parallels with Seneca see nn82, 93, and 118 below.

87

37 Cf the advice in *Rhetorica ad Herennium* 2.12.18: when a wider application of
the law is proposed the speaker must discuss 'whether the absence of a
text concerning the matter here involved was intentional because the framer
was unwilling to make any provision ...' See also n107 below.

38 By ratiocination (*ratiocinando*), a process discussed by Cicero in *De inventione*
2.50.148ff. Cf Quintilian 7.8.3–7.

39 Cf *Tyrannicida* 12.

88

40 Cf Cicero's advice on how to refute arguments from analogy: the speaker
must point out 'that the cases compared differ in kind, nature, meaning,
importance, time, place, person, or repute' (*De inventione* 2.50.151).

41 Erasmus elaborates on this point in his *Laus matrimoniae*, referring to specific
laws; cf CWE 25 132–3.

42 Cf Plato *Crito* 51A–C.

43 This analogy is used extensively by Plato, eg *Republic* 544Cff; it also occurs in
Pseudo-Quintilian *Declamationes minores* 329.

89

44 Ovid in the *Metamorphoses* 1.89ff; cf especially line 90: 'Without law they
observed truthfulness and justice.'

45 A literary commonplace; cf eg Horace *Epistles* 1.6.16: '... virtue by itself sufficient'; Silius Italicus *Punica* 13.663: 'Virtue is its own fairest reward.'

46 Echoes of Virgil *Georgics* 3.9 and Horace *Odes* 4.3.22

47 The speaker pauses artfully, since the claimant has brought this very accusation against him (see 77 above).

90

48 Cf *Tyrannicida* 16: 'I am not unstained with blood ... he was a harsher tyrant
... and what's more important, he was heir and successor to everything.'

49 Cf *Tyrannicida* 11.
50 Quoting *Tyrannicida* 22: '... the old man prostrate upon him ... the blood of both intermingled.'

91
51 *Tyrannicida* 18: 'I knew that he would lay down his life at once, if not through his love, then at all events through his despair.'
52 An augur predicted the future by observing the flight of birds, a haruspex by inspecting the entrails of sacrificed animals.
53 Ie not certain proof, but one that must be made plausible based on the motive of action, the character of the agent, and the nature of the act. Cf Cicero *De inventione* 2.4.16.
54 In the following Erasmus attacks his opponent's arguments because they are not in accord with generally accepted views of the qualities characterizing old men and tyrants. For the standard descriptions (part of the orator's *ethopoieia*) see Aristotle's *Rhetoric* 2.11 (1388b31–1390b13), *Politics* 5.11 (1313aff), and Horace *Ars poetica* 156ff. Quintilian 5.10.17 declines to discuss them in detail and refers the reader to Aristotle. In Lucian's *Phalaris* 7, the tyrant complains about what he considers an unfair image of tyrants.

92
55 See n113 below.
56 See n76 below.
57 Proverbial wisdom; cf *Adagia* I ii 2: *Simile gaudet simili*.

93
58 According to one of the best-known Stoic doctrines, to be virtuous is to live by the dictates of reason.
59 *Adagia* IV iii 94: *Aquam igni miscere*
60 Prometheus, a Greek demigod, usually portrayed as a master craftsman, is said to have fashioned man out of clay.
61 One of the Argonauts in Greek myth; he was so sharp-sighted that he could see through the earth.

94
62 Cf Cicero *De republica* 2.16.48: 'There is no more noisome, hideous ... or loathsome animal' and ibidem: 'He surpasses beasts in the monstrousness of his character.'
63 *Adagia* I i 30: *Factum stultus cognoscit*
64 Cf Cicero *De officiis* 2.7.25: 'Oh wretched man, who trusts a barbarian and a branded slave more than his wife!'

95
65 A mythological race who fought against the gods
66 *Dira cupido*, a Virgilian expression; cf *Aeneid* 6.373, 721.
67 Reminiscent of Ovid *Metamorphoses* 1.148–9: 'Sons inquired into their father's years before the time. / Piety lay vanquished.'
68 The Greek Erinyes and their Roman equivalent, the Furies, were avenging

spirits who disturbed the mind of murderers. Their attributes were snake-hair, fiery eyes, poisonous breath, torches, whips, and double axes.

96

69 Greek deity, half goat and half man, who could induce 'panic' or nightmares
70 Quoting *Tyrannicida* 8
71 *Tyrannicida* 20: 'I had myself composed the whole plot of the tragedy.' Lucian uses the word *poietes*, 'poet' or 'maker' of the tragedy.
72 Echoing *Tyrannicida* 20: '… what the tyrant no doubt did and what he said before his end'

97

73 Title of Athene, goddess of wisdom; Erasmus alludes to a scene in Homer *Iliad* 1.264–6 in which the goddess holds back Achilles:
Behind she stood, and by the golden hair
Achilles seized, to him alone confessed.
A sable cloud concealed her from the rest.
74 Echoing *Tyrannicida* 8
75 *Iliad* 16.672

98

76 See also below 'common sense, custom, nature.' According to Cicero (*De inventione* 1.20.29) these were the prerequisites of plausibility: '… if the story fits the nature of the actors in it, the habits of the ordinary people, and the beliefs of the audience.'
77 Cf the characteristic in Aristotle *Rhetoric* 2.13 (1389b31), 1890a11 and the echo in Horace *Ars poetica* 171.

99

78 A reference to the proverbial device of *deus ex machina*; cf *Adagia* I i 58.
79 *Tyrannicida* 19: 'When the tyrant wished to die and at this moment found himself unarmed, this sword of mine was of service to him.'
80 *Tyrannicida* 19; see n10 above.
81 *Adagia* I vii 57: *In silvam ligna ferre*
82 Cf Seneca *Controversiae* 3.6: 'Certainly a tyrant always carries a sword with him.'

100

83 Cf Quintilian 4.3.7: it is a question of definition 'whether the man who forces a tyrant to kill himself can be considered a tyrannicide' and 7.3.32: the accuser will argue that 'the man whose act leads to another's death is the cause of his death,' whereas the defence will argue that 'only he who *willingly* commits an act that must *necessarily* lead to another's death is the cause of the death.' The examples cited are similar to Erasmus': an old man who commits suicide thinking his son is dead; a man who dies after eating food at a banquet given by his friend.
84 See n9 above.
85 Quoting *Tyrannicida* 12

101

86 The case is discussed by Quintilian 4.2.13. The two men exchanged arms after a single combat (Homer *Iliad* 7.206ff); Ajax later committed suicide using the sword that had originally belonged to Hector.

87 Such a case is discussed in Pseudo-Quintilian *Declamationes minores* 253.

88 According to Homer *Iliad* 9.106 ff

102

89 *Adagia* I v 10: *Non tam ovum ovo simile*

103

90 Erasmus may have been thinking of the several methods tried by Nero in attempts on his mother's life. They are described by Suetonius *Nero* 34.2–3.

91 Cf Cicero *De inventione* 2.37.99, where similar terms are used: 'It could have been avoided ... foreseen ... guarded against ... this should not be called ignorance or chance or necessity, but laziness, carelessness, and folly.' Cf *Rhetorica ad Herennium* 2.16.24.

92 *Tyrannicida* 11

104

93 This argument is also used by Seneca *Controversiae* 4.7: 'I shall honour the spontaneous tyrannicide, I shall not honour the lucky man or one who is forced to act.'

105

94 Not a regular practice in antiquity, but there are references to irregular burial (Aeschines 3.244) and denial of burial (Servius on *Aeneid* 12.603).

95 Ie that a reward is owed him for killing the son

96 A promontory in northern Scotland, part of the land formation on the Orkney Islands (*Orcades*)

106

97 Following the popular misconception of his time Erasmus says 'kings.'

107

98 Cf Aristotle *Rhetoric* 2.13 (1390a11–12) 'Their desires have slackened.'

99 Aristotle (*Politics* 5.11, 1314A) and Plato (*Republic* 9.572D–576B) list similar characteristics.

100 Cf Plato *Republic* 8.566A: '... transformed from a man into a wolf.'

109

101 The proverbial form was *Multi regum aures atque oculi* 'Many are the kings' ears and eyes' (*Adagia* I ii 2).

102 The Titans rose up in revolt against the gods. Briareus is said to have had a hundred hands and fifty heads. Enceladus was the most powerful of the Titans. According to myth, his death caused Aetna to erupt in flames.

103 A monster that sprouted two new heads for every one cut off. It was one of Hercules' labours to destroy her.

110

104 *Adagia* I i 53: *Suo ipsius laqueo captus est*
105 On this issue in court speeches see Cicero *De inventione* 2.40.116; Quintilian 3.6.87–9.
106 Cf Longus 3.23; the nymph was torn in pieces by mad shepherds, but Earth covered up the remains, which continue to utter sounds.

111

107 Cf Cicero *De inventione* 2.40.120: 'It will help greatly to show how the lawgiver would have written it if he had wished the opponent's interpretation to be carried out or adopted.'
108 Ie one that bends; cf the proverbial fight with a leaden sword (*Adagia* II v 10).

112

109 According to Draco's law; this right was extended to include offences against a man's mother, sister, or daughters.
110 Cf Plato *Laws* 869D–E.

114

111 *Adagia* I ii 6: *Malum malo medicari*

115

112 This analogy is best known from Plato, who developed it in his *Republic* (cf especially 8.563 ff).
113 Cf Aristotle *Politics* 5.11 (1314a33, 39–40): tyrants try to make their rule appear 'kingly' and 'cleverly play the part of royalty.'

117

114 Such a case is described in Pseudo-Quintilian *Declamationes minores* 345 and 383.

118

115 The god Apollo delivered oracles from his altar on the island of Delos, where he was born.
116 Cf Quintilian 7.4.22–3: one must take into consideration 'how it was done, by poison or the sword ... again, we must consider the immediate object ... whether it was done in hope of subsequent profit.'
117 Such a case is discussed in Pseudo-Quintilian *Declamationes minores* 321.

119

118 Seneca *Controversiae* 4.7 presents this argument against an adulterous tyrannicide: 'The Roman people does not approve of defeating the enemy with poison or by treacherous means.'
119 At least five thousand, according to Valerius Maximus *Facta ac dicta memorabilia* 2.8.1

120

120 Cf Seneca *Epistulae morales* 4.8: 'Whoever disdains danger to his own life is master over yours.'

121

121 *Adagia* I vii 69: *Intempestiva benevolentia nihil a simultate differt*
122 *Adagia* I viii 44: *Atheniensium inconsulta temeritas*

122

123 Erasmus uses the rhetorical device of prosopopeia (impersonation) as recommended by Quintilian 9.2.29–33 and *Rhetorica ad Herennium* 4.53.66.

123

124 A slip for 'us'
125 A water-clock was used to measure the length of a speaker's discourse. See
Cicero *Tusculan Disputations* 2.27.67.

A COMMENTARY ON OVID'S *NUT-TREE* / *IN
NUCEM OVIDII*

Introductory note

126

1 A.G. Lee 'The authorship of the *Nux*' in *Ovidiana* ed N.G. Herescu (Paris
1958) 457–71; L.P. Wilkinson *Ovid Recalled* (Cambridge 1955); R.J. Tarrant
'Pseudo-Ovid' in *Texts and Transmission: A survey of the Latin Classics* ed L.D.
Reynolds (Oxford 1983) 285–6. Erasmus refers to the author as Ovid at
150, 151, 159, 162, 164, 166 below.
2 It is not mentioned in the various *accessus* published by R.B.C. Huygens
Accessus ad auctores rev ed (Leiden 1970), or G. Przychocki 'Accessus Ovi-
diani' *Rozprawy Akademii Umiiejetnosci* 3rd series, 4 (Cracow 1911) 65–126, or
B. Nogara 'Di alcune vite e commenti medioevali di Ovidio' in *Miscellanea
Ceriani* (Milan 1910). More recently, see Frank T. Coulson, 'Hitherto Unedited
Medieval and Renaissance Lives of Ovid (1)' *Mediaeval Studies* 49 (1987)
152–207.
3 Allen Ep 1397:13 (to Johannes Faber, 21 November 1523)
4 The Latin text is in ASD I-1 145–74. My footnotes are derived almost entirely
from ASD. I am grateful to Dr. M. Winterbottom for assistance on some
details of the translation.

Dedicatory letter

127

1 Not extant
2 Actually, it is the consonants *sigma* and *tau* that do the arguing in Lucian's *The
Complaint of the Consonants*. They address their complaint to the vowels as
judges, who have no lines. Erasmus' memory may have been deceived by the
common Latin title of the work, *Judicium vocalium*.
3 Erasmus' memory deceives him again: it is not in Homer that the *Argo* speaks
but rather in Apollonius of Rhodes' *Argonautica* 1.525.

4 Pythagoras believed the soul to be a fallen divinity condemned to a cycle of
  reincarnation as man, animal, or plant.
5 Dodona was the site of an ancient oracle of Zeus in the mountain of Epirus.
  The god's will was divined from the rustling of the leaves of the sacred
  oak.
6 *Adagia* I v 36; cf I v 35.
7 An ugly, foul-mouthed man who railed at Agamemnon until beaten into
  silence by Odysseus; cf *Iliad* 2.212ff.
8 By Quintilian 10.1.98. The tragedy is not extant.
9 Cf *Adagia* I vii 3
10 Cf CEBR II 97, 452–5.

128
11 The mountain in Boeotia was sacred to Apollo and the Muses.
12 Cornelia, daughter of Scipio Africanus and mother of the famous reform
  politicians Tiberius and Gaius Gracchus (second century BC), whose education in Greek culture she supervised. She was considered the model of
  Roman matronhood.

A Commentary on Ovid's *Nut-tree*

129
1 Erasmus' analysis of the poem is based on Roman rhetorical theory, particularly Quintilian's *Institutio oratoria*. A forensic (*judiciale*) theme is distinguished from the epideictic (praise) and the deliberative (philosophical) types;
  cf Quintilian 3.4.12–16.
2 The *causa* is the whole action or case; the *status* is the basis on which it rests; a
  basis of *qualitas* (quality) is one in which the defendant admits the facts but
  claims that he was in the right; see Quintilian 3.6.1 and 10. Similarly, the
  Rhetorica ad Herennium 1.14.24: 'An issue is juridical when there is agreement on the act, but the right or wrong of the act is in question.'
3 An early Greek mock-heroic poem, ed. T.W. Allen *Homeri opera* v 3rd ed
  (Oxford 1946)
4 For these technical terms, see Quintilian 4.2 (*narratio*) and 4 (*propositio*), also
  3.9 and 4.5, 26; *Ad Herennium* 1.3 and 8–9, 2.18.

130
5 *Works and Days* 1
6 *Pharsalia*
7 *Ars poetica* 136–7.
8 Cf Cicero *De inventione* 1.15.20; Quintilian *Institutio oratoria* 4.1.5.
9 4.5.26

131
10 *Ars amatoria* 3.381–2
11 *Georgics* 2.1–2
12 *De viris illustribus* PL 23 631–760

13 *Ars amatoria* 1.1–2
14 *Heroides* 16.1–2

132
15 *Amores* 2.6.1–2
16 *Amores* 1.14.1–2
17 *Amores* 1.9.1–2; the poem is addressed to 'Atticus,' but I have translated this 'friend' for the metre.
18 *Eclogues* 8.1
19 Bion *Epitaph on Adonis* 1–2, ascribed to Theocritus in some early sixteenth-century editions
20 Virgil's First Eclogue, which is in dramatic form
21 *Idyll* 1
22 2.5.1–2
23 Erasmus translated a number of Lucian's dialogues.

133
24 That is, the provoker can still sue the person whom he provoked; the walnut, however, has not even been guilty of provocation.
25 *Adagia* iii iii 8

134
26 *Against Antonius Raudensis*; in the 1512 edition this comment is on fol 14r, sig C 2r. Valla says that the use of *reatus* for *peccatum* and of *reus* for *nocens* is not an ancient one.
27 That is, *obicere crimen* but not *admittere scelus*
28 Cf Job 10:33.
29 *Aeneid* 1.150
30 *Metamorphoses* 1.141

135
31 That is, the argument rests on the definition (*finis*) of *peccare* (wrongdoing).
32 The Latin is: *In fine mutatur vocabulum.* I take it to refer to the logical sequence X = A; X = B; therefore A = B.
33 *Naturalis historia* 21.17.34, 19.3.18, 18.39.140
34 Cited by Pliny *Naturalis historia* 15.3.11
35 Pliny *Naturalis historia* 16.49.116; in fact Pliny says that the *arbutus* (strawberry-tree) bears more fruit in the upper part, and the walnut and marisca fig lower down.

136
36 Mynors (152) notes that *proveniente* is the correct reading.
37 Exodus 13.2

137
38 *Catachresis* ('abuse'); Erasmus means the use of 'Bacchus' for 'wine.'
39 *Georgics* 2.82
40 *Remedia amoris* 175–6

138

41 *Epistles* 1.10.24

42 That is, in eclipse; Juvenal *Satires* 6.443

43 Mynors (154 n1) cites Willem Heda's chronicle (1521) for an account of this 'event.'

44 Cf Pliny *Naturalis historia* 8.68.169.

139

45 *Naturalis historia* 13.7.31

46 *Naturalis historia* 17.37.216–40 (diseases), 17.39.246–8 (remedies)

47 This comment interrupts the argument and is perhaps misplaced.

48 Cf Gen 16.

49 Mynors (155 n18) notes that this oak stood in the Petersplatz at Basel until 1632. 'Maximilian dined in its shade, in company with his father Frederick III, early in September 1473.'

140

50 *Naturalis historia* 12.3.6–12.6.13

51 *Naturalis historia* 17.18.89. I have been unable to locate the Columella reference. The only hint is in *De arboribus* 22.3, where he says that walnuts must be planted a hand's breadth apart.

52 *Phormio* 667

53 On Terence *Adelphi* 855

54 *Phormio* 68

55 *Carmina* 1.28.31

141

56 3.18.2–7

57 See the next paragraph.

58 See 169 below.

59 *Naturalis historia* 24.1.1

60 Pliny *Naturalis historia* 15.24.87 says that the Greek names show that walnuts came from Persia, 'for their best species is called "Persian" and *basilicon.*'

61 *Saturnalia* 3.18.11–12 is the sole source for this fragment of the *Moretum* by Suevius, which is not to be confused with the Pseudo-Virgilian *Moretum.*

62 *Cornucopiae* (Venice: Aldus 1499) 293:13ff; the *Cornucopiae* is a kind of encyclopedia. Erasmus is right: Macrobius is not referring to the peach (*persica malus*), but to a kind of walnut known as the 'Persian.' See n60 above; Athenaeus (cited in nn90–1 below) says that walnuts (τὰ Περσικὰ 'Persians') cause headaches.

63 *Satires* 2.4.34; Macrobius (*Saturnalia* 3.18.13) does not, in fact, identify the *terentina* [sic] with the walnut; he cites Horace and suggests that Horace may have made a mistake.

64 Cf eg Virgil *Eclogues* 8.30.

142

65 *Naturalis historia* 16.50.114–16, 15.24.91

66 Juvenal *Satires* 15.70

67 'So many early editions of Ovid; the right reading is *vterum vitiat*' (Mynors 157 n33).

143
68 *Noctes Atticae* 12.1.8
69 *Naturalis historia* 16.15.118
70 Ibidem

145
71 Pliny *Naturalis historia* 15.30.102–3 (not 25). Modern editions of Pliny (Loeb, Budé) have *Lutatia* for Erasmus' *Actia*.

146
72 *Phormio* 333–4
73 *Satires* 10.19: 'Only the empty-handed traveller will sing in the face of the robber.'
74 Mynors (160 n21) notes that the authoritative manuscripts read *cur* 'why.'

147
75 Cf Quintilian 7.2 *passim*.
76 *Epistles* 1.2.27
77 *Nux* line 17 (139 above)
78 *Elegantiae* 2.1.
79 *Nux* line 6 (135 above)

148
80 Cf Pliny *Naturalis historia* 28.4.18.
81 3.9.9–15

149
82 *Georgics* 2.398, 401
83 Pliny *Naturalis historia* 17.11.64; Palladius (fourth century AD) *De agricultura* 2.15.15
84 Ibidem. Pliny does not in fact mention this feature of the walnut.
85 *Naturalis historia* 17.39.246

150
86 1.106–10.
87 *Naturalis historia* 17.31.139–40 and 17.40.249.
88 135 above

151
89 *Elegantiae* 4.28: *iuglans ... nec poma dicuntur sed nuces*.
90 *The Deipnosophists* 2.53C. A Bodleian copy of the Aldine edition of 1514 (shelf-mark Auct. 1 R. inf. 1.1) belonged to Erasmus, and against this passage (sig B4v) is a marginal note *iuglans* (walnut) in Erasmus' hand.
91 Athenaeus says that Διὸς βάλανοι ('Zeus' acorns,' also called 'Heracleot nuts,' that is, 'filberts, hazel-nuts') and τὰ Περσικὰ ('Persians,' that is, 'walnuts')

cause headaches. See also Pliny *Naturalis historia* 15.24.86–8: *caryon a capitis gravedine* (*caryon* is named for the headache), that is, from Greek κάρα 'head.'

92 *Naturalis historia* 16.6.15. Erasmus is playing on *iu-glans* and *glans* 'acorn'; the Spanish acorn is a sweet kind of fruit from the *quercus ilex*.

93 In 1508

94 *De re rustica* 143.3

95 *Adagia* I v 35, also used 127 above

96 *Satires* 1.10

97 *Epigrams* 14 (*Apophoreta* 'Table-gifts').1.12

152

98 Mynors notes (163 n35) that several fifteenth-century Ovid texts read *dilaminat*, and (164 n3) that 'the Aldine Ovid of 1502 reads *dilaniat*; in the 1515 edition it is *diuerberat*.'

99 In line 95

100 Of Naucratis, grammarian (second century AD); in his *Onomasticon* 9.103, he mentions the use of acorns in a children's game. The rules of 'nuts' are not clear.

101 *Satires* 2.3.171

102 *Epigrams* 14 (*Apophoreta* 'Table-gifts').18

103 Martial *Epigrams* 13 (*Xenia* 'Guest-gifts').1.7–8

153

104 *Satires* 2.3.248

154

105 *Satires* 3.50

106 Quintilian 8.4.3

155

107 See 151–2 above; Pliny *Naturalis historia* 15.24.86–9

108 *Satires* 1.11

109 *Naturalis historia* 8.8.25

157

110 Cited by Aulus Gellius *Noctes Atticae* 20.1.49

111 Cf Virgil *Aeneid* 3.55–6.

158

112 Cited by Quintilian 9.3.17

113 *Epistles* 1.20.25; *Odes* 4.12.20

159

114 In line 117 the early editions (such as Froben) have *mutantibus* (ie, neither *nutantibus* nor *vitantibus*); the error mentioned in the commentary should perhaps be *mutantibus*, not *nutantibus*.

161

115 The interpretation is based on Quintilian 3.6.10: 'When the accused says,

"Admitting that I did it, I was right to do it" he makes the *basis* one of quality.' See also 3.6.32 and 41–2.

162
116 *Elegantiae* 6.64.481 (not 484)
117 Ie Augustus Caesar; Caesar became the generic name for all emperors.

163
118 Referring to Ovid's exile
119 *Adagia* I i 69

164
120 Cf Quintilian 3.6.30ff (conjecture), 5.9.8–90 (indications).
121 *Naturalis historia* 15.24.87
122 Quintilian 5.9.9 uses this example.
123 *Naturalis historia* 16.85–9.234–40

165
124 Virgil *Aeneid* 4.25

166
125 *Naturalis historia* 8.47.109; the term 'castor oil' was later transferred to vegetable oil.
126 Cf Pliny *Naturalis historia* 32.13.26.
127 Cf Pliny *Naturalis historia* 32.5.11.
128 Wrongly credited with a *Halieutica*
129 Anemones, for example
130 *Aeneid* 2.146–7

167
131 Erasmus' interpretation is over-subtle; the poem does not imply burning *in situ*.

168
132 *Georgics* 1.175
133 *Adagia* I iv 2

169
134 *Naturalis historia* 24.1.1
135 *Naturalis historia* 16.78.212
136 *Naturalis historia* 16.31.76 (not 19)
137 *Naturalis historia* 15.24.86; 141 above

COMMENTARY ON TWO HYMNS OF PRUDENTIUS / *COMMENTARIUS IN DUOS HYMNOS PRUDENTII*

Introductory note

172

1 Johannes Bergman *Aurelii Prudentii Clementis Carmina* CSEL 61 (Vienna 1926) v
2 The most convenient edition of Prudentius is by H.J. Thomson, Loeb Classical Library, 2 vols (London / Cambridge 1949–53; repr 1961–2).
3 See for example Adolf Katzenellenbogen *Allegories of the Virtues and Vices in Mediaeval Art* (London 1939; repr New York 1964).
4 Thomson I 94–115
5 The fullest account of the hymns is by Josef Szöverffy *Die Annalen der lateinischen Hymnendichtung* I (Berlin 1964), 78–94; see also F.J.E. Raby *A History of Christian-Latin Poetry from the Beginnings to the Close of the Middle Ages* 2nd ed (Oxford 1953) 44–71.
6 Bergman CSEL 61 xlviii–liv

Dedicatory letter

173

1 This dedicatory letter (Ep 1404) was translated by R.A.B. Mynors.
2 None has survived.
3 Cf Cyril of Jerusalem *Catechetical Sermons* 19.1.
4 William Roper (c 1496–1578) was the son of John Roper of Kent, a close legal associate of Sir Thomas More. A lawyer himself, William became chief clerk of the Court of King's Bench in 1524, an office that he retained until 1577. By 1518 he had entered the household of Thomas More, whose daughter Margaret he married in July 1521.
5 Thomas Roper (d 1598) his parents' eldest son. He studied law and in 1577 succeeded his father as chief clerk of the Court of King's Bench.
6 Apollo as father of the Muses and patron of all higher learning and culture. The image of Christ as the new Apollo was common among the Italian humanists but rare in Erasmus, who was uncomfortable with such similes.
7 Catherine of Aragon. Calliope was the Muse of epic poetry and of eloquence.
8 Erasmus probably had in mind not only married couples such as the Peutingers of Augsburg but also learned women like Willibald Pirckheimer's sisters and daughters.
9 Margaret's sisters and their companions
10 Cf Allen Ep 1404 introduction: 'It is evident that the year-date here is a year beginning at Christmas,' ie 1523 by our calendar.

Commentary on Prudentius' Hymn on the Nativity

174

1 Ambrose is mentioned as the so-called father of Latin hymnody; he wrote his hymns in iambic dimeters. Here Erasmus uses the first quatrain of Ambrose's *Deus, creator omnium* to illustrate his point. Ambrose bequeathed to the Middle Ages the pattern of four-line stanzas for hymns.
2 *Iam lucis* is the hymn for Prime, now unattributed; see eg Walpole no 81. The second example is line 2 of Prudentius' hymn on the Nativity (176 below).

3 *vividum* F; *invidum* LB

175
4 Matt 24:12
5 Cf Herodotus 2.41, 65, 67, 74 of the Egyptians.
6 Cf Herodotus 1.216, 3.38.
7 Cf 4 Kings (RSV 2 Kings) 23:10.
8 That is, natural law, contrasted in the next sentence with Mosaic law
9 Matt 15:14
10 Isa 9:2; 'sat' is the LB reading (*sedebat*), but the Clementine Vulgate has *ambulabat* 'walked.' In Luke 1:79 it is *sedent*.
11 Luke 1:78–9; cf Ps 111 (RSV 112):4
12 John 8:12
13 Rom 5:12

176
14 Ovid *Amores* 2.9.41
15 *Carmen saeculare* 11
16 Ezek 43:4
17 The point of calling Prudentius 'our Pindar' is that just as Pindar was famous for his choral hymns in praise of ancient gods, so Prudentius successfully composed hymns suitable for congregational singing in praise of the Christian God. Erasmus may have been prompted to the name of Pindar by Horace, who implicitly presents himself as a Latin Pindar in *Odes* 4.2.1.

178
18 *Epodes* 2.40
19 The thought is traditional. The Son of God is the Word, which is taken in through the ear of the Virgin and then made incarnate. A succinct illustration of the point is found in Arundel Lyric 17.21–24: 'naturam decipit / que verbo concipit, / dum, quod auris recipit, / intus incarnatur' (*The Oxford Poems of Hugh Primas and the Arundel Lyrics* ed C.J. McDonough, Toronto 1984, 100)
20 Erasmus repeats this view in his *Annotationes* on Luke 2, note 28, labelling the belief *pia credulitas* (LB VI 235C).

179
21 Isa 53:8
22 Wording of the Nicene Creed
23 *quidam* F; *quidem* LB
24 Plato *Soph* 263E
25 Ps 26 (RSV 27):9
26 Ps 16 (RSV 17):1 etc
27 Acts 7:50; cf Isa 66.2.
28 Acts 13:22
29 Ps 33:16 (RSV 34:15)
30 Luke 1:51
31 Acts 7:49

32 *Elegantiae* 2.21

180
33 Hymn 23 in Walpole 123–6; it is a cento of *Cathemerinon* 9.
34 *aut* F; *ut* LB

181
35 Gen 1:3
36 Heb 1:2
37 *Metamorphoses* 1.7–9

182
38 Prov 8:29–30. *fundamenta* F; *fundamento* LB
39 For this method of calculation see Isidore of Seville *Etymologiae* 5.39.26.
40 Ps 39:7–8 (RSV 40:6–7)
41 Isa 52:6

183
42 Eg Augustus
43 Rom 5:12

184
44 Luke 15:4–7
45 Luke 10:30–37

185
46 Eg the Arians
47 *Eclogues* 4.61

186
48 Cf *Nux*, 139 above.
49 Virgil's *Eclogue* 4 was thought to refer to Christ; Ovid refers to the ages in *Metamorphoses* 1.89–150.
50 *Eclogues* 4.5–7
51 Eph 4:22
52 Rev 21:5; cf Isa 43:19.
53 Isa 9:6, 8:22

187
54 A sound similar to the Latin word *vae* 'woe'
55 *Naturalis historia* 7.1.1–2
56 1 Pet 2:2, the reading for Easter Sunday
57 *Eunuchus* 688

188
58 Isa 11:6–8
59 Joel 3:18
60 Amos 9:13

61 *Eclogues* 4.18–25
62 2 Cor 2:14–16.
63 Cf *Adagia* II iii 35.

189

64 Amphion through the power of his lyre drew stones together to build the walls of Thebes; see Hyginus *Fabulae* 6–7. For Orpheus specifically associated with the movement of oak-trees, see Ovid *Metamorphoses* 10.90–91.
65 On the etymology of 'Saxon-saxum' see Fulcoius Ep 1.27 (text in M.L. Colker 'Fulcoii Belvacensis Epistula' *Traditio* 10 [1954] 209).
66 Hos 2:4
67 Rom 4:17
68 Matt 3:9; Luke 3:8
69 *Aeneid* 6.471
70 Virgil *Eclogues* 4.30

190

71 Virgil *Eclogues* 4.2
72 *Naturalis historia* 12.30–2.55–65
73 For the transition of power from Saturn to Jupiter, see Ovid *Metamorphoses* 1.113–14.
74 Isa 1:3

191

75 Cf John 12:15.
76 Sallust *Bellum Catilinae* 1.1
77 Ps 50:12 (RSV 51:10)

192

78 No specific quotation is intended; the sentiments are common in the Psalms.
79 Cf Ovid *Fasti* 4.757.
80 1 Cor 10:4

193

81 The LB text of the poem reads *mentibus* (104), but Erasmus (like F) clearly had *fletibus*, as is seen below.
82 John 19:37, echoing Zech 12:10
83 Matt 24:30; Mark 13:26

194

84 1 Cor 15:52
85 2 Pet 3:7, 10

195

86 Mark 15:14, etc

A Short Commentary on Prudentius' Hymn on Jesus' Epiphany

196
1 *Illis* LB; *Illic* F and Loeb Prudentius (ie, 'there [you] will be allowed')
2 1 Pet 1:24
3 1 Cor 1:31

197
4 John 8:12

198
5 Sir 27:12
6 Num 24:17
7 *Georgics* 1, 246
8 *Tristia* 4.3.1–2

199
9 *Naturalis historia* 2.22.89
10 *Naturalis historia* 2.22.89–90

200
11 Cf Pliny 2.37.101.
12 Cf Plato *Timaeus* 41E.
13 *Etymologium magnum* sv *seiraino*

201
14 Matt 2:2

203
15 Gen 22:16–17
16 Isa 11:1
17 Isa 11:4
18 Cf Virgil *Aeneid* 12.66 (*subiecit*); *Georgics* 3.241 (*subiectat*).
19 Cf Virgil *Aeneid* 5.158, Ovid *Metamorphoses* 4.707; in prose Pliny *Naturalis historia* 12.2.5.

204
20 The Latin here has 'head,' but this is not an English idiom.
21 There is no noun modifying *quod* in the Latin.

205
22 In the text of the poem, LB and F have *puero* incorrectly; Loeb has *puer*. In the commentary, F has *puero, puer o legendum est*, but LB has *puero, puer legendum est*. As Erasmus clearly regarded *o* as an incorporated gloss, the LB reading must be correct. The sense is not affected, as *puer* is vocative with or without *o*.
23 Matt 28:18
24 *Quo* Loeb; *Quod* LB, F. The reading *quod* makes 'sepulchre' the subject of 'broke,' very awkwardly. The commentary is not affected.

206

25 Mic 5:2
26 Ps 2:7–8

207

27 Erasmus' point here is not clear. Classical Latin *adire* and *cernere* (used here by Prudentius) mean 'claim (an inheritance)'; Erasmus may be thinking of *decernere* 'decide by battle.'
28 Cf Matt 2:16: *iratus* 'angry.'

208

29 Erasmus is explaining the use of *nuntium* 'messenger' to mean 'news.'
30 From Sedulius' *A solis ortus cardine*, in Walpole no 31:29–32

209

31 Erasmus is here interpreting what he sees as a play on words: the infants have just been 'poured out' (*effusa*) from their mothers' wombs, just after their lives or souls (*animae*) have been 'poured in' (*infundendo*).
32 *Epiphonema rei narratae*; see Quintilian 8.5.11.

211

33 Rom 12:1
34 2 Tim 4:6
35 Ie to avoid the hiatus. It would mean 'before whose altar.'

212

36 Exod 1:15 – 2:10
37 In both poem and commentary LB has *praeceptor(em)* 'ruler, adviser,' but Erasmus' gloss '*restitutorem*' shows that his text of the poem (like F and Loeb) must have read *receptor(em)*.
38 *iusserat* LB, F; *ius erat* Loeb. The commentary is not affected.
39 Prudentius is also ambiguous, as he could mean that mothers were not allowed to take away their sons, but the story in Exodus clearly requires 'raise.'

213

40 Rom 2:1; Deut 11:18
41 *Tanti per* F; *Tantisper* LB

214

42 Cf *Liber interpretationum hebraicorum nominum* ed Paul Anton de Lagarde in *Onomastica sacra* 2nd ed (Göttingen 1887; repr Corpus christianorum series latina 72 [Turnhout 1959]) 143:28–9
43 *Baptismum* F; *Baptismus* LB
44 Exod 17:8–16

215

45 Josh 3ff

46 Josh 4
47 Rev 21:14
48 Ps 113 (RSV 114):3, 5

216
49 Matt 2:6 (Mic 5:2)
50 Matt 2:2

217
51 'Ancestral smoky images' is the object of 'abjured,' of which the subject is 'cruel progeny ... whoever moulded ...'; the word-order is that of the hymn.
52 Judg 6:25–32
53 Rom 14:8
54 Cf 1 Thess 4:13–17.

TRANSLATIONS FROM GALEN / *EX GALENO VERSA*

Introductory note

220
1 *Exhortatio ad bonas artes, praesertim medicinam; De optimo docendi genere; Qualem oporteat esse medicum.* Titles vary slightly from one edition to the next; this wording follows the Basel edition of 1526.
2 For the dedicatory letter (Allen Ep 1698) see below 224. On Jan Antonin of Košice see below 224 n1.
3 224 below
4 For more details see nn20, 21, 24, 27, 32, and 33 below.
5 Comparisons between Erasmus' translation and these contemporary or earlier versions will be found in the notes to the text. The quotations from Niccolò da Reggio (Regius) whose translation appeared in Pincio's edition, are taken from the text edited by A. Brinkmann, *Galeni de optimo docendi genere libellus,* Programm zur Feier des Gedächtnisses des Stifters der Universität König Friedrich Wilhelm III (Bonn 1914); the quotations from Bellisarius, whose translation appeared in the Giunta edition, come from M. Beaudouin 'Le *Protrepticus* de Galien et l'édition de Jamot (1583)' *Revue de philologie* 22 (1898) 233–45.
6 This translation is based on the text in ASD I-1 (Amsterdam 1969) 629–69, ed with an introduction and commentary by J.H. Waszink, to whose notes I am indebted for much useful information. Erasmus' translations are also discussed by L. Elaut 'Erasme traducteur de Galien' *Bibliothèque d'Humanisme et Renaissance* 20-1 (1958) 36–44 and E. Rummel *Erasmus as a Translator of the Classics* (Toronto 1985) 109–20. For the Greek text see volume 1 of the Teubner edition (Leipzig 1884) ed J. Marquardt and I.V. Mueller. The *Exhortation* has been edited separately, with a commentary, by G. Kaibel, *Galeni Protreptici quae supersunt* (Berlin 1894). See also J. Walsh 'Galen's Exhortation to the Study of the Arts, Especially Medicine' *Medical Life* 37 (1930) 507ff; this

contains an attractive, but rather free, English translation. The reader should be aware that several passages are paraphrased and others omitted altogether. The Greek text of *The Best Kind of Teaching* has recently been published with an Italian translation by A. Barigazzi *Favorino di Arelate, Opere* (Florence 1966) 179ff.

221

7 Waszink shows that the Aldine edition was the only text available to Erasmus, ie, that he had no opportunity to collate manuscripts (see ASD I–1 632).

8 Cf dedicatory letter 224 below. Cf also Epp 1707:3, 1713:30.

9 See Waszink's assessment of Erasmus' corrections in ASD I–1 632–3.

10 Epp 188:66–7, 177:114–15 (quoting Cicero)

222

11 ASD I-1 643:8, 645:13, 642:10 etc

12 See n17 below.

13 Erasmus adds objects to complete the construction of a verbal phrase (eg ASD I-1 643:2, 648:12) or introduces a relative clause for support: *basis autem cui insistit* 'the base *on which he stands*' (641:5; cf 640:26); *ii qui sequuntur Fortunam* 'those *who follow* Fortuna' (641:9). These clauses have no corresponding phrase in the Greek text, but are necessary for the Latin construction. The compressed Greek phrase ναυαγήσαντι συνεκκολυμβήσει, whose conciseness through compounding cannot be paralleled either in Latin or in English, is skilfully unfolded into *nave fracta simul enatant cum possessore* 'float up together with their owner after the ship has been wrecked' (642:26).

14 ASD I-1 655:21–2 (in Greek type), 656:2, 668:8 (transliterated)

15 ASD I-1 666:17, 650:21, 641:21 (used by Plautus in *Aulularia* 3.5.39)

16 *Basis* (ASD I-1 640:14) is used by Cicero *In Verrem* 2.2.63; *nothus* (644:23) is legitimized by Quintilian 3.6.97; *oeconomus* (656:23) occurs in *Codex Iustiniani* 1.3.33.

17 ASD I-1 645:7, 647:11, 656:19–20 etc

18 *Quid aliud fructus ferunt* (ASD I-1 644:12); *qui docendi munus profitetur* (662:24)

19 *Ciceronianus* LB I 1007D / CWE 28 412

20 ASD I-1 643:8, 649:4

21 See *Exhortation* n7.

223

22 See eg *The Best Kind of Teaching* n12 and n34; *The Best Physician* n2.

23 See *Exhortation* n16 and n25; *The Best Kind of Teaching* n29.

24 See n5 above.

25 Ep 211:77–82

Dedicatory letter

224

1 The recipient of Ep 1698 was a Hungarian physician who had rendered medical services to Erasmus during his stay in Basel. See also n3 below.

2 Chaplain at the Hungarian court. See Allen Ep 1660:16ff for a glowing recommendation accorded him by Jan Antonin of Košice.
3 Antonin had received a public invitation to practise medicine in Basel, but settled in Cracow. Later on he became personal physician to King Sigismund I.
4 Horace *Odes* 4.11.23–4
5 The Greek text contained many corrupt passages. See introduction n4.
6 See n3 above.
7 Henckel had sent Erasmus a golden measuring spoon adorned with a figure of the martyr St Sebastian. Erasmus likens his enemies and their slanderous accusations to the darts of Diocletian's archers who killed St Sebastian.
8 Krzysztof Szydłowiecki, count of Cracow, had sent Erasmus a golden horologe, measuring spoon, and fork (see Allen Ep 1752:7).
9 Erasmus uses the poetic Greek phrase ἀπερείσια θῶρα.

Exhortation to Study the Liberal Arts

225

1 *Anima*, translating the Greek term *psyche*, which covers emotional processes
2 *Affectuum capacem*, literally 'capable of emotions,' is an odd translation for Greek ἐνδιάθετον 'deepseated, residing in the mind,' ie 'of thought or conception.'
3 *Institutione* 'instruction' is a misleading translation for Greek προαιρέσει 'intention.' It shifts the Greek antithesis chance/design to one of nature/ instruction. One is tempted to emend *institutione* to read *instituto* 'by design,' but Erasmus repeats the idea expressed here in much the same terms in *De pueris* LB I 491D.
4 The phrase 'which ... plastic' is added by Erasmus because *figendi*, which he uses to translate Greek πλάττειν 'model' is ambiguous. *Fingere* can mean 'fashioning' in the sense of 'modelling,' but can also denote other creative activities, notably 'composing' a literary work.
5 This is a somewhat awkward rendition of a well-balanced Greek sentence.
6 Frag 292 Snell
7 Erasmus seems to emphasize that man's achievement was his own – the Greek gives no such indication. Galen describes philosophy as the 'greatest of divine goods.' Erasmus omits 'divine,' perhaps 'to avoid too high a qualification of pagan philosophy' (Waszink ASD I-1 640:5n).
8 Cf Pausanias 4.30.6.
9 This whole passage is freely, but most skilfully, translated to reflect the epic mood of the Greek passage. Just as Galen's words recall Homeric phrases, so Erasmus reproduces Virgilian language (cf *Aeneid* 1.69).

226

10 The phrase 'when he is ... troubles' is an expanded translation of Galen's ἐν τοιαύταις περιστάσεσι 'in such difficulties.'
11 The phrase 'on which she stands' is added by Erasmus.

12 The effect of Greek ἄγει καὶ φέρει 'drives and carries' is doubled in the Latin translation.

13 Greek ὅτ 'οὐδὲν ὄφελος 'because of no use' is translated twice, first by *frustra* 'in vain,' then by the lengthy *cum hinc iam nulla sit illius utilitas*, literally 'since they no longer derive any benefit from this source.'

14 *Rationis* 'reason' translates Greek λόγου, which can mean 'speech, word' as well. Cf Hesiod *Works and Days* 77; *Adagia* III vii 95: 'he has great force of expression.'

15 Cf Pausanias 7.22.2. Mercury can also signify ambiguity and changeability; cf *Adagia* III vii 95; *De copia* CWE 24 642–3.

16 The phrase 'supported on all sides by its four corners' is added by Erasmus to explain *tessara* 'cube.'

17 Galen says 'sometimes they also adorn [κοσμοῦσιν] the god himself with this figure.' By rendering κοσμοῦσιν as *repraesentant* 'represent' Erasmus obscures the meaning of the sentence.

18 King of Lydia 560–547 BC. His wealth was proverbial (see *Adagia* I vi 74). He was overthrown by Cyrus (see n22 below). His fate is related by Herodotus 1.29–33.

19 Tyrant of Samos c 538–522 BC. He fell into the hands of a hostile satrap, Oroites, who had him crucified. Cf Herodotus 3.125.

20 A river in Lydia that carried gold in its stream; see Pliny *Naturalis historia* 5.110; *Adagia* I vi 75.

21 A reference to the well-known ring story; see Herodotus 3.42.

22 Persian king, 559–529 BC, killed in a battle against the Massagetes, a neighbouring tribe. Cf Herodotus 1.214.

23 King of Troy; according to the *Iliupersis* Priam was killed by Neoptolemos. Galen, however, says that he was 'bound.' This may be a reference to the fact that he was, in his youth, captured by Heracles.

24 Dionysius II of Syracuse was overthrown by his brother-in-law, Dion, in 555 BC. The reversal of his fortunes is proverbial (see *Adagia* I i 83). He ended up as a schoolteacher in Corinth.

25 The phrase 'in very different positions' is added by Erasmus to explain the contrast.

26 Erasmus' translation of Greek *demagogoi* as *oratores* is weak. *Orator* does not have the same negative connotation as *demagogos*. Compare Cicero *Brutus* 49.182 and *De oratore* 1.46.202 where the good *orator* is contrasted with the ranting and haranguing demagogue, termed *clamator*, *causidicus*, or *rabula*.

227

27 Aristippus was a Greek philosopher of the fourth century BC, the founder of the Cyrenaic school. The anecdote is recorded by Diogenes Laertius 6.1.6.

28 Sophocles *Oedipus Colonus* 3–4

29 The phrase 'with their ... owner' is added by Erasmus.

228

30 The phrase 'into his service' is added by Erasmus.

31 Both sayings are cited as those of Diogenes by Diogenes Laertius 6.2.47 and

60. Kaibel (32) suggests that the expression may go back to Antisthenes, ie, that 'Demosthenes' should read 'Antisthenes.'

32 Greek ἐὰν οὕτως τύχῃ ... 'if it comes to pass that ...' is translated twice, once by *si sic acciderit* 'if it so happens' and again by *forte* 'by chance.'

33 Euripides *Phoenissae* 404-5; the second verse is a laboured translation of a corrupt text. The meaning in Euripides: 'A curse is poverty, no sustenance my noble name.'

229

34 *Menexenus* 247B

35 Erasmus writes *Sthenei*, repeating Galen's error. The quotation comes from Homer *Iliad* 4.405.

36 A florid translation for a succinct Greek phrase. See introductory note 222.

37 The phrase 'than those ... origin' is added by Erasmus.

38 Erasmus uses the term *nothus* 'bastard.' The Greek is more general: 'reviled for his origin.' This is a reference to Themistocles' mother, who was Thracian.

39 Anacharsis was numbered among the Seven Sages. His witty reply is quoted by Diogenes Laertius 1.104.

40 The phrase 'with greater attention and concentration' is added by Erasmus.

41 A Greek poet and physician to the Macedonian king Antigonos Gonatas (fl 270 BC).

42 Stoic philosopher (d 208 BC)

43 Athenian demagogues who came to power after Pericles' death. They were strongly opposed to peace with Sparta. Cleon died in battle against Brasidas (422 BC); Hyperbolus was ostracized and killed in exile (411 BC).

230

44 Frag 83 Snell and *Olympian Odes* 6.152

45 Solon. See Plutarch *Solon* 22.

46 Erasmus keeps this sentence in the imperfect tense, whereas Greek has the gnomic aorist denoting a general statement: 'Since all art is practised ...,' many men neglect ...' Compare 236 'were perfectly proportioned ...' where Erasmus commits the same error.

47 Frag *Adespota* 174 Nauck

48 Cf Herodotus 1.32.

49 Frag 928 Nauck

50 Cf Mimnermus frag 1.4 Diels.

51 Frag 50 Lobel-Page

52 Source unknown

53 In Greek χαλεπόν 'grievous, troublesome' clearly modifies 'storm.' The Latin is ambiguous, since both 'storm' and 'old age' are feminine nouns. LB and ASD punctuation suggests that *molesta* 'grievous' modifies 'old age,' and indeed *molesta* does not seem particularly suited to describe a storm.

54 The word 'oncoming' is added by Erasmus, perhaps as an echo of *imminens* 'threatening,' which occurs in Solon's words quoted shortly before.

55 Homer *Iliad* 14.32

56 *Iliad* 5.429, 6.490, 2.673-5 (paraphrases)

57 The so-called 'mirror of Socrates'; cf Diogenes Laertius 2.33.

231

58 Homer *Odyssey* 8.174, 170–3

59 Epode, the part of an ode sung after the strophe and antistrophe

60 Cf Diogenes Laertius 6.2.32; the same action is attributed to Aristippus at 2.75.

61 One would expect 'he,' as indeed the Greek suggests.

62 Erasmus read μὴ σκοπούμενον 'not considering, not to mention,' but the correct reading is μὴ σκοτούμενον 'without getting dizzy' [ie while turning cartwheels], as translated by Bellisarius: *sic ut non offundantur caligines* (Beaudouin 40).

63 Both were famous for their miniature sculptures (see Pliny *Naturalis historia* 4.36.43).

64 Galen's attitude toward athletics may have been influenced by his experience as physician to the gladiators at Pergamon or his service to the brutish emperor Commodus, who considered himself a reincarnation of Hercules.

65 The famous antecedent for this complaint is Xenophanes (frag 2.6–12 Diels-Kranz): 'The athlete may have more honours in the eyes of the people, he may occupy the illustrious seat of honour at the games, get public mainte-nance and a valuable gift, yet I am worthier than he, for my wisdom is preferable to the strength of horses and men.'

232

66 Galen says 'because of the benefit derived from their arts.' Erasmus may have read εὕρεσιν 'discovery' or something similar for Galen's εὐεργεσίαν 'bene-ficial act.'

67 The Pythian god is Apollo, who gave oracular replies at Delphi.

68 See Plato *Apology* 21A.

69 Herodotus 1.65

70 Cf Plutarch 'The Divine Vengeance' 560E.

233

71 Frag 282.1–9 Nauck

72 Euripides ibidem 16–18

73 Euripides ibidem 19–23 .

74 Erasmus uses *affectio* to translate Greek διάθεσις; *habitudo* for Greek ἕξις. Διάθεσις is a transient state, a stage in a development; ἕξις denotes a perma-nent state.

75 *Nutriment* 34 (Loeb)

234

76 Greek τῶν πολλῶν 'of the many' does not refer to witnesses, but to the 'common people.' Galen says 'they rely on the praises of the common people and from them derive vain glory.'

77 Phryne was a fourth-century BC courtesan renowned for both her beauty and her wit.

78 The phrase 'artfully made horror masks' translates Greek μορμολυκεῖα, liter-ally 'hobgoblins.'

79 Cf Plato *Republic* 533D.

80 *Aphorisms* 1.3 (Loeb)
81 *Epidem* 6.4.18 (Littré). Erasmus' translation does not recapture the succinct-ness and parallel sound of ἀκορίη τροφῆς, ἀοκνίη πόνων.
82 Proverbial expression. See *Adagia* III vii 39.

235
83 Hippocrates *Epidem* 6.6.2 (Littré)
84 *Iliad* 24.677–9, the last verse is changed to suit the author's purpose.
85 Galen says 'scrape their backs with oleander.' Kaibel (51) suggests that this refers to a medication used against scabies. He cites Vegetius *Mulomedicina* 2.135.7.
86 *Aphorisms* 2.51
87 See n75 above.
88 Prayers, personified as the daughters of Zeus, described thus in Homer *Iliad* 9.503
89 *Fossis cavati* 'hollow,' literally 'surrounded by trenches,' translates Greek περιορωρυγμένοι, literally 'dug out around.' Cf Plato *Republic* 533D: 'The eye of the soul is sunk (κατωρύγμενος) in barbaric mire.'

236
90 The translations for the Greek terms have been added by Erasmus.
91 Erasmus read ἀπὸ γῆς μίας, ie 'common ground.' The correct reading is ἀπὸ πηχῆς μίας 'from one fountain-head.' Cf Bellisarius: *ab uno fonte* (Beaudouin 240).
92 Erasmus must have read ἰσχυρότατον (nominative singular neuter), literally 'strongest,' ie 'this is the strongest point.' Galen says ἰσχυρότατοι (nominative plural masculine, referring to the athletes), '*they* are the strongest.' It remains unclear from where Erasmus took the phrase *ad rem publicam* 'to the public.'
93 See n73 above.
94 Reading *pueris … natis*. Cf Bellisarius: *imbecilliores nuper natis infantibus* (Beaudouin 240).

237
95 The phrase 'hold up their heads' is added by Erasmus.
96 This is the meaning of the Greek sentence; Erasmus' translation is confusing.
97 Famous wrestler and Olympic victor in the sixth century BC
98 κατὰ μῆκος 'lengthwise'; omitted by Erasmus
99 Unable to get free, he was attacked and killed by a pack of wolves.
100 Literally 'the state of the Greeks' (*Graecorum rem publicam*). *Res publica* is a very 'Roman' way of translating Galen's τὸ κοινὸν, which denotes a loose association of city states.
101 See Herodotus 7.140ff.
102 Euripides frag 200.3–4 Nauck
103 Erasmus did not recognize the technical meaning of ἐντείνας 'putting into verse'; he used the literal meaning 'stretching,' ie 'long.'
104 The terms *dolichon* and *diaulum* are paraphrased by Erasmus to clarify their meaning.

238

105 Galen adds ἐν πόσιν 'in the footrace.'
106 See 227 above.

The Best Kind of Teaching

240

1 Born in Arelate, France, in the second half of the first century AD, Favorinus settled in Rome, where his skill in sophistic argumentation made him famous. He wrote numerous essays on paradoxical subjects (eg *In Praise of Fever*), none of which are extant.

2 The Academy was founded by Plato, but departed considerably from his doctrine at various points in its history. Under the leadership of Carneades (d 129 BC) the school was known for its sceptical philosophy.

3 Erasmus transliterates the Greek term.

4 The two phrases translate one Greek term, ἀοριστία.

5 Galen says 'to pass judgment before they have learned a scientific method of judgment.' Compare Regius' pedestrian, but accurate, rendition: *absque quod doceantur prius scientiale iudicatorium*.

6 Favorinus' *Peri tes Akademikes diatheseos* is also mentioned by Aulus Gellius 20.1.9.

7 *Pros Epikteton*, ie *Against Epictetus*, was answered by Galen with a defence of Epictetus (not extant).

8 The correct title (as given by Galen) is *Alcibiades*. The preposition belongs to the sentence structure.

9 Erasmus retains the Greek terms and adds Latin translations.

10 The phrase 'which some people use' is added by Erasmus.

11 The Stoics defined 'apprehensive impression' as a perception 'caused by existing objects and imaged and stamped in the subject in accordance with that existing object' (Sextus Empiricus, *Against the Logicians* 1.248). Carneades objected to the last clause, saying that 'impressions are produced by non-real objects just as by real ones' (ibidem 1.402).

12 Erasmus misconstrued the Greek, which says 'and "apprehension" and "apprehensive impression" correspondingly,' ie, 'apprehension' corresponds to 'knowledge' and 'apprehensive imagination' to 'knowable impression,' as translated by Regius: *sed proportionaliter esse his comprehensionem et comprehensibilem fantasiam*.

13 Cf Sextus Empiricus *Against the Logicians* 2.18f for the Sceptics' position: 'But everything apparent is not true (for what is experienced in sleep or in madness is not true).' A criterion is therefore needed to distinguish between true and false appearances: 'This criterion is either apparent to all or non-evident. But if it is apparent, since not every apparent thing is true ... this too will need to be tested by another apparent thing, and that again by a different one, and so we go on *ad infinitum*.'

241

14 Followers of the sceptic philosopher Pyrrho, who taught in the fourth century BC

15 Cf Sextus Empiricus *Against the Logicians* 2.53–4 on the judgment of sick and healthy persons: 'One ought not to trust one condition more than the other.' Similarly on sane and insane persons, ibidem 57ff.

16 Chrysippus (c 280–207 BC) was head of the Academy.

17 Theophrastus (c 370–285 BC), pupil and successor of Aristotle in the Peripatetic school

18 One would expect 'each' for Greek ἕκαστον. Regius uses *singulum* 'each single.'

19 Galen says 'if they grant us any sensation through natural criteria (φυσικοῖς κριτηρίοις).' Erasmus' text omitted κριτηρίοις, and he connected φυσικοῖς (which can mean both 'physical' and 'physician') with ἡμῖν 'us.'

20 In what follows Erasmus made the best he could of a thoroughly corrupted text. His complaint that he had to 'guess' rather than translate is most relevant here. The emended sentence bears a decidedly Erasmian stamp. It is a comment on teaching methods not unlike *De pueris* CWE 26 310, 332–3, 345, rather than a demand for training in logical reasoning as intended by Galen. The text as established by Barigazzi runs (181:2–4): 'Something else is needed: craftsmen should be required to teach their disciples immediately to reason – or as the common people call it, "cast one's vote."' This is also the general meaning of Regius' version.

   Repetitione translates Greek ἀπαιτήσεως, literally 'a demanding back,' in this particular context, 'demanding answers in reply to questions,' ie, making the student repeat or recall what he has been taught. For this notion of *repetere* see *De pueris* 508B, where Erasmus uses *exigendo* and *repetendo* in the sense of 'testing' and 'asking to repeat' respectively.

21 The negative is Erasmus' conjecture; modern editors have accepted the positive adverb *eutheos* 'immediately' and connected it with the following clause, ie educators must immediately introduce their students to a process of reasoning.

22 *Considerationem* 'scrutiny, consideration' is a peculiar translation for Greek λογίζεσθαι 'to reason' (Barigazzi 187: *ragionare*). The objective genitive *eorum quae tradita sunt* 'of what has been handed down' has no equivalent in the Greek text, and one suspects that Erasmus added it. If his purpose was clarification, he was not very successful, for it is not immediately clear whether *tradita* refers to the knowledge transmitted by the teacher or the precepts handed down by previous generations.

23 *Ad calculum vocare* 'reckoning' is Erasmus' translation of ψηφίζειν 'to cast one's vote.' On the meaning of this phrase see *Adagia* I v 55. Regius uses the postclassical *discutere* 'to investigate, separate mentally.'

24 Modern editors read οὗτοι 'these' and interpret Greek to mean 'or'; Erasmus read αὐτοί 'the same' and translated ἤ as 'as,' literally, 'the people who suspend judgment ... are the same as those who reject ...'

25 See n2 above.

26 Carneades argued that the concept of the line was not apprehensible, therefore 'the principles of geometry are unfounded and as these are abolished, no other geometrical theorem can subsist' (Sextus Empiricus *Against the Grammarians* 92).

242

27 Erasmus gives a literal translation of a corrupt passage. His text did not contain the adverb προσηκόντως, 'rightly,' modifying 'admitting,' which occurs in other manuscripts. Also, modern editors have eliminated ὡς 'as,' thereby arriving at the meaning 'Favorinus is right in admitting ...' This is a suitable apodosis to round off the protasis 'if any Academic philosopher ...'

28 This is an obscure translation of a corrupt text. Regius omits the passage altogether. Modern editors have accepted Sauppe's emendation εἰ διδάσκει 'if he teaches' for ἐδίδασκεν 'he taught.'

29 The phrases describing the purpose of the tools have been added by Erasmus.

30 Cf Sextus Empiricus *Against the Logicians* 2.410. He discounts such arguments as 'plausible illustrations'; they cannot be used as rigorous proofs because they deal with corporeal things, while 'proof is incorporeal.'

31 Erasmus says *qui docendi munus profitetur*, literally 'one who engages in the profession of teaching,' an emphatic translation for simple Greek διδάσκαλος 'teacher.'

243

32 This sentence is badly corrupted in Greek. Erasmus' literal translation remains an agglomeration of clauses without clear grammatical structure or unity of thought. He writes: 'Tantum hoc stude, ut sophistas doceas nullam nobis a natura insitam vim iudicandi. Deinde fortassis impudenter nobis, inquit, et sensum et intellectum, quibus evidenter iudicamus de vero, concedet aliquis, cupiens nos in logicis frustranea spe volutari.' The first sentence does not make sense in the context. The Greek text has been variously emended by modern editors, mainly with the purpose of making 'sophists' the subject (cf Barigazzi 183:8). The second sentence introduces a view opposite to that of the first one. Because it lacks a proper transition and does not clearly indicate the author of these statements, modern editors have assumed a lacuna after 'impudent.'

33 Literally 'he said that nothing could be known from that source (*inde ... unde*).' Erasmus' construction shows that he read ὅθεν 'whence,' which has been emended by Marquardt (introductory note n6 above) to read δῆθεν 'indeed.' The modern reading allows for a smoother flow of the sentence.

34 Erasmus' Latin is misleading; he phrases this clause in a negative form: *nullum esse iudicium naturae* 'that there is *no* natural power of judgment.' One would expect a connecting participle: *dicentes* 'saying.'

35 In the passage 'I shall ... with you' Erasmus is content to give a literal translation of the Greek text, but the words are rather abrupt and a lacuna or corruption has been assumed by modern editors.

36 Erasmus diverges from the Greek text, which has 'left off speaking.'

244

37 Literally 'that the right method is right' with εὐθεῖαν 'right' being repeated. The variant μίαν 'one' found in some texts for the second produces a more agreeable reading: 'that there is only one correct method.'

38 Cf Heraclitus' famous saying: 'The path up and down is one and the same' (frag 60 Diels-Kranz).

39 The variant *se* 'he' (reflexive), which is found in some texts, may be preferable: 'that he is blind but still able ...'

40 Cf 241 above. Erasmus' wording is somewhat obscure, reflecting a possible lacuna. Cf Regius' much fuller translation: 'Some are so deficient that they deny us any power of judgment, that they deny the principle "if A ..."'

41 Erasmus translates ἀπιστίαν 'distrust,' 'incredibility,' which makes for an awkward construction in Latin. In the manuscripts we find διδασκαλίαν ἀπιστίαν (ie two nouns side by side: 'teaching,' 'distrust'). Barigazzi omits the second noun, arriving at the meaning 'it makes no difference in teaching judgment.' He notes (185:21 apparatus) that Regius translated *qualiscumque sit* [ie *doctrinatio* 'whatever teaching'] and conjectures that the original text perhaps had διδασκαλίαν ὁποίάν τιν' 'whatever teaching.'

42 A reference to Plato's doctrine of intellectual leadership. Cf *Republic* 412C–D; *Laws* 964D–E.

43 Only fragments of this work are extant.

The Proper Physician

245

1 Cf Hippocrates *Regimen* 1.2 (Loeb).

2 In Greek there are two pairs of ὁ μεν ... οἱ δε 'the one ... the others' referring to Hippocrates on the one hand and his self-styled followers on the other hand. Erasmus does not acknowledge this division in his translation and attributes both sets of opinions to the would-be disciples of Hippocrates.

3 This sudden switch from plural to singular is due to the error pointed out in the preceding note.

4 Cf Hippocrates *Ancient Medicine* 20, 22 (Loeb); Plato *Phaedrus* 270B.

5 For this demand see Plato *Phaedrus* 270D.

6 *Ante cognoscere* is a literal translation of Greek προγιγνώσκειν 'diagnose.' Erasmus evidently felt the need to represent the prefix *pro* in Latin. The Hippocratic corpus contains a treatise *Prognostikon* 'Diagnosis.' This passage contains verbal echoes from the first chapter of this treatise.

7 The Hippocratic corpus contains a treatise *Peri diaites* 'Regimen.'

8 Cf Galen *Natural Faculties* 1.2.

246

9 This is the general meaning of the Greek text – Erasmus' Latin is obscure. See Waszink ASD I-1 666:7–9n: 'Erasmus has not seen that what follows after εὑρίσκων ... is an acc. cum inf. and that a new sentence begins in θατέρου. In consequence of this, the Latin sentence does not run.'

10 The Latin text has *hanc coronam* 'this crown.' Very likely *hanc* is a misprint for *hunc* 'him.'

11 *Natura ... compositus*. The phrase suggests that Erasmus read φυσικὴν 'physical,' 'natural' for ψυχικὴν 'intellectual,' which is found in all the Greek manuscripts.

12 Phidias was a famous sculptor of the Periclean age.

13 A renowned painter, contemporary of Alexander the Great

14 Either the Persian king Artaxerxes I (d 424) or more likely his son and successor by the same name – but neither is expressly linked with Hippocrates in extant sources.

15 Perdiccas II, king of Macedon, whom Hippocrates reputedly cured of his passionate attachment to a woman

16 Cranon, a city in Thessaly, and Thasos, an island off Thrace, are places visited by Hippocrates on his journeys.

247

17 An island off the south-west coast of Asia Minor, birthplace of Hippocrates

18 Hippocrates' colleague and son-in-law

19 The Hippocratic corpus contains a treatise on this topic entitled *Airs, Waters, Places.*

20 Erasmus must have read ἐπάκτιοις 'on the shore' instead of ἐπακτοῖς 'brought in.' The Greek reads: 'the community which uses water that has been brought in ...'

21 The phrase 'an abundance of' is added by Erasmus.

22 The following passage reflects the theories of pre-Socratic philosophers, which were discussed by Hippocrates in *The Nature of Man.* In his commentary on this work (3.93 Chartrè) Galen explains that the 'first nature' consists of primary elements, ie fire, water, air, and earth; blood, flesh, and bones are of the 'second nature' or 'primary composition' of elements also called ὁμοιομερῆ 'similar,' a term going back to Anaxagoras; the 'third nature' is the 'secondary composition' of elements, which comprises the members and internal organs of the body. Diseases are divided in classes corresponding to this order. Cf Galen *Natural Faculties* 1.2.6, 2.8; cf Plato *Timaeus* 82Aff.

23 Erasmus transliterates the Greek term (see previous note) and adds an explanation.

24 Erasmus' word order in this sentence is awkward. He places the relative clause after *philosophus*, making the philosopher rather than the physician the antecedent.

248

25 Erasmus' translation of this passage does not correspond to the Greek, which has the following meaning (diverging phrases in italics): '... contending that a physician must indeed be temperate and modest, that he must despise money and be just, but that it is not necessary for him to be a philosopher; *and that he must* know the nature of bodies ... and the methods of treatment, *but need not* be versed in logical reasoning? Are you not ashamed to quarrel about terms *when you have conceded* the facts?'

26 Greek καὶ μὴν ὀψὲ μέν is rendered in Latin by an equally cumbersome *quamquam id sero quidem*, literally 'although this is indeed late.'

27 Erasmus omits σωφρονήσαντα, ie 'to be reasonable and ...'

28 Waszink in his commentary (ASD I-1 669:9–10n) calls this sentence a 'somewhat free translation.' More likely it is an error. The Greek means 'we must practise philosophy before anything else.'

THE TONGUE / *LINGUA*

Introductory note

250

1 Ep 1593 to Krzysztof Szydłowiecki
2 Allen Ep 1558:69–155 (the dedication of Erasmus' translation of six homilies of Chrysostom)
3 Cf Epp 1540 (January) and 1574 from Botzheim in Constance, 1584 (July) to Adrianus Cornelii Barlandus (in which Erasmus comments, 'I see human life reverting to the barbarism of the Turks ... a bloody drama is being enacted by our peasants here. I do not know what will be the outcome of the tragedy'), and 1599 to Berquin. In October (Ep 1633) he estimates the casualties at 100,000, for which he holds Luther largely responsible. See G.R. Elton *Reformation Europe* (London 1963) 57–60.
4 He obtained a dispensation from abstention from meat (Ep 1547), and Clement VII granted him the privilege of writing his own will (Ep 1588).
5 Ep 1537; cf later Ep 1636.
6 Allen Ep 1538:15–17
7 For Botzheim through the offices of Sadoleto (Ep 1555); for Pierre Toussain, with his bishop (Ep 1618)
8 Cf *Lingua* 347–67.
9 Cf Ep 1579 from Béda in May, answered by Erasmus's Ep 1581 of 15 June; this was returned undelivered and dispatched again with Ep 1596 in late August, to be answered by Béda in October (Ep 1642).
10 Cf Allen Ep 1579 introduction and Erasmus' letter to Berquin (Ep 1599) in July reproaching him for bringing trouble on Erasmus with his indiscreet versions. See A. Renaudet *Etudes Erasmiennes* (Paris 1959) 240–50.
11 Ep 1581:790–804

251

12 Ep 1591
13 On Theoderici see CEBR III 318. For his pamphlet *Apologia in eum librum quem ab anno Erasmus Roterodamus de confessione edidit* see below 348 and n221.
   Ep 1582 was addressed 'To the Theologians of Louvain', but Erasmus names in the letter the dean Nicolas Coppin, Jan Driedo, Godschalk Rosemondt and Willem of Vianen.
14 Cf Ep 1585 (to Maximilianus Transsilvanus, at the court in Brussels):79–81 and Ep 1621 to Pierre Barbier in October of this year. Latomus' work was *De trium linguarum et studii theologici ratione dialogus* (Antwerp: Hillen 1519).
15 'The Treatment of Speech in Medieval Ethical and Courtesy Literature' *Rhetorica* 4-1 (1986) 21–50
16 PL 88 597–719
17 PL 80 942–3
18 See Jeannine Fohlen 'Un Apocryphe de Sénèque mal connu: le *De Verborum Copia*' *Medieval Studies* 42 (1980) 139–211. For Martin's *Formula vitae honestae* see *Martini episcopi Bracarensis opera omnia* ed Claude W. Barlow (New Haven 1950) 204–50. I owe all references to the article of Johnston cited above.

19 Valerianus *De oris insolentia, De otiosis verbis* PL 52 706–12
20 *Super epistulas catholicas: Expositio super divi Jacobi epistolam* PL 93 26–30
21 *Commentarius in Ecclesiasticum* 4.13–14 PL 109 894–900
22 *Sermones de diversis* 17 (*De triplici custodia manus linguae et cordis*) PL 183 583–7.
   Johnston refers to the survey of Paul F. Gehl 'Mystical Language Models
   in Monastic Educational Psychology' *Journal of Medieval Studies* 14 (1984)
   210–43.

252

23 PL 102 801–5
24 Pars 6 (*De silentio clericorum*) PL 203 943–1026
25 PL 176 928–52
26 On Peraldus' *Summa* see Morton W. Bloomfield *The Seven Deadly Sins: An
   Introduction to the History of a Religious Concept* (East Lansing, Michigan 1952)
   124. I owe the next three references to Bloomfield's work.
27 The *Somme le Roy* (1279) was translated into Middle English as *The Book of Vices
   and Virtues*. For the section on sins of the tongue see Early English Text
   Society o s 217 (Oxford 1942) 54–68.
28 Bloomfield 129
29 *Bibliotheca mundi seu Speculi maioris Vicentii Burgundi* ... 2.4.122–77 and
   1.31.92–3 (Douai: Baltazaris Belleri 1624)
30 *Summa theologiae* 2.2.72–6
31 *Summa theologiae* 2.2.110–16
32 *De inventione* 1.2.2–3; *De oratore* 1.33, 2.31; *De officiis* 1.50
33 Cf the dedicatory letter (260 below) on the land where Astraea, spirit
   of justice, may still linger, though she has been driven out of western
   Europe.

253

34 Cf Ep 1622 (October) to Hieronim Łaski; Ep 1652 from Critius, then bishop of
   Przemyśl. See Allen VI 236 for a list of works of Erasmus published in Poland
   through 1525.
35 Note that Ep 1658 (January 1526) from Erasmus Schets praising the
   Lingua precedes the Antwerp publication. He must have received from
   Erasmus complimentary copies both of it and of the *apologia* against
   Sutor.
36 Cf 345 below. The printer had evidently given this sum of money in Venetian
   ducats, which to him at least meant the most important gold coin then
   circulating in Europe. But Erasmus was here referring to the Roman province
   of Asia (ie the western region of modern Turkey, then largely Greek), in
   the first century BC when, of course, no such coin existed. He thus requested
   that the correct monetary term, *talents*, be used. The *talent* (from the Greek
   τάλαντον, a pair of scales) was originally a Greek silver weight containing 60
   minae = 6,000 drachmai.
37 Cf ASD IV 224.
38 On Erasmus and Vives see Y. Charlier *Erasme et l'amitié* (Paris 1977)
39 Marcel Bataillon *Erasmo y España* 2nd ed (Mexico City 1966) 311; ASD IV
   226

254

40 See W.K.C. Guthrie, *History of Greek Philosophy* III-1 *The Sophists* (Cambridge 1971) 25, 44, 168, 180–1.

41 *De inventione* 1.5; *De oratore* 1.32. In *Tusculan Disputations* 5.5 Cicero makes the same claim for philosophy – the other aspect of *logos*.

255

42 347–67 below

43 Cf 355–6, 356, 360, and 362. Cf Romans 12.14, quoted at 365 and used resumptively at 396.

44 412 below

45 1 Cor 13:1

256

46 Cf 360 below.

47 The theme of venom, already associated by Erasmus with calumny in a letter of 1522 (Allen Ep 1310:24–8), appears on the first page of the *Lingua*; the Psylli, introduced at 321, reappear as a metaphor for Christian preachers at 403.

48 Eg the Greek idiom repeated without point from 295–333, the duplicate explanation of the Greek avenging goddesses at 309 and 351, and the unrelated double use of Hesiodic proverbs on the bad neighbour at 281 and 363, and on evil counsel at 313 and 340. Other repetitions such as the resumption of the imagery from *Adagia* from 273 to 279–80, the development of the story of Pyrrhus and the drunken soldier from 278 to 291, or of Augustus and the young man at court from 294 to 386, are deliberate continuations.

49 Cf 324–5 below.

50 Cf 319–22 below.

51 Cf 274–7, 300–14 below.

52 Cf 273–4 below.

53 *Ecclesiastes sive de ratione concionandi*, published August 1535. See now Robert G. Kleinhans in *Essays on the Works of Erasmus* ed deMolen (Yale University Press 1978) 243–54.

54 For a list of the most significant typographical errors and misreadings of the Greek ligatures see Joseph IJsewijn 'Castigationes Erasmianae' *Humanistica Lovaniensia* 31 (1982) 211–16.

55 Thus the coarse language of the translation from Martial (282 below) is faithful to Martial's idiom and intent.

Dedicatory letter

257

1 This dedicatory letter is Ep 1593. Chancellor of Poland since 1515, Szydłowiecki had been educated at the court of Casimir IV. In 1515 he was appointed count of Cracow, and later (1527) castellan. There is no evidence of his acquaintance with Erasmus before this dedication. He was known as an advocate of peace and a man of letters.

The preface derives its theme and many details of its argument from
Plutarch's short essay *Animine an corporis affectiones sint peiores* (*Moralia*
500B–502A), which argues that sicknesses of the soul are far worse than those
of the body. Like Plutarch, Erasmus starts from Homer's verdict that man
is the most wretched of all animals (*Iliad* 17.446–7), but Erasmus amplifies this
with other ancient sayings on the hardships of human life before proceeding to introduce Plutarch's main thesis (257–8). Plutarch subordinated the
issue of physical pain in order to stress the issue of cure: both Plutarch
and Erasmus argue that mental ills are more harmful than physical disease
because they are unrecognized by the sufferer, so that the prerequisite of
recovery, acknowledgment of the need for cure, is lacking. Erasmus has
reorganized much of Plutarch's illustrative material, bringing forward
Plutarch's example contrasting the victim of gout who welcomes the
physician and the madman who resists aid; he has similarly anticipated
Plutarch's account of how men misrepresent their own vices. Erasmus then
leaves Plutarch, and draws the information which is the basis for most of
his subsequent statements from the books of Pliny's *Naturalis historia* which
deal with medicine and disease.

2 Homer *Iliad* 17.446–7; *Odyssey* 18.130–1
3 Erasmus' main sources for this saying, according to his version in *Adagia* II iii
49, are Lactantius *Divinae institutiones* 3.19.3, Cicero, Pliny *Naturalis historia*
7.4, and Plutarch *Consolatio ad Apollonium*, *Moralia* 115B. According to Cicero
Tusculan Disputations 1.114, Silenus was captured by Midas, and in return
for his release advised the king that 'it was best by far for man never to have
been born, but the nearest good to this was to die as soon as possible.' The
anecdote is Greek; for a recent study see M.E. Hubbard 'The Capture of
Silenus' *Proceedings of the Cambridge Philological Society* 201 (1975) 53–62
4 Pliny the Elder (d 79 AD), in the volume of his *Naturalis historia* dealing with
human life, 7.168: 'Nature has granted man no better gift than the shortness of life.' Erasmus was preparing the text of this work for the Froben
edition (Basel: March 1525) at the same time that he was working on *Lingua*
(cf Allen Ep 1544). He had annotated the work somewhat earlier (1516) but
may have contributed to the notes composed by Beatus Rhenanus in 1525
and published by Froben separately from the edition in March 1526.
5 Pythagoras' saying in Lucian's *Gallus* 20 was previously quoted by Erasmus
with the Homeric quotation above (n2) in *Moriae encomium* CWE 27 108.
6 Cf *Adagia* I i 8; Cicero *Ad familiares* 16.24.1.
7 Cf Pliny *Naturalis historia* 26.9; for the unknown and new varieties see ch 4 of
the same book.

258
8 Perhaps suggested to Erasmus by the work *Laus podagrae* addressed to him in
1525 by his friend Willibald Pirckheimer. This was an adaptation of Lucian's
Podagra; see H. Rupprich 'Willibald Pirckheimer' in Gerald Strauss ed *Prerefor-
mation Germany* (London 1972) 410–11.
9 Horace (*Satires* 2.3.30) records this of the lethargic patient.
10 On Erasmus' suffering with gallstones see H. Brabant 'Erasme, ses maladies
et ses médecins' *Colloquia Erasmiana Turonensia* I 547; he first contracted

the affliction in Venice in 1507 and suffered two severe attacks early in 1525 while composing *Lingua* (cf Epp 1543, 1548, 1558, 1560, and 1564).

11 *Naturalis historia* 7.170
12 Pliny *Naturalis historia* 26.3
13 Pliny *Naturalis historia* 26.7–8
14 Pliny (ibidem) describes this unidentified disease as a growth between the toes.

259

15 See Brabant (n10 above); Erasmus himself suffered an attack when in London in 1511.
16 See Brabant ibidem 542–4 and 'Epidémies et médecins' *Colloquia Erasmiana Turonensia* I 515–87, especially 522–4 for contemporary writing on the causes of syphilis. As a disease caused by lapses in morality, it forms a natural transition in Erasmus' moralizing argument to diseases strictly of the mind.
17 Pliny *Naturalis historia* 20.141, 30.28
18 Pliny *Naturalis historia* 26.2

260

19 Literally the words are applied here to the punishment of heretics, but at least the first two practices permit analogy with cautery and surgery, the two most drastic forms of medical treatment then known.
20 Nephew of Archbishop Jan Łaski of Gniezno, Jan Łaski met Erasmus in Basel while on his travels with his brother Hieronim (cf Ep 1622) and opened correspondence with him. He had been living in Erasmus' house since October 1524 (Ep 1502:8n) and left for Italy on October 1525, having bought the reversion of Erasmus' library after his death (on which see Allen VI Appendix 19 504:38–42).
21 Goddess of justice and the last of the gods to leave the earth at the close of the golden age; cf Virgil *Eclogues* 4.6 and *Georgics* 2.473–4; Ovid *Metamorphoses* 1.149–50.

[*The tongue: its nature and capacity*]

262

1 For the adage, proverbial of dispute over a triviality, see *Adagia* I iii 52, III ii 32.
2 To justify the importance of this work to his readers, Erasmus stresses the tremendous ambivalence of man's tongue, which has as great a power to do evil as to perform its proper function of doing good. He begins with an analogy which will recur throughout the work, comparing the tongue to drugs which can serve both as a remedy and a poison. Themes touched on here that will be developed later include the *a fortiori* argument from the wisdom of pagan antiquity to the greater wisdom found in the Scriptures and the higher standard which is therefore required of Christians; the power of a misused tongue to harm even its owner; and an inductive argument from the power of all valued objects to do harm in proportion to their capacity

for good. As animals can be tamed and children disciplined, so Erasmus hopes to teach the discipline of the tongue.

3 Carneades, head of the New Academy in the second century BC, and Chrysippus, successor to Zeno and Cleanthes as head of the Stoic sect in the third century BC, were both praised by Cicero, Erasmus' authority here, for their skill in argumentation. Their works were not known to him directly, and survive only in excerpts.

4 Erasmus recalls this anecdote from Plutarch *De garrulitate* 'On Talkativeness' 506C, one of his main sources for this work. The anecdote is attributed to Amasis and Bias at *Moralia* 138C.

263

5 On the fertility of Africa see Pliny *Naturalis historia* 17.31 and 41 and 18.94.

6 The antithesis of honey and gall is conventional; cf Apuleius *Florida* 18.29.7, which adds the second pairing (good soil/weeds).

7 Pliny *Naturalis historia* 29.70 reports on *theriaci*, medicinal pills made from viper's venom.

8 This attribute of Fortune is relatively undeveloped in antiquity, but cf Cicero *In Pisonem* 10; Virgil *Aeneid* 6.748–9; Tibullus 1.5.69–70. For its evolution in the Middle Ages see H.R. Patch *The Goddess Fortuna in Mediaeval Literature* (Cambridge 1927) 149–77.

264

9 Cf *Adagia* I i 72, where Erasmus refers this belief to Empedocles, quoting Plutarch *Moralia* 474B.

10 Plato apparently denies this at *Republic* 391C–E; no evil can come from the gods, and therefore it cannot come from the true heroes, as children of the gods.

11 This story is told at Plutarch *Themistocles* 2; Erasmus himself has added Alcibiades, Caesar (whom he here as often elsewhere calls Caius Caesar), and Alexander.

12 After he crossed the Rubicon and was marching on Rome in 49 BC. The story is found in Plutarch *Cato* 63 and *Moralia* 810C.

13 Cicero raises the issue of the power of human action to avert the evils foretold by the stars in *De divinatione* 2.89–100; it is central to Erasmus' treatise *De libero arbitrio*, published a year earlier (1524) than the *Lingua*. See C. Trinkhaus 'The Problem of Free Will in the Renaissance and Reformation' *Journal of the History of Ideas* 10 (1949) 51–62.

14 Again influenced by Pliny, who lists in *Naturalis historia* 28.30 drugs derived from living creatures

265

15 Hellenistic philosophy and Stoic theory in particular taught a teleological interpretation of man's nature, whereby his differential feature of speech was seen as his special gift, along with reason itself. For the argument from man's upright position to his function of contemplation and analysis, especially of the heavens, cf *De natura deorum* 2.140. The double consideration of aesthetics and utility (dignity ... convenience) is also characteristic of

Stoic teleology, in which 'the forethought of Nature' (Greek *Pronoia*) is our controlling Providence, equated with the supreme deity.

16 In content and details of phrasing Erasmus reveals his debt for this physiological sketch to Cornelius Celsus *De medicina* 4.1.

17 For the relationship of tongue and heart or mind in rhetorical theory, cf Cicero *De oratore* 3.65.

18 Cf Aristotle *Historia animalium* 1.11 (492b28–35).

266

19 Cf Cicero *De divinatione* 2.136 and Celsus (n16 above), who gives *aspera arteria* and *stomachus* as the conventional names. Cicero and Celsus both describe in detail the function of the epiglottis, which Celsus calls 'a tiny tongue.'

267

20 See Aristotle *Historia animalium* 2.12 (504a35–65).

21 On the formation of sounds by the tongue seen as a *plectrum* cf Cicero *De natura deorum* 2.149.

22 For a similar list cf *De pronuntiatione* CWE 26 404.

23 A favourite story of Erasmus' encyclopaedic sources; cf Valerius Maximus 8.7.16; Pliny *Naturalis historia* 7.88; Quintilian 11.2.56.

24 Traditionally the riddle proposed by the sphinx and answered by Oedipus; cf *Adagia* II iii 9.

268

25 Although this fish is described by Aristotle *Historia animalium* 2.14 505b19 and by Pliny *Naturalis historia* 9.79, Pliny does not use the name *remora*: Erasmus' source for the name is the commentary on Terence by Donatus, which describes the fish's behaviour at *Andria* 739 and *Eunuchus* 302.

26 According to Herodotus (1.85; cf Valerius Maximus 5.4.6), Croesus king of Lydia had a mute son, who recovered his voice when he cried out in fear as a Persian soldier threatened his father's life.

27 James 1:19

28 On the tongue-tied cf *De pronuntiatione* CWE 26 404.

29 There is no such statement in the surviving text of *De lingua latina*; ASD refers to the comment on *ligula* at 7.107, but it is more likely that like many of Erasmus' allusions, this reference to Varro comes at second hand through Gellius or Quintilian.

30 Cf Plutarch *De garrulitate* 'On Talkativeness,' *Moralia* 503C; cf also the recurring Homeric phrase (*Iliad* 4.350, 9.409, etc).

[*Undisciplined use of the tongue: talkativeness*]

269

1 The following anecdote is the first of several borrowed by Erasmus from Aulus Gellius' discussion of talkativeness in *Noctes Atticae* 1.15. Cato the Censor (d 146 BC) is much quoted by Erasmus for his tough moral precepts

and for his wit and invective; the *Disticha Catonis*, which Erasmus edited, were falsely attributed to him. Caelius is otherwise unknown.

2 This word survives only in an anonymous quotation in Pollux *Onomasticon* 2.108.

3 Part of the opening of Cicero's poem on his consulship, quoted by Quintilian 11.1.24, who reports that the line was criticized. The preference for 'sense without eloquence' derives from Cicero *De oratore* 3.142, quoted by Gellius on talkativeness, 1.15 (cf 269 n1 above).

4 'Utter mindless sound' is part of Virgil's description of the phantom of Turnus in *Aeneid* 10.640. Could Erasmus have thought the tag was part of Virgil's description of the sibyl possessed by Apollo in book 6?

270

5 While Gellius also alludes to Thersites in his discussion of talkativeness, Erasmus develops the allusion in far greater detail, with his own commentary on the Homeric context (*Iliad* 2.212–14). For the contrast of the common soldier Thersites' loudmouthed insubordination with the eloquence of the three princely models Menelaus, Ulysses, and Nestor, see also the early *Oratio de virtute amplectenda* 3–13 in this volume.

6 Cf Hesiod *Works and Days* 694.

7 *Iliad* 2.224

8 Cf Plutarch *Cicero* 5 and *Moralia* 204F.

9 *Iliad* 9.442–3; the book number in Erasmus' text is mistaken. The quotation is used by Cicero *De oratore* 3.59 to affirm the mutual dependence of eloquence and action.

10 The three Greek leaders were adopted by the rhetorical tradition as representatives of the three styles of oratory; cf Cicero *Brutus* 40 (on Nestor and Ulysses, paraphrasing *Iliad* 1.247–9, 3.221–3) and 50 (on Menelaus, paraphrasing *Iliad* 3.213–14); also Pliny *Letters* 1.20 (contrasting them with Thersites); Quintilian 12.10.64; Gellius 6.14.7.

271

11 This quotation from Euripides *Bacchae* 386 is discussed by Gellius 1.15 on talkativeness.

272

12 The comic dramatist, contemporary of Aristophanes, whose works survive only in quotations, such as this excerpt from Gellius 1.15

13 Erasmus cites Sallust *Catiline* 5.5 with the variant reading *loquentia* given by Gellius 1.15.18 on the authority of Probus.

14 The works of this Sicilian comic playwright are lost, except for maxims and fragments such as this line from Gellius 1.15.15.

15 Erasmus misrepresents Gellius' quotation (1.15.18 again) from Aristophanes *Frogs* 837f; as Gellius says, the passage refers to archaic grandiloquence, and if Erasmus had returned to Gellius' source he would have realized that the lines are a grossly unfair portrait of Aeschylus by his younger rival Euripides. Erasmus quotes a different text from that in our better manuscripts

and the Homeric scholiasts, which replaces the negative form 'who cannot be out-talked' with the positive 'overtalking.'

16 Here Erasmus works into his Aristophanic theme material from his own *Adagia*; for the third word, and the string of opprobrious synonyms, see *Adagia* II vii 44.

273

17 All these comparisons are found in the *Adagia*: the turtledove I v 30 CWE 31 410; the cicada I ix 100 CWE 32 232–3; the reef III vi 53; the surf II ix 32; the psaltery II vii 44.

18 Also included in the *Adagia*. Archytas of Tarentum, the fourth century BC Pythagorean philosopher, supposedly invented a rattle so as to keep children from breaking household objects, according to Aristotle *Politics* 8.5 (1340B); cf *Adagia* II vii 44.

The windgong of Dodona (*Adagia* I i 7 CWE 31 55–6), a device used to add mystery to the responses of the oracle at Dodona in Epirus, and the piper Arrhabius (or perhaps simply Arab piper) are mentioned in *Adagia* I vii 32 CWE 32 86. Both occur in a well-known passage from Libanius *Narrationes* 26 (Foerster VIII 49) together with comparisons to pigeons and magpies and the other animal sounds listed by Erasmus here. Libanius, three of whose declamations Erasmus translated in his youth, was one of the authors from whose texts he taught himself Greek (see Erika Rummel *Erasmus as a Translator of the Classics* [Toronto 1985] 21–2), and it would be natural for Erasmus to adapt the protests of the character in Libanius' narration (the model for Morose in Ben Johnson's *Silent Woman*). For the phrase 'a word-spewer,' see *Adagia* I vii 32 CWE 32 86; the Daulian rook, *Adagia* III vi 88; Tellenicus' echo, *Adagia* IV iii 32 (Erasmus admits that he does not know the origin of the phrase); the bath-attendant, *Adagia* I vi 44 CWE 32 34.

19 *Adagia* I iii 3: *Citra vinum temulentia* CWE 31 236–7. According to Plutarch *Moralia* 679A the philosopher Theophrastus coined this phrase as a nickname for the gossip of the barbers' shops. Erasmus develops the implied analogy between tipsiness and loquacity at length 277–80 below.

20 Cf *De pronuntiatione* CWE 26 406 and n179; *Adagia* II x 2, quoting Christ's words from Matt 6:7 and offering another derivation, probably based on guesswork, from a poet Battus, who included many repetitious phrases in his hymns. The story given here derives from and partially quotes Ovid *Metamorphoses* 2.702–7, but Erasmus read a different text of 2.702 (*erant et erant*) from modern editions; only the text he read makes Battus repeat himself (see also *Annotationes in Matthaeum* 6:7 LB VI 35E).

274

21 Erasmus is again working from Ovid *Metamorphoses* (11.180–94); cf *Adagia* I iii 67 CWE 31 291; Midas' 'asses ears' were a punishment sent by Apollo for the king's defects as an adjudicator in a song contest between Apollo and Marsyas. The purple turbans are an echo of Ovid *Metamorphoses* 11.181.

22 Horace *Epistles* 2.1.63

23 The contrast of Attic oratory with the verbose and excitable Asiatic style is a

feature of Roman rhetorical theory; cf Cicero *Brutus* 51, *Orator* 25, Quintilian
12.10.16–19.

24 Cicero dedicated both *Brutus* and *Orator* to M. Junius Brutus the tyrannicide.
For the *Orator* as a response to Brutus' criticism of the ideal expressed in
the earlier work see *Orator* 35–6; for his criticism of Cicero's own style see
Quintilian 12.10.12; Tacitus *Dialogus de oratoribus* 18.5–6.

275

25 This is the first of several passages drawn from Plutarch *De garrulitate* and the
Apophthegmata Laconica (*Moralia* 208B–236E). Erasmus translated and augmented Plutarch's various books of apophthegms under the same classifications in his own *Apophthegmata*.

26 Plutarch *Instituta Laconica*, *Moralia* 239D, where, however, the name given is
Cephisophon

27 Cleomenes was king of Sparta c 510–480 BC. The two anecdotes are told by
Plutarch *Apophthegmata Laconica*, *Moralia* 223D, 224C; Erasmus misattributes
the second, which is ascribed to Labotas by Plutarch.

28 Cf Plutarch *De garrulitate*, *Moralia* 503B.

29 Archelaus was not a Spartan but king of Macedonia; cf Plutarch *Moralia* 509A,
177A.

30 Cf *Adagia* II i 92, II x 49.

31 An Athenian general and statesman of the fourth century BC noted for his
austerity. For the anecdotes see Plutarch *Phocion* 5 and 23; Erasmus
Apophthegmata LB IV 219–20.

276

32 See Plutarch *Moralia* 217E.

33 King of Sparta c 427–399 BC; both anecdotes are drawn from Plutarch *Moralia*
215F, 216A.

34 Erasmus himself had composed such a panegyric (CWE 27 1–75) when he was
seeking the patronage of the house of Veere.

35 Agesilaus succeeded his half-brother Agis (above) as king of Sparta; for this
anecdote cf Plutarch *Moralia* 208C.

36 Cf Plutarch *Moralia* 208B; the man is otherwise unknown.

277

37 The celebrated bore of Horace *Satires* 1.9. The quotation is line 10.

38 This metaphor is found both in Plato *Timaeus* 69D and Cicero *De senectute* 44,
Erasmus' probable source.

39 Cf Seneca *De ira* 1.1.

40 Here Erasmus takes up Plutarch's argument again (cf *Moralia* 504A); for the
saying 'He's getting drunk on his own talk' cf Plutarch: 'It is talk which
converts the influence of wine into drunkenness.'

278

41 Terence *Eunuchus* 727

42 This story is found in Plutarch *Pyrrhus* 8 and *Moralia* 184D; Valerius Maximus
5.1.3; Quintilian 6.3.10. It is repeated by Erasmus at 291 below.

43 Cf Plutarch *Moralia* 503F; Leutsch-Schneidewin *Paroemiographi Graeci* I 313, II 219, 687.
44 Cf Gellius 15.2 on Plato's recommendations in the *Laws*; Plato *Laws* 637A, 647E, 666A, 671B.
45 According to Greek tradition the Lapiths were a wild tribe of Thessaly who could not carry their drink. They started a war with the centaurs when they became drunk at the wedding of their king, Peirithous.

279
46 *Aeneid* 4.522–8. Erasmus has substituted *demulcent* 'soothe' in 528 for the reading of the Virgil manuscripts *lenibant* 'eased.'

280
47 Latin *conticinium*, a rare word discussed by Varro *De lingua latina* 6.7 and 7.79
48 See Martial 4.80.1 (where however the name given is Maro) and 6.78; 'the Phrygian' may in fact refer to the man's name, 'a man called Phryx.'
49 These cauldrons were designed to catch the wind and create awesome sounds to enhance the ancient Greek oracle. See *Adagia* I i 7, I iii 28.
50 The portico at Olympia which gave out a sevenfold echo, also mentioned in *Adagia* I i 7 CWE 31 56 citing Plutarch *Moralia* 502D
51 As at *Adagia* I vii 32 Erasmus illustrates the saying from Horace *Satires* 1.3.1–3. The words 'dreadful tribe' are an approximation: I can assign no meaning or source to the Greek phrase printed in LB II 669E and ASD IV 256:629–30, where the adjective *euthunos* is out of place and must be a corruption of the text.
52 Cf Ovid *Metamorphoses* 12.46–7, describing the dwelling of personified *Fama* or Rumour.
53 Horace *Ars poetica* 476

281
54 Not so much a sash as the cords which passed around and bound the breasts; to say that a girl wore Venus' girdle implied that she was sexually irresistible. Compare *Adagia* II ii 36, where Erasmus traces the notion back to *Iliad* 14.215ff, where Hera requests the girdle as a charm with which to seduce the father of the Gods, Zeus.
55 Cf *Adagia* IV iv 9, III viii 56. In classical lore the man who was seen by the wolf before he caught sight of it was struck dumb. Cf Terence *Adelphi* 537; Virgil *Eclogues* 9.54; Pliny *Naturalis historia* 8.80.
56 Cf Hesiod *Works and Days* 346; but Hesiod is concerned with the bad effect upon a farmer's crops and livestock of a neighbour who neglects his responsibilities.
57 This tale is told by Plutarch *Themistocles* 18 and *Moralia* 185E.
58 Thraso in Terence's *Eunuchus*, a favourite illustration of Erasmus, is the soldier who boasts of his wit and charm in conversation.

282
59 Martial 3.44, one of several poems against the poetic bore Ligurinus
60 Erasmus converts into indirect speech Persius 1.54, followed by 53.

61 Pliny's enemy and rival, the prosecutor M. Regulus, forced large numbers of friends and clients to listen to him reciting the eulogy of his dead son; Pliny *Epistles* 4.7.

283

62 Horace *Ars poetica* 385. The 'cedar bookchest' may be an allusion to including the book in the official holdings of the Palatine library.

63 Frag 233 West. The line was known to Erasmus from Plutarch *Moralia* 503B.

64 Philoxenus, the court musician of Dionysius, the fourth century BC tyrant of Syracuse, was sent by Dionysius to the quarries in punishment for condemning the tyrant's bad tragedies. Plutarch *Moralia* 334C; Cicero *Tusculan Disputations* 5.63.

65 Horace uses a metaphor from gladiatorial combat to defend himself against the bore of *Satires* 1.9.29.

66 Quoting Thraso (see n58 above) and his parasite Gnatho in Terence *Eunuchus* 421–2.

67 *Adagia* I ii 49; cf Erasmus *Apophthegmata* LB IV 147. The phrase first appears in Plato *Gorgias* 498A.

68 Reported by Plutarch *Moralia* 504C

69 Such comparative criticism of Homer and Virgil was known to Erasmus from the fifth book of Macrobius' *Saturnalia*, in which passages from Virgil are compared with their models in Homer and other Greek sources.

70 See Plutarch *Moralia* 216F.

71 Erasmus' source is Quintilian (12.10, 12), who both reports and refutes the accusation against Cicero.

284

72 For direct comparison of the style of Demosthenes and Cicero see Quintilian 10.1.105–9 (of which some phrases are echoed by Erasmus here) and Pseudo-Longinus *On the Sublime* 13.4.

73 Erasmus means the censor M. Porcius Cato (d 146 BC) and his great-grandson of the same name, who led the republican opposition to Caesar after Pompey's death and died at Utica. The anecdote of Cato the Elder comes from Plutarch *Cato Maior* 12 and is included in Erasmus' *Apophthegmata* LB IV 263.

74 See Plutarch *Cato Minor* 5; a rather different appraisal of the younger Cato's oratory is given by Cicero *Brutus* 118–9. The phrase 'never leaped forth to speak' echoes Horace *Epistles* 1.19.7–8.

75 On Phocion see 275 n31 above and 303, 345, 396 below.

76 Cf Plutarch *Moralia* 503B.

77 Sounds imitating snickering laughter, found at Aristophanes' *Plutus* 895

285

78 A reprise of the epigram of Martial against Ligurinus quoted 282 above.

79 Cf *Adagia* II i 65.

80 Juvenal 3.152

81 The supposed speaker of Horace *Satires* 2.3: Erasmus adapts line 75.

[*The benefits of silence and of careful use of the tongue*]

286

1 Cf *Adagia* I vii 18, I vii 19 CWE 32 77–8; Erasmus explains the ox as a coin bearing an ox-emblem, so that this idiom, like the silver quinsy, would refer to the results of bribery. This is the account given by Pollux *Onomasticon* 9.61.

2 *Adagia* I ix 1 CWE 32 179–80. According to tradition the inhabitants of Amyclae, weary of repeated false alarms that the Spartans were invading, passed a law forbidding anyone to report an invasion; as a result the Spartans captured and destroyed the village unchallenged.

3 This saying is ascribed to the poet Simonides by Plutarch *Moralia* 515A; cf *Moralia* 10F and 125D. For the attribution to Xenocrates see Valerius Maximus 7.2 ext 6.

4 Horace *Epistles* 1.18.17

5 Erasmus groups with the legislation of Solon for Athens in the first decade of the sixth century BC and that of the Spartan reformer Lycurgus from the seventh or eighth century the official codification of Roman law performed by the *decemviri* in 451–450 BC known as the Twelve Tables. 'Amongst honest men ... dealings' is a quotation from these tables, found at Cicero *Topica* 66.

6 Plato *Republic* 391A–E protests against Homer depicting kings and heroes who were the sons of the gods acting ignobly; cf Horace *Odes* 4.2.13: *reges ... deorum sanguis*.

7 Erasmus reiterates a traditional complaint in the classical sources, from Plato (*Laws* 700) and Aristotle (*Politics* 7.7.6–11, 1342a 15–634) to Horace (*Ars poetica* 202–19). The simultaneous degeneration of eloquence and music is even parodied at the beginning of Petronius' *Satyricon*. On this recurring theme see G.W. Williams *Tradition and Originality in Roman Poetry* (Oxford 1968) 337–9.

8 Cf Erasmus' criticisms in *Annotationes* on 1 Cor 14, note 26 LB VI 731F–732B.

9 Cf Plutarch *Moralia* 220D, where however the manuscripts give a different form of this unfamiliar name; cf also Plutarch *Agis* 10.

287

10 The medical writings attributed to Hippocrates (from the fifth century BC) are here compared favourably with the works of Galen (second century AD), some of which Erasmus had translated (see in this volume 225–48). Similarly Erasmus rates the style of Socrates, judged by the speeches of Socrates in Plato's dialogues, above that of Chrysippus, the third-century Stoic philosopher, whose work Erasmus could only have known in fragmentary form or at second hand from Cicero's adverse opinions of Chrysippus' style (cf *De oratore* 1.50; *Brutus* 120–1).

11 Juvenal 11.108

12 Cf Plutarch *Moralia* 502E.

288

13 Plutarch *Moralia* 220A; a similar story is told of Bias by Plutarch at *Moralia*

503F, where it is followed by the story given here by Erasmus about Zeno the Eleatic philosopher.

14 Plutarch *Moralia* 218B; the 'rhetorician' is presumably the fifth-century geographer Hecataeus of Miletus.

15 There is no such claim in Alcibiades' speeches in the *Symposium*, but he does praise Socrates for his self-control in flight from Potidaea at *Symposium* 221B.

16 An eccentric estimate of Horace, perhaps based on *Satires* 1.6.56–7 recounting his first meeting with Maecenas, where he declares that he spoke little, 'as was his habit.'

17 Filistus is reported by Donatus' *Vita Vergiliana* 77 as one of the contemporary detractors of Virgil. The name Pero in the next sentence is a misspelling of Paro, cited at Donatus 61.

18 Donatus' *Vita Vergiliana* 185, 189–91 (Rostagni) lists the *Aeneomastix* of P. Carvilius [*sic*] Pictor, the *Furta* 'Plagiarisms' of Perellius [*sic*] Faustus (misread by Erasmus' source?), and the *Homoeotetes* 'Likenesses' of G. Octavius Avitus, a work comparing passages adapted by Virgil with their Greek and Roman epic models.

289

19 The root of Greek *axiomata* is the verb *axioun*, to think worthy, claim as right.

20 The pre-Socratic philosopher Heraclitus of Ephesus; Plutarch *Moralia* 511C. This story is followed, as in Erasmus' adaptation, by the tale of the Scythian king Scylarus (Scilourus in Plutarch).

21 The story concerning the Roman general and rebel commander in Spain killed in 72 BC is told in Valerius Maximus 7.3.6.

290

22 Cf Plutarch *Moralia* 225F; cf 3A.

23 Cf Livy 1.54, but the story is a classic Greek anecdote also told of Thrasyboulos and Periander.

24 Cleanthes was a Stoic teacher of the third century BC; the story is told by Cicero of Zeno, the founder of Stoicism, at *Orator* 113.

25 Erasmus recalls his earlier illustrations of Laconic speech at 274–5. The anecdote about Archidamus (Archidamus III, son of Agesilaus) comes from Plutarch *Moralia* 219A.

26 See Plutarch *Moralia* 511A; also *Moralia* 233E for a variant. The next story recalling the fate of the tyrant Dionysius the Younger in exile precedes this anecdote in Plutarch. Erasmus cites these anecdotes together at *Adagia* I i 83 CWE 31 125–6.

27 The story of Demetrius Poliorketes is told more fully in Plutarch *Demetrius* 42, whereas *Moralia* 511A gives only the riposte.

28 Plutarch *Moralia* 213A and *Agesilaus* 14

291

29 Erasmus repeats with a new twist the anecdote told at *Moralia* 549F.

30 These words are attributed to Leonidas on the eve of the battle of Thermopylae by Cicero *Tusculan Disputations* 1.101; Valerius Maximus 3.2 ext 3; Plutarch *Moralia* 225D.

31 The anecdote first appears in Herodotus 1.88.
32 This statesman and general, who gave Thebes her brief hegemony of Greece in the fourth century BC, was much admired by Plutarch. Cf *Moralia* 194B; but many other ancient sources for the anecdote would be known to Erasmus, such as Cicero *De inventione* 1.33 and 38 and Nepos *Life of Epaminondas* 8.
33 Erasmus' account is based on Livy 38.51 and the variant version in Aulus Gellius 4.18.

292

34 Cf Cicero *De oratore* 2.229; the anecdote can be found in Gellius 12.12.4.
35 Erasmus seems to be referring to the speech of M. Terentius in Tacitus *Annals* 6.8. It is not clear why he attributes this speech to Crispinus, or which Crispinus he has in mind.
36 The story comes from Plutarch *Aristides* 22.
37 The anecdote is found at Augustine *De civitate Dei* 4.4.25.
38 Plutarch *Pompey* 10; note that Plutarch calls the man Sthenis, but he would be known to Erasmus as Sthenius from Cicero's prosecution of Verres, in which he is a leading witness.

293

39 Plutarch *Dion* 21; modern editors believe that the name should be read as Theste.
40 Scaurus, leader of the conservatives in the senate, was prosecuted in 90 or 89 BC by the radical tribune Varius; see Quintilian 5.12.10.
41 This anecdote about the fourth-century Athenian general follows that of Scaurus in Quintilian 5.12.10.
42 The contrast between Demosthenes and Phocion is drawn from Plutarch *Demosthenes* 10; the allusion to Phocion's hatchet is also found in *Phocion* 5.
43 A much quoted line from Euripides *Phoenissae* 469

[*The evils of an undisciplined tongue*]

294

1 Appropriateness was one of the four virtues of oratory advocated by Theophrastus. Cf Cicero *De oratore* 3.210–12 for the application of this principle to the circumstances of oratory.
2 See *Adagia* II iii 5.
3 The tale of Augustus comes from Macrobius' collection of the emperor's wit, *Saturnalia* 2.2.19, and is included in Erasmus' *Apophthegmata* LB IV 209. (See 386 below).
4 I have not been able to find the source of this anecdote.
5 From the *Historiae Augustae scriptores* 22.5

295

6 Plutarch *Moralia* 173C–D
7 Valerius Maximus 7.2.11; for a similar comment by Aristotle on Callisthenes see Plutarch *Alexander* 54.

8 Plutarch *Moralia* 174A

9 Although Dion, guardian of Dionysius the Younger, had Plato invited to Syracuse by the tyrant, both Plato and Dion were ill-treated and expelled; according to tradition Plato was even enslaved, and ransomed by a former pupil; cf Diogenes Laertius 3.19–21 and Plutarch *Dion* 6.

10 Again from Plutarch *Moralia* 179C–D

11 I have not been able to find the source of this anecdote.

12 Cf Plutarch *Moralia* 70C, 606C; *Demosthenes* 20.

13 Erasmus is quoting Horace *Satires* 2.1.77–8, itself an image for the envy of the backbiter, but he has replaced Horace's word 'jars upon' by the stronger 'breaks them,' stressing the damage caused by malice by itself.

14 The same proverbial phrase is quoted again at 333 below. Paradoxically its only source is the Roman Cassius, writing to Cicero, *Ad familiares* 15.19.4.

15 Plutarch *Moralia* 176D. The editor of ASD (270:1129) has erroneously printed *verbis quidem* as narrative instead of quotation.

16 Again, Plutarch *Moralia* 223C

17 Erasmus borrows his literary history, with an acknowledgment in his imitative phraseology, from Horace *Epistles* 2.1.48–9. The description of the Cynics as acting without respect for persons, occasions, or circumstances brings Erasmus' argument back to the topic of propriety, which he introduced at 293 above.

296

18 This story, derived from a political speech by the Elder Cato, is told by Aulus Gellius 1.23; when the boy told his mother that the senate was going to legislate that each man might take two wives, his mother told her friends, who mounted a demonstration that was laughed to scorn by the senators; as a reward the boy was invited to attend all meetings of the senate. His name Papirius is misspelled by our editions of Erasmus, probably influenced by the word *papyrus*.

19 Erasmus here calls Plutarch's essay *libello de nugacitate*, a different Latin title from the traditional *De garrulitate*. The reference is to *Moralia* 507B–508B. In the Greek version the bird is a lark; note that the proverbial analogy with new vessels in the next paragraph is also taken from Plutarch.

297

20 Although Erasmus does not acknowledge his source, this story also comes from Plutarch *De garrulitate*, following the previous one at 508C. This is a distortion of the story of Fabius Maximus, friend of Augustus, as told by Tacitus *Annals* 1.5.

298

21 Cf *Adagia* IV iv 89, II x 21.

22 A Sicilian moralist and playwright whose work survives only in quotations; these would be known to Erasmus from several sources, in this case Lucian *Hermotimus* 47 (Epicharmus fr 250 CGF).

23 Plutarch *Cato Maior* 9

24 A recurring saying in both Greek and Roman moralists. Despite the reference

to Cicero, Erasmus' immediate source must be Aulus Gellius, for Cicero *De amicitia* 59 attributes the adage to Bias, whereas Gellius 1.3, discussing the views of Cicero and his sources, ascribes it to Chilon. See however Aulus Gellius 17.14, who fathers it on Publilius Syrus the mime-writer; Erasmus includes it in his *Apophthegmata* LB IV 361.

25 Cicero's brother Quintus bargained for pardon from Caesar in 49 BC by accusing Cicero himself, to such an extent that even Caesar was shocked.

26 Erasmus quotes lines 109–10 and 112.

27 An echo of Erasmus' earlier use at 286 of Horace *Epistles* 1.18.71

28 Again from Plutarch 507A

299

29 An excerpt from Virgil's famous description of rumour, *Aeneid* 4.175f, also used by Erasmus at *Apophthegmata* LB IV 234; in the corresponding place in Plutarch's account (507A) Plutarch quotes a similar excerpt from Greek poetry.

30 Quoted by Plutarch *Moralia* 510C (Epicharmus frag 274 CGF)

31 Erasmus' position on the oath led to his orthodoxy being questioned; cf his defence at LB IX 834C–840D that precisely the man with the highest religious scruples will object most strongly to taking an oath.

300

32 Plutarch *Moralia* 508D; cf Aristotle, *Historia animalium* 5.33 (558a25–31).

33 A proverbial phrase; cf Terence *Phormio* 506; Otto *Sprichwörter* 199; *Adagia* I v 25.

34 Plutarch *Moralia* 175B

301

35 Plutarch *Moralia* 183E

36 Actually Erasmus is again using Plutarch *De garrulitate* (*Moralia* 506D), but seems to be trying to conceal his continuous use of the same source for so many successive anecdotes.

37 The stories about Antigonus and Eumenes follow the anecdote about Metellus at *Moralia* 506D–E; see also *Moralia* 182A.

38 Cf *Adagia* I vii 55.

302

39 These sayings of Agathocles, the fourth-century general and ruler of Syracuse, do not illustrate the need for discretion in warfare so much as 'increasing its cost in bloodshed.' They are found together in Plutarch *Moralia* 176E–F.

40 See Plutarch *Sulla* 13–14.

41 Plutarch *Moralia* 174C

42 Plautus *Aulularia* 455, probably paraphrased here rather than inadvertently misquoted; Plautus has 'We hired your services and not your speech.'

43 *Aeneid* 11.389; Drances is represented as an untrustworthy adviser of King Latinus.

44 *Aeneid* 9.635. Here the Trojans, counter-attacking, ironically shout back at their enemies the abuse ('twice defeated') which had been hurled at them earlier in the book.

45 The story is an anecdote about Phocion, not Epaminondas, in Plutarch *Phocion* 7.

303
46 Plutarch *Phocion* 25; cf *Moralia* 188F.
47 Plutarch *Phocion* 9
48 Again Plutarch *Moralia* 200E
49 Erasmus is probably referring to events leading up to the Holy League against France of Julius II, Ferdinand of Aragon, Venice, the emperor Maximilian, and Henry VIII in October 1511; see Ep 239 from Ammonio for the first report, and *Julius exclusus* CWE 27 172–3 and 185 for a satirical interpretation of these events.
50 Erasmus adopts a tribal name from Caesar's *Bellum Gallicum* to represent the people of Hainault; this occasion cannot be identified.
51 Neither the occasion nor the papal nunzio can be identified, but it can hardly have been Erasmus' respected friend Ammonio.

304
52 It is unlikely that Erasmus knew anything of these men beyond the words of his source, Plutarch *Moralia* 510B. Plutarch cites his own source, Demosthenes *De falsa legatione* 265 inaccurately: for Philocrates he is quoting another allegation of Demosthenes made in the same speech (229).
53 Erasmus is alluding to the king of Persia, often called simply 'the King' by Greek writers. Euphorbus and Philagrus betrayed Eretria to Darius in 490 BC.
54 Plutarch *De garrulitate*, *Moralia* 504B, Erasmus' continuing source for this material, quotes in tragic trimeters from Sophocles, but the play cannot be identified.
55 *Odyssey* 19.210–11. Again Erasmus is adapting Plutarch *Moralia* 506A.

305
56 *Odyssey* 19.494; here Erasmus has corrected Plutarch's inaccurate quotation.
57 Erasmus has added these illustrations from *Odyssey* 9.366 and 13.253–4.
58 There is no passage in the *Odyssey* that matches this allusion.
59 *Aeneid* 1.209, when he must reassure his comrades after the storm
60 The Carians in *Iliad* 2.867
61 Erasmus quotes Ovid *Remedia amoris* 697–8; where Ovid reads the singular *puellae* 'his girl,' Erasmus has the plural.
62 Erasmus recalls Plato *Symposium* 221B.
63 Here Erasmus has embellished Plutarch's account of the night crossing of the Taurus mountains (*Moralia* 510B) with a Virgilian allusion (*Eclogues* 9.36) and details from the similar narrative of Pliny (*Naturalis historia* 10.60). Cf *Adagia* III vi 68.

306
64 Adapted from Horace *Epistles* 1.17.50–1
65 Plutarch *Moralia* 217C–D (Antalcidas) and 229D (Lysander)
66 Again *Moralia* 234A

67 Cf *Adagia* I vii 1.
68 Horace *Epistles* 1.5.25, also quoted in *Adagia* I vii 1

307

69 Martial 1.27.7, quoting the famous Greek lyric tag μισῶ μνάμονα συμπόταν
70 Cf Herodotus 1.8.13; for the evolution of the Gyges legend see K.F. Smith
'The Tale of Gyges' *American Journal of Philology* 23 (1902) 261–82, 361–87.
71 Plutarch *Lycurgus* 15
72 Erasmus returns to the theme of confession, anticipated briefly in the context
of the pagan mysteries of Samothrace at 306. His own writings on the
subject of confession were controversial; see *Modus confitendi* LB V 145–71 and
Declarationes ad censuras Lutetiae vulgatas LB IX 923A–F.
73 Prov 31:4, the first of a series of quotations from Proverbs and the Old Testament books attributed to Solomon. I translate all quotations from the Vulgate
in this work with the equivalent passage in the Douai version, except where
Erasmus has deliberately modified the text. Erasmus resumes quotation
from these books on a larger scale at 324.

308

74 See Matt 14:3.
75 *Moralia* 353B
76 Otto Ribbeck, *Comicorum Latinorum Reliquiae* (Leipzig 1855) 310 quotes a
variant (*absentem laedit, cum ebrio qui litigat*) from medieval sources. Erasmus
himself edited the *Sententiae* (London 1514) and recognized that many of
the sayings attributed to the mime-writer Publilius (not Publius) Syrus were
later accumulations.
77 Erasmus puts the practical obligations of the priest towards man even higher
than the obligation of reverence for God's sacrament. For similar denunciations of priests drunk while administering the sacraments see Ἰχθυοφαγία 'A
Fish Diet' ASD I-3 11:1175f.
78 An echo of the proverbial phrase in Terence *Eunuchus* 1024. Cf *Adagia* I iii 65.

309

79 Plutarch *Moralia* 509F
80 The Erinyes, often called *Dirae* or *Furiae* by the Romans (cf *Adagia* I vii 1)
pursued murderers, especially those who had murdered their own kin.
Erasmus is adapting Plutarch's moral comment in Roman terms.
81 Again from *Moralia* 509D–F
82 Pliny, Erasmus' main source for knowledge of medicinal substances, reports
this use of wine as an antidote for hemlock in *Naturalis historia* 27.50;
Plutarch also attributes this quality to hemlock at *Moralia* 61C.

310

83 *Moralia* 508D–F. Erasmus has replaced *Kallinikos* 'noble in victory' by
Kallimachos 'noble in battle,' but otherwise translated Plutarch phrase for
phrase, except that he has inserted the sentence 'if he had been able,' which
is Plutarch's epilogue, before the climax of his tale.
84 Another anecdote from *De garrulitate, Moralia* 505C. The Heptachalcis is a

region of Athens from which there is access to the Ceramicus (Potter's Quarter).

311

85 *Moralia* 505C–D. This anecdote follows the preceding one in Plutarch also. The story is quite unrelated to Tacitus' and Suetonius' report of the conspiracy of Piso against Nero in 65 BC, but may refer to another less known conspiracy.

86 Cf Plutarch *Cicero* 42. Cicero's Philippic orations against Mark Antony during his consulship in 44 BC drove Antony from Rome but provoked Cicero's inclusion among the proscribed by the triumvirs in the following year. Antony had the hands and head of the orator impaled and hung over a city gate, giving rise to a whole rhetorical tradition of deliberative speeches put into the mouth of Cicero (Seneca Rhetor *Controversiae* 6 and 7).

87 Plutarch *Moralia* 505D

88 *Moralia* 505D–E. This follows the anecdote about Zeno. The story is a late accretion found in Pausanias (1.23.1) and Athenaeus (596f) to the original tradition of the murder of Hipparchus, brother of Hippias, tyrant of Athens, by the lovers Harmodius and Aristogeiton in 514/3 BC.

312

89 M. Antonius was grandfather of Mark Antony the triumvir; he was accused of incest (that is, sacrilegious intercourse) with a vestal virgin in 113 BC; Erasmus' source for this and the next story of Plotius Plancus is Valerius Maximus 6.8.1 and 5.

90 Plutarch *Moralia* 208c

91 Again from *De garrulitate*, *Moralia* 508F

92 *Moralia* 509A, again following the previous anecdote in Plutarch

313

93 This anecdote is modelled on the classical story of Tarquin and Attus Navius the augur in Valerius Maximus 1.4.1, but unlike the Roman story, the British one ends in the triumph of the ruler.

94 The story of Perilaus [*sic*] is told by Plutarch *Moralia* 315C; Lucian *Phalaris* 1; and Pliny *Naturalis historia* 34.89.

95 From Hesiod *Works and Days* 266; this is quoted in the Latin form and developed at 340 below. Cf *Adagia* I ii 14 CWE 31 155–7.

96 Cf Hesiod *Works and Days* 361–2.

314

97 This odd saying, found at Theocritus *Idyll* 10.11, is used by Erasmus as an analogy for letting a money-hungry monarch discover a source of taxation.

98 *Quomodo adulator ab amico internoscatur* 'How to Tell a Flatterer from a Friend' *Moralia* 48E–74E, translated by Erasmus in 1515 LB IV 1–22

99 Cf 1 Cor 14:25.

315

100 An anecdote told by Plutarch of Eudamidas, king of Sparta, *Moralia* 192B and 220D, and of the Spartan official Panthoedas at 230C.

NOTES TO PAGES 315–318

101 At Luke 10:28

102 Cf Isa 8:22; Matt 4:16.

103 Erasmus' connection of thought proceeds through the double reference of the Greek word *hypocrites* 'actor' and 'dissimulator.' Roman (but not Greek) law excluded professional actors from even minor offices like that of town councillor.

316

104 Erasmus quotes the reply of the pimp Dorio, accused of breaking his contract in Terence *Phormio* 525.

105 Cf Deut 22:5; Erasmus treats the theme of acting and hypocrisy again 326–8 below.

106 Erasmus is recalling Horace *Epistles* 1.17.59, in which the tale of the beggar illustrates the effects of deceit in exploiting generosity.

107 The Franciscans had repeatedly spread rumours of Erasmus' death; cf Allen Ep 2154:1–2.

108 I have not found this reference.

317

109 Aulus Gellius 1.21.4 reports this as the most sacred form of oath in early Rome; the procedure is described by Polybius 3.25. See also 331 below.

110 The story is told in all four Gospels: Matt 26:69–75; Mark 14:66–72; Luke 22:55–62; John 18:25–7.

111 On Erasmus' quarrel with the Augustinians and his indulgence from Julius II compare the letter to Lambertus Grunnius, Ep 447:575–83. See also Ἰχθυοφαγία 'A Fish Diet' ASD I-3 523:1031–9, 535:1488–1500 (Thompson *Colloquies* 343, 356) on the Franciscan and Augustinian rule about girdles.

[*The evils of a vicious tongue*]

318

1 Erasmus here draws on ancient lore on poisons, partly from plants and partly from reptiles (venoms in the modern sense); the mythical nature of some of his material, especially that drawn from Lucan's epic (see 318–19 n4 below) shows that he is more concerned with the moral and rhetorical potential of the topic than its application.

2 This is quoted from the early Roman code of the Twelve Tables by Pliny *Naturalis historia* 28.17.

3 *Georgics* 2.128; *Eclogues* 7.27

4 The Greek name *dipsas* means thirst-maker, and this creature is described with four other reptiles listed by Erasmus, the *seps* centipede, *prester* scorpion, *iaculum* dart, and basilisk, in the fantastic account given by Lucan *Bellum civile* 9.718–723 of the horrors of the African desert. They are also individually mentioned in different passages of Pliny's *Naturalis historia* identified in nn5, 6, 11, and 12 immediately below.

319

5 See Pliny *Naturalis historia* 20.12, where it is described as elongated, with hairy feet, and exceptionally poisonous.

6 Cf Pliny *Naturalis historia* 11.87.

7 See Plutarch *Moralia* 65D–F for Alexander's flattering courtiers.

8 Mentioned by Pliny *Naturalis historia* 20.50 and 24.117

9 Isa 22:13; cf 1 Cor 15:32.

10 Pliny *Naturalis historia* 29.65

320

11 Lucan 9.720; Pliny *Naturalis historia* 8.76, 29.66

12 Pliny *Naturalis historia* 8.78, 29.66 and Festus 28 Lindsay: 'Basilisk is the name of a kind of serpent, either because it has a white mark on its head like a diadem, or because other varieties of snake flee from its attack.'

13 Probably the sting-ray as at Pliny 9.44; this is not mentioned under this name in Pliny but see Plato *Meno* 80A, 84B; Aristotle *Historia animalium* 2.13 (505a4); Plutarch *Moralia* 978C.

14 Pliny (n10 above) is Erasmus' source for Varro on the efficacy of urine.

15 Pliny *Naturalis historia* 27.4

16 Erasmus derives this list of antidotes chiefly from Lucan 9.916–21, listing *ebulum* (dwarf-elder) *galbanum* (*ferula galbaniflora*) *tamarix* (tamarisk) *costus* (*saussurea lappa*) *panacea* (*curula bubula*) *centaurea* (centaury or gentian) *peucedanum* (sulphur-wort) *thapsos* (Pliny's *thapsia*, the drias plant?) *habrotonum* (hellebore or southernwood) *larix* (larch) and powdered antler.

17 On the uses of *galbanum* see Virgil *Georgics* 3.415 and 4.264; Pliny 12.126 reports that this herb (for which scholars can give no modern equivalent) drives away serpents; Virgil uses it for driving off *Chelydri* (a kind of water-snake) but also for attracting bees. Erasmus' description of the tamarisk may be a paraphrase of Lucan's epithet 'of scanty leaf.'

321

18 See Pliny 16.64.

19 Cf Lucan 9.921 and Pliny 28.163, who reports the use of this ash for other purposes also.

20 Pliny reports the special immunity of the Psylli to snake-bite in *Naturalis historia* 7.14, 21.78, 28.30; Lucan (9.922–37) describes how they cured snake-bite by spells and by sucking out the venom. Erasmus make them a symbol of the Christian preacher who heals the poisoned mind in his concluding exhortation at 403, 404.

21 So also Pliny 29.98; he comments on the fatal unconsciousness induced by asp-bite at 29.65.

22 Erasmus here reports correctly the evidence of Pliny and Plutarch, which he mistakenly applied to the drinking of aconite (see 309 n82 above).

23 See Pliny *Naturalis historia* 19.91 and 95.

24 This reference is too general to be identified.

25 Pliny *Naturalis historia* 11.87

26 Pliny *Naturalis historia* 29.105

322

27 Pliny *Naturalis historia* 29.67

28 Pliny *Naturalis historia* 15.45 denies that the peach was ever poisonous, but quotes the tradition that it became safe to eat only when transplanted to Egypt.

29 Not the *sorbus* or service-tree, whose fruits are edible, as Pliny attests, *Naturalis historia* 15.84–5

30 On poisonous honey see Pliny *Naturalis historia* 21.75 and 77.

31 Pliny *Naturalis historia* 8.122 claims that the chameleon is harmless.

32 On vipers see 300 n32 and Pliny *Naturalis historia* 29.69; on aconite Pliny ibidem 27.5 and 8.

33 Cf Pliny *Naturalis historia* 25.123.

34 See 320 n12 above.

35 Plutarch *Moralia* 727B–728B

36 On the scorpion see 319, 321 above and nn6 and 23. Erasmus refers to the magic spear of Achilles, cut from wood on Mount Pelion, which wounded Telephus, king of Mysia; the king was told by an oracle that the rust of the spear which wounded him would cure his wound (Propertius 2.1.64; Ovid *Metamorphoses* 12.112).

323

37 This paragraph summarizing the destruction brought on society by the slander of an evil tongue leads, by means of the imaginary interlocutor's demand for a cure, to a new denunciation of slander and treachery based on quotations drawn from the Bible. After a general introduction on the speech of God at the creation, made incarnate in Christ as God's Word (323), Erasmus argues his case on the authority of the Old Testament, using predominantly Ecclesiasticus (called Sirach in his text) Proverbs, Ecclesiastes, and the Psalms (323–6), which he expands with a fuller commentary and pagan parallels.

38 Matt 12:36

39 A reinterpretation of Gen 1:3 and 1:7

324

40 Job 32:18–20

41 Job 33:14

42 Sir 4:34 (RSV 4:29). Note that I follow LB's reading *linguam*, not that of ASD *lingua*.

43 Prov 17:27

44 Prov 18:13

45 Eccles 3:7

46 Amos 5:13

47 Zech 2:13

48 Ps 64:2 (RSV 65:1)

49 Sir 19:11

50 Sir 19:8–10

51 Sir 19:28 (RSV 20:1)

52 Sir 20:5–7

53 Sir 20:20 (RSV 20:18)

54 Sir 20:22 (RSV 20:26)
55 Prov 26:9

325
56 Sir 26:18 (RSV 26:15)
57 Sir 32:9–11 (RSV 32:7)
58 Prov 11:13
59 Sir 13:14 (RSV 13:11)
60 A secular allusion, Horace *Epistles* 1.18.69
61 Sir 20:13
62 Sir 21:17 (RSV 21:14)
63 Sir 21:19 (RSV 21:16)
64 Sir 21:28 (RSV 21:25)
65 Cited by Seneca *Epistulae morales* 114.1 to introduce his discussion of corrupt style
66 Isa 32:6
67 Sir 21:29 (RSV 21:26)
68 Sir 23:17 (RSV 23:13)
69 Prov 10:19
70 Prov 13:3
71 Cf Sir 26:28 (RSV 26:29).
72 Eccles 10:12–13
73 Cf 1 Tim 6:4 and 2:11–12; Eph 4:29–31.

326
74 Cf 1 Cor 14:34–5.
75 A saying from Apuleius *Florida* 2, quoted in *Adagia* III vi 24, which falsely attributes it to Plato's *Charmides*. It is a favourite quotation with Erasmus; cf *Apophthegmata* LB IV 162.
76 Cf *Adagia* I ii 21.
77 Prov 26:28

327
78 Prov 30:8, continued by Erasmus with 30:9
79 Erasmus' source for the beliefs of Stoics and Peripatetics alike on this subject is Cicero *De natura deorum* 1–2, in which speakers from both schools attack the Epicurean theory of divine indifference to human fortunes. Cf 336 below.
80 Acts 18:3 and 2 Thess 3:8
81 1 Cor 11:1
82 John 8:44

328
83 Hos 4:1–3
84 James 1:5–8

329
85 The two excerpts are slightly modified from Jer 23:14 and 17, with the first person of the Vulgate converted into the third person of reported speech.

Other variants: *adulterantium* for *adulterorum*, *impiis ac blasphemiis* for *his qui blasphemant me locutus est Dominus, pax erat vobis* (surely a printer's error) for *erit vobis*.

86 Not a quotation, but a conflation from memory of Matt 17:6 and Mark 9:18
87 Cf Phil 2:10.
88 Paul in 2 Cor 11:2–3
89 2 Cor 11:13
90 2 Cor 11:14
91 Gen 3:4–5

330
92 A reference to the earlier pronouncement, Gen 2:17
93 Cf *Iliad* 2.8f.
94 In 3 Kings (RSV 1 Kings) 22 the false advice of Ahab's prophets led him to the disastrous battle against Syria (Erasmus's Assyria) at Ramoth-gilead.
95 Cf Job 13:4.
96 Jer 9:5

331
97 Under the general concept of blasphemy Erasmus illustrates an ascending scale of abuse of speech by Christians, measured against their special status in relation to God. The argument, which started from the behaviour of pagans in swearing by pagan deities (a topic already briefly handled at 317), moves to condemn *a fortiori* lying and swearing in Christians. To tell a lie is a violation of one's faith; to swear by God's name risks the hazard of perjury in an unwitting false statement if it is done often, while to swear knowingly to what is false is more than perjury, it is blasphemy. For the Christian is consecrated by the sacrament of Christ's blood, and so is more sacred than pagan priests. Erasmus moves on to greater forms of blasphemy: perjury in order to deceive another and taking God's name in vain. After a digression on the relation of man towards man Erasmus shifts to a condemnation of those who are so proud of pagan learning that they deny the holiness of God's prophets and apostles; his climax is the man who shows contempt for the Holy Scriptures. All this leads up to an important distinction by means of which Erasmus will vindicate himself. It would, he argues, be blasphemy to equate the authority of the Fathers of the church with that of the Scriptures; for it is legitimate to disagree with the Fathers on matters of detail, though it would be little short of blasphemy to abuse them. As for the Scriptures, one may be pardoned for error in misinterpreting them, but to distort them wilfully is to incur a charge of blasphemy. This leaves open to Erasmus the freedom to disagree with the Fathers' interpretation of the Scriptures on grounds of inaccuracy.
98 Cf Matt 5:34. Erasmus uses the divine prohibition to frame, here and at 332 (n107) below, an extended argument *a fortiori* from the pagan injunctions against swearing to the evil of swearing for a Christian, since the practice of swearing increases the risk of knowingly or unwittingly swearing to falsehood. For the same argument in shorter form compare Allen Ep 1581 11:726–32 (to Béda in June 1525) and Ἰχθυοϕαγία 'A Fish Diet' ASD I-3

513:664–5 and 528:1220–1 / Thompson *Colloquies* 329, 348. Erasmus' pagan illustrations are predominantly drawn in this section from Plutarch *Quaestiones Romanae* (*Moralia* 263D–291C).

99 See 333 n109 for this practice. Here the context requires not simply men who swore (*iurassent*) but either the verb forswore (*peierassent*) or an adverbial qualifier, since it was no dishonour to swear this oath in good faith. For the sanction against perjury included in Roman oaths see Plutarch *Moralia* 275C.

100 This oath was a favourite with Socrates according to Aristophanes *Birds*.

101 The claim of Hippolytus in Euripides *Hippolytus* 612, condemned even by Euripides' contemporaries; cf Aristophanes *Frogs* 1471.

102 Erasmus reflects the recurring assumption of Roman elegy (eg Ovid *Amores* 2.7.27–8 and 8.18–20) that lovers' oaths were exempt from the usual standards of honesty.

103 Erasmus quotes Plutarch *Moralia* 271B–C.

104 Plutarch discusses the restrictions governing the *flamen dialis* at *Moralia* 274B, 275C, 276D, and 289E–292C; Erasmus was also familiar with the outline of the rules binding this priest given by Gellius 10.15.

332

105 Again from Plutarch *Moralia* 275E; cf also Plutarch *Alcibiades* 41.

106 Cf Gal 6:7

107 Cf Matt 5:37; James 5:12.

108 James 4:15

333

109 Cf 331 n99 above.

110 Erasmus paraphrases Horace's description of the city gossip at *Epistles* 1.15.30.

111 Eccles 10:20

112 Not Jer but Ezek 35:12–13

113 An allusion to 2 Kings (RSV 2 Sam) 1:21

114 Ps 113 (RSV 114):4

115 Rom 12:14

334

116 2 Cor 13:3; see also 402 below.

117 Erasmus argues for proper respect towards temporal government, if only to avoid provoking disobedience in the common people (335), since it is unchristian to answer evil for evil. He concludes with a recommendation which could be called a Christianized version of the Aristotelian mixed constitution, in which kings and people are held in balance by the small aristocratic element of older, more established citizens. To this element corresponds in Erasmus' account the church hierarchy, the ecclesiastical and secular councils, and the city fathers of the leading communities. To abuse any man appointed by God, or any Christian as such (335) leads to the worst extreme of blasphemy. For another contemporary Erasmian discussion of human ordinances cf the colloquy Ἰχθυοφαγία 'A Fish Diet' ASD I-3 509–19: 494–888.

118 Rom 13:1
119 Exod 22:28
120 Acts 23:5
121 Cf 1 Cor 7:13.
122 Cf 1 Cor 7:20–2.
123 Cf Rom 13:1–7.

335
124 *Adagia* I ii 5 CWE 31 149–50
125 See 1 Pet 2:13.
126 Jude 1:8

336
127 Cf 402 above.
128 Pss 13 (RSV 14):1–2, 52 (RSV 53):1–2
129 Mal 3:14–15
130 Exod 32:4
131 Erasmus goes on to allegorize the idolatry of the golden calf and of the pagans towards the Olympian gods, to whom mythology attributed vicious and immoral behaviour, to interpret as idolatry any surrender to a ruling passion that will displace God in man's heart; thus avarice makes a god out of money and greed of man's stomach, and as each man yields to a base desire he can be seen as worshipping a pagan idol, Venus, Comus, or Bacchus.
132 According to Hesiod *Theogony* 453–506 Cronos, fearing that his son would seize power from him, ate his male children, but when his wife Rhea conceived Zeus she brought him to birth secretly in a cave on Mount Ida in Crete; when Zeus grew up he defeated Cronos and seized power on Olympus (the castration is suppressed in Hesiod's narrative). This was followed by the unsuccessful attack of the Titans against Zeus and the Olympians (*Theogony* 668–721).

337
133 Eph 5:5
134 Phil 3:3
135 Matt 6:25; Luke 16:19. Erasmus discusses this text on the conflict between devotion to God and mammon in the colloquy *Convivium religiosum* ASD I-3 258–61.
136 1 Cor 8:5–6

338
137 Ezek 36:23, and cf 37:23 and 27.
138 The Vulgate text of the Lord's Prayer, Matt 6:9
139 A transition from the subject of blasphemy to the deceitful use of the tongue in flattery (false praise) or backbiting and false accusation, which Erasmus sees as equivalent to murder by violence or poison
140 2 Kings (RSV 2 Sam) 16:7
141 Hos 7:16
142 Job 2:9

143 Tob 2:16
144 Erasmus has changed the order of the people's cries, quoting Mark 15:32 before 15:29.
145 Matt 27:43
146 Job 5:21
147 Cf 1 Tim 3:3.
148 *Adagia* I iii 53 CWE 31 280–1

339
149 Gen 26:20
150 Erasmus' interpretation of calumny is partly based on the special sense of the term in Roman law, where it was applied to vexations and unsubstantiated prosecutions. 'False accusations' whose falseness is known to the accuser are far more common outside the courts, hence the parade of illustrations which follows; again he begins with the least vicious form, contentiousness in private.
151 Prov 21:9
152 Prov 19:13
153 Prov 24:24
154 Isa 3:12
155 Prov 1:10

340
156 Prov 26:22, 25
157 Eccles 7:6
158 Sir 37:23 (RSV 37:20)
159 Ps 140 (RSV 141):5
160 Erasmus conflates Ezek 13:10 (misquoted) with 13:17–18.
161 Ps 119 (RSV 120):2–3
162 2 Kings (RSV 2 Sam) 20:8–10, if Ammon is a mistake for Amasa.
163 Judg 16:4
164 Matt 26:49
165 2 Kings (RSV 2 Sam) 13:1–19
166 3 Kings (RSV 1 Kings) 21:5–25
167 2 Chron 10:1–19; 3 Kings (RSV 1 Kings) 12:1–19
168 See 313 and n95 above.

341
169 Dan 6:1–24
170 Cf Sir 27:30 (RSV 27:27); 37:9.
171 This is the transition to slander anticipated at 328 above. The Greek *diabole*, related to *diabolos*, the name of Satan the slanderer, introduces the equation of slander with the devil's works. For Erasmus' equation of slanderer with the devil see eg *Annotationes in Novum Testamentum* on Matt 4 note 1 LB VI 22F or *Responsio ad annotationes Lei* LB IX 284B.
172 Cf Isa 9:6.
173 Gen 3:4; cf 329 n91 above.
174 Job 1:11

175 The passage is a conflation of Ps 56:5 (RSV 57:4) with Ps 13:3 (Vulg); 'he' must refer to David, the psalmist.
176 From Plutarch *Moralia* 221C
177 Ps 56:5 (RSV 57:4)
178 Jer 18:8
179 James 3.6

342
180 Erasmus lists out of chronological sequence here three Julio-Claudian emperors from the first century AD, two military political leaders of the first century BC (Marius and Sulla), and two of the tyrant families of Syracuse ruling between the fifth and third centuries BC.
181 Gen 39:14–15
182 Dan 13 (*Apocrypha* Susanna)
183 Gen 37:2; but the Vulgate and modern versions of this passage declare that Joseph informed on his brothers.
184 Gen 37:18–28 and 42:6–25
185 Gen 37:3
186 In *Homiliae* 61.2 (PG 54 525). Erasmus was already editing Chrysostom, publishing the *De sacerdotibus* and *De orando* in the same year as *Lingua, Conciunculae* in 1526, and *Lucubrationes* in 1527. His edition of the complete works came out in 1530; see Allen Ep 2359 for Erasmus' opinion of the importance and merit of this Father of the church.
187 Cf PL 23 1045 on Gen 37, which passes over this discrepancy.
188 Gen 39:7

343
189 2 Kings (RSV 2 Sam) 2:12–28; cf 340 and n162 above for another instance of Joab's treachery.
190 Although Erasmus' text and the Vulgate both read *benedixit* 'blessed,' the sense requires the opposite, 'maledixit.'
191 3 Kings (RSV 1 Kings) 21:9–10; cf 340 and n166 above.
192 2 Kings (RSV 2 Sam) 11:7–18
193 Henry II, who quarrelled with Thomas Becket over the rights of the church, and is held responsible for his murder by the churches of Rome and Canterbury
194 Plutarch *Alexander* 89
195 *Adagia* I ii 9, from Horace *Satires* 2.3.321
196 Plutarch *Moralia* 202E, also *Sulla* 6 and 14

344
197 The story is first found in Caesar's *Bellum civile* 3.103. For Theodotus' role see Plutarch *Pompey* 78, 80.
198 Plutarch *Brutus* 33

345
199 Plutarch *Antony* 24. The sum of two hundred thousand talents given in the third edition of *Lingua* (August 1526; cf Allen Ep 1621) corrects the careless substitution of ducats in the first two editions.

200 See 340 above; 3 Kings (RSV 1 Kings) 12:1–19 or 2 Chron 10:1–19.
201 At *Iliad* 2.371
202 In 4 Kings (RSV 2 Kings) 5:1–14
203 Despite the transition promised at 340 Erasmus had lapsed into illustrating
the bad (or good) counsel given to princes. Returning to slander against
the innocent he illustrates it from the unjust prosecutions of Socrates (based
on Socrates' own defence in the *Apology* of Plato), Phocion (told in Plutarch
Phocion 31–5), the ostracism of Aristides (told in Plutarch *Aristides* 7–8), and
the trials of Epaminondas and Scipio, which he had already touched on at
291 above. Erasmus again lists these virtuous pagans (with the two Catos and
Brutus) at *Philodoxus* ASD I-3 668:39–42 / Thompson *Colloquies* 481 as
examples of noble men victimized by envy.
204 John 19:15
205 Jer 18:18
206 Cf Phil 2:10.
207 See Acts 7.11–60.

346
208 By his Jewish enemies in Acts 24:5
209 Chrysostom was deprived of his bishopric and twice exiled from Constanti-
nople; see V. Campenhausen *Die griechischen Kirchenväter* (Stuttgart 1967).
210 The prefaces to his biblical translations (cf PL 28 and 29), the works against
Jovinianus, Vigiliantius, and John of Jerusalem, and the *Apologia adversus
libros Rufini* (PL 23 211–404).
211 Cf *Adagia* II iv 8: *Zoili*, where Erasmus links Zoilus, the Alexandrian critic of
Homer, nicknamed *Homeromastix*, and Pero, whom he calls *Virgiliomastix*
(on Pero see 288 n17 above). Mevius or Maevius is the figure cursed by
Horace in *Epodes* 10, but according to Servius on *Georgics* 1.210 it was Virgil
not Horace whom Maevius attacked. 'Ibis,' the name of the Egyptian bird
which fed on dung, is the title of a poem by Ovid, heaping curses on an
unnamed enemy.
212 For this citizen of Ephesus who burned down the temple of Artemis to attain
notoriety see also Allen Ep 1967:52–3 and the colloquy *Philodoxus* 'The
Lover of Glory' ASD I-3 668:22–4 / Thompson *Colloquies* 480. Of the ancient
sources for the burning of the temple of Artemis in 335 BC only Strabo
14.1.21 names the incendiary; Cicero *De natura deorum* 2.69 and Plutarch
Alexander 3 do not name him, and Gellius 2.6.18 claims that the council of
Ephesus decreed that his name should be obliterated.
213 The Athenian demagogue who inflamed the people against Alcibiades, until
the coalition of Alcibiades with his conservative opponent Nicias turned
the public vote of ostracism against their common enemy Hyperbolus, who
went into exile in 416 BC. See Plutarch *Aristides* 7, which is Erasmus' source
for the procedure of ostracism and its abandonment after this date. For
Aristophanes' jokes against Hyperbolus cf *Pax* 681–90.

347
214 See Plutarch *Comparatio Ciceronis et Demosthenis* for the occasion, during
Cicero's defence of Murena against Cato.

215 Cicero's accusation of Verres, governor of Sicily, on behalf of the oppressed subjects of Rome is his only published prosecution; he did, however, prosecute and secure the conviction of the tribune Pompeius Rufus in 52 BC.

216 Livy 39.40 reports that he was continually involved as defendant or prosecutor, and wore down his enemies with his oratory.

217 Plutarch *Aemilius Paulus* 5

348

218 In 61 BC, when Clodius Pulcher was prosecuted for violating the female rites of the Good Goddess, held in Caesar's house, allegedly in pursuit of his affair with Caesar's wife. See Plutarch *Caesar* 10 and *Moralia* 206B.

219 Deut 19:21

220 Erasmus will have read in Gellius 2.22.24 that Aristotle (*Meteorologica* 2.6 / 364b14–15) attributed to this wind the power of attracting rain-clouds.

221 Cf Erasmus' complaints in Allen Ep 1581:396–410 (June 1525), his reply to Béda against the work of Vincentius Theoderici of Harlem, *Apologia in eum librum quem ab anno Erasmus Roterodamus de confessione edidit per Godefridum Ruysium Taxandrum Theologum* (Antwerp: March 1525), and see introductory note nn13, 14.

349

222 Juvenal 1.57

223 Erasmus may have in mind Pierre Cousturier (Le Couturier or Petrus Sutor), the Carthusian who published a pamphlet censuring all modern translations of the Bible in December 1524; see Renaudet *Etudes Erasmiennes* (Paris 1939) 237–44. Sutor was one of a group of theologians of the Sorbonne who had recently prohibited the publication of Berquin's translations of Erasmus' *De modo orandi, Encomium matrimonii*, the colloquy *Inquisitio de fide*, and *Querela pacis* (May and June 1525). Erasmus replied to Sutor in a pamphlet *Adversus Petri Sutoris quondam theologi Sorbonici nunc monachi Cartusiani debacchationem apologia* (August 1525). In a letter to Béda soon after Sutor's publication (Allen Ep 1571, April 1525), Erasmus quotes Sutor's abuse of himself as a heretic and his conclusion that all biblical translations are heretical and blasphemous (lines 33–41). See also Ep 1687 (August 1526) to the Carthusian prior Willem Bibaut (Bibaucus).

224 Matt 5:44–5

225 Matt 5:3, 10:9–10

226 The quotation conflates Jer 9:8 and 9, reading present *extendunt* for Vulgate *extenderunt*.

227 Here and in what follows Erasmus is quoting fragments of Ps 9 (H):7–10 (RSV 10:7–10). Here the Vulgate reads 'cuius maledictione os plenum est et amaritudine et dolo sub lingua eius labor et dolor. Sedet in insidiis ...'

228 Ps 68:10 (RSV 69:9); John 2:17, reading *domus tuae* with LB and the Vulgate; ASD reads *domus dei* without textual comment.

229 Ps 9 (H): 8–10 (RSV 10:8–9)

230 Matt 4:20

350

231 The first reference in this work to a recurring theme; cf 353–62 below.

232 Ps 13 (RSV 14):3
233 Cf *Adagia* IV i 1: *Dulce bellum inexpertis* LB 2.951f, and the separate treatise *De bello turcico* of 1530.
234 Ps 13 (RSV 14):5, continuing the quotation in the preceding paragraph
235 Prov 25:18

351
236 Prov 28:17
237 Repeated from 309 above
238 Eccles 4:1-3; but Erasmus' text is nearer to a paraphrase than a reproduction of the Vulgate.
239 Sir 26:5-7
240 Hos 13:14

352
241 The fable is told in Horace *Epistles* 1.10 35-8.
242 Lev 19:16, followed by 19:11
243 Prov 24:9
244 Erasmus partly quotes and partly paraphrases Horace *Satires* 1.4.95 and 99-100; *sed magis amica veritas* echoes the proverbial *amicus Plato sed magis amica veritas* from Ammonius' *Vita Aristotelis*.

353
245 Cf Allen Ep 1610:139-142 for a preliminary hint of this topic.
246 Erasmus, or his printer, is in error. The distich is usually attributed to Augustus (*divus Augustus*, not *Augustinus*); see Walther 19416A.

354
247 Erasmus indignantly recalls the abuse of himself and others as heretics quoted in Allen Ep 1581 (to Béda): 355f (see also 361 below). For another more discreet contemporary attack on the theologians see Ἰχθυοφαγία 'A Fish Diet' ASD I-3 509:518-9 / Thompson *Colloquies* 329).
248 Perhaps a reference to criticisms of Erasmus' annotation on Luke 2; cf LB IX 152 B-C against Lee and 807B against Sutor.

355
249 See 350 above; Erasmus treats this theme at length in the colloquy *Exsequiae seraphicae* 'The Seraphic Funeral' ASD I-3 686-99 / Thompson *Colloquies* 503-16; see also Ep 447:554-60.
250 Cf *Adagia* I vii 73 and Erasmus' accusations against Béda in LB IX 448E.
251 1 Cor 13:5
252 Acts 18:3; Paul worked with tentmakers in Corinth.

356
253 The theologians abominated all pagan learning. So above 352, Erasmus reports them as declaring they were not allowed to study rhetoric.
254 For Erasmus' views on the status of confession as a sacrament see *Exomologesis* LB V 145f.
255 Eccles 10:11

357

256 Reading *negant* for ASD *negat*, to match the plural *fingunt* in the same sentence

358

257 With this complaint cf Allen Ep 1581:377–84 (June 1525) on the Dominican friar who attacked Erasmus at Louvain while he was away in Calais.

258 The attacks on members of the various orders for their adherence to rules of clothing and violation of the ten commandments return to the accusations of Ἰχθυοφαγία 'A Fish Diet' ASD I-3 523:1031–9 and 535–6:1488–50 / Thompson *Colloquies* 343, 356; see also Ep 447 575–83.

259 Cf Ἰχθυοφαγία 'A Fish Diet' ASD I-3 524:1070–82 / Thompson *Colloquies* 344.

359

260 Gal 5:15

261 Matt 7:16

262 Sir 21:30

360

263 This passage is close to Erasmus' argument in the paraphrase on Mark 2:27, which was labelled Lutheran by Béda; cf Erasmus' defence LB IX 645Dff, and on pious fasting cf LB VII 179Bff.

264 Cicero *De oratore* 1.150

265 Ps 13:3 (Vulg); cf 341 and 350 above.

266 Gen 3:12–13

361

267 Luke 18:11

268 The rascally prosecutor and troublemaker of Terence's play *Phormio*. This sentence introduces a repetition of the theme treated at 316 above.

269 Cf Catullus 22.21, Persius 4.24, and the fable told by Phaedrus 4.10. Men who carried their baggage on their backs would be unaware how disreputable it looked.

270 A favourite Erasmian phrase; cf *Annotationes* on Luke 1 note 53 LB VI 226C; Ep 1352:127–8.

362

271 Cf 1 Cor 10.7–10; Eph 4:17–19.

272 An allusion to 1 Pet 1:14

273 As in Rom 11:7

274 Eg 2 Cor 11:13

275 The action *in quadruplum*, on which see Gellius 11.18.11, Erasmus' probable source, and *Digest* 4.2.14, 2.8.5

363

276 Ps 140 (RSV 141):4

277 Prov 4:24

278 Prov 6:16–19

279 Thales was an Ionian mathematician and philosopher of the sixth century BC, traditionally included among the 'Seven Sages' of the Greek canon.
280 Sir 21:31 (RSV 28)
281 Hesiod *Works and Days* 346, quoted 281 above
282 Sir 28:15 (RSV 13)
283 Plutarch *Moralia* 208D; compare Xenophon *Agesilaus* 11.4.

364
284 Plutarch tells the anecdotes of Antigonus and of Augustus and the Thracian in connection with the legend of Tarpeia (364 below) in *Romulus* 17.
285 See Plutarch *Solon* 21.

365
286 2 Cor 12:20–1
287 Rom 12:14
288 Sir 37:21 (RSV 37:18)
289 Prov 18:21
290 Hesiod *Works and Days* 707–8
291 Erasmus returns to his imagery of poison and antidote from 319. For the asp see 319 n10; for panacea as the name of a specific herb 320.
292 Prov 10:11
293 1 Cor 15:33; the Greek verse is traditionally attributed to Menander (see Menander frag 187 Koerte). Erasmus has given his own Latin adaptation in correct comic verse.
294 Walther 601A; it is also drawn from an unidentified Greek comedy.

366
295 Prov 15:1
296 1 Kings (RSV 1 Sam) 25:32–3. For the provocation offered by Nabal see 10–13 of the same chapter.
297 Zenobius 2.99, Diogenianus 2.24
298 Mercury, or the Greek Hermes, was conceived as the patron of eloquence and civilizer of men. Cf Horace *Odes* 1.10.1–4; in another related legend Mercury taught the poet-singer Amphion to play the lyre, and his music inspired all the stones to come together to build the walls of Thebes.
299 James 3:2–4

367
300 James 3:5–12; see above 341 n179.
301 Ps 11:3 (RSV 12:2)
302 James 1:26
303 The story comes from Plutarch *De garrulitate, Moralia* 505A.
304 Diogenes Laertius 6.2.4

[*The usefulness of a good tongue and remedies against an evil tongue*]

368
1 *Adagia* I x 73 CWE 32 266–7

2 Another echo of Plutarch *De garrulitate, Moralia* 503B
3 1 Cor 5:11

369
4 1 Cor 7:12, 20–4
5 1 Cor 7:13
6 James 3:6; cf 367 above.
7 Prov 16:27–8
8 Ps 13:3 (Vulg), a recurring text; cf 350, 360 above.
9 Deut 32:32
10 Cf Virgil *Aeneid* 6.239–42, explaining the name of Avernus (Aornos) from its volcanic gases, which drove away bird life.

370
11 Ps 5:11 (RSV 9
12 Prov 22:14
13 Prov 23:27
14 Sir 3:27 (RSV 3:24)
15 Ezek 2:6
16 Acts 28:3–5
17 Their march is narrated in Lucan 9.587–940; for the local creatures that beset them see above 318–20 n4.
18 Verses 13–14
19 Mark 16:17

371
20 Prov 5:1–8
21 Avianus fable 29, told at *Adagia* I viii 30

372
22 Isa 5:20
23 I know of no evidence for such masks in *commedia dell'arte*, but they were a feature of carnivals (as illustrated by the mask worn by Leopold Mozart in the film *Amadeus*).
24 Prov 8:13
25 Sir 5:17 (RSV 14)
26 1 Tim 3:8
27 Reported by Plutarch *Cato Minor* 6
28 Plutarch *Moralia* 236c; Erasmus *Apophthegmata* LB IV 141E

373
29 An echo of Horace *Epistles* 1.19
30 The author of this reply is presumably Thomas More, who was in Bruges on royal affairs in 1520.

374
31 Erasmus quotes the Greek word ἀπροσδιόνυσον 'nothing to do with Dionysus'; cf *Adagia* II iv 57: *Nihil ad Bacchum* . Ancient opinion differed as to

the origin of the phrase but generally associated it with the function of drama as an act of worship to Dionysus. Cf Plutarch *Moralia* 615B.

32 *Adagia* I iv 87: *Surdo canis* CWE 31 376–7; cf Virgil *Eclogues* 10.8.
33 *Adagia* I ii 9
34 Lucian *Symposium* 12–13
35 Plutarch *Cato Major* 21

375
36 Terence *Phormio* 1040–1
37 *Heautontimorumenos* 213–15
38 Plautus *Asinaria* 833
39 Juvenal 14.47
40 Plutarch *Cato Major* 20
41 Sir 7:26 (RSV 24)
42 Cf Cicero *De officiis* 1.129.

376
43 *Adagia* II i 49: *Falces postulabam*; cf Zenobius 83.
44 *Moralia* 511D; Piso here is M. Pupius Piso, consul of 61 BC.

377
45 Terence *Phormio* 793
46 At 312 above
47 Plautus *Cistellaria* 121
48 A self-satisfied dandy mocked in *Catullus* 22

378
49 *Adagia* I vii 26 CWE 32 82–3
50 *Adagia* II ii 44; Plutarch *Moralia* 513E
51 Plutarch *Cato Minor* 19
52 The elder Pliny, according to his nephew, Pliny the Younger, *Epistles* 3.5.10
53 The Phrygian and Lydian modes were particularly associated with wanton and emotional music, and so earned the disapproval of Plato in *Republic* 399F.
54 Julius Caesar, according to Plutarch *Caesar* 17; Pliny *Naturalis historia* 7.91

379
55 Plutarch *Moralia* 136D
56 *Adagia* IV ix 27
57 *Historiae Augustae scriptores* (*Heliogabalus*) 29.4
58 Erasmus himself composed a colloquy, *Senatulus, sive* Γυναικοσυνέδριον 'The Lower House, or *The Council of Women*,' on this theme; cf ASD I-3 629–34 (1529) / Thompson *Colloquies* 441–6. Syriamira in our texts is a corruption of the name of Heliogabalus' Syrian aunt, Mammaea, perhaps arising from a printer's confusion with Semiramis. Erasmus' words come virtually unchanged from the text of *Historiae Augustae scriptores* (*Heliogabalus*) 29.4.

380
59 Plutarch *Moralia* 186D; cf *Alcibiades* 9.

60 Erasmus' patron, William Warham, archbishop of Canterbury from 1503 to his death in 1532, lord chancellor of England from 1504 to 1515, and chancellor of Oxford University from 1506

61 Mal 2:6–7

62 An allusion to Matt 5:13, in which Christ calls his disciples the salt of the earth

63 Mal 2:8–9

64 Eugenius III, pope from 1145 to 1153, was a disciple of St Bernard of Clairvaux, who addressed to him a work *De consideratione libri quinque ad Eugenium III.*

381

65 Sir 12:13 (RSV 13–14)

66 *Battologia* is here used of physical stammering, but elsewhere Erasmus invokes the use of the word in the gospel to denote empty talk.

67 The argument here is repeated from 273 above.

68 See *Adagia* II ix 1, where the Greek proverb 'more foolish than Morychus' is derived from Zenodotus' story of the Sicilian statue of Bacchus placed outside his temple and facing away from it, hence ostensibly concerned with other men's affairs instead of his own sanctuary.

69 Foolish acquaintances made fun of by *Martial* 4.37 and 78 (Afer) and 7.10 (Ollus).

382

70 The essay *De garrulitate*, on which Erasmus has drawn substantially in the *Lingua*

71 *De ira* 2.29

72 In the Hannibalic war Rome suffered repeated defeats in pitched battles until Q. Fabius Maximus was named dictator and adopted a new tactic of dogging Hannibal's march while avoiding battle; from the success of this technique he was known as Fabius Cunctator, 'the delayer.'

73 *Adagia* I i 1 CWE 31 29–30, attributed to Cato the Elder

74 Cf *Adagia* II v 60: *Dum nimium properant.* Plato refers to this as a familiar proverb at *Politicus* 264B.

75 *Adagia* IV v 68

383

76 A fragment from an unknown play, 775N Nauck

77 Terence *Phormio* 441–7

384

78 See Plutarch *Themistocles* 11; at *Moralia* 185B the same comment is credited to Adeimantus the Corinthian; cf Herodotus 8.59.

79 This announcement was typical of the Greek Sophists such as Gorgias attacked by Plato for their lack of intellectual honesty.

385

80 James 1:19

386

81 Quintilian 11.3.158

82 *Iliad* 2.317, used as evidence by Quintilian in the passage cited in n81 above
83 A back reference to the anecdote told at 294 above

387
84 Plutarch *Demosthenes* 68
85 Plutarch *Moralia* 205E.
86 Sir 32:9–13 (RSV 7–9), previously quoted at 325 above
87 Literally 'a headless speech'; the phrase comes from Plato's *Phaedrus* 264C.
88 Plato *Euthydemus* 273E

388
89 In the *Epistula ad Pisones* (*Ars poetica* 174). The double-yolked egg is that in which Helen was born to Leda; according to some versions of the myth she and her divine brothers the Dioscuri were hatched from the same egg.
90 Cf Lucian *Alexander* 54.
91 *Adagia* I iii 51 CWE 31 277–8 cites this from Lucian's *Demonax*.
92 *Adagia* II vii 4. Aristotle is alleged to have begun to teach rhetoric because he thought it a disgrace to keep silent if such as Isocrates dared to give instruction. Cf Cicero *De oratore* 3.141.
93 One of the precepts inscribed over the doorway of the Delphic oracle was supposedly 'Know thyself.'

389
94 The example is drawn from *Moralia* 512F. For Socrates' endurance of cold and sleeplessness see Alcibiades' praise in *Symposium* 211B.
95 Plutarch *Moralia* 207C

390
96 Terence *Hecyra* 729–30
97 At *Iliad* 1.207 she prevents Achilles from striking his commander in chief, Agamemnon, in a fit of anger.
98 Cf Rom 12:14; this is repeated 396 n128 below.
99 *Curculio* 121f
100 Cf Plutarch *De garrulitate, Moralia* 513F; couches, lamps, girdles are all apostrophized in love poems of the Palatine Anthology; for the ring cf Ovid *Amores* 2.15.
101 For example Corydon in Virgil's *Eclogue* 2 or Gallus as shepherd in *Eclogue* 10

391
102 Again, the essay *De garrulitate, Moralia* 514C
103 Ibidem 513D; Erasmus *Apophthegmata* LB 4 155E
104 For the guidelines and criteria applied in deliberative oratory cf eg Cicero *De inventione* 2.52, 157–8; Quintilian 3.8.22.
105 Plutarch *Pericles* 8. The reference to 'thunder and lightning' is adapted from Aristophanes *Acharnians* 531, cited by Plutarch.
106 This is the solemn opening of Cicero's speech *Pro Murena*.

392
107 I have not been able to identify this reference.

166 A blend of Acts 5:9 and 2 Cor 13:3
167 Mark 16:17; cf Acts 2:4, 10:46.
168 Mark 16:18; cf 370 n19

[*Christian use of the tongue*]

1 Mark 16:17–18

403
2 Pliny *Naturalis historia* 7.15, 28.19; for the Psylli see 321 n20. Erasmus' analogy between Christian preachers and the Psylli immediately following this is modelled on Lucan's account (*Bellum civile* 9.922–37) of their healing methods.
3 Erasmus lists the orders as if they were in some sense schismatic; besides Dominicans and Franciscans, his special enemies, Erasmus lists Benedictines, Cistercians, Augustinians, Carthusians, and Brigittines. (On St Bruno, founder of the Carthusian order, see the *New Catholic Encyclopaedia* II 837–8; for St Bridget of Sweden, ibidem 798–9). He repeats the comment in his enumeration of the schools of theology, 407 and n29 below.

404
4 Gal 4:20
5 See K.H. Ringstorf *Paulus und die älteste Römische Christenheit* Studia Evangelica II, (Berlin 1964) 447–64.
6 Cf Eph 4:22–4.

405
7 Matt 24:3; Mark 13:4; Luke 21:7; but Erasmus' wording is closer to Acts 1:6.
8 Cf Ps 18:2 (RSV 19:1)
9 Ps 67:24 (RSV 68:23)
10 John 19:15; see 345 n204 above.
11 Mark 15:29; cf Matt 27:40.
12 Cf Acts 15:1.
13 Luke 16:21
14 Cf Acts 7:51 and Paul's treatment of unchristian behaviour as uncircumcised in Rom 2:26–7.
15 1 Cor 13:1
16 Ibidem 11
17 Cf Isa 1:20, 40:5, 58:14.
18 Job 11:5
19 Cf 2 Cor 12:2.

406
20 John 6:69
21 Luke 9:55
22 Luke 22:24
23 Acts 1:6 (modified)
24 Cf Acts 2:11, 2:4, 4:32.

25 Phil 2:1–3

407
26 1 Cor 1:9–10
27 For the church as the body of Christ see Rom 12:4–5, 1 Cor 12:12–31, Eph 4:15–16, Col 3:15.
28 1 Cor 1:12
29 Erasmus represents the schismatic tendencies of contemporary theology by several overlapping classifications. Thus Transalpine and Cisalpine are merely geographical labels to distinguish French from Italian tradition, no doubt an echo of the great schism between Rome and Avignon; similarly the references to the schools of Paris and Cologne are intended to evoke the theologians of the Sorbonne and perhaps the followers of Konrad Kollin, the distinguished Thomist teacher in Cologne. But the allusion to Scotists, Thomists, and Ockhamists groups with the mainstream of the scholastic tradition two later phases, which interpreted theology on different ontological principles, the followers of Duns Scotus (c 1266–1308), the Scottish Franciscan, and of William of Ockham (c 1285–1347), also a Franciscan, and Scotus' contemporary at Oxford. These scholars developed on divergent lines scholastic teaching as it had come down to them from St Thomas Aquinas (c 1225–75), the great Dominican Doctor of the church. (For the main features of Scotist theology see the *New Catholic Encyclopedia* IV 1104–6; on the teachings of Ockham, ibidem XIV 932–5; and on the development of Thomism up to Erasmus' time, ibidem XIV 130–3.) The antithesis of nominalists and realists largely coincides with the division between the followers of Ockham's nominalism and the moderate Aristotelian realism of St Thomas (see *New Catholic Encyclopedia* X 484 and XII 111–12). The new schools of the German reformers are represented by Luther and Andreas Rudolf Bodenstein von Karlstadt (c 1480–1541). The latter began as a Thomist theologian, but after writing a work against the evils of the papal court, published 151 theses attacking the Catholic doctrines of grace and free will, besides a mass of unorthodox exegetical work on the Scriptures; he had recently (1524) been expelled from Wittenberg, and fled to join the Anabaptists. Finally, the names *evangelista* and *papista* had become virtual battle-cries in the confrontation between the reformers and the papacy by the time that *Lingua* was composed.
30 These are not biblical citations, but Erasmus' own comparison of the divided church to the house and city 'divided against itself' (Matt 12:25; Mark 3:24–5) and the divided body of Christ that should be a unity.
31 Cf 1 Esdras (RSV Ezra) 9:1–2, 10:2 and 17–44. Note that 9:2 lists the daughters of Ammon and Moab but not Azotus as recorded here.
32 Cf 3 Kings (RSV 1 Kings) 11:1–4.

408
33 Matt 3:2, the words of John the Baptist.
34 Punished in Acts 5.1–10 for withholding part of their money from the common funds of the Christian community
35 This probably refers to 2 Kings (RSV 2 Sam) 24:10–25.
36 Isa 59:11–13

37 Jer 15:15
38 Dan 9:4

409
39 Job 39:34–5 (RSV 40:4–5)
40 1 Pet 5:6
41 Matt 6:7; cf 325 above.
42 Matt 12:36
43 1 Tim 6:4; cf 325 above.
44 Ps 36 (RSV 37):30
45 Cf Col 4:6.
46 Cf Eph 4:29.
47 Phil 4:8
48 Cf Phil 4:9.

410
49 Eph 4:31
50 Eph 5:19
51 2 Tim 4:2

411
52 Isa 50:4
53 Cf Isa 42:3.
54 Jer 1:9–10
55 Isa 49:2
56 Ibidem

412
57 Cf 1 Cor 13:1, cited 405 n15.

WORKS FREQUENTLY CITED

SHORT-TITLE FORMS

INDEX

WORKS FREQUENTLY CITED

This list provides bibliographical information for works referred to in short-title form in this volume. For Erasmus' writings see the short-title list, pages 522–5.

Allen   P.S. Allen, H.M. Allen, and H.W. Garrod eds *Opus epistolarum Des. Erasmi Roterodami* (Oxford 1906–58) 11 vols and index

ASD   *Opera omnia Desiderii Erasmi Roterodami* (Amsterdam 1969–   )

Barigazzi   A. Barigazzi ed and trans *Favorino di Arelate: Opere* (Florence 1966)

Beaudouin   M. Beaudouin 'Le Protepticus de Galien' *Revue de philologie* n s 22 (1898) 233–45

Brabant   H. Brabant 'Erasme, ses maladies et ses médecins' in *Colloquia Erasmiana Turonensia* ed J.-C. Margolin 2 vols (Toronto 1972) I 539–68

CEBR   P.G. Bietenholz and T.B. Deutscher eds *Contemporaries of Erasmus: A Biographical Register of the Renaissance and Reformation* 3 vols (Toronto 1985–7)

CGF   G. Kaibel ed *Comicorum Graecorum fragmenta* (Berlin 1899)

CSEL   *Corpus scriptorum ecclesiasticorum latinorum* (Vienna-Leipzig 1866–   )

Curtius   E.R. Curtius *European Literature and the Latin Middle Ages* trans W.R. Trask (New York 1953)

CWE   *Collected Works of Erasmus* (Toronto 1974–   )

Diels-Kranz   H. Diels and W. Kranz eds *Die Fragmente der Vorsokratiker* (Berlin 1934–7)

Ferguson *Opuscula*   W.K. Ferguson ed *Erasmi opuscula: A Supplement to the Opera omnia* (The Hague 1933)

Holborn   A. and H. Holborn *Desiderius Erasmus Roterodamus: Ausgewählte Werke* (Munich 1933; repr 1974)

Kaibel   G. Kaibel ed *Galeni protreptici quae supersunt* (Berlin 1963)

LB   J. Leclerc ed *Desiderii Erasmi Roterodami opera omnia* (Leiden 1703–6; repr 1961–2) 10 vols

Lobel-Page

E. Lobel and D. Page eds *Poetarum Lesbiorum fragmenta* (Oxford 1955)

Nauck

A. Nauck ed *Tragicorum Graecorum fragmenta* (Leipzig 1856)

Otto *Sprichwörter*

A. Otto *Die Sprichwörter und sprichwörtlichen Redensarten der Römer* (Leipzig 1890)

Pauly-Wissowa

A. Pauly and G. Wissowa eds *Realencyclopädie der classischen Altertumswissenschaft* (Stuttgart 1893–1963)

PL

J.P. Migne ed *Patrologiae cursus completus ... series latina* (Paris 1844–1902) 221 vols

Reedijk

C. Reedijk ed *The Poems of Desiderius Erasmus* (Leiden 1956)

Ribbeck

Otto Ribbeck ed *Comicorum Latinorum reliquiae* (Leipzig 1855)

Thompson *Colloquies*

Craig R. Thompson ed and trans *The Colloquies of Erasmus* (Chicago and London 1965)

Walpole

A.S. Walpole *Early Latin Hymns* (Cambridge 1922)

Walther

H. Walther *Proverbia Sententiaeque Latinitatis Medii Aevi* 6 vols (Göttingen 1963–9)

Yale CWM

The Complete Works of St Thomas More (New Haven 1961–   )

SHORT-TITLE FORMS FOR ERASMUS' WORKS

Titles following colons are longer versions of the same, or are alternative titles. Items entirely enclosed in square brackets are of doubtful authorship. For abbreviations, see Works Frequently Cited.

Adagia: Adagiorum chiliades 1508 (Adagiorum collectanea for the primitive form, when required) LB II / ASD II-4, 5, 6 / CWE 30–6
Admonitio adversus mendacium: Admonitio adversus mendacium et obtrectationem LB X
Annotationes in Novum Testamentum LB VI
Antibarbari LB X / ASD I-1 / CWE 23
Apologia ad Caranzam: Apologia ad Sanctium Caranzam, or Apologia de tribus locis, or Responsio ad annotationem Stunicae ... a Sanctio Caranza defensam LB IX
Apologia ad Fabrum: Apologia ad Iacobum Fabrum Stapulensem LB IX
Apologia adversus monachos: Apologia adversus monachos quosdam hispanos LB IX
Apologia adversus Petrum Sutorem: Apologia adversus debacchationes Petri Sutoris LB IX
Apologia adversus rhapsodias Alberti Pii: Apologia ad viginti et quattuor libros A. Pii LB IX
Apologia contra Latomi dialogum: Apologia contra Iacobi Latomi dialogum de tribus linguis LB IX
Apologiae contra Stunicam: Apologiae contra Lopidem Stunicam LB IX / ASD IX-2
Apologia de 'In principio erat sermo' LB IX
Apologia de laude matrimonii: Apologia pro declamatione de laude matrimonii LB IX
Apologia de loco 'Omnes quidem': Apologia de loco 'Omnes quidem resurgemus' LB IX
Apologia invectivis Lei: Apologia qua respondet duabus invectivis Eduardi Lei *Opuscula*
Apophthegmata LB IV
Appendix respondens ad Sutorem LB IX
Argumenta: Argumenta in omnes epistolas apostolicas nova (with Paraphrases)
Axiomata pro causa Lutheri: Axiomata pro causa Martini Lutheri *Opuscula*

Carmina varia LB VIII
Catalogus lucubrationum LB I
Christiani hominis institutum, carmen LB V
Ciceronianus: Dialogus Ciceronianus LB I / ASD I-2 / CWE 28
Colloquia LB I / ASD I-3
Compendium vitae Allen I / CWE 4
[Consilium: Consilium cuiusdam ex animo cupientis esse consultum] *Opuscula*

De bello turcico: Consultatio de bello turcico (in Psalmi)
De civilitate: De civilitate morum puerilium LB I / CWE 25
Declamatio de morte LB IV
Declamatiuncula LB IV

Declarationes ad censuras Lutetiae vulgatas: Declarationes ad censuras Lutetiae
  vulgatas sub nomine facultatis theologiae Parisiensis LB IX
De concordia: De amabili ecclesiae concordia (in Psalmi)
De conscribendis epistolis LB I / ASD I-2 / CWE 25
De constructione: De constructione octo partium orationis, or Syntaxis LB I / ASD I-4
De contemptu mundi: Epistola de contemptu mundi LB V / ASD V-1 / CWE 66
De copia: De duplici copia verborum ac rerum LB I / CWE 24
De immensa Dei misericordia: Concio de immensa Dei misericordia LB V
De libero arbitrio: De libero arbitrio diatribe LB IX
De praeparatione: De praeparatione ad mortem LB V / ASD V-1
De pueris instituendis: De pueris statim ac liberaliter instituendis LB I / ASD I-2 /
  CWE 26
De puero Iesu: Concio de puero Iesu LB V / CWE 29
De puritate tabernaculi: De puritate tabernaculi sive ecclesiae christianae (in Psalmi)
De ratione studii LB I / ASD I-2 / CWE 24
De recta pronuntiatione: De recta latini graecique sermonis pronuntiatione LB I /
  ASD I-4 / CWE 26
Detectio praestigiarum: Detectio praestigiarum cuiusdam libelli germanice scripti
  LB X / ASD IX-1
De tedio Iesu: Disputatiuncula de tedio, pavore, tristicia Iesu LB V
De vidua christiana LB V / CWE 66
De virtute amplectenda: Oratio de virtute amplectenda LB V / CWE 29
[Dialogus bilinguium ac trilinguium: Chonradi Nastadiensis dialogus bilinguium ac
  trilinguium] Opuscula / CWE 7
Dilutio: Dilutio eorum quae Iodocus Clithoveus scripsit adversus declamationem
  suasoriam matrimonii
Divinationes ad notata Bedae LB IX

Ecclesiastes: Ecclesiastes sive de ratione concionandi LB V
Elenchus in N. Bedae censuras LB IX
Enchiridion: Enchiridion militis christiani LB V / CWE 66
Encomium matrimonii (in De conscribendis epistolis)
Encomium medicinae: Declamatio in laudem artis medicae LB I / ASD I-4 / CWE 29
Epigrammata LB I
Epistola ad Dorpium LB IX / CWE 3
Epistola ad fratres Inferioris Germaniae: Responsio ad fratres Germaniae Inferioris
  ad epistolam apologeticam incerto autore proditam LB X
Epistola ad graculos: Epistola ad quosdam imprudentissimos graculos LB X
Epistola apologetica de Termino LB X
Epistola consolatoria: Epistola consolatoria virginibus sacris LB V
Epistola contra pseudevangelicos: Epistola contra quosdam qui se falso iactant
  evangelicos LB X / ASD IX-1
Epistola de esu carnium: Epistola apologetica ad Christophorum episcopum
  Basiliensem de interdicto esu carnium LB IX / ASD IX-1
Exomologesis: Exomologesis sive modus confitendi LB V
Explanatio symboli: Explanatio symboli apostolorum sive catechismus LB V / ASD V-1
Expositio concionalis (in Psalmi)
Expostulatio Iesu LB V

Formula: Conficiendarum epistolarum formula (see De conscribendis epistolis)

Hymni varii LB V
Hyperaspistes LB X

In Nucem Ovidii commentarius LB I / ASD I-1 / CWE 29
In Prudentium: Commentarius in duos hymnos Prudentii LB V / CWE 29
Institutio christiani matrimonii LB V
Institutio principis christiani LB IV / ASD IV-1 / CWE 27

[Julius exclusus: Dialogus Julius exclusus e coelis *Opuscula*] CWE 27

Lingua LB IV / ASD IV-1 / CWE 29
Liturgia Virginis Matris: Virginis Matris apud Lauretum cultae liturgia LB V / ASD V-1

Methodus (see Ratio)
Modus orandi Deum LB V / ASD V-1
Moria: Moriae encomium LB IV / ASD IV-3 / CWE 27

Novum Testamentum: Novum Testamentum 1519 and later (Novum instrumentum
    for the first edition, 1516, when required) LB VI

Obsecratio ad Virginem Mariam: Obsecratio sive oratio ad Virginem Mariam in
    rebus adversis LB V
Oratio de pace: Oratio de pace et discordia LB VIII
Oratio funebris: Oratio funebris Berthae de Heyen LB VIII / CWE 29

Paean Virgini Matri: Paean Virgini Matri dicendus LB V
Panegyricus: Panegyricus ad Philippum Austriae ducem LB IV / ASD IV-1 / CWE 27
Parabolae: Parabolae sive similia LB I / ASD I-5 / CWE 23
Paraclesis LB V, VI
Paraphrasis in Elegantias Vallae: Paraphrasis in Elegantias Laurentii Vallae LB I /
    ASD I-4
Paraphrasis in Matthaeum, etc (in Paraphrasis in Novum Testamentum)
Paraphrasis in Novum Testamentum LB VII / CWE 42-50
Peregrinatio apostolorum: Peregrinatio apostolorum Petri et Pauli LB VI, VII
Precatio ad Virginis filium Iesum LB V
Precatio dominica LB V
Precationes LB V
Precatio pro pace ecclesiae: Precatio ad Iesum pro pace ecclesiae LB IV, V
Progymnasmata: Progymnasmata quaedam primae adolescentiae Erasmi LB VIII
Psalmi: Psalmi, or Enarrationes sive commentarii in psalmos LB V / ASD V-2, 3
Purgatio adversus epistolam Lutheri: Purgatio adversus epistolam non sobriam
    Lutheri LB IX

Querela pacis LB IV / ASD IV-2 / CWE 27

Ratio: Ratio seu Methodus compendio perveniendi ad veram theologiam (Methodus

for the shorter version originally published in the Novum instrumentum of 1516)
LB V, VI

Responsio ad annotationes Lei: Liber quo respondet annotationibus Lei LB IX

Responsio ad collationes: Responsio ad collationes cuiusdam iuvenis geronto-
didascali LB IX

Responsio ad disputationem de divortio: Responsio ad disputationem cuiusdam
Phimostomi de divortio LB IX

Responsio ad epistolam Pii: Responsio ad epistolam paraeneticam Alberti Pii, or
Responsio ad exhortationem Pii LB IX

Responsio ad notulas Bedaicas LB X

Responsio ad Petri Cursii defensionem: Epistola de apologia Cursii LB X

Responsio adversus febricantis libellum: Apologia monasticae religionis LB X

Spongia: Spongia adversus aspergines Hutteni LB X / ASD IX-1

Supputatio: Supputatio calumniarum Natalis Bedae LB IX

Tyrannicida: Tyrannicida, declamatio Lucianicae respondens LB I / CWE 29

Virginis et martyris comparatio LB V

Vita Hieronymi: Vita divi Hieronymi Stridonensis *Opuscula*

Index

In this index references to the text and to the notes are separated by a slash. References to the notes are identified by the number of the page on which the reference occurs and by note number.